11-22-00

D0078802

Data Structures, Algorithms, and Applications in Java

Sartaj Sahni

University of Florida

Boston Burr Ridge, IL Dubuque, IA Madison, WI New York San Francisco St. Louis
Bangkok Bogotá Caracas Lisbon London Madrid Mexico City Milan New Delhi
Seoul Singapore Sydney Taipei Toronto

McGraw-Hill Higher Education
A Division of The McGraw-Hill Companies

DATA STRUCTURES, ALGORITHMS, AND APPLICATIONS IN JAVA

This book is printed on acid-free paper.

1 2 3 4 5 6 7 8 9 0 DOC/DOC 9 0 9 8 7 6 5 4 3 2 1 0 9

ISBN 0-07-109217-X

Publisher: *Tom Casson*
Executive editor: *Elizabeth A. Jones*
Developmental editor: *Emily J. Gray*
Senior marketing manager: *John T. Wannemacher*
Senior project manager: *Beth Cigler*
Senior production supervisor: *Heather D. Burbridge*
Freelance design coordinator: *Pam Verros*
Supplement coordinator: *Betty Hadala*
New media developer: *Christopher Styles*
Printer: *R. R. Donnelley & Sons Company*

Library of Congress Cataloging-in-Publication Data
Sahni, Sartaj
    Data Structures, algorithms, and applications in Java / Sartaj Sahni.
        p. cm.
    ISBN 0-07-109217-X
    1. Java (computer program language)
    2. Data structures (Computer science)
    3. Computer algorithms.
    4. Application software-development.
    I. Title.
  QA76.73.J38S24 2000
  005.74–dc21   99-33211
http://www.mhhe.com

To my mother,
      Santosh

My wife,
      Neeta

and my children,
      Agam, Neha, and Param

PREFACE

The study of data structures and algorithms is fundamental to computer science and engineering. A mastery of these areas is essential for us to develop computer programs that utilize computer resources in an effective manner. Consequently, all computer science and engineering curriculums include one or more courses devoted to these subjects. Typically, the first programming course introduces students to basic data structures (such as stacks and queues) and basic algorithms (such as those for sorting and matrix algebra). The second programming course covers more data structures and algorithms. The next one or two courses are usually dedicated to the study of data structures and algorithms.

The explosion of courses in the undergraduate computer science and engineering curriculums has forced many universities and colleges to consolidate material into fewer courses. At the University of Florida, for example, we offer a single one-semester undergraduate data structures and algorithms course. Students coming into this course have had a one-semester course in Java programming and another in discrete mathematics/structures.

Data Structures, Algorithms, and Applications in Java has been developed for use in programs that cover this material in a unified course as well as in programs that spread out the study of data structures and algorithms over two or more courses. The book is divided into three parts. Part I, which consists of Chapters 1 through 4, is intended as a review of Java programming concepts and of methods to analyze and measure the performance of programs. Students who are familiar with programming in C should be able to read Chapter 1 and bridge the gap between C and Java. Although Chapter 1 is not a primer on Java, it covers most of the Java constructs with which students might have become rusty. These concepts include documentation comments, parameter passing, overloaded methods, recursion, classes, inheritance, and throwing and catching exceptions. In Chapter 1 and throughout the remainder of the book, we have followed a naming convention that is identical to that used in Java's packages—class and interface names begin with a capital letter, the names for constants (or final data members) are capitalized, and all other names begin with a lowercase letter. Chapters 2 and 3 are a review of methods to analyze the performance of a program—operation counts, step counts, and asymptotic notation (big oh, omega, theta, and little oh). Chapter 4

v

reviews methods to measure performance experimentally. This chapter also has a brief discussion of how cache affects measured run times. The applications considered in Chapter 2 explore fundamental problems typically studied in a beginning programming course—simple sort methods such as bubble, selection, insertion, and rank (or count) sort; sequential search; polynomial evaluation using Horner's rule; and matrix operations such as matrix addition, transpose, and multiply. Chapter 3 examines binary search. Even though the primary purpose of Chapters 2 through 4 is to study performance analysis and measurement methods, these chapters also ensure that all students are familiar with a set of fundamental algorithms.

Chapters 5 through 17 form the second part of the book. These chapters provide an in-depth study of data structures. Chapters 5 through 7 form the backbone of this study by examining various methods of representing data—array, linked, and simulated pointer. These three chapters develop Java classes to represent the linear list data structure, using each representation method. We compare the different representation schemes with respect to their effectiveness in representing linear lists by presenting experimental data. The remaining chapters on data structures use the representation methods of Chapters 5 through 7 to arrive at representations for other data structures such as arrays and matrices (Chapter 8), stacks (Chapter 9), queues (Chapter 10), dictionaries (Chapters 11, 15, and 16), binary trees (Chapter 12), priority queues (Chapter 13), tournament trees (Chapter 14), and graphs (Chapter 17).

In our treatment of data structures, we have attempted to maintain compatibility with similar or identical structures that are available in the package `java.util`. For example, the linear list data structure that is the subject of Chapter 5 is modeled after the class `java.util.ArrayList`. The public methods of our linear list classes use the same names as used by corresponding methods of `ArrayList`. Further, our implementations are functionally equivalent to the corresponding methods of `ArrayList`—our methods have the same parameters, return the same values, and throw the same exceptions. Because of the compatibility between our classes and those of Java, you can replace the use of any of the classes developed in this book with the corresponding class in `java.util` without affecting the correctness of the application.

The third part of this book, which comprises Chapters 18 through 22 (Chapters 21 and 22 are available from the Web site for this book), is a study of common algorithm-design methods. The methods we study are greedy (Chapter 18), divide and conquer (Chapter 19), dynamic programming (Chapter 20), backtracking (Chapter 21), and branch and bound (Chapter 22). Two lower-bound proofs (one for the minmax problem and the other for sorting) are provided in Section 19.4; approximation algorithms for machine scheduling (Section 13.6.2), bin packing (Section 14.5), and the 0/1 knapsack problem (Section 18.3.2) are also covered. NP-hard problems are introduced, informally, in Section 13.6.2.

A unique feature of this book is the emphasis on applications. Several real-world applications illustrate the use of each data structure and algorithm-design method developed in this book. Typically, the last section of each chapter is dedicated to applications of the data structure or design method studied earlier in the chapter. In many cases additional applications are also introduced early in the chapter. We have drawn applications from various areas—sorting (bubble, selection, insertion, rank, heap, merge, quick, bin, radix, and topological sort); matrix algebra (matrix addition, transpose, and multiplication); electronic design automation (finding the nets in a circuit, wire routing, component stack folding, switch-box routing, placement of signal boosters, crossing distribution, and backplane board ordering); compression and coding (LZW compression and Huffman coding); computational geometry (convex hull and closest pair of points); simulation (machine shop simulation); image processing (component labeling); recreational mathematics (Towers of Hanoi, tiling a defective chessboard, and rat in a maze); scheduling (LPT schedules); optimization (bin packing, container loading, 0/1 knapsack, and matrix multiplication chains); statistics (histogramming, finding the minimum and maximum, and finding the kth smallest); and graph algorithms (spanning trees, components, shortest paths, max clique, bipartite graph covers, and traveling salesperson). Our treatment of these applications does not require prior knowledge of the application areas. The material covered in this book is self-contained and gives students a flavor for what these application areas entail.

By closely tying the applications to the more basic treatment of data structures and algorithm-design methods, we hope to give the student a greater appreciation of the subject. Further enrichment can be obtained by working through the more than 800 exercises in the book and from the associated Web site.

WEB SITE

The URL for the Web site for this book is

```
http://www.mhhe.com/sahnijava
```

From this Web site you can obtain all the programs in the book together with sample data and generated output. The sample data are not intended to serve as a good test set for a given program; rather they are just something you can use to run the program and compare the output produced with the given output.

The Web site also includes animations of several of the abstract data types, data structure implementations, and applications. These animations were developed by Christopher Bobo. Solutions to many of the exercises that appear in each chapter, codes for these solutions, sample tests and solutions to these tests, additional applications, and enhanced discussions of some of the material covered in the text also appear in the Web site.

ICONS

We have used several icons throughout the book to highlight various features. The icon for a section that provides a bird's-eye view of the chapter contents is

The icon for the explanation of a Java language construct is

The icon for the treatment of an application is

The icon for a topic on which more material can be found at the Web site is

Some of the exercises have been labeled with the symbol

The star denotes an exercise whose solution requires development beyond what is done in the chapter. As a result, these exercises are somewhat harder than those without the symbol.

HOW TO USE THIS BOOK

There are several ways in which this book may be used to teach the subject of data structures and/or algorithms. Instructors should make a decision based on the background of their students, the amount of emphasis instructors want to put on applications, and the number of semesters or quarters devoted to the subject. We give a few of the possible course outlines below. We recommend that the assignments require students to write and debug several programs, beginning with a collection of short programs and working up to larger programs as the course progresses. Students should read the text at a pace commensurate with classroom coverage of topics.

TWO-QUARTER SCHEDULE—QUARTER 1
One week of review. Data structures and algorithms sequence.

Week	Topic	Reading
1	Review of Java and program performance.	Chapters 1–4. Assignment 1 given out.
2	Array-based representation.	Chapter 5. Assignment 1 due.
3	Linked representation.	Sections 6.1–6.4. Assignment 2 given out.
4	Bin sort, simulated pointers, and equivalence classes.	Sections 6.5.1, 7.1–7.6, and 7.7.1. Assignment 2 due.
5	Arrays and matrices.	Chapter 8. Examination.
6	Stacks and queues.	Chapters 9 and 10. Assignment 3 given out.
7	Skip lists and hashing.	Chapter 11. Assignment 3 due.
8	Binary and other trees.	Sections 12.1–12.8. Assignment 4 given out.
9	Union-find application. Heaps and heap sort.	Sections 12.9.2, 13.1–13.4, and 13.6.1. Assignment 4 due.
10	Leftist trees, Huffman codes, and tournament trees.	Sections 13.5 and 13.6.3 and Chapter 14.

TWO-QUARTER SCHEDULE—QUARTER 2
Data structures and algorithms sequence.

Week	Topic	Reading
1	Binary search trees. Either AVL or red-black trees. Histogramming.	Chapters 15 and 16. Assignment 1 given out.
2	Graphs.	Sections 17.1–17.7. Assignment 1 due.
3	Graphs.	Sections 17.8 and 17.9. Assignment 2 given out.
4	The greedy method.	Sections 18.1–18.3.5. Assignment 2 due.
5	The greedy method and the divide-and-conquer method.	Sections 18.3.6 and 19.1. Assignment 3 given out.
6	Divide-and-conquer applications.	Section 19.2. Examination.
7	Solving recurrences, lower bounds, and dynamic programming.	Sections 19.3, 19.4, and 20.1. Assignment 3 due.
8	Dynamic-programming applications.	Sections 20.2.1 and 20.2.2. Assignment 4 given out.
9	Dynamic-programming applications.	Sections 20.2.3–20.2.5. Assignment 4 due.
10	Backtracking and branch-and-bound methods.	Chapters 21 and 22.

SEMESTER SCHEDULE
Two weeks of review. Data structures course.

Week	Topic	Reading
1	Review of Java.	Chapter 1. Assignment 1 given out.
2	Review of program performance.	Chapters 2–4.
3	Array-based representation.	Chapter 5. Assignment 1 due.
4	Linked representation.	Sections 6.1–6.4. Assignment 2 given out.
5	Bin sort, simulated pointers, and equivalence classes.	Sections 6.5.1, 7.1–7.6, and 7.7.1.
6	Arrays and matrices.	Chapter 8. Assignment 2 due. First examination.
7	Stacks and queues. One or two applications.	Chapters 9 and 10. Assignment 3 given out.
8	Skip lists and hashing.	Chapter 11.
9	Binary and other trees.	Sections 12.1–12.8. Assignment 3 due.
10	Union-find application.	Section 12.9.2. Assignment 4 given out. Second examination.
11	Priority queues, heap sort, and Huffman codes.	Chapter 13.
12	Tournament trees and bin packing.	Chapter 14. Assignment 4 due.
13	Binary search trees. Either AVL or red-black trees. Histogramming.	Chapters 15 and 16. Assignment 5 given out.
14	Graphs.	Sections 17.1–17.7.
15	Graphs. Shortest paths.	Sections 17.8, 17.9, 18.3.5, and 20.2.3. Assignment 5 due.
16	Minimum-cost spanning trees. Merge sort and quick sort.	Sections 18.3.6, 19.2.2, and 19.2.3.

SEMESTER SCHEDULE
One week of review. Data structures and algorithms course.

Week	Topic	Reading
1	Review of program performance.	Chapters 1–4.
2	Array-based representation.	Chapter 5. Assignment 1 given out.
3	Linked representation and simulated pointers.	Chapters 6 and 7.
4	Arrays and matrices.	Chapter 8. Assignment 1 due.
5	Stacks and queues. One or two applications.	Chapters 9 and 10. Assignment 2 given out.
6	Skip lists and hashing.	Chapter 11. Assignment 2 due. First examination.
7	Binary and other trees.	Sections 12.1–12.8. Assignment 3 given out.
8	Union-find application. Heaps and heap sort.	Sections 12.9.2, 13.1–13.4, and 13.6.1.
9	Leftist trees, Huffman codes, and tournament trees.	Sections 13.5 and 13.6.3 and Chapter 14. Assignment 3 due.
10	Binary search trees. Either AVL or red-black trees. Histogramming.	Chapters 15 and 16. Assignment 4 given out. Second examination.
11	Graphs.	Sections 17.1–17.7.
12	Graphs and the greedy method.	Sections 17.8, 17.9, 18.1, and 18.2. Assignment 4 due.
13	Container loading, 0/1 knapsack, shortest paths, and spanning trees.	Section 18.3. Assignment 5 given out.
14	Divide-and-conquer method.	Chapter 19.
15	Dynamic programming.	Chapter 20. Assignment 5 due.
16	Backtracking and branch-and-bound methods.	Chapters 21 and 22.

ACKNOWLEDGMENTS

This book would not have been possible without the assistance, comments, and suggestions of many individuals. I am deeply indebted to the following reviewers for their valuable comments, which have resulted in a better manuscript:

George Ledin	Sonoma State University
David Poplawski	Michigan Tech
Lily Hou	Carnegie Mellon University
Archer Harris	James Madison University
Gregory Speegle	Baylor University
Eleni Stroulia	University of Alberta
Ho Kuen Ng	San Jose State University

Special thanks go to the students in my data structures and algorithms class who provided valuable feedback and helped debug the manuscript. Additionally, I am grateful to the following individuals at the University of Florida for their contributions: Chris Bobo, Joachim Hammer, Gayathri Venkataraman, and Liang Zhong.

The McGraw-Hill book team has been a pleasure to work with. Everyone contributed immensely to the quality of the final manuscript. The members of this team are Heather Burbridge, Beth Cigler, Emily Gray, Betsy Jones, and Pam Verros.

Finally, I am indebted to the copy editor, June Waldman, for having done an excellent job.

Sartaj Sahni
Gainesville
July 1999

CONTENTS IN BRIEF

CONTENTS

PART III   ALGORITHM-DESIGN METHODS

WEB CONTENTS

JAVA REVIEW

BIRD'S-EYE VIEW

Well, folks, we are about to begin a journey through the world of data structures, algorithms, and computer programs that solve many real-life problems. The program development process will require us to (1) represent data in an effective way and (2) develop a suitable step-by-step procedure (or algorithm) that can be implemented as a computer program. Effective data representation requires expertise in the field of data structures, and the development of a suitable step-by-step procedure requires expertise in the field of algorithm design methods.

Before you embark on the study of data structures and algorithm design methods, you need to be a proficient Java programmer and an adept analyst of computer programs. These essential skills are typically gained from introductory Java and discrete structures courses. The first four chapters of this book are intended as a review of these skills, and much of the material covered in these chapters should already be familar to you.

In this first chapter we discuss some features of the Java language. However, this chapter is not intended as a Java primer, and we do not cover basic constructs such as assignment statements, `if` statements, and looping statements. This chapter covers the following Java language features, which you should review:

- Documentation comments.

- Initial values for primitive data types.

- Parameter passing in Java.

- Method overloading.

- Throwing, handling, and defining exceptions.

- Classes and interfaces.

- Public, protected, and private class members.

- Inheritance and method overriding.

- Writing generic methods.

- Recursive methods.

Many of the codes developed in this book, particularly those for data structures, are developed as generic codes, which means they can be used with any data type that is not a primitive data type of Java. Although it would have been easier to develop these codes for a specific primitive data type such as `int`, we have not done so because this book emphasizes code reuse and applications. Our applications are able to use the generic code with no change. To write generic code, it is necessary to define Java interfaces such as `Computable` and `Operable`. To read the code samples in the remaining chapters, you will need to be familiar with the interfaces given in Section 1.13.

Additional Java features that may not have been covered in a first Java course are introduced in later chapters as needed. Chapter 1 also includes codes for the following applications:

- Finding the roots of a quadratic function.

- Generating all permutations of n items.

- Finding the maximum of n elements.

Chapter 1 concludes with tips on how to test and debug a program. Visit the Web site for this book

```
http://www.mhhe.com/sahnijava
```

to see a sample debugging session using Java's debugger `jdb`.

1.1   INTRODUCTION

Some of the questions we should ask when examining a computer program are

- Is it correct?

- How easy is it to read the program and understand the code?

- Is the program well documented?

- How easy is it to make changes to the program?

- How much memory is needed to run the program?

- For how long will the program run?

- How general is the code? Will it solve problems over a large range of inputs without modification?

- Can the code be compiled and run on a variety of computers or are modifications needed to run it on different computers?

The relative importance of some of these questions depends on the application environment. For example, if we are writing a program that is to be run once and discarded, then correctness, memory and time requirements, and the ability to compile and run the code on a single computer are the dominating considerations. Regardless of the application, the most important attribute of a program is correctness. An incorrect program, no matter how fast, how general, or how well documented, is of little use (until it is corrected). Although we do not explicitly dwell on techniques to establish program correctness, we provide informal proofs of correctness and implicitly develop programming habits conducive to the production of correct codes. The goal is to teach techniques that will enable you to develop correct, elegant, and efficient solutions.

Before we can begin the study of these techniques, we must review some essential aspects of the Java language, techniques to test and debug programs, and techniques to analyze and measure the performance of a program. This chapter focuses on the first two items. Chapters 2 through 4 review performance analysis and measurement techniques.

1.2   STRUCTURE OF A JAVA PROGRAM

1.2.1   Stand-Alone Programs and Applets

Every Java program is a class, and every class may contain data and method (or function) members. Although a Java class may also contain members that are themselves classes, we will not need this capability until we get to Chapter 5. A stand-alone Java program must have a method whose name is `main`, and a Java applet must have a method whose name is `init`. Stand-alone programs may be executed (or run) by typing in the command

```
java ProgramName
```

where `ProgramName` is the name of the Java stand-alone program. When a stand-alone Java program is executed, its `main` method is invoked. Java applets must be embedded in Hypertext Markup Language (HTML) files and executed through an applet viewer or a Web browser. When a Java applet is executed, its `init` method is invoked.

1.2.2   Packages

After you write a large number of Java programs, you probably will not want to keep them all in the same directory or folder. Java allows you to organize your programs (or classes) into **packages**. Each package defines a directory or folder that can contain as many programs as you wish. Some of the packages that come with java are `java.awt` (the Abstract Windowing Toolkit package; contains programs/classes to create and use graphical objects), `java.io` (contains classes useful for input and output of data), `java.lang` (contains wrapper classes such as `Integer`, `String`, and `Boolean`), and `java.util` (contains classes to manipulate time and date objects, dictionaries, vectors, etc.). The package name `java.lang` refers to all programs in the directory `java/lang` (or `java\lang`, depending on the convention your computer uses to specify a path).

Program 1.1 gives a stand-alone Java program that consists of just one method (i.e., the method `main`), which outputs a message that welcomes you to this text. *In this book, all names (other than those for classes and constants) begin with a lowercase letter.* The classes and packages that come with Java also use this convention.

The first line of Program 1.1 states that this program is a member of the package `misc`, and the second line states that the name of this program/class is `Welcome`. That is, the code of Program 1.1 is stored in a file whose name is `Welcome.java`, and this file is in the directory `misc`.

We will put each class that we develop in this book into one of the six packages: `applications`, `dataStructures`, `wrappers`, `exceptions`, `utilities`, and `misc`. Therefore, when you unzip the source code file you download from the Web site for this book

```
http://www.mhhe.com/sahnijava
```

the codes will be found in six directories. The names of these directories are the same as the package names. The package `applications` contains all the application codes (e.g., codes to sort, find a path in a maze, and schedule machines) developed in this text; codes for the data structures developed in this book are in the package `dataStructures`; wrapper classes such as `MyInteger` are in the package `wrappers`;

```
package misc;

public class Welcome
{
    public static void main(String [] args)
    {
        System.out.println("Welcome to the text Data Structures,");
        System.out.println("Algorithms, and Applications in Java");
        System.out.println("by Sartaj Sahni");
        System.out.println("Hope you enjoy the text.");
    }
}
```

Program 1.1 A welcome program

exception classes that are defined in this book are in the package `exeptions`; the interfaces we define to support generic codes (see Section 1.13) are in the package `utilities`, as are codes to swap elements in an array and to find the maximum element in an array; and codes that do not fit into any of these categories appear in the package `misc`. Because of our extensive use of document comments (see Section 1.4), a complete catalog of all packages, classes, methods, and so on is available as HTML files that you can browse to locate any code developed in this book. These HTML files are also in the source code zip file. The package directories also contain the compiled versions of the Java programs and sample input and output files. These files enable you to run the programs in this book without compiling the source code yourself.

1.2.3   Importing Classes and Packages

Imagine that you are writing a program and you need to invoke a method that is contained in some other program. You can do so by providing enough of the path to this method as the Java compiler needs to uniquely locate the method. For example, the line

```
System.out.println("Welcome to the text Data Structures,");
```

invokes the method `println` that is defined in the class `PrintStream`, which is a class in Java's package `java.io`. How does the Java compiler figure out that the method `java.io.PrintStream.println` is intended? The Java compiler first locates the class `System`, which is in the package `java.lang`. Next the compiler determines that `out` is a data member (or field) of the class `java.lang.System` and that the data type of `out` is `PrintStream`, which is in the package `java.io`.

The compiler then determines that `java.io.PrintStream` has a method `println` that has a single parameter of type `String`. Bingo—the intended method has been located! Pretty cool!

Although Java automatically searches the package `java.lang` for classes you may have referenced in your program, to get Java to search any other package, you must import that package into your program via an `import` statement. The statement

```
import java.io.*;
```

imports the entire package `java.io`, and the statement

```
import java.io.PrintStream;
```

imports only the class `PrintStream` that is in the package `java.io`.

Although you can put as many `import` statements as you want in your program, all `import` statements must immediately precede the `class` statement. So in Program 1.1 we would place our `import` statements (if any) between the `package` and `class` statements.

1.2.4   Superclasses and Subclasses

Java classes enjoy a hierarchical relationship similar to the hierarchical relationship among the administrative staff of a corporation. Just as a corporation has its board of directors at the top (or root) of the hierachy, division presidents at the next level of the hierarchy, vice presidents below presidents, and so on, the Java class hierarchy has the class `java.lang.Object` at the root and classes such as `String`, `Number`, `Throwable`, `InputStream`, and `OutputStream` at the next level of the hierarchy. Figure 1.1 shows the class hierarchy for a few of Java's many classes. The shaded classes are in the package `java.lang`; the remaining classes are in the package `java.io`.

Suppose that `A` and `B` are two Java classes and there is a line or edge between the two in the hierarchy diagram (e.g., in Figure 1.1 there is an edge between the classes `Object` and `String`; there is no edge between the classes `InputStream` and `PrintStream`). Further, suppose that `A` is one level higher in the hierarchy (i.e., closer to the root) than is `B`. We say that `A` is the **superclass** of `B`; `B` **derives** from `A`. In Figure 1.1 `Throwable` is the superclass of the classes `Exception` and `Error`; `OutputStream` is the superclass of `FileOutputStream` and `FilterOutputStream`; `Integer` and `Double` derive from `Number`; and `Exception` and `Error` derive from `Throwable`.

Class `B` is a subclass of class `A` if `B` either derives from `A` or from a class that is a subclass of `A`. In Figure 1.1 the classes `Number`, `String`, `Throwable`, `InputStream`, and `OutputStream` are subclasses of `Object` because each derives from `Object`. The classes `Exception` and `Error` are subclasses of `Object` because each derives from `Throwable`, which is a subclass of `Object`; `Exception` and `Error` are also subclasses

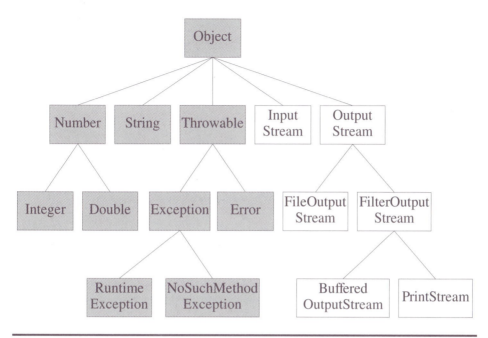

Figure 1.1 Hierarchy for a few Java classes

of Throwable; RuntimeException and NoSuchMethodException are subclasses of Exception, Throwable, and Object.

Class A is an **ancestor** of class B iff B is a subclass of A. In Figure 1.1 Object and Number are the ancestors of Integer.

All classes (including those you may define but excluding java.lang.Object) are subclasses of java.lang.Object. Every class, other than java.lang.Object has a superclass. No class has more than one superclass. You can specify the superclass of a class that you define by using the extends clause in the class header as shown below.

```
public class Welcome extends NameOfSuperClass
```

When no extends clause is provided in the class header (as was the case in Program 1.1), the superclass defaults to java.lang.Object. When defining a new class, you must choose its superclass carefully; this choice determines which data members and methods the new class inherits (see Section 1.10).

You can prevent people from extending a class by using the final attribute as is done below.

```
public final class Welcome
```

Java's wrapper classes `Boolean`, `Byte`, `Character`, `Double`, `Integer`, `Long`, and `Short`, for example, are declared as `final` classes. Therefore, you cannot extend these classes. Although it is difficult to imagine why you would want to prevent people from extending a particular class, the Java compiler is able to generate more efficient bytecode when it knows that certain classes cannot be extended. So if you want your code to run faster and you are quite sure no one will want to extend your class, use the `final` attribute on the class header.

EXERCISES

1. How many classes can a Java class derive from (i.e., extend)? Why?

2. List the subclasses of `OutputStream` that are shown in Figure 1.1.

1.3   THE JAVA COMPILER AND VIRTUAL MACHINE

Before you can execute a Java program, you must compile it. The compilation process translates your Java source code into something called Java **bytecode** (or J-code). It is a lot easier and more efficient to execute the bytecode than it is to execute the original source code. When the program `ProgramName` is compiled, the program source code is read from the file `ProgramName.java`, and the complied bytecode is written in the file `ProgramName.class`.

The compilation process for programming languages such as C and C++ translates from source code into the native language of the computer on which you intend to execute the program. The compiled C or C++ program runs directly on your computer. Consequently, compiled C and C++ programs run very fast. Java bytecode, on the other hand, is not the native language for any computer. Java bytecode may be viewed as the native language for a virtual computer—the Java Virtual Machine (JVM). The Java interpreter serves as a buffer between your Java program and the computer on which this program is to run. This interpreter runs the bytecode version of a program on your computer. Since Java programs are not run in native mode, they run slower than equivalent programs written in C and C++. In fact, some Java programs may run 100 times, or more, slower than equivalent C or C++ programs.

Do not despair; all is not lost. Although you might be discouraged by the performance of interpreted Java programs relative to that of native mode C and C++ programs, Java programs have advantages of their own:

- Java bytecode can be run on any computer that supports the JVM. Since the JVM is supported by virtually all computers, Java bytecode is truly portable. Java has delivered on its promise, "write once, run anywhere." Compiled C or C++ code, on the other hand, can be run only on the computer (or computer family) for which it was compiled. So although we can run the same Java bytecode on Sun, IBM (and IBM compatible), and Apple computers, we must compile C and C++ programs separately for each. Because of differences among the C and C++ compilers available on different computers (and even among compilers for the same computer), a C or C++ program that compiles on one computer may not compile on another.

- Java bytecodes tend to be more compact than compiled and C and C++ codes. In fact, the size of the Java bytecode of a program is usually about one-half that of the compiled code for the equivalent C or C++ program.

- Since Java bytecode is run interpretively by the JVM, every instruction in the code can be validated. This approach allows the JVM to provide a much higher level of security than can be provided when a program is run in native mode.

The performance of a Java program may be enhanced through the use of **just-in-time (JIT) compilers**. These compilers translate from Java bytecode to the native language of the computer on which you want to run the code. Typically, Java bytecode will be downloaded from a server, on which the bytecode resides, to a client computer where the code is to be run; a JIT residing on the client computer will translate the bytecode into native code. The Java class `java.lang.Compiler` contains methods that allow you to specify which classes in the bytecode are to be translated into native code. Java version 1.2, for example, has a JIT compiler.

Another product that will really turbocharge your Java applications is a Java microprocessor. Java bytecode is the native language of a Java microprocessor. If you install a Java microprocessor on your computer, your Java bytecodes will run in native mode on the Java microprocessor. When run in this fashion, your Java programs could well run faster than equivalent C or C++ programs.

1.4   DOCUMENTATION COMMENTS

Java provides three ways to write comments in your programs. Two of these—comments beginning with a double slash (//) and going to the end of the line and comments beginning with /* and ending with */—allow you to write comments that are completely ignored by the Java compiler and by all other Java processors. The third way—comments beginning with /** and ending with */—enables you to write comments that are processed by Java's document generation program `javadoc`. These comments are called **documentation comments**.

When the command `javadoc *` is executed, documentation is created for the packages and Java programs in the current directory. This documentation is in the form of several HTML files that can be viewed with a browser such as Netscape or Explorer. These files include an index of all names used in the packages, a list of all classes in each package, and so on. The best way to see the capabilities of `javadoc` is to view the HTML files available from the Web site for this book. These HTML files were produced by `javadoc`.

When producing the documentation, `javadoc` processes documentation comments and includes these in the generated HTML documentation files. A documentation comment may include one or more documentation tags that `javadoc` uses to format the documentation it produces. Documentation tags begin with the @ symbol and must appear as the first item of a documentation line. Although `javadoc` understands several tags, the tags `@throws`, `@param`, and `@return` are the only ones used in this book. These three tags can be used only in a document comment that precedes a method definition. Figure 1.2 illustrates the use of these tags within a document comment, and Figure 1.3 gives the resulting documentation.

```
/** Method to find the position of the largest integer.
  * @param a is the array containing the integers
  * @param n gives the position of the last integer
  * @throws IllegalArgumentException when n < 0
  * @return position of max element in a[0:n] */
public static int max(int [] a, int n)
{
    implementation of max comes here
}
```

Figure 1.2 Example of a document comment

```
public static int max(int a[],
                      int n)
    Method to find the position of the largest integer.
```

Parameters
        a-is the array containing the integers
        n-gives the position of the last integer

Returns:
        position of max element in a[0:n]

Throws:
        IllegalArgumentException - when n < 0

Figure 1.3 Documentation produced by the document comment of Figure 1.2

1.5   DATA TYPES

The Java language supports a rich set of primitive data types such as `int`, `float`, and `char`. The complete set of Java primitive data types, the default (or initial) value of variables of each of these primitive data types, the space allocated to each, and the range of allowable values for each are given in Figure 1.4. The ranges for `double`, `float`, and `long` are approximate.

Type	Default	Space (bits)	Range
boolean	false	1	[true, false]
byte	0	8	$[-128, 127]$
char	\u0000	16	$[\backslash u000, \backslash uFFFF]$
double	0.0	64	$\pm 4.9 * 10^{-324}$ to $\pm 1.8 * 10^{308}$
float	0.0	32	$\pm 1.4 * 10^{-45}$ to $\pm 3.4 * 10^{38}$
int	0	32	$[-2, 147, 483, 648, 2, 147, 483, 647]$
long	0	64	$\pm 9.2 * 10^{17}$
short	0	16	$[-32768, 32767]$

Figure 1.4 Java's primitive data types

Java also provides nonprimitive data types such as `Byte`, `Integer`, `Boolean`, and `String`. Although you can create your own nonprimitive data types (see Section 1.8), you cannot create your own primitive data types. An **object** is an instance of a primitive or nonprimitive data type. We will use the terms *object* and *instance* interchangeably.

There is an important difference in the way Java handles primitive and nonprimitive data types. When you declare a variable that is of a primitive data type, an instance (or object) of that data type with value equal to the default value is created. So, for example, the statement

```
int theInt;
```

creates an instance of the data type `int`; the name of this instance is **theInt**; and the instance is assigned the default value (0) for the data type `int`. The statement

```
String theString;
```

does not create an instance of the data type `String`. Rather, it creates an object that can reference (you may think of a reference as being a memory address) a string. The name of the created reference object is **theString**, and its initial value is **null**. An object of type reference is allocated 32 bits; and **null** is the default initial value for all objects of type reference.

String objects are created by statements such as

```
theString = new String("Welcome");
String s = new String("Bye");
```

The first statement assumes that the data type of `theString` has been previously declared. This first statement stores `Welcome` somewhere in your computer's memory and sets the value of `theString` to the memory address where `Welcome` was stored. The second statement declares `s` to be an object that can reference a string, stores `Bye` somewhere in the memory of your computer, and sets `s` to be the memory address where `Bye` was stored. Objects of other nonprimitive data types are created in a similar fashion.

1.6   METHODS

1.6.1   Parameters

A **method** is a function or procedure to perform a well-defined task. Consider the Java method `abc` (Program 1.2). This method computes the expression `a+b*c+b/c` for the case when `a`, `b`, and `c` are integers. The result is also an integer.

```
public static int abc(int a, int b, int c)
   {return a+b*c+b/c;}
```

Program 1.2 Compute an integer expression

In Program 1.2 `a`, `b`, and `c` are the **formal parameters** of the method `abc`. Each is of type integer. If the method is invoked by the statement

```
z = abc(2,x,y)
```

then `2`, `x`, and `y` are the **actual parameters** that correspond to `a`, `b`, and `c`, respectively. When the invocation `abc(2,x,y)` is executed, `a` is assigned the value 2, `b` is assigned the value of `x`, and `c` is assigned the value of `y`. In case `x` and/or `y` are not of type `int`, then a type conversion between their type and `int` is performed prior to the assignment of values to `b` and `c` (provided such a type conversion is defined). For example, if `x` is of type `float` and has the value 3.8, then `b` is assigned the value 3.

In Java all method parameters are **value parameters**. Consequently, at run time the value of each actual parameter is copied into the corresponding formal parameter before the method is executed. If the actual and formal parameters are of different data types, a type conversion is performed from the type of the actual parameter to that of the value formal parameter if such a type conversion is defined. When a method terminates, formal parameter values are not copied back into the actual parameters. Consequently, *method invocation does not change the actual parameters that correspond to value formal parameters*. Therefore, introducing the statement

```
b = a + c;
```

just before the `return` statement of Program 1.2 does not change the value of the actual parameter (i.e., x when the invocation is `abc(2, x, y)`) that corresponds to the formal parameter b.

1.6.2   Overloaded Methods

The **signature** of a method is defined by the data types of the method's formal parameters and the number of formal parameters. The signature of the method `abc` of Program 1.2 is `(int, int, int)`. Java allows you to define two or more methods with the same name provided no two methods with the same name have the same signature. The ability to define several methods with the same name is called **method overloading**. Because of the availablity of method overloading, we can write a program that includes both the method `abc` of Program 1.2 and the method `abc` of Program 1.3.

```
public static float abc(float a, float b, float c)
    {return a+b*c+b/c;}
```

Program 1.3 Compute a floating-point expression

By matching the signature used by a method invocation statement to the signature in a method definition, the Java compiler can determine which of the overloaded methods is meant.

EXERCISES

3. Explain why the `swap` method of Program 1.4 fails to swap (i.e., interchange) the values of the integer actual parameters that correspond to the formal parameters x and y.

```
/** Swap the integers x and y */
public static void swap(int x, int y)
{
    int temp = x;
    x = y;
    y = temp;
}
```

Program 1.4 Incorrect method to swap two integers

4. Do the following headers define methods with different signatures? Why?

   (a) `public int abc(int a, int b, int c)`

   (b) `public float abc(int a, int b, int c)`

5. Suppose we have defined a class `AB` that contains both class methods `abc` given in Programs 1.2 and 1.3. Which `abc` method is invoked by each of the following statements placed inside the `main` method of `AB`? Which will result in a compile-time error? Why?

   (a) `System.out.println(abc(1, 2, 3);)`

   (b) `System.out.println(abc(1.0F, 2.0F, 3.0F);)`

   (c) `System.out.println(abc(1, 2, 3.0F);)`

   (d) `System.out.println(abc(1.0, 2.0, 3.0);)`

   (e) `System.out.println(abc(1.0F, 2.0F, 3.0);)`

1.7 EXCEPTIONS

1.7.1 Throwing an Exception

Exceptions are used to signal the occurrence of errors. For example, if `c = 0` in Program 1.2, then the evaluation of the expression `a+b*c+b/c` results in an integer division by 0. An integer division by 0 causes Java to throw the exception `ArithmeticException`. Exceptions of this type may also be thrown when other exceptional conditions arise during artithmetic operations. Three other types of exceptions that Java may throw are `ArrayIndexOutOfBoundsException` (thrown when an array index is less than 0 or greater than or equal to the array size), `IllegalArgumentException` (thrown when an argument or parameter to a method is illegal), and `IOException` (thrown when an exceptional condition arises during input and output).

We can write Java programs that check for exceptional conditions other than those checked for by the Java interpreter. For example, the task performed by method `abc` (Program 1.2) may be defined only when each of its three parameters is greater than 0. In this case we would modify the code of Program 1.2 to first check that the values of `a`, `b`, and `c` are actually > 0. If one or more of these parameters is ≤ 0, we can signal an exceptional condition by throwing an `IllegalArgument` exception. Program 1.5 does this.

The code of Program 1.5 can throw an exception of type `IllegalArgumentException`. We can make this fact explicit by changing the method header from

```
public static int abc(int a, int b, int c)
```

to

```
public static int abc(int a, int b, int c)
{
   if (a <= 0 || b <= 0 || c <= 0)
      throw new IllegalArgumentException
            ("All parameters must be > 0");
   else
      return a + b * c + b / c;
}
```

Program 1.5 Throwing an exception

```
public static int abc(int a, int b, int c)
   throws IllegalArgumentException
```

However, you are not required to include a `throws` clause in the header because `IllegalArgumentException` is a subclass of the Java class `RuntimeException`. Only subclasses of `Throwable` that are not a subclass of either `RuntimeException` or `Error` must be declared in a `throws` clause (see Figure 1.1 for a portion of the Java class hierarchy). The type `IOException`, for example, is a subclass of `Exception` (which in turn is a subclass of `Throwable`) but is not a subclass of either `RuntimeException` or `Error`. Methods that throw exceptions of type `IOException` or any of its subclasses must declare the types of the thrown exceptions (or a superclass of the thrown exception type) in a `throws` clause.

1.7.2 Handling Exceptions

Exceptions that might be thrown by a piece of code can be handled by enclosing this code within a `try` block. The `try` block is then followed by zero or more `catch` blocks. Each `catch` block has a parameter or argument whose type is `Throwable` or a subclass of `Throwable`. A `catch` block typically contains code to recover from the exception that has occurred, or if recovery is not possible, the code in the `catch` block prints out an error message. The `catch` blocks may optionally be followed by a `finally` block. Program 1.6 shows an example of the `try-catch-finally` construct. The method `abc` that is invoked within the `try` block is the one given in Program 1.5.

In Program 1.6 two `catch` blocks follow the `try` block. The parameter of the first `catch` block is `e`, and its type is `IllegalArgumentException`. The parameter of the second `catch` block is also `e`. However, the type for the second `catch` block's parameter is `Throwable`. A `catch` block can catch exceptions whose type is the same as that of the `catch` block's parameter or whose type is a subclass of this type. Therefore, the first `catch` block catches exceptions of type `IllegalArgumentException`

```
public static void main(String [] args)
{
   try {System.out.println(abc(2, -3, 4));}
   catch (IllegalArgumentException e)
   {// a bad argument was passed to abc
      System.out.println
         ("The parameters to abc were 2, -3, and 4");
      System.out.println(e);
   }
   catch (Throwable e)
   {// some other exception occurred
      System.out.println(e);
   }
   finally
   {// this code gets executed whether or not
    // an exception is thrown in the try block
      System.out.println("Thanks for trying this program");
   }
}
```

Program 1.6 Catching an exception

or any of the subclasses of `IllegalArgumentException`; the second `catch` block catches exceptions of type `Throwable` or any of its subclasses. Since all Java exceptions are subclasses of `Throwable`, the second `catch` block will catch every exception, no matter what its type.

When the code within a `try` block terminates with no exception, we bypass the `catch` blocks and enter the `finally` block. When an exception is thrown, normal execution of the `try` block terminates and we enter the first `catch` block that can catch an exception of the type thrown. Following the execution of the code within this matching `catch` block, we enter the `finally` block. If no `catch` block matches the thrown exception type, the code in the `finally` block is executed; then the exception propagates through the hierarchy of nested enclosing `try` blocks to the first `catch` block in this hierarchy that can handle the exception. If the exception is not caught by any `catch` block, the Java interpreter outputs an exception message and terminates the program. Note that as an exception propagates through nested `try` blocks, the `finally` clauses of these `try` blocks are executed.

When Program 1.6 executes, `abc` throws an exception of type `IllegalArgument-Exception`. This exception causes `abc` to execute and the `try` block to terminate (the output method `System.out.println` in the `try` block is not invoked). Since the type of the exception thrown by `abc` is the same as that of the first `catch` block's parameter, the first catch block is entered. The parameter e is assigned the value All parameters must be > 0, and the code within the catch block is executed. Following the execution of this code, the code in the finally block is executed. Figure 1.5 gives the output generated by Program 1.6.

```
The parameters to abc were 2, -3, and 4
java.lang.IllegalArgumentException: All parameters must be > 0
Thanks for trying this program
```

Figure 1.5 Output from Program 1.6

1.8   YOUR VERY OWN DATA TYPE

1.8.1   The Class Currency

Despite the richness of Java's data types, many of the applications we develop in this text require data types that do not come with Java. You can define your own data types by using the class construct. Suppose you wish to deal with instances of type Currency. Instances of type Currency have the componenets: sign (plus or minus), dollars, and cents. Two examples are $2.35 (sign is plus, 2 dollars, and 35 cents) and −$6.05 (sign is minus, 6 dollars, and 5 cents). Some of the operations we wish to perform on instances of type Currency follow:

- Set their value.

- Determine the components (i.e., sign, dollar amount, and number of cents).

- Add two instances of type Currency.

- Increment the value of an instance.

- Output.

Instances of type Currency may be represented by using the three variables sign, dollars, and cents. These variables, respectively, represent the three components of a Currency instance. The data types of these three variables are boolean, long, and byte, respectively. The boolean variable sign has value true iff (if and only if) the sign component of the Currency instance is plus.

We may define a Java class Currency whose data members (i.e., fields) include the variables sign, dollars, and cents. The method members of this class will include a method for each of the operations we wish to perform on an object of type Currency. Program 1.7 gives the outline for the class.

The first line of Program 1.7 states that this program is a member of the package applications, and the second line, which is the **class header**, states that we

```
package applications;

public class Currency
{
    // data and method members of Currency come here
}
```

Program 1.7 Outline of the file for the class Currency

are defining a class (or program) whose name is Currency. Since the class header does not have an extends clause, the class Currency, by default, extends the class java.lang.Object. The keyword public is an **access modifier** that makes the class Currency accessible by or visible to all other classes. Without this modifier, the class Currency would be visible only to other classes within the package that contains Currency (i.e., the package applications). Other access modifiers supported by Java are private and protected. We will talk about these in Sections 1.8.2 and 1.9. The class definition (or implementation) is enclosed in braces ({}). Within these braces we place the data and method members of the class.

1.8.2   The Data Members of Currency

Program 1.8 gives the data members and some of the method members of Currency. We have defined five data members PLUS, MINUS, sign, dollars, and cents. PLUS and MINUS are of type boolean. They have been initialized to true and false, respectively. The keyword final in the declaration of these two data members means that the values of PLUS and MINUS cannot be changed. Therefore, these two data members are actually constants. *By convention, the names of constants are in uppercase.* The keyword static in the declaration of PLUS and MINUS means that these two members are **class data members**. A class data member is associated with the entire class rather than with individual instances of a class. Therefore, each class has exactly one copy of each of its class data members. The access modifier public causes the data members PLUS and MINUS to be visible to all classes. Without this access modifier, these constants would be visible only to classes within the package applications.

The remaining data members—sign, dollars, and cents—are not declared as static data members. Therefore, these data members are **instance data members**. That is, each instance of the data type Currency will have its own copy of these data members. The access modifier private used in the declaration of sign, dollars, and cents means that these data members are visible only within the class Currency (i.e., within the braces that contain the data and method members of Currency). Therefore, the data members sign, dollars, and cents are

```
// class constants
public static final boolean PLUS = true;
public static final boolean MINUS = false;

// instance data members
private boolean sign;
private long dollars;
private byte cents;

// constructors
/** initialize instance to
 * theSign $ theDollars.theCents
 * @throws IllegalArgumentException when theDollars < 0
 * or theCents < 0 or theCents > 99 */
public Currency(boolean theSign, long theDollars, byte theCents)
{
   sign = theSign;

   if (theDollars < 0)
      throw new IllegalArgumentException
            ("Dollar value must be >= 0");
   else
      dollars = theDollars;

   if (theCents < 0 || theCents > 99)
      throw new IllegalArgumentException
            ("Cents must be between 0 and 99");
   else
      cents = theCents;
}

/** initialize instance to $0.00 */
public Currency()
   {this(PLUS, 0L, (byte) 0);}

/** initialize with double */
public Currency(double theValue)
   {setValue(theValue);}
```

Program 1.8 Data members and constructors for the class Currency hidden within the class. Data hiding is an important principle of object-oriented programming. Since the instance data members are closely tied to the implementation of a class, an important benefit of hiding these data members is that we can later change the implementation (in particlular, we can change the instance data members) without requiring any changes in the programs that make use of class instances.

1.8.3   The Method Members of `Currency`

The declaration of the data members is followed by the declaration and implementation of the method members. We have divided the method members of `Currency` into the following categories: constructor methods, accessor methods, mutator methods, an output method, arithmetic methods, and a `main` method. Constructor methods are invoked automatically when a class instance is created. These methods are used to initialize instance data members. Accessor methods return the value of data members, and mutator methods change data member values. The output method is named `toString` because Java uses a method by this name to convert a class instance into its output format (see Section 1.10 for an explanation of this process). The arithmetic methods perform various arithmetic operations (such as add and subtract) on class instances. The `main` method is present in all stand-alone Java applications. If we attempt to execute the class `Currency`, this execution will invoke the member method `main`.

1.8.4   The Constructors of `Currency`

In Program 1.8 the constructor methods for our class follow the declaration of the data members. A constructor method always has the same name as the class of which it is a constructor, and a constructor method never returns a value. As you can see in Program 1.8, our class `Currency` has three constructors. The header for the first of these constructors is

```
public Currency(boolean theSign, long theDollars, byte theCents)
```

The method name is `Currency` (the same as the class name), and the method has three formal parameters: `theSign`, `theDollars`, and `theCents`. When this constructor is invoked, the value of the actual parameters is assigned to the formal parameters. The code for the constructor verifies that these values are permissible values for the instance data members `dollars` and `cents`. In case the values are permissible, the data members are set to the given values. When one or more of the given values is illegal, an `IllegalArgumentException` exception is thrown.

The header for the second constructor is

```
public Currency()
```

This constructor initializes the newly created `Currency` instance to have the value +$0.00. The statement

```
this(PLUS, 0L, (byte) 0);
```

invokes the first constructor using the actual parameters `PLUS`, a 0 of type `long`, and a 0 of type `byte`. The header for the third constructor is

```
public Currency(double theValue)
```

This version of the constructor is used to initialize the currency value by providing a value of type `double` (e.g., −2.20 or 6.97). The initialization is done by the mutator method `setValue`, which is defined later.

The signatures for our three constructor methods are (`boolean, long, byte`), (), and (`double`). Since the three signatures are different, we have a valid use of method overloading.

1.8.5   Creating Instances of `Currency`

To create a `Currency` object, we must first declare a variable that can hold a reference to such an object. The statement

```
Currency g, h, i, j;
```

declares four variables `g`, `h`, `i`, and `j` that can hold references to objects of type `Currency`. These variables, like all reference variables in Java, have the default initial value `null`. Once we have declared `Currency` variables as above, we can create instances of `Currency` by using the Java method `new` and a `Currency` constructor as below.

```
g = new Currency();
h = new Currency(PLUS, 3L, (byte) 50);
i = new Currency(-2.50);
j = new Currency();
```

The variables `g` and `j` reference two different `Currency` objects having the value $0.0, `h` references a `Currency` object with value +$3.50, and `i` references a `Currency` object with value −$2.50. The method `new` allocates memory for the object to be created and invokes the appropriate constructor for the object. We also can create and initialize the four `Currency` objects `g` through `j` by using the statement

```
Currency g = new Currency(),
         h = new Currency(PLUS, 3L, (byte) 50),
         i = new Currency(-2.50),
         j = new Currency();
```

A one-dimensional array of type currency may be created as below.

```
Currency[] balance = new Currency[10];
```

This statement does not actually create 10 `Currency` objects. Rather, it first declares a variable `balance` of type `Currency[]`; then using the method `new`, an array that can hold 10 references to objects of type `Currency` is dynamically allocated (i.e., the array is allocated at run time rather than at compile time); and finally, the 10 references are set to their default value `null`. To create 10 objects with the initial value $0.00, we will need to also execute the following `for` loop:

```
for (int m = 0; m < 10; m++)
   balance[m] = new Currency();
```

When the Java method `new` is invoked, it allocates memory for the object that is to be created. If sufficient memory is not available to create the new object, an error of type `OutOfMemoryError` is thrown.

1.8.6   The Accessor Methods of `Currency`

We define three accessor methods `getSign`, `getDollars`, and `getCents` for our class. Program 1.9 gives the codes for these methods. Depending on the nature of the class you define, you may or may not need to provide an accessor method for each of the instance data members.

```
/** @return sign */
public boolean getSign()
   {return sign;}

/** @return dollars */
public long getDollars()
   {return dollars;}

/** @return cents */
public byte getCents()
   {return cents;}
```

Program 1.9 Accessors for the class `Currency`

1.8.7   The Mutator Methods of `Currency`

Mutator methods allow the user to set or change the characteristics (typically, these are stored in the data members) of an object. Program 1.10 gives a variety of mutator methods for our currency class. The first version of the overloaded mutator method `setValue` adds 0.005 while computing the number of cents. This method allows for possible small errors in the internal computer representation of a floating-point number. These errors result from the fact that some floating-point numbers do not have an exact binary representation. The second version of `setValue` allows you to assign the value of one `Currency` object to another.

1.8.8   Invoking Methods and Accessing Data Members

Like a data member, a method may be either a class method (i.e., a static method) or an instance method. The methods of Programs 1.2 through 1.6 are class methods, whereas all methods of the class `Currency` other than the method `Currency.main` are instance methods. There is an important difference between how we invoke class methods and instance methods. Class methods are invoked using the method name and the actual parameters for the method invocation. For example, the method `abc` of Program 1.2 may be invoked as below.

```
z = abc(2,x,y)
```

Here `x` and `y` are integer variables. To invoke an instance method, we must additionally provide the class instance the method is to work on.

Suppose that we have created and initialized the `Currency` objects g through j as above. To determine the number of cents in the objects referenced by g and h (or more simply, in the objects g and h), we can use the syntax given below.

```
byte gCents = g.getCents();
byte hCents = h.getCents();
```

In object-oriented programming, we perform operations on objects. In the above statements, we perform the method `getCents` on the objects g and h. The use of the data member `cents` in the `return` statement of the code for `getCents` refers to the `cents` data member of the object g when `getCents` is invoked by `g.getCents()` and to the `cents` data member of object h when the invocation is `h.getCents()`. When writing the code for a member method, we can explicitly reference the object that is being worked on (i.e., the object that invoked the method) by using the name `this`. So, for example, we could have written the code for `getCents` as

```
return this.cents
```

This syntax means return the `cents` data member of the object `this`.

In the second `setValue` mutator method, we have a need to access the data members of two different objects `this` (i.e., the invoking object) and `x` (the formal parameter of type `Currency`). To access the members of `x`, we use the syntax

```
/** set sign = theSign */
public void setSign(boolean theSign)
   {sign = theSign;}

/** set dollars = theDollars
  * @throws IllegalArgumentException when theDollars < 0 */
public void setDollars(long theDollars)
{
   if (theDollars < 0)
      throw new IllegalArgumentException
             ("Dollar value must be >= 0");
   else
      dollars = theDollars;
}

// code for setCents is on the Web site

/** set sign, dollars, and cents */
public void setValue(double theValue)
{
   if (theValue < 0)
   {
      sign = MINUS;
      theValue = -theValue;
   }
   else
      sign = PLUS;

   dollars = (long) theValue; // extract integral part

   // get two decimal digits
   cents = (byte) ((theValue + 0.005 - dollars) * 100);
}

public void setValue(Currency x)
{
   sign = x.sign;
   dollars = x.dollars;
   cents = x.cents;
}
```

Program 1.10 Mutators for the class Currency

x.<member name>. So, for example, x.dollars refers to the dollars data member of the object x. Recall that since the data member dollars is a private data member, the syntax x.dollars can be used only within the definition of the class Currency. Note also that we could have written the statement

```
cents = x.cents;
```

as

```
this.cents = x.cents;
```

When a member method of a class is to perform a task on an instance of that class, the member method should be developed as an instance method. Class methods (i.e., static methods) should be used only for tasks that are not performed on instances of the class of which the method is a member. Some classes such as java.lang.Math simply provide a mechanism to group a collection of methods. It does not make sense for us to create instances of these classes. Therefore, these classes have no instance data or method members; all members are class (i.e., static) members.

1.8.9   Output and Arithmetic Methods for Currency

Program 1.11 gives the output and arithmetic methods for our currency class. Java outputs objects using the method toString, which is defined in the Java class Object. Since the class Object is the root class for all other classes, we can get Java to output our objects any way we want by redefining the method toString in our class. Such a redefining of toString overrides any other definition of toString as far as objects of type Currency are concerned. See Section 1.10 for more about overriding methods.

The method add sums the currency amounts of the invoking object and x and then returns the result. The method increment adds the currency amount x to the invoking object.

1.8.10   The Method main

Every stand-alone Java application must be defined as a class and must include a method with the header

```
public static void main(String [] args)
```

Inclusion of such a method allows you to execute an application (Currency in our case) by typing

```
java application.Currency a1 a2 ...
```

```
/** convert to a string */
public String toString()
{
   if (sign == PLUS)
      {return "$" + dollars + "." + cents;}
   else
      {return "-$" + dollars + "." + cents;}
}

// arithmetic methods
/** @return this + x */
public Currency add(Currency x)
{
   // convert this to a long
   long a1 = dollars * 100 + cents;
   if (sign == MINUS)
      a1 = -a1;

   // convert x to a long
   long a2 = x.dollars * 100 + x.cents;
   if (x.sign == MINUS)
      a2 = -a2;

   long a3 = a1 + a2;

   // convert result to Currency object
   Currency answer = new Currency();
   if (a3 < 0)
   {
      answer.sign = MINUS;
      a3 = -a3;
   }
   else
      answer.sign = PLUS;
   answer.dollars = a3 / 100;
   answer.cents = (byte) (a3 - answer.dollars * 100);

   return answer;
}
```

Program 1.11 Output and arithmetic methods for the class Currency (continues)

```
/** @return this incremented by x */
public Currency increment(Currency x)
{
   setValue(add(x));
   return this;
}
```

Program 1.11 Output and arithmetic methods for the class `Currency` (concluded)

Here a1,a2, ··· are command line arguments that are passed to the `main` method via the array `args`. The use of the keyword `static` in the header for the `main` method indicates that the `main` method is a class method rather than an instance method (just as a `static` data member is a class data member rather than an instance data member). Class, or `static`, methods are invoked differently from instance methods. When a class method is invoked, there is no invoking object. Therefore, the syntax

<object name> . <method name(actual parameters)>

is not used. The syntax used to invoke a class method is

method name(actual parameters)

For example, to invoke the class method `Math.sqrt`, which is a method in Java's `Math` package, we could use the syntax

```
e = Math.sqrt(d);
```

where `d` and `e` are of type `double`.

Even though the class `Currency` has not been developed with a specific application in mind, we can include a `main` method. This `main` method can serve as a test of the class implementation. Program 1.12 gives a sample test code for the class.

EXERCISES

6. Since the default value for the data type `boolean` is `false` (see Figure 1.4), is it really necessary to explicitly initialize `MINUS` as is done in Program 1.8? If not, do you see any merit to doing the initialization nonetheless?

7. (a) What are the maximum and minimum currency values permissible when the representation of Program 1.8 is used?

   (b) What are the maximum and minimum currency values permissible when the representation of Program 1.8 is used and the data types of `dollars` and `cents` are changed to `int`?

```
public static void main(String [] args)
{
    // test constructors
    Currency g = new Currency(),
             h = new Currency(PLUS, 3L, (byte) 50),
             i = new Currency(-2.50),
             j = new Currency();

    // test toString
    System.out.println("The initial values are " + g +
                       " " + h + " " + i + " " + j);
    System.out.println();

    // test mutators
    // first make g nonzero
    g.setDollars(2);
    g.setSign(MINUS);
    g.setCents((byte) 25);
    i.setValue(-6.45);
    System.out.println("New values are " + g + " " + i);
    System.out.println();

    // do some arithmetic
    j = h.add(g);
    System.out.println(h + " + " + g + " = " + j);

    System.out.print(i + " incremented by " + h + " is ");
    i.increment(h);
    System.out.println(i);

    j = i.add(g).add(h);
    System.out.println(i + " + " + g + " + " + h +
                       " = " + j);
    System.out.println();

    j = i.increment(g).add(h);
    System.out.println(j);
    System.out.println(i);
}
```

Program 1.12 A sample test method for the class Currency

(c) If method add (Program 1.11) is used to add two currency amounts, what are their largest possible values so that no error occurs when converting from type currency to type long as is done to set a1 and a2?

8. Enhance the class Currency by adding the following public member methods:

   (a) input() inputs a currency value from the standard input stream and assigns it to the invoking object.

   (b) subtract(x) subtracts the value of the currency object x from that of the invoking object and returns the result.

   (c) percent(x) returns a currency object whose value is x percent of the value of the invoking object. x is a floating-point number.

   (d) multiply(x) returns the currency object that results from multiplying the invoking object and the floating-point number x.

   (e) divide(x) returns the currency object that results from dividing the invoking object by the floating-point number x.

   Implement all member methods and test their correctness using suitable test data.

9. Write a Java class for the data type Length. An instance of Length has the data members sign, inches, feet, and yards with $0 \leq$ inches < 12, $0 \leq$ feet < 3, and yards ≥ 0. If you prefer, you may do this exercise using the data members sign, millimeters, centimeters, and meters. Your class must include one or more constructors, methods to input and output, and methods to access and modify each component, add and subtract two instances, multiply an instance by an integer, and multiply an instance by a currency amount that is the cost per yard (or meter). Test your code.

10. Write a Java class for the data type Weight. An instance of Weight has the data members sign, ounces, pounds, and tons with $0 \leq$ ounces < 16, $0 \leq$ pounds < 2240, and tons ≥ 0 (note that 1 ton = 2240 pounds). If you prefer, you may do this exercise using the data members sign, grams, kilograms, and metricTons. Your class must provide one or more constructors, methods to input and output, and methods to access and modify each component, add and subtract two instances, multiply an instance by an integer, and multiply an instance by a currency amount that is the cost per pound (or kilogram). Test your code.

1.9   ACCESS MODIFIERS

The class Currency defined in Section 1.8.1 illustrated most of the basic concepts that relate to classes. When defining the data and method members of this class, we used the access or visibility modifiers `public` and `private`. In addition to these two access modifiers, Java provides a third modifier, `protected`. When no access modifier is explicitly used, the default visibility controls apply. Figure 1.6 summarizes the visibility controls provided by each access modifier when a data or method member of class C is declared using one of these modifiers.

Access Modifier	Member Visibility
default	member is visible only to classes in the same package
private	member is visible only within the class C
protected	member is visible to all classes in the same package and to subclasses of C in other packages
public	member is visible to all classes in all packages

Figure 1.6 Visibility controls for a member of class C

Information hiding and encapsulation are two of the cornerstones of object-oriented programming. Information is encapsulated within a class and may be hidden from all or portions of the world outside of the encapsulating class by using the appropriate access modifier. The ability to encapsulate and hide information enables us to guarantee the integrity of our data as well as to make changes in the implementation details of our data and method members without requiring any change in the programs from which these details were hidden.

By using the `private` access modifier, we can let the user see only what he or she needs to see while we hide the remaining information (generally having to do with implementation details). *Although Java syntax permits you to declare data members as* `public` *members, good software-engineering practice discourages this practice.* An exception, of course, is class data members, such as PLUS and MINUS in the class `Currency`, which are declared with the `final` attribute. These data members are constants that no one can change.

By making the instance data members of the class `Currency` private, we deny access to these members to all code that is external to the class. So a user of instances of the class `Currency` cannot change the values of these private data members using statements such as

```
h.cents = 20;
h.dollars = 100;
h.sign = PLUS;
```

These data members are changed only by method members of the class `Currency`. We can assure the integrity of the instance data members by writing the member methods so that they leave behind valid values if they begin with valid data member values. Our codes for the constructor and mutator methods validate the data before using it. The remaining methods have the property they leave behind valid data if they start with valid data. As a result, the codes for methods such as `add` and `toString` do not need to verify that the number of cents is, in fact, between 0 and 99. If the data members are declared as `public` members, their integrity cannot be assured. The user might (erroneously) set `cents` equal to 305, which would cause methods such as `toString` to malfunction. As a result, all member methods would need to validate the data before proceeding with their tasks. This validation would slow down the codes and also make them less elegant.

1.10   INHERITANCE AND METHOD OVERRIDING

When you write a new class, it comes with a lot of baggage. This baggage consists of the members of the superclass of your new class. We say that the new class **inherits** the members of its superclass. Inheritance means that each instance of the new class has its own copy of the instance data members of the superclass in addition to the instance data members defined for the new class. In addition, on each instance of the new class we can perform the methods defined in both the new class and the superclass. Equivalently, we may regard the `extends` clause as implementing the "IsA" relationship. Each instance of a class is also an instance of every ancestor class. In Figure 1.1 an `Integer` is a `Number`, and a `Number` is an `Object`. An instance of a class may be cast into an instance of any of its ancestor classes.

The superclass for the class `Currency`, defined in Section 1.8.1, is `Object`. Therefore, `Currency` inherits the members of `Object`. Since `Object` has no data members, the only instance data members associated with a `Currency` object are `sign`, `dollars`, and `cents`.

The class `Object` has several instance methods associated with it. Two of these are `equals` and `toString`. The headers for these two methods are

```
public boolean equals(Object theObject);
public String toString();
```

The method `Object.equals` returns the value `true` iff the values (i.e., the memory addresses) of `this` and `theObject` are the same; `Object.toString` returns the string representation of the memory address stored in `this`.

Even though we have not defined the method `Currency.equals` in Section 1.8.1, it is permissible to write a statement such as

```
if (currA.equals(currB))
   {System.out.println("The values are the same");}
```

The class currency inherits the method `equals` from its superclass `Object`. The data type of `currB` is `Currency`, which is a subclass of `Object`. Since an object can be cast into an instance of its superclass, the Java compiler can cast `currB` into an instance of `Object`. With this type conversion, we have a match with the signature of the inherited `equals` method. Therefore, the expression `currA.equals(currB)` causes the invocation of the inherited method `Object.equals`. This invocation does not have the desired result because `Object.equals` compares the memory addresses referenced by `currA` and `currB`, rather than the `sign`, `dollars`, and `cents` members of these currency objects. As a result, unless `currA` and `currB` reference the same instance, `Object.equals` returns the value `false`. We may remedy this problem by defining a method `Currency.equals`, which has the same signature as `Object.equals`. The method `Currency.equals` will override the inherited method `Object.equals`. Consequently, the expression `currA.equals(currB)` will invoke `Currency.equals` rather than `Object.equals`.

The method `Currency.toString`, defined in Section 1.8.1, has the same signature as the inherited method `Object.toString`. Therefore, `Currency.toString` overrides `Object.toString`. This is fortunate because when you execute an output statement such as

```
System.out.println(theCurrency);
```

the method `println` makes the invocation `theCurrency.toString()` to obtain the string that is to be output. Since `Currency.toString` overrides the inherited `Object.toString`, the invocation `theCurrency.toString()` invokes `Currency.toString` rather than `Object.toString()`. If we omit `Currency.toString()` from the implementation of `Currency`, then `Object.toString()` would be invoked and the memory address stored in `theCurrency` would be output.

When the header for a method includes the `final` attribute, as is shown below,

```
public final boolean equals(Object theObject);
```

the method cannot be overridden; `static` and `private` methods cannot be overridden either. Since you cannot extend a class declared with the `final` attribute, you cannot override its methods. As is the case for `final` classes, declaring a method `final` allows the Java compiler to better optimize the bytecode.

Note that since the superclass of a class inherits the members of its superclass, and so on, each class actually inherits the members of all the classes on the derivation hierachy path from the root to your new class. In Figure 1.1 the class `RuntimeException`, for example, inherits the members of `Exception`, `Throwable`, and `Object`.

EXERCISES

11. Consider the following Java classes: `Vehicle`, `Bicycle`, `Airplane`, `Automobile`, `Ship`, `BoeingJet`, `Boeing727`, `Boeing747`, `Boeing767`, `AirbusJet`, `Airbus300`, `Airbus320`, `GMCar`, `FordCar`, `ToyotaCar`, `MercedesCar`, `FordTaurus`, `ToyotaCamry`, and `ToyotaCorolla`. Develop a suitable hierarchy for these classes (see Figure 1.1). Your hierarchy should implement the "IsA" relationship. For example, a `ToyotaCamry` is a `ToyotaCar` but is not an `Airplane`.

12. Do Exercise 11 for the following classes: Shape, Polygon, Circle, Triangle, Quadrilateral, Pentagon, Hexagon, IsosclesTriangle, EquilateralTriangle, Rectangle, and Square. Explain how inheritance will enable you to simplify the development of codes to input, output, and compute the area and perimeter of instances of these classes.

13. (a) Write a program that uses two different currency objects (see Section 1.8.1) x and y that have the same dollar value. Your program should print the value of x.equals(y). Verify that the output is false. Why is this the case?

    (b) Now enhance the class Currency of Section 1.8.1 by adding the method equals that checks whether two currency values are equal by comparing their values. Your method should have the same signature as Object.equals. Run the program of part (a) using this version of Currency and verify that the output is now true.

14. (a) Write a class Square that has the single instance data member length. Your class should include at least one constructor. Additionally, you should include instance methods to access and change the value of length; methods area and perimeter that, respectively, return the area and perimeter of the square; a method to output the length of the square; and a method printAP to print the area and perimeter of the square. The last method should invoke area and perimeter to determine the values that are to be output. Test your code.

    (b) Now develop the class SquareTrack that extends the class Square. Figure 1.7 shows an instance of a SquareTrack. Your class should have only one instance data member—trackWidth; the data member Square.length is inherited. You should include at least one constructor and methods to access and change the track width. You should override the methods Square.area (the area of the track is the area of the solid part of Figure 1.7) and Square.perimeter (the perimeter of a track is the sum of the perimeters of the outer and inner squares of Figure 1.7). The method Square.printAP as well as the methods to access and change the square's length are to be inherited. Test your code.

1.11 Currency REVISITED

Suppose that many application codes have been developed using the class Currency of Program 1.8. Now we desire to change the representation of a currency object to one that results in faster codes for the more frequently performed operations of add and increment and hence speed the application codes. Since the user interacts with the class Currency only through the public members of Currency, changes made to the private members do not affect the correctness of the application codes.

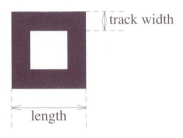

track width

length

Figure 1.7 A square track

Hence we can change the `private` members without making any changes in the applications!

The new representation of a currency object has just one `private` data member, `amount`, which is of type `long`. The number 132 represents $1.32, while −20 represents −$0.20. Program 1.13 gives some of the methods of the new version of `Currency`. (The complete code is available from the Web site.) We have given the new version of `Currency` a new name `CurrencyAsLong` because we need a new file name (and hence a new class name) if both versions are to be members of the same package. In practice, we could simply discard the old version and give the new version the same class and file name.

Although the headers of all public methods are the same in both implementations of the currency class, the `getSign` accessor method may not return the same value in both classes. When the currency amount is $0.00, the new implementation cannot distinguish between −$0.00 and +$0.00. Program 1.13 documents this difference.

If you examine the full code for `CurrencyAsLong`, you will notice that the new implementation provides an additional mutator method. The inclusion of this additional method does not affect application codes written for the old implementation, but does allow an added capability that can be used by new application codes.

Notice that if the new version is given the same class name `Currency` as the old version has, we can use the `main` method as given in Program 1.12 with no change at all! *As indicated earlier, an important benefit of hiding the implementation details from the user is that we can replace old representations with new more efficient ones without changing the application codes.*

Since we have changed the name of the class to `CurrencyAsLong`, we need to change all occurrences of `Currency` in Program 1.12 to `CurrencyAsLong` to get a `main` method that can be used within the class `CurrencyAsLong` for test purposes.

```
/** return this + x */
public CurrencyAsLong add(CurrencyAsLong x)
   {return new CurrencyAsLong(amount + x.amount);}

/** return this incremented by x */
public CurrencyAsLong increment(CurrencyAsLong x)
{
   amount += x.amount;
   return this;
}

/** @return sign
  * For this to work properly amount must be nonzero. */
public boolean getSign()
{
   if (amount < 0)
      return MINUS;
   else
      return PLUS;
}

/** @return dollars */
public long getDollars()
{
   if (amount < 0)
      return - amount / 100;
   else
      return amount / 100;
}

/** Set the sign of amount to theSign.
  * For this to work properly amount must be nonzero. */
public void setSign(boolean theSign)
{
   // change the sign as necessary
   if ((amount < 0 && theSign == PLUS) ||
       (amount > 0 && theSign == MINUS))
      amount = -amount;
}
```

Program 1.13 Some methods of CurrencyAsLong

EXERCISES

15. Do Exercise 8 using the implementation of Program 1.13.

16. Do Exercise 10 using a single data member `ounces` (or `grams`) of type `long`). Public methods common to the two exercises should have the same headers.

17. Do Exercise 9 using a single data member `inches` (or `millimeters`) of type `long`. Public methods common to the two exercises should have the same headers.

1.12   DEFINING AN EXCEPTION CLASS

Often, when you need to throw an exception, you can throw an exception of one of the standard types defined in Java. At times, however, you will want to define your own exception types. In this book, for example, we define our own exception type `MyInputException`, which is a subclass of `RuntimeException`. Exceptions of type `MyInputException` are thrown by methods of the class `MyInputStream`, which is an input class we have defined for use with this book. You can get the code for this class (as well as for all other classes developed in this book) from the Web site for this book. We have defined our own input class `MyInputStream` because Java's standard input methods throw exceptions that are subclasses of `IOException`. As indicated in Section 1.7.1, exceptions of type `IOException` and any of its subclasses must be declared in the `throws` clause of all methods that might throw these exceptions. Therefore, virtually all methods that perform input must either contain `catch` blocks to handle the input exceptions that might potentially be thrown or must declare the unhandled exceptions in a `throws` clause. This requirement makes our code rather cluttered and cumbersome. Since `MyInputException` is a subclass of `RuntimeException`, we can use the methods of `MyInputStream` and not bother with catching or declaring exceptions (unless we want to).

Program 1.14 gives the typical syntax used to define an exception type. Exception subclasses include a default constructor as well as a constructor with a `String` formal parameter. The `String` formal parameter corresponds to the message that is to be associated with the exception that has occurred. The statement `super()` invokes the constructor for the superclass `RuntimeException`.

The code for the class `MyInputStream` can be obtained from the Web site for this book. Methods in this class basically catch the exceptions of type `IOException` thrown by Java's input methods and throw exceptions of type `MyInputException` in their place.

```
public class MyInputException
      extends RuntimeException
{
   public MyInputException()
      {super();}
   public MyInputException(String message)
      {super(message);}
}
```

Program 1.14 Defining an exception class

1.13 GENERIC METHODS

Programs 1.2 and 1.3 differ only in the data types of the formal parameters and the return value. Rather than write a new version of the code for every possible data type of the formal parameters and return value, we wish to write a generic code that is independent of this data type.

Although it is not possible to write generic methods to work with actual parameters of any of the Java primitive data types, generic methods can be written to work with actual parameters of the type `Object` or of any subclass of `Object`. In particular, we can write generic methods that will work with the wrapper classes of Java (e.g., `Integer`, `Float`, and `Double`) because these wrapper classes are subclasses of `Object`.

At times the effort needed to write a generic method is almost the same as that needed to write a nongeneric one. For example, Program 1.15 gives a method to swap the integers stored in positions `i` and `j` of a one-dimensional array `a`.

```
public static void swap(int [] a, int i, int j)
{
   // Don't bother to check that indexes i and j
   // are in bounds. Java will do this and throw
   // an ArrayIndexOutOfBoundsException if i or
   // j is out of bounds.
   int temp = a[i];
   a[i] = a[j];
   a[j] = temp;
}
```

Program 1.15 Swap the integers in a[i] and a[j]

Program 1.16 gives a generic method to swap the objects referenced by a[i] and a[j]. Note that the method of Program 1.16 cannot be used to swap a[i] and a[j] when the type of a is one of the primitive data types of Java. In particular, Program 1.16 cannot be used in place of Program 1.15 to swap the integers stored at two array positions. Program 1.16 can be used whenever we wish to swap two elements in an array of type Object or any subclass of Object.

```
public static void swap(Object [] a, int i, int j)
{
   Object temp = a[i];
   a[i] = a[j];
   a[j] = temp;
}
```

Program 1.16 Swap the object references a[i] and a[j]

Although the transition from the nongeneric swap method of Program 1.15 to the generic swap method of Program 1.16 involves a reatively painless process, a similar transition from Program 1.2 to a corresponding generic method requires considerable effort.

1.13.1   The Interface Computable

A Java interface is a list of zero or more static final data members (i.e., constants) and zero or more method headers (with no method implementation provided). Program 1.17 gives the Computable interface, which contains several method headers but no constants.

Like a class, an interface defines a data type. So Program 1.17 defines the data type Computable. Although you can define methods that have formal parameters whose data type is Computable, you cannot create an instance of the data type Computable. When a class ImplementingClass implements all methods of Computable and declares itself as a class that implements the interface Computable, the instances of ImplementingClass may be cast into the data type Computable.

If we wish to write a generic method that involves arithmetic operations such as add, multiply, and divide, we can set up our generic method so that its parameters are of type Computable. The generic method can then be invoked using actual parameters of any data type that implements the interface Computable.

1.13.2   The Generic Method abc

Having defined a suitable interface Computable for generic methods that involve arithmetic operations, we can define a generic version of the abc method of Programs 1.2 and 1.3. Program 1.18 gives the code.

```
public interface Computable
{
    /** @return this + x */
    public Object add(Object x);

    /** @return this - x */
    public Object subtract(Object x);

    /** @return this * x */
    public Object multiply(Object x);

    /** @return quotient of this / x */
    public Object divide(Object x);

    /** @return remainder of this / x */
    public Object mod(Object x);

    /** @return this incremented by x */
    public Object increment(Object x);

    /** @return this decremented by x */
    public Object decrement(Object x);

    /** @return the additive zero element */
    public Object zero();

    /** @return the multiplicative identity element */
    public Object identity();
}
```

Program 1.17 The interface Computable

```
public static Computable abc(Computable a, Computable b, Computable c)
{
    Computable t = (Computable) a.add((Computable) b.multiply(c));
    return (Computable) t.add((Computable) b.divide(c));
}
```

Program 1.18 Compute an expression using a generic method

The generic method of Program 1.18 cannot be invoked with actual parameters that are of any of the primitive data types defined in Java as these primitive data types are not subclasses of `Object`. Additionally, these primitive data types do not implement the interface `Computable`.

1.13.3   The Interface `java.lang.Comparable`

Generic methods that require you to compare two instances of an object may be written using the method `compareTo`, which is the sole member of the interface `java.lang.Comparable`. `x.compareTo(y)` returns a negative integer when $x < y$; 0 when $x = y$; and a positive integer when $x > y$.

1.13.4   The Interface `Operable`

Some of the generic methods we develop require that the methods of both the `Computable` and the `java.lang.Comparable` interface be implemented. The interface `Operable` (Program 1.19), which contains no constants or methods, achieves this objective. An interface that has no constants or methods is called a **marker interface**.

```
public interface Operable extends Computable, Comparable
{}
```

Program 1.19 The interface `Operable`

1.13.5   The Interfaces `Zero` and `CloneableObject`

Two of the other interfaces we use in this book are `Zero` and `CloneableObject`. The interface `Zero` includes the method `zero`, which returns the zero element (i.e., the additive zero) for the class, and the method `equalsZero`, which returns the value `true` iff `this` equals the zero element of the class.

The interface `CloneableObject` includes only the method `clone()`, which returns a clone (replica) of the object `this`. To see the difference between cloning an object and simply making a copy of a reference to an object, suppose that variables `x` and `y` are of type `Currency` (Program 1.8). The code

```
x = new Currency(3.42);
y = x;
y.setValue(6.25);
System.out.println(x);
```

first creates an object of type `Currency` that has the value $3.42; the variable x contains a reference to this newly created object; see Figure 1.8(a). Next the reference to the newly created `Currency` object is copied into y, and we have the configuration of Figure 1.8(b). The third line changes the value of the object referenced by y to \$6.25; see Figure 1.8(c). Since both x and y reference the same object, the value of the object referenced by x is also changed to \$6.25. The value output by line 4 of the code is \$6.25.

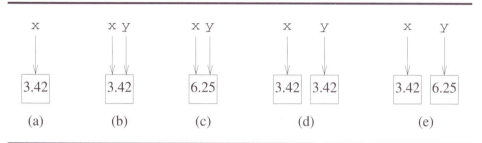

Figure 1.8 Copying a reference vs. cloning an object

Suppose that we have defined a method `clone` for `Currency` and that line 2 of the above code is changed to

```
y = x.clone();
```

Now, when line 2 is executed, a new object of type `Currency` that has the same value as does x is created by `clone`. Figure 1.8(d) shows the configuration following line 2. When line 3 changes the value of the object referenced by y, we get the configuration shown in Figure 1.8(e). Consequently, line 4 now outputs the value \$3.42.

1.13.6   The Wrapper Class `MyInteger`

We now proceed to define the class `MyInteger`, which implements the interfaces `Operable`, `Zero`, and `CloneableObject`. The class `MyInteger` is also a subclass of the class `Object`.

The class `MyInteger` has a single instance variable `value`, which is the value of the integer represented by an instance of `MyInteger`. It would be natural to define `MyInteger` as a subclass of the Java wrapper class `Integer`. This, however, is not possible because the class `Integer` is defined as a `final` class, and so it cannot be extended. Therefore, we define `MyInteger` from scratch as in Program 1.20. Program 1.20 shows only some of the methods of `MyInteger`. The remaining methods needed to complete the implementation of the interface `Operable` are similar to those given in Program 1.20.

```
public class MyInteger
       implements Operable, Zero, CloneableObject
{
    // value of the integer
    private int value;

    // constructor
    public MyInteger(int theValue)
       {value = theValue;}

    // a Computable interface method
    /** @return this + x */
    public Object add(Object x)
       {return new MyInteger(value + ((MyInteger) x).value);}

    // Comparable interface method
    /** @return -1 if this < x,
     *           0 if this == x,
     *           1 if this > x */
    public int compareTo(Object x)
    {
        int y = ((MyInteger) x).value;
        if (value < y) return -1;
        if (value == y) return 0;
        return 1;
    }
}
```

Program 1.20 The wrapper class MyInteger (only some methods are shown)

1.13.7   Using Data Types and Methods as Parameters

The ability to use a data type or a method as an actual or formal parameter of a method is an important tool when writing generic code. Suppose we wish to develop a class Array1D whose instances are one-dimensional arrays (see Figure 1.9).

The method inputArray inputs the number n of elements that are to be in a, creates an array a of size n, and then inputs the n elements and stores them in the newly created array. The difficulty in writing the code for this method is that the data type of the n elements that are to be input is unknown and may change from one invocation of inputArray to the next. We can overcome this difficulty by making the element data type a parameter of the method inputArray. Let us call this formal parameter theClass. The data type of theClass is Class, which is a

```
public class Array1D
{
    // instance data member
    Object [] a;

    // method of Array1D
    public void inputArray()
    {
        // code for inputArray comes here
    }
}
```

Figure 1.9 Pseudocode for `Array1D`

class defined in the package `java.lang`. We can get an object of type `Class` that describes any primitive data type as well as any data type that is derived from the class `Object` using the syntax

```
Class typeOfInt = int.class;
Class typeOfFloat = float.class;
Class typeofMyInteger = MyInteger.class;
Class typeOfCurrency = Currency.class;
```

In addition to knowing the data type of the elements that are to be input, the method `inputArray` must know (1) where to input the data from (i.e., from the standard input stream of the computer, from a specific file, etc.) and (2) how to input an element of the specified type (e.g., to input an element of type `Currency`, we must input a sign, a dollar value, and a cents value; to input an element of type `MyInteger`, only an integer is to be input). We can handle item (1) by making the input stream from where the data is to be obtained a parameter of `inputArray`. Figure 1.10 shows the form that we expect `inputArray` will take.

For item (2), we require that each data type implement a public static method `input(MyInputStream stream)`, which inputs an instance of that data type from the input stream `stream` and returns the instance that was input. Program 1.21 shows such a method for the class `MyInteger`. `readInteger` is a member method of `MyInputStream`. This method reads and returns an integer.

We can invoke the `input` method of the specified data type and save, in the array `a`, the element that was input. To get a reference to the input method of the desired class, we use the method `java.lang.Class.getMethod`, which returns an object of type `Method`. The class `Method` is one of the classes in the package `java.lang.reflect`. The method `getMethod` has two parameters. The first parameter, `name`, is of type `String` and specifies the name of the method (in our case

```
/** input elements of type theClass from stream */
public void inputArray(Class theClass, MyInputStream stream)
{
    input the value of n from stream;
    a = new Object [n];
    for (int i = 0; i < n; i++)
        input a[i] using the input method for data type theClass;

}
```

Figure 1.10 Pseudocode for `inputArray`

```
/** input from the given input stream */
public static MyInteger input(MyInputStream stream)
{
    System.out.println("Enter an integer value");
    return new MyInteger(stream.readInteger());
}
```

Program 1.21 `MyInteger.input`

input), and the second parameter, `parameterTypes`, is an array of type `Class`, which gives the signature of the method whose name is `name`. The statements

```
Class [] parameterTypes = {MyInputStream.class};
Method inputMethod = theClass.getMethod("input", parameterTypes);
```

set `inputMethod` so that it refers to the input method of the class `theClass`. To actually execute this input method, we must use the method `Method.invoke` as shown below.

```
Object [] inputMethodArgs = {stream};
a[i] = inputMethod.invoke(null, inputMethodArgs);
```

The first parameter of `invoke` is the instance on which the method being invoked is to operate. Whenever the method being invoked is a static method, this first parameter is `null`. The second parameter of `invoke` is an array that contains the actual parameters for the invocation. Program 1.22 gives the Java code for the method `inputArray`.

We have enclosed the code in a `try` block because the methods `getMethod` and `invoke` throw exceptions that are not of a type that is a subclass of `RuntimeExeption`

```
public void inputArray(Class theClass, MyInputStream stream)
{
    try
    {
        // get the proper method to be used to read in the values
        Class [] parameterTypes = {MyInputStream.class};
        Method inputMethod = theClass.getMethod("input", parameterTypes);

        // input number of elements and create an array of that size
        System.out.println("Enter number of elements");
        int n = stream.readInteger();
        a = new Object [n];

        // input the elements
        Object [] inputMethodArgs = {stream};
        for (int i = 0; i < n; i++)
        {
            System.out.println("Enter element " + (i+1));
            a[i] = inputMethod.invoke(null, inputMethodArgs);
        }
    }
    catch (Exception e)
    {
        System.out.println(e);
        throw new IllegalArgumentException("Array1D.inputArray");
    }
}
```

Program 1.22 The method inputArray

(for example, exceptions of the types NoSuchMethodException and IllegalAccess-Exception may be thrown). Therefore, we must either catch these exceptions within the method inputArray or we must declare, in the header of inputArray, that exceptions of these types may flow through inputArray. In Program 1.22 we catch the exceptions that might be thrown by getMethod and invoke (as well as by any other method or operation) and throw, in their place, an exception of type IllegalArgumentException, which is a subclass of RuntimeException.

An alternative implementation of inputArray results if we replace the parameter theClass with the parameter inputMethod. Program 1.23 gives the alternative implementation.

```
public void inputArray(Method inputMethod, MyInputStream stream)
{
   try
   {
      // input number of elements and create an array of that size
      System.out.println("Enter number of elements");
      int n = stream.readInteger();
      a = new Object [n];

      // input the elements
      Object [] inputMethodArgs = {stream};
      for (int i = 0; i < n; i++)
      {
         System.out.println("Enter element " + (i+1));
         a[i] = inputMethod.invoke(null, inputMethodArgs);
      }
   }
   catch (Exception e)
   {
      System.out.println(e);
      throw new IllegalArgumentException("Array1D.inputArray");
   }
}
```

Program 1.23 An alternative implementation of the method `inputArray`

EXERCISES

18. Write the public method `MyInteger.input()` to input an integer and assign it to `this.value`. The input is from the standard input device (normally a keyboard). Give the user three attempts to enter a valid integer before your method quits unsuccessfully. If unsuccessful, you should throw an exception of type `MyInputException` (see Program 1.14). Test your method.

19. Write a public method `clone` for the class `Currency` (Program 1.8).

20. Write a generic static method to determine whether the elements in the one-dimensional array `a` are in sorted order (i.e., `a[i]` $\leq$ `a[i+1]`, $0 \leq i <$ `a.length-1`). Your method should return `false` if `a` is not sorted and `true` if it is. The formal parameter to your method is an array of type `Comparable`. Test your code.

21. Write a generic static method that returns the sum of the elements in the one-dimensional array a. Your implementation should work for all data types that implement the interface Computable. Test your code.

22. Let a be a two-dimensional array of type Comparable and let theThreshold be of the same data type as a. Write a generic static method binarize that returns a two-dimensional array b of type boolean such that b[i][j] = true iff a[i][j] >= theThreshold. Test your code.

1.14   GARBAGE COLLECTION

Each time you invoke the method new, storage is allocated to you. The statements

```
int [] a = new int[500000];
Currency c = new Currency();
```

allocate space for an integer array and an instance of Currency. The integer array requires $500{,}000 * 4 = 2{,}000{,}000$ bytes plus 4 bytes for the array length, and the instance of Currency needs space for a boolean, a long, and a byte.

After several invocations of new, you are likely to run out of memory, and at this time Java's garbage collector is invoked. The garbage collector scours memory to salvage what is not in use and make this not-in-use memory available for reuse. The garbage collector determines which bytes of memory are not in use by checking the references in your program variables. For example, a references a block of 2,000,000+ bytes, and c references a block of about 10 bytes. Memory that is not referenced by your program is determined to be garbage (i.e., not in use) and reclaimed for reallocation by new.

If at some point in your program, you decide you no longer need the array a and the Currency object c, you can cause the space occupied by these variables to be garbage collected by setting the references to null as is done below.

```
a = null;
c = null;
```

Although there may not be much benefit in doing this for c, making it possible to reclaim the 2,000,000+ bytes allocated to a could save you from an OutOfMemoryError error (new gives an error of this type when it cannot allocate enough memory for the object you wish to create).

If the array a is of type Currency (instead of int), then each element of a is a 4-byte reference to a Currency object. If all 500,000 Currency objects have been created, then the total space used by a and the 500,000 Currency objects is about 7 megabytes (MB). Setting a to null when a is no longer needed allows the garbage collector to reclaim the 7 MB of memory the program no longer needs.

1.15   RECURSION

A **recursive method** invokes itself. In **direct recursion** the code for method f contains a statement that invokes f, whereas in **indirect recursion** method f invokes a method g, which invokes a method h, and so on until method f is again invoked. Before delving into recursive Java methods, we examine two related concepts from mathematics—recursive definitions of mathematical functions and proofs by induction.

1.15.1   Recursive Functions

In mathematics we often define a function in terms of itself. For example, the factorial function $f(n) = n!$, for n an integer, is defined as follows:

$$f(n) = \begin{cases} 1 & n \leq 1 \\ nf(n-1) & n > 1 \end{cases} \qquad (1.1)$$

This definition states that $f(n)$ equals 1 whenever n is less than or equal to 1; for example, $f(-3) = f(0) = f(1) = 1$. However, when n is more than 1, $f(n)$ is defined recursively, as the definition of f now contains an occurrence of f on the right side. This use of f on the right side does not result in a circular definition, as the parameter of f on the right side is smaller than that on the left side. For example, from Equation 1.1 we obtain $f(2) = 2f(1)$. From Equation 1.1 we also obtain $f(1) = 1$, and substituting for $f(1)$ in $f(2) = 2f(1)$, we obtain $f(2) = 2$. Similarly, from Equation 1.1 we obtain $f(3) = 3f(2)$. We have already seen that Equation 1.1 yields $f(2) = 2$. So $f(3) = 3 * 2 = 6$.

For a recursive definition of $f(n)$ (we assume direct recursion) to be a complete specification of f, it must meet the following requirements:

- The definition must include a **base** component in which $f(n)$ is defined directly (i.e., nonrecursively) for one or more values of n. For simplicity, we assume that the domain of f is the nonnegative integers and that the base covers the case $0 \leq n \leq k$ for some constant k. (It is possible to have recursive definitions in which the base covers the case $n \geq k$ instead, but we encounter these definitions less frequently.)

- In the **recursive component** all occurrences of f on the right side should have a parameter smaller than n so that repeated application of the recursive component transforms all occurrences of f on the right side to occurrences of f in the base.

In Equation 1.1 the base is $f(n) = 1$ for $n \leq 1$; in the recursive component $f(n) = nf(n-1)$, the parameter of f on the right side is $n-1$, which is smaller than n. Repeated application of the recursive component transforms $f(n-1)$ to

$f(n-2)$, $f(n-3)$, $\cdots$, and finally to $f(1)$ which is included in the base. For example, repeated application of the recursive component gives the following:

$$f(5) = 5f(4) = 20f(3) = 60f(2) = 120f(1)$$

Notice that each application of the recursive component gets us closer to the base. Finally, an application of the base gives $f(5) = 120$. From the example, we see that $f(n) = n(n-1)(n-2)\cdots 1$ for $n \geq 1$.

As another example of a recursive definition, consider the Fibonacci numbers that are defined recursively as below:

$$F_0 = 0, \quad F_1 = 1, \quad F_n = F_{n-1} + F_{n-2} \text{ for } n > 1 \qquad (1.2)$$

In this definition, $F_0 = 0$ and $F_1 = 1$ make up the base component, and $F_n = F_{n-1} + F_{n-2}$ is the recursive component. The function parameters on the right side are smaller than n. For Equation 1.2 to be a complete recursive specification of F, repeated application of the recursive component beginning with any value of $n > 1$ should transform all occurrences of F on the right side to occurrences in the base. Since repeated subtraction of 1 or 2 from an integer $n > 1$ reduces it to either 0 or 1, right-side occurrences of F are always transformed to base occurrences. For example, $F_4 = F_3 + F_2 = F_2 + F_1 + F_1 + F_0 = 3F_1 + 2F_0 = 3$.

1.15.2   Induction

Now, we turn our attention to the second concept related to recursive computer functions—proofs by induction. In a proof by induction, we establish the validity of a claim such as

$$\sum_{i=0}^{n} i = n(n+1)/2, n \geq 0 \qquad (1.3)$$

by showing that the claim is true for one or more base values of n (generally, $n = 0$ suffices); we assume the claim is true for values of n from 0 through m where m is an arbitrary integer greater than or equal to the largest n covered in the base; and finally using this assumption, we show the claim is true for the next value of n (i.e., $m + 1$). This methodology leads to a proof that has three components—**induction base**, **induction hypothesis**, and **induction step**.

Suppose we are to prove Equation 1.3 by induction on n. In the induction base we establish correctness for $n = 0$. At this time the left side is $\sum_{i=0}^{0} i = 0$, and the right side is also 0. So Equation 1.3 is valid when $n = 0$. In the induction hypothesis we assume the equation is valid for $n \leq m$ where m is an arbitrary integer ≥ 0. (For the ensuing induction step proof, it is sufficient to assume that Equation 1.3 is valid only for $n = m$.) In the induction step we show that the equation is valid for $n = m+1$. For this value of n, the left side is $\sum_{i=0}^{m+1} i$, which equals $m+1+\sum_{i=0}^{m} i$.

From the induction hypothesis we get $\sum_{i=0}^{m} i = m(m+1)/2$. So when $n = m+1$, the left side becomes $m + 1 + m(m+1)/2 = (m+1)(m+2)/2$, which equals the right side.

At first glance, a proof by induction appears to be a circular proof—we establish a result assuming it is correct. However, a proof by induction is not a circular proof for the same reasons that a recursive definition is not circular. A correct proof by induction has an induction base similar to the base component of a recursive definition, and the induction step proves correctness using correctness for smaller values of n. Repeated application of the induction step reduces the proof to one that is solely in terms of the base.

1.15.3   Recursive Methods

Java allows us to write recursive methods. A proper recursive method must include a base component. The recursive component of the method should use smaller values of the method parameters so that repeated invocation of the method results in parameters equal to those included in the base component.

Example 1.1 [Factorial] Program 1.24 gives a Java recursive method that uses Equation 1.1 to compute n!. The base component covers the cases when $n \leq 1$. Consider the invocation `factorial(2)`. To compute `2*factorial(1)` in the `else` statement, the computation of `factorial(2)` is suspended and `factorial` invoked with n = 1. When the computation of `factorial(2)` is suspended, the program state (i.e., values of local variables and value formal parameters, bindings of reference formal parameters, location in code, etc.) is saved in a recursion stack. This state is restored when the computation of `factorial(1)` completes. The invocation `factorial(1)` returns the value 1. The computation of `factorial(2)` resumes, and the expression $2 * 1$ is computed.

```
public static int factorial(int n)
{
   if (n <= 1)
      return 1;
   else
      return n * factorial(n - 1);
}
```

Program 1.24 Recursive method to compute n!

When computing `factorial(3)`, the computation is suspended when the `else` statement is reached so that `factorial(2)` may be computed. We have already seen how the invocation `factorial(2)` works to produce the result 2. When the computation of `factorial(2)` completes, the computation of `factorial(3)` resumes and the expression $3 * 2$ is computed.

Because of the similarity between the code of Program 1.24 and Equation 1.1, the correctness of the code follows from the correctness of the equation. ∎

Example 1.2 The generic method `Sum` (Program 1.25) computes the sum of elements `a[0]` through `a[n-1]` (abbreviated `a[0:n-1]`). When `a.length` is 0, the method returns the value `null`. When `n > a.length`, an `ArrayIndexOutOfBounds-Exception` is thrown by the Java interpreter. Our code of Program 1.25 doesn't bother to catch this or any other exception that might be thrown.

```
public static Computable sum(Computable [] a, int n)
{
    if (a.length == 0) return null;
    Computable sum = (Computable) a[0].zero();
    for (int i = 0; i < n; i++)
        sum.increment(a[i]);
    return sum;
}
```

Program 1.25 Add a[0:n-1]

Program 1.26 is a recursive method to compute the sum of the elements `a[0:n-1]`. The driver method `recursiveSum` verifies that `a.length > 0` and invokes the recursive method `rSum`, which does the actual sum computation. By breaking the code into two methods, we are able to avoid making the check `a.length > 0` more than once. The code for `rSum` results from a recursive formulation of the problem— when `n` is 0, the sum is 0; when `n` is greater than 0, the sum of `n` elements is the sum of the first `n − 1` elements plus the last element. ∎

Example 1.3 [Permutations] Often we wish to examine all permutations of n distinct elements to determine the best one. For example, the permutations of the elements a, b, and c are abc, acb, bac, bca, cba, and cab. The number of permutations of n elements is $n!$.

Although developing a nonrecursive Java method to output all permutations of n elements is quite difficult, we can develop a recursive one with modest effort. Let $E = \{e_1, \cdots, e_n\}$ denote the set of n elements whose permutations are to be generated; let E_i be the set obtained by removing element i from E; let $perm(X)$ denote the permutations of the elements in set X; and let $e_i.perm(X)$ denote the permutation list obtained by prefixing each permutation in $perm(X)$ with element e_i. For example, if $E = \{a, b, c\}$, then $E_1 = \{b, c\}$, $perm(E_1) = (bc, cb)$, and $e_1.perm(E_1) = (abc, acb)$.

```
public static Computable recursiveSum(Computable [] a, int n)
{// Driver for true recursive method rsum.
   if (a.length > 0)
      return rSum(a, n);
   else return null;  // no elements to sum
}


private static Computable rSum(Computable [] a, int n)
{
   if (n == 0) return (Computable) a[0].zero();
   else return (Computable) rSum(a, n - 1).add(a[n-1]);
}
```

Program 1.26 Recursive code to add a[0:n-1]

For the recursion base, we use $n = 1$. Since only one permutation is possible when we have only one element, $perm(E) = (e)$ where e is the lone element in E. When $n > 1$, $perm(E)$ is the list $e_1.perm(E_1)$ followed by $e_2.perm(E_2)$ followed by $e_3.perm(E_3) \cdots$ followed by $e_n.perm(E_n)$. This recursive definition of $perm(E)$ defines $perm(E)$ in terms of n $perm(X)$s, each of which involves an X with $n - 1$ elements. Both the base component and recursive component requirements of a complete recursive definition are satisfied.

When $n = 3$ and $E = (a, b, c)$, the preceding definition of $perm(E)$ yields $perm(E) = a.perm(\{b, c\}), b.perm(\{a, c\}), c.perm(\{b, a\})$. From the recursive definition $perm(\{b, c\})$ is $b.perm(\{c\}), c.perm(\{b\})$. So $a.perm(\{b, c\})$ is $ab.perm(\{c\})$, $ac.perm(\{b\}) = ab.c, ac.b = (abc, acb)$. Proceeding in a similar way, we obtain $b.perm(\{a, c\})$ is $ba.perm(\{c\}), bc.perm(\{a\}) = ba.c, bc.a = (bac, bca)$ and $c.perm(\{b, a\})$ is $cb.perm(\{a\}), ca.perm(\{b\}) = cb.a, ca.b = (cba, cab)$. So $perm(E) = (abc, acb, bac, bca, cba, cab)$.

Notice that $a.perm(\{b, c\})$ is actually the two permutations abc and acb. a is the prefix of these permutations, and $perm(\{b, c\})$ gives their suffixes. Similarly, $ac.perm(\{b\})$ denotes permutations whose prefix is ac and whose suffixes are the permutations $perm(\{b\})$.

Program 1.27 transforms the preceding recursive definition of $perm(E)$ into a Java method. This code outputs all permutations whose prefix is list[0:k-1] and whose suffixes are the permutations of list[k:m]. The invocation Perm(list,0,n-1) outputs all n! permutations of list[0:n-1]. With this invocation, k is 0 and m is n-1. So the prefix of the generated permutations is null, and their suffixes are the permutations of list[0:n-1]. When k equals m, there is only one suffix list[m], and now list[0:m] defines a permutation that is to be output. When k < m, the else clause is executed. Let E denote the elements in list[k:m] and let E_i be the set obtained by removing $e_i = $ list[i] from E. The first swap in the for loop has the effect of setting list[k] $= e_i$ and list[k+1:m] $= E_i$. Therefore, the following call to perm computes $e_i.perm(E_i)$. The second swap restores list[k:m] to its state prior to the first swap.

```
/** perm(x, 0, n) outputs all permutations of x[0:n] */
public static void perm(Object [] list, int k, int m)
{// Generate all permutations of list[k:m].
   int i;
   if (k == m)
   {// list[k:m] has one permutation, output it
      for (i = 0; i <= m; i++)
         System.out.print(list[i]);
      System.out.println();
   }
   else
   // list[k:m] has more than one permutation
   // generate these recursively
      for (i = k; i <= m; i++)
      {
         MyMath.swap(list, k, i);
         perm(list, k+1, m);
         MyMath.swap(list, k, i);
      }
}
```

Program 1.27 Recursive method for permutations

Figure 1.11 shows the progress of Program 1.27 when invoked with k = 0, m = 2, and list[0:2] = [a, b, c]. The figure shows the contents of list[0:2] immediately after each call to perm, as well as immediately after the second swap is done following a return from perm. The unshaded entries denote list[0:k-1], and the shaded entries denote list[k:m]. Configuration numbers are shown outside the array. Each edge of Figure 1.11 is traversed twice during the execution of perm(list, 0, 2): once when a call to perm is made in the for loop and once when a return from perm is made.

We begin with configuration 1. The first swap done in the for loop has no effect on the array; configuration 2 shows the state just after perm is invoked from within the for loop. From configuration 2 we move to configuration 3. Configuration 3 is output because, in this configuration, k = m. Following this output, we make a return and execute the second swap statement in the for loop. As a result, we restore configuration 2. From configuration 2 we move forward to configuration 4,

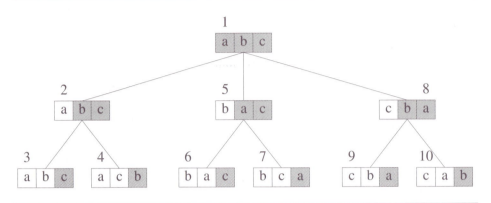

Figure 1.11 Generating the permutations of abc

and the permutation `acb` is output. Then we back up through earlier configurations until we can move forward again. We back up through configurations 2 and 1. From configuration 1 we move forward to configurations 5 and 6. The sequence of configurations encountered in the complete execution is 1, 2, 3, 2, 4, 2, 1, 5, 6, 5, 7, 5, 1, 8, 9, 8, 10, 8, 1. ■

EXERCISES

23. Write a nonrecursive method to compute $n!$. Test your method.

24. (a) Write a recursive method to compute the Fibonacci number F_n. Test your code.

    (b) Show that your code for part (a) computes the same F_i more than once when it is invoked to compute F_n for any $n > 2$.

    (c) Write a nonrecursive method to compute the Fibonacci number F_n. Your code should compute each Fibonacci number just once. Test your code.

25. Consider the function f, which is defined in Equation 1.4. n is a nonnegative integer.

$$f(n) = \begin{cases} n/2 & n \text{ is even} \\ f(3n + 1) & n \text{ is odd} \end{cases} \tag{1.4}$$

    (a) Use Equation 1.4 to manually compute $f(5)$ and $f(7)$.

(b) Identify the base and recursive components of the function definition. Show that repeated application of the recursive component transforms the occurrence of f on the right side to the occurrence of f in the base component.

(c) Write a recursive method to compute $f(n)$. Test your code.

(d) Use your proof for part (b) to arrive at a nonrecursive method to compute f. Your code should have no loops. Test your code.

26. [Ackermann's Function] Equation 1.5 defines Ackermann's function. In this definition, i and j are integers that are $geq 1$.

$$A(i, j) = \begin{cases} 2^j & i = 1 \text{ and } j \geq 1 \\ A(i-1, 2) & i \geq 2 \text{ and } j = 1 \\ A(i-1, A(i, j-1)) & i, j \geq 2 \end{cases} \qquad (1.5)$$

(a) Use Equation 1.5 to manually compute $A(1, 2)$, $A(2, 1)$, and $A(2, 2)$.

(b) Identify the base and recursive components of the function definition.

(c) Write a recursive method to compute $A(i, j)$. Test your code.

27. [GCD] The **greatest common divisor (GCD)** of two nonnegative integers x and y is 0 when exactly one of them is 0. When at least one of x and y is nonzero, their GCD, $gcd(x, y)$, is the greatest integer that evenly divides both. So $gcd(0, 0) = 0$, $gcd(10, 0) = gcd(0, 10) = 10$, and $gcd(20, 30) = 10$. Euclid's GCD algorithm is a recursive algorithm that is believed to date back to 375 B.C.; it is perhaps the earliest example of a recursive algorithm. Euclid's algorithm implements the recursive definition given in Equation 1.6.

$$gcd(x, y) = \begin{cases} x & y = 0 \\ gcd(y, x \bmod y) & y > 0 \end{cases} \qquad (1.6)$$

In Equation 1.6 **mod** is the modulo operator that is implemented in Java as the operator %. $x \bmod y$ is the remainder of x/y.

(a) Use Equation 1.6 to manually compute $gcd(20, 30)$ and $gcd(112, 42)$.

(b) Identify the base and recursive components of the function definition. Show that repeated application of the recursive component transforms the occurrence of gcd on the right side to the occurrence of gcd in the base component.

(c) Write a recursive method to compute $gcd(x, y)$. Test your code.

28. Write a generic recursive method to determine whether element x is one of the elements in the array `a[0:n-1]`.

29. [Subset Generation] Write a generic recursive method to output all subsets of n elements. For example, the subsets of the three-element set $\{a, b, c\}$ are $\{\}$ (empty set), $\{a\}$, $\{b\}$, $\{c\}$, $\{a, b\}$, $\{a, c\}$, $\{b, c\}$, and $\{a, b, c\}$. These subsets may be denoted by the 0/1 vector sequence 000, 100, 010, 001, 110, 101, 011, and 111, respectively (a 0 means that the corresponding element is not in the subset, and a 1 means that it is). So it is sufficient that your method output all 0/1 sequences of length n.

30. [Gray Code] The **Hamming distance** between two vectors is the number of positions in which the vectors differ. For example, the Hamming distance between 100 and 010 is 2. A (binary) Gray code is a subset sequence in which the Hamming distance between every pair of consecutive vectors (also called codes) is 1. The three-element subset sequence given in Exercise 29 is not a Gray code. However, the three-element subset sequence 000, 100, 110, 010, 011, 111, 101, 100 is a Gray code. This sequence also has the property that the first and last vectors differ in exactly one place. In some applications of subset sequences, the cost of going from one subset to the next depends on the Hamming distance between these two subsets. In these applications, we desire a subset sequence that is a Gray code. A Gray code may be compactly represented by giving the sequence of positions in which the vectors of the code change. For the three-element Gray code given above, the position change sequence is 1, 2, 1, 3, 1, 2, 1. Let $g(n)$ be the position change sequence for a Gray code for n elements. Equation 1.7 gives a recursive definition for $g(n)$.

$$g(n) = \begin{cases} 1 & n = 1 \\ g(n-1), n, g(n-1) & n > 1 \end{cases} \qquad (1.7)$$

(a) Use Equation 1.6 to manually compute $g(4)$.

(b) Identify the base and recursive components of the function definition. Show that repeated application of the recursive component transforms both occurrences of g on the right side to the occurrence of g in the base component.

(c) Write a recursive method to compute $g(n)$. Test your code.

1.16   TESTING AND DEBUGGING

1.16.1   What Is Testing?

As indicated in Section 1.1, correctness is the most important attribute of a program. Because providing a mathematically rigorous proof of correctness for even a small program is quite difficult, we resort to a process called **program testing** in which we execute the program on the target computer using input data, called **test data**, and compare the program's behavior with the expected behavior. If these two behaviors are different, we have a problem with the program. Unfortunately, however, even if the two behaviors are the same, we cannot conclude that the program is correct, as the two behaviors may not be the same on other input data. By using many sets of input data and verifying that the observed and expected behaviors are the same, we can increase our confidence in the correctness of the program. By using all possible input data, we can verify that the program is correct. However, for most practical programs, the number of possible input data is too large to perform such exhaustive testing. The subset of the input data space that is actually used for testing is called the **test set**.

Example 1.4 [Quadratic Roots] A **quadratic function** (or simply a **quadratic**) in x is a function that has the form

$$ax^2 + bx + c$$

where the values of a, b, and c are real numbers and $a \neq 0$. $3x^2 - 2x + 4$, $-9x^2 - 7x$, $3.5x^2 + 4$, and $5.8x^2 + 3.2x + 5$ are examples of quadratic functions. $5x + 3$ is not a quadratic function.

The **roots** of a quadratic function are the values of x at which the function value is 0. For example, the roots of $f(x) = x^2 - 5x + 6$ are 2 and 3, as $f(2) = f(3) = 0$. Every quadratic has exactly two roots, and these roots are given by the formula:

$$\frac{-b \pm \sqrt{b^2 - 4ac}}{2a}$$

For the function $f(x) = x^2 - 5x + 6$, $a = 1$, $b = -5$, and $c = 6$. Substituting these into the above formula, we get

$$\frac{5 \pm \sqrt{25 - 4 * 1 * 6}}{2} = \frac{5 \pm 1}{2}$$

So the roots of $f(x)$ are $x = 3$ and $x = 1$.

When $d = b^2 - 4ac = 0$, the two roots are the same; when $d > 0$, the two roots are different and real numbers; and when $d < 0$, the two roots are different and complex numbers. In this last case each root has a *real* part and an *imaginary* part.

```
public static void outputRoots(double a, double b, double c)
{
   if (a == 0)
      throw new IllegalArgumentException
               ("Coefficient of x^2 must be nonzero");

   double d = b * b - 4 * a * c;
   if (d > 0) {// two real roots
               double sqrtd = Math.sqrt(d);
               System.out.println
               ("There are two real roots " +
               (-b + sqrtd) / (2 * a) + " and " +
               (-b - sqrtd) / (2 * a));
               }
   else if (d == 0)
            // both roots are the same
            System.out.println
            ("There is only one distinct root " + -b / (2 * a));
         else {//  complex conjugate roots
            System.out.println("The roots are complex");
            System.out.println("The real part is " + -b / (2 * a));
            System.out.println("The imaginary part is " +
               Math.sqrt(-d) / (2 * a));
            }
}
```

Program 1.28 Compute and output the roots of the quadratic $ax^2 + bx + c$

The real part is $real = -b/(2a)$, and the imaginary part is $imag = \sqrt{-d}/(2a)$. The complex roots are $real + imag * i$ and $real - imag * i$ where $i = \sqrt{-1}$.

The method `outputRoots` (Program 1.28) computes and outputs the roots of a quadratic. We shall not attempt a formal correctness proof for this method. Rather, we wish to establish correctness by testing. The number of possible inputs is the number of different triples (a, b, c) with $a \neq 0$. Even if we restrict a, b, and c to 16-bit nonnegative integers, the number of possible input triples is too large for us to test the program on all inputs. With 16 bits per integer, there are 2^{16} different values for b and c and $2^{16} - 1$ for a (recall that a cannot be 0). The number of different triples is $2^{32}(2^{16} - 1)$. If our target computer can test at the rate of 1,000,000 triples per second, it would take almost 9 years to complete! A faster computer executing at the rate of 1,000,000,000 triples per second would take almost 3 days. So a practical test set can contain only a small subset of the entire space of input data.

If we run the program using the data set $(a, b, c) = (1, -5, 6)$, the roots 2 and 3 are output. The program behavior agrees with the expected behavior, and we conclude that the program is correct for this input. However, verifying agreement between observed and expected behavior on a proper subset of the possible inputs does not prove that the program works correctly on all inputs.   ■

Since the number of different inputs that can be provided to a program is generally very large, testing is often limited to a very small subset of the possible inputs. Testing with this subset cannot conclusively establish the correctness of the program. As a result, *the objective of testing is not to establish correctness, but to expose the presence of errors.* The test set must be chosen so as to expose any errors that may be present in the program. Different test sets can expose different errors in a program.

Example 1.5 The test data $(a, b, c) = (1, -5, 6)$ causes `outputRoots` to execute the code for the case when there are two real roots. If the roots 2 and 3 are output, we can have some confidence that the statements executed during this test are correct. Notice that an erroneous code could still give the correct results. For example, if we omitted the `a` from the expression for `d` and mistakenly typed

```
double d = b * b - 4 * c;
```

the value of `d` is the same for our test data because `a` $= 1$. Since the test data $(1, -5, 6)$ did not execute all statements of the code, we have less confidence in the correctness of the statements that are not executed.

The test set $\{(1, -5, 6), (1, 3, 2), (2, 5, 2)\}$ can expose errors only in the first seven lines of `outputRoots`, as each triple in this test set executes only these seven lines of code. However, the test set $\{(1, -5, 6), (1, -8, 16), (1, 2, 5)\}$ causes all statements of `outputRoots` to execute and so has a better chance of exposing the errors in the code.   ■

1.16.2   Designing Test Data

When developing test data, we should keep in mind that the objective of testing is to expose the presence of errors. If data designed to expose errors fails to expose any errors, then we may have confidence in the correctness of the program. To tell whether or not a program malfunctions on given test data, we must be able to verify the correctness of the program behavior on the test data.

Example 1.6 For our quadratic roots example, the behavior on any test data may be verified in one of two ways. First, we might know the roots of the test quadratic. For example, the roots of the quadratic with $(a, b, c) = (1, -5, 6)$ are 2 and 3. We can verify the correctness of Program 1.28 on the test data $(1, -5, 6)$ by comparing the output roots with the correct roots 2 and 3. Another possibility is to substitute

the roots produced by the program into the quadratic function and verify that the function value is 0. So if our program outputs 2 and 3 as the roots, we compute $f(2) = 2^2 - 5 * 2 + 6 = 0$ and $f(3) = 3^2 - 5 * 3 + 6 = 0$. We can implement these verification methods as computer programs. In the first the test program inputs the triple (a, b, c) as well as the expected roots and then checks the computed roots against the expected ones. For the second method we write code to evaluate the quadratic at the computed roots and verify that the result is 0.   ■

We can evaluate any candidate test data using the following criteria:

- What is these data's potential to expose errors?

- Can we verify the correctness of the program behavior on this data?

Techniques for test data development fall into two categories: black box methods and white box methods. In a **black box method**, we consider the program's function, not the actual code, when we develop test data. In a **white box method**, we examine the code in an attempt to develop test data whose execution results in a good coverage of the program's statements and execution paths.

Black Box Methods

The most popular black box methods are I/O partitioning and cause-effect graphing. This section elaborates on the I/O partitioning method only. In this method we partition the input and/or output data space into classes. The data in different classes cause the program to exhibit qualitatively different behaviors, while data in the same class cause qualitatively similar behaviors. The quadratic roots example has three different qualitiative behaviors: the roots are complex, the roots are real and distinct, and the roots are real and the same. We can use these three behaviors to partition the input space into three classes. Data in the first class cause the first kind of behavior; data in the second cause the second kind of behavior; and data in the third cause the third kind of behavior. A test set should include at least one input from each class.

White Box Methods

White box methods create test data based on an examination of the code to be generated. The weakest condition we can place on a test set is that it results in each program statement being executed at least once. This condition is called **statement coverage**. For our quadratic roots example, the test set $\{(0,1,2), (1,-5,6), (1,-8,16), (1,2,5)\}$ causes all statements in Program 1.28 to execute. So this test set provides statement coverage. The test set $\{(0, 1, 2), (1,-5,6), (1,3,2), (2,5,2)\}$ does not provide statement coverage.

In **decision coverage** we require the test set to cause each conditional in the program to take on both true and false values. The code of Program 1.28 has three conditionals: a == 0, d > 0, and d == 0. In decision coverage we require at least one set of test data for which a == 0.0 is true and at least one for which it is false. We also require at least one test data for which d > 0 is true and at least one for which it is false; there should also be at least one set of test data for which d == 0 is true and at least one for which it is false.

Example 1.7 [Maximum Element] Program 1.29 returns the position of the largest element in the array a[0:n]. The program finds this position by scanning the array from positions 0 to n, using variable positionOfCurrentMax to keep track of the position of the largest element seen so far. The data set {(a,-1), (a,4)} with a[0:4] = [2, 4, 6, 8, 9] provides statement coverage, but not decision coverage, as the condition a[positionOfCurrentMax].compareTo(a[i]) < 0 never becomes false. When a[0:4] = [4, 2, 6, 8, 9]}, we get both decision and statement coverage.

■

```
public static int max(Comparable [] a, int n)
{
    if (n < 0)
        throw new IllegalArgumentException
            ("MyMath.max: Cannot find max of zero elements ");

    int positionOfCurrentMax = 0;
    for (int i = 1; i <= n; i++)
        if (a[positionOfCurrentMax].compareTo(a[i]) < 0)
            positionOfCurrentMax = i;
    return positionOfCurrentMax;
}
```

Program 1.29 Finding the position of the largest element in a[0:n]

We can strengthen the decision coverage criterion to require each clause of each conditional to take on both true and false values. This strengthened criterion is called **clause coverage**. A **clause** is formally defined to be a Boolean expression that contains no Boolean operator (i.e., &&, ||, !). The expressions $x > y$, $x + y < y * z$, and c (where c is of type Boolean) are examples of clauses. Consider the statement

```
if ((C1 && C2) || (C3 && C4)) S1;
else S2;
```

where C1, C2, C3, and C4 are clauses and S1 and S2 are statements. Under the decision coverage criterion, we need to use one test set that causes ((C1 && C2) || (C3 && C4)) to be true and another that results in this conditional being false.

Clause coverage requires us to use a test set that causes each of the four clauses C1 through C4 to evaluate to true at least once and to false at least once.

We can further strengthen clause coverage to require testing for all combinations of clause values. In the case of the conditional ((C1 && C2)||(C3 && C4)), this strengthening requires the use of 16 sets of test data: one for each truth combination of the four conditions. However, several of these combinations may not be possible.

If we sequence the statements of a program in their order of execution by a certain set of test data, we get an execution path. Different test data may yield different execution paths. Program 1.28 has only four execution paths—lines 1 through 3 (lines are numbered beginning with the line if (a == 0.0), blank lines are not numbered); 1, 4 through 10; lines 1, 4, 5, 11 through 14; and lines 1, 4, 5, 11, 15 through 20. The number of execution paths of Program 1.29 grows as n increases. When $n < 0$, there is just one execution path—1, 2, 3; when $n = 0$, there is again just one path—lines 1, 4, 5, 8; when $n = 1$, there are two paths—lines 1, 4, 5, 6, 5, 8 and 1, 4, 5, 6, 7, 5, 8; and when $n = 2$, there are four paths—1, 4, 5, 6, 5, 6, 5, 8; 1, 4, 5, 6, 7, 5, 6, 5, 8; 1, 4, 5, 6, 5, 6, 7, 5, 8; and 1, 4, 5, 6, 7, 5, 6, 7, 5, 8. For a general n, $n \geq 0$, the number of execution paths is 2^n.

Execution path coverage requires the use of a test set that causes all execution paths to be executed. For the quadratic roots code, statement coverage, decision coverage, clause coverage, and execution path coverage are equivalent requirements. But for Program 1.29, statement coverage, decision coverage, and execution path coverage are different, and decision and clause coverage are equivalent.

Of the white box coverage criteria we have discussed, execution path coverage is generally the most demanding. A test set that results in total execution path coverage also results in statement and decision coverage. It may, however, not result in clause coverage. Total execution path coverage often requires an infinite number of test data or at least a prohibitively large number of test data. Hence total path coverage is often impossible in practice.

Many exercises in this book ask you to test the correctness of your codes. The test data you use should at least provide statement coverage. Additionally, you should test for special cases that could cause your program to malfunction. For example, a program designed to sort $n \geq 0$ elements should be tested with $n = 0$ and 1 in addition to other values of n. If such a program uses an array a[0:99], it should also be tested with $n = 100$. $n = 0$, 1, and 100 represent the boundary conditions empty, singleton, and full.

1.16.3   Debugging

Testing exposes the presence of errors in a program. Once a test run produces a result different from the one expected, we know that something is wrong with the program. The process of determining and correcting the cause of the discrepancy between the desired and observed behaviors is called **debugging**. Although a thorough study of debugging methods is beyond the scope of this book, we do provide some suggestions for debugging.

- Try to determine the cause of an error by logical reasoning. If this method fails, then you may wish to perform a program trace (using a debugger such as jdb; see the Web site) to determine when the program started performing incorrectly. This approach becomes infeasible when the program executes many instructions with that test data and the program trace becomes too long to examine manually. In this case you must try to isolate the part of the code that is suspect and obtain a trace of this part.

- Do not attempt to correct errors by creating special cases. The number of special cases will soon become very large, and your code will look like a dish of spaghetti. Errors should be corrected by first determining their cause and then redesigning your solution as necessary.

- When correcting an error, be certain that your correction does not result in errors where there were none before. Run your corrected program on the test data on which it originally worked correctly to ensure that it still works correctly on these data.

- When testing and debugging a multimethod program, begin with a single method that is independent of the others. This method would typically be an input or output method. Then introduce additional methods one at a time, testing and debugging the larger program for correctness. This strategy is called **incremental testing and debugging**. When this strategy is used, the cause of a detected error can reasonably be expected to lie in the most recently introduced method.

EXERCISES

31. Show that test sets that provide statement coverage for Program 1.28 also provide decision and execution path coverage.

32. Develop a test set for Program 1.29 that provides execution path coverage for the for loop when n = 3.

33. How many execution paths are in Program 1.25?

34. How many execution paths are in method rSum of Program 1.26?

1.17   REFERENCES AND SELECTED READINGS

A good introduction to programming in Java can be found in the texts *Java Gently* by J. Bishop, Second Edition, Addison-Wesley, Menlo Park, CA, 1998 and *The Java Programming Language* by K. Arnold and J. Gosling, Addison-Wesley, Menlo Park,

CA, 1998. *Java in a Nutshell*, by D. Flanagan, O'Reilly & Associates, Cambridge, MA, is a good Java reference.

You can download Java documentation as well as the latest Java compiler from `http://www.javasoft.com:80/products/jdk`, and you can use SUN's JDK through Windows95/98/NT by downloading a program such as Kawa from `http://www.tek-tools.com/kawa`. Online Java tutorials are available from `http://www.sun.com/docs/books`.

To learn more about Java microprocessors, see the paper "PicoJava: A Direct Execution Engine for Java Bytecode" by H. McGhan and M. O'Conner, *IEEE Computer*, October 1998, 22–30.

The Art of Software Testing by G. Myers, John Wiley, New York, NY, 1979 and *Software Testing Techniques* by B. Beizer, Second Edition, Van Nostrand Reinhold, New York, NY, 1990 have more thorough treatments of software testing and debugging techniques.

CHAPTER 2

PERFORMANCE ANALYSIS

BIRD'S-EYE VIEW

The most important attribute of a program is correctness. A program that does not correctly perform the task it was designed to do is of little use. However, correct programs may also be of little use. This is the case, for example, when a correct program takes more memory than is available on the computer it is to run on as well as when a correct program takes more time than the user is willing to wait. We use the term *program performance* to refer to the memory and time requirements of a program. To appreciate the need for good data structures and algorithm design methods, you must be able to evaluate the performance of a program.

This chapter focuses on paper-and-pencil methods to determine the memory and time requirements of a program. The operation count and step-count approaches to estimate run time are developed, and the notions of best-case, worst-case, and average run time are introduced. A more advanced measure of run time—amortized complexity—is developed in the Web site for this book. You should not attempt to read the material on amortized complexity until you have completed Chapter 10.

Chapter 3 reviews asymptotic notations such as big oh, omega, theta, and little oh, which make up the lingua franca for performance analysis. The use of asymptotic notation often simplifies the analysis. Chapter 4 shows you how to measure the actual run time of a program by using a clocking method.

65

Many application codes are developed in this chapter. These applications, which will prove useful in later chapters, include

- Searching an array of elements for an element with a specified characteristic.

- Sorting an array of elements. Codes for the rank (or count) sort, selection sort, bubble sort, and insertion sort methods are developed.

- Evaluating a polynomial using Horner's rule.

- Performing matrix operations such as add, transpose, and multiply.

2.1   WHAT IS PERFORMANCE?

By the **performance of a program**, we mean the amount of computer memory and time needed to run a program. We use two approaches to determine the performance of a program. One is analytical, and the other experimental. In **performance analysis** we use analytical methods, while in **performance measurement** we conduct experiments.

The **space complexity** of a program is the amount of memory it needs to run to completion. We are interested in the space complexity of a program for the following reasons:

- If the program is to be run on a multiuser computer system, then we may need to specify the amount of memory to be allocated to the program.

- For any computer system, we would like to know in advance whether or not sufficient memory is available to run the program.

- A problem might have several possible solutions with different space requirements. For instance, one Java compiler for your computer might need only 1 MB of memory, while another might need 4 MB. The 1 MB compiler is the only choice if your computer has less than 4 MB of memory. Even users whose computers have the extra memory will prefer the smaller compiler if its capabilities are comparable to those of the bigger compiler. The smaller compiler leaves the user with more memory for other tasks.

- We can use the space complexity to estimate the size of the largest problem that a program can solve. For example, we may have a circuit simulation program that requires $10^6 + 100(c + w)$ bytes of memory to simulate circuits with c components and w wires. If the total amount of memory available is $4 * 10^6$ bytes, then we can simulate circuits with $c + w \leq 30,000$.

The **time complexity** of a program is the amount of computer time it needs to run to completion. We are interested in the time complexity of a program for the following reasons:

- Some computer systems require the user to provide an upper limit on the amount of time the program will run. Once this upper limit is reached, the program is aborted. An easy way out is to simply specify a time limit of a few thousand years. However, this solution could result in serious fiscal problems if the program runs into an infinite loop caused by some discrepancy in the data and you actually get billed for the computer time used. We would like to provide a time limit that is just slightly above the expected run time.

- The program we are developing might need to provide a satisfactory real-time response. For example, all interactive programs must provide such a response. A text editor that takes a minute to move the cursor one page down or one page up will not be acceptable to many users. A spreadsheet program that takes several minutes to reevaluate the cells in a sheet will be satisfactory only to very patient users. A database management system that allows its users adequate time to drink two cups of coffee while it is sorting a relation will not find too much acceptance. Programs designed for interactive use must provide satisfactory real-time response. From the time complexity of the program or program module, we can decide whether or not the response time will be acceptable. If not, we need to either redesign the algorithm or give the user a faster computer.

- If we have alternative ways to solve a problem, then the decision on which to use will be based primarily on the expected performance difference among these solutions. We will use some weighted measure of the space and time complexities of the alternative solutions.

EXERCISES

1. Give two more reasons why analysts are interested in the space complexity of a program.

2. Give two more reasons why analysts are interested in the time complexity of a program.

2.2   SPACE COMPLEXITY

2.2.1   Components of Space Complexity

The space needed by a program has the following components:

- *Instruction space*
  Instruction space is the space needed to store the compiled version of the program instructions.

- *Data space*
  Data space is the space needed to store all constant and variable values. Data space has two components:

  1. Space needed by constants (for example, the numbers 0 and 1 in Programs 1.24 and 1.25) and simple variables (such as a, b, and c in Program 1.2).

  2. Space needed by dynamically allocated objects such as arrays and class instances.

- *Environment stack space*

  The environment stack is used to save information needed to resume execution of partially completed methods. For example, if method `fun1` invokes method `fun2`, then we must at least save a pointer to the instruction of `fun1` to be executed when `fun2` terminates.

Instruction Space

The amount of instruction space that is needed depends on factors such as

- The compiler used to compile the program into machine code.

- The compiler options in effect at the time of compilation.

- The target computer.

The compiler is a very important factor in determining how much space the resulting code needs. Figure 2.1 shows three possible codes for the evaluation of `a+b+b*c+(a+b-c)/(a+b)+4`. These codes need a different amount of space, and the compiler in use determines exactly which code will be generated.

Even with the same compiler, the size of the generated program code can vary. For example, a compiler might provide the user with optimization options. These could include code-size optimization as well as execution-time optimization. In Figure 2.1, for instance, the compiler might generate the code of Figure 2.1(b) in nonoptimization mode. In optimization mode, the compiler might use the knowledge that `a+b+b*c = b*c+(a+b)` and generate the shorter and more time-efficient code of Figure 2.1(c). The use of the optimization mode will generally increase the time needed to compile the program.

The example of Figure 2.1 brings to light an additional contribution to the space requirements of a program. Space is needed for temporary variables such as `t1`, `t2`, $\cdots$, `t6`.

Another option that can have a significant effect on program space is the overlay option in which space is assigned only to the program module that is currently executing. When a new module is invoked, it is read in from a disk or other device, and the code for the new module overwrites the code of the old module. So program space corresponding to the size of the largest module (rather than the sum of the module sizes) is needed.

Since Java programs are compiled into code for the Java Virtual Machine, the target computer configuration does not affect the code size. However, when a JIT compiler is used, some or all classes are compiled into code for the target machine. The configuration of the target computer can affect the size of the compiled code. If the computer has floating-point hardware, then floating-point operations will translate into one machine instruction per operation. If this hardware is not installed, then code to simulate floating-point computations will be generated.

```
        LOAD   a            LOAD   a            LOAD   a
        ADD    b            ADD    b            ADD    b
        STORE t1            STORE t1            STORE t1
        LOAD   b            SUB    c            SUB    c
        MULT   c            DIV    t1           DIV    t1
        STORE t2            STORE t2            STORE t2
        LOAD   t1           LOAD   b            LOAD   b
        ADD    t2           MUL    c            MUL    c
        STORE t3            STORE t3            ADD    t2
        LOAD   a            LOAD   t1           ADD    t1
        ADD    b            ADD    t3           ADD    4
        SUB    c            ADD    t2
        STORE t4            ADD    4
        LOAD   a
        ADD    b
        STORE t5
        LOAD   t4
        DIV    t5
        STORE t6
        LOAD   t3
        ADD    t6
        ADD    4
          (a)                (b)                (c)
```

Figure 2.1 Three equivalent codes

Data Space

The Java language specifies the space allocated for simple variables and constants (see Figure 1.4). We can obtain the space requirement of an array by multiplying the array size and the space needs of a single array element.

Consider the following array declarations:

```
double[] a = new double [100];
int[][] maze = new int [rows][cols];
```

When computing the space allocated to an array, we shall be concerned only with the space allocated for the array elements. Therefore, we ignore the space allocated to store the array size, type, and so on. The array a has space for 100 elements of type double, each taking 8 bytes (1 byte = 8 bits). The total space allocated to the array is therefore 800 bytes. The array maze has space for rows*cols elements of type int. The total space taken by this array is 4*rows*cols bytes.

Environment Stack

Beginning performance analysts often ignore the space needed by the environment stack because they don't understand how methods (and in particular recursive ones) are invoked and what happens on termination. Each time a method is invoked the following data are saved on the environment stack:

- The return address.

- The values of all local variables and formal parameters in the method being invoked (necessary for recursive methods only).

Each time the recursive method rSum (Program 1.26) is invoked, whether from recursiveSum or from the else clause of rSum, the current values of a and n and the program location to return to on completion are saved in the environment stack.

It is worth noting that some compilers may save the values of the local variables and formal parameters for both recursive and nonrecursive methods, while others may do so for recursive methods alone. So the compiler in use will affect the amount of space needed by the environment stack.

Summary

The space needed by a program depends on several factors. Some of these factors are not known at the time the program is conceived or written (e.g., the computer or the compiler that will be used). Until these factors have been determined, we cannot make an accurate analysis of the space requirements of a program.

We can, however, determine the contribution of those components that depend on characteristics of the problem instance to be solved. These characteristics typically include factors that determine the size of the problem instance (e.g., the number of inputs and outputs or magnitude of the numbers involved) being solved. For example, if we have a program that sorts n elements, we can determine space requirements as a function of n. For a program that adds two $n \times n$ matrices, we may use n as the instance characteristic, and for one that adds two $m \times n$ matrices, we may use m and n as the instance characteristics.

The size of the instruction space is relatively insensitive to the particular problem instance being solved. The contribution of the constants and simple variables to the data space is also independent of the characteristics of the problem instance to be solved except when the magnitude of the numbers involved becomes too large for the chosen data type. At this time we will need to either change the data type or rewrite the program using multiprecision arithmetic and then analyze the new program.

The space needed by some of the dynamically allocated memory may also be independent of the problem size. The environment stack space is generally independent of the instance characteristics unless recursive methods are in use. When recursive methods are in use, the instance characteristics will generally (but not always) affect the amount of space needed for the environment stack.

The amount of stack space needed by recursive methods is called the **recursion stack space**. For each recursive method this space depends on the space needed by the local variables and the formal parameters, the maximum depth of recursion (i.e., the maximum number of nested recursive calls), and the compiler being used. For Program 1.26 recursive calls get nested until n equals 0. At this time the nesting resembles Figure 2.2. The maximum depth of recursion for this program is therefore n+1. A smart compiler would replace a recursive call that is the last statement of a method (known as tail recursion) by equivalent iterative code. This technique could reduce, even eliminate, the recursion stack space.

```
rSum(a,n)
    rSum(a,n-1)
        rSum(a,n-2)
              .
              .
              .
        rSum(a,1)
            rSum(a,0)
```

Figure 2.2 Nesting of recursive calls for Program 1.26.

We can divide the total space needed by a program into two parts:

- A fixed part that is independent of the instance characteristics. This part typically includes the instruction space (i.e., space for the code), space for simple variables, space for constants, and so on.

- A variable part that consists of the dynamically allocated space (to the extent that this space depends on the instance characteristics); and the recursion stack space (insofar as this space depends on the instance characteristics).

The space requirement of any program P may therefore be written as

$$c + S_P(\text{instance characteristics})$$

where c is a constant that denotes the fixed part of the space requirements and S_P denotes the variable component. An accurate analysis should also include the space needed by temporary variables generated during compilation (refer to Figure 2.1). This space is compiler dependent and, except in the case of recursive methods, independent of the instance characteristics. We will ignore the space needs of these compiler-generated variables.

When analyzing the space complexity of a program, we will concentrate solely on estimating S_P (instance characteristics). For any given problem we need to first determine which instance characteristics to use to measure the space requirements. The choice of instance characteristics is very problem specific, and we will resort to examples to illustrate the various possibilities. Generally speaking, our choices are limited to quantities related to the number and magnitude of the inputs to and outputs from the program. At times we also use more complex measures of the interrelationships among the data items.

2.2.2 Examples

Example 2.1 Consider Program 1.2. Before we can determine S_P, we must select the instance characteristics to be used for the analysis. Suppose we use the magnitudes of a, b, and c as the instance characteristic. Since a, b, and c are of type int, 4 bytes are allocated to each of the formal parameters. In addition, space is needed for the code. Neither the data space nor the instruction space is affected by the magnitudes of a, b, and c. Therefore, S_{abc}(instance characteristics) = 0. ∎

Example 2.2 [Sequential Search] Program 2.1 examines the elements of the array a from left to right to see whether one of these elements equals x. If an element equal to x is found, the method returns the position of the first occurrence of x. If the array has no element equal to x, the method of Program 2.1 returns −1. For Program 2.1 to work correctly, you must override the method java.lang.equals, which simply compares two object references for equality. The overriding method must compare the objects rather than the references to the objects.

```
/** Search the unordered array a for x.
  * CAUTION: Object.equals must be overriden for this
  * method to work correctly
  * @return position of x if found; -1 otherwise */
public static int sequentialSearch(Object [] a, Object x)
{
   int i;
   for (i = 0; i < a.length && !x.equals(a[i]); i++);
   if (i == a.length) return -1;
   else return i;
}
```

Program 2.1 Sequential search

We wish to obtain the space complexity of Program 2.1 in terms of the instance characteristic a.length. Although we need space for the formal parameters a and x, the constants 0 and −1, and the code, the space needed is independent of a.length. Therefore, $S_{sequentialSearch}$(a.length) = 0.

Note that the array a must be large enough to hold the a.length elements being searched. The space needed by this array (4*a.length bytes for the Object references plus the space for the a.length objects) is, however, allocated in the method where the actual parameter corresponding to a is declared and initialized. As a result, we do not add the space requirements of this array into the space requirements of the method sequentialSearch. ■

Example 2.3 For method sum (Program 1.25), suppose we are interested in measuring space requirements as a function of the number of elements to be summed. Space is required for the formal parameters a and n, the local variables i and sum, the constant 0, and the instructions. The amount of space needed does not depend on the value of n, so $S_{sum}(n) = 0$. ■

Example 2.4 Consider the method rSum (Program 1.26). As in the case of sum, assume that the instances are characterized by n. Further, assume that $0 \le n <$ a.length. The recursion stack space includes space for the formal parameters a and n and the return address. In the case of a, a reference (4 bytes) is saved, while in the case of n, a value of type int (also 4 bytes) is saved on the recursion stack. If we assume that the return address also takes 4 bytes, we determine that each call to rSum requires 12 bytes of recursion stack space. Since the depth of recursion is n+1, the recursion stack space needed is 12(n+1) bytes. So $S_{rSum}(n) = 12(n+1)$.
     Program 1.25 has a smaller space requirement than does Program 1.26. ■

Example 2.5 [Factorial] The space complexity of Program 1.24, which computes the factorial function, is analyzed as a function of n rather than as a function of the number of inputs (one) or outputs (one). The recursion depth is max{n,1}. The recursion stack saves a return address (4 bytes) and the value of n (4 bytes) each time factorial is invoked. No additional space that is dependent on n is used, so $S_{factorial}(n) = 8 * \max\{n,1\}$. ■

Example 2.6 [Permutations] Program 1.27 outputs all permutations of a list of elements. With the initial invocation perm(list,0,n-1), the depth of recursion is n. Since each recursive call requires 20 bytes of recursion stack space (4 for each of return address, list, k, m, and i), the recursion stack space needed is 20n bytes, so $S_{perm}(n) = 20n$. ■

EXERCISES

3. Compile a sample Java program using two Java compilers. Is the code length (the length of the generated .class file) the same or different?

4. List additional factors that may influence the space complexity of a program.

5. Using the data provided in Figure 1.4, determine the number of bytes needed by the following arrays:

   (a) `double y[3]`
   (b) `int matrix[10][100]`
   (c) `double x[100][5][20]`
   (d) `float z[10][10][10][5]`
   (e) `boolean a[2][3][4]`
   (f) `long b[3][3][3][3]`

6. Program 2.2 gives a recursive method `rSearch` that searches the elements of the array `a[0:lastPosition]` for the element `x`. If `x` is found, the method returns the position of `x` in `a`. Otherwise, the method returns -1. Determine $S_P(n)$, where $n = $ `lastPosition+1`.

```
/** Recursively search a[0:lastPosition] for x.
 * CAUTION: Object.equals must be overriden for this
 * method to work correctly */
private static int rSearch(int lastPosition)
{
   if (lastPosition < 0)
      return -1;
   if (x.equals(a[lastPosition]))
      return lastPosition;
   return rSearch(lastPosition - 1);
}
```

Program 2.2 Recursive sequential search method

7. Write a nonrecursive method to compute $n!$ (see Example 1.1). Compare the space requirments of your nonrecursive method and those of the recursive version (Program 1.24).

2.3   TIME COMPLEXITY

2.3.1   Components of Time Complexity

The time complexity of a program depends on all the factors that the space complexity depends on. A program will run faster on a computer capable of executing

10^9 instructions per second than on one that can execute only 10^7 instructions per second. The code of Figure 2.1(c) will require less execution time than the code of Figure 2.1(a). Some compilers will take less time than others to generate the corresponding computer code. Smaller problem instances will generally take less time than larger instances.

The time taken by a program P is the sum of the compile time and the run (or execution) time. The compile time does not depend on the instance characteristics. Also, we can assume that a compiled program will be run several times without recompilation. Consequently, we will concern ourselves with just the run time of a program. This run time is denoted by t_P(instance characteristics).

Because many of the factors t_P depends on are not known when a program is conceived, it is reasonable to only estimate t_P. If we knew the characteristics of the compiler to be used, we could determine the number of additions, subtractions, multiplications, divisions, compares, loads, stores, and so on that the code for P would make. Then we could obtain a formula for t_P. Letting n denote the instance characteristics, we might have an expression for $t_P(n)$ of the form

$$t_P(n) = c_a ADD(n) + c_s SUB(n) + c_m MUL(n) + c_d DIV(n) + \cdots \qquad (2.1)$$

where c_a, c_s, c_m, and c_d respectively denote the time needed for an addition, subtraction, multiplication, and division, and ADD, SUB, MUL, and DIV are functions whose value is the number of additions, subtractions, multiplications, and divisions that will be performed when the code for P is used on an instance with characteristic n. To determine the operation times (i.e., c_a, c_s, etc.), we would need to know whether a JIT compiler will be used just prior to code execution or whether the code will be run interpretively on the JVM.

The fact that the time needed for an arithmetic operation depends on the type (int, float, double, etc.) of the numbers in the operation makes obtaining such an exact formula more cumbersome. So we must separate the operation counts by data type.

Fine-tuning Equation 2.1 as described above still does not give us an accurate formula to predict run time because today's computers do not necessarily perform arithmetic operations in sequence. For example, computers can perform an integer operation and a floating-point operation at the same time. Further, the capability to pipeline arithmetic operations and the fact that modern computers have a memory hierarchy (Section 4.5) means that the time to perform m additions isn't necessarily m times the time to perform 1.

Since the analytical approach to determine the run time of a program is fraught with complications, we attempt only to estimate run time. Two more manageable approaches to estimating run time are (1) identify one or more key operations and determine the number of times these are performed and (2) determine the total number of steps executed by the program.

2.3.2 Operation Counts

One way to estimate the time complexity of a program or method is to select one or more operations, such as add, multiply, and compare, and to determine how many of each is done. The success of this method depends on our ability to identify the operations that contribute most to the time complexity. Several examples of this method follow.

Example 2.7 [Max Element] Program 1.29 returns the position of the largest element in the array `a[0:n]`. When $n \geq 0$, the time complexity of Program 1.29 can be estimated by determining the number of comparisons made between elements of the array `a`. Note that this number also equals the number of times the method `compareTo` is invoked. When $n \leq 0$, the `for` loop is not entered. So no comparisons between elements of `a` are made. When $n > 0$, each iteration of the `for` loop makes one comparison between two elements of `a`, and the total number of element comparisons is n. Therefore, the number of element comparisons is $\max\{n, 0\}$. The method `max` performs other comparisons (for example, each iteration of the `for` loop is preceded by a comparison between `i` and `n`) that are not included in the estimate. Other operations such as initializing `pos` and incrementing the `for` loop index `i` are also not included in the estimate. If we included these other operations into our count, the count would increase by a constant factor.

Notice that our analysis has implicitly assumed that $n \leq$ `a.length`. When $n >$ `a.length`, Program 1.29 throws an exception of the type `IndexOutOfBounds-Exception`, and the number of element comparisons is not $\max\{n, 0\}$. In our future analyses we also implicitly assume that no exceptions or errors, other than those explicitly thrown by our code, are thrown. ∎

Example 2.8 [Polynomial Evaluation] Consider the polynomial $P(x) = \sum_{i=0}^{n} c_i x^n$. If $c_n \neq 0$, $P(x)$ is a polynomial of degree n. Program 2.3 gives one way to compute $P(x)$ for a given value of x. When `coeff.length` ≥ 1, the time complexity can be estimated by determining the number of additions (i.e., invocations of `increment`) and multiplications performed inside the `for` loop. We will use the degree $n =$ `coeff.length - 1` as the instance characteristic. The `for` loop is entered a total of n times, and each time we enter the `for` loop one addition and two multiplications are done. (This operation count excludes the add performed each time the loop variable `i` is incremented.) The number of additions is n, and the number of multiplications is $2n$.

Horner's rule evaluates $P(x)$ as shown below.

$$P(x) = (\cdots (c_n * x + c_{n-1}) * x + c_{n-2}) * x + c_{n-3}) * x \cdots) * x + c_0$$

So $P(x) = 5 * x^3 - 4 * x^2 + x + 7$ is computed as $((5 * x - 4) * x + 1) * x + 7$. The corresponding Java method is given in Program 2.4. Using the same measure as

```
public static Computable valueOf(Computable [] coeff, Computable x)
{
   if (coeff.length < 1)
      throw new IllegalArgumentException
              ("must have >= 1 coefficient");

   Computable y = (Computable) coeff[0].identity(),   // x^0
               value = coeff[0];                       // coeff[0] * x^0

   // add remaining terms to value
   for (int i = 1; i < coeff.length; i++)
   {
      y = (Computable) y.multiply(x);   // y = x^i

      // add in next term
      value.increment(y.multiply(coeff[i]));
   }

   return value;
}
```

Program 2.3 Evaluating a polynomial

used for Program 2.3, we estimate the complexity of Program 2.4 as n additions and n multiplications. Since Program 2.3 performs the same number of additions but twice as many multiplications as does Program 2.4, we expect Program 2.4 to be faster. ∎

Example 2.9 [Ranking] The **rank** of an element in a sequence is the number of smaller elements in the sequence plus the number of equal elements that appear to its left. For example if the sequence is given as the array a = [4, 3, 9, 3, 7], then the ranks are r = [2, 0, 4, 1, 3]. Method **rank** (Program 2.5) computes the ranks of the elements in the array a. We can estimate the complexity of **rank** by counting the number of comparisons between elements of a. These comparisons are done in the if statement. When r.length < a.length, the number of comparisons is 0. Assume that r.length ≥ a.length. For each value of i, the number of element comparisons is i. Let n = a.length be the number of elements in a. The total number of element comparisons is $1 + 2 + 3 + \cdots + n - 1 = (n - 1)n/2$ (see Equation 1.3).

Note that our complexity estimate excludes the overhead associated with the for loops, the cost of initializing the array r, and the cost of incrementing r each time two elements of a are compared. ∎

```
public static Computable valueOf(Computable [] coeff, Computable x)
{
   if (coeff.length < 1)
      throw new IllegalArgumentException
               ("must have >= 1 coefficient");

   // compute value
   Computable value = coeff[coeff.length - 1];
   for (int i = coeff.length - 2; i >= 0; i--)
   {
      value = (Computable) value.multiply(x);
      value = (Computable) value.increment(coeff[i]);
   }

   return value;
}
```

Program 2.4 Horner's rule for polynomial evaluation

```
public static void rank(Comparable [] a, int [] r)
{// Rank the objects in a[].
   // make sure rank array is large enough
   if (r.length < a.length)
      throw new IllegalArgumentException
            ("length of rank array cannot " +
             "be less than the number of objects");

   // set all ranks to zero
   for (int i = 0; i < a.length; i++)
      r[i] = 0;

   // compare all pairs of objects
   for (int i = 1; i < a.length; i++)
      for (int j = 0; j < i; j++)
         if (a[j].compareTo(a[i]) <= 0) r[i]++;
         else r[j]++;
}
```

Program 2.5 Computing ranks

Example 2.10 [Rank Sort] Once the elements have been ranked using Program 2.5, they may be rearranged in nondecreasing order so that a[0] ≤ a[1] ≤ ⋯ ≤ a[a.length-1] by moving elements to positions corresponding to their ranks. If we have space for an additional array u, we can use the method **rearrange** given in Program 2.6.

```
private static void rearrange(Comparable [] a, int [] r)
{
    // create an additional array u
    Comparable [] u = new Comparable [a.length];

    // move references to correct place in u
    for (int i = 0; i < a.length; i++)
        u[r[i]] = a[i];

    // move back to a
    for (int i = 0; i < a.length; i++)
        a[i] = u[i];
}
```

Program 2.6 Rearranging elements using an additional array

Assume that the invocation of **new** succeeds in allocating space to the array u. The number of element moves performed during the execution of method **rearrange** is $2n$ (recall that $n =$ a.length). The complete sort requires $(n - 1)n/2$ comparisons and $2n$ element reference moves This method of sorting is known as **rank** or **count** sort. An alternative method to rearrange the elements is considered later (Program 2.11). This alternative method does not use an additional array such as u. ■

Example 2.11 [Selection Sort] Example 2.10 examined one way to rearrange the elements in an array a so that a[0] ≤ a[1] ≤ ⋯ ≤ a[a.length-1]. Let $n =$ a.length. An alternative strategy is to determine the largest element and move it to a[$n - 1$], then determine the largest of the remaining $n - 1$ elements and move it to a[$n - 2$], and so on. Figure 2.3(a) shows an example in which selection sort is used to sort the six-element array a[0:5] = [6, 5, 8, 4, 3, 1]. Shaded array positions designate the, as yet, unsorted part of the array. A heavy bar over an array position marks the maximum element, and a light bar marks the position into which the maximum element is to move.

Line 1 of the figure shows the initial configuration; the entire array is considered unsorted, the maximum element is in a[2], and this maximum element is to be

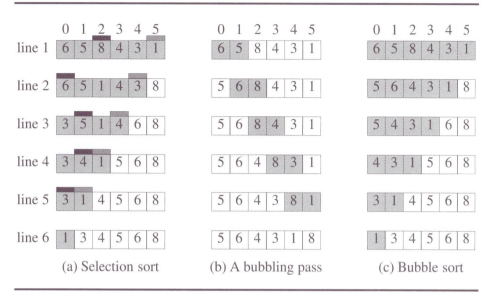

	0 1 2 3 4 5
line 1	6 5 8 4 3 1
line 2	6 5 1 4 3 8
line 3	3 5 1 4 6 8
line 4	3 4 1 5 6 8
line 5	3 1 4 5 6 8
line 6	1 3 4 5 6 8

(a) Selection sort

	0 1 2 3 4 5
line 1	6 5 8 4 3 1
line 2	5 6 8 4 3 1
line 3	5 6 8 4 3 1
line 4	5 6 4 8 3 1
line 5	5 6 4 3 8 1
line 6	5 6 4 3 1 8

(b) A bubbling pass

	0 1 2 3 4 5
line 1	6 5 8 4 3 1
line 2	5 6 4 3 1 8
line 3	5 4 3 1 6 8
line 4	4 3 1 5 6 8
line 5	3 1 4 5 6 8
line 6	1 3 4 5 6 8

(c) Bubble sort

Figure 2.3 Selection and bubble sort

moved to `a[5]`. The move is accomplished by swapping the elements at the positions designated by the bars. Following the swap, we need concern ourselves only with sorting the elements `a[0:4]` because `a[5]` is known to contain the maximum element. Line 2 shows the configuration after the swap; the maximum element of `a[0:4]` is `a[0]`, and this element is to be swapped with `a[4]`. Line 3 shows the result. Line 6 shows the result following three more stages of find the max and swap. At this time the unsorted part of the array (`a[0:0]`) has a single element that is known to be less than or equal to the other elements in the array. So the entire array is sorted.

Program 2.7 gives the Java method, `selectionSort`, which implements the above strategy. Program 1.29 gave the method `max`. We can estimate the complexity of `selectionSort` by counting the number of element comparisons made. From Example 2.7 we know that each invocation `max(a,size)` results in `size-1` comparisons being made. So the total number of comparisons is $1 + 2 + 3 + \cdots + n - 1$ $= (n - 1)n/2$. The number of element reference moves is $3(n - 1)$. Selection sort uses the same number of comparisons rank sort uses (Example 2.10) but requires 50 percent more element reference moves. We consider another version of selection sort in Example 2.16. ∎

```
public static void selectionSort(Comparable [] a)
{
   for (int size = a.length; size > 1; size--)
   {
      // find max object in a[0:size-1]
      int j = MyMath.max(a, size-1);

      // move max object to right end
      MyMath.swap(a, j, size - 1);
   }
}
```

Program 2.7 Selection sort

Example 2.12 [Bubble Sort] Bubble sort is another simple way to sort elements. This sort employs a "bubbling strategy" to get the largest element to the right. In a bubbling pass, pairs of adjacent elements are compared. The elements are swapped in case the one on the left is greater than the one on the right. Suppose we have six integers in the order [6, 5, 8, 4, 3, 1] (see line 1 of Figure 2.3(b)). First the 6 and the 5 are compared and swapped to get the sequence shown in line 2. Next the 6 and 8 are compared, and no swap takes place. Then 8 and 4 are compared (line 3) and swapped; line 4 shows the result. The next comparison is between 8 and 3, and the two are swapped. The last comparison is between 8 and 1; these are swapped to get the configuration shown in line 6. The bubbling pass is now complete. At the end of the bubbling pass, we are assured that the largest element is in the right-most position.

The method **bubble** (Program 2.8) performs a bubbling pass over a[0:n-1]. The number of comparisons between pairs of elements of a is n-1.

```
private static void bubble(Comparable [] a, int n)
{
   for (int i = 0; i < n - 1; i++)
      if (a[i].compareTo(a[i+1]) > 0)
         MyMath.swap(a, i, i + 1);
}
```

Program 2.8 A bubbling pass

Since **bubble** causes the largest element to move to the right-most position, it can be used in place of **max** in **selectionSort** (Program 2.7) to obtain a new sorting method (Program 2.9). The number of element comparisons is $(n-1)n/2$ (again, $n = $ a.length) as it is for selectionSort. Figure 2.3(c) shows an initial array configuration as well as the array configuration after each bubbling pass.   ∎

```
public static void bubbleSort(Comparable [] a)
{
   for (int i = a.length; i > 1; i--)
      bubble(a, i);
}
```

Program 2.9 Bubble sort

2.3.3   Best, Worst, and Average Operation Counts

In the examples so far, the operation counts were nice functions of fairly simple instance characteristics like the number of inputs and/or outputs. Some of our examples would have been more complicated if we had chosen to count some other operations. For example, the number of swaps performed by bubble (Program 2.8) depends not only on the instance characteristic n but also on the particular values of the elements in the array a. The number of swaps varies from a low of 0 to a high of $n-1$. Since the operation count isn't always uniquely determined by the chosen instance characteristics, we ask for the best, worst, and average counts. The average operation count is often quite difficult to determine. As a result, in several of the following examples we limit our analysis to determining the best and worst counts.

Example 2.13 [Sequential Search] We are interested in determining the number of comparisons between x and the elements of a during an execution of the sequential search code of Program 2.1. A natural instance characteristic to use is $n = $ a.length. Unfortunately, the number of comparisons isn't uniquely determined by n. For example, if $n = 100$ and x $=$ a[0], then only 1 comparison is made. However, if x isn't equal to any of the a[]s, then 100 comparisons are made.

A search is **successful** when x is one of the a[]s. All other searches are **unsuccessful**. Whenever we have an unsuccessful search, the number of comparisons is n. For successful searches the best comparison count is 1, and the worst is n. For the average count assume that all array elements are distinct and that each is searched for with equal frequency. The average count for a successful search is

$$\frac{1}{n} \sum_{i=1}^{n} i = (n+1)/2 \qquad\qquad ∎$$

Example 2.14 [Insertion into a Sorted Array] You are to insert a new element into a sorted array so that the result is also a sorted array. For example, when you insert 3 into a[0:4] = [2,4,6,8,9], the result is a[0:5] = [2,3,4,6,8,9]. The insertion may be done by beginning at the right end and successively moving array elements one position right until we find the location for the new element. Figure 2.4(a) illustrates the process. In our example we moved 9, 8, 6, and 4 one position right and inserted 3 into the now-vacant spot a[1].

	0	1	2	3	4	5
line 1	2	4	6	8	9	
line 2	2	4	6	8		9
line 3	2	4	6		8	9
line 4	2	4		6	8	9
line 5	2		4	6	8	9
line 6	2	3	4	6	8	9

(a) Insert

0	1	2	3	4	5
3	0	4	5	2	1
d	a	e	f	c	b

0	1	2	3	4	5
5	0	4	3	2	1
f	a	e	d	c	b

0	1	2	3	4	5
1	0	4	3	2	5
b	a	e	d	c	f

0	1	2	3	4	5
0	1	4	3	2	5
a	b	e	d	c	f

(b) In-place rearrange

0	1	2	3	4	5
0	1	4	3	2	5
a	b	e	d	c	f

0	1	2	3	4	5
0	1	4	3	2	5
a	b	e	d	c	f

0	1	2	3	4	5
0	1	2	3	4	5
a	b	c	d	e	f

0	1	2	3	4	5
0	1	2	3	4	5
a	b	c	d	e	f

(c) In-place rearrange

Figure 2.4 Insert and rearrange

Program 2.10 implements the above strategy to insert an element x into a sorted array a[0:n-1].

We wish to determine the number of comparisons made between x and the elements of a. The natural instance characteristic to use is the number n of elements initially in a. For the analysis assume that a.length $\geq$ n+1. The best or minimum number of comparisons is 1, which happens when the new element x is to be inserted at the right end. The maximum number of comparisons is n, which happens when x is to be inserted at the left end. For the average assume that x has an equal chance of being inserted into any of the possible n+1 positions. If x is eventually inserted into position i+1 of a, i $\geq$ 0, then the number of comparisons is n-i. If x is inserted into a[0], the number of comparisons is n. So the average count is

$$\frac{1}{n+1}\left(\sum_{i=0}^{n-1}(n-i)+n\right) \;=\; \frac{1}{n+1}\left(\sum_{j=1}^{n}j+n\right)$$

```
public static void insert(Comparable [] a, int n, Comparable x)
{
    if (a.length < n + 1)
        throw new IllegalArgumentException
                ("array not large enough");

    // find proper place for x
    int i;
    for (i = n - 1; i >= 0 && x.compareTo(a[i]) < 0; i--)
        a[i+1] = a[i];

    a[i+1] = x;   // insert x
}
```

Program 2.10 Inserting into a sorted array

$$= \frac{1}{n+1}(\frac{n(n+1)}{2} + n)$$
$$= \frac{n}{2} + \frac{n}{n+1}$$

So the average count is almost 1 more than half the worst-case count. ■

Example 2.15 [Rank Sort Revisited] Suppose the elements of an array have been ranked using method **rank** (Program 2.5, Example 2.9). We can perform an in-place rearrangement of elements into sorted order by examining the array positions one at a time beginning with position 0. If we are currently examining position i and r[i] = i, then we may advance to the next position. If r[i] ≠ i, then we swap the elements in positions i and r[i]. This swap moves the element previously in position i into its correct sorted position. The swap operation is repeated at position i until the element that belongs in position i in the sorted order is swapped into position i. Then we advance i to the next position.

Parts (b) and (c) of Figure 2.4 show how the above rearrangement strategy works. The initial array is a[0:5] = [d,a,e,f,c,b]. Element ranks are shown above the elements. So the initial rank array is r[0:5] = [3,0,4,5,2,1]. We begin at array position 0. Since r[0] ≠ 0, a[0] and a[r[0]] = a[3] are to be swapped. The configurations of parts (b) and (c) of Figure 2.4 have a heavy bar above the position a[i] being examined (initially, i = 0) and a light bar above the position a[r[i]] where a[i] is to move to. When r[a[i]] = i, the figure has only a heavy bar above a[i]. Shaded array positions denote elements that are not in their proper place (i.e., elements with r[i] ≠ i).

We begin with `i = 0` and swap elements `a[i]` and `a[r[i]]` = `a[3]`; `r[0]` and `r[3]` are also swapped. This process results in the second configuration. Notice that `a[3]` now contains the proper element and `r[3]` = 3. Next elements `a[0]` and `a[r[0]]` = `a[5]`) together with their ranks are swapped to get the third configuration of Figure 2.4(b). When `a[0]` and `a[r[0]]` = `a[1]` (and their ranks) are swapped, we get the fourth configuration. Now `r[0]` = 0, and we increment `i` to the next position 1. The new configuration is shown at the top of Figure 2.4(c). Since `r[i]` = `r[1]` = 1, we advance `i` to the next position 2 (see the second configuration of Figure 2.4(c)). Now `a[i]` = `a[2]` and `a[r[2]]` = `a[4]` (as well as their ranks) are swapped. Following the swap, `r[2]` = 2. Even though the rearrangement is complete at this time, our code will not be able to detect this and we continue to advance `i` to the right, making sure that each element is in its proper position. So `i` is advanced to the next position 3 (see the third configuration of Figure 2.4(c)). Then `i` is advanced to positions 4 and 5.

Program 2.11 gives the in-place rearrangement method `rearrange`.

```
private static void rearrange(Comparable [] a, int [] r)
{// In-place rearrangement into sorted order.
   for (int i = 0; i < a.length; i++)
      // get proper element reference to a[i]
      while (r[i] != i)
      {
         int t = r[i];
         MyMath.swap(a, i, t);
         MyMath.swap(r, i, t);
      }
}
```

Program 2.11 In-place rearrangement of elements

Let n = `a.length`. The number of swaps performed varies from a low of 0 (when the elements are initially in sorted order) to a high of $2(n-1)$. Notice that each swap involving the `a[]`s moves at least one element into its sorted position (i.e., element `a[i]`). So after at most $n-1$ swaps, all n elements must be in sorted order. Exercise 20 establishes that this many element swaps may be needed on certain inputs. Hence the number of swaps is 0 in the best case and $2(n-1)$ in the worst case (includes rank swaps). When this rearrangement method is used in place of the one in Program 2.6, the worst-case execution time increases because we need more element reference moves (each swap requires three moves). However, the space requirements are reduced.   ■

Example 2.16 [Selection Sort Revisited] A shortcoming of the selection sort code of Program 2.7 is that it continues to work even after the elements have been sorted. For example, the `for` loop iterates $n-1$ ($n =$ `a.length`) times, even though the array may be sorted after the second iteration. To eliminate the unnecessary iterations, during the scan for the largest element we can check to see whether the array is already sorted. Program 2.12 gives the resulting selection sort method. Here we have incorporated the loop to find the largest element directly into method `selectionSort`, rather than write it as a separate method.

```
public static void selectionSort(Comparable [] a)
{// Early-terminating version of selection sort.
   boolean sorted = false;
   for (int size = a.length; !sorted && (size > 1); size--)
   {
      int pos = 0;
      sorted = true;

      // find largest
      for (int i = 1; i < size; i++)
         if (a[pos].compareTo(a[i]) <= 0)
            pos = i;
         else
            sorted = false; // out of order

      MyMath.swap(a, pos, size - 1);
   }
}
```

Program 2.12 Early-terminating version of selection sort

Figure 2.5(a) shows the progress of Program 2.12 when started with `a[0:5]` = `[6,5,4,3,2,1]`. In the first iteraton of the outer `for` loop, `size` = 6 and the line `sorted = false` is executed when i = 1, 2, 3, 4, and 5. So following the swap of `a[0]` and `a[5]`, which results in the configuration of line 2, the outer `for` loop is reentered with `size = 5`. This time the line `sorted = false` is executed when i = 2, 3, and 4. Therefore, following the swap of `a[1]` and `a[4]`, the outer `for` loop is reentered; this time `size` = 4. Now the line `sorted = false` is executed when i = 4, and following the swap of `a[2]` and `a[3]`, the outer `for` loop is reentered. This time we are working with the array configuration of line 4; the line `sorted = false` is not executed, and execution of the outer `for` loop terminates. On the initial data of line 1 of Figure 2.5(a), the early terminating version makes one less pass than it does when started with the data shown in line 1 of Figure 2.3(a).

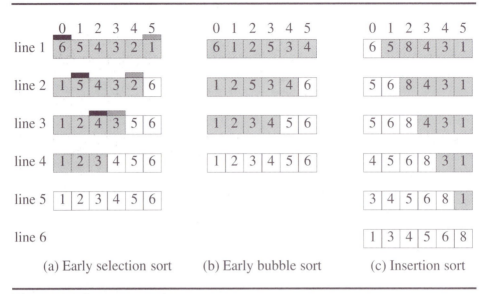

(a) Early selection sort   (b) Early bubble sort   (c) Insertion sort

Figure 2.5 Sorting examples

The best case for the early-terminating version of selection sort arises when the array a is sorted to begin with. Now the outer for loop iterates just once, and the number of comparisons between elements of a is $n - 1$. In the worst case the outer for loop is iterated until size $= 1$ and the number of comparisons is $(n - 1)n/2$. The best- and worst-case number of swaps remains the same as for Program 2.7. Notice that in the worst case we expect the early-terminating version to be slightly slower because of the additional work to maintain the variable sorted. ■

Example 2.17 [Bubble Sort Revisited] As in the case of selection sort, we can devise an early-terminating version of bubble sort. If a bubbling pass results in no swaps, then the array is in sorted order and no further bubbling passes are necessary. Program 2.13 gives the early-terminating version of bubble sort.

Line 1 of Figure 2.5(b) shows an instance on which at least one swap is done when going from line 1 to line 2 (the invocation bubble(a,6)) and in going from line 2 to line 3 (the invocation bubble(a,5)). No swaps are done in the invocation bubble(a,4), and so the sort terminates following this invocation.

The worst-case number of comparisons made by Program 2.13 is unchanged from the original version (Program 2.9). The best-case number of comparisons is $n - 1$, where $n = $ a.length. ■

```
private static boolean bubble(Comparable [] a, int n)
{
    boolean swapped = false; // no swaps so far
    for (int i = 0; i < n - 1; i++)
        if (a[i].compareTo(a[i+1]) > 0)
        {
            MyMath.swap(a, i, i + 1);
            swapped = true; // swap was done
        }
    return swapped;
}


public static void bubbleSort(Comparable [] a)
{
    for (int i = a.length; i > 1 && bubble(a, i); i--);
}
```

Program 2.13 Early-terminating bubble sort

Example 2.18 [Insertion Sort] Program 2.10 can be used as the basis of a method to sort n elements. Since an array with one element is a sorted array, we start with an array that contains just the first of the n elements to be sorted. By inserting the second element into this one-element array, we get a sorted array of size 2. The insertion of the third element yields a sorted array of size 3. Continuing in this way, we obtain a sorted array of size n.

Line 1 of Figure 2.5(c) shows the unsorted array a[0:5]. We start with a sorted segment a[0:0]; the remaining elements a[1:5] define the unsorted segment. The unsorted segment is the shaded segment in Figure 2.5(c). First a[1] is inserted into the sorted segment a[0:0] to get the configuration of line 2; a[0:1] is now the sorted segment, and a[2:5] is the unsorted segment. Next a[2] is inserted into the sorted segment, and we get line 3 of the figure. a[0:2] becomes the sorted segment, and a[3:5] is the unsorted segment. After three more inserts, the entire array is sorted.

Method insertionSort (Program 2.14) implements this strategy. The method Insert.insert was given in Program 2.10. Actually, we can embed the code of insert directly into the sort method to get the insertion sort version of Program 2.15.

Both versions perform the same number of comparisons. In the best case the number of comparisons is $n-1$, and in the worst case it is $(n-1)n/2$. Once again, $n = $ a.length.   ■

```
public static void insertionSort(Comparable [] a)
{
   for (int i = 1; i < a.length; i++)
      Insert.insert(a, i, a[i]);
}
```

Program 2.14 Insertion sort

```
public static void insertionSort(Comparable [] a)
{
   for (int i = 1; i < a.length; i++)
   { // insert a[i] into a[0:i-1]
      Comparable t = a[i];

      // find proper place for t
      int j;
      for (j = i - 1; j >= 0 && t.compareTo(a[j]) < 0; j--)
         a[j+1] = a[j];

      a[j+1] = t;  // insert t = original a[i]
   }
}
```

Program 2.15 Another version of insertion sort

2.3.4   Step Counts

As noted in some of the examples on operation counts, the operation-count method of estimating time complexity omits accounting for the time spent on all but the chosen operations. In the **step-count** method, we attempt to account for the time spent in all parts of the program/method. As was the case for operation counts, the step count is a function of the instance characteristics. Although any specific instance may have several characteristics (e.g., the number of inputs, the number of outputs, the magnitudes of the inputs and outputs), the number of steps is computed as a function of some subset of these. Usually we choose the characteristics that are of interest to us. For example, we might wish to know how the computing (or run) time (i.e., time complexity) increases as the number of inputs increases. In this case the number of steps will be computed as a function of the number of inputs alone. For a different program we might want to determine how the computing time increases as the magnitude of one of the inputs increases. In this case the number of steps will be computed as a function of the magnitude of this input alone. Thus before the step count of a program can be determined, we need to know exactly which characteristics of the problem instance are to be used. These characteristics define not only the variables in the expression for the step count but also how much computing can be counted as a single step.

After the relevant instance characteristics have been selected, we can define a step. A **step** is any computation unit that is independent of the selected characteristics. Thus 10 additions can be one step; 100 multiplications can also be one step; but n additions, where n is an instance characteristic, cannot be one step. Nor can $m/2$ additions or $p + q$ subtractions, where m, p, and q are instance characteristics, be counted as one step.

Definition 2.1 *A **program step** is loosely defined to be a syntactically or semantically meaningful segment of a program for which the execution time is independent of the instance characteristics.* ∎

The amount of computing represented by one program step may be different from that represented by another. For example, the entire statement

```
return a+b+b*c+(a+b-c)/(a+b)+4;
```

can be regarded as a single step if its execution time is independent of the instance characteristics we are using. We may also count a statement such as

```
x = y;
```

as a single step.

We can determine the number of steps that a program or method takes to complete its task by creating a global variable count with initial value 0. Next we introduce statements into the program to increment count by the appropriate amount. Therefore, each time a statement in the original program or method is executed, count is incremented by the step count of that statement. The value of count when the program or method terminates is the number of steps taken.

Example 2.19 When statements to increment count are introduced into Program 1.25, the result is Program 2.16. The change in the value of count by the time this program terminates is the number of steps executed by Program 1.25.

Program 2.17, which is a simplified version of Program 2.16, determines only the change in the value of count. We see that for every initial value of count, both Programs 2.16 and 2.17 compute the same final value for count. Assume that $0 \leq n <$ a.length. In the for loop of Program 2.17, the value of count increases by a total of 2n. If count is 0 to start with and if a.length $\neq 0$, then count will be 2n+4 on termination. Therefore, each invocation of sum (Program 1.25) executes a total of 2n+4 steps when $0 \leq n <$ a.length. When a.length is 0, Program 1.25 executes just one step. ∎

```
public static Computable sum(Computable [] a, int n)
{
    count++; // for conditional and return
    if (a.length == 0) return null;
    Computable sum = (Computable) a[0].zero();
    count++; // for preceding statement
    for (int i = 0; i < n; i++)
    {
        count++; // for the for statement
        sum.increment(a[i]);
        count++; // for increment
    }
    count++; // for last execution of for statement
    count++; // for return
    return sum;
}
```

Program 2.16 Counting steps in Program 1.25

```
public static Computable sum(Computable [] a, int n)
{
    count++;
    if (a.length == 0) return null;
    for (int i = 0; i < n; i++)
        count += 2;

    count += 3;
    return null;
}
```

Program 2.17 Simplified version of Program 2.16

Example 2.20 When we introduce statements to increment count into method rSum (Program 1.26), we obtain Program 2.18. Note that since Program 1.26 is a recursive method, it requires space for the recursion stack. Thus the method can fail to complete its task for lack of sufficient memory for the recursion stack; that is, an error of the type OutOfMemoryError may be thrown. For the step-count analysis, we will assume that the method rSum does not throw an OutOfMemoryError. We shall also assume that $0 \le n <$ a.length, and so an IndexOutOfBoundsException is not thrown either.

```
public static Computable recursiveSum(Computable [] a, int n)
{// Driver for true recursive method rsum.
   count++; // for if-else statement
   if (a.length > 0)
      return rSum(a, n);
   else return null;   // no elements to sum
}


private static Computable rSum(Computable [] a, int n)
{
   if (n == 0)
   {
      count++; // for conditional and return
      return (Computable) a[0].zero();
   }
   else
   {
      count++;   // for conditional, rSum invocation,
                 // add, and return
      return (Computable) rSum(a, n - 1).add(a[n-1]);
   }
}
```

Program 2.18 Counting steps in Program 1.26

Let $t_{rSum}(n)$ be the increase in the value of count between the time method rSum of Program 2.18 is invoked by method recursiveSum and the time rSum returns to recursiveSum. We see that $t_{rSum}(0) = 1$. When n > 0, count increases by 1 plus whatever increase results from the invocation of rSum from within the else clause. From the definition of t_{rSum}, it follows that this additional increase is $t_{rSum}(n-1)$. So if the value of count is 0 initially, its value at the time of termination is $1 + t_{rSum}(n-1)$, n > 0.

When analyzing a recursive program for its step count, we often obtain a recursive formula for the step count (such as $t_{rSum}(n) = 1 + t_{rSum}(n-1)$, n > 0 and $t_{rSum}(0) = 1$). This recursive formula is referred to as a **recurrence equation** (or simply as a **recurrence**). We can solve this recurrence by repeatedly substituting for t_{rSum} as shown:

$$
\begin{aligned}
t_{rSum}(n) &= 1 + t_{rSum}(n-1) \\
&= 1 + 1 + t_{rSum}(n-2)
\end{aligned}
$$

$$
\begin{aligned}
&= \quad 2 + t_{rSum}(n-2) \\
&\quad \vdots \\
&= \quad n + t_{rSum}(0) \\
&= \quad n + 1, \quad n \geq 0
\end{aligned}
$$

So the step count for method rSum (Program 1.26) is n+1. Therefore, the step count for recursiveSum is n+2 when $0 \leq n <$ a.length.   ■

Comparing the step counts of Programs 1.25 and 1.26, we see that the count for Program 1.26 is less than that for Program 1.25. However, we cannot conclude that Program 1.25 is slower than Program 1.26, because a step doesn't correspond to a definite time unit. A step of recursiveSum may take more time than a step of sum, so recursiveSum might well be (and we expect it to be) slower than sum.

The step count is useful in that it tells us how the run time for a program changes with changes in the instance characteristics. From the step count for sum, we see that if n is doubled, the run time will also double (approximately); if n increases by a factor of 10, we expect the run time to increase by a factor of 10; and so on. So we expect the run time to grow *linearly* in n.

Rather than introduce statements to increment count, we can build a table in which we list the total number of steps that each statement contributes to count. We can arrive at this figure by first determining the number of steps per execution (s/e) of the statement and the total number of times (i.e., frequency) each statement is executed. Combining these two quantities gives us the total contribution of each statement. We can then add the contributions of all statements to obtain the step count for the entire program. This approach to obtaining the step count is called **profiling**.

The s/e of a statement is the amount by which count *changes as a result of the execution of that statement.* An important difference between the step count of a statement and its s/e is illustrated by the following example. The statement

```
x = sum(a,m);
```

has a step count of 1, while the total change in count resulting from the execution of this statement is actually 1 plus the change resulting from the invocation of sum (i.e., 2m+4). Therefore, the s/e of the above statement is 1+2m+4 = 2m+5.

Figure 2.6 lists the number of steps per execution and the frequency of each of the statements in method sum (Program 1.25). The total number of steps required by the program is 2n+4. Note that the frequency of the for statement is n+1 and not n because i has to be incremented to n before the for loop can terminate.

Program 2.19 transposes a rows × rows matrix a[0:rows-1][0:rows-1]. Recall that b is the transpose of a iff (if and only if) b[i][j] = a[j][i] for all i and j.

Statement	s/e	Frequency	Total steps
`public static Computable sum(···)`	0	0	0
`{`	0	0	0
`    if (a.length == 0) return null;`	1	1	1
`    Computable sum = (Computable) a[0].zero();`	1	1	1
`    for (int i = 0; i < n; i++)`	1	$n+1$	$n+1$
`        sum.increment(a[i]);`	1	n	n
`    return sum;`	1	1	1
`}`	0	0	0
Total			$2n+4$

Figure 2.6 Step count for Program 1.25

```
public static void transpose(int [][] a, int rows)
{
   for (int i = 0; i < rows; i++)
      for (int j = i+1; j < rows; j++)
      {
         // swap a[i][j] and a[j][i]
         int t = a[i][j];
         a[i][j] = a[j][i];
         a[j][i] = t;
      }
}
```

Program 2.19 Matrix transpose

Figure 2.7 gives the step-count table. Let us derive the frequency of the second `for` statement. For each value of `i`, this statement is executed `rows-i` times. So its frequency is

$$\sum_{i=0}^{rows-1} (rows - i) = \sum_{q=1}^{rows} q = rows(rows + 1)/2$$

The frequency for each of the executable statements in the second `for` loop is

$$\sum_{i=0}^{rows-1} (rows - i - 1) = \sum_{q=0}^{rows-1} q = rows(rows - 1)/2$$

Statement	s/e	Frequency	Total steps
`public static void transpose(···)`	0	0	0
`{`	0	0	0
`    for (int i = 0; i < rows; i++)`	1	$rows + 1$	$rows + 1$
`        for (int j = i+1; j < rows; j++)`	1	$rows(rows + 1)/2$	$rows(rows + 1)/2$
`        {`	0	0	0
`            // swap a[i][j] and a[j][i]`	0	0	0
`            int t = a[i][j];`	1	$rows(rows - 1)/2$	$rows(rows - 1)/2$
`            a[i][j] = a[j][i];`	1	$rows(rows - 1)/2$	$rows(rows - 1)/2$
`            a[j][i] = t;`	1	$rows(rows - 1)/2$	$rows(rows - 1)/2$
`        }`	0	0	0
`}`	0	0	0
Total			$2rows^2 + 1$

Figure 2.7 Step count for Program 2.19

In some cases the number of steps per execution of a statement varies from one execution to the next, for example, for the assignment statement of method **inef** (Program 2.20). Method **inef** is a very inefficient way to compute the prefix sums $b[j]$.

$$b[j] = \sum_{i=0}^{j} a[i] \text{ for } j = 0, 1, \cdots, n - 1$$

```
public static int [] inef(int [] a)
{
    // create an array for the prefix sums
    int [] b = new int [a.length];

    // compute the prefix sums
    for (int j = 0; j < a.length; j++)
        b[j] = MyMath.sum(a, j + 1);

    return b;
}
```

Program 2.20 Inefficient prefix sums

For the analysis we will assume that there is sufficient memory to create the array b. Let n = a.length. The step count for sum(a,m) has already been determined to be 2m+4 (see Example 2.19). Therefore, the number of steps per execution of the assignment statement `b[j]` = `MyMath.sum(a, j + 1)` of method `inef` is $2j+7$. To arrive at this step count, we have added 1 to the step count of method `sum` to account for the cost of invoking the method `sum` and of assigning the method value to `b[j]`. The frequency of this assignment statement is n = `a.length`. But the total number of steps resulting from this statement is not $(2j+6)n$. Instead, the number of steps is

$$\sum_{j=0}^{n-1}(2j + 7) = n(n + 6)$$

Figure 2.8 gives the complete analysis for this method.

Statement	s/e	Frequency	Total steps
`public static int [] inef(int [] a)`	0	0	0
`{`	0	0	0
`    // create an array for the prefix sums`	0	0	0
`    int [] b = new int [a.length];`	n	1	n
	0	0	0
`    // compute the prefix sums`	0	0	0
`    for (int j = 0; j < a.length; j++)`	1	$n+1$	$n+1$
`        b[j] = MyMath.sum(a, j + 1);`	$2j+7$	n	$n(n+6)$
`        return b;`	1	1	1
`}`	0	0	0
Total			$n^2 + 8n + 2$

Figure 2.8 Step count for Program 2.20

The notions of best, worst, and average operation counts are easily extended to the case of step counts. Examples 2.21 and 2.22 illustrate these notions.

Example 2.21 [Sequential Search] Figures 2.9 and 2.10 show the best- and worst-case step-count analyses for method `sequentialSearch` (Program 2.1). In both figures n = `a.length`.

For the average step-count analysis for a successful search, we assume that the n values in `a` are distinct and that in a successful search, `x` has an equal probability of being any one of these values. Under these assumptions the average step count for a successful search is the sum of the step counts for the n possible successful searches divided by n. To obtain this average, we first obtain the step count for the case `x` = `a[j]` where `j` is in the range $[0, n − 1]$ (see Figure 2.11).

Now we obtain the average step count for successful searches:

$$\frac{1}{n}\sum_{j=0}^{n-1}(j + 4) = (n + 7)/2$$

Statement	s/e	Frequency	Total steps
public static int sequentialSearch(···)	0	0	0
{	0	0	0
int i;	1	1	1
for (i = 0; i < a.length && !x.equals(a[i]); i++);	1	1	1
if (i == a.length) return -1;	1	1	1
else return i;	1	1	1
}	0	0	0
Total			4

Figure 2.9 Best-case step count for Program 2.1

Statement	s/e	Frequency	Total steps
public static int sequentialSearch(···)	0	0	0
{	0	0	0
int i;	1	1	1
for (i = 0; i < a.length && !x.equals(a[i]); i++);	1	$n+1$	$n+1$
if (i == a.length) return -1;	1	1	1
else return i;	1	0	0
}	0	0	0
Total			$n+3$

Figure 2.10 Worst-case step count for Program 2.1

Statement	s/e	Frequency	Total steps
public static int sequentialSearch(···)	0	0	0
{	0	0	0
int i;	1	1	1
for (i = 0; i < a.length && !x.equals(a[i]); i++);	1	$j+1$	$j+1$
if (i == a.length) return -1;	1	1	1
else return i;	1	1	1
}	0	0	0
Total			$j+4$

Figure 2.11 Step count for Program 2.1 when x = a[j]

This value is a little more than half the step count for an unsuccessful search.

Now suppose that successful searches occur only 80 percent of the time and that each a[i] still has the same probability of being searched for. The average step count for SequentialSearch is

.8 * (average count for successful searches) + .2 * (count for an unsuccessful search)

$$= .8(n + 7)/2 + .2(n + 3)$$
$$= .6n + 3.4$$

∎

Example 2.22 [Insertion into a Sorted Array] The best- and worst-case step counts for method `insert` (Program 2.10) are obtained in Figures 2.12 and 2.13, respectively. Our best-case analysis assumes that an exception is not thrown.

Statement	s/e	Frequency	Total steps
`public static void insert(···)`	0	0	0
`{`	0	0	0
`  if (a.length < n + 1)`	1	1	1
`    throw new IllegalArgumentException`	1	0	0
`      ("Insert.insert: array not large enough");`			
`  // find proper place for x`	0	0	0
`  int i;`	1	1	1
`  for (i = n - 1; i >= 0 && x.compareTo(a[i]) < 0; i--)`	1	1	1
`    a[i+1] = a[i];`	0	0	0
`  a[i+1] = x;`	1	1	1
`}`	0	0	0
Total			4

Figure 2.12 Best-case step count for Program 2.10 assuming no exception is thrown

Statement	s/e	Frequency	Total steps
`public static void insert(···)`	0	0	0
`{`	0	0	0
`  if (a.length < n + 1)`	1	1	1
`    throw new IllegalArgumentException`	1	0	0
`      ("Insert.insert: array not large enough");`			
`  // find proper place for x`	0	0	0
`  int i;`	1	1	1
`  for (i = n - 1; i >= 0 && x.compareTo(a[i]) < 0; i--)`	1	$n + 1$	$n + 1$
`    a[i+1] = a[i];`	1	n	n
`  a[i+1] = x;`	1	1	1
`}`	0	0	0
Total			$2n + 4$

Figure 2.13 Worst-case step count for Program 2.10

For the average step count, assume that x has an equal chance of being inserted into any of the possible n+1 positions. If x is eventually inserted into position j, $j \geq 0$, then the step count is 2n-2j+4. So the average count is

$$
\begin{aligned}
\frac{1}{n+1} \sum_{j=0}^{n} (2n - 2j + 4) &= \frac{1}{n+1}[2\sum_{j=0}^{n}(n-j) + \sum_{j=0}^{n} 4] \\
&= \frac{1}{n+1}[2\sum_{k=0}^{n} k + 4(n+1)] \\
&= \frac{1}{n+1}[n(n+1) + 4(n+1)] \\
&= \frac{(n+4)(n+1)}{n+1} \\
&= n+4
\end{aligned}
$$

The average count is 2 more than half the worst-case count.   ∎

EXERCISES

8. According to the analysis in Example 2.8, Program 2.3 makes four additions and eight multiplications when evaluating the polynomial $3x^4 + 4x^3 + 5x^2 + 6x + 7$, and Program 2.4 makes four additions and four multiplications. Identify these additions and multiplications for the case $x = 2$. Do this by showing the precise numbers that are being added or multiplied.

9. Give the rank array r for the case when a[0:8] = [3, 2, 6, 5, 9, 4, 7, 1, 8] (see Example 2.9).

10. Consider the selection sort method of Program 2.7. Draw a figure similar to Figure 2.3(a) for the case when a[0:6] = [3, 2, 6, 5, 9, 4, 8].

11. Consider the bubbling pass method of Program 2.8. Draw a figure similar to Figure 2.3(b) for the case when a[0:6] = [3, 2, 6, 5, 9, 4, 8].

12. For the bubble sort method of Program 2.9, draw a figure similar to Figure 2.3(c) for the case when a[0:6] = [3, 2, 6, 5, 9, 4, 8].

13. Suppose that we are to insert 3 into the sorted array a[0:6] = [1, 2, 4, 6, 7, 8, 9]. Draw a figure similar to Figure 2.4(a). Your figure should show the progress of Program 2.10.

14. The array a[0:8] = [g, h, i, f, c, a, d, b, e] is to be sorted using a rank sort. The ranks are determined to be r[0:8] = [6, 7, 8, 5, 2, 0, 3, 1, 4]. Draw a figure similar to Figures 2.4(b) and (c) to show the progress of the in-place rearrangment method of Program 2.11.

15. (a) Suppose that the array a[0:9] = [9, 8, 7, 6, 5, 4, 3, 2, 1, 0] is sorted using the early-terminating version of selection sort (Program 2.12). Draw a figure similar to Figure 2.5(a) to show the progress of the sort method.

    (b) Do part (a) for the case when a[0:8] = [8, 4, 5, 2, 1, 6, 7, 3, 0].

16. The array a[0:9] = [4, 2, 6, 7, 1, 0, 9, 8, 5, 3] is sorted using the early-terminating version of bubble sort (Program 2.13). Draw a figure similar to Figure 2.5(b) to show the progress of the sort method.

17. The array a[0:9] = [4, 2, 6, 7, 1, 0, 9, 8, 5, 3] is to be sorted using insertion sort (Program 2.14). Draw a figure similar to Figure 2.5(c) to show the progress of the sort method.

18. How many additions (i.e., invocations of increment) are done in the for loop of method sum (Program 1.25)?

19. How many multiplications are performed by the method factorial (Program 1.24)?

20. Create an input array a that causes method rearrange (Program 2.11) to do $n - 1$ element reference swaps and $n - 1$ rank swaps; $n = $ a.length.

21. How many additions are performed between pairs of array elements by method add (Program 2.21)?

```
public static void add (int [][] a, int [][] b, int [][] c,
                        int rows, int cols)
{
   for (int i = 0; i < rows; i++)
      for (int j = 0; j < cols; j++)
         c[i][j] = a[i][j] + b[i][j];
}
```

Program 2.21 Matrix addition

22. How many swap operations are performed by method transpose (Program 2.19)?

23. Determine the number of multiplications done by method squareMultiply (Program 2.22), which multiplies two n × n matrices.

```
public static void squareMultiply(int [][] a, int [][] b,
                                  int [][] c, int n)
{
   for (int i = 0; i < n; i++)
      for (int j = 0; j < n; j++)
      {
         int sum = 0;
         for (int k = 0; k < n; k++)
            sum += a[i][k] * b[k][j];
         c[i][j] = sum;
      }
}
```

Program 2.22 Multiply two n × n matrices

```
public static void multiply(int [][] a, int [][] b, int [][] c,
                            int m, int n, int p)
{
   for (int i = 0; i < m; i++)
      for (int j = 0; j < p; j++)
      {// compute c[i][j]
         int sum = 0;
         for (int k = 0; k < n; k++)
            sum += a[i][k] * b[k][j];
         c[i][j] = sum;
      }
}
```

Program 2.23 Multiply an m × n and an n × p matrix

24. Determine the number of multiplications done by method `multiply` (Program 2.23), which multiplies an m × n matrix and an n × p matrix.

25. Determine the number of `swap` operations performed by method `perm` (Program 1.27).

26. Method `minMax` (Program 2.24) determines the locations of the minimum and maximum elements in an array a. Let $n =$ `a.length` be the instance characteristic. What is the number of comparisons between elements of a? Program 2.25 gives an alternative method to determine the locations of the minimum and maximum elements. What are the best-case and worst-case

numbers of comparisons between elements of a? What can you say about the expected relative performance of the two methods?

```java
public class MinMaxPair
{
    public int min;
    public int max;

    // constructor
    public MinMaxPair(int theMin, int theMax)
    {
        min = theMin;
        max = theMax;
    }
}

public static MinMaxPair minMax(Comparable [] a)
{
    if (a.length < 1)
        throw new IllegalArgumentException
                ("Cannot find min and max of zero elements");

    // guess that a[0] is min and max
    MinMaxPair p = new MinMaxPair(0,0);

    // update guess
    for (int i = 1; i < a.length; i++)
    {
        if (a[p.min].compareTo(a[i]) > 0) p.min = i;
        if (a[p.max].compareTo(a[i]) < 0) p.max = i;
    }
    return p;
}
```

Program 2.24 Finding the minimum and maximum

27. How many comparisons between the a[]s and x are made by the recursive method rSearch (Program 2.2)?

28. Program 2.26 gives an alternative iterative sequential search method. What is the worst-case number of comparisons between x and the elements of a? Compare this number with the corresponding number for Program 2.1. Which method should run faster? Why?

```
public static MinMaxPair minMax(Comparable [] a)
{
    if (a.length < 1)
        throw new IllegalArgumentException
                ("Cannot find min and max of zero elements");

    // guess that a[0] is min and max
    MinMaxPair p = new MinMaxPair(0,0);

    // update guess
    for (int i = 1; i < a.length; i++)
        if (a[p.min].compareTo(a[i]) > 0) p.min = i;
        else if (a[p.max].compareTo(a[i]) < 0) p.max = i;
    return p;
}
```

Program 2.25 Another method to find the minimum and maximum

```
public static int sequentialSearch(Object [] a, Object x)
{
    a[a.length - 1] = x; // assume extra position available
    int i;
    for (i = 0; !x.equals(a[i]); i++);

    if (i == a.length - 1) return -1;
    else return i;
}
```

Program 2.26 Another sequential search method

29. (a) Introduce statements to increment count at all appropriate points in
        Program 2.27.

    (b) Simplify the resulting program by eliminating statements. Both the sim-
        plified program and the program of part (a) should compute the same
        value for count.

    (c) What is the exact value of count when the program terminates? You
        may assume that the initial value of count is 0.

    (d) Use the frequency method to determine the step count for Program 2.27.
        Clearly show the step-count table.

```
public static void d(int [] x, int n)
{
   for (int i = 0; i < n; i += 2)
      x[i] += 2;
   int i = 1;
   while (i <= n/2)
   {
      x[i] += x[i+1];
      i++;
   }
}
```

Program 2.27 Method for Exercise 29

30. Do Exercise 29 for each of the following methods:

   (a) max (Program 1.29).

   (b) minMax (Program 2.24).

   (c) minMax (Program 2.25). Determine the worst-case step count.

   (d) factorial (Program 1.24).

   (e) valueOf (Program 2.3).

   (f) valueOf (Program 2.4).

   (g) rank (Program 2.5).

   (h) perm (Program 1.27).

   (i) sequentialSearch (Program 2.26). Determine the worst-case step count.

   (j) selectionSort (Program 2.7). Determine the best- and worst-case step counts.

   (k) selectionSort (Program 2.12). Determine the best- and worst-case step counts.

   (l) insertionSort (Program 2.14). Determine the worst-case step count.

   (m) insertionSort (Program 2.15). Determine the worst-case step count.

   (n) bubbleSort (Program 2.9). Determine the worst-case step count.

   (o) bubbleSort (Program 2.13). Determine the worst-case step count.

   (p) add (Program 2.21).

   (q) squareMultiply (Program 2.22).

31. Do Exercise 29 parts (a), (b), and (c) for the following methods:

   (a) transpose (Program 2.19).

(b) `inef` (Program 2.20).

32. Determine the average step counts for the following methods:

    (a) `sequentialSearch` (Program 2.2).

    (b) `sequentialSearch` (Program 2.26).

    (c) `insert` (Program 2.10).

33. (a) Do Exercise 29 for Program 2.23.

    (b) Under what conditions will it be profitable to interchange the two outermost `for` loops?

34. Compare the worst-case number of element reference moves made by methods `selectionSort` (Program 2.12), `insertionSort` (Program 2.15), `bubbleSort` (Program 2.13), and rank sort using Program 2.11.

35. Must a program exhibit its worst-case time behavior and worst-case space behavior at the same time (i.e., for the same input)? Prove your answer.

36. Use repeated substitution to solve the following recurrences (see Example 2.20).

(a) $t(n) = \begin{cases} 2 & n = 0 \\ 2 + t(n-1) & n > 0 \end{cases}$

(b) $t(n) = \begin{cases} 0 & n = 0 \\ 1 & n = 1 \\ 1 + t(n-2) & n > 0 \end{cases}$

(c) $t(n) = \begin{cases} 0 & n = 0 \\ 2n + t(n-1) & n > 0 \end{cases}$

(d) $t(n) = \begin{cases} 1 & n = 0 \\ 2 * t(n-1) & n > 0 \end{cases}$

(e) $t(n) = \begin{cases} 1 & n = 0 \\ 3 * t(n-1) & n > 0 \end{cases}$

CHAPTER 3

ASYMPTOTIC NOTATION

BIRD'S-EYE VIEW

Chapter 2 showed you how to analyze the space and time complexities of a program. The methods of that chapter are somewhat cumbersome because they attempt to obtain exact counts, rather than estimates. In this chapter we review asymptoic notation, which is used to make statements about program performance when the instance characteristics are large. When we use this notation, we need only estimate the step count. Although the big oh notation is the most popular asymptotic notation used in the performance analysis of programs, the omega, theta, and little oh notations also are in common use.

Asymptotic notation is first introduced in an informal manner in Section 3.2. The informal treatment of this section is adequate to follow all the analyses done in this book. A more rigorous treatment is presented in Section 3.3. You may omit Section 3.3 and not face any dire consequences.

The use of asymptotic notation is illustrated through the applications developed in Chapters 1 and 2. Additionally, an important and efficient search method—binary search of a sorted array—is developed and analyzed in this chapter. This search method is also available as the method `java.util.arrays.binarySearch`.

107

3.1   INTRODUCTION

Two important reasons to determine operation and step counts are (1) to predict the growth in run time as the instance characteristics increase and (2) to compare the time complexities of two programs that perform the same task. When using operation counts, we focus on certain "key" operations and ignore all others. Therefore, you must be very cautious when using an operation count for either of the above purposes. For example, a program may do $2n$ comparisons, but the total number of computation steps could be $6n^2 + 8n$. It would be incorrect to use the comparison count of $2n$ to conclude that the run time grows linearly in n. It would also be incorrect to conclude that a program that makes $2n$ comparisons is faster than a program, for the same task, that makes $3n$ comparisons; the $3n$ comparison program may actually do less total work than is done by the $2n$ comparison program.

The operation count method accounts for only some of the work that is done in a program. Step counts attempt to overcome this deficiency by accounting for all work. However, the notion of a step is inexact. Both the instructions x = y and x = y+z+(x/y) count as one step. Therefore, two analysts may arrive at $4n^2 + 6n + 2$ and $7n^2 + 3n + 4$ as the step count for the same program. We cannot conclude that the run time will grow as either $4n^2 + 6n + 2$ or $7n^2 + 3n + 4$, because any step count of the form $c_1 n^2 + c_2 n + c_3$, where $c_1 > 0$, c_2, and c_3 are constants, could be a correct step count for the program. Because of the inexactness of what a step stands for, the exact step count isn't very useful for comparative purposes either. However, when the difference in the step counts of two programs is very large as in $3n + 3$ versus $900n + 10$. We might feel quite safe in predicting that the program with step count $3n + 3$ will run in less time than the one with step count $900n + 10$.

We can use the step count to accurately predict the growth in run time for large instance sizes (i.e., in the asymptote as n approaches infinity) and to predict the relative performance of two programs when the instance size becomes large. Suppose that the step count of a program is determined to be $c_1 n^2 + c_2 n + c_3$, $c_1 > 0$. When n becomes large, the $c_1 n^2$ term will be much larger than the remaining terms $c_2 n + c_3$. The ratio of these two expressions is $r(n) = (c_2 n + c_3)/(c_1 n^2) = c_2/(c_1 n) + c_3/(c_1 n^2)$. Figure 3.1 plots $r(n)$ for the case $c_1 = 1$, $c_2 = 2$, and $c_3 = 3$. Even though $r(n)$ never equals 0 for any finite n, $r(n)$ gets closer and closer to 0 as we make n bigger and bigger.

Regardless of the values of $c_1 > 0$, c_2, and c_3, the ratio $r(n)$ approaches 0 as n approaches infinity; that is,

$$\lim_{n \to \infty} \left(\frac{c_2}{c_1 n} + \frac{c_3}{c_1 n^2} \right) = 0$$

So for large n, $c_2 n + c_3$ is insignificant when compared to $c_1 n^2$, and run time may be approximated by the $c_1 n^2$ term. Let n_1 and n_2 be two large values of n. We conclude that

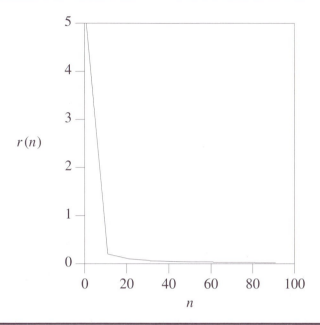

Figure 3.1 Plot of $r(n) = 2/n + 3/n^2$

$$\frac{t(n_1)}{t(n_2)} \approx \frac{c_1 n_1^2}{c_1 n_2^2} = \left(\frac{n_1}{n_2}\right)^2$$

Therefore, the run time is expected to increase by a factor of 4 (approximately) when the instance size is doubled; the run time increases by a factor of 9 when the instance size is tripled; and so on. To make this conclusion, all we need to know is that the biggest term in the step count is an n^2 term; the value of the coefficient c_1 is irrelevant to the conclusion.

Suppose that programs A and B perform the same task. Assume that John has determined the step counts of these programs to be $t_A(n) = n^2 + 3n$ and $t_B(n) = 43n$. It is entirely possible that Mary's analysis of the same programs yields $t_A(n) = 2n^2 + 3n$ and $t_B(n) = 83n$. In fact, assuming that John's analysis is correct, all other correct analyses would result in $t_A(n) = c_1 n^2 + c_2 n + c_3$ and $t_B(n) = c_4 n$, where c_1, c_2, c_3, and c_4 are constants, $c_1 > 0$, and $c_4 > 0$.

To see what conclusion we can draw about the relative performance of programs A and B knowing that the constant coefficients may vary from analyst to analyst, examine the plot of Figure 3.2. First, look at the curves for John's analysis, $t_A(n) = n^2 + 3n$ and $t_B(n) = 43n$. We conclude that for $n < 40$, program A is faster; for

$n > 40$, program B is faster; and $n = 40$ is the break-even point between the two programs. Now suppose that the analysis had instead concluded that $t_B(n) = 83n$. In this case we would conclude that for $n < 80$, program A is faster; for $n > 80$, program B is faster; and $n = 80$ is the break-even point between the two programs. Our conclusion that program B is faster than program A for large n does not change; only the break-even point changes.

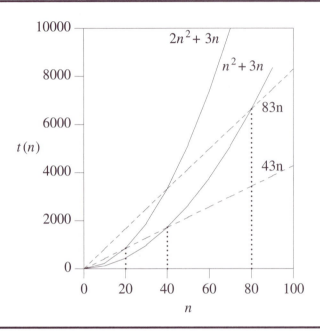

Figure 3.2 Comparing run time functions

What if John's analysis had concluded $t_A(n) = 2n^2 + 3n$? From Figure 3.2, we see that regardless of whether $t_B(n) = 43n$ or $83n$, program B remains faster than program A when n is suitably large ($n > 20$ when $t_B(n) = 43n$ and $n > 40$ when $t_B(n) = 83n$).

To arrive at the conclusion that program B is faster than program A when n is large, all we need to know is that the biggest term in the step count for program A is an n^2 term while that for program B is an n term; the values of the coefficients c_1 through c_4 are irrelevant to this conclusion. Asymptotic analysis focuses on determining the biggest terms (but not their coefficients) in the complexity function.

3.2   ASYMPTOTIC NOTATION

3.2.1   Big Oh Notation (O)

Definition 3.1 *Let $p(n)$ and $q(n)$ be two nonnegative functions. $p(n)$ is* **asymptotically bigger** *($p(n)$ asymptotically dominates $q(n)$) than the function $q(n)$ iff*

$$\lim_{n \to \infty} \frac{q(n)}{p(n)} = 0 \tag{3.1}$$

$q(n)$ is **asymptotically smaller** *than $p(n)$ iff $p(n)$ is asymptotically bigger than $q(n)$. $p(n)$ and $q(n)$ are* **asymptotically equal** *iff neither is asymptotically bigger than the other.*   ■

Example 3.1 Since

$$\lim_{n \to \infty} \frac{10n + 7}{3n^2 + 2n + 6} = \frac{10/n + 7/n^2}{3 + 2/n + 6/n^2} = 0/3 = 0$$

$3n^2 + 2n + 6$ is asymptotically bigger than $10n + 7$ and $10n + 7$ is asymptotically smaller than $3n^2 + 2n + 6$. A similar derivation shows that $8n^4 + 9n^2$ is asymptotically bigger than $100n^3 - 3$, and that $2n^2 + 3n$ is asymptotically bigger than $83n$. $12n + 6$ is asymptotically equal to $6n + 2$.   ■

In the following discussion the function $f(n)$ denotes the time or space complexity of a program as a function of the instance characteristic n. Since the time or space requirements of a program are nonnegative quantities, we assume that the function f has a nonnegative value for all values of n. Further, since n denotes an instance characteristic, we assume that $n \geq 0$. The function $f(n)$ will, in general, be a sum of terms. For example, the terms of $f(n) = 9n^2 + 3n + 12$ are $9n^2$, $3n$, and 12. We may compare pairs of terms to determine which is bigger (see Definition 3.1). The biggest term in the example $f(n)$ is $9n^2$.

Figure 3.3 gives the terms that occur frequently in a step-count analysis. Although all the terms in Figure 3.3 have a coefficient of 1, in an actual analysis, the coefficients of these terms may have a different value.

We do not associate a logarithmic base with the functions in Figure 3.3 that include $\log n$ because for any constants a and b greater than 1, $\log_a n = \log_b n / \log_b a$. So $\log_a n$ and $\log_b n$ are asymptotically equal.

Using Definition 3.1, we obtain the following ordering for the terms of Figure 3.3 ($<$ is to be read as "is asymptotically smaller than"):

$$1 < \log n < n < n \log n < n^2 < n^3 < 2^n < n!$$

Term	Name
1	constant
$\log n$	logarithmic
n	linear
$n \log n$	$n \log n$
n^2	quadratic
n^3	cubic
2^n	exponential
$n!$	factorial

Figure 3.3 Commonly occurring terms

Asymptotic notation describes the behavior of the time or space complexity for large instance characteristics. Although we will develop asymptotic notation with reference to step counts alone, our development also applies to space complexity and operation counts. The terms *time complexity* and *step count* are used as synonyms. When the instance characteristic is described by a single variable, say n, asymptotic notation describes the complexity using a single term, the asymptotically biggest term in the step count.

The notation $f(n) = O(g(n))$ (read as "$f(n)$ is big oh of $g(n)$") means that $f(n)$ is asymptotically smaller than or equal to $g(n)$. Therefore, in an asymptotic sense $g(n)$ is an upper bound for $f(n)$. You may use this as a working definition of "big oh"; a formal definition is provided in Section 3.3.1.

Example 3.2 From Example 3.1 and the working definition of big oh, it follows that $10n + 7 = O(3n^2 + 2n + 6); 100n^3 - 3 = O(8n^4 + 9n^2); 12n + 6 = O(6n + 2); 3n^2 + 2n + 6 \neq O(10n + 7);$ and $8n^4 + 9n^2 \neq O(100n^3 - 3)$. ∎

Although Example 3.2 uses the big oh notation in a correct way, it is customary to use $g(n)$ functions that are **unit terms** (i.e., $g(n)$ is a single term whose coefficient is 1) except when $f(n) = 0$. In addition, it is customary to use, for $g(n)$, the smallest unit term for which the statement $f(n) = O(g(n))$ is true. When $f(n) = 0$, it is customary to use $g(n) = 0$.

Example 3.3 The customary way to describe the asymptotic behavior of the functions used in Example 3.2 is $10n + 7 = O(n); 100n^3 - 3 = O(n^3); 12n + 6 = O(n); 3n^3 + 2n + 6 \neq O(n);$ and $8n^4 + 9n^2 \neq O(n^3)$. ∎

In asymptotic complexity analysis, we determine the biggest term in the complexity; the coefficient of this biggest term is set to 1. The unit terms of a step-count function are step-count terms with their coefficients changed to 1. For example, the unit terms of $3n^2 + 6n \log n + 7n + 5$ are n^2, $n \log n$, n, and 1; the biggest unit term is n^2. So when the step count of a program is $3n^2 + 6n \log n + 7n + 5$, we say that its asymptotic complexity is $O(n^2)$.

Example 3.4 In Example 2.19, we determined that $t_{\mathsf{sum}}(n) = 2n + 4$ when $n =$ `a.length` > 0. Since the biggest unit term in $t_{\mathsf{sum}}(n)$ is n, $t(n) = O(n)$, when $n > 0$.

   Since $t_{\mathsf{rSum}}(n) = n + 1$, $n \geq 1$ (see Example 2.20), $t_{\mathsf{rSum}}(n) = O(n)$, $n \geq 1$.

   The step count for Program 2.19 is $2rows^2 + 1$ (see Figure 2.7). The biggest unit term is $rows^2$. Therefore, $t_{\mathsf{transpose}}(rows) = O(rows^2)$. ∎

   Notice that $f(n) = O(g(n))$ is not the same as $O(g(n)) = f(n)$. In fact, saying that $O(g(n)) = f(n)$ is meaningless. The use of the symbol $=$ is unfortunate, as this symbol commonly denotes the equals relation. We can avoid some of the confusion that results from the use of this symbol (which is standard terminology) by reading the symbol $=$ as "is" and not as "equals."

Definition 3.2 *Let $t(m,n)$ and $u(m,n)$ be two terms. $t(m,n)$ is asymptotically bigger than $u(m,n)$ (equivalently, $u(m,n)$ is asymptotically smaller than $t(m,n)$) iff either*

$$\lim_{n \to \infty} \frac{u(m,n)}{t(m,n)} = 0 \ and \ \lim_{m \to \infty} \frac{u(m,n)}{t(m,n)} \neq \infty$$

or

$$\lim_{n \to \infty} \frac{u(m,n)}{t(m,n)} \neq \infty \ and \ \lim_{m \to \infty} \frac{u(m,n)}{t(m,n)} = 0$$ ∎

   We may obtain a working definition of big oh for the case of functions in more than one variable as follows.

- Let $f(m,n)$ be the step count of a program. From $f(m,n)$ remove all terms that are asymptotically smaller than at least one other term in $f(m,n)$.

- Change the coefficients of all remaining terms to 1.

Example 3.5 Consider $f(m,n) = 3m^2n + m^3 + 10mn + 2n^2$. $10mn$ is smaller than $3m^2n$ because

$$\lim_{n \to \infty} \frac{10mn}{3m^2n} = \frac{10}{3m} \neq \infty \ and \ \lim_{m \to \infty} \frac{10mn}{3m^2n} = \lim_{m \to \infty} \frac{10}{3m} = 0$$

   None of the remaining terms is smaller than another. Dropping the $10mn$ term and changing the coefficients of the remaining terms to 1, we get $f(m,n) = O(m^2n + m^3 + n^2)$. ∎

3.2.2   Omega (Ω) and Theta (Θ) Notations

Although the big oh notation is the most frequently used asymptotic notation, the omega and theta notations are sometimes used to describe the asymptotic complexity of a program. We provide a working definition of these notations in this section. See Sections 3.3.2 and 3.3.3 for a more formal definition.

The notation $f(n) = \Omega(g(n))$ (read as "$f(n)$ is omega of $g(n)$") means that $f(n)$ is asymptotically bigger than or equal to $g(n)$. Therefore, in an asymptotic sense, $g(n)$ is a lower bound for $f(n)$. The notation $f(n) = \Theta(g(n))$ (read as "$f(n)$ is theta of $g(n)$") means that $f(n)$ is asymptotically equal to $g(n)$.

Example 3.6 $10n+7 = \Omega(n)$ because $10n+7$ is asymptotically equal to n; $100n^3 - 3 = \Omega(n^3)$; $12n+6 = \Omega(n)$; $3n^3 + 2n + 6 = \Omega(n)$; $8n^4 + 9n^2 = \Omega(n^3)$; $3n^3 + 2n + 6 \neq \Omega(n^5)$; and $8n^4 + 9n^2 \neq \Omega(n^5)$.

$10n+7 = \Theta(n)$ because $10n+7$ is asymptotically equal to n; $100n^3 - 3 = \Theta(n^3)$; $12n + 6 = \Theta(n)$; $3n^3 + 2n + 6 \neq \Theta(n)$; $8n^4 + 9n^2 \neq \Theta(n^3)$; $3n^3 + 2n + 6 \neq \Theta(n^5)$; and $8n^4 + 9n^2 \neq \Theta(n^5)$.

Since $t_{\text{sum}}(n) = 2n+4$ when $n \neq 0$ (see Example 2.19) and $2n+4$ is asymptotically equal to n, $t_{\text{sum}}(n) = \Theta(n)$ for $n \neq 0$.

Since $t_{\text{rSum}}(n) = n+1$, $n \geq 1$ (see Example 2.20) and $n+1$ asymptotically equals n, $t_{\text{rSum}}(n) = \Theta(n)$, $n \geq 1$.

The step count for Program 2.19 is $2rows^2 + 1$ (see Figure 2.7), and $2rows^2 + 1$ asymptotically equals $rows^2$. Therefore, $t_{\text{transpose}}(rows) = \Theta(rows^2)$.

The best-case step count for SequentialSearch (Program 2.1) is 4 (Figure 2.9), the worst-case step count is $n + 3$, and the average step count is $0.6n + 3.4$. So the best-case asymptotic complexity of SequentialSearch is $\Theta(1)$, and the worst-case and average complexities are $\Theta(n)$. It is also correct to say that the complexity of SequentialSearch is $\Omega(1)$ and $O(n)$ because 1 is a lower bound (in an asymptotic sense) and n is an upper bound (in an asymptotic sense) on the step count.

From Figures 2.12 and 2.13, it follows that $4 \leq t_{\text{insert}}(n) \leq 2n + 4$. Therefore, $t_{\text{insert}}(n)$ is both $\Omega(1)$ and $O(n)$. ∎

At times it is useful to interpret $O(g(n))$, $\Omega(g(n))$, and $\Theta(g(n))$ as being the following sets:

$O(g(n)) = \{f(n) | f(n) = O(g(n))\}$

$\Omega(g(n)) = \{f(n) | f(n) = \Omega(g(n))\}$

$\Theta(g(n)) = \{f(n) | f(n) = \Theta(g(n))\}$

Under this interpretation, statements such as $O(g_1(n)) = O(g_2(n))$ and $\Theta(g_1(n)) = \Theta(g_2(n))$ are meaningful. When using this interpretation, it is also convenient to read $f(n) = O(g(n))$ as "f of n is in (or is a member of) big oh of g of n" and so on.

The working definitions of big oh, omega, and theta are all you need to understand the analyses done in this book. The next section contains a more formal treatment of asymptotic notation that will help you with more complex analyses.

EXERCISES

1. Use Equation 3.1 to show that $p(n)$ is asymptotically bigger than $q(n)$ for the following functions:

   (a) $p(n) = 3n^4 + 2n^2$, $q(n) = 100n^2 + 6$

   (b) $p(n) = 6n^{1.5} + 12$, $q(n) = 100n$

   (c) $p(n) = 7n^2 \log n$, $q(n) = 10n^2$

   (d) $p(n) = 17n^2 2^n$, $q(n) = 100n2^n + 33n$

2. Express the following step counts using big oh notation. Your $g(n)$ function should be the smallest possible unit term.

   (a) $2n^3 - 6n + 30$

   (b) $44n^{1.5} + 33n - 200$

   (c) $16n^2 \log n + 5n^2$

   (d) $31n^3 + 17n^2 \log n$

   (e) $23n2^n - 3n^3$

3. Use the working definition of big oh and Equation 3.1 to show the following:

   (a) $2n + 7 \neq O(1)$

   (b) $12n^2 + 8n + 7 \neq O(n)$

   (c) $5n^3 + 6n^2 \neq O(n^2)$

   (d) $15n^3 \log n + 16n^2 \neq O(n^3)$

4. Express the step counts of Exercise 2 using omega notation.

5. Use the working definition of omega and Equation 3.1 to show the following:

   (a) $2n + 7 \neq \Omega(n^2)$

   (b) $12n^2 + 8n + 7 \neq \Omega(n^3)$

   (c) $5n^3 + 6n^2 \neq \Omega(n^3 \log n)$

   (d) $15n^3 \log n + 16n^2 \neq \Omega(n^4)$

6. Express the step counts of Exercise 2 using theta notation.

7. Let $t(n)$ be the step count of a program. Express the following step-count information using asymptotic notation. Use the most appropriate $g(n)$ functions.

(a) $6 \le t(n) \le 20$

(b) $6 \le t(n) \le 2n$

(c) $3n^2 + 1 \le t(n) \le 4n^2 + 3n + 9$

(d) $3n^2 + 1 \le t(n) \le 4n^2 \log n + 3n^2 + 9$

(e) $t(n) \ge 5n^3 + 7$

(f) $t(n) \ge 32n \log n + 77n - 6$

(g) $t(n) = 17n^2 + 3n$

8. Express the following step counts using big oh notation. m and n are instance characteristics.

(a) $7m^2n^2 + 2m^3n + mn + 5mn^2$

(b) $2m^2 \log n + 3mn + 5m \log n + m^2n^2$

(c) $m^4 + n^3 + m^3n^2$

(d) $3mn^2 + 7m^2n + 4mn + 8m + 2n + 16$

3.3   ASYMPTOTIC MATHEMATICS (OPTIONAL)

3.3.1   Big Oh Notation (O)

The big oh notation describes an upper bound on the asymptotic growth rate of the function f.

Definition 3.3 [Big oh] $f(n) = O(g(n))$ *iff positive constants c and n_0 exist such that $f(n) \le cg(n)$ for all n, $n \ge n_0$.*   ∎

The definition states that the function f is at most c times the function g except possibly when n is smaller than n_0. Here c is some positive constant. Thus g is an upper bound (up to a constant factor c) on the value of f for all suitably large n (i.e., $n \ge n_0$). Figure 3.4 illustrates what it means for a function $g(n)$ to upper bound (up to a constant factor c) another function $f(n)$. Although $f(n)$ may be less than, equal to, or greater than $cg(n)$ for several values of n, there must exist a value m of n beyond which $f(n)$ is never less than $cg(n)$. The n_0 in the definition of big oh could be any integer $\ge m$.

When providing an upper-bound function g for f, we will normally use only simple functional forms. These typically contain a single term in n with a multiplicative constant of 1.

Example 3.7 [Linear Function] Consider $f(n) = 3n + 2$. When n is at least 2, $3n + 2 \le 3n + n \le 4n$. So $f(n) = O(n)$. Thus $f(n)$ is bounded from above by a linear function. We can arrive at the same conclusion in other ways. For example,

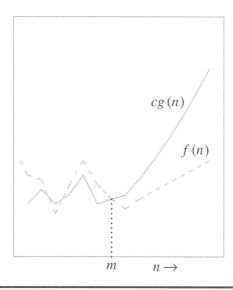

Figure 3.4 $g(n)$ is an upper bound (up to a constant factor c) on $f(n)$

$3n + 2 \leq 10n$ for $n > 0$. Therefore, we can also satisfy the definition of big oh by selecting $c = 10$ and n_0 equal to any integer greater than 0. Alternatively, $3n + 2 \leq 3n + 2n = 5n$ for $n \geq 1$, so we can satisfy the definition of big oh by setting $c = 5$ and $n_0 = 1$. The values of c and n_0 used to satisfy the definition of big oh are not important because we will be saying only that $f(n)$ is big oh of $g(n)$ and in this statement neither c nor n_0 play a role.

For $f(n) = 3n + 3$, we note that for $n \geq 3$, $3n + 3 \leq 3n + n \leq 4n$. So $f(n) = O(n)$. Similarly, $f(n) = 100n + 6 \leq 100n + n = 101n$ for $n \geq n_0 = 6$. Therefore, $100n + 6 = O(n)$. As expected, $3n + 2$, $3n + 3$, and $100n + 6$ are all big oh of n; that is, they are bounded from above by a linear function (for suitably large n). ∎

Example 3.8 [Quadratic Function] Suppose that $f(n) = 10n^2 + 4n + 2$. We see that for $n \geq 2$, $f(n) \leq 10n^2 + 5n$. Now we note that for $n \geq 5$, $5n \leq n^2$. Hence for $n \geq n_0 = 5$, $f(n) \leq 10n^2 + n^2 = 11n^2$. Therefore, $f(n) = O(n^2)$.

As another example of a quadratic complexity, consider $f(n) = 1000n^2 + 100n - 6$. We easily see that $f(n) \leq 1000n^2 + 100n$ for all n. Furthermore, $100n \leq n^2$ for $n \geq 100$. Hence $f(n) < 1001n^2$ for $n \geq n_0 = 100$. So $f(n) = O(n^2)$. ∎

Example 3.9 [Exponential Function] As an example of exponential complexity, consider $f(n) = 6 * 2^n + n^2$. Observe that for $n \geq 4$, $n^2 \leq 2^n$. So $f(n) \leq 6 * 2^n + 2^n = 7 * 2^n$ for $n \geq 4$. Therefore, $6 * 2^n + n^2 = O(2^n)$. ∎

Example 3.10 [Constant Function] When $f(n)$ is a constant, as in $f(n) = 9$ or $f(n) = 2033$, we write $f(n) = O(1)$. The correctness of this is easily established. For example, $f(n) = 9 \leq 9 * 1$; setting $c = 9$ and $n_0 = 0$ satisfies the definition of big oh. Similarly, $f(n) = 2033 \leq 2033 * 1$, and the definition of big oh is satisfied by setting $c = 2033$ and $n_0 = 0$.   ∎

Example 3.11 [Loose Bounds] $3n + 3 = O(n^2)$ as $3n + 3 \leq 3n^2$ for $n \geq 2$. Although n^2 is an upper bound for $3n + 3$, it is not a tight upper bound; we can find a smaller function (in this case linear) that also satisfies the big oh relation.

$10n^2 + 4n + 2 = O(n^4)$ as $10n^2 + 4n + 2 \leq 10n^4$ for $n \geq 2$. Once again, n^4 does not provide a tight upper bound for $100n^2 + 4n + 2$.

Similarly, $6n2^n + 20 = O(n^2 2^n)$, but it is not a tight upper bound because we can find a smaller function, namely, $n2^n$, for which the definition of big oh is satisfied. That is, $6n2^n + 20 = O(n2^n)$.   ∎

Note that the strategy in each of the preceding derivations is to replace the low-order terms by higher-order terms until only a single term remains.

Example 3.12 [Incorrect Bounds] $3n + 2 \neq O(1)$, as there is no $c > 0$ and n_0 such that $3n + 2 \leq c$ for all n, $n \geq n_0$. We can use contradiction to prove this condition formally. Suppose that such a c and n_0 exist. Then $n \leq (c - 2)/3$ for all n, $n \geq n_0$. This is not true for $n > \max\{n_0, (c - 2)/3\}$.

To prove $10n^2 + 4n + 2 \neq O(n)$, suppose the equality holds. That is, $10n^2 + 4n + 2 = O(n)$. There exists a positive c and an n_0 such that $10n^2 + 4n + 2 \leq cn$ for all $n \geq n_0$. Dividing both sides of the relation by n, we get $10n + 4 + 2/n \leq c$ for $n \geq n_0$. This relation cannot be true because the left side increases as n increases, whereas the right side does not change. In particular, we get a contradiction for $n \geq \max\{n_0, (c - 4)/10\}$.

$f(n) = 3n^2 2^n + 4n2^n + 8n^2 \neq O(2^n)$. To prove this inequality, suppose that $f(n) = O(2^n)$. Then a $c > 0$ and an n_0 exist such that $f(n) \leq c * 2^n$ for $n \geq n_0$. Dividing both sides by 2^n, we get $3n^2 + 4n + 8n^2/2^n \leq c$ for $n \geq n_0$. Once again, the left side of the relation is an increasing function of n while the right side is constant. So the relation cannot hold for "large" n.   ∎

As illustrated in Example 3.11, the statement $f(n) = O(g(n))$ states only that $cg(n)$ is an upper bound on the value of $f(n)$ for all n, $n \geq n_0$. It doesn't say anything about how good or tight this bound is. Notice that $n = O(n^2)$, $n = O(n^{2.5})$, $n = O(n^3)$, and $n = O(2^n)$. For the statement $f(n) = O(g(n))$ to be informative, $g(n)$ should be as small a function of n as possible for which $f(n) = O(g(n))$. So although we often say $3n + 3 = O(n)$, we almost never say $3n + 3 = O(n^2)$, even though the latter statement is correct.

Theorem 3.1 obtains a very useful result concerning the order of $f(n)$ (i.e., the $g(n)$ in $f(n) = O(g(n))$) when $f(n)$ is a polynomial in n.

Theorem 3.1 *If* $f(n) = a_m n^m + \cdots + a_1 n + a_0$ *and* $a_m > 0$, *then* $f(n) = O(n^m)$.

Proof $f(n) \leq \sum_{i=0}^{m} |a_i| n^i \leq n^m \sum_0^m |a_i| n^{i-m} \leq n^m \sum_0^m |a_i|$ for $n \geq 1$. So $f(n) = O(n^m)$. ∎

Example 3.13 Let us apply Theorem 3.1 to the functions of Examples 3.7, 3.8, and 3.10. For the three linear functions of Example 3.7, $m = 1$, and so these functions are $O(n)$. For the functions of Example 3.8, $m = 2$, and so all are $O(n^2)$. For the constants of Example 3.10, $m = 0$, so both constants are $O(1)$. ∎

We can extend the strategy used in Example 3.12 to show that an upper bound is incorrect to the case when an upper bound is correct, as shown in the following theorem. *It is usually easier to show* $f(n) = O(g(n))$ *by using this theorem than by using the definition of big oh.*

Theorem 3.2 [Big oh ratio theorem] *Let* $f(n)$ *and* $g(n)$ *be such that* $\lim_{n \to \infty} f(n)/g(n)$ *exists.* $f(n) = O(g(n))$ *iff* $\lim_{n \to \infty} f(n)/g(n) \leq c$ *for some finite constant* c.

Proof If $f(n) = O(g(n))$, then positive c and an n_0 exist such that $f(n)/g(n) \leq c$ for all $n \geq n_0$. Hence $\lim_{n \to \infty} f(n)/g(n) \leq c$. Suppose that $\lim_{n \to \infty} f(n)/g(n) \leq c$. It follows that an n_0 exists for which $f(n) \leq \max\{1, c\} * g(n)$ for all $n \geq n_0$. ∎

Example 3.14 $3n+2 = O(n)$ as $\lim_{n \to \infty} (3n+2)/n = 3$. $10n^2 + 4n + 2 = O(n^2)$ as $\lim_{n \to \infty} (10n^2+4n+2)/n^2 = 10$. $6*2^n + n^2 = O(2^n)$ as $\lim_{n \to \infty} (6*2^n+n^2)/2^n = 6$. $2n^2 - 3 = O(n^4)$ as $\lim_{n \to \infty} (2n^2 - 3)/n^4 = 0$. $3n^2 + 5 \neq O(n)$ as $\lim_{n \to \infty} (3n^2+5)/n = \infty$. ∎

3.3.2   Omega Notation (Ω)

The omega notation, which is the lower-bound analog of the big oh notation, permits us to bound the asymptotic growth rate of f from below.

Definition 3.4 [Omega] $f(n) = \Omega(g(n))$ *iff positive constants* c *and* n_0 *exist such that* $f(n) \geq cg(n)$ *for all* n, $n \geq n_0$. ∎

When we write $f(n) = \Omega(g(n))$, we are saying that f is at least c times the function g except possibly when n is smaller than n_0. Here c is some positive constant. Thus g is a lower bound (up to a constant factor c) on the value of f for all suitably large n (i.e., $n \geq n_0$). Figure 3.5 illustrates what it means for a function $g(n)$ to lower bound (up to a constant factor c) another function $f(n)$. Although $f(n)$ may be less than, equal to, or greater than $cg(n)$ for several values of n, there must exist a value m of n beyond which $f(n)$ is never greater than $cg(n)$. The n_0 in the definition of omega could be any integer $\geq m$.

As in the case of the big oh notation, we normally use only simple functional forms for g.

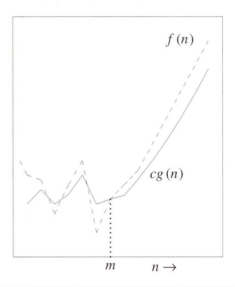

Figure 3.5 $g(n)$ is a lower bound (up to a constant factor c) on $f(n)$

Example 3.15 $f(n) = 3n + 2 > 3n$ for all n. So $f(n) = \Omega(n)$. Also, $f(n) = 3n + 3 > 3n$, and so $f(n) = \Omega(n)$. Since $f(n) = 100n + 6 > 100n$, $100n + 6 = \Omega(n)$. So $3n + 2$, $3n + 3$, and $100n + 6$ are all bounded from below by a linear function.

$f(n) = 10n^2 + 4n + 2 > 10n^2$ for $n \geq 0$. So $f(n) = \Omega(n^2)$. Similarly, $1000n^2 + 100n - 6 = \Omega(n^2)$. Furthermore, since $6 * 2^n + n^2 > 6 * 2^n$, $6 * 2^n + n^2 = \Omega(2^n)$.

Observe also that $3n + 3 = \Omega(1)$; $10n^2 + 4n + 2 = \Omega(n)$; $10n^2 + 4n + 2 = \Omega(1)$; $6 * 2^n + n^2 = \Omega(n^{100})$; $6 * 2^n + n^2 = \Omega(n^{50.2})$; $6 * 2^n + n^2 = \Omega(n^2)$; $6 * 2^n + n^2 = \Omega(n)$; and $6 * 2^n + n^2 = \Omega(1)$.

To see that $3n + 2 \neq \Omega(n^2)$, suppose that $3n + 2 = \Omega(n^2)$. Then positive c and n_0 exist such that $3n + 2 \geq cn^2$ for all $n \geq n_0$. So $cn^2/(3n + 2) \leq 1$ for all $n \geq n_0$. This relation cannot be true because its left side increases to infinity as n becomes large. ∎

As in the case of the big oh notation, there are several functions $g(n)$ for which $f(n) = \Omega(g(n))$. $g(n)$ is only a lower bound (up to a constant factor) on $f(n)$. For the statement $f(n) = \Omega(g(n))$ to be informative, $g(n)$ should be as large a function of n as possible for which the statement $f(n) = \Omega(g(n))$ is true. So although we say that $3n + 3 = \Omega(n)$ and that $6 * 2^n + n^2 = \Omega(2^n)$, we almost never say that $3n + 3 = \Omega(1)$ or that $6 * 2^n + n^2 = \Omega(1)$, even though both these statements are correct.

Theorem 3.3 is the analog of Theorem 3.1 for the omega notation.

Theorem 3.3 *If* $f(n) = a_m n^m + \cdots + a_1 n + a_0$ *and* $a_m > 0$, *then* $f(n) = \Omega(n^m)$.

Proof See Exercise 12.   ∎

Example 3.16 From Theorem 3.3, it follows that $3n + 2 = \Omega(n)$, $10n^2 + 4n + 2 = \Omega(n^2)$, and $100n^4 + 3500n^2 + 82n + 8 = \Omega(n^4)$.   ∎

Theorem 3.4 is the analog of Theorem 3.2, and it is usually easier to show $f(n) = \Omega(g(n))$ by using Theorem 3.4 than by using the definition of omega.

Theorem 3.4 [Omega ratio theorem] *Let $f(n)$ and $g(n)$ be such that $\lim_{n\to\infty} g(n)/f(n)$ exists. $f(n) = \Omega(g(n))$ iff $\lim_{n\to\infty} g(n)/f(n) \le c$ for some finite constant c.*

Proof See Exercise 13.   ∎

Example 3.17 $3n + 2 = \Omega(n)$ as $\lim_{n\to\infty} n/(3n + 2) = 1/3$. $10n^2 + 4n + 2 = \Omega(n^2)$ as $\lim_{n\to\infty} n^2/(10n^2 + 4n + 2) = 0.1$. $6 * 2^n + n^2 = \Omega(2^n)$ as $\lim_{n\to\infty} 2^n/(6 * 2^n + n^2) = 1/6$. $6n^2 + 2 = \Omega(n)$ as $\lim_{n\to\infty} n/(6n^2 + 2) = 0$. $3n^2 + 5 \neq \Omega(n^3)$ as $\lim_{n\to\infty} n^3/(3n^2 + 5) = \infty$.   ∎

3.3.3   Theta Notation (Θ)

The theta notation is used when the function f can be bounded both from above and below by the same function g.

Definition 3.5 [Theta] *$f(n) = \Theta(g(n))$ iff positive constants c_1 and c_2 and an n_0 exist such that $c_1 g(n) \le f(n) \le c_2 g(n)$ for all n, $n \ge n_0$.*   ∎

When we write $f(n) = \Theta(g(n))$, we are saying that f lies between c_1 times the function g and c_2 times the function g except possibly when n is smaller than n_0. Here c_1 and c_2 are positive constants. Thus g is both a lower and upper bound (up to a constant factor c) on the value of f for all suitably large n (i.e., $n \ge n_0$). Another way to view the theta notation is that it says $f(n)$ is both $\Omega(g(n))$ and $O(g(n))$.

Figure 3.6 illustrates what it means for a function $g(n)$ to both upper and lower bound (up to a constant factor) another function $f(n)$. There must exist a value m of n beyond which $f(n)$ lies between $c_1 g(n)$ and $c_2 g(n)$. The n_0 in the definition of theta could be any integer $\ge m$.

As in the case of the big oh and omega notations, we normally use only simple functional forms for g.

Example 3.18 From Examples 3.7, 3.8, 3.9, and 3.15, it follows that $3n + 2 = \Theta(n)$; $3n + 3 = \Theta(n)$; $100n + 6 = \Theta(n)$; $10n^2 + 4n + 2 = \Theta(n^2)$; $1000n^2 + 100n - 6 = \Theta(n^2)$; and $6 * 2^n + n^2 = \Theta(2^n)$.

$10 * \log_2 n + 4 = \Theta(\log_2 n)$ as $\log_2 n < 10 \log_2 n + 4 \le 11 \log_2 n$ for $n \ge 16$. As remarked earlier, $\log_a n$ is $\log_b n$ times a constant, and we write $\Theta(\log_a n)$ simply as $\Theta(\log n)$.

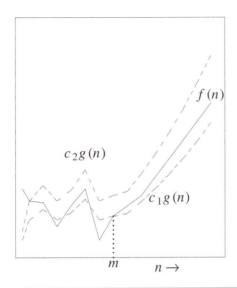

Figure 3.6 $g(n)$ is a lower and upper bound (up to a constant factor) on $f(n)$

In Example 3.12 we showed that $3n + 2 \neq O(1)$. So $3n + 2 \neq \Theta(1)$. Similarly, we may show that $3n + 3 \neq \Theta(1)$ and $100n + 6 \neq \Theta(1)$. Since $3n + 3 \neq \Omega(n^2)$, $3n + 3 \neq \Theta(n^2)$. Since $10n^2 + 4n + 2 \neq O(n)$, $10n^2 + 4n + 2 \neq \Theta(n)$. Also, since $10n^2 + 4n + 2 \neq O(1)$, it is not $\Theta(1)$.

Since $6 * 2^n + n^2$ is not $O(n^2)$, it is not $\Theta(n^2)$. Similarly, $6 * 2^n + n^2 \neq \Theta(n^{100})$; and $6 * 2^n + n^2 \neq \Theta(1)$. ■

As mentioned earlier it is common practice to use only g functions with a multiplicative factor of 1. We almost never say that $3n + 3 = O(3n)$ or $10 = O(100)$ or $10n^2 + 4n + 2 = \Omega(4 * n^2)$ or $6 * 2^n + n^2 = \Omega(6 * 2^n)$ or $6 * 2^n + n^2 = \Theta(4 * 2^n)$, even though each of these statements is true.

Theorem 3.5 *If* $f(n) = a_m n^m + \cdots + a_1 n + a_0$ *and* $a_m > 0$, *then* $f(n) = \Theta(n^m)$.

Proof See Exercise 12. ■

Example 3.19 From Theorem 3.5 it follows that $3n + 2 = \Theta(n)$, $10n^2 + 4n + 2 = \Theta(n^2)$, and $100n^4 + 3500n^2 + 82n + 8 = \Theta(n^4)$. ■

Theorem 3.6 is the analog of Theorems 3.2 and 3.4.

Theorem 3.6 [Theta ratio theorem] *Let* $f(n)$ *and* $g(n)$ *be such that* $\lim_{n \to \infty} f(n)/g(n)$ *and* $\lim_{n \to \infty} g(n)/f(n)$ *exist.* $f(n) = \Theta(g(n))$ *iff* $\lim_{n \to \infty} f(n)/g(n) \leq c$ *and* $\lim_{n \to \infty} g(n)/f(n) \leq c$ *for some finite constant* c.

Proof See Exercise 13.   ■

Example 3.20 $3n + 2 = \Theta(n)$ as $\lim_{n\to\infty}(3n + 2)/n = 3$ and $\lim_{n\to\infty} n/(3n + 2)$
$= 1/3 < 3$; $10n^2 + 4n + 2 = \Theta(n^2)$ as $\lim_{n\to\infty}(10n^2 + 4n + 2)/n^2 = 10$; and
$\lim_{n\to\infty} n^2/(10n^2 + 4n + 2) = 0.1 < 10$. $6*2^n + n^2 = \Theta(2^n)$ as $\lim_{n\to\infty}(6*2^n + n^2)/2^n$
$= 6$ and $\lim_{n\to\infty} 2^n/(6*2^n + n^2) = 1/6 < 6$. $6n^2 + 2 \neq \Theta(n)$ as $\lim_{n\to\infty}(6n^2 + 2)/n$
$= \infty$.   ■

3.3.4   Little Oh Notation (o)

The little oh notation describes a strict upper bound on the asymptotic growth
rate of the function f. Informally, $f(n)$ is little oh of $g(n)$ iff $f(n)$ is asymptotically
smaller than $g(n)$ (recall that $f(n)$ is big oh of $g(n)$ iff $f(n)$ is asymptotically smaller
than or equal to $g(n)$).

Definition 3.6 [Little oh] $f(n) = o(g(n))$ *(read as "f of n is little oh of g of n")*
iff $f(n) = O(g(n))$ *and* $f(n) \neq \Omega(g(n))$.   ■

Example 3.21 [Little oh] $3n + 2 = o(n^2)$ as $3n + 2 = O(n^2)$ and $3n + 2 \neq \Omega(n^2)$.
However, $3n + 2 \neq o(n)$. Similarly, $10n^2 + 4n + 2 = o(n^3)$, but is not $o(n^2)$.   ■

The little oh notation is often used in step-count analyses. A step count of $3n$
$+ o(n)$ would mean that the step count is $3n$ plus terms that are asymptotically
smaller than n. When performing such an analysis, one can ignore portions of the
program that are known to contribute less than $\Theta(n)$ steps.

3.3.5   Properties

The following theorem is useful in computations involving asymptotic notation.

Theorem 3.7 *These statements are true for every real number x, $x > 0$ and for
every real ϵ, $\epsilon > 0$:*

1. *An n_0 exists such that $(\log n)^x < (\log n)^{x+\epsilon}$ for every n, $n \geq n_0$.*

2. *An n_0 exists such that $(\log n)^x < n^\epsilon$ for every n, $n \geq n_0$.*

3. *An n_0 exists such that $n^x < n^{x+\epsilon}$ for every n, $n \geq n_0$.*

4. *For every real y, an n_0 exists such that $n^x(\log n)^y < n^{x+\epsilon}$ for every n, $n \geq$
    n_0.*

5. *An n_0 exists such that $n^x < 2^n$ for every n, $n \geq n_0$.*

Proof Follows from the definition of the individual functions.   ■

Example 3.22 From Theorem 3.7 we obtain the following: $n^3 + n^2 \log n = \Theta(n^3)$; $2^n/n^2 = \Omega(n^k)$ for every natural number k; $n^4 + n^{2.5} \log^{20} n = \Theta(n^4)$; $2^n n^4 \log^3 n + 2^n n^4 / \log n = \Theta(2^n n^4 \log^3 n)$. ∎

Figure 3.7 lists some of the more useful identities involving the big oh, omega, and theta notations. In this table all symbols other than n are positive constants. Figure 3.8 lists some useful inference rules for sums and products.

	$f(n)$	Asymptotic
E1	c	$\oplus(1)$
E2	$\sum_{i=0}^{k} c_i n^i$	$\oplus(n^k)$
E3	$\sum_{i=1}^{n} i$	$\oplus(n^2)$
E4	$\sum_{i=1}^{n} i^2$	$\oplus(n^3)$
E5	$\sum_{i=1}^{n} i^k, k > 0$	$\oplus(n^{k+1})$
E6	$\sum_{i=0}^{n} r^i, r > 1$	$\oplus(r^n)$
E7	$n!$	$\oplus(\sqrt{n}(n/e)^n)$
E8	$\sum_{i=1}^{n} 1/i$	$\oplus(\log n)$

$\oplus$ can be any one of O, Ω, and Θ

Figure 3.7 Asymptotic identities

Figures 3.7 and 3.8 prepare you to use asymptotic notation to describe the time complexity (or step count) of a program.

The definitions of O, Ω, Θ, and o can be extended to include functions of more than one variable. For example, $f(n,m) = O(g(n,m))$ iff positive constants c, n_0, and m_0 exist such that $f(n,m) \leq cg(n,m)$ for all $n \geq n_0$ and all $m \geq m_0$.

EXERCISES

9. Show that the following equalities are correct, using the definitions of O, Ω, Θ, and o only. Do not use Theorems 3.1 through 3.6, or Figures 3.7 and 3.8.

   (a) $5n^2 - 6n = \Theta(n^2)$.

I1 $\{f(n) = \oplus(g(n))\} \rightarrow \sum_{n=a}^{b} f(n) = \oplus(\sum_{n=a}^{b} g(n))$.

I2 $\{f_i(n) = \oplus(g_i(n)), 1 \le i \le k\} \rightarrow \sum_{i=1}^{k} f_i(n) = \oplus(\max_{1 \le i \le k}\{g_i(n)\})$.

I3 $\{f_i(n) = \oplus(g_i(n)), 1 \le i \le k\} \rightarrow \prod_{i=1}^{k} f_i(n) = \oplus(\prod_{i=1}^{k} g_i(n))$.

I4 $\{f_1(n) = O(g_1(n)), f_2(n) = \Theta(g_2(n))\} \rightarrow f_1(n) + f_2(n) = O(g_1(n) + g_2(n))$.

I5 $\{f_1(n) = \Theta(g_1(n)), f_2(n) = \Omega(g_2(n))\} \rightarrow f_1(n) + f_2(n) = \Omega(g_1(n) + g_2(n))$.

I6 $\{f_1(n) = O(g(n)), f_2(n) = \Theta(g(n))\} \rightarrow f_1(n) + f_2(n) = \Theta(g(n))$.

Figure 3.8 Inference rules for $\oplus \in \{O, \Omega, \Theta\}$

    (b) $n! = O(n^n)$.

    (c) $2n^2 2^n + n \log n = \Theta(n^2 2^n)$.

    (d) $\sum_{i=0}^{n} i^2 = \Theta(n^3)$.

    (e) $\sum_{i=0}^{n} i^3 = \Theta(n^4)$.

    (f) $n^{2^n} + 6 * 2^n = \Theta(n^{2^n})$.

    (g) $n^3 + 10^6 n^2 = \Theta(n^3)$.

    (h) $6n^3/(\log n + 1) = O(n^3)$.

    (i) $n^{1.001} + n \log n = \Theta(n^{1.001})$.

    (j) $n^{k+\epsilon} + n^k \log n = \Theta(n^{k+\epsilon})$ for all k and ϵ, $k \ge 0$, and $\epsilon > 0$.

10. Do Exercise 9 using Theorems 3.2, 3.4, and 3.6.

11. Show that the following equalities are incorrect:

    (a) $10n^2 + 9 = O(n)$.

    (b) $n^2 \log n = \Theta(n^2)$.

    (c) $n^2/\log n = \Theta(n^2)$.

    (d) $n^3 2^n + 6n^2 3^n = O(n^3 2^n)$.

12. Prove Theorems 3.3 and 3.5.

13. Prove Theorems 3.4 and 3.6.

14. Prove that $f(n) = o(g(n))$ iff $\lim_{n \to \infty} f(n)/g(n) = 0$.

15. Prove that equivalences E5 to E8 (Figure 3.7) are correct.

16. Prove the correctness of inference rules I1 to I6 (Figure 3.8).

17. Which of the following inferences are true? Why?

(a) $\{f(n) = O(F(n)), g(n) = O(G(n))\} \rightarrow f(n)/g(n) = O(F(n)/G(n))$.

(b) $\{f(n) = O(F(n)), g(n) = O(G(n))\} \rightarrow f(n)/g(n) = \Omega(F(n)/G(n))$.

(c) $\{f(n) = O(F(n)), g(n) = O(G(n))\} \rightarrow f(n)/g(n) = \Theta(F(n)/G(n))$.

(d) $\{f(n) = \Omega(F(n)), g(n) = \Omega(G(n))\} \rightarrow f(n)/g(n) = \Omega(F(n)/G(n))$.

(e) $\{f(n) = \Omega(F(n)), g(n) = \Omega(G(n))\} \rightarrow f(n)/g(n) = O(F(n)/G(n))$.

(f) $\{f(n) = \Omega(F(n)), g(n) = \Omega(G(n))\} \rightarrow f(n)/g(n) = \Theta(F(n)/G(n))$.

(g) $\{f(n) = \Theta(F(n)), g(n) = \Theta(G(n))\} \rightarrow f(n)/g(n) = \Theta(F(n)/G(n))$.

(h) $\{f(n) = \Theta(F(n)), g(n) = \Theta(G(n))\} \rightarrow f(n)/g(n) = \Omega(F(n)/G(n))$.

(i) $\{f(n) = \Theta(F(n)), g(n) = \Theta(G(n))\} \rightarrow f(n)/g(n) = O(F(n)/G(n))$.

3.4   COMPLEXITY ANALYSIS EXAMPLES

In Section 3.2 we saw several examples in which we started with the step count of a program and then arrived at its asymptotic complexity. Actually, we can determine the asymptotic complexity quite easily without determining the exact step count. The procedure is to first determine the asymptotic complexity of each statement (or group of statements) in the program and then add up these complexities. Figures 3.9 to 3.12 determine the asymptotic complexity of several methods without performing an exact step-count analysis. These figures use the following fact that when $f_1(n) = \Theta(g_1(n))$ and $f_2(n) = \Theta(g_2(n))$, then $f_1(n) + f_2(n) = \Theta(\max\{g_1(n), g_2(n)\})$.

Statement	s/e	Frequency	Total Steps
`public static Computable sum(···)`	0	0	$\Theta(0)$
`{`	0	0	$\Theta(0)$
`    if (a.length == 0) return null;`	1	1	$\Theta(1)$
`    Computable sum = (Computable) a[0].zero();`	1	1	$\Theta(1)$
`    for (int i = 0; i < n; i++)`	1	$n+1$	$\Theta(n)$
`        sum.increment(a[i]);`	1	n	$\Theta(n)$
`    return sum;`	1	1	$\Theta(1)$
`}`	0	0	$\Theta(0)$

$$t_{\text{sum}}(n) = \Theta(\max\{g_i(n)\}) = \Theta(n)$$

Figure 3.9 Asymptotic complexity of sum (Program 1.25)

While the analyses of Figures 3.9 through 3.12 are actually carried out in terms of step counts, it is correct to interpret $t_P(n) = \Theta(g(n))$, $t_P(n) = O(g(n))$, or $t_P(n)$

Statement	s/e	Frequency	Total Steps
`public static void transpose(···)`	0	0	$\Theta(0)$
`{`	0	0	$\Theta(0)$
`for (int i = 0; i < rows; i++)`	1	$rows + 1$	$\Theta(rows)$
`for (int j = i+1; j < rows; j++)`	1	$rows(rows + 1)/2$	$\Theta(rows^2)$
`{`	0	0	$\Theta(0)$
`// swap a[i][j] and a[j][i]`	0	0	$\Theta(0)$
`int t = a[i][j];`	1	$rows(rows - 1)/2$	$\Theta(rows^2)$
`a[i][j] = a[j][i];`	1	$rows(rows - 1)/2$	$\Theta(rows^2)$
`a[j][i] = t;`	1	$rows(rows - 1)/2$	$\Theta(rows^2)$
`}`	0	0	$\Theta(0)$
`}`	0	0	$\Theta(0)$

$$t_{\text{transpose}}(rows) = \Theta(rows^2)$$

Figure 3.10 Asymptotic complexity of `transpose` (Program 2.19)

Statement	s/e	Frequency	Total Steps
`public static int [] inef(int [] a)`	0	0	$\Theta(0)$
`{`	0	0	$\Theta(0)$
`// create an array for the prefix sums`	0	0	$\Theta(0)$
`int [] b = new int [a.length];`	1	n	$\Theta(n)$
	0	0	$\Theta(0)$
`// compute the prefix sums`	0	0	$\Theta(0)$
`for (int j = 0; j < a.length; j++)`	1	$n + 1$	$\Theta(n)$
`b[j] = MyMath.sum(a, j + 1);`	$2j + 7$	n	$\Theta(n^2)$
`return b;`	1	1	$\Theta(1)$
`}`	0	0	$\Theta(0)$

$$t_{\text{inef}}(n) = \Theta(n^2)$$

Figure 3.11 Asymptotic complexity of `inef` (Program 2.20)

Statement	s/e	Frequency	Total Steps
`public static int sequentialSearch(···)`	0	0	$\Theta(0)$
`{`	0	0	$\Theta(0)$
`int i;`	1	1	$\Theta(1)$
`for (i = 0; i < a.length && !x.equals(a[i]); i++);`	1	$\Omega(1), O(n)$	$\Omega(1), O(n)$
`if (i == a.length) return -1;`	1	1	$\Theta(1)$
`else return i;`	1	$\Omega(0), O(1)$	$\Omega(0), O(1)$
`}`	0	0	$\Theta(0)$

$$t_{\text{sequentialSearch}}(n) = \Omega(1) \qquad\qquad t_{\text{sequentialSearch}}(n) = O(n)$$

Figure 3.12 Asymptotic complexity of `SequentialSearch` (Program 2.1)

$= \Omega(g(n))$ as a statement about the computing time of program P because each step takes only $\Theta(1)$ time to execute.

After you have had some experience using the table method, you will be in a position to arrive at the asymptotic complexity of a program by taking a more global approach. We elaborate on this method in the following examples.

Example 3.23 [Permutations] Consider the permutation generation code of Program 1.27. Assume that `m = n-1`. When `k = m`, the time taken is cn, where c is a constant. When `k < m`, the `else` clause is entered. At this time the `for` loop is entered `m-k+1` times. Each iteration of this loop takes dt_{perm}(`k+1,m`) time, where d is a constant. So t_{perm}(`k,m`) $= d$(`m-k+1`)t_{perm}(`k+1,m`) when `k<m`. Using the substitution method, we obtain t_{perm}(`0,m`) $= \Theta($(`m+1`)$*$(`m+1`)`!`$) = \Theta($`n*n!`$)$, $n \geq 1$.   ■

Example 3.24 [Binary Search] Program 3.1 is a method to search a sorted array `a` for the element `x`. The Java method `java.util.arrays.binarySearch` is quite similar. The variables `left` and `right` record the two ends of the array to be searched. Initially we are to search between positions 0 and `a.length-1`. So `left` and `right` are initialized to these values. We maintain the following invariant throughout:

$$\text{x is one of a[0:a.length-1] iff x is one of a[left:right]}$$

The search begins by comparing `x` with the element in the middle of the array. If `x` equals this element, the search terminates. If `x` is smaller than this element, then we need only search the left half and so `right` is updated to `middle-1`. If `x` is bigger than the middle element, only the right half needs to be searched and `left` is updated to `middle+1`.

Each iteration of the `while` loop—except the last one—results in a decrease in the size of the segment of `a` that has to be searched (i.e., the portion between `left` and `right`) by a factor of about 2. So this loop iterates $\Theta(\log$ `a.length`$)$ times in the worst case. As each iteration takes $\Theta(1)$ time, the overall worst-case complexity is $\Theta(\log$ `a.length`$)$.   ■

Example 3.25 [Insertion Sort] Program 2.15 uses the insertion sort method to sort $n =$ `a.length` elements. For each value of `i`, the innermost `for` loop has a worst-case complexity $\Theta($`i`$)$. As a result, the worst-case time complexity of Program 2.15 is *at most* $\Theta(1 + 2 + 3 + \cdots + n - 1) = \Theta(n^2)$. The best-case time complexity of Program 2.15 is $\Theta(n)$.   ■

As mentioned in Example 2.7 the analyses performed in this chapter implicitly assume that no exceptions or errors, other than those explicitly thrown by the code

```
public static int binarySearch(Comparable [] a, Comparable x)
{// Search a[0] <= a[1] <= ... <= a[a.length-1] for x.
   int left = 0;
   int right = a.length - 1;
   while (left <= right)
   {
      int middle = (left + right)/2;
      if (x.equals(a[middle]))
         return middle;
      if (x.compareTo(a[middle]) > 0)
         left = middle + 1;
      else
         right = middle - 1;
   }
   return -1; // x not found
}
```

Program 3.1 Binary search

being analyzed, are thrown. If we remove this assumption, the complexity of many codes will change from $\Theta(g(n))$ to $O(g(n))$. Keeping this in mind, almost all of the analyses done in the remainder of the book will yield a big oh result for the complexity of an entire method even though we might see that under some suitable assumptions one or more statements might be executed $\Theta(g(n))$ times.

EXERCISE

18. Determine the asymptotic time complexity of the following methods. Set up a frequency table similar to Figures 3.9 through 3.12.

    (a) `factorial` (Program 1.24).

    (b) `minMax` (Program 2.24).

    (c) `minMax` (Program 2.25).

    (d) `add` (Program 2.21).

    (e) `squareMultiply` (Program 2.22).

    (f) `multiply` (Program 2.23).

    (g) `max` (Program 1.29).

    (h) `valueOf` (Program 2.3).

    (i) `valueOf` (Program 2.4).

(j) `rank` (Program 2.5).

(k) `perm` (Program 1.27).

(l) `selectionSort` (Program 2.7).

(m) `selectionSort` (Program 2.12).

(n) `insertionSort` (Program 2.14).

(o) `insertionSort` (Program 2.15).

(p) `bubbleSort` (Program 2.9).

(q) `bubbleSort` (Program 2.13).

3.5   PRACTICAL COMPLEXITIES

We have seen that the time complexity of a program is generally some function of the instance characteristics. This function is very useful in determining how the time requirements vary as the instance characteristics change. We can also use the complexity function to compare two programs P and Q that perform the same task. Assume that program P has complexity $\Theta(n)$ and that program Q has complexity $\Theta(n^2)$. We can assert that program P is faster than program Q is for "sufficiently large" n. To see the validity of this assertion, observe that the actual computing time of P is bounded from above by cn for some constant c and for all n, $n \geq n_1$, while that of Q is bounded from below by dn^2 for some constant d and all n, $n \geq n_2$. Since $cn \leq dn^2$ for $n \geq c/d$, program P is faster than program Q whenever $n \geq \max\{n_1, n_2, c/d\}$.

One should always be cautiously aware of the presence of the phrase *sufficiently large* in the assertion of the preceding discussion. When deciding which of the two programs to use, we must know whether the n we are dealing with is, in fact, sufficiently large. If program P actually runs in $10^6 n$ milliseconds while program Q runs in n^2 milliseconds and if we always have $n \leq 10^6$, then program Q is the one to use.

To get a feel for how the various functions grow with n, you should study Figures 3.13 and 3.14 very closely. These figures show that 2^n grows very rapidly with n. In fact, if a program needs 2^n steps for execution, then when $n = 40$, the number of steps needed is approximately $1.1*10^{12}$. On a computer performing 1,000,000,000 steps per second, this program would require about 18.3 minutes. If $n = 50$, the same program would run for about 13 days on this computer. When $n = 60$, about 310.56 years will be required to execute the program, and when $n = 100$, about $4*10^{13}$ years will be needed. We can conclude that the utility of programs with exponential complexity is limited to small n (typically $n \leq 40$).

Programs that have a complexity that is a high-degree polynomial are also of limited utility. For example, if a program needs n^{10} steps, then our 1,000,000,000 steps per second computer needs 10 seconds when $n = 10$; 3171 years when $n = 100$; and $3.17*10^{13}$ years when $n = 1000$. If the program's complexity had been

$\log n$	n	$n \log n$	n^2	n^3	2^n
0	1	0	1	1	2
1	2	2	4	8	4
2	4	8	16	64	16
3	8	24	64	512	256
4	16	64	256	4096	65,536
5	32	160	1024	32,768	4,294,967,296

Figure 3.13 Value of various functions

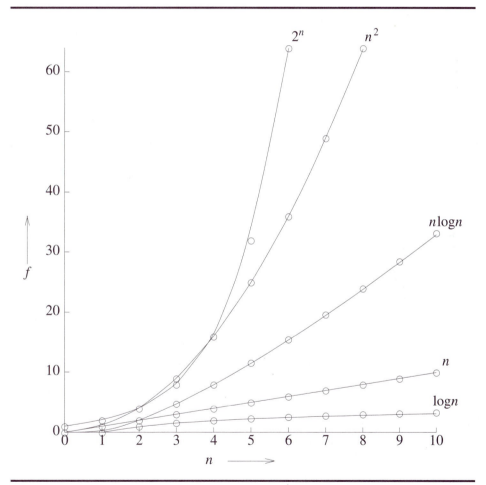

Figure 3.14 Plot of various functions

n^3 steps instead, then the computer would need 1 second when $n = 1000$, 110.67 minutes when $n = 10,000$, and 11.57 days when $n = 100,000$.

Figure 3.15 gives the time that a 1,000,000,000 instructions per second computer needs to execute a program of complexity $f(n)$ instructions. One should note that currently only the fastest computers can execute about 1,000,000,000 instructions per second. From a practical standpoint, it is evident that for reasonably large n (say $n > 100$) only programs of small complexity (such as n, $n \log n$, n^2, and n^3) are feasible. Further, this is the case even if we could build a computer capable of executing 10^{12} instructions per second. In this case the computing times of Figure 3.15 would decrease by a factor of 1000. Now when $n = 100$, it would take 3.17 years to execute n^{10} instructions and $4 * 10^{10}$ years to execute 2^n instructions.

				$f(n)$			
n	n	$n \log_2 n$	n^2	n^3	n^4	n^{10}	2^n
10	.01 μs	.03 μs	.1 μs	1 μs	10 μs	10 s	1 μs
20	.02 μs	.09 μs	.4 μs	8 μs	160 μs	2.84 h	1 ms
30	.03 μs	.15 μs	.9 μs	27 μs	810 μs	6.83 d	1 s
40	.04 μs	.21 μs	1.6 μs	64 μs	2.56 ms	121 d	18 m
50	.05 μs	.28 μs	2.5 μs	125 μs	6.25 ms	3.1 y	13 d
100	.10 μs	.66 μs	10 μs	1 ms	100 ms	3171 y	$4 * 10^{13}$ y
10^3	1 μs	9.96 μs	1 ms	1 s	16.67 m	$3.17 * 10^{13}$ y	$32 * 10^{283}$ y
10^4	10 μs	130 μs	100 ms	16.67 m	115.7 d	$3.17 * 10^{23}$ y	
10^5	100 μs	1.66 ms	10 s	11.57 d	3171 y	$3.17 * 10^{33}$ y	
10^6	1 ms	19.92 ms	16.67 m	31.71 y	$3.17 * 10^7$ y	$3.17 * 10^{43}$ y	

μs = microsecond = 10^{-6} seconds; ms = milliseconds = 10^{-3} seconds; s = seconds; m = minutes; h = hours; d = days; y = years

Figure 3.15 Run times on a 1,000,000,000 instruction per second computer

EXERCISES

19. Let A and B be two programs that perform the same task. Let $t_A(n)$ and $t_B(n)$, respectively, denote their run times. For each of the following pairs, find the range of n values for which program A is faster than program B.

    (a) $t_A(n) = 1000n$, $t_B(n) = 10n^2$.

    (b) $t_A(n) = 2n^2$, $t_B(n) = n^3$.

    (c) $t_A(n) = 2^n$, $t_B(n) = 100n$.

    (d) $t_A(n) = 1000n \log_2 n$, $t_B(n) = n^2$.

20. Redo Figure 3.15 assuming a computer capable of doing 1 trillion instructions per second.

21. Suppose that using a certain program and computer, it is possible to solve problems of size up to $n = N$ in a "reasonable amount of time." Create a table that shows the largest value of n for which solutions can be found in reasonable time using the same program and a computer that is x times as fast. Do this exercise for $x = 10$, 100, 1000, and $1,000,000$ and $t_A(n) = n$, n^2, n^3, n^5, and 2^n.

3.6   REFERENCES AND SELECTED READINGS

The following books provide asymptotic analyses for several programs: *Fundamentals of Computer Algorithms* by E. Horowitz, S. Sahni, and S. Rajasekaran, W. H. Freeman and Co., New York, NY, 1998; *Introduction to Algorithms* by T. Cormen, C. Leiserson, and R. Rivest, McGraw-Hill, New York, NY, 1992; *Compared to What: An Introduction to the Analysis of Algorithms* by G. Rawlins, W. H. Freeman and Co., New York, NY, 1992; and *Algorithms from P to NP. Volume I: Design and Efficiency* by B. Moret and H. Shapiro, Benjamin-Cummings, Menlo Park, CA, 1991.

CHAPTER 4

PERFORMANCE MEASUREMENT

BIRD'S-EYE VIEW

You can analyze and dissect all you like, but the proof of the pudding lies in the tasting. When you try to market an application code, your customer will want to know how many megabytes and seconds its going to take to solve his/her problem on his/her computer. We can get a good handle on the memory requirements from the size of the compiled code and the size of the data space needed. The data space size is usually easy to figure out once you know what size instances the user is interested in solving. Determining the number of seconds the program will run requires you to actually perform experiments and measure run times. This chapter goes through the steps required to perform such an experiment.

The performance of your program depends not only on the number and type of operations you perform but also on the memory access pattern for the data and instructions in your program. Your computer has different kinds of memory—L1 cache, L2 cache, and main memory (for example)—and the time needed to access data from each is quite different. So a program with a large operation count and a small number of accesses to slow memory may take less time than a program with a small operation count and a large number of accesses to slow memory. This phenomenon is demonstrated using the matrix multiplication problem.

4.1   INTRODUCTION

Performance measurement is concerned with obtaining the actual space and time requirements of a program. As noted in earlier sections, these quantities are very dependent on the particular compiler and options used as well as on the specific computer on which the program is run. Unless otherwise stated, all performance values in this book were obtained using a 300 MHz Pentium II PC and Sun's JDK 1.2 Java compiler. Background programs such as screen savers and virus scanners were disabled during performance measurement.

We ignore the space and time needed for compilation because each program (after it has been fully debugged) will be compiled once and then executed several times. However, the space and time needed for compilation are important during program testing when more time may be spent on this task than in actually running the compiled code.

We do not explicitly consider measuring the run-time space requirements of a program for the following reasons:

- The size of the instruction and statically allocated data space are provided by the compiler following compilation, so no measurement techniques are needed to obtain these figures.

- We can get a fairly accurate estimate of the recursion stack space and the space needed by dynamically allocated variables using the analytical methods of the earlier sections.

To obtain the execution (or run) time of a program, we need a clocking mechanism. We will use the Java method `System.currentTimeMillis()`, which returns the present time in milliseconds since midnight (GMT), January 1, 1970.

Suppose we wish to measure the worst-case time requirements of method `insertionSort` (Program 2.15). First we need to

1. Decide on the values of $n = $ `a.length` for which the times are to be obtained.

2. Determine, for each of the above values of n, the data that exhibit the worst-case behavior.

4.2   CHOOSING INSTANCE SIZE

We decide on which values of n to use according to two factors: the amount of timing we want to perform and what we expect to do with the times. Suppose we want to predict how long it will take, in the worst case, to sort an array `a` of n objects using `insertionSort`. From Example 3.25 we know that the worst-case complexity of `insertionSort` is $\Theta(n^2)$; that is, it is quadratic in n. In theory, if we know the times for any three values of n, we can determine the quadratic function that describes the worst-case run time of `insertionSort` and we can obtain the time for all other values of n from this quadratic function. In practice, we need the times for more than three values of n for the following two reasons:

1. Asymptotic analysis tells us the behavior only for sufficiently large values of n. For smaller values of n, the run time may not follow the asymptotic curve. To determine the point beyond which the asymptotic curve is followed, we need to examine the times for several values of n.

2. Even in the region where the asymptotic behavior is exhibited, the times may not lie exactly on the predicted curve (quadratic in the case of `insertionSort`) because of the effects of low-order terms that are discarded in the asymptotic analysis. For instance, a program with asymptotic complexity $\Theta(n^2)$ can have an actual complexity that is $c_1 n^2 + c_2 n \log n + c_3 n + c_4$—or any other function of n in which the highest order term is $c_1 n^2$ for some constant c_1, $c_1 > 0$.

We expect the asymptotic behavior of Program 2.15 to begin for some n that is smaller than 100. So for $n > 100$ we will obtain the run time for just a few values. A reasonable choice is $n = 200, 300, 400, \cdots, 1000$. There is nothing magical about this choice of values. We can just as well use $n = 500, 1000, 1500, \cdots, 10,000$ or $n = 512, 1024, 2048, \cdots, 2^{15}$. The latter choices will cost us more in terms of computer time and probably will not provide any better information about the run time of our method.

For n in the range $[0, 100]$, we will carry out a more refined measurement, as we aren't quite sure where the asymptotic behavior begins. Of course, if our measurements show that the quadratic behavior doesn't begin in this range, we will have to perform a more detailed measurement in the range $[100, 200]$ and so on until we detect the onset of this behavior. Times in the range $[0, 100]$ will be obtained in steps of 10 beginning at $n = 0$.

4.3   DEVELOPING THE TEST DATA

For many programs we can generate manually or by computer the data that exhibit the best- and worst-case time complexity. The average complexity, however, is usually quite difficult to demonstrate. For `insertionSort` the worst-case data for any n are a decreasing sequence such as $n, n-1, n-2, \cdots, 1$. The best-case data are a sorted sequence such as $0, 1, 2, \cdots, n-1$. It is difficult to envision the data that would cause `insertionSort` to exhibit its average behavior.

When we are unable to develop the data that exhibit the complexity we want to measure, we can pick the least (maximum, average) measured time from some randomly generated data as an estimate of the best (worst, average) behavior.

4.4   SETTING UP THE EXPERIMENT

Having selected the instance sizes and developed the test data, we are ready to write a program that will measure the desired run times. For our insertion sort example this program takes the form given in Program 4.1. The measured times are given in Figure 4.1.

```
public static void main(String [] args)
{
    int step = 10;

    System.out.println("The worst-case times, in milliseconds, are");
    System.out.println("n \telapsed time");
    for (int n = 0; n <= 1000; n += step)
    {
        // create element array
        Integer [] a = new Integer[n];

        // initialize array
        for (int i = 0; i < n; i++)
            a[i] = new Integer(n - i);

        long startTime = System.currentTimeMillis();

        // sort the elements
        InsertionSort2.insertionSort(a);

        long elapsedTime = System.currentTimeMillis() - startTime;

        System.out.println(n + "\t" + elapsedTime);

        if (n == 100) step = 100;
    }
}
```

Program 4.1 Program to obtain worst-case run times for insertion sort

Figure 4.1 suggests that no time is needed to sort arrays with 0, 10, 20, 30, 40, 50, 60, 80, 90, 100, 200, 300, 400, or 700 objects; it takes 50 ms to sort 70 objects, even though 700 objects can be sorted in no time; it is quicker to sort 900 objects than to sort 70; and there is no difference in the times to sort 500 and 600 objects. This conclusion, of course, isn't true. The problem is that the time needed is too small for `System.currentTimeMillis()` to measure. Furthermore, all measurements are accurate to within the accuracy of the timimg method `System.currentTimeMillis()`. Although the Java language does not specify the accuracy of this method, let us assume that this method is accurate to within 100

n	Time	n	Time
0	0	100	0
10	0	200	0
20	0	300	0
30	0	400	0
40	0	500	60
50	0	600	50
60	0	700	0
70	50	800	60
80	0	900	50
90	0	1000	110

Times are in milliseconds

Figure 4.1 Times using Program 4.1

milliseconds. Therefore, if the method returns a time of t, the actual time lies between $t - 100$ and $t + 100$. The reported time (see Figure 4.1) for n = 1000 is 110 milliseconds. So the actual time could be anywhere between 10 and 210 milliseconds. If we wish our measurements to be accurate to within 10 percent, `elapsedTime` should be at least 1000 milliseconds. The times in Figure 4.1 do not meet this criterion.

To improve the accuracy of our measurements, we need to repeat the sort several times for each value of n. Since the sort changes the array a, we need to initialize this array before each sort. Program 4.2 gives the new timing program. Notice that now the measured time is the time to sort plus the time to initialize a and the overhead associated with the while loop. Figure 4.2 gives the measured times, and Figure 4.3 is a plot of these times.

We can determine the overhead associated with the while loop and the initialization of the array a by running Program 4.2 without the statement

```
InsertionSort2.insertionSort(a)
```

Figure 4.4 gives the output from this run for selected values of n. Subtracting the overhead time from the time per sort (Figure 4.2) gives us the worst-case time for insertionSort as a function of n. Notice how for larger n the times of Figure 4.2 almost quadruple each time n is doubled. We expect this pattern, as the worst-case complexity is $\Theta(n^2)$.

```
public static void main(String [] args)
{
   int step = 10;

   System.out.println("The worst-case times, in milliseconds, are");
   System.out.println("n \trepetitions \telapsed time \ttime/sort");
   for (int n = 0; n <= 1000; n += step)
   {
      // create element array
      Integer [] a = new Integer[n];

      long startTime = System.currentTimeMillis();
      long counter = 0;
      do
      {
         counter++;
         // initialize array
         for (int i = 0; i < n; i++)
            a[i] = new Integer(n - i);

         // sort the elements
         InsertionSort2.insertionSort(a);
      } while (System.currentTimeMillis( ) - startTime < 1000);

      long elapsedTime = System.currentTimeMillis() - startTime;
      System.out.println(n + "\t" + counter + "\t\t"
         + elapsedTime + "\t\t" + ((float) elapsedTime)/counter);

      if (n == 100) step = 100;
   }
}
```

Program 4.2 Program to obtain times with an accuracy of 10 percent

EXERCISES

1. Why does Program 4.3 not measure run times to an accuracy of 10 percent?

2. Use Program 4.2 to obtain the worst-case run times for the two versions of insertion sort given in Programs 2.14 and 2.15. Use the same values of n as used in Program 4.2. Evaluate the relative merits of using the **insert** method versus incorporating the code for an insert directly into the sort method.

n	Repetitions	Total Time	Time per Sort
0	11273	1050	0.09
10	8842	1050	0.12
20	6891	1040	0.15
30	5126	1040	0.20
40	3890	1050	0.27
50	3093	1040	0.34
60	2426	1040	0.43
70	1928	1050	0.54
80	1577	1040	0.66
90	1309	1040	0.79
100	1109	1050	0.95
200	326	1040	3.19
300	151	1040	6.89
400	85	1050	12.35
500	56	1040	18.57
600	39	1050	26.92
700	29	1040	35.86
800	22	1040	47.27
900	17	1050	61.76
1000	14	1040	74.29

Times are in milliseconds

Figure 4.2 Output from Program 4.2

3. Use Program 4.2 to obtain the worst-case run times for the versions of bubble sort given in Programs 2.9 and 2.13. Use the same values of n as used in Program 4.2. However, you will need to verify that the worst-case data used by Program 4.2 is, in fact, worst-case data for the two bubble sort methods. Present your results as a table with three columns: n, Program 2.9, Program 2.13. What can you say about the worst-case performance of the two bubble sorts?

4. (a) Devise worst-case data for the two versions of selection sort given in Programs 2.7 and 2.12.

   (b) Use a suitably modified version of Program 4.2 to determine the worst-case times for the two selection sort methods. Use the same values of n as used in Program 4.2.

   (c) Present your results as a single table with three columns: n, Program 2.7, Program 2.12.

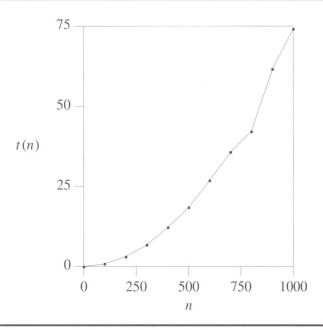

Figure 4.3 Plot of worst-case insertion sort times

n	Repetitions	Total Time	Overhead
0	11291	1040	0.09
10	9620	1040	0.11
50	7055	1040	0.15
100	5242	1040	0.20
500	1711	1050	0.61
1000	915	1040	1.14

Times are in milliseconds

Figure 4.4 Overhead in measurements of Figure 4.2

    (d) What can you say about the worst-case performance of the two selection sorts?

5. This exercise compares the worst-case run times of insertion sort (Program 2.15) and the early-terminating versions of selection sort (Program 2.12) and bubble sort (Program 2.13). To level the playing field, rewrite Program 2.13 as a single method.

```
long counter = 0,
      startTime,
      elapsedTime = 0;
do
{
   counter++;
   startTime = System.currentTimeMillis();

   doSomething();

   elapsedTime += System.currentTimeMillis() - startTime;
} while (elapsedTime < 1000)

System.out.println("Time taken is "
                   + ((float) elapsedTime)/counter);
```

Program 4.3 Inaccurate way to time doSomething

(a) Devise data that show the worst-case behavior of each method.

(b) Using the data of (a) and the timing program of Program 4.2, obtain worst-case run times.

(c) Provide these times both as a single table with columns labeled n, selection sort, bubble sort, and insertion sort and as a single graph showing three curves (one for each method). The x-axis of the graph is labeled by n values, and the y-axis by time values.

(d) What conclusions can you draw about the relative worst-case performance of the three sort methods?

(e) Measure the overheads for each value of n and report these in a table as in Figure 4.4. Subtract this overhead from the times obtained in (b) and present a new table of times and a new graph.

(f) Are there any changes to your conclusions about relative performance as a result of subtracting the overhead?

(g) Using the data you have obtained, estimate the worst-case time to sort 2000; 4000; and 10,000 numbers using each sort method.

6. Modify Program 4.2 so that it obtains an estimate of the average run time of insertionSort (Program 2.15). Do the following:

(a) Sort a random permutation of the numbers 0, 1, $\cdots$, n-1 on each iteration of the while loop. This permutation is generated using a random permutation generator. In case you don't have such a method available, try to write one using a random number generator, or simply generate a random sequence of n numbers.

(b) Set the `while` loop so that at least 20 random permutations are sorted and so that at least 1 second has elapsed.

(c) Estimate the average sort time by dividing the elapsed time by the number of permutations sorted.

Present the estimated average times as a table.

7. Use the strategy of Exercise 6 to estimate the average run times of the bubble sort methods given in Programs 2.9 and 2.13. Use the same values of n as in Program 4.2. Present your results as a table and as a graph.

8. Use the strategy of Exercise 6 to estimate the average run times of the selection sort methods given in Programs 2.7 and 2.12. Use the same values of n as in Program 4.2. Present your results as a table and as a graph.

9. Use the strategy of Exercise 6 to estimate and compare the average run times of the methods of Programs 2.12, 2.13, and 2.15. Use the same values of n as in Program 4.2. Present your results as a table and as a graph.

10. Devise experiments to determine the average time taken by sequential search (Program 2.1) and binary search (Program 3.1) to perform a successful search. Assume that each element of the array being searched is looked for with equal probability. Present your results as a table and as a graph.

11. Devise experiments to determine the worst-case time taken by sequential search (Program 2.1) and binary search (Program 3.1) to perform a successful search. Present your results as a table and as a graph.

12. Determine the run time of method `add` (Program 2.21) for rows = 10, 20, 30, $\cdots$, 100. Present your measured times as a table and as a graph.

13. Java has a sort method `java.util.arrays.sort` that sorts an array. This sort method uses either quick sort (Section 19.2.3) or merge sort (Section 19.2.2) depending on whether the data type of the array being sorted is one of the primitive data types or is a subclass of `Object`. Measure the time Java's sort method takes on best- and worst-case insertion sort data. Compare these times with those for Program 2.15.

14. Determine the run time of method `transpose` (Program 2.19) for rows = 10, 20, 30, $\cdots$, 100. Present your measured times as a table and as a graph.

15. Determine the run time of method `squareMultiply` (Program 2.22) for rows = 10, 20, 30, $\cdots$, 100. Present your measured times as a table and as a graph.

4.5   YOUR CACHE AND YOU

4.5.1   A Simple Computer Model

Consider a simple computer model in which the computer's memory consists of
an L1 (level 1) cache, an L2 cache, and main memory. Arithmetic and logical
operations are performed by the arithmetic and logic unit (ALU) on data resident
in registers (R). Figure 4.5 gives a block diagram for our simple computer model.

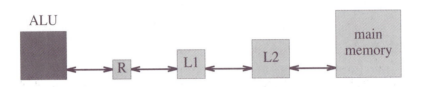

Figure 4.5 A simple computer model

Typically, the size of main memory is tens or hundreds of megabytes; L2 cache
sizes are typically a fraction of a megabyte; L1 cache is usually in the tens of
kilobytes; and the number of registers is between 8 and 32. When you start your
program, all your data are in main memory.

To perform an arithmetic operation such as an add, in our computer model,
the data to be added are first loaded from memory into registers, the data in the
registers are added, and the result is written to memory.

Let one cycle be the length of time it takes to add data that are already in
registers. The time needed to load data from L1 cache to a register is two cycles
in our model. If the required data are not in L1 cache but are in L2 cache, we get
an L1 cache miss and the required data are copied from L2 cache to L1 cache and
the register in 10 cycles. When the required data are not in L2 cache either, we
have an L2 cache miss and the required data are copied from main memory into L2
cache, L1 cache, and the register in 100 cycles. The write operation is counted as
one cycle even when the data are written to main memory because we do not wait
for the write to complete before proceeding to the next operation.

4.5.2   Effect of Cache Misses on Run Time

For our simple model, the statement a = b + c is compiled into the computer
instructions

```
load a; load b; add; store c;
```

where the `load` operations load data into registers and the `store` operation writes
the result of the `add` to memory. The `add` and the `store` together take two cycles.
The two `load`s may take anywhere from 4 cycles to 200 cycles depending on whether

we get no cache miss, L1 misses, or L2 misses. So the total time for the statement
a = b + c varies from 6 cycles to 202 cycles. In practice, the variation in time is
not as extreme because we can overlap the time spent on successive cache misses.

Suppose that we have two algorithms that perform the same task. The first
algorithm does 2000 adds that require 4000 load, 2000 add, and 2000 store operations and the second algorithm does 1000 adds. The data access pattern for the first
algorithm is such that 25 percent of the loads result in an L1 miss and another 25
percent result in an L2 miss. For our simplistic computer model, the time required
by the first algorithm is 2000 ∗ 2 (for the 50 percent loads that cause no cache miss)
+ 1000 ∗ 10 (for the 25 percent loads that cause an L1 miss) + 1000 ∗ 100 (for the
25 percent loads that cause an L2 miss) + 2000 ∗ 1 (for the adds) + 2000 ∗ 1 (for the
stores) = 118,000 cycles. If the second algorithm has 100 percent L2 misses, it will
take 2000 ∗ 100 (L2 misses) + 1000 ∗ 1 (adds) + 1000 ∗ 1 (stores) = 202,000 cycles.
So the second algorithm, which does half the work done by the first, actually takes
76 percent more time than is taken by the first algorithm.

Computers use a number of strategies (such as preloading data that will be
needed in the near future into cache, and when a cache miss occurs, the needed data
as well as data in some number of adjacent bytes are loaded into cache) to reduce
the number of cache misses and hence reduce the run time of a program. These
strategies are most effective when successive computer operations use adjacent bytes
of main memory.

Although our discussion has focussed on how cache is used for data, computers
also use cache to reduce the time needed to access instructions.

4.5.3 Matrix Multiplication

This section is for the skeptics among you who do not believe that on a commercial
computer, a program that performs more operations may actually take less time
than another program that performs fewer operations. We are about to make a
believer out of you.

Program 2.22 is the real program we start with. This program multiplies two
square matrices that are represented as two-dimensional arrays. It performs the
following computation:

$$c[i][j] = \sum_{k=1}^{n} a[i][k] * b[k][j], \ 1 \leq i \leq m, \ 1 \leq j \leq p \qquad (4.1)$$

(You don't need to understand matrix multiplication to follow this demonstra-
tion. Matrix multiplication is described in Section 8.2.1 in case you need reassurance
this is a worthwhile operation.) Program 2.22 is a fairly standard piece of code that
you can find in many books. Program 4.4 is an alternative code that produces the
same two-dimensional array c as is produced by Program 2.22. We observe that
Program 4.4 has two nested for loops that are not present in Program 2.22 and

does more work than is done by Program 2.22 with repect to indexing into the array c. The remainder of the work is the same.

```
public static void fastSquareMultiply(int [][] a, int [][] b,
                                      int [][] c, int n)
{
    for (int i = 0; i < n; i++)
        for (int j = 0; j < n; j++)
            c[i][j] = 0;

    for (int i = 0; i < n; i++)
        for (int j = 0; j < n; j++)
            for (int k = 0; k < n; k++)
                c[i][j] += a[i][k] * b[k][j];
}
```

Program 4.4 Less efficient way than Program 2.22 to multiply square matrices

You will notice that if you permute the order of the three nested `for` loops in Program 4.4, you do not affect the result array c. We refer to the loop order in Program 4.4 as `ijk` order. When we swap the second and third `for` loops, we get `ikj` order. In all, there are $3! = 6$ ways in which we can order the three nested `for` loops. All six orderings result in methods that perform exactly the same number of operations of each type. So you might think all six take the same time. Not so. By changing the order of the loops, we change the data access pattern and so change the number of cache misses. This in turn affects the run time.

In `ijk` order, we access the elements of a and c by rows; the elements of b are accessed by column. Since elements in the same row are in adjacent memory and elements in the same column are far apart in memory, the accesses of b are likely to result in many L2 cache misses when the matrix size is too large for the three arrays to fit into L2 cache. In `ikj` order, the elements of a, b, and c are accessed by rows. Therefore, `ikj` order is likely to result in fewer L2 cache misses and so has the potential to take much less time than taken by `ijk` order.

Figure 4.6 gives the run time for Program 4.4 using `ijk` and `ikj` order as well as for Program 2.22. Figure 4.7 shows the normalized run times (i.e., the time taken by a method divided by the time taken by `ijk` order).

What a surprise: `ikj` order takes 10 percent less time than does `ijk` order when the matrix size is $n = 500$ and 16 percent less time when the matrix size is 2000. Equally surprising is that `ikj` order runs faster than Program 2.22 (by about 5 percent when $n = 2000$). This despite the fact that `ikj` order does more work than is done by Program 2.22. Are you still skeptical?

n	Program 2.22 mult	Program 4.4	
		ijk order	ikj order
500	13.8	15.3	13.7
1000	115.7	127.9	110.5
2000	961.7	1059.1	886.5

Figure 4.6 Run times (in seconds) for matrix multiplication

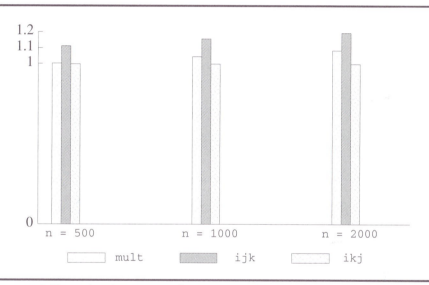

Figure 4.7 Normalized run times for matrix multiplication

The effect that memory hierarchy has on the performance of your code varies with the programming language, compiler, compiler options, and computer configuration. When our Java codes were compiled using the optimize option (i.e., `javac -O fileName.java`), there was no noticeable difference in the run time.

When the programming language was changed from Java to C++, the run times decreased by 20 to 40 percent, the percentage difference between the three matrix multiply codes favored the `ikj` code even more, and compiling with the optimize option produced code that actually ran faster. Figures 4.8 and 4.9 show the results using Borland's C++ compiler.

n	Nonoptimized			Optimized		
	mult	ijk order	ikj order	mult	ijk order	ikj order
500	10.4	12.7	9.4	10.0	11.0	8.4
1000	87.4	110.9	76.9	84.0	96.0	67.8
2000	763.3	931.1	619.3	740.0	811.3	544.5

Figure 4.8 Run times (in seconds) using Borland C++

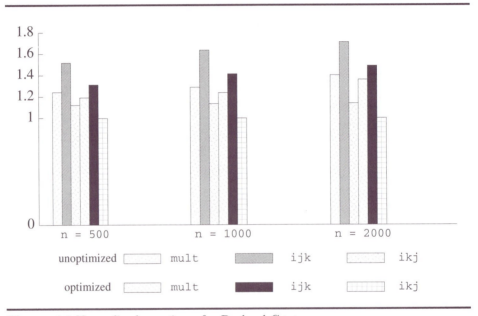

Figure 4.9 Normalized run times for Borland C++

Using the optimization option reduced the run time of the ikj method by 12 percent when n = 2000; the run times for Program 2.22 and the ijk method reduced by 3 percent and 13 percent, respectively. For n = 2000 the optimized codes for Program 2.22 and the ijk method, respectively, took 36 percent and 49 percent more time than did the optimized code for the ikj method. With the optimized code, the ijk method took 49 percent more time than did the ikj method. Your cache is really working to your advantage in the ikj method.

The effect of cache misses is even more dramatic when you run the three matrix multiply codes on a SUN Ultra Sparc II station. For example, the optimized C++ versions of Program 2.22, the ijk method, and the ikj method took 208, 223, and 123 seconds, respectively, when n = 1000. That is, Program 2.22 took 69 percent more time and the `ijk` method took 81 percent more time than the `ikj` method. Optimized C language versions (the `gcc` compiler with `04` option was used) took 322, 329, and 161 seconds, respectively, on an Ultra Sparc II; Program 2.22 took twice the time taken by the `ikj` method.

EXERCISES

16. Repeat the experiment of Figure 4.6 using all six orderings of the three nested `for` loops of Program 4.4. Present your results as a table and as a bar chart.

17. In an alternative implementation of matrix multiplication, we first compute the transpose array `bt[j][k] = b[k][j]`. Equation 4.1 becomes

$$c[i][j] = \sum_{k=1}^{n} a[i][k] * bt[j][k], \ 1 \leq i \leq m, \ 1 \leq j \leq p \qquad (4.2)$$

 (a) Write programs to compute the two-dimensional array `c` by first computing `bt` and then using Equation 4.2. You should have seven programs: one for each of the six permutations of the three nested `for` loops and one that corresponds to Program 2.22.

 (b) Measure the time taken by these seven programs for the cases n = 500, 1000, and 2000.

 (c) Present your results as a table and as a bar chart. Compare these times with those of Exercise 16.

18. Write a program to transpose an $n \times n$ array by blocks. That is, imagine that the array is partitioned into $k \times k$ subarrays (or blocks) and transpose one subarray at a time. Measure the run time of your transpose code for large n; use $k = 2, 4, 8, 16, 32,$ and 64; assume that n is a power of 2. How does the performance of your code compare with that of the transpose code of Program 2.19. Can you explain the relative performance?

4.6   REFERENCES AND SELECTED READINGS

To learn more about how a cache works, see *Computer Organization and Design*, by J. Hennessey and D. Patterson, Second Edition, Morgan Kaufmann Publishers, Inc., San Francisco, CA, 1998, Chapter 7.

CHAPTER 5

LINEAR LISTS—ARRAY REPRESENTATION

BIRD'S-EYE VIEW

We are now ready to begin the study of data structures, which continues through Chapter 17 of this book. Although Chapters 5 through 7 focus on the data structure *linear list*, their primary purpose is to introduce the different ways in which data may be represented or stored in a computer's memory as well as on a disk. In succeeding chapters we study the representation of other popular data structures such as matrices, stacks, queues, dictionaries, priority queues, tournament trees, search trees, and graphs.

The common data representation methods used by Java programs are array based, linked (or pointer based), and simulated pointer. The data structure *linear list* is used to illustrate these representation methods. The current chapter develops the array representation of a linear list, Chapter 6 develops the linked representation of a linear list, and Chapter 7 develops the simulated pointer representation.

Java's linear list classes—`java.util.ArrayList` and `java.util.LinkedList`— are roughly equivalent to our array and linked representations of a linear list; the Java classes have many additional methods though. In our development of the array-based and linked representations of a linear list, we have used the same method names and signatures as used by Java's implementations. This approach will enable you to switch easily to Java's linear list classes.

150

In an array representation, elements are stored in an array; a mathematical formula is used to determine where to store each element. When the element is of a primitive data type, this formula gives the array index where the element resides. For nonprimitive data types, the formula gives the array index where a reference to the element resides. In further discussion we will not explicitly make this distinction between storing an element and storing a reference to an element. In the simplest cases the formula stores successive elements of a list in successive memory locations, and we obtain what is commonly known as the sequential representation of a list.

The data structure concepts introduced in this chapter are

- Abstract data types and their specification as a Java interface.

- Linear lists.

- Changing array length and array doubling.

- Array representation.

- Data structure iterators.

The Java concepts developed in this chapter are

- Abstract classes.

- Member classes.

This chapter also introduces abstract classes. No new array-based applications are introduced in this chapter because several array-based applications were introduced in Chapters 1 through 3.

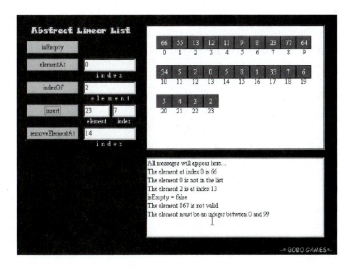

Linear lists come to life—On the Web

5.1   DATA OBJECTS AND STRUCTURES

A **data object** is a set of *instances* or *values*. Some examples are

1. *Boolean* = {*false, true*}

2. *Digit* = {0, 1, 2, 3, 4, 5, 6, 7, 8, 9}

3. *Letter* = {A, B, C, ···, Z, a, b, ···, z}

4. *NaturalNumber* = {0, 1, 2, ···}

5. *Integer* = {0, ±1, ±2, ±3, ···}

6. *String* = {a, b, ···, aa, ab, ac, ···}

Boolean, Digit, Letter, NaturalNumber, Integer, and *String* are data objects. *true* and *false* are the instances of *Boolean*, while 0, 1, ···, and 9 are the instances of *Digit*. We may regard the individual instances of a data object as being either **primitive** (or **atomic**) or composed of instances of another (possibly the same) data object. In the latter case we use the term **element** to refer to the individual components of an instance of an object.

For example, each instance of the data object *NaturalNumber* can be regarded as atomic. In this case we are not concerned with a further decomposition of the instances of this data object. Another view is to regard each instance of a *NaturalNumber* as being composed of several instances of the data object *Digit*. In this view the number 675 comprises the digits 6, 7, and 5 (in that order).

The data object *String* is the set of all possible string instances. Each instance of a string is composed of characters. Some examples of instances are *good, a trip to Hawaii, going down hill,* and *abcabcdabcde*. The first string has the four elements *g, o, o,* and *d* (in that order). Each element is an instance of the data object *Letter*.

The instances of a data object as well as the elements that constitute individual instances are generally related in some way. For example, the natural number 0 is the smallest natural number; 1 is the next; and 2 is the next. In the natural number 675, the most significant digit is 6, the next is 7, and 5 is the least significant digit. In the string *good, g* is the first letter, *o* the second and third, and *d* the last.

In addition to interrelationships, a set of operations (or functions) is generally associated with any data object. These operations may transform one instance of an object into another instance of that object, or into an instance of another data object, or do both these transformations. The operation could simply create a new instance without transforming the instances from which the new one is created. For example, the operation *add* defined on the natural numbers creates a new natural number that is the sum of the two numbers to be added; the two numbers that get added are unaltered.

A **data structure** is a data object together with the relationships that exist among the instances and among the individual elements that compose an instance. These relationships are provided by specifying the operations of interest.

When we study data structures, we are concerned with the representation of data objects (actually of the instances) as well as the implementation of the operations of interest for the data objects. The representation of each data object should facilitate an efficient[1] implementation of the operations.

The most frequently used data objects together with their frequently used operations are already implemented in Java as a primitive data type. The data objects *Integer* (`int`) and *Boolean* (`boolean`), defined above, fall into this category. All other data objects can be represented using the primitive data types and the grouping ability provided by the class, array, and pointer (i.e., reference) features of Java.

5.2   THE LINEAR LIST DATA STRUCTURE

Each instance of the data structure **linear list** (or **ordered list**) is an ordered collection of elements. Each instance is of the form $(e_0, e_1, \cdots, e_{n-1})$ where n is a finite natural number; the e_i items are the elements of the list; the **index** of e_i is i; and n is the list **length** or **size**. The elements may be viewed as atomic, as their individual structure is not relevant to the structure of the list. When $n = 0$, the list is **empty**. When $n > 0$, e_0 is the **zeroth** (or **front**) element and e_{n-1} is the **last** element of the list. We say that e_0 **comes before** (or precedes) e_1, e_1 comes before e_2, and so on. Other than this precedence relation, no other structure exists in a linear list.

Some examples of linear lists are (1) an alphabetized (i.e., ordered by name) list of students in a class; (2) a list of exam scores in nondecreasing order; (3) an alphabetized list of members of Congress; and (4) a list of gold-medal winners in the Olympics men's basketball event ordered by year. With these examples in mind, we see the need to perform the following operations on a linear list:

- Create a linear list.

- Destroy a linear list.

- Determine whether the list is empty.

- Determine the size of the list.

- Find the element with a given index.

- Find the index of a given element.

- Delete or remove an element given its index.

- Insert a new element so that it has a given index.

- Output the list elements in order, left to right.

---

[1]The term *efficient* is used here in a very liberal sense. It includes performance efficiency as well as measures of the complexity of development and maintenance of associated software.

5.2.1   The Abstract Data Type *LinearList*

A linear list may be specified as an **abstract data type** (ADT) in which we provide a specification of the instances as well as of the operations that are to be performed (see ADT 5.1). The ADT specification is independent of any representation and programming language we have in mind. All representations of the ADT must satisfy the specification, and the specification becomes a way to validate the representation. In addition, all representations that satisfy the specification may be used interchangeably in applications of the data type. In ADT 5.1 we have omitted specifying operations to create and destroy instances of the data type. All ADT specifications implicitly include an operation to create an empty instance and, optionally, an operation to destroy an instance.

AbstractDataType *LinearList*
{

    instances
       ordered finite collections of zero or more elements

    operations
       isEmpty() : return `true` if the list is empty, `false` otherwise

       size() : return the list size (i.e., number of elements in the list)

       get(*index*): return the *index*th element of the list

       indexOf(*x*): return the index of the first occurrence of x in the list, return -1 if x is not in the list

       remove(*index*): remove and return the *index*th element, elements with higher index have their index reduced by 1

       add(*index*, *x*): insert x as the *index*th element, elements with index $\geq index$ have their index increased by 1

       output(): output the list elements from left to right

}

ADT 5.1 Abstract data type specification of a linear list

5.2.2   The Interface `LinearList`

Rather than use the informal English approach to specify an ADT as in ADT 5.1, we may use a Java interface as in Program 5.1.

```java
public interface LinearList
{
    public boolean isEmpty();
    public int size();
    public Object get(int index);
    public int indexOf(Object elem);
    public Object remove(int index);
    public void add(int index, Object obj);
    public String toString();
}
```

Program 5.1 Interface specification of a linear list

Although the specification of Program 5.1 is quite similar to that of ADT 5.1, this specification is programming-language dependent. In particular, many of the keywords we have used are defined only in Java, and we have changed the name of the output operation to **toString** because the standard output methods of Java invoke a method by this name for output. On the plus side, if we require every Java class that implements the ADT to also implement the interface **LinearList**, we ensure that every Java implementation of the ADT contains implementations for all methods of the interface.

5.2.3   The Abstract Class `LinearListAsAbstractClass`

Java supports two types of classes—abstract and nonabstract. The default type for a Java class is nonabstract. An abstract class is declared by using the keyword **abstract** in the class header. When the **abstract** keyword is not used in the class header, the defined Java class is nonabstract.

The essential differences between abstract and nonabstract classes are

- An abstract class contains zero or more methods (called *abstract methods*) whose implementation is not provided.

- You cannot create an instance of an abstract class.

An abstract method is specified by using the keyword **abstract** in the method header; and in place of a method body, we have a semicolon. Note that Java allows you to declare a class abstract even though it contains no abstract methods. This capability simply allows you to define a class that cannot be instantiated. Also, note that an interface is almost equivalent to an abstract class, all of whose methods are abstract.

Program 5.2 uses an abstract class to specify the ADT *LinearList*.

```
public abstract class LinearListAsAbstractClass
{
    public abstract boolean isEmpty();
    public abstract int size();
    public abstract Object get(int index);
    public abstract int indexOf(Object theElement);
    public abstract Object remove(int index);
    public abstract void add(int index, Object theElement);
    public abstract String toString();
}
```

Program 5.2 Abstract class specification of a linear list

All the methods of Program 5.2 are abstract. Since an `interface` provides an implementation for no method, all methods of an interface are abstract (though you do not have to use the keyword `abstract` in each method's header).

When the ADT *LinearList* is specified as an abstract class, we require that all implementations of the ADT be declared as subclasses of the abstract class. Since a class that derives from or extends an abstract class is itself abstract (and so cannot be instantiated) unless it provides an implementation for all abstract methods of its superclass, by requiring that every ADT implementation be derived from the abstract class for that ADT, we ensure a complete and consistent (i.e., with the same public methods) implementation of the ADT.

The difference between using an abstract class and an interface is in the flexibility each provides a software developer. An abstract class can define nonconstant data members and nonabstract methods (in addition to constants and abstract methods) that are inherited by its subclasses. In some applications (see Section 17.4), the need for this capability causes us to use an abstract class instead of an interface.

When we wish to define only constants and abstract methods, using an interface gives us more flexibility than using a class because a class can implement many interfaces but can extend at most one class. Consider, for example, the interfaces `Computable` and `Comparable` defined in Section 1.13. Because a class can implement several interfaces, it is possible for us to define classes whose instances can be cast into (1) both `Computable` and `Comparable` or (2) `Computable` but not `Comparable` or (3) `Comparable` but not `Computable`. If we define `Computable` and `Comparable` as abstract classes instead of as interfaces, we will not be able to define a class whose instances can be cast into both `Computable` and `Comparable` unless `Computable` is a subclass of `Comparable` or vice versa. But if we make `Computable` a subclass of

Comparable (or vice versa), then we must give up one of the possiblities (2) and (3).

We do not intend to develop nonabstract methods that are to be inherited by the many linear list classes we develop in this book. However, we will develop at least one linear list class that extends an existing Java class (see Section 5.4; as a result, this linear list implementation cannot also extend an abstract class specification of a linear list). Therefore, we use the interface LinearList of Program 5.1 rather than the abstract class of Program 5.2 to represent our ADT. Our decision to use an interface to specify the ADT *LinearList* also is consistent with the use of the interface java.util.List that specifies a Cadillac version of a linear list.

With the exception of the ADT Graph of Chapter 17, we use interfaces to specify ADTs throughout this book.

EXERCISE

1. Let $L = (a, b, c, d)$ be a linear list. What is the result of each of the following operations?

    (a) *isEmpty*()

    (b) *size*()

    (c) *get*(0), *get*(2), *get*(6), *get*(−3)

    (d) *indexOf*(a), *indexOf*(c), *indexOf*(q)

    (e) *remove*(0), *remove*(2), *remove*(3)

    (f) *add*(0, e), *add*(2, f), *add*(3, g), *add*(4, h), *add*(6, h), *add*(−3, h)

5.3   ARRAY REPRESENTATION

5.3.1   The Representation

In an **array representation**, we use an array to store either the list elements or references to these elements. Although we can pack several instances into a single array (see Section 5.5), it is easier to use a different array for each instance. Individual elements of an instance (or references to these elements) are located in the array using a mathematical formula.

Suppose we decide to use a different one-dimensional array for each list to be represented. The one-dimensional array element has many positions (or locations) element[0] ··· element[element.length-1], and each array position can be used to store a single list element. We need to map the elements of the list to positions in the array. Where does the zeroth element reside? Where does the last element reside? The most natural mapping uses the formula

$$location(i) = i \qquad (5.1)$$

Equation 5.1 states that the ith element of the list (if it exists) is in position i of the array. Figure 5.1(a) shows how the list [5, 2, 4, 8, 1] is stored in the array `element` using the mapping of Equation 5.1. The length of the array is 10, and the size of the list is 5.

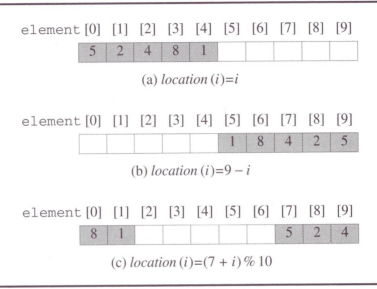

(a) *location* $(i){=}i$

(b) *location* $(i){=}9-i$

(c) *location* $(i){=}(7+i)\,\%\,10$

Figure 5.1 Different ways to map [5, 2, 4, 8, 1] into a one-dimensional array

Although Equation 5.1 is a natural choice for a forumla to map list elements into array positions, other choices are possible. For example, the formula

$$location(i) = \texttt{element.length} - i - 1 \qquad (5.2)$$

stores the list elements backwards beginning at the right end of the array `element`, and the formula

$$location(i) = (location(0) + i)\%\texttt{element.length} \qquad (5.3)$$

stores elements beginning at any position in the array and wraps around to the front of the array, if necessary, to store the remaining elements. Figure 5.1(b) shows how the list [5, 2, 4, 8, 1] is stored when Equation 5.2 is used, and Figure 5.1(c) shows how this list is stored using Equation 5.3 and *location*(0) = 7. Equation 5.3 is used in Chapter 10 to map a queue into a one-dimensional array.

In our array representation of a linear list, we use a one-dimensional array `element`, Equation 5.1, and a variable `size` that keeps track of the number of elements currently in the list. We may remove element e_i from the list by moving elements to its right down by 1. For example, to remove the element $e_1 = 2$ from the list of Figure 5.1(a), we have to move the elements $e_2 = 4$, $e_3 = 8$, and $e_4 = 1$, which are to the right of e_1, to positions 1, 2, and 3 of the array element. Figure 5.2(a) shows the result. The shaded elements were moved.

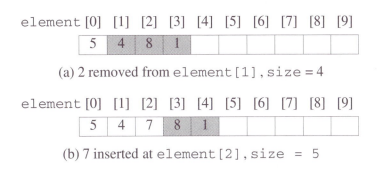

(a) 2 removed from element[1], size = 4

(b) 7 inserted at element[2], size = 5

Figure 5.2 Removing and inserting an element

To insert an element so that it becomes element i of a list, we must first move the existing element e_i (if any) and all elements to its right one position right and then put the new element into position i of the array. For example, to insert 7 as the second element of the list of Figure 5.2(a), we first move elements e_2 and e_3 to the right by 1 and then put 7 into position 2 of the array. Figure 5.2(b) shows the result. The shaded elements were moved.

Before we can write an array-based class that implements the interface Linear-List, we must decide on the data type of the array element and the length of this array. By declaring element to be of type Object, we can use the array element to hold references to elements of any user-defined data type. This method gives us the most general implementation possible. The length of the array element must be large enough to hold the maximum number of elements that might be in the list at any time. This maximum number is often difficult to estimate. To overcome this hurdle, we can ask the user to provide an estimate and then dynamically increase the length of the array element in case the user underestimated.

5.3.2   Changing the Length of a One-Dimensional Array

To increase or decrease the length of a one-dimensional array a that contains elements in positions a[0:n-1], we first define an array of the new length, then copy the n elements from a to the new array, and finally change the value of a so that it references the new array. Program 5.3 gives the method changeLength1D, which performs the first two of these tasks. The method changeLength1D uses three Java methods—newInstance, getComponentType, and arraycopy—with which you may not be familiar.

```
public static Object [] changeLength1D(Object [] a,
                           int n, int newLength)
{// a[0:n-1] is to be copied into new array
   // make sure new length is adequate
   if (n > newLength)
      throw new IllegalArgumentException
              ("new length is too small");

   // allocate a new array of desired length and same type
   Object [] newArray = (Object []) Array.newInstance
              (a.getClass().getComponentType(), newLength);

   // copy from old space to new space
   System.arraycopy(a, 0, newArray, 0, n);

   return newArray;
}

// full array a is to be copied into new array
public static Object [] changeLength1D(Object [] a, int newLength)
   {return changeLength1D(a, a.length, newLength);}
```

Program 5.3 Changing the length of a one-dimensional array

newInstance(componentType, length) is a class (i.e., static) method of the class Array, which is in the java.lang.reflect package. This method creates a new array of length length, and the components of this array are of the type componentType. getComponentType() is an instance method of the class Class, which is in the java.lang package. This method returns the data type of the components of the invoking Class instance. The method arraycopy is a class method of the class System, which is in the package java.lang. This method is described by the comments and header given below.

```
// copy from sourceArray[sourceStart:sourceStart+n-1] to
// destArray[destStart:destStart+n-1]
// sourceArray and destArray may be the same array
arraycopy(Object [] sourceArray, int sourceStart,
         Object [] destArray, int destStart, int number)
```

It takes $\Theta(m)$ time to create an array of length m because all elements of the newly created array are initialized to the default value for the component type. Notice that the invocation of `new` to create the new array may cause an `OutOfMemoryError`, and so the complexity of this invocation of `new` is actually $O(\texttt{newSize})$. If `new` is successful in creating the new array, Program 5.3 spends $\Theta(\texttt{n})$ time copying elements from the source array into the destination array. Therefore, the complexity of Program 5.3 is $O(\texttt{newSize+n}) = O(\texttt{newSize})$.

When an array is used to represent a data structure whose size increases dynamically, the array length is normally doubled whenever the array becomes full. This process is referred to as **array doubling**. When array doubling is used, the total time spent changing the array length is (in an asymptotic sense) no more than the total time spent inserting elements into the data structure (see Theorem 5.1).

5.3.3   The Class `ArrayLinearList`

Constructors for `ArrayLinearList`

We define a Java class `ArrayLinearList` that implements the ADT *LinearList* Equation 5.1. Program 5.4 gives the class header, the instance data members, and the constructors for the class `ArrayLinearList`. Since `ArrayLinearList` implements the interface `LinearList`, the class `ArrayLinearList` must provide an implementation of all the methods of `LinearList`. The class `ArrayLinearList` can, however, contain methods that are not declared in `LinearList`. In particular, our implementation contains two constructor methods. The first of these allows the user to provide an initial capacity for the list, and the second uses a default initial capacity of 10. The complexity of the first constructor is $O(\texttt{initialCapacity})$ and that of the second constructor is $\Theta(1)$.

Linear lists that are represented as arrays may be created using statements similar to those given below.

```
// create a linear list with initial capacity 100
LinearList y = new ArrayLinearList(100);
// create a linear list with the default initial capacity
ArrayLinearList z = new ArrayLinearList();
```

Elementary Methods of `ArrayLinearList`

Program 5.5 gives the implementation of the `isEmpty`, `size`, `get`, and `indexOf` methods. The complexity of the first three of these methods is $\Theta(1)$ and that of the fourth method is $O(\max\{\texttt{size}, 1\})$. For simplicity, we will often write complexities of this form as $O(\texttt{size})$.

```
public class ArrayLinearList implements LinearList
{
   // data members
   protected Object [] element;  // array of elements
   protected int size;           // number of elements in array

   // constructors
   /** create a list with initial capacity initialCapacity
     * @throws IllegalArgumentException when
     * initialCapacity < 1 */
   public ArrayLinearList(int initialCapacity)
   {
      if (initialCapacity < 1)
         throw new IllegalArgumentException
                 ("initialCapacity must be >= 1");
      // size has the default initial value of 0
      element = new Object [initialCapacity];
   }

   /** create a list with initial capacity 10 */
   public ArrayLinearList()
   {// use default capacity of 10
      this(10);
   }
```

Program 5.4 Data members and constructors for `ArrayLinearList`

Removing an Element

To remove or delete the `index`th element from a list, we need to first ascertain that the list contains an `index`th element and then delete this element. If the list does not have an `index`th element, an exception occurs because the ADT *LinearList* (ADT 5.1) doesn't tell us what to do at this time. Therefore, we throw an exception of type `IllegalArgumentException`.

When there is an `index`th element, we can perform the deletion by moving elements `index+1`, `index+2`, $\cdots$, `size-1` down (left) one position and reducing the value of `size` by 1. Method `remove` (Program 5.6) implements the delete/remove operation. We set `element[size]` to `null` to eliminate the reference in `element[size]`. Although this step is not necessary for the remove method to work properly, it is necessary for Java's storage reclamation method—garbage collection—to reclaim free storage.

```
/** @return true iff list is empty */
public boolean isEmpty()
    {return size == 0;}

/** @return current number of elements in list */
public int size()
   {return size;}

/** @throws IndexOutOfBoundsException when
  * index is not between 0 and size - 1 */
void checkIndex(int index)
{
   if (index < 0 || index >= size)
      throw new IndexOutOfBoundsException
         ("index = " + index + "  size = " + size);
}

/** @return element with specified index
  * @throws IndexOutOfBoundsException when
  * index is not between 0 and size - 1 */
public Object get(int index)
{
   checkIndex(index);
   return element[index];
}

/** @return index of first occurrence of theElement,
  * return -1 if theElement not in list */
public int indexOf(Object theElement)
{
   // search element[] for theElement
   for (int i = 0; i < size; i++)
      if (element[i].equals(theElement))
         return i;

   // theElement not found
   return -1;
}
```

Program 5.5 Elementary list operations

```
public Object remove(int index)
{
    checkIndex(index);

    // valid index, shift elements with higher index
    Object removedElement = element[index];
    for (int i = index + 1; i < size; i++)
        element[i-1] = element[i];

    element[--size] = null;    // enable garbage collection
    return removedElement;
}
```

Program 5.6 Remove and return the indexth element

When there is no indexth element, an exception is thrown and the time taken by remove is $\Theta(1)$. When the list has an indexth element, size-index element references are moved, taking $\Theta(\texttt{size-index})$ time. Hence the overall complexity is $O(\texttt{size-index})$.

Inserting an Element

To insert a new element as the indexth element in the list, we need to first move elements index through size-1 one position up (right), then insert the new element in position index, and finally increment size by 1. Program 5.7 gives the complete Java code to insert an element. As you can see, the method doubles the length of the array element in case the array has no space to accommodate the new element that is to be inserted. It takes $\Theta(1)$ time to determine whether an exception is to be thrown, $\Theta(\texttt{size})$ (this is the same as $\Theta(\text{old length})$ and $\Theta(\text{new length})$) time to double the array length if this doubling is necessary, and $\Theta(\texttt{size-index})$ time to shift elements. Therefore, the total time taken by insert is $O(\texttt{size})$.

Why do we double the array length in Program 5.7 and not simply increase the length by 1 or 2 (say)? Although increasing the array length by 1 or 2 every time does not affect the worst-case complexity of an insert (this worst-case complexity remains $\Theta(\texttt{size})$), increasing array length in this way can affect the asymptotic complexity of a sequence of inserts. Suppose we start with an empty list with initial capacity 1 and perform $n = 2^k + 1$ inserts. Assume that the inserts are performed at the end of the list. Therefore, no insert requires a shift of previously inserted elements and the time required to make the n inserts is $\Theta(n)$ plus the time spent increasing the array length. When the array length is always increased by 1, the time spent increasing the array length is $\Theta(\sum_{i=1}^{n-1} i) = \Theta(n^2)$. Therefore, the

```
public void add(int index, Object theElement)
{
   if (index < 0 || index > size)
      // invalid index
      throw new IndexOutOfBoundsException
             ("index = " + index + "  size = " + size);

   // valid index, make sure we have space
   if (size == element.length)
      // no space, double capacity
      element = ChangeArrayLength.changeLength1D(element, 2 * size);

   // shift elements right one position
   for (int i = size - 1; i >= index; i--)
      element[i + 1] = element[i];

   element[index] = theElement;

   size++;
}
```

Program 5.7 Insert `theElement` as `index`th element

total time needed for the n inserts is $\Theta(n^2)$.

If we double the array length as is done in Program 5.7, the total time spent changing the array length is $\Theta(\sum_{i=0}^{k} 2^i) = \Theta(2^{k+1} - 1) = \Theta(n)$. Therefore, the complexity of the n inserts is $\Theta(n)$. In fact, a simple generalization of this analysis shows that when the array length is always increased by a multiplicative factor (from `length` to $c \cdot$`length`, where $c > 1$ is a constant), the total time spent increasing the array length is O(number of inserts) even if `remove` and other operations are mixed in with the insert operations. This analysis leads to Theorem 5.1.

Theorem 5.1 *If we always increase the array length by a constant factor (which is 2 in Program 5.7), the time spent on any sequence of linear list operations increases by at most a constant factor when compared to the time taken for the same set of operations under the assumption that the initial capacity is not an underestimate (note that when this assumption is valid, no time is spent increasing the array length).*

The Method `toString`

Program 5.8 gives the code for `toString`. This method creates a comma separated string that is enclosed in square brackets and contains the linear list elements in index order. The complexity of `ArrayLinnearList.toString` is $O(\text{size})$ under the assumption that the expression `element[i].toString()` takes $O(1)$ time to compute.

```java
/** convert to a string */
public String toString()
{
   StringBuffer s = new StringBuffer("[");

   // put elements into the buffer
   for (int i = 0; i < size; i++)
      if (element[i] == null)
         s.append("null, ");
      else
         s.append(element[i].toString() + ", ");

   if (size > 0)
      s.delete(s.length() - 2, s.length());  // remove last ", "

   s.append("]");

   // create equivalent String
   return new String(s);
}
```

Program 5.8 Converting a linear list into a string

Decreasing the Length of `element`

Although our implementation of a linear list increases the length of `element` as needed, it never reduces its length. Therefore, an array-based linear list whose element array has grown to a length of 1,000,000 (say) will hold on to this much array space until no references to the linear list remain. This status continues even though the list may never again have more than 10 elements in it.

To enable the linear list to free some of the array space when the list size becomes small, we can modify the method `remove` so that it reduces the array length to max{`initialCapacity`, `element.length/2`} whenever `size` < `element.length/4` (say). This strategy is considered in Exercise 14.

Using the Class `ArrayLinearList`

A sample `main` method and the generated output can be found on the Web site.

The Class `FastArrayLinearList`

Many of you have probably noticed that we can replace the `for` loops in the codes for `remove` and `add` by the following statements, respectively:

```
System.arraycopy(element, index + 1, element, index,
                 size - index - 1);
System.arraycopy(element, index, element, index + 1, size - index);
```

Let `FastArrayLinearList` be the class obtained when we make this replacement. We can also refine `add` by combining the array copy done during array doubling with the array copy done to shift the elements `element[index]` through `element[size-1]` right by one. We do not incorporate this refinement.

5.3.4   An Iterator for `ArrayLinearList`

An **iterator** is a class that implements the Java interface `Iterator`, which is in the package `java.util`. This interface specifies a unified mechanism to examine (or enumerate or iterate through) the elements in an object one at a time. The methods in the interface `Iterator` are `hasNext`, `next`, and `remove`. The first of these methods is a `boolean` valued method that returns `true` iff one or more elements remain to be examined. The method `next` returns an unexamined element of the object. This method throws a `NoSuchElementException` in case no unexamined elements remain. The method `remove` deletes the last element that was returned by `next`. In case this last element has already been deleted or if `next` was never invoked, an `IllegalStateException` is thrown. Since the `remove` method is an optional method of `Iterator`, iterator classes that do not implement `remove` throw the exception `UnsupportedOperationException` when `remove` is invoked.

Java also provides a closely related interface `Enumeration`, which has the methods `hasMoreElements` and `nextElement`. We use the interface `Iterator` in this text, rather than `Enumeration`, because the interface `Iterator` is more general and is the basis for the iterators implemented in Java's collections framework.

Using a Top-Level Class

Program 5.9 gives an iterator for `ArrayLinearList`. The instance data member `list` keeps track of the list that is being iterated. This data member is initialized by the constructor. The complexity of each method of our iterator class is $\Theta(1)$.

Although you can instantiate an `ArrayLinearListIterator` directly using the `new` method, it is more common to add an instance method `iterator()` to the class

```
class ArrayLinearListIterator implements Iterator
{
   // data members
   private ArrayLinearList list;  // list to be iterated
   private int nextIndex;         // index of next element

   // constructor
   public ArrayLinearListIterator(ArrayLinearList theList)
   {
      list = theList;
      nextIndex = 0;
   }

   // methods
   /** @return true iff the list has a next element */
   public boolean hasNext()
      {return nextIndex < list.size;}

   /** @return next element in list
     * @exception NoSuchElementException
     * thrown if there is no next element */
   public Object next()
   {
      if (nextIndex < list.size)
         return list.element[nextIndex++];
      else
         throw new NoSuchElementException("No next element");
   }

   /** unsupported method */
   public void remove()
   {
      throw new UnsupportedOperationException
               ("remove not supported");
   }
}
```

Program 5.9 An iterator for the class ArrayLinearList

`ArrayLinearList` that does this instantiation. Program 5.10 gives the implementation of such a method.

```
public Iterator iterator()
   {return new ArrayLinearListIterator(this);}
```

Program 5.10 Instantiating an iterator for the class `ArrayLinearList`

Program 5.11 shows you how to use an iterator to output the elements of a linear list from left to right, obtaining a different format than provided by the `toString` method. A similar construct could be used to obtain the sum of all the elements in the list, and so on.

```
public static void main(String [] args)
{
   // create the list [0, 1, 2, 3, 4]
   ArrayLinearList x = new ArrayLinearList();
   x.add(0, new Integer(4));
   x.add(0, new Integer(3));
   x.add(0, new Integer(2));
   x.add(0, new Integer(1));
   x.add(0, new Integer(0));

   // output using an iterator
   Iterator y = x.iterator();
   while (y.hasNext())
      System.out.print(y.next() + " ");
   System.out.println();
}
```

Program 5.11 Using an iterator

Using a Member Class

There are some disadvantages to using a top-level class to implement an iterator as was done in Program 5.9. Since the iterator class needs access to the instance data members `element` and `size`, these data members cannot be declared as `private` data members. If we use the default visibility level (i.e., package), then should we decide to change the data members used in the representation of a linear list, we will need to examine all classes in the `dataStructures` package; determine which use the data members; and modify these classes to make use of the new data members. When the visibility level is protected, we will need to examine all classes in the same package as well as all derived classes in other packages. Software maintenance becomes much easier if the data members are declared as private members. Also, since the implementation of the iterator is very closely tied to that of the class it iterates, we would like to define the iterator in the same file.

We can accomplish both these objectives—ease of software maintenence and defining the iterator in the same file as the class it iterates—by implementing the iterator class as a member class of ArrayLinearList. Since a member class has the same access privileges as a member method, a member class can access the private data members of the enclosing class. Further, since the code for a member class is placed within the braces that contain the other members of the enclosing class, the member class definition appears in the same file as the one that contains the definition of the enclosing class. Program 5.12 gives partial code for the member class ArrayLinearListIterator of ArrayLinearListWithIterator as well as the new version of the method iterator. The new code is quite similar to the code used when the iterator class was a top-level class (see Programs 5.9 and 5.10). We can use the code of Program 5.11 to iterate the elements of a list by changing ArrayLinearList to ArrayLinearListWithIterator.

```
public class ArrayLinearListWithIterator implements LinearList
{
   // previously discussed methods of ArrayLinearList come here

   // only methods related to iteration are shown
   public Iterator iterator()
      {return new ArrayLinearListIterator();}

   private class ArrayLinearListIterator implements Iterator
   {
      // data member
      private int nextIndex;   // index of next element

      // constructor
      public ArrayLinearListIterator() {}

      // codes for hasNext, next, and remove are the same
      // as when a top-level class
   }
}
```

Program 5.12 An iterator member class

Merits of Using an Iterator

Since all implementations of the interface `LinearList` (Program 5.2) must provide an implementation of the method `get`, application codes can examine the elements of a linear list `x` in left-to-right order using the code

```
int size = x.size();
for (int i = 0; i < size; i++)
   examine(x.get(i));
```

Alternatively, applications may utilize the iterator methods and the code

```
Iterator y = x.iterator();
while (y.hasNext())
   examine(y.next());
```

Which is better? The code using the iterator methods is more general in that it can be used with all data types (not just linear lists) that implement the interface `Iterator` and is often more efficient. For example, when we use the `get` method to examine the elements of an array-based linear list, each invocation of `get` results in validating the index `i` by comparing `i` with both 0 and `size`; `next` compares `nextIndex` with `size` only. Additionally, `get` has one parameter, whereas `next` has none. Other than these differences, the codes for `get` and `next` are quite similar. Consequently, even though both the `get` and iterator methods take $\Theta(\text{size})$ time to access the list elements in the desired order, the iterator method is expected to be slightly faster. In Chapter 6 we will see that when linear lists are represented as chains, the `get` method takes $\Theta(\text{size}^2)$ time, whereas the iterator method takes only $\Theta(\text{size})$ time.

The linear list iterator permits applications to easily access list elements in left-to-right order. For any other access order, we must use the `get` method.

EXERCISES

2. Let L $= (a, b, c, d, e)$ be a linear list that is represented in an array `element` using Equation 5.1. Assume that `element.length` $= 10$. Draw figures similar to Figure 5.2 showing the contents of the array `element` and the value of `size` following each operation in the operation sequence: initial state, $add(0, f)$, $add(3, g)$, $add(7, h)$, $remove(0)$, $remove(4)$.

3. Write a method `changeLength2D` to change the length of a two-dimensional array. You must allow for a change in both dimensions of the array. Test your method.

4. Extend the class `ArrayLinearList` to include a constructor that allows you to specify the amount by which the list capacity (or array length) is to be increased whenever array resizing is needed. When no capacity increment is specified, array doubling is done. Modify `add` to work in this way. Test your code.

5. Extend `ArrayLinearList` to include the method `trimToSize`, which makes the array size equal to the list size. What is the complexity of your method? Test your code.

6. Extend `ArrayLinearList` to include the method `setSize`, which makes the list size equal to the specified size. If the original list size was less than the new one, `null` elements are added, and if the original size was more than the new one, the extra elements are removed. What is the complexity of your method? Test your code.

7. Extend `ArrayLinearList` to include the method `set(theIndex, theElement)`, which replaces the element whose index is `theIndex` with `theElement`. Throw an exception in case `theIndex` is out of range. You should return the old element with the specified index. Test your code.

8. Extend `ArrayLinearList` to include the method `clear`, which makes the list empty. What is the complexity of your method? Test your code.

9. Extend `ArrayLinearList` to include the method `removeRange`, which removes all elements in the specified index range. What is the complexity of your method? Test your code.

10. Extend `ArrayLinearList` to include the method `lastIndexOf`, which returns the index of the right-most occurrence of the specified object. A −1 is returned in case the specified object is not in the list. What is the complexity of your method? Test your code.

11. Write a new version of the method `add` (Program 5.7) that works like the present one when no array resizing is needed. However, when array resizing is needed, the element shifting now done in the `for` loop is done during the copying of elements from the old array to the new array. Comment on the relative complexities of the two versions of `add`.

12. Write an instance method `clone()` for the class `ArrayLinearList`. The method should return a copy of the invoking list. What is the complexity of your method? Test your code.

13. Prove Theorem 5.1.

14. A shortcoming of the class `ArrayLinearList` (Program 5.2) is that it never decreases the length of the array `element`.

(a) Write a new version of this class so that if, following a deletion, the list size drops below `element.length/4`, a smaller array of length max{`element.length/2, initialCapacity`} is allocated and the elements are copied from the old array into the new one.

(b) (Optional) Consider any sequence of n linear list operations beginning with an empty list. Suppose that the total step count is $f(n)$ when the initial capacity equals or exceeds the maximum list size. Show that if we start with an initial capacity of 1 and use array resizing during inserts and removes as described above and in Section 5.3, the new step count is at most $cf(n)$ for some constant c.

15. Prove a theorem analogous to Theorem 5.1 for the case when array length is increased by a constant factor $c > 1$ whenever the array gets full and is reduced by the factor c whenever array occupancy falls below $1/(2c)$ (subject, of course, to the constraint that array length never falls below its initial length).

16. Program 5.8 uses a string buffer s to assemble the string version of a linear list and then converts s into an object of type `String` to obtain the object that is returned by the method. The complexity of the method `StringBuffer.append(x)` is linear in the length of x, and the complexity of `new String(s)` is linear in the length of s.

(a) Show that the complexity of `toString` (Program 5.14) is $O(n)$ where n is the list length. Assume that each list element is a single character and the complexity of `element[i].toString()` is $\Theta(1)$.

(b) Write a new version of the method `toString` in which a string buffer is not used. Instead, assemble the output string using string concatenation operations as are used in Program 1.11. What is the time complexity of the new method? (It should be $O(n^2)$.)

(c) Measure the run time of the two `toString` methods using lists of size 100; 1000; and 10,000. Do the measured times agree with the analyses?

17. Write the interface `IterableLinearList`, which implements the interfaces `LinearList` and `Iterator`.

18. (a) Extend the class `ArrayLinearList` (Program 5.4) to include a method `reverse` that reverses the order of the elements in the list. The reversal is to be done in place (i.e., within the array `element` and without the creation of a new array). Note that before the reversal, the kth element (if it exists) of the list is in `element[k]`; following the reversal the kth element is in `element[size-k-1]`.

(b) The complexity of your method should be linear in `size`. Show that this is the case.

(c) Test the correctness of your code, using your own test data.

(d) Now write another in-place method to reverse an object of type **Array-LinearList**. This method is not a class member and should not access the data members of **ArrayLinearList**. Rather, your method should use the member methods of **ArrayLinearList** to produce the reversed list.

(e) What is the time complexity of your new method?

(f) Compare the run-time performance of the two reversal methods using linear lists of size 1000; 5000; and 10,000.

19. (a) Extend the class **ArrayLinearList** to include a method **leftShift(i)** that shifts the list elements left by **i** positions. If L = [0, 1, 2, 3, 4], then **L.leftShift(2)** results in L = [2, 3, 4].

    (b) What is the time complexity of your method?

    (c) Test your code.

20. In a circular shift operation, the elements of a linear list are rotated clockwise by a given amount. For example, when the elements of L = [0, 1, 2, 3, 4] are shifted circularly by 2, the result is L = [2, 3, 4, 0, 1].

    (a) Describe how you can perform a circular shift using three reversal operations. Each reversal may reverse a portion of the list or reverse the entire list.

    (b) Extend the class **ArrayLinearList** by adding the method **circular-Shift(i)**, which performs a circular shift by **i** positions. The complexity of your method should be linear in the list length.

    (c) Test your code.

21. Extend the class **ArrayLinearList** by adding the method **half()**. The invocation **x.half()** eliminates every other element of **x**. So if **x.size** is initially 7 and **x.element[]** = [2, 13, 4, 5, 17, 8, 29], then following the execution of **x.half()**, **x.size** is 4 and **x.element[]** = [2, 4, 17, 29]. If **x.size** is initially 4 and **x.element[]** = [2, 13, 4, 5], then following the execution of **x.half()**, **x.size** is 2 and **x.element[]** = [2, 4]. If **x** is initially empty, then it is empty following the execution of **x.half()**.

    (a) Write code for the member method **half()**. You should not use any of the other methods of **ArrayLinearList**. The complexity of your code should be $O(\text{size})$.

    (b) Show that the complexity of your code is, in fact, $O(\text{size})$.

    (c) Test your code.

22. Write a method equivalent to the method **half** of Exercise 21. Your method should not be a member of **ArrayLinearList** and should not access any of

the data members of this class either. Rather, accomplish your task by using methods of the interface LinearList. What is the complexity of your method? Test your code.

23. In several applications we need to move back and forth on a list. Extend the iterator class ArrayLinearListIterator (Program 5.12) to include code for the following members:

   (a) reset—Set nextIndex to 0.

   (b) hasPrevious—Return false iff at the zeroth element of the list.

   (c) previous—Return the preceding element and decrement nextIndex by 1.

   Test your code.

24. Let a and b be two objects of type ArrayLinearList.

   (a) Write a member method meld(a,b) to create a linear list that contains elements alternately from a and b, beginning with the zeroth element of a. If you run out of elements in one list, then append the remaining elements of the other list to the list being created. The invocation c.meld(a,b) should make c the melded list. The complexity of your code should be linear in the sizes of the two input lists.

   (b) Show that the complexity of your code is linear in the sum of the sizes of a and b.

   (c) Test your code.

25. Let a and b be objects of type ArrayLinearList. Assume that the elements of a and b are of type Comparable and are in sorted order (i.e., nondecreasing from left to right).

   (a) Write a member method merge(a,b) to create a new sorted linear list that contains all the elements in a and b. The merged list is assigned to the invoking object.

   (b) What is the complexity of your method?

   (c) Test your code.

26. (a) Write the method ArrayLinearList.split(a,b) to create two linear lists a and b. a contains the elements of this that have an even index, and b contains the remaining elements.

   (b) What is the complexity of your method?

   (c) Test your code.

27. Suppose that we are to represent a linear list using Equation 5.3. Rather than store the list size explicitly, we keep variables `first` and `last` that give the locations of the first and last elements of the list.

   (a) Develop a class similar to `ArrayLinearList` for this representation. Write code for all methods. You can make the `remove` and `add` codes more efficient by properly choosing to move either elements to the left or right of the removed/inserted element.

   (b) What is the time complexity of each of your methods?

   (c) Test your code.

28. Write an iterator member-class for your array-based linear list class of Exercise 27.

29. Do Exercise 18 using Equation 5.3 instead of 5.1.

30. Do Exercise 24 using Equation 5.3 instead of 5.1.

31. Do Exercise 25 using Equation 5.3 instead of 5.1.

32. Do Exercise 26 using Equation 5.3 instead of 5.1.

5.4   VECTOR REPRESENTATION

Java provides a class `Vector` in its `java.util` package that uses an array and provides all of the functionality of the class `ArrayLinearList` (plus many additional methods). The length of the array used to implement a `Vector` is dynamically increased as needed. The names we have used for the methods of `LinearList` and `ArrayLinearList` are exactly those used in `Vector` to perform identical operations.

We could have defined our array-based linear list class as a subclass of `Vector`, inheriting the methods of `Vector` (including the iterator methods). Program 5.13 gives the corresponding implementation. What could be easier?

The array-based linear list implementations `ArrayLinearList` and `LinearList-AsVectorSubclass` differ in one important way—they throw exceptions of a different type. While the methods of `ArrayLinearList` throw exceptions of the type `IndexOutOfBoundsException` when a list index is out of bounds, the methods of `Vector` (which are inherited by `LinearListAsVectorSubclass`) throw exceptions of type `ArrayIndexOutOfBoundsException` under this circumstance. This difference means that we cannot replace `ArrayLinearList` with `LinearListAsVectorSubclass`; linear list applications written to catch exceptions of type `IndexOutOfBoundsException` and then take remedial action will fail.

Well, why did we not develop `ArrayLinearList` to throw exceptions of the same type as thrown by `Vector` in the first place? Some of the reasons for the course we took follow.

```
public class LinearListAsVectorSubclass extends Vector
                                   implements LinearList
{
   // constructors
   public LinearListAsVectorSubclass(int initialCapacity)
      {super(initialCapacity);}

   public LinearListAsVectorSubclass()
   {// use default capacity of 10
      this(10);
   }
}
```

Program 5.13 Implementing an array-based linear list as a subclass of `Vector`

- Although throwing exceptions of type `ArrayIndexOutOfBounds` makes good sense in the context of an array implementation, the fact that an array implementation is used has been hidden from the user. Therefore, throwing an exception of this type would leave the user wondering as to the connection between arrays and the linear lists he/she is using. From the user's perspective, it makes more sense for our linear list methods to throw an exception of type `IndexOutOfBoundsException`.

- We shall later see implementations of a linear list that do not employ arrays or `Vectors`. For compatibility reasons, these implementations should throw exceptions of the same type as thrown by array and `Vector` implementations. Yet since these new implementations use no arrays, there is no justification for them to throw exceptions of the type `ArrayIndexOutOfBoundsException`.

- In a real situation the predicament we are in right now—we have two implementations of `LinearList` that differ in the type of exception thrown—cannot be foreseen. The reason is that when we are developing the first implementation (for example, `ArrayLinearList`), we are unaware of the possibility of a simpler implementation such as that of Program 5.13. For example, the next version of the Java language might provide additional classes that make some previously developed user-defined classes obsolete. So our predicament illustrates a situation you might find yourself in several months or years after you have developed some classes. Actually the additional classes provided in future versions of Java may differ from existing user-defined classes that provide similar functionality not only in the types of exceptions thrown but also in the method names and method signatures used.

We now wish to get the benefits of the class Vector and provide a linear list implementation that behaves exactly as does ArrayLinearList. When we do so, we can guarantee that already developed applications that used the old implementation of ArrayLinearList will run the same way with the new implementation (provided, of course, that they did not access the data members of ArrayLinearList).

Our first strategy would be to define a subclass of Vector that inherits the Vector methods such as size, isEmpty, and toString that behave exactly as do the corresponding methods of ArrayLinearList; methods of Vector (e.g., get, remove, and add) that behave differently from those of ArrayLinearList will be overridden by new implementations of these methods. Unfortunately, this is not possible because the methods we wish to override are declared as final methods in the class Vector. Therefore, we cannot define a subclass of Vector that overrides these methods.

However, all is not lost. With some additional effort, we can achieve our objective of using the class Vector to obtain an array-based implementation of the ADT *LinearList* that behaves exactly as does ArrayLinearList. We define a class that is not a subclass of Vector; rather, it has a data member element whose type is Vector. The method implementations are generally simple invocations of the corresponding methods of Vector. Some of the methods need to catch exceptions of type ArrayIndexOutOfBoundsException that are thrown by the corresponding methods of Vector and throw exceptions of type IndexOutOfBoundsException in their place.

Program 5.14 gives the codes for the methods of the array-based linear list class LinearListAsVector in which each instance is represented as a Vector. The constructor invocation

```
element = new Vector(initialCapacity)
```

creates a Vector whose initial capacity is initialCapacity. Since a Vector is represented as an array, the constructor actually creates an array whose length is initialCapacity. If an attempt is made to add more elements to the Vector than its current capacity, the array length is doubled. The class Vector has other constructors as well. One of these has no parameters and constructs an array of default length 10. Another constructor allows you to specify the amount by which the capacity is to be increased whenever there is need for additional capacity.

Notice that even though we have changed the data members of the class, the method headers have remained the same. Therefore, had we declared the data members of ArrayLinearList as private, all applications that use ArrayLinear-List will run just as well with LinearListAsVector. Since the data members of ArrayLinearList are declared protected, applications in the same package (i.e., the package dataStructures) or in classes derived from ArrayLinearList might contain references to the data members of ArrayLinearLists. These applications will fail if they use LinearListAsVector.

```
// data member
protected Vector element;

// constructors
public LinearListAsVector(int initialCapacity)
{
   if (initialCapacity < 1)
      throw new IllegalArgumentException
               ("initialCapacity must be >= 1");
   element = new Vector(initialCapacity);
}

public LinearListAsVector()
{// use default capacity of 10
   this(10);
}

// methods
public boolean isEmpty()
    {return element.isEmpty();}

public int size()
   {return element.size();}

public Object get(int index)
{
   try {return element.get(index);}
   catch (Exception e)
   {
      throw new IndexOutOfBoundsException
               ("index = " + index + "  size = " + size());
   }
}

public int indexOf(Object theElement)
   {return element.indexOf(theElement);}
```

Program 5.14 An array-based linear list implemented using a Vector (continues)

```
public Object remove(int index)
{
   try {return element.remove(index);}
   catch (Exception e)
   {
      throw new IndexOutOfBoundsException
               ("index = " + index + "  size = " + size());
   }
}

public void add(int index, Object theElement)
{
   try {element.add(index, theElement);}
   catch (Exception e)
   {
      throw new IndexOutOfBoundsException
               ("index = " + index + "  size = " + size());
   }
}

public String toString()
   {return element.toString();}
```

Program 5.14 An array-based linear list implemented using a `Vector` (concluded)

EXERCISES

33. A shortcoming of the class `LinearListAsVector` (Program 5.14) is that it never decreases the capacity of the vector `element`. Write a new version of this class so that if, following a deletion, the list size drops below `element.capacity()/4`, the vector capacity is reduced to max{`element.size()`, `initial-Capacity`}.

34. Compare the run-time performance of the classes `ArrayLinearList`, `LinearListAsVectorSubclass`, and `LinearListAsVector`. Do this comparison by performing a sequence of n insert-at-0 operations followed by a sequence of n remove-from-0 operations.

5.5 MULTIPLE LISTS IN A SINGLE ARRAY

Before accepting the array-based representation of a linear list, let us reflect on its merits. Certainly, the operations to be performed on a linear list can be implemented as very simple Java methods. The methods `indexOf`, `remove`, and `add` have a worst complexity that is linear in the size of the individual list. We might regard this complexity as quite satisfactory. (In Chapters 11 and 16 we will see representations that allow us to perform these operations even faster.)

A negative aspect of the array-based representation is its inefficient use of space. Consider the following situation. We are to maintain three lists. We know that the three lists together will never have more than 4097 elements in them at any time. However, it is quite possible for a particular list to have 4097 elements at one time and for another list to have 4097 elements at another time. If we create three instances of `ArrayLinearList`, each with an initial array length of 4097, we will need space for a total of 12,291 elements (or element references) even though we will never have more than 4097 elements at any time. However, using an initial length of 4097 for each array ensures that array resizing will not be required and our program will run as fast as possible. On the other hand, if we create three arrays with initial length 1, then when the length of one of these arrays is to increase from 4096 to 4097, we will need to first create an array of length 8192 and copy 4096 elements into the new array. During the copy, both the 4096 and 8192 length arrays are needed. Therefore, space for at least 12,288 elements is needed.

In many applications of linear lists, the amount of memory used is not an issue because our computer has enough memory for the application to run to completion using the single-list-in-a-single-array representation. However, in applications that use very large lists, the list representations of this chapter may cause the application to fail (for insufficient memory) even though the total number of elements we have is small enough that all elements can be accommodated in the available memory. The application fails because excess memory has been allocated to a particular array or because array doubling fails.

One way to overcome this space requirement problem is to buy more memory. Another possiblity is to map all of our lists into a single array `element` whose length is the maximum possible. In addition, we use two other arrays, `front` and `last`, to index into the array `list`. Figure 5.3 shows three lists represented in the single array `element`. We adopt the convention that the lists are numbered 1 through `m` if there are `m` lists and that `front[i]` is actually one less than the actual position of the zeroth element in list `i`. This convention on `front[i]` makes it easier to use the representation. `last[i]` is the actual position of the last element in list `i`. Notice that with this convention, `last[i]` > `front[i]` whenever the `i`th list is not empty. We shall have `front[i]` = `last[i]` whenever list `i` is empty. So in the example of Figure 5.3, list 2 is empty. The lists are represented in the array in the order 1, 2, 3, $\cdots$, `m` from left to right.

To avoid having to handle the first and last lists differently from others, we define two boundary lists 0 and `m+1` with `front[0]` = `last[0]` = -1 and `front[m+1]` =

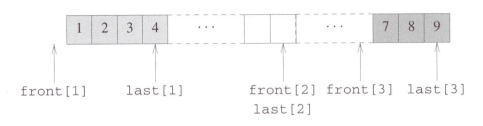

Figure 5.3 Three lists in a single array

`last[m+1]` = `list.length-1`. To insert an element as the `index`th element of list
i, we need to first create space for the new element. If `last[i]` = `front[i+1]`,
then there is no space between lists i and i+1 and we cannot move elements `index`
through the last one up one position. At this time we can check whether it is
possible to move elements 0 through `index-1` of the ith list one position down by
checking the relation `last[i-1]` < `front[i]`. If this relation does not hold, then
we need to either shift some of the lists 1 through i-1 down or some of the lists i+1
through m up and create space for list i to grow. This shifting is possible when the
total number of elements in all the lists is fewer than `list.length`.

Figure 5.4 is a pseudo-Java version of the method to insert an element into list
i. This pseudocode may be refined into compilable Java code.

Although representing several lists in a single array uses space more efficiently
than using a separate array for each list, insertions take more time in the worst case.
In fact, a single insertion could require us to move as many as `list.length-1` elements. The multiple-list-in-a-single-array representation is also quite cumbersome
to implement. A much simpler solution whose space requirement equals that for $2n$
references, where n is the number of elements in all lists together, involves the use
of pointers. This solution is the subject of the next chapter.

EXERCISES

35. Refine Figure 5.4 into a Java method and test its correctness.

36. Write a Java method to insert an element as the *index*th element in list
    i. Assume that a single array represents m lists. If you have to move lists
    to accommodate the new element, your should first determine the amount
    of available space and then move the lists so that each has about the same
    amount of space available for future growth. Test your code.

37. Write a Java method to remove the *index*th element from list i. Assume
    that a single array represents m lists. Test the correctness of your code by
    compiling and executing it.

```
void add(int i, int index, Object element)
{// Insert y as the index'th element in list i.
    size = last[i] - front[i]; // number of elements in list i
    if (index < 0 || index > size)
    throw an exception;
    // Is there space on the right?
    Find the least j, j ≥ i such that last[j] < front[j+1];
    If such a j exists, then move lists i+1 through j and elements index through
      the last one of list i up one position and insert element into list i;
      This move should update appropriate last and first values;

    // Is there space on the left?
    If no j was found above, then find the largest j, j < i such that
    last[j] < front[j+1];
    If such a j is found, then move lists j through i-1
    and elements 1 through index-1 of list i one position left and insert element;
    This move should update appropriate last and first values;

    // Success?
    if (no j was found above) throw an exception;
}
```

Figure 5.4 Pseudocode to insert an element in the many lists per array representation

5.6   PERFORMANCE MEASUREMENT

In this chapter we have developed four array-based classes that implement the interface LinearList—ArrayLinearList (ALL), FastArrayLinearList (FALL), LinearListAsVector (LLAV), and LinearListAsVectorSubclass(LLAVS). All four classes are equally good as far as their space complexity is concerned. Even though all four classes offer the same asymptotic time complexity, their actual run times are likely to be different.

To obtain the actual run times, we must design an experiment. We wish to measure the time taken by the operations get, add, and remove. We expect the times for the indexOf operation to be the same as that for the get operation. Therefore, no separate measurement is made for the indexOf operation.

For the get operation, we measure the total time required for the sequence get(i), $0 \leq i <$ size. Figure 5.5 gives the measured times for size $= 40,000$, and Figure 5.6 shows these times as bar graphs. We expect the time for ArrayLinearList and FastArrayLinearList to be the same because the code is identical. We also expect the times for LinearListAsVector and LinearListAsVectorSubclass to be about the same. Our measurements verify these expectations. However, we see that for the get operation, ArrayLinearList and FastArrayLinearList take about one-third the time taken by LinearListAsVector and LinearListAsVectorSubclass. Exercise 38 explores the reason for this behavior.

operation	ALL	FALL	LLAV	LLAVS
get	5.6 ms	5.6 ms	20.8 ms	18.6 ms
best-case inserts	26.2/14.0 ms	31.2/18.0 ms	51.2/38.9 ms	48.2/36.4 ms
average inserts	70/69 s	5.8/5.8 s	5.8/5.8 s	5.8/5.8 s
worst-case inserts	140/140 s	11.8/11.8 s	11.8/11.8 s	11.8/11.8 s
best-case removes	6.9 ms	8.6 ms	18.4 ms	22.4 ms
average removes	71 s	5.7 s	5.8 s	5.8 s
worst-case removes	142 s	11.7 s	11.8 s	11.8 s

Times for 40,000 operations

Figure 5.5 Time taken by different array-based linear list implementations

For the add operation, we do a sequence of $n = 40,000$ inserts beginning with an empty list and report the total time for the 40,000 inserts. The best case for the insert sequence is when each new element is inserted at the right end of the list; the worst case is when each new element is inserted at the left end. To estimate average behavior, we do the inserts at randomly generated positions of the list. Figure 5.5 gives the insert times in the format TA/TB, where TA is the time when the list is constructed with the default initial capacity of 10 and TB is the time when the initial capacity is $40,000$. For best-case inserts, array doubling increases run time by about 87 precent for ArrayLinearList when compared with the case when no array resizing is done. The times for FastArrayLinearList, LinearListAsVector, and LinearListAsVectorSubclass increase by 73 percent, 32 percent, and 32 percent, respectively, when array resizing is done; this works out to about 12 ms for each class. For the average and worst-case tests, the array resizing time of approximately 12 ms is a negligible part of the total cost. This result is to be expected because array doubling adds $\Theta(n)$ to the cost of n inserts; the cost of n best-case inserts is $\Theta(n)$, and the cost of n worst-case inserts is $\Theta(n^2)$.

Notice the colossal increase in run time from the best-case inserts to the worst-case inserts—the run time for ArrayLinearList jumped from 26.2 ms to 140 seconds, more than a 5300-fold increase. This 5300-fold increase isn't altogether surprising given that n best-case inserts take $\Theta(n)$ time, whereas n worst-case inserts take $\Theta(n^2)$ time. If the constant factors in the best-case and worst-case time expressions are the same (and they are not), we would expect to see the time go up by a factor of almost $n = 40,000$.

The average insert time is approximately half the worst-case insert time. This

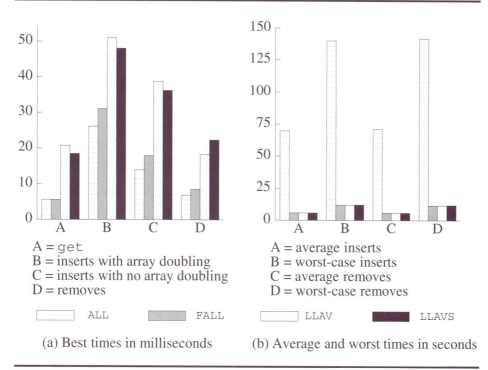

A = get
B = inserts with array doubling
C = inserts with no array doubling
D = removes

ALL   FALL

(a) Best times in milliseconds

A = average inserts
B = worst-case inserts
C = average removes
D = worst-case removes

LLAV   LLAVS

(b) Average and worst times in seconds

Figure 5.6 Plot of run times

result is to be expected because, on average, half the elements have to be moved during an insert; in the worst-case, all elements are moved.

For the average and worst-case insert tests, `ArrayLinearList` took about 12 times the time taken by each of the other three implementations. The use of `arraycopy` in place of a `for` loop to shift array elements reduces the average and worst-case run times of `ArrayLinearList` by a factor of 12! This is quite a performance boost—three cheers for the developers of `arraycopy`.

For the `remove` operation, we start with a list that has $n = 40,000$ elements and do a sequence of n removes. The best case for the remove sequence is when each remove operation removes the element at the right end of the list; the worst case is when each remove operation removes the element at the left end. To estimate average behavior, we do the removes from randomly generated positions of the list. For best-case removes, `ArrayLinearList` is best, but for average and worst-case removes, `ArrayLinearList` takes about 12 times the time taken by each of the remaining three linear list classes. Again, notice that the average remove time is approximately half the worst-case remove time.

So which class should you use? If your primary operation is `get` or if you are doing `adds` and `removes` from the right end of the list (as is the case for the stack data structure of Chapter 9), use `ArrayLinearList`. For other applications of a linear list, use `FastArrayLinearList`. But wait; we have yet to see other linear list implementations. These might be even faster!

EXERCISE

38. [Detective Work] Why is the best-case performance of `ArrayLinearList` and `FastArrayLinearList` better than that of `LinearListAsVector`? Is it because we are super-duper programmers, or is it because `java.util.Vector` has features and capabilities that `FastArrayLinearList` does not have—features that necessarily slow down the methods of `Vector`? For example, several methods of `Vector` are declared as `synchronized` methods. Since Java is a multithreaded language, two independent tasks (or threads) can concurrently manipulate the same instance. When two threads try to insert an element into the same list at the same time, chaos ensues. To avoid this chaos, the inserts are serialized; that is, they are done one after the other rather than concurrently. To prevent methods such as `add` from being executed concurrently by two threads (i.e., to prevent two concurrent inserts), the `add` method is declared as a `synchronized` method.

    Your mission, Sherlock Holmes, is to determine why the best-case performance of `ArrayLinearList` and `FastArrayLinearList` is better than that of `LinearListAsVector`. To resolve this mystery, study the code for `Vector`, which is in the `src.jar` file that comes with Java. Experiment with the codes, modifying codes as needed to test hypotheses. For example, if you think that synchronization is the culprit, add the modifier `synchronized` to the appropriate methods of `ArrayLinearList` and `FastArrayLinearList` and measure run times.

39. The run time of a method that runs in $\Theta(1)$ time can be affected drastically by minor changes in coding style. Put the code of `checkIndex` directly into the `get` and `remove` methods of `ArrayLinearList` and `FastArrayLinearList` (instead of invoking `checkIndex`) and measure the best-case time for the `get` and `remove` methods. How does this result compare with the best-case times for the original code?

5.7   THE CLASS `java.util.ArrayList`

Java's `java.util.ArrayList` (AL) is an array-based implementation of a linear list that implements the interface `java.util.List`. Although Java's implementation is quite similar to `FastArrayLinearList`, Java's implementation provides many additional methods. Furthermore, the linear list iterator provided for the class `ArrayList` implements the interface `java.util.ListIterator`, which allows bidirectional movement along the linear list; it allows you to also add and remove elements from the list as you iterate upon the list.

Figure 5.7 gives the measured run times for `ArrayList`. Despite all the bells and whistles in `ArrayList`, it is quite competitive with `FastArrayLinearList`. `Array-List` is noticeably slower than `FastArrayLinearList` when it comes to best-case inserts because `ArrayList` increases array length by 50 percent, rather than by 100 percent, whenever we run out of space in the element array.

operation	ALL	FALL	AL
get	5.6 ms	5.6 ms	5.6 ms
best-case inserts	26.2/14.0 ms	31.2/18.0 ms	32.5/19.6 ms
average inserts	70/69 s	5.8/5.8 s	5.8/5.8 s
worst-case inserts	140/140 s	11.8/11.8 s	11.8/11.8 s
best-case removes	6.9 ms	8.6 ms	6.0 ms
average removes	71 s	5.8 s	5.7 s
worst-case removes	142 s	11.7 s	11.7 s

Times for 40,000 operations

Figure 5.7 Comparing with `ArrayList` (AL)

EXERCISE

40. [Detective Work] `ArrayList.remove` invokes `arraycopy` only when the removed element was not the right-most element. Conduct an experiment to determine whether this behavior explains why `ArrayList` best-case removes take about 30 percent less time compared to `FastArrayLinearList` best-case removes.

5.8   REFERENCES AND SELECTED READINGS

Additional material on data structures in Java may be found in the texts *Data Structures in Java* by T. Standish, Addison-Wesley, Menlo Park, CA, 1997; *Data Structures and Problem Solving Using Java* by M. Weiss, Addison-Wesley, Menlo Park, CA, 1998; and *Data Structures and Algorithms in Java* by M. Goodrich and R. Tamassia, John Wiley & Sons, New York, NY, 1998.

CHAPTER 6

LINEAR LISTS—LINKED REPRESENTATION

BIRD'S-EYE VIEW

The array-based representation of a linear list is so natural that you may think there is no other reasonable way to represent a linear list. This chapter will dispel any such thought you may have.

In a linked representation, the elements of a list may be stored in any arbitrary set of memory locations. Each element has an explicit pointer or link (the terms *pointer* and *link* are synonyms) that tells us the location (i.e., the address) of the next element in the list. In Java, pointers (links) are represented as object references.

In an array-based representation, the element addresses are determined by using a mathematical formula; and in a linked representation, the element addresses are distributed across the list elements.

The data structure concepts introduced in this chapter are

- Linked representation.

- Chains, circular lists, and doubly linked lists.

- Header nodes.

Note that the class `java.util.LinkedList`, which comes with Java, also implements a linear list using pointers. This class uses a doubly linked list.

The applications developed in this chapter are bin sort (also known as bucket sort), radix sort, and convex hulls. Bin sort and radix sort use chains, and the convex hull application uses a doubly linked list. Using either a bin sort or a radix sort, you can sort n elements in $O(n)$ time provided the key values are in an "appropriate range." Although the sort methods developed in Chapter 2 take $O(n^2)$ time, they do not require the keys to lie in a particular range. Bin sort and radix sort are considerably faster than the sort methods of Chapter 2 when the key values lie in an appropriate range.

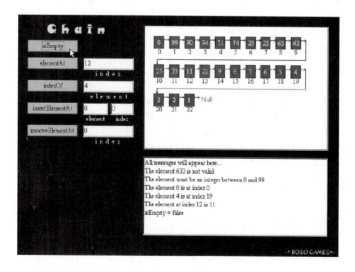

A chain—On the Web

6.1   SINGLY LINKED LISTS AND CHAINS

6.1.1   The Representation

In a linked representation each element of an instance of a data object is represented in a cell or node. The nodes, however, need not be components of an array, and no formula is used to locate individual elements. Instead, each node keeps explicit information about the location of other relevant nodes. This explicit information about the location of another node is called a **link** or **pointer**.

Let $L = (e_0, e_1, \cdots, e_{n-1})$ be a linear list. In one possible linked representation for this list, each element e_i is represented in a separate node. Each node has exactly one link field that is used to locate the next element in the linear list. So the node for e_i links to that for e_{i+1}, $0 \leq i < n - 1$. The node for e_{n-1} has no node to link to and so its link field is `null`. The variable `firstNode` locates the first node in the representation. Figure 6.1 shows the linked representation of the list $L = (e_0, e_1, ..., e_{n-1})$. Links are shown as arrows. To locate the element e_2, for example, we must start at `firstNode`; follow the pointer in `firstNode` to the next node; follow one more pointer to get to the node with e_2. In general, to locate the element with index *theIndex*, we must follow a sequence of *theIndex* pointers beginning at `firstNode`.

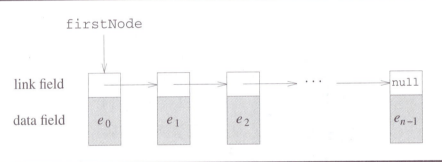

Figure 6.1 Linked representation of a linear list

Since each node in the linked representation of Figure 6.1 has exactly one link, the structure of this figure is called a **singly linked list**. Since the nodes are ordered from left to right, each node (other than the last one) links to the next, and the last node has a `null` link, the structure is also called a **chain**.

To remove the element e_2 whose index is 2 from the chain of Figure 6.2, we do the following (note that e_2 is in the third node of the chain):

- Locate the second node in the chain.

- Link the second node to the fourth node.

firstNode

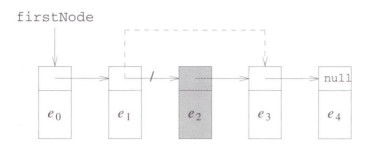

Figure 6.2 Removing e_2 from a 5-node chain

Notice that the removal of the third node from Figure 6.2 automatically decrements the index of the succeeding nodes by 1 (i.e., what were previously the fourth and fifth nodes of the chain become the third and fourth nodes). Because the nodes on a chain are always defined to be those nodes that can be reached following a sequence of pointers beginning at `firstNode`, we do not bother to change the pointer in the removed node (i.e., the former third node of the chain). Since the removed node is no longer reachable from `firstNode`, it is no longer part of the chain.

To insert a new element as the `index`th element in a chain, we need to first locate the `index-1`th element and then insert a new node just after it. Figure 6.3 shows the link changes needed for the two cases `index = 0` and $0 < $ `index` $\le$ `size`. Solid pointers exist prior to the insert, and those shown as broken (or dashed) lines exist following the insert.

firstNode

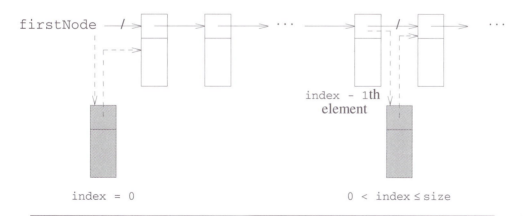

Figure 6.3 Insertion into a chain

6.1.2   The Class `ChainNode`

To represent a linear list as a chain, we define two classes: `ChainNode` and `Chain`. Program 6.1 gives the class `ChainNode`, which defines the data type of the nodes used in Figure 6.1. The data member `element` holds a reference to a list element and is the data field of the node; the data member `next` holds a reference to the next node in the chain and is the node's link field. So we implement links or pointers in Java as references.

```
class ChainNode
{
   // package visible data members
   Object element;
   ChainNode next;

   // package visible constructors
   ChainNode() {}

   ChainNode(Object element)
      {this.element = element;}

   ChainNode(Object element, ChainNode next)
      {this.element = element;
       this.next = next;}
}
```

Program 6.1 Class definition for a chain node

Notice that two of the constructors of `ChainNode` use the syntax `this.element` and `this.next` to access the data members of the constructed instance. This syntax is necessary to distinguish between the data members of the constructed instance and the formal parameters of the constructors because the data members and formal parameters have the same names.

6.1.3   The Class `Chain`

Constructors, isEmpty, and size

The class `Chain` implements a linear list as a singly linked list of nodes in which the last node has the pointer `null`; that is, it implements a linear list as a chain of nodes. Program 6.2 gives the data members and the constructor, `isEmpty`, and `size` methods.

```
public class Chain implements LinearList
{
    // data members
    protected ChainNode firstNode;
    protected int size;

    // constructors
    /** create a list that is empty */
    public Chain(int initialCapacity)
    {
        // the default initial values of firstNode and size
        // are null and 0, respectively
    }

    public Chain()
        {this(0);}

    // methods
    /** @return true iff list is empty */
    public boolean isEmpty()
        {return size == 0;}

    /** @return current number of elements in list */
    public int size()
        {return size;}
```

Program 6.2 Some of the members of the class `Chain`

The instance data members are `firstNode` and `size`. `firstNode` is a pointer (or reference) to the first node (i.e., the node for the zeroth element of the list) in the chain. When the chain has no first node, that is, when the chain is empty, `firstNode` is `null`. `size` gives the number of elements in the list, which equals the number of nodes in the chain.

To create an empty chain, we need merely set the first node pointer `firstNode` to `null`. Unlike the case when a linear list is represented by an array, we do not allocate space for the expected maximum number of elements at the time the chain is created. Therefore, the user does not need to specify an estimate of this maximum size or provide an initial capacity for the list. Nevertheless, we have provided a constructor which has `initialCapacity` as a formal parameter in order to be compatible with the class `ArrayLinearList`. As a result of this compatibility, applications can use either class interchangeably. In particular, an application can create an array of type `LinearList` and initialize the array components using either form of constructor as is shown below.

```
LinearList [] list = new LinearList[4];
list[0] = new ArrayLinearList(20);
list[1] = new ArrayLinearList();
list[2] = new Chain(5);
list[3] = new Chain();
```

Notice that because Java initializes variables of type `Object` or a subclass of `Object` to `null`, the constructors of Program 6.2 do not explicitly set `firstNode` to `null`. The complexity of each constructor is $\Theta(1)$.

The method get

When an array-based representation is used, we locate a list element by evaluating a (usually simple) formula. To find the `index`th element of a chain, however, we must start at the first node and follow the `next` links until we reach the desired node; that is, we must follow `index` number of links. *We cannot access the desired node by performing arithmetic on the value of* `firstNode`. Program 6.3 gives the code. The complexity of `Chain.get` is $O(\text{index})$, while that of `ArrayLinearList.get` is $\Theta(1)$.

The method indexOf

Program 6.4 gives the code for the method `Chain.indexOf`. This code differs from the code for `ArrayLinkedList.indexOf` primarily in the mechanism used to go from one list element to the next. In the case of an array-based list, we go from one element to the next by performing some arithmetic on the location of the current element (when Equation 5.1 is used, we add 1 to the current location to get to the next location). When a chain is used, the only way to go from one node to the next is to follow the link or pointer in the current node. The complexity of `Chain.indexOf` is $O(\text{size})$.

The Method remove

Program 6.5 gives the code for the remove operation. There are three cases to consider:

- `index` < 0 or `index` $\geq$ `size`. In this case the remove operation fails because there is no `index`th element to remove. This case implicitly covers the case when the chain is empty.

- The zeroth element is to be removed from a nonempty chain.

```
/** @throws IndexOutOfBoundsException when
  * index is not between 0 and size - 1 */
void checkIndex(int index)
{
   if (index < 0 || index >= size)
      throw new IndexOutOfBoundsException
         ("index = " + index + "  size = " + size);
}


public Object get(int index)
{
   checkIndex(index);

   // move to desired node
   ChainNode currentNode = firstNode;
   for (int i = 0; i < index; i++)
      currentNode = currentNode.next;

   return currentNode.element;
}
```

Program 6.3 Method to return the indexth element

- An element other that the zeroth is to be removed.

To get a feel for Program 6.5, manually try it on an initially empty list as well as on lists that contain at least one node. In addition, try out values of index, such as index < 0, index = 0 (remove the zeroth element), index = size-1 (remove the last element), index ≥ size, and 0 < index < size-1 (remove an interior element).

The complexity of Chain.remove is $O(\text{index})$, whereas the complexity of Array-LinearList.remove is $O(\text{size-index})$. Therefore, the linked implementation of a linear list is expected to perform better than the array-based list for removals that are done from near the front of the list.

The method add

Insertion and removal work in a similar way. To insert a new element as the indexth one in a chain, we need to first locate the index-1th element and then insert a new node just after it. Program 6.6 gives the code. Its complexity is $O(\text{index})$.

```
public int indexOf(Object theElement)
{
   // search the chain for theElement
   ChainNode currentNode = firstNode;
   int index = 0;  // index of currentNode
   while (currentNode != null &&
           !currentNode.element.equals(theElement))
   {
      // move to next node
      currentNode = currentNode.next;
      index++;
   }

   // make sure we found matching element
   if (currentNode == null)
      return -1;
   else
      return index;
}
```

Program 6.4 Method to return the index of the first occurrence of `theElement`

The Methods `toString` and `iterator`

Program 6.7 gives the code for the `toString` method. This code differs from that for `ArrayLinearList.toString` primarily in its use of the `next` pointer to go from one node to the next. The complexity of `Chain.toString` is the same as that of `ArrayLinearList.toString`, $O(size)$.

The method `Chain.iterator` is identical to the corresponding method for an array-based linear list when the iterator class is a member class (Program 5.12).

The Member Class `ChainIterator`

The code (Program 6.8) for the member iterator class is quite similar to that for the member iterator class for an array-based linear list (Program 5.12).

The difference in run times between using the `get` method and the iterator method to access the linear list elements in left-to-right order is quite dramatic when the list is represented as a chain. The time needed to get the `i`th element using `get` is $\Theta(i)$. Therefore, the `get` method to examine the list elements takes $\Theta(size^2)$ time, whereas the iterator method takes only $\Theta(size)$ time.

```
public Object remove(int index)
{
   checkIndex();

   Object removedElement;
   if (index == 0) // remove first node
   {
      removedElement = firstNode.element;
      firstNode = firstNode.next;
   }
   else
   { // use q to get to predecessor of desired node
      ChainNode q = firstNode;
      for (int i = 0; i < index - 1; i++)
         q = q.next;

      removedElement = q.next.element;
      q.next = q.next.next; // remove desired node
   }
   size--;
   return removedElement;
}
```

Program 6.5 Remove and return the `index`th element

6.1.4   Extensions to the ADT *LinearList*

In some applications of linear lists, we wish to perform operations in addition to those that are part of the abstract data type `LinearList` (ADT 5.1). So it is useful to extend the ADT to include additional functions such as *clear* (remove all elements from the list) and *add(x)* (add element *x* to the end of the list). Program 6.9 gives the interface that corresponds to the extended ADT.

6.1.5   The Class `ExtendedChain`

We will develop a class `ExtendedChain` that provides a linked implementation of the interface `ExtendedLinearList`. The easiest way to arrive at the class `Extended-Chain` is to define it as a subclass of `Chain`. The subclass inherits the members of the superclass and so need implement only those methods that are either not inherited or do not work properly for the subclass.

To efficiently insert an element at the end of a chain, we add a new data member `lastNode` that points to the last node in the chain. Using this pointer, we can

```
public void add(int index, Object theElement)
{
   if (index < 0 || index > size)
      // invalid list position
      throw new IndexOutOfBoundsException
               ("index = " + index + "  size = " + size);

   if (index == 0)
      // insert at front
      firstNode = new ChainNode(theElement, firstNode);
   else
   {   // find predecessor of new element
       ChainNode p = firstNode;
       for (int i = 0; i < index - 1; i++)
          p = p.next;

       // insert after p
       p.next = new ChainNode(theElement, p.next);
   }
   size++;
}
```

Program 6.6 Insert `theElement` as the `index`th element of the chain

append an element to a chain in $\Theta(1)$ time. However, the addition of this new data member requires us to make changes in the implementation of the methods `remove` and `add(index, theElement)` because these methods may change the last node in the chain. When these methods change the last node, they must also update the new data member `lastNode`. Therefore, the class `ExtendedChain` will declare the data member `lastNode`; provide implementations of the methods `remove` and `add(index, theElement)` that will override the corresponding methods of the superclass; and provide implementations for the new methods `clear` and `add(theElement)`.

Program 6.10 gives the code for the class `ExtendedChain`. This code provides no explicit constructor. So only the default constructor

```
public ExtendedChain()
   {super();}
```

is available.

```
/** convert to a string */
public String toString()
{
   StringBuffer s = new StringBuffer("[");

   // put elements into the buffer
   ChainNode currentNode = firstNode;
   while(currentNode != null)
   {
      if (currentNode.element == null)
         s.append("null, ");
      else
         s.append(currentNode.element.toString() + ", ");
      currentNode = currentNode.next;
   }
   if (size > 0)
      s.delete(s.length() - 2, s.length());  // remove last ", "
   s.append("]");

   // create equivalent String
   return new String(s);
}
```

Program 6.7 The method toString

6.1.6   Performance Measurement

Memory Comparison

In an array-based implementation of a linear list, we typically use array doubling when the array gets full and array halving when the array occupancy falls below 25 percent (note that although Java's **Vector** class uses array doubling by default, the class **ArrayList** increases array length by a factor of 1.5). Therefore, a linear list with n elements may reside in an array whose length is between n and $4n$. So space for between n and $4n$ references is needed. When a chain is used, exactly n nodes, each with two reference fields, are alloted to the list. Therefore, the chain representation uses space for $2n$ references. For most applications this difference in the space requirements will not be a deciding factor in selecting the representation to use.

```
private class ChainIterator implements Iterator
{
   // data member
   private ChainNode nextNode;

   // constructor
   public ChainIterator()
      {nextNode = firstNode;}

   // methods
   public boolean hasNext()
      {return nextNode != null;}

   public Object next()
   {
      if (nextNode != null)
      {
         Object elementToReturn = nextNode.element;
         nextNode = nextNode.next;
         return elementToReturn;
      }
      else
         throw new NoSuchElementException("No next element");
   }

   public void remove()
   {
      throw new UnsupportedOperationException
               ("remove not supported");
   }
}
```

Program 6.8 The member class `ChainIterator`

Run-Time Comparison

For the time requirements we expect `Chain.get` to be much slower than the corresponding method of the array-based classes of Chapter 5. We expect this result because the complexity of `Chain.get` is $O(size)$, whereas the complexity of the `get` method of the array-based classes is $\Theta(1)$. This expectation is borne out by experiment. `Chain.get` took 157 seconds to perform the same set of 40,000 operations as performed by `ArrayLinearList` in 5.6 ms—not a commendable showing

```
public interface ExtendedLinearList extends LinearList
{
   public void clear();
   public void append(Object theElement);
}
```

Program 6.9 Interface for extended linear list

for the `Chain` class. Things do not get any better when we compare the times for the insert and remove operations.

Figures 6.4 and 6.5 compare the times taken by `FastArrayLinearList` and `Chain` (for now, regard `IAVL` as a mystery class). Figure 6.5 does not plot the `get` time for `Chain` and the best-case `remove` time for `IAVL` because these times are too large to fit. The worst-case insert and remove times for the class `Chain` are about 13 times that for `FastArrayLinearList`. The linked representation gets a thumbs down as far as standard linear list operations are concerned!

Operation	FastArrayLinearList	Chain	IAVL
get	5.6 ms	157 s	63 ms
best-case inserts	31.2 ms	304 ms	253 ms
average inserts	5.8 s	115 s	392 ms
worst-case inserts	11.8 s	157 s	544 ms
best-case removes	8.6 ms	13.2 ms	1.3 s
average removes	5.8 s	149 s	1.5 s
worst-case removes	11.7 s	157 s	1.6 s

Times for 40,000 operations

Figure 6.4 Time taken by different linear list implementations

The above comparison of insert and remove times isn't entirely fair because the array-based class that was compared uses a finely tuned array copy method provided by Java. In the absence of such a method (which is also used by the classes `Vector` and `ArrayList`), we would get array-based performances close to that of `ArrayLinearList`. The worst-case insert and remove times for `Chain` and `ArrayLinearList` are much closer. Fair or not, Java comes with `arraycopy`, and we ought to use it in our array-based implementation of a linear list.

Even though the insert and remove sequences used in the worst-case test cause our methods to do the maximum work, these sequences do not ensure maximum run time because of the cache effect (Section 4.5). When we start a program, successive calls to `new` give nodes that are adjacent in main memory. Since our worst-case test

```java
public class ExtendedChain extends Chain
                           implements ExtendedLinearList
{
   // data member
   protected ChainNode lastNode;

   // methods
   /** Make the chain empty. */
   public void clear()
   {
      firstNode = lastNode = null;
      size = 0;
   }

   /** add theElement to the right end of the chain. */
   public void add(Object theElement)
   {
      ChainNode y = new ChainNode(theElement, null);
      if (firstNode == null)
         // chain is empty
         firstNode = lastNode = y;
      else
      {   // attach y next to lastNode
         lastNode.next = y;
         lastNode = y;
      }
      size++;
   }

   public Object remove(int index)
   {// overrides Chain.remove
      // code is similar to Chain.remove; see Web site
   }

   public void add(int index, Object theElement)
   {// overrides Chain.add
      // code is similar to Chain.add; see Web site
   }
}
```

Program 6.10 The class ExtendedChain

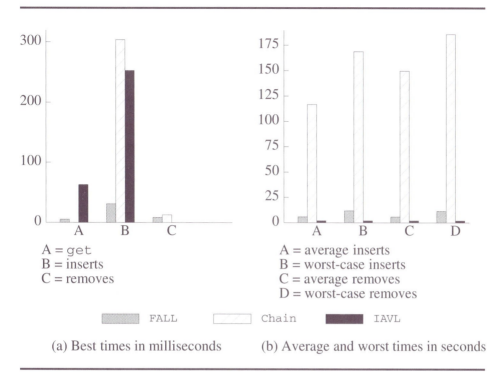

A = get
B = inserts
C = removes

A = average inserts
B = worst-case inserts
C = average removes
D = worst-case removes

FALL   Chain   IAVL

(a) Best times in milliseconds   (b) Average and worst times in seconds

Figure 6.5 Bar chart of run times

does a sequence of inserts to the right end of the chain, the nodes in our worst-case chain are actually adjacent in memory and our worst-case test accesses memory in a fashion that is favored by the cache management strategy (Section 4.5). If we had arranged for our nodes to use memory in a random fashion, we would get many more cache misses and an increased run time.

The fact that the nodes in our worst-case chain are adjacent in memory explains why our measured average run times are substantially more than half the worst-case times even though the worst-case tests do approximately twice as much work. Since the average-case data insert elements at random positions, we jump all over memory as we move from left to right in the chain. This situation creates a nightmare for cache management, and a large number of cache misses occur. Therefore, you should not be surprised if, on your computer, the average test actually takes more time than the worst-case test takes.

Cache effects did not play a role in our comparison of best-case, average, and worst-case times for array-based representation (Section 5.6) because in all tests, the array elements are accessed from left to right and an array occupies a contiguous block of memory.

Are Pointers Any Good?

You are probably wondering whether you have just wasted a lot of time studying pointers. The mystery column of Figure 6.4 labeled `IAVL` has some rather unbelievable numbers in it. These times are for a linear list representation that uses an indexed AVL tree (Exercise 16.20). This representation uses pointers, and as you can see, it knocks the socks off of `FastArrayLinearList` as far as worst-case inserts and removes are concerned. The times reported in Figure 6.4 in the rows labeled best-case, average, and worst-case should be read as the least, next-to-least, and maximum time from the timing runs for insert and remove from the left end of the list; insert and remove from the right end; and random generation of insert and remove indexes. The actual best-case times are slightly smaller, and the actual worst-case times are slightly larger. This amazing performance of indexed AVL trees should keep you eagerly awaiting the arrival of Chapter 16. Incredible as it might sound, other pointer structures developed in Chapter 16 may provide even better performance.

Despite the poor showing of chains in the linear list timing experiments we conducted, chains are more efficient than array-based linear list representations in several linear list applications. Section 6.5 gives a few of these applications. These applications require us to combine multiple lists into one or to remove and insert elements when the node just before the node to be removed or inserted is known because of other work done on the chain.

Two chains may be combined into one by linking the last node of one chain to the first node of the second. If we know both the first and last nodes of a chain, this combining is done in $O(1)$ time. To combine two array-based linear lists into one, we must copy the second into the array used by the first. This copying takes $\theta(\texttt{size of second list})$ time (yes, even using `arraycopy`, the copy takes this much time). When we know the "just before node," the remove and insert operations of a chain run in $O(1)$ time; the complexity of these operations remains $O(\texttt{list size})$ when an array-based representation is used.

EXERCISES

1. Let L = (a, b, c, d, e) be a linear list that is represented as a chain. Draw figures similar to Figure 6.1 showing the chain following each operation in the operation sequence: initial state, $add(0, f)$, $add(3, g)$, $add(7, h)$, $remove(0)$, $remove(4)$.

2. Extend `Chain` to include the method `setSize` that makes the list size equal to the specified size. If the original list size was less than the new one, `null` elements are added at the right end, and if the original size was more than the new one, the extra elements are removed from the right end. What is the complexity of your method? Test your code.

3. Extend `Chain` to include the method `set(theIndex, theElement)` that sets the element whose index is `theIndex` to `theElement`. Throw an exception in case `theIndex` is out of range. What is the complexity of your method? Test your code.

4. Extend `Chain` to include the method `removeRange` that removes all elements in the specified index range. What is the complexity of your method? Test your code.

5. Extend `Chain` to include the method `lastIndexOf` that returns the index of the rightmost occurrence of the specified object. A -1 is returned in case the specified object is not in the list. What is the complexity of your method? Test your code.

6. Write the method `Chain.clone` that makes a copy of a chain. What is the complexity of your method? Test your code.

7. Write a method to convert an array-based linear list into a chain. Your method is a member of neither `ArrayLinearList` nor `Chain`. Use the `get` method of `ArrayLinearList` and the `add` method of `Chain`. What is the time complexity of your method? Test the correctness of your code.

8. Write a method to convert a linear list that is an instance of `Chain` into an equivalent list that is an instance of `ArrayLinearList`. Your method is a member of neither `ArrayLinearList` nor `Chain`.

   (a) First use only the `get` method of `Chain` and the `add` method of `Array-LinearList`. What is the time complexity of your method? Test the correctness of your code.

   (b) Now use a chain iterator. What is the time complexity of the new code? Test your code using your own test data.

9. Add member methods to `Chain` to convert an `ArrayLinearList` to a `Chain` and vice versa. Specifically, write a method `fromList(l)` to convert an array-based linear list `l` into a chain and another method `toList(l)` to convert the chain `this` into an array-based linear list `l`. What is the time complexity of each method? Test the correctness of your code.

10. (a) Extend the class `Chain` to include a method `leftShift(i)` that shifts the list elements left by i positions. If $L = [0, 1, 2, 3, 4]$, then `L.left-Shift(2)` results in $L = [2, 3, 4]$.

    (b) What is the time complexity of your method?

    (c) Test your code.

11. (a) Add a method `reverse` to the class `Chain` to reverse the order of the elements in `x`. Do the reversal in-place and do not allocate any new nodes.

(b) What is the complexity of your method?

(c) Test the correctness of your method by compiling and then executing the code. Use your own test data.

12. Write a nonmember method to reverse a chain. Use the member methods of Chain to accomplish the reversal. What is the complexity of your method? Test the correctness of your method.

13. Let a and b be of type ExtendedChain.

(a) Write a method meld to create a new chain c that contains elements alternately from a and b, beginning with the first element of a. If you run out of elements in one of the chains, then append the remaining elements of the other chain to c. The complexity of your code should be linear in the lengths of the input chains. meld is not a member method of the class ExtendedChain.

(b) Show that your code has linear complexity.

(c) Test the correctness of your method by compiling and then executing the code. Use your own test data.

14. Extend the class Chain by adding the method meld to the class. This method is similar to the method meld of Exercise 13. You should use the same physical nodes used by the chains a and b. Following a call to meld, the input chains a and b are empty.

(a) Write the code for meld. The complexity of your code should be linear in the lengths of initial chains.

(b) Show that your code has linear complexity.

(c) Test the correctness of your code by compiling and then executing the code. Use your own test data.

15. Let a and b be of type ExtendedChain. Assume that the elements of a and b are of type Comparable and are in sorted order (i.e., nondecreasing from left to right).

(a) Write a nonmember method merge to create a new sorted linear list c that contains all the elements in a and b.

(b) What is the complexity of your method?

(c) Test the correctness of your method by compiling and then executing the code. Use your own test data.

16. Redo Exercise 15 but this time extend the class Chain to include the method merge. You should use the same nodes as the two input chains use. Following the merge, the input chains are empty.

17. Let c be of type `ExtendedChain`.

    (a) Write a nonmember method `split` to create two chains a and b. a contains all elements in odd positions of c, and b contains the remaining elements. Your method should not change the chain c.

    (b) What is the complexity of your code?

    (c) Test the correctness of your method by compiling and then executing the code. Use your own test data.

18. Extend the class `Chain` by adding a method `split` that is similar to the method `split` of Exercise 17. However, the new method `split` destroys the input chain `this` and uses its nodes to construct a and b.

19. In a circular shift operation, the elements of a linear list are rotated clockwise by a given amount. For example, when the elements of L = [0, 1, 2, 3, 4] are shifted circularly by 2, the result is L = [2, 3, 4, 0, 1].

    (a) Extend the class `ExtendedChain` by adding the method `circularShift(i)`, which performs a circular shift by i positions.

    (b) Test your code.

20. Let `theChain` be a chain. Suppose that as we move to the right, we reverse the direction of the chain pointers; therefore, when we are at node p, the chain is split into two chains. One is a chain that begins at p and goes to the last node of `theChain`. The other begins at the node 1 that precedes p in `theChain` and goes back to the first node of `theChain`. Initially, p = `theChain.firstNode` and 1 = `null`.

    (a) Draw a chain with six nodes and show the configuration when p is at the third node and 1 is at the second.

    (b) Develop the class `MoveLeftAndRightOnAChain`. The class constructor initializes the data members 1 and p. The public methods of `Move-LeftAndRightOnAChain` are `moveRight`—move 1 and p one node right, `moveLeft`—move 1 and p one node left, `currentElement`—return the element at node p, and `previousElement`—return the element at node 1.

    (c) Test your codes using suitable data.

21. Use the ideas of Exercise 20 to obtain a new version of the class `Chain` of Program 6.2. The new version should permit you to move back and forth on a chain efficiently and to perform the methods of `LinearList` even though the chain may be split into two chains as described in Exercise 20. For this version, add the data members 1 and p as in Exercise 20 and add the following public methods:

(a) reset—Set p to firstNode and l to null.

(b) current()—Return the element pointed to by p; throw an exception if the operation fails.

(c) atEnd—Return true if p is at the last element of the list; return false otherwise.

(d) atFront—Return true if p is at the first element of the list; return false otherwise.

(e) moveToNext—Move p and l one position right; throw an exception if the operation fails.

(f) moveToPrevious—Move p and l one position back; throw an exception if the operation fails.

To implement the add, remove, and indexOf methods efficiently, it will be useful to have another data member currentElement that gives you the index of the element to which p points (i.e., is it element 0, 1, 2, etc., of the list?). Test the correctness of your code using suitable test data.

22. Write code for the class ChainWithSortMethods. This class is a subclass of Chain and it includes the member method insertionSort, which uses insertion sort (see Program 2.15) to reorder the chain elements into nondecreasing order. Do not create new nodes or delete old ones. You may assume that the elements being sorted are of type Comparable.

(a) What is the worst-case time complexity of your method? How much time does your method need if the elements are already in sorted order?

(b) Test the correctness of your method by compiling and then executing the code. Use your own test data.

23. Do Exercise 22 for the following sort methods (see Chapter 2 for descriptions):

(a) Bubble sort.

(b) Selection sort.

(c) Count or rank sort.

6.2   CIRCULAR LISTS AND HEADER NODES

Application codes that result from the use of chains can often be simplified and made to run faster by doing one or both of the following: (1) represent the linear list as a **singly linked circular list** (or simply **circular list**), rather than as a chain, and (2) add an additional node, called the **header node**, at the front. A circular list is obtained from a chain by linking the last node back to the first as

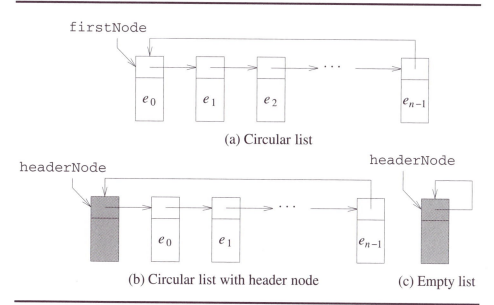

(a) Circular list

(b) Circular list with header node

(c) Empty list

Figure 6.6 Circular linked lists

in Figure 6.6(a). Figure 6.6(b) shows a nonempty circular list with a header node, and Figure 6.6(c) shows an empty circular list with a header node.

The use of header nodes is a very common practice when linked lists are used, as their presence generally leads to simpler and faster programs. Program 6.11 gives the constructor and `indexOf` methods for the class `CircularWithHeader`, which represents a linear list as a circular list with a header node. The constructor creates the configuration for an empty list (Figure 6.6(c)). The complexity of the constructor is $\Theta(1)$ and that of `indexOf` is $O(\texttt{size})$. Although `Chain.indexOf` and `CircularWithHeader.indexOf` have the same complexity, the code for the latter method is slightly simpler. Since `CircularWithHeader.indexOf` avoids the check `current-Node != null` that is made by `Chain.indexOf` on each iteration of its `while` loop, `CircularWithHeader.indexOf` will run slightly faster than `Chain.indexOf` except possibly when we are looking for an element near the left end of the chain.

EXERCISES

24. Compare the run-time performance of the `indexOf` methods of Programs 6.4 and 6.11. Do this for both worst-case and average run times using linear lists of size 100; 1000; 10,000; and 100,000. Present your times in tabular form and in graph form.

```java
public class CircularWithHeader
{
   // data member
   protected ChainNode headerNode;

   // constructor
   /** create a circular list that is empty */
   public CircularWithHeader()
   {
      headerNode = new ChainNode();
      headerNode.next = headerNode;
   }

   /** @return index of first occurrence of theElement,
     * return -1 if theElement not in list */
   public int indexOf(Object theElement)
   {
      // put theElement in header node
      headerNode.element = theElement;

      // search the list for theElement
      ChainNode currentNode = headerNode.next;
      int index = 0;  // index of currentNode
      while (!currentNode.element.equals(theElement))
      {
         // move to next node
         currentNode = currentNode.next;
         index++;
      }

      // make sure we found matching element
      if (currentNode == headerNode)
         return -1;
      else
         return index;
   }
}
```

Program 6.11 Searching a circular linked list that has a header node

25. Develop the class `CircularList`. Objects of this type are circular linked lists, as in Figure 6.6, except the lists do not have a header node. You must implement all the methods defined for the classes `Chain` (Section 6.1.3) and `ExtendedChain` (Section 6.1.5). What is the time complexity of each method? Test the correctness of your code.

26. Do Exercise 11 using circular lists instead of chains.

27. Do Exercise 12 using circular lists instead of chains.

28. Do Exercise 13 using circular lists instead of chains.

29. Do Exercise 15 using circular lists instead of chains.

30. Do Exercise 16 using circular lists instead of chains.

31. Do Exercise 17 using circular lists instead of chains.

32. Do Exercise 18 using circular lists instead of chains.

33. Let x point to an arbitrary node in a circular list.

    (a) Write a method to remove the element in node x. *Hint:* Since we do not know which node precedes x, it is difficult to remove the node x from the list; however, to remove the element in x, it is sufficient to replace the data field (i.e., `element`) of x by the data field of the node y that follows it and then remove the node y. When the element in the last node is removed, the element in the first node becomes the last element.

    (b) What is the complexity of your method?

    (c) Test the correctness of your method by compiling and then executing the code. Use your own test data.

34. Develop the class `CircularListWithHeader`. Objects of this type are circular linked lists, as in Figure 6.6. You must implement all the methods defined for the classes `Chain` (Section 6.1.3) and `ExtendedChain` (Section 6.1.5). What is the time complexity of each method? Test the correctness of your code.

35. Do Exercises 11 and 12 using circular lists with header nodes instead of chains.

36. Do Exercises 13 and 14 using circular lists with header nodes instead of chains.

37. Do Exercises 15 and 16 using circular lists with header nodes instead of chains.

38. Do Exercises 17 and 18 using circular lists with header nodes instead of chains.

6.3   DOUBLY LINKED LISTS

For most applications of linear lists, the chain and/or circular list representations are adequate. However, in some applications it is useful to have a pointer from each element to both the next and previous elements. **A doubly linked list** is an ordered sequence of nodes in which each node has two pointers: `next` and `previous`. The `previous` pointer points to the node (if any) on the left, and the `next` pointer points to the node (if any) on the right. Figure 6.7 shows the doubly linked list representation of the linear list $(1, 2, 3, 4)$.

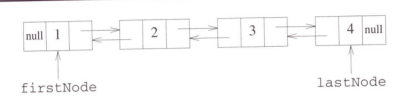

Figure 6.7 A doubly linked list

When defining the Java class `DoublyLinkedList`, we use two instance data members `firstNode` and `lastNode` that, respectively, point to the left-most and right-most nodes of the doubly linked list (see Figure 6.7). A doubly linked list with just one element or node p has `firstNode = lastNode = p`, whereas `firstNode = lastNode = null` for an empty doubly linked list. These conventions are similar to those used for an extended chain (Program 6.10). When a doubly linked list is used, we find the `index`th element by moving from left to right when `index < size/2` and from right to left otherwise. Exercise 39 asks you the develop the code for the class `DoublyLinkedList`.

We can enhance doubly linked lists by adding a header node at the left and/or right ends and by making them circular lists. In a nonempty circular doubly linked list, `firstNode.previous` is a pointer to the right-most node (i.e., `firstNode.-previous = lastNode`), and `lastNode.next` is a pointer to the left-most node. So we can dispense with the variable `lastNode` and simply keep track of the list using the variable `firstNode`.

EXERCISES

39. Develop the class `DoublyLinkedList`. Objects of this type are doubly linked lists with no header node. You must implement all the methods defined for the class `Chain` (Section 6.1.3) as well as for the class `ExtendedChain` (Section 6.1.5). What is the time complexity of each method? Test the correctness of your code.

40. Write a method to join two doubly linked lists into a single doubly linked list. In a join the elements of the second list are appended to the end of those of the first list; the join is destructive in the sense that following the join, the second list becomes empty. Test your code.

41. Do Exercises 11 and 12 using doubly linked lists instead of chains.

42. Do Exercises 13 and 14 using doubly linked lists instead of chains.

43. Do Exercises 15 and 16 using doubly linked lists instead of chains.

44. Do Exercises 17 and 18 using doubly linked lists instead of chains.

45. Develop the class `DoubleCircularList`. Objects of this type are doubly linked circular lists with no header node. You must implement all the methods defined for the class `Chain` (Section 6.1.3) as well as for the class `ExtendedChain` (Section 6.1.5). What is the time complexity of each method? Test the correctness of your code.

46. Do Exercises 11 and 12 using doubly linked circular lists.

47. Do Exercise 40 using doubly linked circular lists.

48. Do Exercises 13 and 14 using doubly linked circular lists.

49. Do Exercises 15 and 16 using doubly linked circular lists.

50. Do Exercises 17 and 18 using doubly linked circular lists.

51. Do Exercise 45 using a header node for the doubly linked circular list. Compare the run time of your class with that of Exercise 45 and `java.util.-` `LinkedList` (this Java class implements a doubly linked circular list with a header node). Perform an experiment similar to that done in Section 6.1.6.

52. Do Exercises 11 and 12 using doubly linked circular lists with header nodes.

53. Do Exercise 40 using doubly linked circular lists with header nodes.

54. Do Exercises 13 and 14 using doubly linked circular lists with header nodes.

55. Do Exercises 15 and 16 using doubly linked circular lists with header nodes.

56. Do Exercises 17 and 18 using doubly linked circular lists with header nodes.

57. To efficiently support moving back and forth on a doubly linked list, we can define a special iterator class, `DoubleIterator`, for doubly linked lists. This class has the instance data member `currentNode` that records our current location in the list. The initial value of `currentNode` is `null`. The public methods are

(a) `DoubleIterator()`—Constructor.

(b) `hasNext()`—Return `true` iff there is no next element.

(c) `hasPrevious()`—Return `true` if there is no previous element.

(d) `next()`—Return next element in list. Throw an exception if there is no next element.

(e) `previous()`—Return previous element in list. Throw an exception if there is no previous element.

Write Java code for the class `DoubleIterator`. Test the correctness of your code using suitable test data.

6.4   GLOSSARY OF LINKED LIST TERMS

This chapter introduced the following important concepts:

- *Chain.* A chain is a singly linked list of nodes. Let x be a chain. x is empty iff `x.firstNode = null`. If x is not empty, then `x.firstNode` points to the first node in the chain. The first node links to the second; the second to the third; and so on. The link (i.e., `next`) field of the last node is `null`.

- *Singly linked circular list.* This type of list differs from a chain only in that now the last node links back to the first. When the circular list x is empty, `x.firstNode = null`.

- *Header node.* A header node is an additional node introduced into a linked list. The use of this additional node generally results in simpler programs, as we can often avoid treating the empty list as a special case. When a header node is used, every list (including the empty list) contains at least one node (i.e., the header node).

- *Doubly linked list.* A doubly linked list consists of nodes ordered from left to right. Nodes are linked from left to right using a pointer field (say) `next`. The right-most node has this field set to `null`. Nodes are also linked from right to left using a pointer field (say) `previous`. The left-most node has this field set to `null`.

- *Circular doubly linked list.* This type of list differs from a doubly linked list only in that now the left-most node uses its `previous` field to point to the right-most node and the right-most node uses its `next` field to point to the left-most node.

6.5   APPLICATIONS

6.5.1   Bin Sort

Suppose that a chain is used to maintain a list of students in a class. Each node has fields for the student's name, Social Security number, score on each assignment and test, and weighted aggregate score of all assignments and tests. Assume that all scores are integers in the range 0 through 100. We are to sort the nodes in order of the aggregate score. This sort takes $O(n^2)$ time (n is the number of students in the class) if we use one of the sort methods of Chapter 2. A faster way to accomplish the sort is to use **bin sort**. In a bin sort the nodes are placed into bins, each bin containing nodes with the same score. Then we combine the bins to create a sorted chain.

Figure 6.8(a) shows a sample chain with 10 nodes. This figure shows only the name and score fields of each node. The first field is the name, and the second is the score. For simplicity, we assume that each name is a single character and that the scores are in the range 0 through 5.

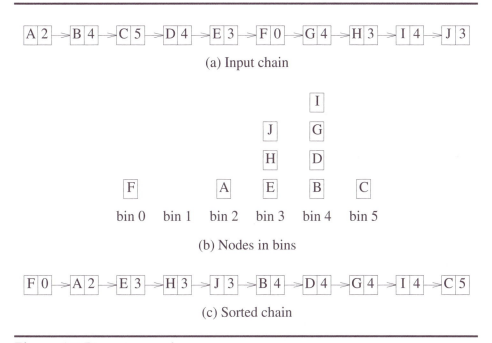

(a) Input chain

(b) Nodes in bins

(c) Sorted chain

Figure 6.8 Bin sort example

We will need six bins, one for each of the possible score values 0 through 5. Figure 6.8(b) shows the 10 nodes distributed into bins by score. We can obtain this distribution by moving down the chain and examining the nodes one at a time.

When a node is examined, it is placed into the bin that corresponds to its score. So the first node is placed into bin 2, the second into bin 4, and so forth. Now if we collect the nodes from the bins, beginning with those in bin 0, we will have a sorted list as shown in Figure 6.8(c).

To implement the bins, we note that each bin is a linear list of nodes. The number of nodes in a bin may vary from 0 to as many as n. Before we begin the node distribution step, all bins are empty.

For bin sort we need to be able to (1) move down the input chain deleting nodes from this chain and adding them to the list for the appropriate bin and (2) collect and concatenate lists from the bins into a single sorted chain. If the input chain is of type `Chain` (Program 6.2), we can do (1) by successively deleting the first element from the chain and inserting it as the first element in the appropriate bin list; we can do (2) by deleting the elements from the bins (beginning with the last bin) and inserting them at the front of an initially empty chain.

We reqire that the elements in the chain have a data member `score`. We define a class `ScoreObject` (Program 6.12) that has only this data member. Other data types that include the member `score` can be defined as subclasses of `ScoreObject`.

```
public class ScoreObject
{
    int score;

    public ScoreObject(int theScore)
        {score = theScore;}
}
```

Program 6.12 The class `ScoreObject`

Program 6.13 gives a possible node structure for student records. In a realistic situation, `StudentRecord` would contain several additional data members. Since our code for the bin sort method makes reference only to the data type `ScoreObject`, it will sort chains of elements whose type is `ScoreObject` or any subclass of `ScoreObject`.

Program 6.14 gives the code for the bin sort method. This code uses a chain for each bin. Although we could have represented each bin as an array-based list, we have used a chain because we plan to develop another bin sort method that is a member of `Chain`. In this new method, it is more efficient to use chains rather than array-based lists because the input and output for the sort is a chain. The code of Program 6.14 assumes that `binSort` is in the same package as `ScoreObject`.

For the complexity analysis, we first note that the bin sort method could terminate prematurely because of an exception or error. For example, the statement

```
Chain[] bin = new Chain[range + 1];
```

```
public class StudentRecord extends ScoreObject
{
    String name;  // student name

    /** constructor */
    public StudentRecord(String theName, int theScore)
    {
        super(theScore);
        name = theName;
    }

    /** convert to a string */
    public String toString()
        {return String.valueOf(score);}
}
```

Program 6.13 Possible node class for bin sort

could fail for lack of sufficient memory. If this statement fails, the method terminates in $\Theta(1)$ time. Assume that no exception or error occurs while the method executes. Now the first for loop takes $\Theta(\mathtt{range})$ time. Each insert and remove performed in the remaining two for loops takes $\Theta(1)$ time. Therefore, the complexity of the second for loop is $\Theta(n)$ where n is the size of the input chain, the complexity of the third for loop is $\Theta(n+\mathtt{range})$, and the overall complexity of binSort (when no exception is thrown) is $\Theta(n+\mathtt{range})$. Accounting for the possibility of an exception or error, the overall complexity is $O(n+\mathtt{range})$.

Bin Sort as a Method of a Subclass of Chain

Efficiency-conscious readers have probably noticed that we can avoid much of the work done by the method binSort by developing binSort as a method of Chain or of a subclass of Chain. This approach enables us to avoid the calls to new made by the invocations of add in Program 6.14. Further, by keeping track of the front and end of each bin chain, we can concatenate the bin chains in the "collection phase," as shown in Program 6.15.

The chain for each bin begins with the node at the bottom of the bin and goes to the node at the top of the bin. Each chain has two pointers, bottom and top, to it. bottom[theBin] points to the node at the bottom of bin theBin, while top[theBin] points to the node at the top of this bin. The initial configuration of empty bins is represented by bottom[theBin] = null for all bins. Since the default initial value of bottom[theBin] is null, Program 6.15 does not explicitly initialize

6.5.2   Radix Sort

The bin sort method of Section 6.5.1 may be extended to sort, in $\Theta(n)$ time, n integers in the range 0 through $n^c - 1$ where $c \geq 0$ is an integer constant. Notice that if we use `binSort` with `range` $= n^c$, the sort complexity will be $\Theta(n + \text{range})$ $= \Theta(n^c)$. Instead of using `binSort` directly on the numbers to be sorted, we will decompose these numbers using some radix r. For example, the number 928 decomposes into the digits 9, 2, and 8 using the radix 10 (i.e., $928 = 9*10^2 + 2*10^1 + 8*10^0$). The most siginificant digit is 9, and the least significant digit is 8; the ones digit is 8, the tens digit is 2, and the hundreds digit is 9. The number 3725 has the radix 10 decomposition 3, 7, 2, and 5; using the radix 60 instead, the decomposition is 1, 2, and 5 (i.e., $(3725)_{10} = (125)_{60}$). In a **radix sort** we decompose the numbers into digits using some radix r and then sort by digits.

Example 6.1 Suppose that we are sorting 10 integers in the range 0 through 999. If we use `binSort` with `range` $= 1000$, then the bin initialization takes 1000 steps, the node distribution takes 10 steps, and collecting from the bins takes 1000 steps. The total step count is 2010. Another approach is

1. Use `binSort` to sort the 10 numbers by their least significant digit (i.e., the ones digit). Since each digit ranges from 0 through 9, we have `range` $= 10$. Figure 6.9(a) shows a sample 10-number chain, and Figure 6.9(b) shows the chain sorted by least significant digit.

2. Use `binSort` to sort the chain from (1) by the next digit (i.e., the tens digit). Again, `range` $= 10$. Since bin sort is a stable sort, elements that have the same second digit remain sorted by the least significant digit. As a result, the chain is now sorted by the two least signficant digits. Figure 6.9(c) shows our chain following this sort.

3. Use `binSort` to sort the chain from (2) by the next digit (i.e., the hundreds digit). (For numbers smaller than 100, the hundreds digit is 0.) Since the sort on the hundreds digit is stable, elements with the same hundreds digit remain sorted on the remaining two digits. As a result, the chain is sorted on the three least significant digits. Figure 6.9(d) shows the chain following this sort.

The preceding sorting scheme describes a radix 10 sort. The numbers to be sorted are decomposed into their decimal (or base 10) digits, and the numbers are sorted on these digits. Since each number has at most three digits, three sort passes are made. Each sort pass uses a bin sort with `range` $= 10$. In each of these three bin sorts, we spend 10 steps in initializing the bins, 10 in distributing the records, and 10 in bin collection. The total number of steps is 90, which is less than when the 10 numbers are sorted using a single bin sort with `range` $= 1000$. The single bin sort scheme is really a radix sort with $r = 1000$.   ∎

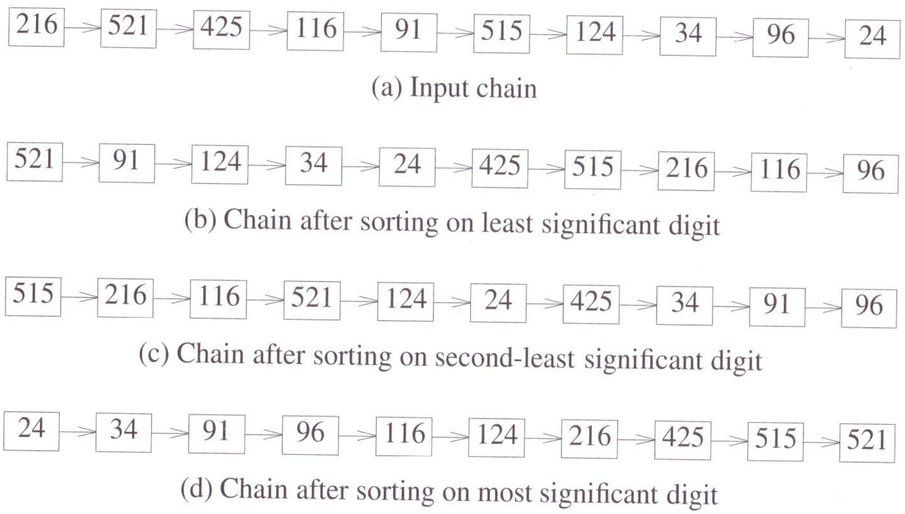

216 →521 →425 →116 → 91 →515 →124 → 34 → 96 → 24

(a) Input chain

521 → 91 →124 → 34 → 24 →425 →515 →216 →116 → 96

(b) Chain after sorting on least significant digit

515 →216 →116 →521 →124 → 24 →425 → 34 → 91 → 96

(c) Chain after sorting on second-least significant digit

24 → 34 → 91 → 96 →116 →124 →216 →425 →515 →521

(d) Chain after sorting on most significant digit

Figure 6.9 Radix sort with $r = 10$ and $d = 3$

Example 6.2 Suppose that 1000 integers in the range 0 through $10^6 - 1$ are to be sorted. Using a radix of $r = 10^6$ corresponds to using `binSort` directly on the numbers and takes 10^6 steps to initialize the bins, 1000 steps to distribute the numbers into bins, and another 10^6 to collect from the bins. The total number of steps is therefore 2,001,000. With $r = 1000$, the sort proceeds as follows:

1. Sort using the three least significant decimal digits of each number and use `range = 1000`.

2. Sort the result of (1) using the next three decimal digits of each number.

Each of the preceding sorts takes 3000 steps, so the sort is accomplished in a total of 6000 steps. When $r = 100$ is used, three bin sorts on pairs of decimal digits are performed. Each of these sorts takes 1200 steps, and the total number of steps needed for the sort becomes 3600. If we use $r = 10$, six bin sorts will be done, one on each decimal digit. The total number of steps will be $6(10 + 1000 + 10) = 6120$. For our example we expect radix sort with $r = 100$ to be most efficient. ∎

We can decompose a number into digits by using the division and mod operators. If we are performing a radix 10 decomposition, then the radix 10 digits may be computed (from least significant to most significant) using the following expressions:

$$x\%10; \quad (x\%100)/10; \quad (x\%1000)/100; \quad \cdots$$

When $r = 100$, these expressions become

$$x\%100; \quad (x\%10000)/100; \quad (x\%1000000)/10000; \quad \cdots$$

For a general radix r, the expressions are

$$x\%r; \quad (x\%r^2)/r; \quad (x\%r^3)/r^2; \quad \cdots$$

When we use the radix $r = n$ to decompose n integers in the range 0 through $n^c - 1$, the number of digits is c. So the n numbers can be sorted using c bin sort passes with `range` $= n$. The time needed for the sort is $\Theta(cn) = \Theta(n)$, as c is a constant.

6.5.3   Convex Hull

A **polygon** is a closed planar figure with three or more straight edges. The polygon of Figure 6.10(a) has six edges, and that of Figure 6.10(b) has eight. A polygon **contains** all points that are either on its edges or inside the region it encloses. A polygon is **convex** iff all line segments that join two points on or in the polygon include no point that is outside the polygon. The polygon of Figure 6.10(a) is convex, while that of Figure 6.10(b) is not. Figure 6.10(b) shows two line segments (broken lines) whose endpoints are on or in the polygon. Both of these segments contain points that are outside the polygon.

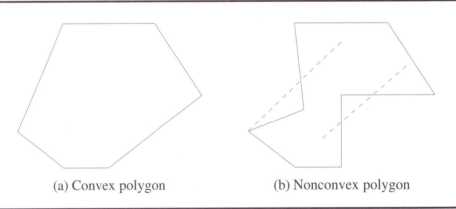

(a) Convex polygon   (b) Nonconvex polygon

Figure 6.10 Convex and nonconvex polygons

The **convex hull** of a set S of points in the plane is the smallest convex polygon that contains all these points. The vertices (i.e., corners) of this polygon are the **extreme points** of S. Figure 6.11 shows 13 points in the plane. The convex hull is the polygon defined by the solid lines. The extreme points have been identified by circles. When all points of S lie on a straight line (i.e., they are colinear), we have a degenerate case for which the convex hull is defined to be the smallest straight line that includes all the points.

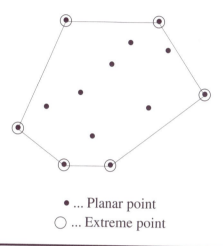

• ... Planar point

◯ ... Extreme point

Figure 6.11 Convex hull of planar points

The problem of finding the convex hull of a set of points in the plane is a fundamental problem in computational geometry. The solutions to several other problems in computational geometry (e.g., find the smallest rectangle that encloses a set of points in the plane) require the computation of the convex hull. In addition, the convex hull finds application in image processing and statistics.

Suppose we pick a point X in the interior of the convex hull of S and draw a vertical line downwards from X (Figure 6.12(a)). Exercise 63 describes how we can select the point X. Let a_i be the (polar) angle made by this line and the line from X to the ith point of S. a_i is measured by going counterclockwise from a point on the vertical line to the line from X to the ith point. Figure 6.12(a) shows a_2. Now let us arrange the points of S into nondecreasing order of a_i. Points with the same polar angle are ordered by distance from X. In Figure 6.12(a) the points have been numbered 1 through 13 in the stated order.

A counterclockwise sweep of the vertical line downwards from X encounters the extreme points of S in order of the polar angle a_i. If u, v, and w are three consecutive extreme points in counterclockwise order, then the counterclockwise angle made by the line segments from u to v and w to v is more than 180 degrees. (Figure 6.12(b) shows the counterclockwise angle made by points 8, 11, and 12.) When the counterclockwise angle made by three consecutive points in the polar order is less than or equal to 180 degrees, then the second of these points is not

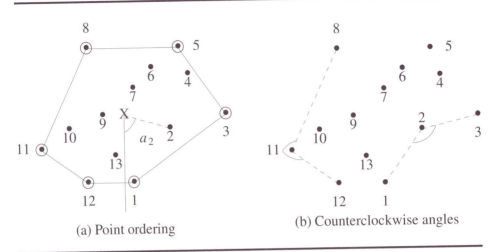

(a) Point ordering   (b) Counterclockwise angles

Figure 6.12 Identifying extreme points

an extreme point. Notice that when the angle made by u, v, and w is less than 180 degrees, if we walk from u to v to w, we make a right turn at v. When we walk counterclockwise around a convex polygon, all our turns are left turns. The observations made so far result in the algorithm of Figure 6.13, which finds the extreme points and convex hull of S.

Step 1 of the algorithm handles the degenerate cases when the number of points in S is 0 or 1, as well as when all points of S are colinear. This step can be done in $O(n)$ time where n is the number of points in S. For the colinearity test, we select any two points and compute the equation of the line through them. Next we examine the remaining $n - 2$ points and determine whether they lie on this line. During this process we can also determine the endpoints of the shortest line that includes all points in case they are colinear.

In step 2 the points are ordered by polar angle and collected into a doubly linked list because in step 3 we will be eliminating points that are not extreme points and also moving backwards on the list. Both operations are straightforward in a doubly linked list. Exercise 63 asks you to explore the use of a singly linked list. Because of the sort, this step takes $O(n^2)$ time if we use any of the sorts from Chapter 2. In Chapters 9 and 14, we will see that we can sort in $O(n \log n)$ time. As a result, the complexity of step 2 is counted as $O(n \log n)$.

In step 3 we repeatedly examine sets of three consecutive points in counterclockwise order and check whether the angle they make is less than or equal to 180 degrees. If it is, then the middle point `rx` is not an extreme point and is eliminated. If the angle exceeds 180 degrees, `rx` may or may not be an extreme point and we advance `x` to the next vertex `rx`. When the `for` loop is exited, every point `x` on the

Step 1: [Handle degenerate cases]
   If S has fewer than three points, return S.
   If all points lie on a straight line, compute the endpoints of the smallest line that includes all points of S and return these two points.

Step 2: [Sort by polar angle]
   Find a point X that is inside the convex hull of S.
   Sort S by polar angle and within polar angle by distance from X.
   Create a doubly linked circular list of points using the above order.
   Let `right` link to the next point in the order and `left` link to the previous point.

Step 3: [Eliminate nonextreme points]
   Let `p` be the point that has the smallest y-coordinate (break a tie, if any, by selecting the one with largest x-coordinate).
   ```
   for (x = p, rx = point to the right of x; x != rx; )
   {
       rrx = point to the right of rx;
       if (angle formed by x, rx, and rrx is ≤ 180 degrees)
       {
          delete rx from the list;
          rx = x; x = point on left of rx;
       }
       else {x = rx; rx = rrx;}
   }
   ```

Figure 6.13 Pseudocode to find the convex hull of S

doubly linked circular list satisfies the property that the angle made by x, rx, and rrx exceeds 180 degrees. Hence all of these points are extreme points. By going around the list using the `right` fields, we traverse the boundary of the convex hull in counterclockwise order. We begin at the point with lowest y, as this point must be in the convex hull.

For the complexity of step 3, we note that following each angle check in the `for` loop either (1) a vertex rx is eliminated and x is moved back one node on the list or (2) x is moved forward on the list. Since the number of eliminated vertices is $O(n)$, x can be moved back at most a total of $O(n)$ nodes. Hence we can be in case (2) only $O(n)$ times, so the `for` loop is iterated $O(n)$ times. Since an angle check takes $\Theta(1)$ time, the complexity of step 3 is $O(n)$. As a result, we can find the convex hull of n points in $O(n \log n)$ time.

EXERCISES

58. Is Program 6.14 a stable sort program?

59. Compare the run times of the bin sort methods given in Programs 6.14 and 6.15. Use $n = 10{,}000$; 50,000; and 100,000. What can you say about the overhead introduced by using the class `Chain`?

60. In this exercise we will extend the class `Chain` to include a method to sort, using the radix sort technique, the elements in a chain into ascending order of the field `score` (see Program 6.15).

   (a) Write an instance method to accomplish the sort using the radix sort method. The radix r and number of digits d in the radix r decomposition are inputs to your method. The complexity of your method should be $O(d(r + n))$. Show that this is the case.

   (b) Test the correctness of your method by compiling and executing it with your own test data.

   (c) Compare the performance of your method with one that performs a linked insertion sort. Do so for $n = 100$; 1000; and 10,000; $r = 10$; and $d = 3$.

61. (a) Write a method to sort n integers in the range 0 through $n^c - 1$ using the radix sort method and $r = n$. The complexity of your method should be $O(cn)$. Show that this is the case. Assume the integers are in a chain; the element type is `MyInteger`.

   (b) Test the correctness of your method.

   (c) Measure the run time of your method for $n = 10$; 100; 1000; and 10,000 and $c = 2$. Present your results in tabular form and in graph form.

62. You are given a pile of n card decks. Each card has three fields: deck number, suit, and face value. Since each deck has at most 52 cards (some cards may be missing from a deck), the pile has at most $52n$ cards. You may assume there is at least one card from each deck. So the number of cards in the pile is at least n.

   (a) Explain how to sort this pile by deck number, within deck number by suit, and within suit by face value. You should make three bin sort passes over the pile to accomplish the sort.

   (b) Write a program to input n and a card pile and to output the sorted pile. You should represent the card pile as a chain. Each card has the fields: `deck`, `suit`, `face`, and `link`. The complexity of your program should be $O(n)$. Show that this is the case.

   (c) Test the correctness of your program.

63. [Convex Hull]

  (a) Let u, v, and w be three points in the plane. Assume that they are not colinear. Write a method to find a point inside the triangle formed by these three points.

  (b) Let S be a set of points in the plane. Write a method to determine whether all the points are colinear. In case they are, your method should compute the endpoints of the shortest line that includes all the points. In case the points are not colinear, then you should find three noncolinear points from the given point set. You can use these three points together with your method for part (a) to determine a point inside the convex hull of S. The complexity of your method should be $O(n)$. Show that this is the case.

  (c) Use the codes of (a) and (b) to refine Figure 6.13 into a Java program that inputs S and outputs the convex hull of S. During input the points may be collected into a doubly linked list that is later sorted by polar angle. For the sort step you may use one of the sort methods of Chapter 2, or if you have access to an $O(n \log n)$ sort, you may use it.

  (d) Write additional convex hull programs that replace the use of a doubly linked list with (i) a chain and (ii) an array-based linear list.

  (e) Test the correctness of your convex hull programs.

64. Do Exercise 63 using a singly linked list. Use the ideas of Exercise 20 to ensure that the **for** loop of step 3 of Figure 6.13 has complexity $O(n)$.

★ 65. Develop a representation for integers that is suitable for performing arithmetic on arbitrarily large integers. The arithmetic is to be performed with no loss of accuracy. Write Java methods to input and output large integers and to perform the arithmetic operations add, subtract, multiply, and divide. The method for division will return two integers: the quotient and the remainder.

★ 66. [Polynomials] A **univariate polynomial** of degree d has the form

$$c_d x^d + c_{d-1} x^{d-1} + c_{d-2} x^{d-2} + \cdots + c_0$$

where $c_d \neq 0$. The c_is are the coefficients, and d, $d-1$, $\cdots$ are the exponents. By definition d is a nonnegative integer. For this exercise you may assume that the coefficients are also integers. Each $c_i x^i$ is a term of the polynomial. We wish to develop a Java class to support arithmetic involving polynomials. For this exercise we will represent each polynomial as a linear list $(c_0, c_1, c_2, \cdots, c_d)$ of coefficients.

Develop a Java class `Polynomial` that should have an instance data member `degree`, which is the degree of the polynomial. It may have other instance data members also. Your polynomial class should support the following operations:

(a) `Polynomial()`—Create the zero polynomial. The degree of this polynomial is 0 and it has no terms. `Polynomial()` is the class constructor.

(b) `degree()`—Return the degree of the polynomial.

(c) `input(inStream)`—Read in a polynomial from the input stream `inStream`. You may assume the input consists of the polynomial degree and a list of coefficients in ascending order of exponents.

(d) `output()`—Output the polynomial. The output format should be the same as the input format.

(e) `add(b)`—Add to polynomial b and return the result polynomial.

(f) `subtract(b)`—Subtract the polynomial b and return the result.

(g) `multiply(b)`—Multiply with polynomial b and return the result.

(h) `divide(b)`—Divide by polynomial b and return the quotient.

(i) `valueOf(x)`—Return the value of the polynomial at point x.

Test your code.

★   67. [Polynomials] Design and code a linked class to represent and manipulate univariate polynomials (see Exercise 66). Assume that the coefficients are integers. Use circular linked lists with header nodes. Each node should have the fields `exp` (exponent), `coeff` (coefficient), and `next` (pointer to next node). In addition to the header node, the circular list representation of a polynomial has one node for each term that has a nonzero coefficient. Terms whose coefficient is 0 are not represented. The terms are in decreasing order of exponent, and the header node has its exponent field set to -1. Figure 6.14 gives some examples.

The external (i.e., for input or output) representation of a univariate polynomial will be assumed to be a sequence of numbers of the form n, e_1, c_1, e_2, c_2, e_3, c_3, $\cdots$, e_n, c_n, where the e_i represent the exponents and the c_i the coefficients; n gives the number of terms in the polynomial. The exponents are in decreasing order; that is, $e_1 > e_2 > \cdots > e_n$.

Your class should support all the methods of Exercise 66. Test the correctness of your code using suitable polynomials.

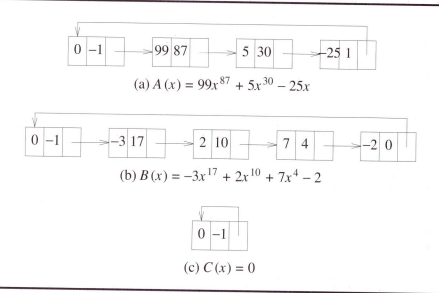

(a) $A(x) = 99x^{87} + 5x^{30} - 25x$

(b) $B(x) = -3x^{17} + 2x^{10} + 7x^4 - 2$

(c) $C(x) = 0$

Figure 6.14 Sample polynomials

CHAPTER 7

LINEAR LISTS—SIMULATED POINTERS

BIRD'S-EYE VIEW

Simulated-pointer representation is very similar to a linked representation. However, we use an array of nodes to represent the available memory, and pointers are represented by integers rather than by Java references. Simulated pointers are essential when we wish to represent linked structures on a disk; they are also useful in certain internal memory applications. To use simulated pointers, we must implement our own memory management scheme—a scheme to keep track of the free nodes in our memory (i.e., array of nodes), to allocate a free node when needed (equivalent to the **new** method of Java), and to reclaim allocated nodes that have become free (Java uses a process called garbage collection).

The data structure concepts introduced in this chapter are

- Simulated-pointer representation.

- Memory management strategies.

In the applications section we show how a machine-scheduling problem and a circuit wiring problem may be modeled by the classical union-find problem. The classical union-find problem is then solved using simulated pointers.

7.1   THE NEED FOR SIMULATED POINTERS

In most applications we can implement the desired linked representations using dynamic allocation (i.e., Java's method **new**) and Java references. Memory allocated via the **new** method and that is no longer in use by a program is automatically reclaimed using a process called garbage collection (see Section 7.4). Some applications where the use of Java references as pointers is not suitable are given in the following examples.

Example 7.1 [Disk Storage] Here is a simple way to manage disk storage. When a disk is formatted, it is partitioned into blocks (or allocation units) of a predetermined size *blockSize* (say 32 KB). Each block has an index from which the exact location of that disk block can be determined. When a file whose size is *fileSize* is to be stored, it is allocated $\lceil fileSize/blockSize \rceil$ blocks; these blocks are linked together to form a chain; the *nextBlock* pointer in each block is the index of the next block in the chain; and an entry (name of file, index of first block in chain) is made in the file allocation table that keeps track of all files on the disk. When a file is deleted, the blocks allocated to the file become free.

Java pointers cannot be used because Java pointers are internal memory addresses and not addresses of disk memory.   ■

Example 7.2 [Data Structure Backup] How would you back up a chain of integers that you might need next week? You would move down the chain from left to right and write each chain element (i.e., integer) to disk. This process of writing every element of the data structure in some sequential order is called **serialization**. You would not write the **next** pointer in each chain node because this pointer is a memory address; the address of the next node on the chain. To recover your chain next week, you would read back the serialized version and reconstruct the chain. This process is called **deserialization**. The memory addresses available for reconstruction would generally be different from those used by the original chain.

Serializing and deserializing a chain is quite easy because a chain represents a linear list that is, itself, a sequentially ordered collection of elements. Imagine that you have a data structure in which each node has five pointers going any which way they please. You can build a fairly intricate arrangement (much like a nice bowl of spaghetti) of nodes using five pointers per node. Serializing and deserializing your data structure could be both time-consuming and a chore likely to give you a headache. In addition to writing out the elements in a sequential order, you will need to capture the pointer information so that you can reconstruct the linked structure.

When simulated pointers are used, we can simply write out the entire simulated memory (which is a one-dimensional array). When the simulated memory is read back, presto, the linked data structure comes back too.   ■

Example 7.3 [External Data Structures] Although this book focuses primarily on data structures that reside in internal memory—internal memory data structures—some data structures such as the B-tree of Section 16.4.3 are intended for data that reside on a disk. These data structures require pointers that cannot be Java references because these pointers refer to addresses on a disk.   ■

Although these three examples involve data that are to be stored on a disk, some internal memory applications also benefit from the use of simulated pointers. One such application—the union-find problem—is developed in Sections 7.7 and 12.9.2. Another application—bipartite covers—is developed in Section 18.3.4.

7.2   SIMULATING POINTERS

We describe how to simulate pointers in internal memory. The techniques readily extend to disk storage. We implement linked lists using an array of nodes and simulate Java references by integers that are indexes into this array. Our linked data structures reside within this array. Therefore, to back up our data structures, for example, we need merely back up the contents of each node as it appears from left to right in the node array. To recover, we read back the node contents in left-to-right order and reestablish the node array.

Suppose we use an array `node` whose data type is `SimulatedNode` (Program 7.1). The type `SimulatedNode` differs from the data type `ChainNode` only in the data type of the member `next`—in `ChainNode` the member `next` is a Java reference, whereas in `SimulatedNode`, `next` is an `int`.

```
class SimulatedNode
{
   // package visible data members
   Object element;
   int next;

   // package visible constructors
   SimulatedNode() {}

   SimulatedNode(int next)
      {this.next = next;}
}
```

Program 7.1 Data type of nodes using simulated pointers

The nodes `node[0]`, `node[1]`, $\cdots$, `node[numberOfNodes-1]` are available for our linked data structures. We will refer to `node[i]` as node `i`, and we will use the integer -1 to play the role of `null`.

We may construct a simulated chain (i.e., a singly linked list of nodes that uses integer pointers; the last node's pointer is -1) `c` that consists of nodes 5, 2, and 7 (in that order) in the following way:

- set `c.firstNode` $= 5$ (pointer to first node on the simulated chain c is of type `int`)

- set `node[5].next` $= 2$ (pointer to second node on simulated chain)

- set `node[2].next` $= 7$ (pointer to next node)

- set `node[7].next` $= -1$ (indicating that node 7 is the last node on the chain).

Figure 7.1(a) shows a 10-node memory array `node` with our three-node simulated chain. The shaded nodes are the in-use nodes, and the unshaded ones are the free nodes. Simulated chain drawings such as the one in Figure 7.1(a) are hard to follow because they do not visually display the linear ordering of the chain nodes. We therefore draw simulated chains the same way as when Java references are used (Figure 7.1(b)); the nodes are drawn in their left-to-right list order, and simulated pointers are drawn as arrows.

node	[0]	[1]	[2]	[3]	[4]	[5]	[6]	[7]	[8]	[9]
next			7			2		-1		
element			e_1			e_0		e_2		

(a) Three-node simulated chain with `c.firstNode` $= 5$

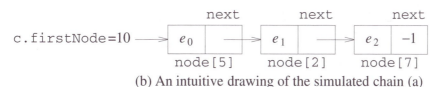

(b) An intuitive drawing of the simulated chain (a)

Figure 7.1 Simulated chain with three nodes

7.3   MEMORY MANAGEMENT

When we use simulated pointers, we must find a way to do some of the things that Java does for us when references are used as pointers. For example, we must be able to allocate a node for use (i.e., do the equivalent of the `new` method of Java) and reclaim previously allocated nodes that are no longer being used. A **memory management system** provides for three tasks—create a collection of nodes, allocate a node as needed, and reclaim nodes that are no longer in use.

Although memory management for nodes with different sizes is rather complex, memory management for nodes of the same size is fairly simple. The node array of Figure 7.1(a), for example, deals with fixed-size nodes (their data type is `SimulatedNode`, and each instance of this data type is 8 bytes long). We limit our development of methods to allocate and reclaim memory to a simple scheme for nodes of a fixed size.

The scheme we will develop deviates philosophically from that used by Java in the way memory is reclaimed; while Java relies on garbage collection, our scheme will require the user to explicitly reclaim memory that he/she no longer needs. This explicit reclaiming of memory is done by invoking a memory deallocation method.

In our simple memory management scheme, nodes that are not in use (nodes 0, 1, 3, 4, 6, 8, and 9 in Figure 7.1(a)) are kept in a **storage pool** from where they may be allocated for use as needed. Initially, this pool contains all nodes `node[0:numberOfNodes-1]` that are to be managed. `allocateNode` takes a node out of this pool and makes this node available to the user; the user may free a node that was in use by invoking the method `deallocateNode`, which puts a node back into the pool. The method `allocateNode` is functionally equivalent to the `new` method of Java. Since Java reclaims dynamically allocated storage that is no longer in use by a garbage collection process, Java does not have a method equivalent to `deallocateNode`.

Even though a general simulated-pointer system includes methods to initialize the storage pool and to allocate and deallocate nodes, many applications of simulated pointers need none or only some of these three methods. For example, our applications of simulated pointers in Sections 7.7 and 12.9.2 require none of these methods.

We will develop two classes `SimulatedSpace1` and `SimulatedSpace2` that implement memory management schemes for the case of equal size nodes. In `SimulatedSpace1`, all free nodes are on a simulated chain; in `SimulatedSpace2`, only free nodes that have been used at least once are on this chain. This difference in the organization of the storage pool mainly influences the time it takes to initialize the pool.

7.3.1   The Class `SimulatedSpace1`

In this implementation of a memory management system, the storage pool is set up as a simulated chain of nodes (as in Figure 7.2). This chain is called the **available space list**. It contains all nodes that are currently free. `firstNode` is a variable of type `int` that points to the first node on this chain. When a node is deallocated, it is added to the chain of free nodes; when a node is to be allocated for use, a node is removed from the free node chain. Additions to and removals from the chain of free nodes are made at the front.

Figure 7.2 Available space list

The class `SimulatedSpace1` has the data members `firstNode` (integer pointer to first node on available space list) and `node` (array of type `SimulatedNode`). The class also has a constructor method that allocates the array `node` and initializes the available space list, the method `allocateNode` that allocates the first node on the available space list (in case the available space list is empty, `allocateNode` first doubles the array size and puts the additional nodes created by this doubling on to the available space list), and the method `deallocateNode` that returns a previously allocated node to the available space list.

Since all nodes are initially free, the available space list contains `numberOfNodes` nodes at the time it is created. The class contructor (Program 7.2) initializes the available space list. Programs 7.3 and 7.4 perform the `allocateNode` and `deallocateNode` operations.

```
public SimulatedSpace1(int numberOfNodes)
{
   node = new SimulatedNode [numberOfNodes];

   // create nodes and link into a chain
   for (int i = 0; i < numberOfNodes - 1; i++)
      node[i] = new SimulatedNode(i + 1);

   // last node of array and chain
   node[numberOfNodes - 1] = new SimulatedNode(-1);
   // firstNode has the default initial value 0
}
```

Program 7.2 Initialize available space list

The time complexity of the constructor is $O(\texttt{numberOfNodes})$. The complexity of `allocateNode` is $\Theta(1)$ except when it becomes necessary to double the size of the array `node`. When array doubling is necessary, the complexity of `allocateNode` is $O(\texttt{node.length})$. From the analysis that resulted in Theorem 5.1, it follows that

```
public int allocateNode(Object element, int next)
{// Allocate a free node and set its fields.
   if (firstNode == -1)
   {   // double number of nodes
       node = (SimulatedNode []) ChangeArrayLength.
             changeLength1D(node, 2 * node.length);

       // create and link new nodes
       for (int i = node.length / 2;
            i < node.length - 1; i++)
          node[i] = new SimulatedNode(i + 1);
       node[node.length - 1] = new SimulatedNode(-1);

       firstNode = node.length / 2;
   }

   int i = firstNode;         // allocate first node
   firstNode = node[i].next;  // firstNode points to
                              // next free node
   node[i].element = element;
   node[i].next = next;
   return i;
}
```

Program 7.3 Allocate a node using simulated pointers

```
public void deallocateNode(int i)
{// Free node i.
   // make i first node on free space list
   node[i].next = firstNode;
   firstNode = i;

   // remove element reference so that space can be garbage collected
   node[i].element = null;
}
```

Program 7.4 Deallocate a node with simulated pointers

the time required to allocate n nodes is $\Theta(n)$. The complexity of `deallocateNode` is $\Theta(1)$.

7.3.2   The Class `SimulatedSpace2`

We can reduce the run time of the constructor (Program 7.2) by maintaining two available space lists. One contains all free nodes that haven't been used yet. The second contains all free nodes that have been used at least once. Whenever a node is deallocated, it is put onto the second list. When a new node is needed, we provide it from the second list if this list is not empty. Otherwise, we attempt to provide the new node from the first list. Let the integer variables `first1` and `first2`, respectively, point to the front of the first and second space lists. Because of the way nodes are allocated, the nodes on the first list are `node[i]`, `first1` $\le$ `i` $<$ `node.length`. The code for `SimulatedSpace2` is available from the Web site.

7.3.3   Evaluation of Simulated Memory Management

We make the following observations:

- When the single list scheme is in use, simulated chains can be built by explicitly setting the link field only in the last node because the appropriate link values are already present in the remaining nodes (see Figure 7.2). This advantage can also be incorporated into the dual available space list scheme by writing a method `getNodes(n)` that provides a chain with `n` nodes on it. This method will explicitly set links only when nodes are taken from the first available space list.

- An entire chain of nodes can be freed efficiently using either of these schemes. For instance, if we know the front `f` and end `e` of a chain, all nodes on it are freed by the following statements:

```
node[e].next = firstNode;
firstNode = f;
```

  When the nodes of a simulated chain are deallocated in this way, garbage collection of the memory used by the objects referenced by the `element` fields of the nodes is not enabled. To enable garbage collection of this space, we must set the `element` fields of the freed nodes to `null`.

- If `theList` is a simulated circular list, then all nodes on it are deallocated in $\Theta(1)$ time by using Program 7.5. `S` is the simulated space used by the circular lists. Figure 7.3 shows the link changes that take place. Note that in this code `theList.firstNode` points to the first node in the circular list `theList`, `secondNode` points to the second node of `theList`, and `firstNode` points the first node of the available space list (a single space list is assumed).

```
public void deallocateCircular(SimulatedCircularList theList)
{// Deallocate all nodes in the circular list theList.
   if (theList.firstNode != -1)
   {// theList is not empty
      int secondNode = S.node[theList.firstNode].next;
      S.node[theList.firstNode].next = firstNode;
      firstNode = secondNode;
      theList.firstNode = -1;   // theList is now empty
   }
}
```

Program 7.5 Deallocate a circular list

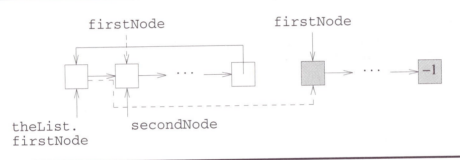

Figure 7.3 Deallocating a circular list

7.4   COMPARISON WITH GARBAGE COLLECTION

The use of garbage collection, as is done in Java, to reclaim free storage and the use of a method such as `deallocateNode` represent two fundamentally different approaches to memory management. In the garbage collection method, memory that was in use but has subsequently become free is returned to the storage pool by a program called the **garbage collector**. Garbage collectors typically perform two tasks—identify free memory (this task is called **marking**) and return the identified free memory to the storage pool.

A third task—garbage compaction—is often associated with garbage compaction. In garbage compaction data in memory that is in use are relocated so that the in-use memory forms a contiguous block of memory and the free memory forms another contiguous block. Garbage compaction is often done following garbage collection or whenever an invocation of **new** determines that even though the requested memory size is no more than the amount of free memory, enough contiguous memory is not available. For example, an invocation of `new` may request 80 bytes of contiguous memory when the free memory consists of three blocks of size 50, 60, and 70. So even though we have 180 bytes of free memory, we do not have 80 bytes of contiguous memory. To remedy the problem, a garbage compactor is invoked. Following garbage compaction, the free memory makes up a single block of 180 contiguous bytes from which an 80-byte subblock may be allocated.

A garbage collector might always be running in the background (while your program runs in the foreground), constantly looking for memory that has become free and reclaiming this free memory. Alternatively, the collector may be invoked whenever an invocation of `new` determines that the current request for memory cannot be met from the free memory in the storage pool. We assume this alternative mode.

When garbage collection is used to reclaim free memory, the user does not have the burden of determining when portions of memory are no longer needed by his/her program and explicitly invoking a method to deallocate this free memory. However, this freedom comes at a significant cost should the garbage collector ever be invoked. The time a garbage collector takes to to identify the free memory is proportional to the size of the total memory allocated to the program, not to the amount of memory that is actually free or being reclaimed. Therefore, in a program that uses 1,000,000 nodes, a garbage collector would take about 1,000,000 steps to reclaim free memory even if only one node is free. The time taken by a garbage compactor is proportional to the number of bytes of memory (not the number of nodes) that is in use.

When the `deallocateNode` method is used, the user incurs the burden of explicitly freeing memory that his/her program no longer needs. The time required to free this memory is proportional to the amount of memory being freed (in some cases large amounts of memory can be freed in a single step), rather than to the total amount of memory available to the program or the amount of memory that is in use. Typically, when a garbage collector is invoked, only a small fraction of the total number of nodes is free. Therefore, programs that use the `deallocateNode` methodology often, though not always, run faster than programs that rely on a garbage collector. Even though it takes less time to free memory by explicit calls to a memory deallocator such as `deallocateNode`, your program may have no use for the memory that has been explicitly freed. In this case the garbage collection method works better because the garbage collector is not invoked and no time is spent reclaiming free memory.

Programs that rely on a garbage collector often run faster if more memory is made available to them. This is because by making more memory available, we can reduce (even eliminate) the number of times the garbage collector is invoked. The run time of programs that explicitly free memory using a deallocator is generally insensitive to the total amount of memory that is available.

7.5   SIMULATED CHAINS

7.5.1   The Class `SimulatedChain`

We may define a class, `SimulatedChain`, for simulated chains that use the simulated space S (see Program 7.6, which gives the data members and some methods; the complete code is available from the Web site). S is declared as a `static` data member rather than as an instance data member so that all simulated chains share the same simulated space.

7.5.2   Performance Measurement

The table of Figure 7.4 compares the asymptotic complexity of performing various operations on a linear list, using array-based and linked (either Java references or simulated pointers) representations. Since the asymptotic complexity of each operation is the same when Java references and simulated pointers are used, the table contains a single row for both.

	Method		
Representation	get	remove	add
array based	$\Theta(1)$	$O(n-k)$	$O(n-k)$
linked list (Java & simulated)	$O(k)$	$O(k)$	$O(k)$

n = number of elements in the linear list
k = value of `index`

Figure 7.4 Comparison of representation methods

By using the method `binarySearch` (Program 3.1), we can search an array-based sorted list in $O(\log n)$ time. This search takes $O(n)$ time when a linked representation is used.

Simulated chains get a thumbs down as far as run-time performance is concerned. Our run-time measurements used the same experimental setup as we used for array-based and linked representations of linear lists (see Sections 5.6 and 6.1.6). Figure 7.5 gives the measured times. Cache effects (Section 4.5) have finally caught up with us—the average test for removes took more time than the worst-case test, even though the worst-case test did twice as much work.

Despite the discouraging performance of simulated chains as a representation for linear lists, simulated chains remain useful for other applications (see Sections 7.7, 12.9.2, and 18.3.4).

```
public class SimulatedChain implements LinearList
{
   // data members
   protected int firstNode;
   protected int size;
   public static SimulatedSpace1 S = new SimulatedSpace1(10);

   // constructors
   public SimulatedChain(int initialCapacity)
   {
      firstNode = -1;
      // size has the default initial value 0
   }

   // methods
   /** @return index of first occurrence of elem,
     * return -1 if elem not in list */
   public int indexOf(Object elem)
   {
      // search the chain for elem
      int currentNode = firstNode;
      int index = 0;  // index of currentNode
      while (currentNode != -1 &&
             !S.node[currentNode].element.equals(elem))
      {
         // move to next node
         currentNode = S.node[currentNode].next;
         index++;
      }

      // make sure we found matching element
      if (currentNode == -1) return -1;
      else return index;
   }

   // remaining methods on Web site
}
```

Program 7.6 The class SimulatedChain

`deallocateNode` are invoked 1,000,000 times each. But `new` is invoked only 50 times. The time savings from the 999,950 calls to `new` that are not made plus the savings from the significantly reduced garbage collection effort are more than the cost of the 1,000,000 calls to each of `allocateNode` and `deallocateNode`.

The described modifications do not always result in a reduction in run time. For example, suppose we make 1,000,000 inserts, follow these with 1,000,000 removes, and then terminate the program. The original version of `Chain` makes 1,000,000 calls to `new`; the modified version makes 1,000,000 calls to each of the methods `new`, `allocateNode`, and `deallocateNode`.

The performance enhancement strategy just described also may be applied to the linked classes developed in later chapters.

EXERCISE

6. Develop the class `ManagedChain` that includes all the public instance methods of the class `Chain` (Program 6.2). The class `ManagedChain` includes class methods to allocate and deallocate nodes. The storage pool is initially empty; simulated pointers are not used. The allocate method `allocateNode` allocates a node from the storage pool whenever the storage pool is not empty. When the storage pool is empty, it gets a node by invoking the Java method `new`. The `remove` method should return the freed node to the storage pool, and the `add` method should invoke `allocateNode` rather than `new`.

   (a) Test the correctness of your code.
   (b) Comment on the relative merits of using the classes `ManagedChain` and `Chain` to represent a collection of chains.

7.7   APPLICATION—UNION-FIND PROBLEM

7.7.1   Equivalence Classes

Suppose we have a set $U = 1, 2, \cdots, n$ of n elements and a set $R = (i_1, j_1)$, $(i_2, j_2), \cdots, (i_r, j_r)$ of r relations. The relation R is an **equivalence relation** iff the following conditions are true:

- $(a, a) \in R$ for all $a \in U$ (the relation is reflexive).

- $(a, b) \in R$ iff $(b, a) \in R$ (the relation is symmetric).

- $(a, b) \in R$ and $(b, c) \in R$ imply that $(a, c) \in R$ (the relation is transitive).

Often when we specify an equivalence relation R, we omit some of the pairs in R. The omitted pairs may be obtained by applying the reflexive, symmetric, and transitive properties of an equivalence relation.

Example 7.4 Suppose $n = 14$ and $R = \{(1,11),\ (7,11),\ (2,12),\ (12,8),\ (11,12),\ (3,13),\ (4,13),\ (13,14),\ (14,9),\ (5,14),\ (6,10)\}$. We have omitted all pairs of the form (a, a) because these pairs are implied by the reflexive property. Similarly, we have omitted all symmetric pairs. Since $(1,11) \in R$, the symmetric property requires $(11,1) \in R$. Other omitted pairs are obtained by applying the transitive property. For example, $(7,11)$ and $(11,12)$ imply $(7,12)$. ∎

Two elements a and b are equivalent if $(a, b) \in R$. An **equivalence class** is defined to be a maximal set of equivalent elements. *Maximal* means that no element outside the class is equivalent to an element in the class. Since it is not possible for an element to be in more than one equivalence class, an equivalence relation partitions the universe U into disjoint classes.

Example 7.5 Consider the equivalence relation of Example 7.4. Since elements 1 and 11, and 11 and 12 are equivalent, elements 1, 11, and 12 are equivalent. They are therefore in the same class. These three elements do not, however, form an equivalence class, as they are equivalent to other elements (e.g., 7). So $\{1, 11, 12\}$ is not a maximal set of equivalent elements. The set $\{1, 2, 7, 8, 11, 12\}$ is an equivalence class. The relation R defines two other equivalence classes: $\{3, 4, 5, 9, 13, 14\}$ and $\{6, 10\}$. Notice that the three equivalence classes are disjoint. ∎

In the **offline equivalence class** problem, we are given n and R and are to determine the equivalence classes. From the definition of an equivalence class, it follows that each element is in exactly one equivalence class. In the **online equivalence class** problem, we begin with n elements, each in a separate equivalence class. We are to process a sequence of the operations: (1) `combine(a,b)` $\cdots$ combine the equivalence classes that contain elements `a` and `b` into a single class and (2) `find(theElement)` $\cdots$ determine the class that currently contains element `the-Element`. The purpose of the find operation is to determine whether two elements are in the same class. Hence the find operation is to be implemented to return the same answer for elements in the same class and different answers for elements in different classes.

We can write the combine operation in terms of two `find`s and a `union` that actually takes two different classes and makes one. So `combine(a,b)` is equivalent to

```
classA = find(a);
classB = find(b);
if (classA != classB)
   union(classA, classB);
```

Notice that with the find and union operations, we can add new relations to R. For instance, to add the relation (a, b), we determine whether a and b are already in the same class. If they are, then the new relation is redundant. If they aren't, then we perform a `union` on the two classes that contain a and b.

In this section we are concerned primarily with the online equivalence problem, which is more commonly known as the **union-find** problem. Although the solutions developed in this section are rather simple, they are not the most efficient. Faster solutions are developed in Section 12.9.2. A fast solution for the offline equivalence problem is developed in Section 9.5.5.

7.7.2   Applications

The following examples show how a machine-scheduling problem and a circuit-wiring problem may be modeled as online equivalence class problems. A version of the circuit wiring problem may be modeled as an offline equivalence class problem.

Example 7.6 A certain factory has a single machine that is to perform n tasks. Task i has an integer release time r_i and an integer deadline d_i. The completion of each task requires one unit of time on this machine. A **feasible schedule** is an assignment of tasks to time slots on the machine such that task i is assigned to a time slot between its release time and deadline and no slot has more than one task assigned to it.
Consider the following four tasks:

Task	A	B	C	D
Release time	0	0	1	2
Deadline	4	4	2	3

Tasks A and B are released at time 0, task C is released at time 1, and task D is released at time 2. The following task-to-slot assignment is a feasible schedule: do task A from 0 to 1; task C from 1 to 2; task D from 2 to 3; and task B from 3 to 4 (see Figure 7.6).

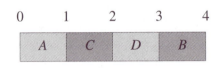

Figure 7.6 A schedule for four tasks

An intuitively appealing method to construct a schedule is

1. Sort the tasks into nonincreasing order of release time.

2. Consider the tasks in this nonincreasing order. For each task determine the free slot nearest to, but not after, its deadline. If this free slot is before the task's release time, fail. Otherwise, assign the task to this slot.

Exercise 9 asks you to prove that the strategy just described fails to find a feasible schedule only when such a schedule does not exist.

The online equivalence class problem can be used to implement step (2). For this step, let d denote the latest deadline of any task. The usable time slots are of the form "from $i - 1$ to i" where $1 \leq i \leq d$. We will refer to these usable slots as slots 1 through d. For any slot a, define $near(a)$ as the largest i such that $i \leq a$ and slot i is free. If no such i exists, define $near(a) = near(0) = 0$. Two slots a and b are in the same equivalence class iff $near(a) = near(b)$.

Prior to the scheduling of any task, $near(a) = a$ for all slots, and each slot is in a separate equivalence class. When slot a is assigned a task in step (2), $near$ changes for all slots b with $near(b) = a$. For these slots the new value of $near$ is $near(a - 1)$. Hence when slot a is assigned a task, we need to perform a $\texttt{union}$ on the equivalence classes that currently contain slots a and $a - 1$. If with each equivalence class e we retain, in $nearest[e]$, the value of $near$ of its members, then $near(a)$ is given by $nearest[\texttt{find}(a)]$. (Assume that the equivalence class name is taken to be whatever the $\texttt{find}$ operation returns.)   ■

Example 7.7 [From Wires to Nets] An electronic circuit consists of components, pins, and wires. Figure 7.7 shows a circuit with the three components A, B, and C. Each wire connects a pair of pins. Two pins a and b are **electrically equivalent** iff they are either connected by a wire or there is a sequence $i_1, i_2, \ldots i_k$ of pins such that $a, i_1; i_1, i_2; i_2, i_3; \cdots; i_{k-1}, i_k;$ and i_k, b are all connected by wires. A **net** is a maximal set of electrically equivalent pins. *Maximal* means that no pin outside the net is electrically equivalent to a pin in the net.

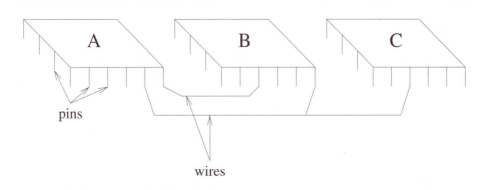

Figure 7.7 A three-chip circuit on a printed circuit board

Consider the circuit shown in Figure 7.8. In this figure only the pins and wires have been shown. The 14 pins are numbered 1 through 14. Each wire may be described by the two pins that it connects. For instance, the wire connecting pins

1 and 11 is described by the pair (1,11), which is equivalent to the pair (11,1). The set of wires is {(1,11), (7,11), (2,12), (12,8), (11,12), (3,13), (4,13), (13,14), (14,9), (5,14), (6,10)}. The nets are {1, 2, 7, 8, 11, 12}, {3, 4, 5, 9, 13, 14} and {6, 10}.

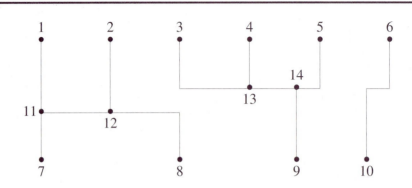

Figure 7.8 Circuit with pins and wires shown

In the **offline net finding problem**, we are given the pins and wires and are to determine the nets. This problem is modeled by the offline equivalence problem with each pin being a member of U and each wire a member of R.

In the **online** version we begin with a collection of pins and no wires and are to perform a sequence of operations of the form (1) add a wire to connect pins a and b and (2) find the net that contains pin a. The purpose of the find operation is to determine whether two pins are in the same net or in different nets. This version of the net problem may be modeled by the online equivalence class problem. Initially, there are no wires, and we have $R = \phi$. The net find operation corresponds to the equivalence class find operation and adding a new wire (a, b) corresponds to combine(a, b), which is equivalent to union(find(a), find(b)).   ■

7.7.3   First Union-Find Solution

A simple solution to the online equivalence class problem is to use an array equivClass and let equivClass[i] be the class that currently contains element i. The methods to initialize, union, and find take the form given in Program 7.7. n is the number of elements. n and equivClass are both assumed to be class (i.e., static) data members. To unite two different classes, we arbitrarily pick one of these classes and change the equivClass values of all elements in this class to correspond to the equivClass values of the elements of the other class. Note that the inputs to union are equivClass values (i.e., the results of a find operation) and not element indexes. Even though union works correctly when a redundant union (i.e., one in which classA = classB), we make the assumption that redundant unions are not performed. The initialize and union methods have complexity $\Theta(n)$ (we assume that `new` does not throw an exception when invoked by `initialize`), and the complexity of `find` is $\Theta(1)$. From Examples 7.6 and 7.7, we see that in any application of these methods, we will perform one initialization, u unions, and f finds. The time needed for all of these operations is $\Theta(n+u*n+f) = \Theta(u*n+f)$.

```
public class UnionFindFirstSolution
{
   static int [] equivClass;
   static int n;   // number of elements

   /** initialize numberOfElements classes with one element each */
   static void initialize(int numberOfElements)
   {
      n = numberOfElements;
      equivClass = new int [n + 1];
      for (int e = 1; e <= n; e++)
         equivClass[e] = e;
   }

   /** unite the classes classA and classB */
   static void union(int classA, int classB)
   {// assume classA != classB
      for (int k = 1; k <= n; k++)
         if (equivClass[k] == classB)
            equivClass[k] = classA;
   }

   /** find the class that contains theElement */
   static int find(int theElement)
      {return equivClass[theElement];}
}
```

Program 7.7 Union-find methods using arrays

7.7.4   Second Union-Find Solution

The time complexity of the union operation can be reduced by keeping a chain for each equivalence class because now we can find all elements in a given equivalence class by going down the chain for that class, rather than by examining all `equivClass` values. In fact, if each equivalence class knows its size, we can choose to change the `equivClass` values of the smaller equivalence class and perform the union operation even faster. By using simulated pointers, we get quick access to the node that represents element e. We adopt the following conventions:

- **EquivNode** is a class with data members **equivClass**, **size**, and **next**. Program 7.8 gives the code for this class.

```
class EquivNode
{
   int equivClass;    // element class identifier
   int size;          // size of class
   int next;          // pointer to next element in class

   /** constructor */
   EquivNode(int theClass, int theSize)
   {
      equivClass = theClass;
      size = theSize;
      // next has the default value 0
   }
}
```

Program 7.8 The class EquivNode

- An array **node[1:n]** of type **EquivNode** is used to represent the n elements together with the equivalence class chains.

- **node[e].equivClass** is both the value to be returned by **find(e)** and a pointer to the first node in the chain for the equivalence class **node[e].equiv-Class**.

- **node[e].size** is defined only if e is the first node on a chain. In this case **node[e].size** is the number of nodes on the chain that begins at **node[e]**.

- **node[e].next** gives the next node on the chain that contains node e. Since the nodes in use are numbered 1 through n, a **null** pointer can be simulated by 0 rather than by −1.

Program 7.9 gives the new code for **initialize**, **union**, and **find**.

Since an equivalence class is of size $O(n)$, the complexity of the union operation is $O(n)$ when chains are used. The complexity of the initialization and find operations remain $O(n)$ and $\Theta(1)$, respectively. To determine the complexity of performing one initialization and a sequence of u unions and f finds, we will use the following lemma.

```
public class UnionFindSecondSolution
{
   static EquivNode [] node; // array of nodes
   static int n;             // number of elements

   /** initialize numberOfElements classes with one element each */
   static void initialize(int numberOfElements)
   {
      n = numberOfElements;
      node = new equivNode [n + 1];

      for (int e = 1; e <= n; e++)
         // node[e] is initialized so that its equivClass is e,
         // size is 1, and next is 0
         node[e] = new equivNode(e,1);
   }

   /** unite the classes classA and classB */
   static void union(int classA, int classB)
   {// assume classA != classB
      // make classA smaller class
      if (node[classA].size > node[classB].size)
      {// swap classA and classB
         int t = classA;
         classA = classB;
         classB = t;
      }

      //  change equivClass values of smaller class
      int k;
      for (k = classA; node[k].next != 0; k = node[k].next)
         node[k].equivClass = classB;
      node[k].equivClass = classB; // last node in chain

      // insert chain classA after first node in chain classB
      // and update new chain size
      node[classB].size += node[classA].size;
      node[k].next = node[classB].next;
      node[classB].next = classA;
   }
}
```

Program 7.9 Union-find methods using chains (continues)

```
static int find(int theElement)
   {return node[theElement].equivClass;}
}
```

Program 7.9 Union-find methods using chains (concluded)

Lemma 7.1 *If we start with n classes that have one element each and perform u nonredundant unions, then*

1. *No class has more than $u + 1$ elements.*

2. *At least $n - 2u$ singleton classes remain.*

3. *$u < n$.*

Proof See Exercise 7.   ∎

The complexity of the initialize and f finds is $O(\mathbf{n}+f)$. For the u nonredundant unions, we note that the cost of each union is Θ(size of smaller class). During the union elements are moved from the smaller class to the bigger one. The complexity of a single union is O(number of elements moved), and the complexity of all u unions is O(total number of element moves). Following a union operation, each element that is moved to a new class ends up in a class whose size is at least twice that of the class the element was in before the union operation (because elements move from an initially smaller class into an initially bigger class). Therefore, since at the end no class has more than $u + 1$ elements (Lemma 7.1(1)), no element can be moved more than $\log_2(u + 1)$ times during the u unions. Furthermore, from Lemma 7.1(2), at most $2u$ elements can move (because the elements left in singleton classes have never moved). So the total number of element moves cannot exceed $2u \log_2(u + 1)$. As a result, the time needed to perform the u unions is $O(u \log u)$. The complexity of the initialization and the sequence of u unions and f finds is therefore $O(\mathbf{n}+u \log u+f)$.

EXERCISES

7. Prove Lemma 7.1.

8. Write a Java program for the online net finding problem of Example 7.7. Model the problem as the online equivalence class problem and use the chain method. Test the correctness of your program.

9. Prove that the strategy outlined in Example 7.6 fails to find a feasible schedule only when such a schedule does not exist.

10. Compare the run-time performance of Programs 7.7 and 7.9.

11. Develop a version of Program 7.9 in which the simulated chains are replaced by array-based linear lists.

    (a) Test your code.

    (b) What is the time complexity of your new implementation?

    (c) Compare the performance of Program 7.9 and your new implementation.

12. Develop a version of Program 7.9 in which the chains use Java references rather than simulated pointers. To access the node for element i in $O(1)$ time, keep an array *theNode* such that *theNode*$[i]$ is a pointer to the node that represents element i.

    (a) Test your code.

    (b) What is the time complexity of your new implementation?

    (c) Compare the performance of Program 7.9 and your new implementation.

13. Write a Java program for the scheduling problem of Example 7.6. Model the problem as the online equivalence class problem and use the chain method. Test the correctness of your program.

CHAPTER 8

ARRAYS AND MATRICES

BIRD'S-EYE VIEW

In practice, data are often available in tabular form. Although arrays are the most natural way to represent tabular data, we can often reduce both the space and time requirements of our programs by using a customized representation. This reduction is possible, for example, when a large portion of the table entries are 0.

This chapter begins by examining the row-major and column-major representations of a multidimensional array. These representations map a multidimensional array into a one-dimensional array.

The data object matrix is often represented as a two-dimensional array. However, matrices are normally indexed beginning at 1 rather than 0. Matrices also support operations such as add, multiply, and transpose, which are not supported by Java's two-dimensional arrays. Therefore, we develop another class `Matrix` that conforms more closely to the data object matrix.

We also consider the representation of matrices with special structures—diagonal, tridiagonal, triangular, and symmetric matrices. Using customized array representations, we can reduce the space requirements of these matrices considerably when compared to the space used by the natural two-dimensional array representation. The customized representations also result in reduced run times for most operations.

The final section of this chapter develops array and linked representations for sparse matrices (i.e., matrices with a large number of 0s) in which the positions of the 0s do not necessarily define a regular pattern.

254

8.1 ARRAYS

8.1.1 The Abstract Data Type

Each instance of an array is a set of pairs of the form (index, value). No two pairs in this set have the same index. The operations performed on the array follow.

- *Get an element*—Gets the value of the pair that has a given index.

- *Set an element*—Adds a pair of the form (index, value) to the set, and if a pair with the same index already exists, deletes the old pair.

These two operations define the abstract data type *Array* (ADT 8.1).

AbstractDataType *Array*
{
    instances
        set of (index, value) pairs, no two pairs have the same index

    operations
      get(index) : return the value of the pair with this index

set(index, value) : add this pair to set of pairs, overwrite existing pair (if any) with
                the same index

}

ADT 8.1 Abstract data type specification of an array

Example 8.1 The high temperature (in degrees Farenheit) for each day of last week may be represented by the following array:

$$high = \{(\text{Sunday}, 82), (\text{Monday}, 79), (\text{Tuesday}, 85), (\text{Wednesday}, 92),$$
$$(\text{Thursday}, 88), (\text{Friday}, 89), (\text{Saturday}, 91)\}$$

Each pair of the array is composed of an index (day of week) and a value (the high temperature for that day). The name of the array is *high*. We can change the high temperature recorded for Monday to 83 by performing the following operation:

$$set(\text{Monday}, 83)$$

We can determine the high temperature for Friday by performing this operation:

$$get(\text{Friday})$$

An alternative array to represent the daily high temperature is

$$high = \{(0, 82), (1, 79), (2, 85), (3, 92), (4, 88), (5, 89), (6, 91)\}$$

In this array the index is a number rather than the name of the day. The numbers $(0, 1, 2, \cdots)$ replace the names of the days of the week (Sunday, Monday, Tuesday, $\cdots$). ∎

8.1.2   Indexing a Java Array

Arrays are a standard data structure in Java. The index (also called **subscript**) of an array in Java must be of the form

$$[i_1][i_2][i_3]\cdots[i_k]$$

where each i_j is a nonnegative integer. If k is one, the array is a one-dimensional array, and if k is two, it is a two-dimensional array. i_1 is the first coordinate of the index, i_2 the second, and i_k the kth. A 3-dimensional array `score`, whose values are of type integer, may be *created* in Java using the statement

$$\texttt{int [][][] score = new int } [u_1][u_2][u_3]$$

where the u_is are integer-valued expressions. With such a declaration, indexes with i_j in the range $0 \le i_j < u_j$, $1 \le j \le 3$ are permitted. So the array can hold a maximum of $n = u_1 u_2 u_3$ values. Since each value in the array `score` is of type `int`, 4 bytes are needed for each. The memory `sizeOf(score)` needed for the entire array is therefore $4n$ bytes. The Java compiler reserves this much memory for the array. This memory begins at byte *start* (say) and extends up to and including byte *start* + `sizeOf(score)` -1.

Java also initializes every element of an array to the default value for the data type of the array's components (Figure 1.4). The time complexity of the statement

$$\texttt{int [][][] score = new int } [u_1][u_2][u_3]$$

is $O(u_1 u_2 u_3)$ because an error of type `OutOfMemoryError` is generated when we do not have enough memory to accommodate the array; when we have enough memory for the array, it takes $\Theta(u_1 u_2 u_3)$ time to set the array elements to their default values.

8.1.3   Row- and Column-Major Mappings

Some applications of arrays require us to arrange the array elements into a serial or one-dimensional order. For example, the elements of an array can be output or input only one element at a time. Therefore, we must decide on the order in which the array elements are output or input. In Sections 8.3 and 8.4, we will see several types of two-dimensional tables (matrices) that we will map into a one-dimensional array. To accomplish this mapping, we convert the two-dimensional arrangement of the table elements into a one-dimensional arrangement.

Let n be the number of elements in a k-dimensional array. The serialization of the array is done using a mapping function, which maps the array index $[i_1][i_2][i_3] \cdots [i_k]$ into a number $map(i_1, i_2, \cdots, i_k)$ in the range $[0, \ n-1]$ such that array element with index $[i_1][i_2][i_3] \cdots [i_k]$ is mapped to position $map(i_1, i_2, \cdots, i_k)$ in the serial order.

When the number of dimensions is 1 (i.e., $k = 1$), the function

$$map(i_1) = i_1 \tag{8.1}$$

is used. When the number of dimensions is 2, the indexes may be arranged into a table with indexes that have the same first coordinate forming a row of the table and those with the same second coordinate forming a column (see Figure 8.1).

[0][0]	[0][1]	[0][2]	[0][3]	[0][4]	[0][5]
[1][0]	[1][1]	[1][2]	[1][3]	[1][4]	[1][5]
[2][0]	[2][1]	[2][2]	[2][3]	[2][4]	[2][5]

Figure 8.1 Tabular arrangement of indexes for `int score[3][6]`

The mapping is obtained by numbering the indexes by row beginning with those in the first (i.e., top) row. Within each row numbers are assigned from left to right. The result is shown in Figure 8.2(a). This way of mapping the positions in a two-dimensional array into a number in the range 0 through $n-1$ is called **row major**. The numbers are assigned in row-major order. Figure 8.2(b) shows an alternative scheme, called **column major**. In column-major order the numbers are assigned by column beginning with the left column. Within a column the numbers are assigned from top to bottom.

When row-major order is used, the mapping function is

$$map(i_1, i_2) = i_1 u_2 + i_2 \tag{8.2}$$

where u_2 is the number of columns in the array. To verify the correctness of Equation 8.2, note that by the time the index $[i_1][i_2]$ is numbered in the row-major

ing either a row- or column-major mapping. The two-dimensional array x[3][5] of ints that was considered above could be mapped into a 15-element array

```
int [] b = new int [15];
```

using either a row-major or column-major mapping. In this case a single contiguous block of memory large enough to hold 15 ints and an array length is used. The total memory required drops from 88 bytes to 64 bytes.

To access a[i][j], we must use the two-dimensional mapping function (Equation 8.2 in case a row-major mapping is used) to compute an index u and then access b[u] using the one-dimensional mapping function. Depending on whether it takes more or less time to use the one-dimensional mapping function to fetch a pointer and then follow this pointer or to compute the two-dimensional mapping function, Java's array representation scheme could be slower or faster than using a row- or column-major mapping.

8.1.6   Irregular Two-Dimensional Arrays

A two-dimensional array is regular in the sense that every row has the same number of elements. For example, every row of the 3×6 array score of Figure 8.1 has six elements. When two or more rows of an array have a different number of elements, we call the array **irregular**. Irregular arrays may be created and used as illustrated in Program 8.1. Notice that the only difference between regular and irregular arrays in that an irregular array may have rows whose length is different, whereas in a regular array all rows have the same length. The elements in regular and irregular arrays are accessed in the same way.

EXERCISES

1. (a) List the indexes of score[2][3][2][2] in row-major order.

   (b) Develop the row-major mapping function for a four-dimensional array.

2. Develop the row-major mapping function for a five-dimensional array.

3. Develop the row-major mapping function for a k-dimensional array.

4. (a) List the indexes of score[2][3][4] in column-major order. Note that now all indexes with the third coordinate equal to 0 are listed first, then those with this coordinate equal to 1, and so on. Indexes with the same third coordinate are listed in order of the second, and those with the same last two coordinates in order of the first.

   (b) Develop the column-major mapping function for a three-dimensional array.

5. (a) List the indexes of score[2][3][2][2] in column-major order.

```
public static void main(String [] args)
{
    int numberOfRows = 5;

    // define the size of each of the five rows
    int [] size = {6, 3, 4, 2, 7};

    // declare a two-dimensional array variable
    // and allocate the desired number of rows
    int [][] irregularArray = new int [numberOfRows][];

    // now allocate space for the elements in each row
    for (int i = 0; i < numberOfRows; i++)
        irregularArray[i] = new int [size[i]];

    // use the array like any regular array
    irregularArray[2][3] = 5;
    irregularArray[4][6] = irregularArray[2][3] + 2;
    irregularArray[1][1] += 3;

    // output selected elements
    System.out.println(irregularArray[2][3]);
    System.out.println(irregularArray[4][6]);
    System.out.println(irregularArray[1][1]);
    System.out.println(irregularArray[3][1]);
}
```

Program 8.1 Creating and using an irregular two-dimensional array

(b) Develop the column-major mapping function for a four-dimensional array (see Exercise 4).

6. Develop the column-major mapping function for a k-dimensional array.

7. We wish to map the elements of a two-dimensional array beginning with the bottom row and within a row from left to right.

   (a) List the indexes of score[3][5] in this order.

   (b) Develop the mapping function for score$[u_1][u_2]$.

8. We wish to map the elements of a two-dimensional array beginning with the right column and within a column from top to bottom.

(a) List the indexes of score[3][5] in this order.

(b) Develop the mapping function for score$[u_1][u_2]$.

9. A two-dimensional $m \times n$ array has mn elements.

   (a) Determine the amount of memory used when these mn elements are stored using a two-dimensional Java array and when they are stored in a one-dimensional array using row-major mapping. Assume that the elements are of type int. First do this exercise for the case $m = 10$ and $n = 2$ and then for general m and n.

   (b) How large can the ratio of the two memory requirements get?

10. A three-dimensional $m \times n \times p$ array has mnp elements.

   (a) Determine the amount of memory used when these mnp elements are stored using a three-dimensional Java array and when they are stored in a one-dimensional array using row-major mapping. Assume that the elements are of type int. First do this exercise for the case $m = 10$, $n = 4$, and $p = 2$ and then for general m, n, and p.

   (b) How large can the ratio of the two memory requirements get?

   (c) When is one scheme expected to provide faster element access than the other?

11. A four-dimensional $m \times n \times p \times q$ array has $mnpq$ elements.

   (a) Determine the amount of memory used when these $mnpq$ elements are stored using a four-dimensional Java array and when they are stored in a one-dimensional array using row-major mapping. Assume that the elements are of type int.

   (b) How large can the ratio of the two memory requirements get?

12. A k-dimensional $u_1 \times u_2 \times \cdots \times u_k$ array has $u_1 u_2 \cdots u_k$ elements.

   (a) Determine the amount of memory used when these $u_1 u_2 \cdots u_k$ elements are stored using a k-dimensional Java array and when they are stored in a one-dimensional array using row-major mapping. Assume that the elements are of type int.

   (b) How large can the ratio of the two memory requirements get?

   (c) When is one scheme expected to provide faster element access than the other?

8.2 MATRICES

8.2.1 Definitions and Operations

An $m \times n$ **matrix** is a table with m rows and n columns (Figure 8.4). m and n are the **dimensions** of the matrix.

	col 1	col 2	col 3	col 4
row 1	7	2	0	9
row 2	0	1	0	5
row 3	6	4	2	0
row 4	8	2	7	3
row 5	1	4	9	6

Figure 8.4 A 5×4 matrix

Example 8.2 Matrices are often used to organize data. For instance, in an effort to document the assets of the world, we might first produce a list of asset types of interest. This list could include mineral deposits (silver, gold, etc.); animals (lions, elephants, etc.); people (physicians, engineers, etc.); and so on. We can determine the amount of each asset type present in the country. The data can be presented as a table with one column for each country and one row for each asset type. The result is an asset matrix with a number of columns n equal to the number of countries and a number of rows m equal to the number of asset types. We use the notation $M(i, j)$ to refer to the element in row i and column j of matrix M, $1 \leq i \leq m$, $1 \leq j \leq n$. If row i represents cats and column j represents the United States, then $asset(i, j)$ would be the number of cats in the United States.

Figure 8.5(a) shows an asset matrix for four countries; the assets listed in this matrix are platinum, gold, and silver. Country B has $asset(1, 2) = 5$ units of platinum, $asset(2, 2) = 2$ units of gold, and $asset(3, 2) = 10$ units of silver.

Figure 8.5(b) shows a matrix that gives the value of one unit of each asset type for three different economic scenarios. Under scenario 3 a unit of platinum is worth $value(1, 3) = \$50$; a unit of gold is worth $value(2, 3) = \$40$; and a unit of silver is worth $value(3, 3) = \$2$. ∎

The operations most commonly performed on matrices are transpose, addition or sum, and multiplication or product. The transpose of an $m \times n$ matrix M is an $n \times m$ matrix M^T with the property

$$M^T(i, j) = M(j, i), \ 1 \leq i \leq n, \ 1 \leq j \leq m$$

asset	country			
	A	B	C	D
platinum	2	5	1	0
gold	6	2	3	8
silver	0	10	50	30

(a) *asset*

asset	scenario		
	1	2	3
platinum	20	15	50
gold	15	12	40
silver	1	1	2

(b) *value*

Figure 8.5 Asset and value matrices

The sum of two matrices is defined only when the two matrices have the same dimensions (i.e., the same number of rows and the same number of columns). The sum of two $m \times n$ matrices A and B is a third $m \times n$ matrix C such that

$$C(i,j) = A(i,j) + B(i,j), \ 1 \leq i \leq n, \ 1 \leq j \leq m \tag{8.3}$$

The product $A * B$ of an $m \times n$ matrix A and a $q \times p$ matrix B is defined only when the number of columns in A equals the number of rows in B, that is, $n = q$. When $n = q$, the product is an $m \times p$ matrix C with the property

$$C(i,j) = \sum_{k=1}^{n} A(i,k) * B(k,j), \ 1 \leq i \leq m, \ 1 \leq j \leq p$$

Example 8.3 Consider the asset matrix described in Example 8.2. Suppose that the data are being accumulated by two agencies and neither duplicates the work of the other. The result is two $m \times n$ matrices: *asset1* and *asset2*. To get the desired asset matrix, we add the two matrices *asset1* and *asset2*.

Next suppose we have another matrix *value* (as in Figure 8.5(b)) that is an $m \times s$ matrix. *value*(i,j) is the value of one unit of asset i under scenario j. Let $CV(i,j)$ be the value of the assets of country i under scenario j. Using the data of Figure 8.5, we see that the value of the assets held by country B under scenario 3 is

$$
\begin{aligned}
CV(2,3) \quad = \quad & \text{(amount of platinum} * \text{value of platinum)} \\
& + \text{(amount of gold} * \text{value of gold)} \\
& + \text{(amount of silver} * \text{value of silver)} \\
= \quad & asset(1,2) * value(1,3) + asset(2,2) * value(2,3) \\
& + asset(3,2) * value(3,3) \\
= \quad & 5 * 50 + 2 * 40 + 10 * 2 \\
= \quad & 350
\end{aligned}
$$

We see that CV is an $n \times s$ matrix and that

$$
CV(i,j) = \sum_{k=1}^{m} asset(k,i) * value(k,j) = \sum_{k=1}^{m} asset^T(i,k) * value(k,j)
$$

So CV satisfies the equation

$$
CV = asset^T * value
$$

Figure 8.6(a) gives the transpose of the asset matrix of Figure 8.5(a), and Figure 8.6(b) gives the CV matrix that corresponds to the asset and value matrices of Figure 8.5. ∎

	p	g	s
A	2	6	0
B	5	2	10
C	1	3	50
D	0	8	30

(a) $asset^T$

	1	2	3
A	130	102	340
B	140	109	350
C	115	101	270
D	150	126	380

(b) $CV = asset^T * value$

Figure 8.6 Example for matrix transpose and product

Java methods to compute the transpose of a matrix and to add and multiply two matrices represented as two-dimensional arrays were considered in Chapter 2 (Programs 2.21, 2.19, 2.22, and 2.23, respectively).

8.2.2   The Class `Matrix`

A `rows` × `cols` matrix M all of whose elements are integer may be represented as a two-dimensional integer array

```
int x[rows][cols];
```

with $M(i,j)$ being stored as `x[i-1][j-1]`. This representation requires the user to write applications using array indexes that differ from matrix indexes by 1. Alternatively, we may define the array `x` as

```
int x[rows + 1][cols + 1];
```

and not use the array positions $[0][*]$ and $[*][0]$. In this section we consider an alternative representation in which the elements of matrix M are mapped into a one-dimensional array in row-major order.

The class `Matrix` uses a one-dimensional array `element` to store, in row-major order, the `rows * cols` elements of a `rows` × `cols` matrix. Program 8.2 gives the data members and the constructor for the class. Notice that the constructor allows you to create a 0×0 matrix as well as matrices for which both `rows` > 0 and `cols` > 0.

```java
public class Matrix implements CloneableObject
{
    // data members
    int rows, cols;      // matrix dimensions
    Object [] element;   // element array

    // constructor
    public Matrix(int theRows, int theColumns)
    {
        // code to validate theRows and theColumns comes here

        // create the matrix
        rows = theRows;
        cols = theColumns;
        element = new Object [rows * cols];
    }
}
```

Program 8.2 Data members and constructor for the class `Matrix`

Program 8.3 gives the code for the clone and copy methods. The `clone` method creates a new matrix with references to clones (i.e., replicas) of the elements in the matrix that was cloned. The `copy` method, on the other hand, does not create new versions of the matrix elements. It simply creates a new matrix that references the same elements as the matrix that was copied.

```
/** @return a clone of the matrix */
public Object clone()
{
   // create a new matrix
   Matrix x = new Matrix(rows, cols);

   // copy each element of this into x
   for (int i = 0; i < rows * cols; i++)
      x.element[i] = ((CloneableObject) element[i]).clone();

   return x;
}

/** copy the references in m into this */
public void copy(Matrix m)
{
   if (this != m) // not a copy to self
   {
      rows = m.rows;
      cols = m.cols;
      element = new Object [rows * cols];

      // copy each reference
      for (int i = 0; i < rows * cols; i++)
         element[i] = m.element[i];
   }
}
```

Program 8.3 The clone and copy methods for `Matrix`

The *get* and *set* operations specified in the abstract data type *Array* (ADT 8.1) are implemented by the Java methods `get` and `set` (Program 8.4).

Program 8.5 gives the code for matrix addition. Since matrices have been mapped into one-dimensional arrays, we can add two matrices using a single `for` loop rather than two nested `for` loops as were used in Program 2.21. The codes for matrix operations such as increment (increase the value of each matrix entry by the same amount) and subtraction are similar to that for matrix addition.

The loop structure of the matrix multiplication code (Program 8.6) is similar to

```
/** @throws IndexOutOfBoundsException when i < 1
  * or j < 1 or i > rows or j > cols */
void checkIndex(int i, int j)
{
   if (i < 1 || j < 1 || i > rows || j > cols)
      throw new IndexOutOfBoundsException
                 ("i = " + i + " j = " + j +
                  " rows = " + rows + " cols = " + cols);
}

/** @return the element this(i,j)
  * @throws IndexOutOfBoundsException when i or j invalid */
public Object get(int i, int j)
{
   checkIndex(i, j);
   return element[(i - 1) * cols + j - 1];
}

/** set this(i,j) = newValue
  * @throws IndexOutOfBoundsException when i or j invalid */
public void set(int i, int j, Object newValue)
{
   checkIndex(i, j);
   element[(i - 1) * cols + j - 1] = newValue;
}
```

Program 8.4 Get and set methods for Matrix

that of Program 2.23. There are three nested `for` loops. The innermost loop uses Equation 8.3 to compute the (i,j)th element of the product matrix. When we enter the innermost loop, `element[ct]` is the first element of row i and `m.element[cm]` the first of column j. To go to the next element of row i, `ct` is to be incremented by 1 because in row-major order the elements of a row occupy consecutive positions. To go to the next element of column j, `cm` is to be incremented by `m.cols`, as consecutive elements of a column are `m.cols` positions apart in row-major order. When the innermost loop completes, `ct` is positioned at the end of row i and `cm` is at the end of column j. For the next iteration of the `for j` loop, `ct` needs to be at the start of row i and `cm` at the start of the next column of `m`. The resetting that occurs after the innermost loop completes positions `ct`. When the `for j` loop completes, `ct` should be set to the position of the first element of the next row and `cm` to that of the first element of the first column.

```
/** @return this + m
 * @throws IllegalArgumentException when matrices are incompatible */
public Matrix add(Matrix m)
{
    if (rows != m.rows || cols != m.cols)
        throw new IllegalArgumentException
                    ("The matrices are incompatible");

    // create result matrix w
    Matrix w = new Matrix(rows, cols);
    int numberOfTerms = rows * cols;
    for (int i = 0; i < numberOfTerms; i++)
        w.element[i] = ((Computable) element[i]).add(m.element[i]);

    return w;
}
```

Program 8.5 Matrix addition

Complexity

The complexity of the matrix constructor is $O(\texttt{row*cols})$ because all elements of the constructed matrix are initialized to `null`. The asymptotic complexity of the methods `clone`, `copy`, `add`, and `toString` are also $O(\texttt{row*cols})$ if we assume that the times to clone a matrix term, add two matrix terms, and convert a matrix entry into a string are all $\Theta(1)$. The matrix multiplication code has the complexity $O(\texttt{row*cols*m.cols})$.

EXERCISES

13. (a) What is the transpose of the matrix of Figure 8.4?

     (b) What is the product of the matrix of Figure 8.4 and the transpose?

14. Do Exercise 13 using the matrix of Figure 8.2(b).

15. Add code for the methods `decrement` (decrease each matrix entry by a specified amount), `input` (input a matrix), `multiplyByConstant` (multiply each matrix entry by a specified value), and `divideByConstant` to the class `Matrix`. Test your methods.

16. To the class `Matrix` add a public member `transpose()` that returns the transpose of `this`. Test your code.

```
public Matrix multiply(Matrix m)
{
   if (cols != m.rows)
      throw new IllegalArgumentException
               ("the matrices are incompatible");

   Matrix w = new Matrix(rows, m.cols);  // result matrix

   // define cursors for this, m, and w
   // initial values give location of (1,1) element
   int ct = 0, cm = 0, cw = 0;

   // compute w(i,j) for all i and j
   for (int i = 1; i <= rows; i++)
   {// compute row i of result
      for (int j = 1; j <= m.cols; j++)
      {// compute first term of w(i,j)
         Computable sum =  (Computable) ((Computable)element[ct])
                           .multiply(m.element[cm]);
         // add in remaining terms
         for (int k = 2; k <= cols; k++)
         {
            ct++;  // next term in row i of this
            cm += m.cols;  // next in column j of m
            sum.increment(((Computable) element[ct]).multiply
                          (m.element[cm]));
         }
         w.element[cw++] = sum;  // save w(i,j)

         // reset to start of row and next column
         ct -= cols - 1;
         cm = j;
      }
      // reset to start of next row and first column
      ct += cols;
      cm = 0;
   }
   return w;
}
```

Program 8.6 Matrix multiplication

17. (a) Develop the class `MatrixAs2DArray` in which a matrix is represented as a two-dimensional array. Your class should include all methods of `Matrix` as well as method to transpose a matrix.

    (b) Test your methods.

    (c) Compare the performance of the matrix addition and multiplication methods of the classes `Matrix` and `MatrixAs2DArray`. Do this comparison by making actual run-time measurements. What can you say about the merits of using the row-major mapping instead of a two-dimensional array?

8.3   SPECIAL MATRICES

8.3.1   Definitions and Applications

A **square** matrix has the same number of rows and columns. Some special forms of square matrices that arise frequently are

- **Diagonal.** M is diagonal iff $M(i,j) = 0$ for $i \neq j$; see Figures 8.7(a) and 8.8(a).

- **Tridiagonal.** M is tridiagonal iff $M(i,j) = 0$ for $|i-j| > 1$; see Figures 8.7(b) and 8.8(b).

- **Lower triangular.** M is lower triangular iff $M(i,j) = 0$ for $i < j$; see Figures 8.7(c) and 8.8(c).

- **Upper triangular.** M is upper triangular iff $M(i,j) = 0$ for $i > j$; see Figures 8.7(d) and 8.8(d).

- **Symmetric.** Matrix M is symmetric iff $M(i,j) = M(j,i)$ for all i and j; see Figure 8.8(e).

Example 8.4 Consider the six cities Gainesville, Jacksonville, Miami, Orlando, Tallahassee, and Tampa, which are all in Florida. We may number these cities 1 through 6 in the listed order. The distance between pairs of these cities may be represented using a 6×6 matrix *distance*. The ith row and column of this matrix represent the ith city, and $distance(i,j)$ is the distance between city i and city j. Figure 8.9 shows the distance matrix. Since $distance(i,j) = distance(j,i)$ for all i and j, the distance matrix is symmetric. ∎

Example 8.5 Suppose we have a stack of n cartons with carton 1 at the bottom and carton n at the top. Each carton has width w and depth d. The height of the ith carton is h_i. The volume occupied by the stack is $w * d * \sum_{i=1}^{n} h_i$. In the **stack**

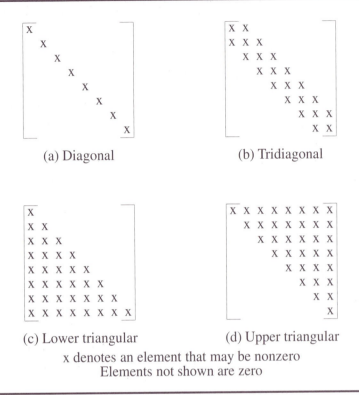

(a) Diagonal   (b) Tridiagonal

(c) Lower triangular   (d) Upper triangular

x denotes an element that may be nonzero
Elements not shown are zero

Figure 8.7 Location of nonzero elements in special matrices

folding problem, we are permitted to create substacks of cartons by selecting a fold point i and creating two adjacent stacks. One has cartons 1 through i and the other cartons $i + 1$ through n. By repeating this folding process, we may obtain several stacks of cartons. If we create s stacks, the width of the arrangement is $s * w$, its depth is d, and the height h is the height of the tallest stack. The volume of the space needed for the stacks is $s * w * d * h$. Since h is the height of a stack of boxes i through j for some i and j, $i \le j$, the possible values for h are given by the $n \times n$ matrix H where $H(i,j)$ is 0 for $i > j$ and is $\sum_{k=i}^{j} h_k$ for $i \le j$. Since the height of each carton is > 0, an $H(i,j)$ value of 0 indicates an infeasible stack height. Figure 8.10(a) shows a five-carton stack. The numbers inside each rectangle give the carton height. Figure 8.10(b) shows a folding of the five-carton stack into three stacks. The height of the largest stack is 7. The matrix H is an upper-triangular matrix, as shown in Figure 8.10(c). One application of the stack folding problem is to the folding of a stack of electronic components so as to minimize the area occupied by the folded stack (see Web site for Chapter 20).   ∎

```
2  0  0  0        2  1  0  0        2  0  0  0
0  1  0  0        3  1  3  0        5  1  0  0
0  0  4  0        0  5  2  7        0  3  1  0
0  0  0  6        0  0  9  0        4  2  7  0
```

    (a) Diagonal   (b) Tridiagonal   (c) Lower triangular

```
2  1  3  0        2  4  6  0
0  1  3  8        4  1  9  5
0  0  1  6        6  9  4  7
0  0  0  0        0  5  7  0
```

      (d) Upper triangular   (e) Symmetric

Figure 8.8 4×4 special matrices

	GN	JX	MI	OD	TL	TM
GN	0	73	333	114	148	129
JX	73	0	348	140	163	194
MI	333	348	0	229	468	250
OD	114	140	229	0	251	84
TL	148	163	468	251	0	273
TM	129	194	250	84	273	0

GN = Gainesville	OD = Orlando
JX = Jacksonville	TL = Tallahassee
MI = Miami	TM = Tampa

Distance in miles

Figure 8.9 A distance matrix (source: Rand McNally Road Atlas)

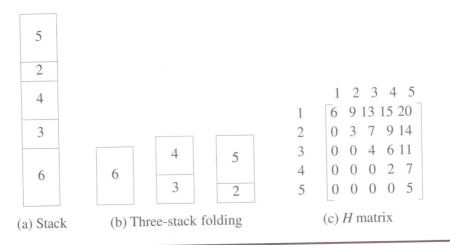

(a) Stack   (b) Three-stack folding   (c) *H* matrix

Figure 8.10 Stack folding

8.3.2   Diagonal Matrices

One way to represent a rows × rows diagonal matrix D is to use a two-dimensional array created as

```
Object [][] element = new Object [rows][rows]
```

and use element[i-1][j-1] to represent $D(i, j)$. This representation requires space for rows^2 objects, and it takes $O(\text{rows}^2)$ time to create the array. However, since a diagonal matrix contains at most rows nonzero entries, we may use a one-dimensional array created as

```
Object [] element = new Object [rows]
```

and use element[i-1] to represent $D(i, i)$. The elements of the matrix D that are not represented in the array are all known to be zero. This representation leads to the Java class DiagonalMatrix (Programs 8.7 through 8.9).

Notice that the constructor sets element[0:rows-1] to zero. Since the constructor does not create a clone of zero for each position of element, all entries of element initially reference the same object zero. Therefore, we must be careful not to use the methods increment and decrement of the interface Computable on a zero element of the diagonal. If we increment a diagonal element that has value zero, all elements with value zero (including DiagonalMatrix.zero) will get incremented.

The complexity of the constructor is $O(\text{rows})$ and that of the methods get and set is $\Theta(1)$.

```
public class DiagonalMatrix
{
   // data members
   int rows;              // matrix dimension
   Object zero;           // zero element
   Object [] element;     // element array

   // constructor
   public DiagonalMatrix(int theRows, Object theZero)
   {
      // validate theRows
      if (theRows < 1)
         throw new IllegalArgumentException("number of rows must be > 0");

      // create and initialize the matrix
      rows = theRows;
      zero = theZero;
      element = new Object [rows];
      for (int i = 0; i < rows; i++)
         element[i] = zero;
   }
```

Program 8.7 The data members and constructor for `DiagonalMatrix`

```
public Object get(int i, int j)
{
   // code to validate i and j comes here

   // determine element to return
   if (i == j)
      return element[i-1];  // diagonal element
   else
      return zero;          // nondiagonal element
}
```

Program 8.8 Get method for `DiagonalMatrix`

```
public void set(int i, int j, Object newValue)
{
    // code to validate i and j comes here

    if (i == j)
        // save the diagonal element
        element[i - 1] = newValue;
    else
        // nondiagonal element, newValue must be zero
        if (!((Zero) newValue).equalsZero())
            throw new IllegalArgumentException
                    ("nondiagonal elements must be zero");
}
```

Program 8.9 Set method for `DiagonalMatrix`

8.3.3   Tridiagonal Matrix

In a `rows` × `rows` tridiagonal matrix T, the nonzero elements lie on one of the three diagonals:

1. Main diagonal—for this, $i = j$.

2. Diagonal below main diagonal—for this, $i = j + 1$.

3. Diagonal above main diagonal—for this, $i = j - 1$.

The number of elements on these three diagonals is $3*\text{rows} - 2$. We can use a one-dimensional array `element` with $3*\text{rows} - 2$ positions to represent T. Only the elements on the three diagonals are explicitly stored. Consider the 4×4 tridiagonal matrix of Figure 8.8(b). There are 10 elements on the main diagonal and the diagonals just above and below the main diagonal. If these elements are mapped into `element` by rows, then `element[0:9]` = $[2, 1, 3, 1, 3, 5, 2, 7, 9, 0]$; if the mapping is by columns, `element` = $[2, 3, 1, 1, 5, 3, 2, 9, 7, 0]$; and if the mapping is by diagonals beginning with the lowest, then `element` = $[3, 5, 9, 2, 1, 2, 0, 1, 3, 7]$. As we can see, there are several reasonable choices for the mapping of T into `element`. Each requires a different code for the `get` and `set` methods. Suppose that the class `TridiagonalMatrix` maps by diagonals. The data members and constructor are quite similar to those of the class `Diagonal`. Program 8.10 gives the code for `get`; the code for `set` is similar and is on the Web site.

An alternative space-efficient representation of a tridiagonal array is considered in Exercise 25. This alternative representation uses an irregular array (see Section 8.1.6).

```
public Object get(int i, int j)
{
   // code to validate i and j comes here

   // determine element to return
   switch (i - j)
   {
      case 1: // lower diagonal
               return element[i - 2];
      case 0: // main diagonal
               return element[rows + i - 2];
      case -1: // upper diagonal
               return element[2 * rows + i - 2];
      default: return zero;
   }
}
```

Program 8.10 The method get for a tridiagonal matrix

8.3.4 Triangular Matrices

In an n-row lower-triangular matrix (Figure 8.7(c)), the nonzero region has one element in row 1, two in row 2, $\cdots$, and n in row n; and in an n-row upper-triangular matrix, the nonzero region has n elements in row 1, $n-1$ in row 2, $\cdots$, and one in row n. In both cases the total number of elements in the nonzero region is

$$\sum_{i=1}^{n} i = n(n+1)/2$$

Both kinds of triangular matrices may be represented by using a one-dimensional array of size $n(n+1)/2$. Consider a lower-triangular matrix L mapped into a one-dimensional array element. Two possible ways to do the mapping are by rows and by columns. If the mapping is done by rows, then the 4×4 lower-triangular matrix of Figure 8.8(c) has the mapping element[0:9] = [2, 5, 1, 0, 3, 1, 4, 2, 7, 0]. The column mapping results in element = [2, 5, 0, 4, 1, 3, 2, 1, 7, 0].

Consider element $L(i,j)$ of a lower-triangular matrix. If $i < j$, the element is in the zero region. If $i \geq j$, the element is in the nonzero region. In a row mapping, the element $L(i,j)$, $i \geq j$, is preceded by $\sum_{k=1}^{i-1} k$ nonzero region elements that are in rows 1 through $i-1$ and $j-1$ such elements from row i. The total number of nonzero region elements that precede it in a row mapping is $i(i-1)/2 + j - 1$.

24. Is the product of two tridiagonal matrices neccessarily tridiagonal?

25. Develop the class `TridiagonalAsIrregularArray` in which a tridiagonal matrix is represented using a two-dimensional array `element`. When representing an $n \times n$ matrix, rows 0 and $n-1$ of `element` have two positions each; the remaining rows have three positions each. See Section 8.1.6 to determine how to create such an array. Your class must include all methods included in the class `TridiagonalMatrix`.

    (a) Test your code.

    (b) Comment on the relative merits of the one-dimensional array representation as used in the class `TridiagonalMatrix` and the irregular array representation as used in `TridiagonalAsIrregularArray`.

26. Develop the class `LowerTriangleAsIrregularArray` in which a lower-triangular matrix is represented using a two-dimensional array `element`. When representing an $n \times n$ matrix, row i of element has i positions. See Section 8.1.6 to determine how to create such an array. Your class must include all methods included in the class `LowerTriangularMatrix`.

    (a) Test your code.

    (b) Comment on the relative merits of the one-dimensional array representation as used in the class `LowerTriangularMatrix` and the irregular array representation as used in `LowerTriangleAsIrregularArray`.

27. Develop the Java class `UpperTriangularMatrix` analogous to Program 8.11 for the case of an upper-triangular matrix. Include constructor, get, and set methods.

28. Extend the class `LowerTriangularMatrix` by including public member methods to input, output, add, and subtract lower-triangular matrices. What is the time complexity of each method?

29. Extend the class `LowerTriangularMatrix` by adding a public method `transpose` that returns the transpose of the lower-triangular matrix `this`. The transpose is an instance of the class `UpperTriangularMatrix`. What is the time complexity of your code?

30. Let A and B be two $n \times n$ lower-triangular matrices. The total number of elements in the lower triangles of the two matrices is $n(n+1)$. Devise a scheme to represent both triangles in an array `element[n+1][n]`. [*Hint:* If you join the lower triangle of A and the upper triangle of B^T, you get an $(n+1) \times n$ matrix.] Write the get and set functions for both A and B. The complexity of each should be $\Theta(1)$.

31. Write a method to multiply two lower-triangular matrices that are members of the class `LowerTriangularMatrix` (Program 8.11). The result matrix is to be stored in a two-dimensional array. What is the time complexity of your method?

32. Write a method to multiply a lower-triangular and an upper-triangular matrix mapped into one-dimensional arrays by rows. The result matrix is in a two-dimensional array. What is the time complexity of your method?

33. Suppose that symmetric matrices are stored by mapping the lower-triangular region into one-dimensional arrays by rows. Develop a Java class `LowerSymmetricMatrix` that includes public methods for the get and set operations. The complexity of your methods should be $\Theta(1)$.

34. In an $n \times n$ **C-matrix**, all terms other than those in row 1, row n, and column 1 (see Figure 8.11)) are zero. A C-matrix has at most $3n - 2$ nonzero terms. A C-matrix may be compactly stored in a one-dimensional array by first storing row 1, then row n, and then the remaining column 1 elements.

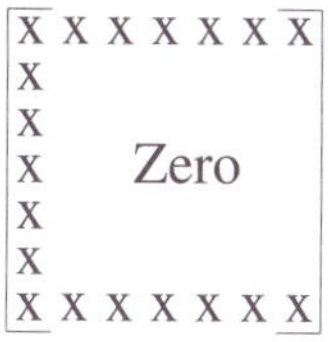

$$
\begin{array}{|l|}
\hline
\text{X X X X X X X} \\
\text{X} \\
\text{X} \\
\text{X} \qquad \text{Zero} \\
\text{X} \\
\text{X} \\
\text{X X X X X X X} \\
\hline
\end{array}
$$

x denotes a possible nonzero
All other terms are zero

Figure 8.11 A C-matrix

(a) Give a sample 4×4 C-matrix and its compact representation.

(b) Show that an $n \times n$ C-matrix has at most $3n - 2$ nonzero terms.

(c) Develop a class `CMatrix` that represents an $n \times n$ C-matrix in a one-dimensional array `element` as above. You should include the constructor and get and set public members.

35. An $n \times n$ square matrix M is an **antidiagonal** matrix iff all entries $M(i, j)$ with $i + j \neq n + 1$ equal zero.

(a) Give a sample of a 4×4 antidiagonal matrix.

(b) Show that the antidiagonal matrix M has at most n nonzero entries.

(c) Devise a way to represent an antidiagonal matrix in a one-dimensional array of size n.

(d) Use the representation of (c) to arrive at the code for the Java class `AntidiagonalMatrix` that includes public members for the get and set operations.

(e) What is the time complexity of your get and set codes?

(f) Test your code.

36. An $n \times n$ matrix T is a **Toeplitz matrix** iff $T(i,j) = T(i-1, j-1)$ for all i and j, $i > 1$ and $j > 1$.

(a) Show that a Toeplitz matrix has at most $2n - 1$ distinct elements.

(b) Develop a mapping of a Toeplitz matrix into a one-dimensional array of size $2n - 1$.

(c) Use the mapping of (b) to obtain a Java class `ToeplitzMatrix` in which a Toeplitz matrix is mapped into a one-dimensional array of size $2n - 1$. Include public members for the get and store operations. The complexity of each should be $\Theta(1)$.

(d) Write a public member to multiply two Toeplitz matrices stored as in (b). The result is stored in a two-dimensional array. What is the time complexity of your code?

⋆ 37. A **square band matrix** $D_{n,a}$ is an $n \times n$ matrix in which all the nonzero terms lie in a band centered around the main diagonal. The band includes the main diagonal and $a - 1$ diagonals below and above the main diagonal (Figure 8.12).

(a) How many elements are in the band matrix $D_{n,a}$?

(b) What is the relationship between i and j for elements $d_{i,j}$ in the band of $D_{n,a}$?

(c) Assume that the band of $D_{n,a}$ is mapped into a one-dimensional array b by diagonals, starting with the lowest diagonal. Figure 8.13 shows the representation for band matrix $D_{4,3}$ of Figure 8.12.

Develop a formula for the location of an element $d_{i,j}$ in the lower band of $D_{n,a}$ (location(d_{10}) = 2 in the example above).

(d) Develop the Java class `SquareBandMatrix` that uses the mapping of (c); include methods for the get and set operations. What is the time complexity of each method? Test your code.

(e) Develop the class `SquareBandAsIrregularArray` that uses a two-dimensional array `element` in which each row has as many positions as the width of the band at that row. For example, `element[0].width` equals a; include methods for the get and set operations. What is the time complexity of each method? Test your code.

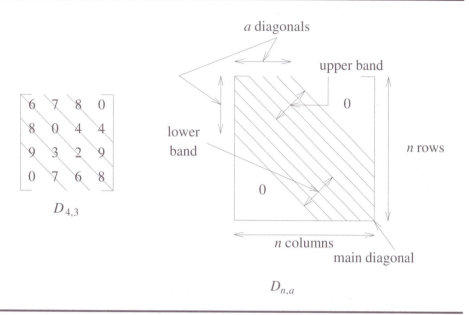

Figure 8.12 Square band matrix

b[0]	b[1]	b[2]	b[3]	b[4]	b[5]	b[6]	b[7]	b[8]	b[9]	b[10]	b[11]	b[12]	b[13]
9	7	8	3	6	6	0	2	8	7	4	9	8	4
d_{20}	d_{31}	d_{10}	d_{21}	d_{32}	d_{00}	d_{11}	d_{22}	d_{33}	d_{01}	d_{12}	d_{23}	d_{02}	d_{13}

Figure 8.13 Representation for matrix $D_{4,3}$ of Figure 8.12

(f) What are the relative merits/demerits of the two representations used in (d) and (e)?

8.4   SPARSE MATRICES

8.4.1   Motivation

An $m \times n$ matrix is said to be **sparse** if "many" of its elements are zero. A matrix that is not sparse is **dense**. The boundary between a dense and a sparse matrix is not precisely defined. Diagonal and tridiagonal $n \times n$ matrices are sparse. Each has $O(n)$ nonzero terms and $O(n^2)$ zero terms. Is an $n \times n$ triangular matrix sparse? It has at least $n(n-1)/2$ zero terms and at most $n(n+1)/2$ nonzero terms.

For the representation schemes in this section to be competitive over the standard two-dimensional array representation, the number of nonzero terms will need to be less than $n^2/3$ and in some cases less than $n^2/5$. In this context we will classify triangular matrices as dense.

Sparse matrices such as diagonal and tridiagonal matrices have sufficient structure in their nonzero regions that we can devise a simple representation scheme whose space requirements equal the size of the nonzero region. In this section we are concerned with sparse matrices with an irregular or unstructured nonzero region.

Example 8.6 A supermarket is conducting a study of the mix of items purchased by its customers. For this study, data are gathered for the purchases made by 1000 customers. These data are organized into a matrix, *purchases*, with $purchases(i, j)$ being the quantity of item i purchased by customer j. Suppose that the supermarket has an inventory of 10,000 different items. The *purchases* matrix is therefore a $10,000 \times 1000$ matrix. If the average customer buys 20 different items, only about 20,000 of the 10,000,000 matrix entries are nonzero. However, the distribution of the nonzero entries does not fall into any well-defined structure.

The supermarket has a $10,000 \times 1$ matrix, *price*. $price(i)$ is the selling price of one unit of item i. The matrix $spent = purchases^T * price$ is a 1000×1 matrix that gives the amount spent by each customer. If a two-dimensional array is used to represent the matrix *purchases*, an unnecessarily large amount of memory is used and the time required to compute *spent* is also unnecessarily large. ∎

8.4.2   Representation Using a Single Linear List

The nonzero entries of an irregular sparse matrix may be mapped into a linear list in row-major order. For example, the nonzero entries of the 4×8 matrix of Figure 8.14(a) in row-major order are 2, 1, 6, 7, 3, 9, 8, 4, 5.

```
0 0 0 2 0 0 1 0
0 6 0 0 7 0 0 3
0 0 0 9 0 8 0 0
0 4 5 0 0 0 0 0
```

terms	0	1	2	3	4	5	6	7	8
row	1	1	2	2	2	3	3	4	4
col	4	7	2	5	8	4	6	2	3
value	2	1	6	7	3	9	8	4	5

(a) A 4×8 matrix   (b) Its linear list representation

Figure 8.14 A sparse matrix and its linear list representation

To reconstruct the matrix structure, we need to record the originating row and column for each nonzero entry. So each element of the array into which the sparse matrix is mapped needs to have three fields: `row` (the row of the matrix entry), `col` (the column of the matrix entry), and `value` (the value of the matrix entry). For this purpose we define the class `MatrixTerm` that has these three data members.

The nonzero entries of the matrix of Figure 8.14(a) may be stored in a linear list `terms` in row-major order as shown in Figure 8.14(b). The row labeled `terms` gives the list index of a matrix term. In addition to storing the nonzero entries of the matrix, we need to store the number of rows and columns in the matrix.

Suppose that our linear list `terms` is an instance of `ArrayList`. If we assume that the nine nonzero elements of Figure 8.14(a) are stored as `int`s, the linear list representation requires 8 (for number of rows and columns) + 9 * 12 (each nonzero element requires the storage of its row, column, and value; 4 bytes each) = 116 bytes. This count ignores the additional space needed to store the number of elements in `terms` and the capacity of `terms`. If we had represented our matrix using a 4 × 8 array, the space used would have been 32 * 4 = 128 bytes (ignoring the space needed to store the matrix dimensions). The space saving achieved by the linear list representation isn't much in this case. However, for the matrix *purchase* (see our supermarket example, Example 8.6), the array-based representation takes approximately 60,000 * 4 = 240,000 bytes, whereas the two-dimensional array representation needs approximately 10,000,000 * 4 = 40,000,000 bytes. The space saving is 39,760,000 bytes! A corresponding amount of time is saved creating the linear list representation over initializing a two-dimensional array.

The linear list representation of a sparse matrix does not lead to efficient implementations of the get and set operations. The get operation takes $O(\log$ [number of nonzero entries]) time when an array-based linear list and binary search are used. The set operation takes O(number of nonzero entries) time because we may need to move this many entries to make room for the new term. Both opertions take O(number of nonzero entries) time when a linked linear list is used. Each of these operations takes $\Theta(1)$ time using the standard two-dimensional array representation. However, matrix operations such as transpose, add, and multiply can be performed efficiently.

The Class SparseMatrixAsExtendedArrayList

Based on our experiments of Section 6.1.6, we are motivated to use an array-based representation for `terms`. We would like to use the class `ArrayList`. However, this class is missing a method `setSize`, which we need in this application. (This method, which is available in the class `Vector`, adds `null` elements to the right end or removes elements from the right end, as necessary, to make the list size equal to a specified value.) To overcome this deficiency, we extend `ArrayList` to include a `setSize` method. The extended class is called `ExtendedArrayList`.

Program 8.12 gives the data members and constructors for the class `SparseMatrixAsExtendedArrayList`, which uses the row-major mapping of a sparse matrix into an `ExtendedArrayList`. Notice that the constructors require the user to provide the zero element for the data type of the matrix. This zero element could be used during output, for example, because only nonzero elements are stored explicitly. The zero element is also useful in case we need to determine the data type of the matrix elements.

```
// data members
int rows;        // number of rows in matrix
int cols;        // number of columns in matrix
Object zero;     // zero element
ExtendedArrayList terms;   // list of nonzero terms

// constructors
public SparseMatrixAsExtendedArrayList(int theRows, int theColumns,
                          int estimatedMaxSize, Object theZero)
{
   // code to validate theRows and theColumns comes here

   rows = theRows;
   cols = theColumns;
   zero = theZero;
   terms = new ExtendedArrayList(estimatedMaxSize);
}

/** use a default estimated maximum size of 1 */
public SparseMatrixAsExtendedArrayList(int theRows, int theColumns,
                          Object theZero)
   {this(theRows, theColumns, 1, theZero);}

/** defaults are rows = cols = estimatedMaxSize = 1 */
public SparseMatrixAsExtendedArrayList(Object theZero)
   {this(1, 1, 1, theZero);}
```

Program 8.12 Data members and constructors of SparseMatrixAsExtended-ArrayList

Program 8.13 converts a sparse matrix into a string. This conversion is done by using an iterator to sequence through the elements in the **ExtendedArrayList** in left-to-right order. This order gets the nonzero matrix elements in row-major order. If the output string is printed or displayed on a screen, we will see one matrix term per line. Notice that we can replace the use of the iterator and the **while** loop with the single statement

```
s.append(terms.toString());
```

This statement will put the terms into a bracket-enclosed, comma-separated string.

We cannot use this statement to output one term per line with no commas in the output string.

```java
public String toString()
{
   StringBuffer s = new StringBuffer();

   // put matrix characteristics into s
   s.append("rows = " + rows + "  columns = " + cols + "\n");
   s.append("number of nonzero terms = " + terms.size() + "\n");

   // put terms, one per line into s
   // use an ExtendedArrayList iterator
   Iterator y = terms.iterator();
   while (y.hasNext())
      s.append(y.next().toString() + "\n");

   // create equivalent String
   return new String(s);
}
```

Program 8.13 Convert a sparse matrix into a string

Program 8.14 inputs the sparse matrix entries in row-major order and sets up the internal representation. Exercise 42 considers refinements of this code.

Matrix Transpose

Program 8.15 gives the code for the **transpose** method. We first create a sparse matrix instance t such that t.terms has a capacity equal to the number of nonzero entries in the matrix being transposed; t will eventually be the transpose of this. Even though the list t.terms is empty now, we set its size equal to the number of nonzero entries it will eventually have. This step is necessary so that we can use the methods of ArrayList to place entries into arbitrary positions in t.terms. If we do not change the size of t.terms in this manner, then we must grow the linear list one element at a time. As we will see, when we transpose a sparse matrix, the zeroth element of the matrix being transposed may be the sixth (say) element of the transpose. We cannot insert an element at position 6 of a linear list unless the list size is currently 6 or more. By beginning with a list whose size equals its capacity (even though all elements are null), we can essentially use the list as a one-dimensional array. The element in any position of the list can be assigned a new value using the method set.

```
public static SparseMatrixAsExtendedArrayList input(Object theZero,
                                     MyInputStream stream)
{
   Method inputMethod;
   Object [] inputMethodArgs = {stream};
   Class [] parameterTypes = {MyInputStream.class};
   try
   {
      // get the proper method to be used to read in the values
      inputMethod = theZero.getClass().
                    getMethod("input", parameterTypes);

      // create a default matrix for input
      SparseMatrixAsExtendedArrayList x =
           new SparseMatrixAsExtendedArrayList(theZero);

      // input matrix characteristics
      System.out.println("Enter number of rows, columns, " +
                         "and nonzero terms");
      x.rows = stream.readInteger();
      x.cols = stream.readInteger();
      int size = stream.readInteger();
      x.terms = new ExtendedArrayList(size);

      // should validate input values here, left as an exercise

      // input the nonzero terms
      for (int i = 0; i < size; i++)
      {
         System.out.println("Enter row and column of term " + (i+1));
         MatrixTerm newTerm = new MatrixTerm();
         newTerm.row = stream.readInteger();
         newTerm.col = stream.readInteger();
         newTerm.value = inputMethod.invoke(null, inputMethodArgs);
         // should validate input, left as an exercise

         x.terms.add(i, newTerm);  // put into the EAL
      }
      return x;
   }
```

Program 8.14 Input a sparse matrix (continues)

```
    catch (Exception e)
    {System.out.println(e); throw new IllegalArgumentException
        ("SparseMatrixAsExtendedArrayList.input");
    }
}
```

Program 8.14 Input a sparse matrix (concluded)

Next we create two arrays `colSize` and `rowNext`. `colSize[i]` is the number of nonzero entries of the input matrix `this` that are in column i, and `rowNext[i]` denotes the index in `t` for the next nonzero term that is in row i of the transpose. For the sparse matrix of Figure 8.14(a), `colSize[1:8]` = [0, 2, 1, 2, 1, 1, 1, 1]. Prior to the generation of any entries in the transpose matrix, `rowNext[1:8]` = [0, 0, 2, 3, 5, 6, 7, 8].

`colSize` is computed in the first `while` loop by simply examining each term of the input matrix using an iterator. `rowNext` is computed in the `for` loop. In this `for` loop, `rowNext[i]` is set to be the number of entries in rows 0 through `i-1` of the transpose matrix `t`, which is equal to the number of entries in columns 0 through `i-1` of the input matrix `this`. Finally, in the last `while` loop, the nonzero entries are copied from the input matrix to their correct positions in `t`.

Although Program 8.15 is more complex than its counterpart for matrices stored as two-dimensional arrays (see Program 2.19), for matrices with many zero entries, Program 8.15 is faster. It is not too difficult to see that computing the transpose of the *purchases* matrix of Example 8.6 using the linear list representation and method `transpose` is much faster than using a two-dimensional array representation and the transpose function of Program 2.19. The time complexity of `transpose` is $O(\texttt{cols+terms.size()})$.

Adding Two Matrices

Our code to add two matrices uses the top-level nested class `TIPair`, which has the data members `term` (a nonzero term of the matrix) and `index` (the row-major index of the term plus the number of columns in the matrix; it is slightly easier to compute this quantity than it is to compute the row-major index alone).

The add method for sparse matrices uses the method `nextPair` (Program 8.16), which returns the next term in a matrix (the next term is found by using the iterator `iter`) and the index of this term. The value `null` is returned in case there is no next term in the matrix.

The code of Program 8.17 computes `w = this + m` and then returns the matrix `w`. The result matrix `w` is produced by scanning the entries of the two input matrices from left to right. This scan is done using two iterators—`it` (for the matrix `this`)

```
/** @return the transpose of this
  * matrix values are not cloned */
public SparseMatrixAsExtendedArrayList transpose()
{
   int size = terms.size();  // number of nonzero terms
   // create result matrix
   SparseMatrixAsExtendedArrayList t =
         new SparseMatrixAsExtendedArrayList(cols,
                                     rows, size, zero);
   // make it look like t has size elements already
   t.terms.setSize(size);

   // initialize to compute transpose
   // default initial values are 0
   int [] colSize = new int[cols + 1];
   int [] rowNext = new int[cols + 1];

   // find number of entries in each column of this
   // use an ExtendedArrayList iterator
   Iterator y = terms.iterator();
   while (y.hasNext())
      colSize[((MatrixTerm) y.next()).col]++;

   // find the starting point of each row of t
   // rowNext[1] is 0 by default
   for (int i = 2; i <= cols; i++)
      rowNext[i] = rowNext[i - 1] + colSize[i - 1];

   // perform the transpose copying from this to t
   // initialize iterator
   y = terms.iterator();
   while (y.hasNext())
   {
      MatrixTerm x = (MatrixTerm) y.next();
      MatrixTerm w = new MatrixTerm(x.col, x.row, x.value);
      int j = rowNext[x.col]++; // position in t
      // change the element at j
      t.terms.set(j, w);
   }
   return t;
}
```

Program 8.15 Transpose a sparse matrix

```
static TIPair nextPair(Iterator iter, int columns)
{
   if (iter.hasNext())
   {
      MatrixTerm t = (MatrixTerm) iter.next();
      // row-major index plus number of columns in matrix
      int index = t.row * columns + t.col;
      return new TIPair(t, index);
   }
   else return null;
}
```

Program 8.16 Method to return the next term and its index

and im (for the matrix m). Let tPair.term and mPair.term, respectively, denote the terms of the matrices this and m that we are currently examining. On each iteration of the while loop, we need to determine whether the position in w of the term tPair.term is before, at the same place as, or after that of mPair.term. We can make this determination by comparing the row-major index of these two terms. However, it is actually simpler to compute and compare the row-major index plus the number of columns in the matrix, as we do in method nextPair (Program 8.16).

The first while loop of the method add is iterated at most terms.size() + m.terms.size() times, as on each iteration the iterator it for this or the iterator im for m or both advance by one element. The second while loop is iterated at most terms.size() times, while the third is iterated $O(m.terms.size())$ times. Also, each iteration of each loop takes constant time. So the complexity of add is $O(\text{terms.size()}+\text{m.terms.size()})$. If the two matrices this and m were represented as two-dimensional arrays, it would take $O(rows*cols)$ time to add them. When terms.size()+m.terms.size() is much less than rows*cols, the sparse matrix representation results in a faster implementation.

8.4.3   Representation Using Many Linear Lists

An alternative sparse matrix representation results when we store the nonzero entries in each row in a separate linear list. In exploring this alternative, we use linked lists; array-based lists may be used instead (Exercise 52).

The Representation

We link together the nonzero entries in each row to form a chain (called a row chain) as shown by the unshaded nodes of Figure 8.15.

```
public SparseMatrixAsExtendedArrayList
        add(SparseMatrixAsExtendedArrayList m)
{
   // verify compatibility
   if (rows != m.rows || cols != m.cols)
      throw new IllegalArgumentException
            ("the matrices are incompatible");

   // create result matrix
   SparseMatrixAsExtendedArrayList w =
         new SparseMatrixAsExtendedArrayList(rows, cols, zero);

   // define iterators for this and m
   Iterator it = terms.iterator();
   Iterator im = m.terms.iterator();
   TIPair tPair = nextPair(it, cols);  // a pair from this
   TIPair mPair = nextPair(im, cols);  // a pair from m

   // move through this and m adding like terms
   while (tPair != null && mPair != null)
      if (tPair.index < mPair.index)
      {// term from this comes first in row-major order
         MatrixTerm q = tPair.term;
         w.terms.add(w.terms.size(),
                     new MatrixTerm(q.row, q.col, q.value));
         tPair = nextPair(it, cols);
      }
      else if (tPair.index == mPair.index)
          {// both in same position
             // append to w only if sum is not zero
             Zero sum = (Zero) ((Computable) tPair.term.value)
                                     .add(mPair.term.value);
             if (!sum.equalsZero())
                w.terms.add(w.terms.size(),
                new MatrixTerm(tPair.term.row, tPair.term.col, sum));
             tPair = nextPair(it, cols);
             mPair = nextPair(im, cols);
          }
```

Program 8.17 Adding two sparse matrices (continues)

```
          else
          {// term from m comes first in row-major order
             MatrixTerm q = mPair.term;
             w.terms.add(w.terms.size(),
                         new MatrixTerm(q.row, q.col, q.value));
             mPair = nextPair(im, cols);
          }

   // copy over remaining terms from this
   if (tPair != null)
   {
      MatrixTerm q = tPair.term;
      w.terms.add(w.terms.size(),
                  new MatrixTerm(q.row, q.col, q.value));
   }
   while (it.hasNext())
   {
      MatrixTerm q = (MatrixTerm) it.next();
      w.terms.add(w.terms.size(),
                  new MatrixTerm(q.row, q.col, q.value));
   }

   // copy over remaining terms from m
   if (mPair != null)
   {
      MatrixTerm q = mPair.term;
      w.terms.add(w.terms.size(),
                  new MatrixTerm(q.row, q.col, q.value));
   }
   while (im.hasNext())
   {
      MatrixTerm q = (MatrixTerm) im.next();
      w.terms.add(w.terms.size(),
                  new MatrixTerm(q.row, q.col, q.value));
   }
   return w;
}
```

Program 8.17 Adding two sparse matrices (concluded)

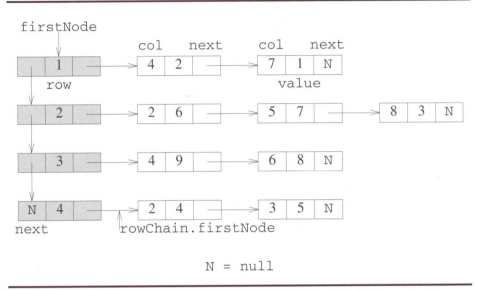

N = null

Figure 8.15 Linked representation of matrix of Figure 8.14(a)

Each unshaded node represents a nonzero term of the sparse matrix. Each node in a row chain has the fields (data members) `element` and `next`. The `element` field of a node in a row chain has two subfields—`col` (the column number for the term) and `value` (the value of the term). Figure 8.16(a) shows the structure of a node on a row chain. Subfields of `element` are not shaded.

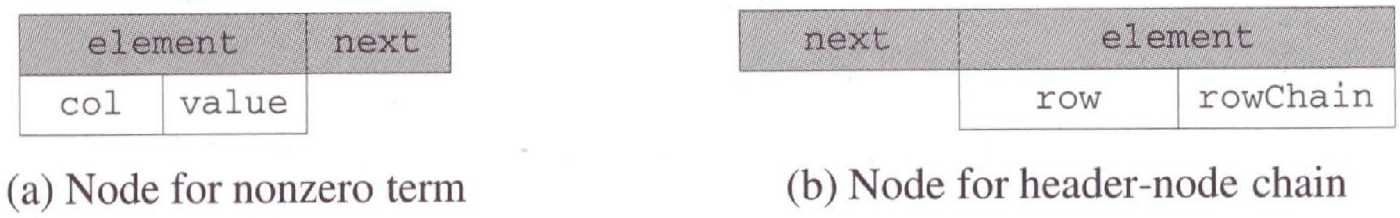

(a) Node for nonzero term   (b) Node for header-node chain

Figure 8.16 Node structures in linked sparse matrix representation

Row chains are created only for rows that have at least one nonzero term. The nodes on a row chain are linked in ascending order of their `col` value. The row chains (i.e., unshaded chains) are collected together by using another chain (called the header-node chain) as shown by the shaded nodes of Figure 8.15. Like a node on a row chain, a node on the header-node chain has two fields—`element` and `next`. The `element` field of a node on the header-node chain has two subfields—`row` (row number for corresponding row chain) and `rowChain` (the chain of unshaded nodes;

`rowChain.firstNode` points to the first unshaded node). Figure 8.16(b) shows the structure of a node on the header-node chain.

The nodes on the header-node chain are linked together in ascending order of their `row` value. Each node on the header-node chain may be viewed as the header node of a row chain. An empty header-node chain represents a matrix with no nonzero terms.

Element Types

The class `RowElement` defines a data type suitable for the elements of a row chain. Its data members are `col` (column index of the term) and `value` (value of the term). The class `HeaderElement` defines a corresponding class for elements in the header-node chain. Its data members are `row` (index of row) and `rowChain` (the actual chain, data type is `ExtendedChain`).

The Class `LinkedSparseMatrix`

The class that uses the representation of Figure 8.15 is called `LinkedSparseMatrix`. The row chains and header-node chain of Figure 8.15 are actually represented as instances of `ExtendedChain` because we will need to append (i.e., add at the right end) elements to these chains. In an `ExtendedChain` (Program 6.10) an element can be appended in $\Theta(1)$ time, whereas it takes $\Theta(\text{size of chain})$ time to append to an instance of `Chain` (Program 6.2). Java's doubly linked circular list class `Linked-List` may be used instead of `ExtendedChain`, though we do not need the doubly linked capability.

The data members and constructors for `LinkedSparseMatrix` are almost the same as those for `SparseMatrixAsExtendedArrayList`; the exception is that the data member `terms` is replaced by `headerChain`, which is of type `ExtendedChain`. The codes for the `toString` and `input` methods also are similar to the corresponding codes for `SparseMatrixAsExtendedArrayList`. These similar codes are on the Web site.

The Method `LinkedSparseMatrix.transpose`

For the transpose operation, we use bins to collect the terms of the input matrix `this` that belong in the same row of the result. `bin[i]` is a chain for the terms of row `i` of the result matrix `t`. In the nested `while` loops of Program 8.18, we examine the terms of `this` in row-major order by going down the header-node chain of the input matrix and making a left-to-right traversal of each row chain. We move along the header-node and row chains by using an iterator `ih` for the header-node chain and another iterator `ir` for the row chain. Each term encountered in this ordered traversal of the matrix `this` is appended to the bin chain for its row in the result. The bin chains are collected together in the `for` loop to create the header-node chain of the result.

CHAPTER 9

STACKS

BIRD'S-EYE VIEW

Stacks and queues are, perhaps, the most frequently used data structures. Both are restricted versions of the linear or ordered list data structure studied extensively in Chapters 5 through 7. In fact, stacks are so widely used that the Java language provides an array-based implementation, the class `java.util.Stack`, which is derived from the class `java.util.Vector`. We will study stacks in this chapter and queues in the next. Even though Java provides an implementation of a stack, we obtain our own stack implementations just to learn how to implement a stack.

The stack data structure is obtained from a linear list by restricting the insertions and removals to take place from the same end. As a result, a stack is a last-in-first-out (LIFO) structure. Since a stack is a special kind of linear list, it is natural to derive stack classes from corresponding linear list classes. Therefore, we may derive an array-based stack class from any of the array-based linear list representations of Chapter 5; a linked-stack class may be derived from the class `Chain` (Program 6.2). Although these derivations simplify the programming task, they result in code that incurs a significant run-time penalty. Since a stack is a very basic data structure that many applications employ, we also develop array-based and linked-stack classes from scratch (i.e., not derived from any other class). These latter classes provide improved run-time performance over their derived counterparts.

Six application codes that make use of stacks are also developed. The first is a simple program to match left and right parentheses in an expression. The second is the classical Towers of Hanoi problem in which we move disks one at a time from a source tower to a destination tower using one intermediary tower; each tower operates as a stack. The third application uses stacks to represent shunting tracks in a railroad yard. The objective is to rearrange the cars in a train into the desired order. The fourth application is from the computer-aided design of circuits field. In this application we use a stack to determine whether a switch box can be feasibly routed. The fifth application revisits the offline equivalence class problem introduced in Section 7.7.1. A stack enables us to determine the equivalence classes in linear time. The final application considered in this chapter is the classical rat-in-a-maze problem in which we are to find a path from the entrance of a maze to its exit. You are urged to go through this application very carefully, as its treatment in this chapter illustrates many software-engineering principles. Additional stack applications appear in later chapters.

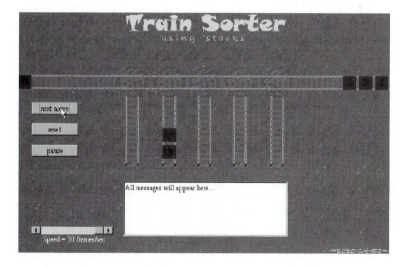

Rearrange railroad cars—On the Web

9.1 DEFINITION AND APPLICATIONS

Definition 9.1 *A* **stack** *is a linear list in which insertions (also called additions and pushes) and removals (also called deletions and pops) take place at the same end. This end is called the* **top***; the other end of the list is called the* **bottom***.* ■

Figure 9.1(a) shows a stack with four elements. Suppose we wish to add element E to the stack of Figure 9.1(a). This element will have to be placed on top of element D, giving us the configuration of Figure 9.1(b). If we are to delete an element from the stack of Figure 9.1(b), it will be element E. Following the deletion, the configuration of Figure 9.1(a) results. If we perform three successive deletions on the stack of Figure 9.1(b), the stack of Figure 9.1(c) results.

```
                              E ←top
    D←top                     D
    C                         C
    B                         B              B←top
    A←bottom                  A←bottom       A←bottom
       (a)                       (b)            (c)
```

Figure 9.1 Stack configurations

From the preceding discussion, we see that a stack is a LIFO list. Lists of this type appear frequently in computing.

Example 9.1 [Stacks in the Real World]

- If you examine the paper tray of your printer (or copy machine), you will see that the next sheet that gets used is the one at the top; when you add a sheet to the paper tray, you add it to the top. So the paper tray maintains a stack of paper; the paper tray works in a LIFO manner. This LIFO behavior of the paper tray is quite convenient when you want to do that occasional letter on a preprinted letterhead sheet or you want to print the next page on a preprinted form—you simply put the letterhead sheet or form at the top of the paper tray and smile when the printer prints on the desired sheet.

- Walk into a cafeteria, and you'll see a stack of trays. When you get into the food line, you pick up a tray from the top of this stack (unless, of course, you spot a new tray not too far from the top); when the tray stack is replenished, trays are added at the top of the stack. So barring anomalous behavior (like picking up a new tray that is not at the stack top), the tray stack in a cafeteria operates just like the stack data structure we have defined—the tray stack works in a LIFO manner.

- The next time you are in a college bookstore at the start of a term, observe any pile of heavy text books. Each student who needs the book removes and purchases the book at the top of the pile. When the pile gets sufficently low, a bookstore employee mysteriously appears and adds books to the top of the pile. The book pile works in a LIFO manner—the pile is a stack.   ■

Example 9.2 [Recursion] How does your computer run a recursive method? Recursive methods are correctly executed using a **recursion stack**. When a method is invoked, a return address (i.e., the location of the program instruction to execute once the invoked method completes) and the values of all local variables and formal parameters of the invoked method are stored on the recursion stack. When a `return` is executed, the values of local variables and formal parameters are restored to their values prior to the method invocation (these prior values are at the top of the recursion stack) and program execution resumes from the return address, which is also at the top of the stack.

Suppose the recursive sum program (Program 1.26) is invoked from the method `outerMethod` using the statement

```
y = rSum(x,2);
```

This statement is compiled into code to invoke `rSum` and is followed by code to store the value returned by `rSum` into `y`. Let l_1 be the address of the first instruction in the code to store the returned value into `y`. The `else` clause of Program 1.26 is compiled into code to invoke `rSum`, followed by code to invoke `add`, followed by code to typecast the value returned by `add` into the datatype `Computable`, followed by code to return this typecast value. Let l_2 be the address of the first instruction in the code to invoke `add`.

When the invocation `rSum(x,2)` is made from `outerMethod`, the return address (l_1) and the the values of the formal parameters and local variables of `rSum` are saved on the recursion stack as a tuple of the form

(return address, values of formal parameters, values of local variables)

Since `a` and `n` have their default values at this time, the tuple (l_1, `null`, 0) is added to the recursion stack (note that `rSum` has no local variables) and the formal parameters of `rSum` are assigned their new values. The parameter `a` is assigned the value $r(x)$, which denotes the reference in `x`, and `n` is assigned the value 2. Execution continues with the first instruction of `rSum`.

When `rSum` is invoked from its `else` clause, the tuple (l_2, $r(a) = r(x)$, 2) is added to the stack; the formal parameters of `rSum` are assigned their new values ($r(a) = r(x)$ and 1); and we continue with the first instruction of `rSum`. The `else` clause is entered again, and (l_2, $r(a) = r(x)$, 1) is added to the stack; the formal parameters are assigned their new values ($r(a) = r(x)$ and 0); and we proceed to the first instruction of `rSum`. Now since `n` equals 0, the value 0 is to be returned by rSum. How do we know whether we should return to l_1 or to l_2? This determination is made by removing the top tuple from the stack. The stack contents (from bottom to top) are

$$[(l_1, \texttt{null}, 0), (l_2, r(x), 2), (l_2, r(x), 1)]$$

The top tuple $(l_2, r(x), 1)$ is removed from the stack, the values of the formal parameters and local variables of the method we are exiting (i.e., rSum) are reset (a is reset to $v(x)$ and n is reset to 1), and we continue with the instruction at l_2. The sum 0 + x[0] is computed, and another return executed. At this time the recursion stack looks like this:

$$[(l_1, \texttt{null}, 0), (l_2, r(x), 2)]$$

The top tuple $(l_2, r(x), a)$ is removed from the stack, a is reset to $v(x)$, n is reset to 2, the computed sum 0 + a[0] is to be returned, and we continue with the instruction at l_2. This time a[1] is added to 0 + a[0], the top tuple $(l_1, \texttt{null}, 0)$ is removed from the stack, a is set to null, n is set to 0, the value 0 + a[0] + a[1] is to be returned, and we continue at l_1. ■

EXERCISES

1. The following sequence of operations is done on an initially empty stack: push A, push B, pop, push T, push T, push U, pop, pop, push A, push D. Draw figures similar to those of Figure 9.1 to show the stack configuration after each operation.

2. Do Exercise 1 for the operation sequence: push S, push S, push T, push U, pop, pop, push A, push L, push G, pop, push C, push A, push B, pop, pop.

3. Identify three additional real-world applications of a stack.

4. Show the contents of the recursion stack following each invocation of and each return from the method rSum (Program 1.26). The initial invocation is rSum(x,3).

5. Show the contents of the recursion stack following each invocation of and each return from the method factorial (Program 1.24). The initial invocation is factorial(3).

6. Show the contents of the recursion stack following each invocation of and each return from the method perm (Program 1.27). The initial invocation is perm(x, 0, 2).

9.2   THE ABSTRACT DATA TYPE

The ADT stack is specified in ADT 9.1. We have chosen the stack operation names to be the same as the method names used in the class `java.util.Stack`. The specification of the *push* operation differs from the method `java.util.Stack.-push`; our operation returns nothing, but Java's `push` method returns the item added to the stack. There is no reason for the *push* operation to return its input x.

AbstractDataType *Stack*
{
    instances
        linear list of elements; one end is called the *bottom*; the other is the *top*;

    operations
      empty() : Return `true` if the stack is empty, return `false` otherwise;

      peek() : Return the top element of the stack;

    push(x) : Add element x at the top of the stack;

      pop() : Remove the top element from the stack and return it;
}

ADT 9.1 The abstract data type stack

Program 9.1 gives the Java interface that corresponds to the *Stack* abstract data type.

```
public interface Stack
{
    public boolean empty();
    public Object peek();
    public void push(Object theObject);
    public Object pop();
}
```

Program 9.1 The Java interface `Stack`

9.3   ARRAY REPRESENTATION

Since a stack is a linear list with the restriction that additions and deletions take place at the same end, we may use any of the linear list representations of Section 5.3.

When we identify the stack top with the right end of the array-based linear list, the `push` and `pop` operations correspond to the best case for linear list inserts and removes. Consequently, both operations take $O(1)$ time.

9.3.1   Implementation as a Subclass

The experimental results of Section 5.6 indicate that the best stack performance (which corresponds to best-case insert and remove from a linear list) is expected when we derive from `ArrayLinearList`. Program 9.2 gives the class `DerivedArrayStack`, which is a subclass of `ArrayLinearList`. Other derived array-based stack classes such as `DerivedVectorStack`, which is a subclass of `Vector`, may be obtained by replacing all occurrences of `DerivedArrayStack` by `DerivedVectorStack` and changing the clause `extends ArrayLinearList` to `extends Vector`.

The first constructor for `DerivedArrayStack` simply invokes the constructor for the superclass `ArrayLinearList`, which allocates a one-dimensional array whose capacity (length) is `initialCapacity`. The second (i.e., default) constructor invokes the first constructor with an actual parameter value of 10. The codes for the remaining methods of `DerivedArrayStack` are also straightforward.

Complexity of `DerivedArrayStack` Methods

The complexity of the first constructor method is $O(\texttt{initialCapacity})$ because it takes $\Theta(\texttt{initialCapacity})$ time to initialize the array `ArrayLinearList.element`. The complexity of `push` is $\Theta(1)$ except when the addition of an element requires us to increase the capacity of the stack. In this latter case the complexity is $O(\texttt{capacity})$. The complexity of each of the remaining methods is $\Theta(1)$.

Comments on `DerivedArrayStack`

The codes for `peek` and `pop` check whether the stack is empty before they invoke the inherited method `super.get`. Since `super.get` will throw an exception when invoked with an empty stack, we can eliminate the stack empty check from `peek` and `push` without affecting the program outcome. Although the elimination of this check would reduce the run time of `peek` and `push`, the message output when an exception is thrown will pertain to a problem with an array-based linear list and not a stack. Such a message will bewilder the user who has no knowledge of the fact that `DerivedArrayStack` is implemented as a subclass of `ArrayLinearList`. An alternative is to replace the check for an empty stack by a `try-catch` construct in which the `catch` block catches the exception thrown by `super.get` and throws a new and meaningful exception in its place. Program 9.3 shows the code for the method `peek` when we use this alternative. The corresponding class is called `DerivedArrayStackWithCatch`.

Note that the codes for the `DerivedArrayStack` methods access only the public methods of `ArrayLinearList`. Consequently, we can obtain array-based stack im-

```
public class DerivedArrayStack extends ArrayLinearList
                               implements Stack
{
   // constructors
   /** create a stack with the given initial capacity */
   public DerivedArrayStack(int initialCapacity)
      {super(initialCapacity);}

   /** create a stack with initial capacity 10 */
   public DerivedArrayStack()
      {this(10);}

   // methods
   /** @return true iff stack is empty */
   public boolean empty()
      {return isEmpty();}


   /** @return top element of stack */
   public Object peek()
   {
      if (empty())
         throw new EmptyStackException();
      return get(size() - 1);
   }

   /** add theElement to the top of the stack */
   public void push(Object theElement)
      {add(size(), theElement);}

   /** remove top element of stack and return it */
   public Object pop()
   {
      if (empty())
         throw new EmptyStackException();
      return remove(size() - 1);
   }
}
```

Program 9.2 An array-based stack class derived from `ArrayLinearList`

```
public Object peek()
{
   try {return get(size() - 1);}
   catch (IndexOutOfBoundsException e)
   {
      throw new EmptyStackException();
   }
}
```

Program 9.3 Implementation of peek using the try-catch construct

plementations that are subclasses of ArrayList and Vector by making very simple changes to the code for DerivedArrayStack. In fact, if we do not wish to change the name of the stack class, we need only change the extends clause! Had our methods of DerivedArrayStack used the data members of ArrayLinearList, it would take a lot more effort to develop array-based stack implementations that are subclasses of other array-based linear list classes. The reason is that even though these other classes have the same public methods, they have different data members.

Although the class DerivedArrayStack implements the interface Stack faithfully, DerivedArrayStack is unable to enforce the stack LIFO discipline. This condition occurs because, in addition to the methods of DerivedArrayStack, the user can perform the public methods of ArrayLinearList on a stack instance. For example, the following instruction sequence, which adds the element 2 to the bottom of the stack, is perfectly legal.

```
DerivedArrayStack s = new DerivedArrayStack();
s.push(new Integer(1));
s.add(0, new Integer(2));
```

In fact, when you define an instance of java.util.stack, you can perform any method of Vector on that instance.

To enforce the LIFO discipline, you can override the methods of ArrayLinearList by defining methods in DerivedArrayStack that have the same signature as the undesired methods of ArrayLinearList. The corresponding members of DerivedArrayStack throw an UnsupportedMethodException in case they are invoked. For example, we may override ArrayLinearList.add with the following code for DerivedArrayStack.add.

```
public void add(int index, Object obj)
{
   throw new UnsupportedOperationException
            ("operation Stack.add is not supported");
}
```

Another way to enforce the LIFO discipline is to define a stack class whose superclass is `Object` rather than one of the linear list classes defined in Chapter 5. This stack class could use a data member `stack` of type `ArrayLinearList` and define the stack methods in terms of operations on the linear list `stack`. The code would be quite similar to that of Program 9.2 and would suffer the same performance penalties. Alternatively, the data member `stack` could be an array of type `Object`, and the code for the `Stack` interface methods would not employ any method of `LinearList`. We explore this alternative in the next subsection.

9.3.2   The Class `ArrayStack`

When we obtain a stack class by extending a linear list class as was done in Program 9.2, we pay a performance penalty. For example, whenever we add an element to a stack, the `push` method invokes `ArrayLinearList.add` and the header of a `for` loop intended to shift certain elements one position right is executed. The execution of this header is unnecessary because when we add an element to a stack, the element is always added to the right end of the linear list and so we never need to shift elements right by one position.

One way to arrive at a faster implementation of an array-based stack is to not derive from any linear list class. This approach also helps to enforce the LIFO discipline because our new implementation need permit only the methods of the `Stack` interface to be performed on a stack object. Program 9.4 gives the class `ArrayStack`, which uses a one-dimensional array `element` to store the stack elements. The bottom element is stored in `element[0]`, and the top element in `element[top]`. The asymptotic complexity of each method of `ArrayStack` is the same as that of the corresponding method of `DerivedArrayStack`.

9.3.3   Performance Measurement

Even though the array-based stack classes `ArrayStack` (AS), `DerivedArrayStack` (DAS), `DerivedArrayStackWithCatch` (DASWC), `DerivedVectorStack` (DVS), and `java.util.Stack` (Stack) implement all methods of the stack interface so as to have the same asymptotic complexity, the observed performance of the methods is expected to be different for each class. We may use the results of Figure 5.5 to predict the performance of these stack classes.

- The performance of `Stack` is expected to be close to the best-case performance of `LinearListAsVectorSubclass` (LLAVS) because the superclass for both of these classes is `Vector`; best-case linear list inserts and removes correspond to stack push and pop operations. Let an n-sequence be a sequence of n best-case inserts (or pushes), followed by n gets (or peeks), followed by n best-case removes (or pops). Since LLAVS took $48.2 + 18.6 + 22.4 = 89.2$ ms to perform a 40,000-sequence when the initial capacity of the linear list was 10, we expect

```
public class ArrayStack implements Stack
{
   int top;           // current top of stack
   Object [] stack;   // element array

   /** create a stack with the given initial capacity */
    * @throws IllegalArgumentException when initialCapacity < 1 */
   public ArrayStack(int initialCapacity)
   {
      if (initialCapacity < 1)
         throw new IllegalArgumentException
               ("initialCapacity must be >= 1");
      stack = new Object [initialCapacity];
      top = -1;
   }

   /** create a stack with initial capacity 10 */
   public ArrayStack() {this(10);}

   /** @return true iff stack is empty */
   public boolean empty() {return top == -1;}

   /** @return top element of stack
     * @throws EmptyStackException when the stack is empty */
   public Object peek()
   {
      if (empty())
         throw new EmptyStackException();
      return stack[top];
   }

   /** add theElement to the top of the stack */
   public void push(Object theElement)
   {
      // increase array size if necessary
      if (top == stack.length - 1)
         stack = ChangeArrayLength.changeLength1D(stack, 2 * stack.length);

      // put theElement at the top of the stack
      stack[++top] = theElement;
   }
```

Program 9.4 The class ArrayStack (continues)

```
/** remove top element of stack and return it
 * @throws EmptyStackException when the stack is empty */
public Object pop()
{
   if (empty())
      throw new EmptyStackException();
   Object topElement = stack[top];
   stack[top--] = null;    // enable garbage collection
   return topElement;
}
```

Program 9.4 The class `ArrayStack` (concluded)

that `Stack` will take approximately 89.2 ms for a 40,000-sequence. Since the time for an n-sequence is linear in n, we expect a 500,000-sequence to take $89.2 * 500,000/40,000 = 1.12$ seconds.

- DVS and DAS are expected to take more time to perform an n-sequence than `Stack` and `ArrayLinearList`, respectively, take because the derived classes incur the overhead of checking for conditions that would cause their superclasses to throw an exception.

- `ArrayStack` is expected to take less time to perform an n-sequence than `ArrayLinearList` takes because of the reduced overhead. So `ArrayStack` with an initial capacity of 10 is expected to take less than $(26.2 + 5.6 + 6.9) * 500,000/40,000 = 0.48$ second for a 500,000-sequence. We expect `Stack` to take about $1.12/0.48 = 2.3$ times the time taken by `ArrayStack`.

- We expect DASWC to be faster than DAS because the `try-catch` construct is free (except when an exception is thrown), whereas the `if-else` construct has a nonzero cost. DASCW is, however, expected to be slower than `ArrayStack` because of the extra overheads incurred in invoking and executing the methods of `ArrayLinearList`.

- Given the expected difference in the run times of `ArrayStack` and `Stack` and the fact that the overhead incurred by DASWC and DAS is expected to be less than this difference, our expected ordering of the performance of the array-based stack classes is (from fastest to slowest) `ArrayStack`, DASWC, `Stack`, and DAS.

Figure 9.2 gives the measured times to perform a 500,000-sequence, and Figure 9.3 shows these time as a bar chart. For all stack classes except `java.util.Stack`, we obtained the run times for the cases: (1) start with a stack having the default capacity 10 and (2) start with a stack whose initial capacity is 500,000. We did not try (2) for `java.util.Stack` because this class does not have a constructor that allows us to specify an initial capacity.

	initialCapacity	
Class	10	500,000
`ArrayStack`	0.44	0.22
`DerivedArrayStack`	0.60	0.38
`DerivedArrayStackWithCatch`	0.55	0.33
`DerivedVectorStack`	1.27	1.04
`Stack`	1.15	–

Times are in seconds

Figure 9.2 Time taken by different array-based stack implementations

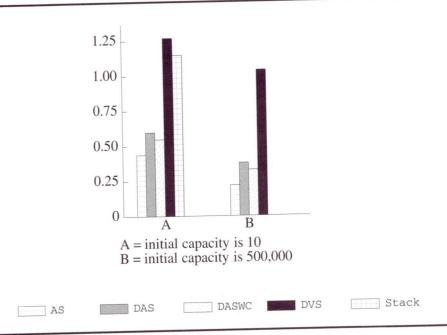

A = initial capacity is 10
B = initial capacity is 500,000

AS   DAS   DASWC   DVS   Stack

Figure 9.3 Stack run times in seconds

Our run-time experiment confirms our predictions on the relative ordering of the stack classes, and the observed times for `ArrayStack` and `Stack` are quite close to those we predicted. `Stack` took 2.6 times the time taken by `ArrayStack` to perform a 500,000-sequence. The performance ratio jumps to 5.2 when we start with an `ArrayStack` whose capacity is 500,000 (this jump is due mainly to the fact that `Stack` does not allow you to specify an initial capacity and so dynamic increase of the array length cannot be avoided).

Another interesting (and expected) observation is that the time spent resizing the array (this is just the difference in the time taken when the initial capacity is 10 and when it is 500,000) is approximately the same for all implementations (approximately 0.2 second). The time spent on array resizing is about 50 percent of the total time taken by `ArrayStack` when we start with an array having the default length 10.

EXERCISES

7. (a) Extend the stack ADT by adding functions to
    i. Determine the size (i.e., number of elements) of the stack.
    ii. Input a stack.
    iii. Convert a stack into a string suitable for output.
    iv. Split a stack in two. The first contains the bottom half elements, and the second the remaining elements.
    v. Combine two stacks by placing all elements of the second stack on top of those in the first. The relative order of elements from the second stack is unchanged.

   (b) Define the interface `ExtendedStack` that extends the interface `Stack` (Program 9.1) and includes the methods that correspond to the functions of (a).

   (c) Develop the classes `ExtendedDerivedArrayStack` and `ExtendedArrayStack` that implement the interface `ExtendedStack` and are, respectively, subclasses of `DerivedArrayStack` and `ArrayStack`.

   (d) Test the correctness of your codes.

8. Consider the class `ArrayStack`. Show that even though it is possible for an individual `push` operation to take Θ(capacity) time, the time taken by any sequence of n stack operations is $O(n)$.

9. Consider the class `ArrayStack`.

   (a) As implemented in Program 9.4, the capacity of a stack can increase but not decrease. To use space more efficiently, modify the implementation of `pop` so that you decrease the capacity to one-half of the current capacity whenever a `pop` reduces the stack occupancy below one-fourth of capacity.

   (b) Show that even though it is possible for an individual `push` and `pop` operation to take Θ(capacity) time, the time taken by any sequence of n stack operations is $O(n)$.

9.4   LINKED REPRESENTATION

Although the array representation of a stack considered in the previous section is both elegant and efficient, it is wasteful of space when multiple stacks are to coexist. The reasons are the same as those cited in Section 5.5 for the inefficiency of the separate arrays for separate lists representation. An exception is when only two stacks are to coexist. We can maintain space and time efficiency by pegging the bottom of one stack at position 0 and the bottom of the other at position `length-1` of a one-dimensional array. The two stacks grow toward the middle of the array (see Figure 9.4). When more than two stacks are to be represented, the multiple lists in a single array representation may be adapted to the case of multiple stacks. While this adaptation results in a space-efficient implementation, the worst-case `push` time becomes $O(\text{length})$ rather than $\Theta(1)$. The `pop` time remains $\Theta(1)$.

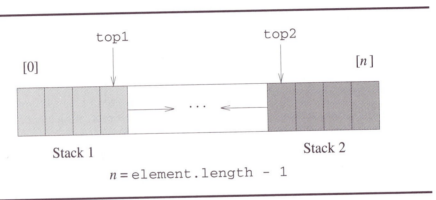

Figure 9.4 Two stacks in an array

Multiple stacks can be represented efficiently by using a chain for each stack. This representation incurs a space penalty of one pointer (`next`) field for each stack element. However, each stack operation can be performed in $\Theta(1)$ time.

When using a chain to represent a stack, we must decide which end of the chain corresponds to the stack top. If we associate the right end of the chain with the stack top, then the stack operations `peek`, `push`, and `pop` are implemented using invocations to the chain methods `get(size() - 1)`, `add(size(), x)`, and `remove(size() - 1)`. Each of these chain operations takes $O(\text{size}())$ time. On the other hand, if we associate the left end of the chain with the stack top, then the chain operations to use are `get(0)`, `add(0, x)`, and `remove(0)`. Each of these operations takes $\Theta(1)$ time. This analysis shows that we should use the left end of the chain to represent the stack top.

9.4.1   The Class `DerivedLinkedStack`

The code for the class `DerivedLinkedStack`, which is a subclass of `Chain` (Program 6.2) and which implements the interface `Stack`, may be obtained from the code for `DerivedArrayStack` (Program 9.2) by replacing the clause `extends Array-LinearList` with the clause `extends Chain`; replacing all occurences of the name `DerivedArrayStack` with the name `DerivedLinkedStack`; and changing the actual parameter to all uses of the methods `get`, `remove`, and `add` to 0 so that these operations take place at the left end of the chain. What could be easier? By using the object-oriented programming principles of information hiding and encapsulation, we have greatly simplified program development. The complexity of each method of `DerivedLinkedStack` (including the constructor and `push` methods) is $\Theta(1)$.

9.4.2   The Class `LinkedStack`

As was the case with the class `ArrayStack` (Program 9.4), we can improve the run-time performance by customizing the code and not deriving our linked-stack class from any other class. Program 9.5 gives the customized code.

9.4.3   Performance Measurement

`DerivedLinkedStack` and `LinkedStack` took 3.2 and 2.96 seconds, respectively, to perform a 500,000-sequence. Comparing with the times reported in Figure 9.2, we see that `LinkedStack` not only requires more memory than does `ArrayStack` but also takes 7 times the time `ArrayStack` takes when started with a capacity of 10 and 15 times the time taken when the array stack's initial capacity is 500,000. The use of pointers provides no benefit when we represent a single stack.

EXERCISE

10. In some stack applications the elements to be put on a stack are already in nodes of type `ChainNode`. For these applications it is desirable to have the methods `pushNode(ChainNode theNode)`, which adds `theNode` to the top of the stack (notice that no call to `new` is made), and `popNode`, which removes and returns the top node of the stack.

    (a) Write code for these methods

    (b) Test your code.

    (c) Compare the peformance of a 500,000-sequence that uses `pushNode` and `peekNode` with a 500,000-sequence that uses `push` and `peek`.

11. Develop the class `ExtendedLinkedStack` to extend `LinkedStack` and implement the interface `ExtendedStack` (see Exercise 7).

```java
public class LinkedStack implements Stack
{
   protected ChainNode topNode;

   /** create an empty stack */
   public LinkedStack(int initialCapacity)
   {
      // the default initial value of topNode is null
   }

   public LinkedStack() {this(0);}

   /** @return true iff stack is empty */
   public boolean empty() {return topNode == null;}

   /** @return top element of stack
     * @throws EmptyStackException when the stack is empty */
   public Object peek()
   {
      if (empty())
         throw new EmptyStackException();
      return topNode.element;
   }

   /** add theElement to the top of the stack */
   public void push(Object theElement)
      {topNode = new ChainNode(theElement, topNode);}

   /** remove top element of stack and return it
     * @throws EmptyStackException when the stack is empty */
   public Object pop()
   {
      if (empty())
         throw new EmptyStackException();
      Object topElement = topNode.element;
      topNode = topNode.next;
      return topElement;
   }
}
```

Program 9.5 Customized linked stack

12. Compare the performance of the array-based stack classes used in Figure 9.2 and the linked classes `DerivedLinkedStack` and `LinkedStack`. Do this by performing an alternating sequence of 500,000 `push` and `pop` operations. For the array-based classes start with the default initial capacity. Does array doubling occur in your experiment? Why?

9.5   APPLICATIONS

9.5.1   Parenthesis Matching

Problem Description

In this problem we are to match the left and right parentheses in a character string. For example, the string `(a*(b+c)+d)` has left parentheses at positions 0 and 3 and right parentheses at positions 7 and 10. The left parenthesis at position 0 matches the right at position 10, while the left parenthesis at position 3 matches the right parenthesis at position 7. In the string `(a+b))(`, the right parenthesis at position 5 has no matching left parenthesis, and the left parenthesis at position 6 has no matching right parenthesis. Our objective is to write a Java program that inputs a string and outputs the pairs of matched parentheses as well as those parentheses for which there is no match. Notice that the parenthesis matching problem is equivalent to the problem of matching braces ({ and }) in a Java program.

Solution Strategy

We observe that if we scan the input expression from left to right, then each right parenthesis is matched to the most recently seen unmatched left parenthesis. This observation motivates us to save the position of left parentheses on a stack as they are encountered in a left-to-right scan. When a right parenthesis is encountered, it is matched to the left parenthesis (if any) at the top of the stack. The matched left parenthesis is deleted from the stack.

Java Implementation

Program 9.6 gives the Java code.

Complexity

The time complexity of Program 9.6 is $O(n)$ where n is the length of the input expression. To see this, note that the program performs $O(n)$ `push` and $O(n)$ `pop` operations. Even though the complexity of an individual `push` operation is $O(\text{capacity})$ (because of array doubling), the complexity of $O(n)$ `push` operations is $O(n)$. The complexity of each `pop` operation is $O(1)$. Therefore, the complexity of $O(n)$ `pop` operations is $O(n)$.

```
public static void printMatchedPairs(String expr)
{
   ArrayStack s = new ArrayStack();
   int length = expr.length();

   // scan expression expr for ( and )
   for (int i = 0; i < length; i++)
      if (expr.charAt(i) == '(')
         s.push(new Integer(i));
      else
         if (expr.charAt(i) == ')')
         try
         {// remove location of matching '(' from stack
            System.out.println(s.pop() + "   " + i);
         }
         catch (Exception e)
         {// stack was empty, no match exists
            System.out.println("No match for right parenthesis"
                                   + " at " + i);

         }

   // remaining '(' in stack are unmatched
   while (!s.empty())
      System.out.println("No match for left parenthesis at "
                            + s.pop());
}
```

Program 9.6 Program to output matched parentheses

9.5.2   Towers of Hanoi

Problem Description

The **Towers of Hanoi** problem is fashioned after the ancient Tower of Brahma ritual. According to legend, when the world was created, there was a diamond tower (tower 1) with 64 golden disks (Figure 9.5). The disks were of decreasing size and were stacked on the tower in decreasing order of size from bottom to top. Next to this tower are two other diamond towers (towers 2 and 3). Since the time of creation, Brahman priests have been attempting to move the disks from tower 1 to tower 2, using tower 3 for intermediate storage. As the disks are very heavy, they can be moved only one at a time. In addition, at no time can a disk be on top of a smaller disk. According to legend, the world will come to an end when the priests have completed their task.

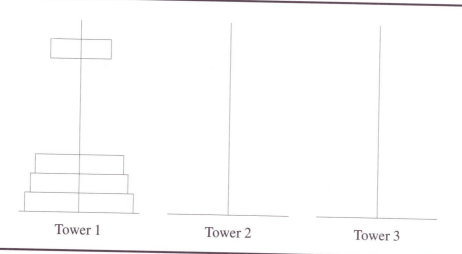

Figure 9.5 Towers of Hanoi

In the Towers of Hanoi problem, we are given n disks and three towers. The disks are initially stacked on tower 1 in decreasing order of size from bottom to top. We are to move the disks to tower 2, one disk at a time, such that no disk is ever on top of a smaller one. You may wish to attempt a solution to this problem for $n = 2, 3$, and 4 before reading further.

Solution Strategy

A very elegant solution results from the use of recursion. To get the largest disk to the bottom of tower 2, we move the remaining $n - 1$ disks to tower 3 and then move the largest to tower 2. Now we are left with the task of moving the $n - 1$ disks from tower 3 to tower 2. To perform this task, we can use towers 1 and 2. We can safely ignore the fact that tower 2 has a disk on it because this disk is larger than the disks being moved from tower 3. Therefore, we can place any disk on top of the disk on tower 2.

First Implementation

Program 9.7 gives recursive Java code for this solution. The initial invocation is `towersOfHanoi(n, 1, 2, 3)`. The correctness of Program 9.7 is easily established.

```
public static void towersOfHanoi(int n, int x, int y, int z)
{// Move the top n disks from tower x to tower y.
 // Use tower z for intermediate storage.
   if (n > 0)
   {
      towersOfHanoi(n-1, x, z, y);
      System.out.println("Move top disk from tower " + x +
                         " to top of tower " + y);
      towersOfHanoi(n-1, z, y, x);
   }
}
```

Program 9.7 Recursive method for Towers of Hanoi

Complexity

The time taken by Program 9.7 is proportional to the number of lines of output generated, and the number of lines output is equal to the number of disk moves performed. Examining Program 9.7, we obtain the following recurrence for the number of moves, $moves(n)$:

$$moves(n) = \begin{cases} 0 & n = 0 \\ 2moves(n-1)+1 & n > 0 \end{cases}$$

This recurrence may be solved by using the substitution method of Chapter 2 (see Example 2.20). The result is $moves(n) = 2^n - 1$. We can show that $2^n - 1$ is, in fact, the least number of moves in which the disks can be moved. Since $n = 64$ in the Tower of Brahma, the Brahman priests will need quite a few years to finish their task. From the solution to the above recurrence, we conclude that the time complexity of `towersOfHanoi` is $\Theta(2^n)$ provided the method runs to completion.

Second Implementation

The output from Program 9.7 gives us the disk-move sequence needed to move the disks from tower 1 to tower 2. Suppose we wish to show the state (i.e., the disks together with their order bottom to top) of the three towers following each move. To show this state, we must store the state of the towers in memory and change the state of each as disks are moved. Following each move, we can output the tower states to an output device such as the computer screen, printer, or video recorder.

Since disks are removed from each tower in a LIFO manner, each tower may be represented as a stack. The three towers together contain exactly n disks at any time. Using linked stacks, we can get by with space for n elements. If array-based stacks are used, towers 1 and 2 must have a capacity of n disks each, while tower 3 must have a capacity of $n - 1$. Therefore, we need space for a total of $3n - 1$ disks. As our earlier analysis has shown, the time complexity of the Towers of Hanoi problem is exponential in n. So using a reasonable amount of computer time, the problem can be solved only for small values of n (say $n \leq 30$). For these small values of n, the difference in space required by the array-based and linked representations is sufficiently small that either may be used. Since the array-based implementations of a stack run faster that the linked implementations, we use an array-based implementation.

The code of Program 9.8 uses array-based stacks. `towersOfHanoi(n)` is just a preprocessor for the recursive method `showTowerStates`, which is modeled after the method of Program 9.7. The preprocessor creates the three stacks `tower[1:3]` that will store the states of the three towers. The disks are numbered 1 (smallest) through n (largest). Since the disks are modeled as integers, the disk numbers cannot be stored on a stack unless their data type is converted from `int` to a wrapper type for `int`. We can use either of the types `Integer` or `MyInteger` for this purpose. The initial configuration has all n disks in `tower[1]`; the remaining two towers have no disk. After constructing this initial configuration, the preprocessor invokes the method `showTowerStates`.

9.5.3   Rearranging Railroad Cars

Problem Description

A freight train has n railroad cars. Each is to be left at a different station. Assume that the n stations are numbered 1 through n and that the freight train visits these stations in the order n through 1. The railroad cars are labeled by their destination. To facilitate removal of the railroad cars from the train, we must reorder the cars so that they are in the order 1 through n from front to back. When the cars are in this order, the last car is detached at each station. We rearrange the cars at a shunting yard that has an *input track*, an *output track*, and k holding tracks between the input and output tracks. Figure 9.6(a) shows a shunting yard with $k = 3$ holding tracks $H1$, $H2$, and $H3$. The n cars of the freight train begin in the input track and are to end up in the output track in the order 1 through n from right to left. In Figure 9.6(a), $n = 9$; the cars are initially in the order 5, 8, 1, 7, 4, 2, 9, 6, 3 from back to front. Figure 9.6(b) shows the cars rearranged in the desired order.

Solution Strategy

To rearrange the cars, we examine the cars on the input track from front to back. If the car being examined is the next one in the output arrangement, we move it directly to the output track. If not, we move it to a holding track and leave it there until it is time to place it in the output track. The holding tracks operate in a LIFO manner as cars enter and leave these tracks from the top. When rearranging cars, only the following moves are permitted:

```
public class TowersOfHanoiShowingStates
{
   // data member
   private static ArrayStack [] tower;   // the towers are tower[1:3]

   /** n disk Towers of Hanoi problem */
   public static void towersOfHanoi(int n)
   {// Preprocessor for showTowerStates

      // create three stacks, tower[0] is not used
      tower = new ArrayStack[4];
      for (int i = 1; i <= 3; i++)
         tower[i] = new ArrayStack();

      for (int d = n; d > 0; d--) // initialize
         tower[1].push(new Integer(d));   // add disk d to tower 1

      // move n disks from tower 1 to 2 using 3 as
      // intermediate tower
      showTowerStates(n, 1, 2, 3);
   }

   public static void showTowerStates(int n, int x, int y, int z)
   {// Move the top n disks from tower x to tower y.
    // Use tower z for intermediate storage.
      if (n > 0)
      {
         showTowerStates(n-1, x, z, y);
         Integer d = (Integer) tower[x].pop();   // move d from top
                                                  // of tower x to
         tower[y].push(d);                        // top of tower y
         System.out.println("Move disk " + d + " from tower "
                         + x + " to top of tower " + y);
         // output statement should be replaced by showState() when
         // showState method has been implemented
         showTowerStates(n-1, z, y, x);
      }
   }
}
```

Program 9.8 Towers of Hanoi using stacks

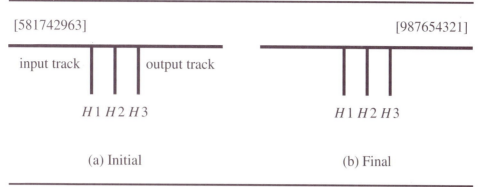

[581742963]   [987654321]

input track   output track

H1 H2 H3   H1 H2 H3

(a) Initial   (b) Final

Figure 9.6 A three-track example

- A car may be moved from the front (i.e., right end) of the input track to the top of one of the holding tracks or to the left end of the output track.

- A car may be moved from the top of a holding track to the left end of the output track.

Consider the input arrangement of Figure 9.6(a). Car 3 is at the front and cannot be output yet, as it is to be preceded by cars 1 and 2. So car 3 is detached and moved to the holding track $H1$. The next car, car 6, is also to be moved to a holding track. If car 6 is moved to $H1$, the rearrangement cannot be completed because car 3 will be below car 6. However, car 3 is to be output before car 6 and so must leave $H1$ before car 6 does. So car 6 is put into $H2$. The next car, car 9, is put into $H3$ because putting it into either $H1$ or $H2$ will make it impossible to complete the rearrangement. *Notice that whenever the car labels in a holding track are not in increasing order from top to bottom, the rearrangement cannot be completed.* The current state of the holding tracks is shown in Figure 9.7(a).

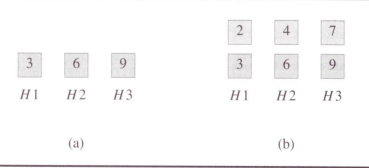

				2	4	7
3	6	9		3	6	9
H1	H2	H3		H1	H2	H3

(a)   (b)

Figure 9.7 Track states

have both been seen, we are unable to complete the processing of the first region defined by this net, as pin 4's routing has to cross the boundary. As a result, when we complete the examination of all pins, the stack will not be empty.

Java Implementation and Complexity

Program 9.13 gives a Java method that implements this strategy. This method assumes that the number of pins is even and that each pin has a net number. So for the example in Figure 9.8(c), the input array net is [1, 2, 2, 1, 3, 3, 4, 4]. The complexity of the program is $O(n)$ where n is the number of pins.

```java
/** determine whether the switch box is routable
  * @param net[0..net.length-1] array of pin to net assignments
  * @param n number of pins */
public static boolean checkBox(int [] net, int n)
{
    int n = net.length;    // number of pins
    ArrayStack s = new ArrayStack();

    // scan nets clockwise
    for (int i = 0; i < n; i++)
        // process pin i
        if (!s.empty())
            // check with top net
            if (net[i] == net[((Integer) s.peek()).intValue()])
                // net[i] is routable, delete from stack
                s.pop();
            else s.push(new Integer(i));
        else s.push(new Integer(i));

    // any unrouted nets left?
    if (s.empty())
    {// no nets remain
        System.out.println("Switch box is routable");
        return true;
    }

    System.out.println("Switch box is not routable");
    return false;
}
```

Program 9.13 Switch box routing

9.5.5   Offline Equivalence Class Problem

Problem Description

The offline equivalence problem was defined in Section 7.7. The inputs to this problem are the number of elements n, the number of relation pairs r, and the r relation pairs. We are to partition the n elements into equivalence classes.

Solution Strategy

The solution is in two phases. In the first phase we input the data and set up n lists to represent the relation pairs. For each relation pair (i, j), i is put on $list[j]$ and j is put on $list[i]$.

Example 9.3 Suppose that $n = 9$, $r = 11$, and the 11 relation pairs are (1, 5), (1, 6), (3, 7), (4, 8), (5, 2), (6, 5), (4, 9), (9, 7), (7, 8), (3, 4), and (6, 2). The nine lists are

$$
\begin{aligned}
list[1] &= [5, 6] \\
list[2] &= [5, 6] \\
list[3] &= [7, 4] \\
list[4] &= [8, 9, 3] \\
list[5] &= [1, 2, 6] \\
list[6] &= [1, 2, 5] \\
list[7] &= [3, 9, 8] \\
list[8] &= [4, 7] \\
list[9] &= [4, 7]
\end{aligned}
$$

Element order within a list is not important.   ■

In the second phase, the equivalence classes are identified by first locating an element that has not been output as part of an equivalence class. This element becomes the **seed** for the next equivalence class. The seed is output as the first member of the next equivalence class. From the seed we identify all other members of the class as follows. The seed is put onto a list, *unprocessedList*, of elements that are in the same equivalence class as the seed and whose lists have yet to be processed. We remove an element i from *unprocessedList* and process $list[i]$. All elements on $list[i]$ are in the same equivalence class as the seed; elements on $list[i]$ that haven't already been identified as class members are output and added to *unprocessedList*. This process of removing an element i from *unprocessedList* and then outputting and adding elements in $list[i]$ that haven't already been output to *unprocessedList* continues until the *unprocessedList* becomes empty. At this time we have completed a class, and we proceed to find a seed for the next class.

Example 9.4 Consider the data of Example 9.3. Let 1 be the first seed; 1 is output as part of a new class and is also added to *unprocessedList*. Next 1 is removed from *unprocessedList*, and *list*[1] is processed. The elements 5 and 6 that are in *list*[1] are output as part of the same class as element 1; 5 and 6 are also added to *unprocessedList*. Either 5 or 6 is removed from *unprocessedList*, and its list is processed. Suppose that 5 is removed. The elements 1, 2, and 6 that are in *list*[5] are examined. Since 1 and 6 have already been output, we ignore them. Element 2 is output and added to *unprocessedList*. When the remaining elements (6 and 2) that are in *unprocessedList* are removed and processed, no additional element is output or added to *unprocessedList*; this list becomes empty, and we have identified an equivalence class.

To find another equivalence class, we search for a seed—an element not yet output. Element 3 has not been output and is used as the seed for the next class. Elements 3, 4, 7, 8, and 9 are output as part of this next class. Since no seeds remain, we have found all the classes.   ■

Java Implementation

To proceed with an implementation, we must select a representation for *list* and *unprocessedList*. The operations performed on *list* are to insert and examine all elements. Since it doesn't matter where elements are inserted in *list*, any linear list or stack representation may be used. We select a specific linear list or stack representation based on which is expected to provide the best space and time performance.

The total number of elements in all n of the lists *list*$[1 : n]$ is $2r$. Therefore, as far as space requirements go, all our array-based linear list and stack classes require space for between $2r$ and $4r$ references (because of array doubling, the allocated array length may be up to two times the number of elements). Our linked classes require space for $4r$ references. Our run-time performance studies of linear list and stack implementations (see Sections 5.6, 6.1.6, 9.3.3, and 9.4.3) show that the linked implementations of these data structures are slower than their array-based counterparts. Since these linked representations also require more space, we eliminate them from further consideration as far the offline equivalence class problem is concerned.

The fastest linear list representation we have is `ArrayLinearList` (Section 5.3.3). By inserting new elements at the right end of a list, our application will exhibit the best-case time performance for `ArrayLinearList`. However, if we use an `Array-Stack`, we will do slightly better. We may examine the elements of a stack by removing them one at a time. For performance reasons *unprocessedList* is also implemented as an `ArrayStack`.

Program 9.14 gives a two-part program for the offline equivalence problem. In the first part, n, r, and the r pairs are input, and the stack for each of the n elements constructed. The stack `list[i]` for element i contains all elements j such that (i,j) or (j,i) is an input relation pair. An `ArrayIndexOutOfBounds` exception is thrown if a pair (a, b) with either a or b not in the range [1, n] is input because a and b are used as indexes into the array `list` and `list[0]` is `null`. Exercise 29 asks you to modify the code so as to explicitly validate the input relations.

The second part of the program outputs the equivalence classes. For the second part we maintain an array `out` such that `out[i]` = `true` iff element i has been output as a member of some equivalence class. A stack `unprocessedList` assists in locating all elements of an equivalence class. This stack holds all elements that have been output as part of the current class and that may lead to additional elements of the class. To find the seed for the next equivalence class, we scan the array `out` for an element not yet output. If there is no such element, then there is no next class. If such an element is found, it begins the next class.

Complexity

Part 1 of the program (input and initialize the array `list[]`) of relation pairs takes $O(n+r)$ time (this analysis allows for the possiblity that an exception may be thrown during input). For part 2, under the assumption that no exception occurs, we note that since each of the n elements is output exactly once, each is added to `unprocessedList` once and deleted from `unprocessedList` once. So the total time spent pushing and popping elements from `unprocessedList` is $\Theta(n)$. Finally, when an element j is removed from `unprocessedList`, all elements on `list[j]` are examined by popping then off of `list[j]`. Each element in each `list[j]` is popped exactly once. So the time required to pop and examine all elements on all lists `list[1:n]` is $\Theta(r)$ (note that the total number of elements on all lists `list[1:n]` is $2*r$ following the input phase). Allowing for the possibility that an exception may occur, we conclude that the overall complexity of Program 9.14 is $O(n+r)$. The complexity when no exception occurs is $\Theta(n+r)$.

Since every program for the offline equivalence class problem must examine each relation and element at least once, it is not possible to solve the offline equivalence problem in less than $O(n+r)$ time.

9.5.6   Rat in a Maze

Problem Description

A **maze** (Figure 9.9) is a rectangular area with an entrance and an exit. The interior of the maze contains walls or obstacles that one cannot walk through. In our mazes these obstacles are placed along rows and columns that are parallel to the rectangular boundary of the maze. The entrance is at the upper-left corner, and the exit is at the lower-right corner.

Suppose that the maze is to be modeled as an $n \times m$ matrix with position (1,1) of the matrix representing the entrance and position (n, m) representing the exit. n and m are, respectively, the number of rows and columns in the maze. Each

```java
public static void main(String [] args)
{
    // define the input stream to be the standard input stream
    MyInputStream keyboard = new MyInputStream();

    // input the number of elements, n
    System.out.println("Enter number of elements");
    int n = keyboard.readInteger();
    if (n < 2)
    {
        System.out.println("Too few elements");
        System.exit(1);    // terminate
    }

    // input the number of relations, r
    System.out.println("Enter number of relations");
    int r = keyboard.readInteger();
    if (r < 1)
    {
        System.out.println("Too few relations");
        System.exit(1);
    }

    // create an array of empty stacks, list[0] not used
    ArrayStack [] list = new ArrayStack [n + 1];
    for (int i = 1; i <= n; i++)
        list[i] = new ArrayStack();

    // input the r relations and put on stacks
    for (int i = 1; i <= r; i++)
    {
        System.out.println("Enter next relation/pair");
        int a = keyboard.readInteger();
        int b = keyboard.readInteger();
        list[a].push(new Integer(b));
        list[b].push(new Integer(a));
    }
```

Program 9.14 Offline equivalence class program (continues)

```
// initialize to output equivalence classes
ArrayStack unprocessedList = new ArrayStack();
boolean [] out = new boolean [n + 1];
// default boolean value is false

// output equivalence classes
for (int i = 1; i <= n; i++)
  if (!out[i])
  {// start of a new class
      System.out.print("Next class is: " + i + " ");
      out[i] = true;
      unprocessedList.push(new Integer(i));
      // get rest of class from unprocessedList
      while (!unprocessedList.empty())
      {
          int j = ((Integer) unprocessedList.pop()).intValue();

          // elements on list[j] are in the same class
          while (!list[j].empty())
          {
              int q = ((Integer) list[j].pop()).intValue();
              if (!out[q])  // q not yet output
              {
                  System.out.print(q + " ");
                  out[q] = true;
                  unprocessedList.push(new Integer(q));
              }
          }
      }
      System.out.println();
  }

  System.out.println("End of list of equivalence classes");
}
```

Program 9.14 Offline equivalence class program (concluded)

maze position is described by its row and column intersection. The matrix has a 1 in position (i, j) iff there is an obstacle at the corresponding maze position. Otherwise, there is a 0 at this matrix position. Figure 9.10 shows the matrix representation of the maze of Figure 9.9. The **rat-in-a-maze** problem is to find a path from the

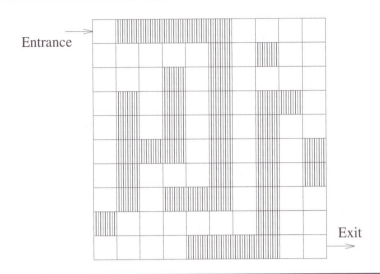

Entrance

Exit

Figure 9.9 A maze

$$
\begin{matrix}
0 & 1 & 1 & 1 & 1 & 1 & 0 & 0 & 0 & 0 \\
0 & 0 & 0 & 0 & 0 & 1 & 0 & 1 & 0 & 0 \\
0 & 0 & 0 & 1 & 0 & 1 & 0 & 0 & 0 & 0 \\
0 & 1 & 0 & 1 & 0 & 1 & 0 & 1 & 1 & 0 \\
0 & 1 & 0 & 1 & 0 & 1 & 0 & 1 & 0 & 0 \\
0 & 1 & 1 & 1 & 0 & 1 & 0 & 1 & 0 & 1 \\
0 & 1 & 0 & 0 & 0 & 1 & 0 & 1 & 0 & 1 \\
0 & 1 & 0 & 1 & 1 & 1 & 0 & 1 & 0 & 0 \\
1 & 0 & 0 & 0 & 0 & 0 & 0 & 1 & 0 & 0 \\
0 & 0 & 0 & 0 & 1 & 1 & 1 & 1 & 0 & 0 \\
\end{matrix}
$$

Figure 9.10 Matrix representation of maze of Figure 9.9

entrance to the exit of a maze. A **path** is a sequence of positions, none of which is blocked, and such that each (other than the first) is the north, south, east, or west neighbor of the preceding position (Figure 9.11).

You are to write a program to solve the rat-in-a-maze problem. You may assume that the mazes for which your program is to work are square (i.e., $m = n$) and are sufficiently small so that the entire maze can be represented in the memory of the target computer. Your program will be a stand-alone product that will be used directly by persons wishing to find a path in a maze of their choice.

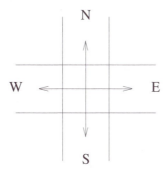

Figure 9.11 The four options for a move from any position in the maze

Design

We will use the top-down modular methodology to design the program. It is not too difficult to see the three aspects to the problem: input the maze, find a path, and output the path. We will use one program module for each task. A fourth module that displays a welcome message and identifies the program and its author is also desirable. While this module is not directly related to the problem at hand, the use of such a module enhances the user-friendliness of the program.

The module that finds the path does not interact directly with the user and will therefore contain no help facility and will not be menu driven. The remaining three modules interact with the user, and we need to expend some effort designing their user interface. The user interface should make the user want to use your program rather than competing programs.

Let us begin with the welcome module. We wish to display a message such as

Welcome To
RAT IN A MAZE
©Joe Bloe, 2000

While displaying this message might seem like a trivial task, we can use various design elements to obtain a pleasing effect. For example, the message can be multi-colored to take advantage of the user's color display. The three lines of the welcome display need to be positioned on the screen, and we can change the character size from one line to the next (or even from character to character). The welcome message can be introduced on the display with a reasonable time lapse between the introduction of one character and the next. Alternatively, the time lapse can be very small. In addition, we might consider the use of sound effects. We also need to determine the duration for which the message is to be displayed. It should be displayed long enough so that the user can read it, but not long enough to leave the user yawning. As you can see, the design of the welcome message (and the whole user interface in general) requires strong artistic skills.

For the input module we must decide whether we want the input as a matrix of 0s and 1s or whether we will display a maze of the desired size and then ask the user to click a mouse at the squares that contain an obstacle. We must also decide on the colors to use, whether we will have audio during input, and so on.

The input module can also verify that the entrance and exit of the maze are not blocked. If they are, then no path exists. In all likelihood the user made an error in input. The following discussion assumes that the input module performs this verification and that the entrance and exit are not blocked.

Once again, we see that what initially appeared to be a simple task (read in a matrix) is actually quite complex if we want to do it in a user-friendly way.

The output module design involves essentially the same considerations as the design of the input module.

Program Plan

The design phase has already pointed out the need for four program modules. We also need a root (or main) module that invokes these four modules in the following sequence: welcome module, input module, find path module, and output module.

Our program will have the modular structure of Figure 9.12. Each program module can be coded independently. The root module will be coded as the method `main`; the welcome, input, find path, and output path modules will each be a single private method.

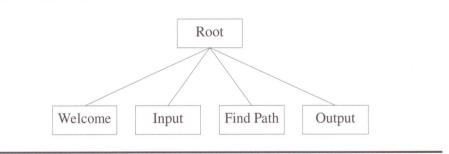

Figure 9.12 Modular structure of rat-in-a-maze program

At this point we see that our program is going to have the form given in Figure 9.13.

Program Development

Substantial data structure and algorithm issues arise in the development of the path-finding module only. Consequently, we will develop just this module here.

```
// private static method welcome
// private static method inputMaze
// private static method findPath
// private static method outputPath

public static void main(String [] args)
{
    welcome();
    inputMaze();
    if (findPath()) outputPath();
    else System.out.println("No path");
}
```

Figure 9.13 Form of rat-in-a-maze program

Exercise 31 asks you to develop the remaining modules. Without thinking too much about the coding of the path-finding module, we can arrive at the Java pseudocode given in Figure 9.14. This code is readily seen to be correct. Unfortunately, we cannot present it to a computer in this form, and we need to refine the pseudocode into pure Java code.

```
private static boolean findPath()
{
    Search the maze for a path to the exit;
    if (a path is found) return true;
    else return false;
}
```

Figure 9.14 First version of findPath

Before attempting a refinement of Figure 9.14 that will get us closer to Java code, let us figure out how we are to search the maze for a path. We begin with the entrance as our present position. If the present position is the exit, then we have found a path and we are done. If we are not at the exit, then we block the present position (i.e., place an obstacle there) so as to prevent the search from returning here. Next we see whether there is an adjacent maze position that is not blocked. If so, we move to this new adjacent position and attempt to find a path from there to the exit. If we are unsuccessful, we attempt to move to some other unblocked adjacent maze position and try to find a path from there. To facilitate this move, we save the current position on a stack before advancing to a new adjacent position.

If all adjacent unblocked positions have been tried and no path is found, there is no path from entrance to exit in the maze.

Let us use the above strategy on the maze of Figure 9.9. We begin with the position (1,1) on the stack and move to its only unblocked neighbor (2,1). The position (1,1) is blocked to prevent the search path from moving through this position later. From (2,1) we can move to (3,1) or (2,2). Suppose we decide to move to (3,1). Prior to the move, we block (2,1) and add it to the stack. From (3,1) we may move to either (4,1) or (3,2). If we move to (4,1), (4,1) gets blocked and added to the stack. From (4,1) we move to (5,1), (6,1), (7,1), and (8,1). The path cannot be extended from (8,1). Our stack now contains the path from (1,1) to (8,1). To try another path, we back up to (7,1) by deleting this position from the stack. As there are no unblocked positions adjacent to (7,1), we back up to (6,1) by deleting this position from the stack. In this way we back up to position (3,1) from which we are again able to move forward (i.e., move to (3,2)). Notice that the stack always contains the path from the entrance to the current position. If we reach the exit, the entrance-to-exit path will be on the stack.

To refine Figure 9.14, we need representations for the maze, which is a matrix of zeros and ones, each maze position, and the stack. Let us consider the maze first. The maze is naturally represented as a two-dimensional array `maze` of type `byte`. (Since each array position can take on only one of the values 0 and 1, we could use the data type `boolean` and represent the value 1 by `true` and the value 0 by `false`. This approach would reduce the space required for the array `maze` to one-eighth.) Position (i,j) of the maze matrix corresponds to position [i][j] of the array `maze`.

From interior (i.e., nonboundary) positions of the maze, four moves are possible: right, down, left, and up. From positions on the boundary of the maze, either two or three moves are possible. To avoid having to handle positions on the boundaries of the maze differently from interior positions, we will surround the maze with a wall of obstacles. For an $m \times m$ maze, this wall will occupy rows 0 and $m + 1$ and columns 0 and $m + 1$ of the array `maze` (see Figure 9.15).

All positions in the maze are now within the boundary of the surrounding wall, and we can move to four possible positions from each position (some of these four positions may have obstacles). By surrounding the maze with our own boundary, we have eliminated the need for our program to handle boundary conditions, which significantly simplifies the code. This simplification is achieved at the cost of a slightly increased space requirement for the array `maze`.

Each maze position is described by its row and column index, which are, respectively, called the row and column coordinates of the position. We may define a class `Position` with private members `row` and `col` and use objects of type `Position` to keep track of maze positions. The stack, `path`, that maintains the path from the entrance to the current position may be represented as an array-based stack. An $m \times m$ maze with no blockages can have paths with as many as m^2 positions (see Figure 9.16(a)).

```
1  1  1  1  1  1  1  1  1  1  1  1
1  0  1  1  1  1  1  0  0  0  0  1
1  0  0  0  0  0  1  0  1  0  0  1
1  0  0  0  1  0  1  0  0  0  0  1
1  0  1  0  1  0  1  0  1  1  0  1
1  0  1  0  1  0  1  0  1  0  0  1
1  0  1  1  1  0  1  0  1  0  1  1
1  0  1  0  0  0  1  0  1  0  1  1
1  0  1  0  1  1  1  0  1  0  0  1
1  1  0  0  0  0  0  0  1  0  0  1
1  0  0  0  0  1  1  1  1  0  0  1
1  1  1  1  1  1  1  1  1  1  1  1
```

Figure 9.15 Maze of Figure 9.9 with wall of 1s around it

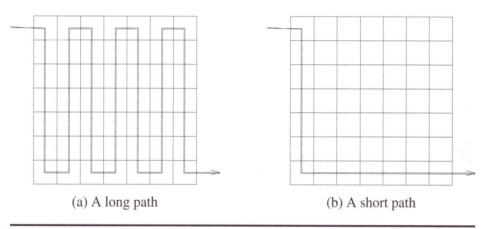

(a) A long path   (b) A short path

Figure 9.16 Paths in a maze with no blockages

Since no path repeats a position and the maze has only m^2 positions, no path can have more than m^2 positions. Further, as the last position on a path is not stored on the stack, at most $m^2 - 1$ positions can get stacked. Notice that a maze with no blockages always has a path with at most $2m$ positions between any two points (see, for example, Figure 9.16(b)). However, we have no assurance at this time that our path finder will find the shortest path.

We can now refine Figure 9.14 and obtain Figure 9.17, which is closer to being a Java program.

```
boolean findPath()
{// Find a path from (1,1) to the exit (m,m).
   Initialize wall of obstacles around maze;

   // initialize variable to keep track of
   // our current position in the maze
   here.row = 1;
   here.col = 1;

   maze[1][1] = 1;  // prevent return to entrance

   // search for a path to the exit
   while (not at exit) do
   {
       find a neighbor to move to;
       if (there is such a neighbor)
       {
          add position here to path stack;
          // move to and block neighbor
          here = neighbor;
          maze[here.row][here.col] = 1;
       }
       else
       {
          // cannot move forward, backup
          if (path empty) return false;
          back up to position here, which is at top of path stack;
       }
   }
   return true;
}
```

Figure 9.17 Refined version of Figure 9.14

Now we need to tackle the problem of determining a neighbor of position **here**
that can be moved to. The task of trying out alternative moves is simplified if
we select from the options available at any position in some systematic way. For
example, we may first attempt to move right, then down, then left, and finally
up. Once an option has been selected, we need to know the coordinates of the
position to move to. These coordinates are easily computed by maintaining a table
of offsets as in Figure 9.18. The moves right, down, left, and up have, respectively,

been numbered 0, 1, 2, and 3. In the table of Figure 9.18, offset[i].row and offset[i].col, respectively, give the amounts to be added to the row and col coordinates of the present position to move to the adjacent position in direction i. For example, if we are at position (3, 4), then the position on the right has row coordinate 3+offset[0].row = 3 and column coordinate 4+offset[0].col = 5.

Move	Direction	offset[move].row	offset[move].col
0	right	0	1
1	down	1	0
2	left	0	−1
3	up	−1	0

Figure 9.18 Table of offsets

To avoid moving to positions that we have been through before, we place an obstacle (i.e., set maze[i][j] = 1) at each position maze[i][j] that we move to.

Incorporating these refinements into the code of Figure 9.17 results in the Java code of Program 9.15. In the code of Program 9.15, the variable size contains the number m of rows and columns in the maze.

The method findPath begins by creating an empty stack path. It then initializes the array of offsets and builds a wall of obstacles around the maze. In the while loop we attempt to advance the path forward from the current position here by trying the move options in the following order: right, down, left, and up. If we are able to move forward, the present location is stored on the stack path and a forward move is made. If a forward move isn't possible, we try to back up to a previous position. If there is no position to back up to (i.e., the stack is empty), there is no path to the exit. Otherwise, we can back up. Once we back up to the top position on the stack (next), we need to move forward by trying the next move option. This option can be computed from the positions next and here. Notice that here is a neighbor of next. In fact, at some previous time in the program, we moved from next to here, and this move was the last move made from next. The next move option to try is correctly computed by the following code:

```
if (next.row == here.row)
    option = 2 + next.col - here.col;
else option = 3 + next.row - here.row;
```

For the time complexity analysis, we see that in the worst case we may move to each unblocked position of the input maze. Each such position may get added to the stack at most three times. (Each time we move forward from a position, it is added to the stack; at most three forward moves are possible from any position.) Hence each position may be removed from the stack at most three times. Further,

```
/** find a path from (1,1) to the exit (size, size)
  * @return true if successful, false if impossible */
private static boolean findPath()
{
   path = new ArrayStack();

   // initialize offsets
   Position [] offset = new Position [4];
   offset[0] = new Position(0, 1);    // right
   offset[1] = new Position(1, 0);    // down
   offset[2] = new Position(0, -1);   // left
   offset[3] = new Position(-1, 0);   // up

   // initialize wall of obstacles around maze
   for (int i = 0; i <= size + 1; i++)
   {
      maze[0][i] = maze[size + 1][i] = 1; // bottom and top
      maze[i][0] = maze[i][size + 1] = 1; // left and right
   }

   Position here = new Position(1, 1);
   maze[1][1] = 1; // prevent return to entrance
   int option = 0; // next move
   int lastOption = 3;

   // search for a path
   while (here.row != size || here.col != size)
   {// not at exit
      // find a neighbor to move to
      int r = 0, c = 0;    // row and column of neighbor
      while (option <= lastOption)
      {
         r = here.row + offset[option].row;
         c = here.col + offset[option].col;
         if (maze[r][c] == 0) break;
         option++; // next option
      }
```

Program 9.15 Code to find a path in a maze (continues)

```
    // was a neighbor found?
    if (option <= lastOption)  // yes
    {// move to maze[r][c]
        path.push(here);
        here = new Position(r, c);
        // set to 1 to prevent revisit
        maze[r][c] = 1;
        option = 0;
    }
    else
    {// no neighbor to move to, back up
        if (path.empty()) return false;  // no place to back up to
        Position next = (Position) path.pop();
        if (next.row == here.row)
            option = 2 + next.col - here.col;
        else option = 3 + next.row - here.row;
        here = next;
    }
  }

  return true;  // at exit
}
```

Program 9.15 Code to find a path in a maze (concluded)

at each position $\Theta(1)$ time is spent examining its neighbors. So the time complexity is $O(unblocked)$ where *unblocked* is the number of unblocked positions in the input maze. This complexity is $O(\mathtt{size}^2) = O(m^2)$.

When you get to Section 17.8.4 you'll see that the strategy used by findPath is really a depth-first search, and when you get to Chapter 21, you'll see that depth-first search is just a special case of a more general strategy called backtracking. So findPath is really an application of depth-first search, backtracking, and stacks.

EXERCISES

13. Write a program to determine whether or not a character string has an un-matched parenthesis. You should not use a stack. Test your code. What is the time complexity of your program?

14. Write a version of Program 9.6 that looks for matched pairs of parenthe-ses and matched pairs of brackets ([and]). In the string (a+[b*(c-d)-+f]), the matched pairs are (0,14), (3,13), and (6,10); and in the string

(a+[b*(c-d]+f)), there is a nesting problem because the left parenthesis at 6 should be matched by a right parenthesis before a left bracket is encountered. Test your code.

15. Do Exercise 14 for the case when you have parentheses, brackets, and braces ({ and }).

16. Manually determine the sequence of disk moves for the four-disk Tower of Hanoi problem.

17. Establish the correctness of Program 9.7 by induction on the number of disks.

18. Assume that the Towers of Hanoi disks are labeled 1 through n with the smallest disk being disk 1. Modify Program 9.7 so that it also outputs the label of the disk that is being moved. This modification requires a simple change to the output statement. Do not make any other changes.

19. Write code for the showState method of Program 9.8 assuming that the output device is a computer screen. If necessary, use the methods of Vector to access the disks on a tower in a convenient manner. You will need to introduce a time delay so that the display does not change too rapidly. Show each disk in a different color.

20. The Towers of HaHa problem is like the Towers of Hanoi problem. However, the disks are numbered 1 through n; odd-numbered disks are red, and even-numbered ones are yellow. The disks are initially on tower 1 in the order 1 through n from top to bottom. The disks are to be moved to tower 2, and at no time should a disk sit on top of a disk that has the same color. The initial and final disk order are the same.

    (a) Write a program to move the disks from tower 1 to tower 2 using tower 3 for intermediate storage.

    (b) How many disk moves does your program make?

★ 21. Investigate the Towers of Hanoi problem under the assumption that you have $k > 1$ intermediate towers. The availability of more towers reduces the number of moves needed. For example, when the number of intermediate towers is $n - 1$, a total of $2n - 1$ disk moves suffices. A good place to start is the case when two intermediate towers are available.

22. (a) You have a railroad shunting yard with three shunting tracks that operate as stacks. The initial ordering of cars is 3, 1, 6, 7, 2, 8, 5, 4. Draw figures similar to Figures 9.6 and 9.7 to show the configuration of the shunting tracks, the input track, and the output track following each car move made by the solution of Section 9.5.3.

    (b) Do part (a) for two shunting tracks.

23. In our solution to the railroad car rearrangement problem (Section 9.5.3), we use k array-based stacks to represent k holding tracks. How large can each stack get? What is the total stack space required?

★ 24. (a) Does Program 9.10 succeed in rearranging the cars whenever it is possible to do this rearrangement using k tracks?

   (b) The total number of car moves required is $n +$ (number of cars moved to a holding track). Suppose that the initial car arrangement can be rearranged using k tracks and Program 9.10. Does Program 9.10 perform the rearrangement using the minimum number of moves? Prove your answer.

25. Develop a program for the railroad car rearrangement problem under the assumption that holding track i can hold at most s_i cars, $1 \leq i \leq k$.

26. Walk through Program 9.13 for the case when the nets are (1, 6), (2, 5), (3, 4), (7, 10), (8, 9), (12, 13), and (11, 14). Show the stack configuration after the examination of each pin.

27. In the switch box routing application, we noted that processing can stop when two pins of the same net get on to the stack. Write a new version of checkBox that does this. The time complexity of your new method should be $O(n)$ where n is the number of pins. You may assume that the net numbers are 1 through $n/2$. How large a stack do you need?

28. Do the following for the offline equivalence class problem:

   (a) Give the lists $list[1 : n]$ for the case when $n = 9$, $r = 9$, and the input relation pairs are (1, 3), (4, 2), (3, 8), (6, 7), (5, 8), (6, 2), (1, 5), (4, 7), and (9, 7).

   (b) Walk through the second phase of the solution strategy using the lists of part (a). Provide an explanation of your progress as is done in Example 9.4.

29. Program 9.14 does not validate the relations as they are input. Rather, it relies on the subsequent indexing into the array list to catch errant input. Modify this program so that it makes sure that each a and b that is input is in the range [1, n] and throws an exception of type MyInputException whenever this is not the case.

30. (a) Modify Program 9.14 so that list[] is an array of type ArrayLinear-List rather than ArrayStack. Use a linear list iterator to examine the elements on a linear list in phase 2 of the program.

   (b) Experimentally compare the performance of Program 9.14 and your new code.

31. Complete the rat-in-a-maze code. Write a pleasing Java program by doing the following:

    (a) Write a `welcome` method that incorporates graphics and audio.

    (b) Write a robust `inputMaze` method. For example, there may not be enough memory to create the array `maze`. Check for this condition and output an error message. Also provide user prompts for input.

    (c) Write the `outputPath` method to output the path from the maze to the exit (not from the exit to the entrance).

    Test your codes using sample mazes.

32. Modify the code for the rat-in-a-maze problem so that the code works for mazes in which you are allowed to move to the north, northeast, east, southeast, south, southwest, west, and northwest neighbors of a position. Test the correctness of the modified code using suitable mazes.

33. Develop a better bound than $m^2 - 1$ for the maximum size of the stack `path`.

34. The strategy used to find a path in a maze is really a recursive one. From the present position we find a neighbor to move to and then determine whether there is a path from this neighbor to the exit. If so, we are done. If not, we find another neighbor to move to. Use recursion to find a path in a maze. Test the correctness of your code using suitable mazes.

★ 35. Study the rat-in-a-maze animation that is on the Web site for this book.

    (a) Identify heuristics you could program into the rat-in-a-maze program to select the next move in a more intelligent fashion than is done in Program 9.15. For example, should you preferentially follow along a wall of blocked positions looking for a break in the wall?

    (b) Modify Program 9.15 to incorporate your heuristics.

    (c) Test the correctness of the new code.

    (d) Compare the run-time performance of the new code and that of Program 9.15.

36. You are given an array, `data[]`, of integers. Your task is to compute another integer array `lastAsBig[]`. Informally, `lastAsBig[i]` gives you the nearest position to the left where the data value is at least as big. For example, when `data[] = [6, 2, 3, 1, 7, 5]`, `lastAsBig[] = [-1, 0, 0, 2, -1, 4]`. More formally, `lastAsBig[i]` is the largest integer j such that j < i and data[j] ≥ data[i]. In case no there is no such j, then `lastAsBig[i] = -1`.

    One application of `lastAsBig` is in weather reporting. Let `data[i]` be the high temperature recorded in Gainesville in day i of the current year. If `lastAsBig[i]` is -1, then we have not seen a temperature this high earlier in the year. When `lastAsBig[i]` $\neq -1$, `lastAsBig[i]` gives the last time this year that the temperature was this high; $i -$ `lastAsBig[i]` gives the number of days since the temperature was this high (this year).

(a) Give two more applications for `lastAsBig`.

(b) Write a method to compute `lastAsBig` that uses a stack. The time complexity of your method should be $O($`data.length`$)$.

(c) Test your method.

9.6   REFERENCES AND SELECTED READINGS

The switch box routing algorithm is from Hsu and Pinter. It is described in the papers "General River Routing Algorithm" by C. Hsu, *ACM/IEEE Design Automation Conference*, pages 578–583, 1983 and "River-Routing: Methodology and Analysis" by R. Pinter, *Third Caltech Conference on VLSI*, March 1983.

CHAPTER 10

QUEUES

BIRD'S-EYE VIEW

A queue, like a stack, is a special kind of linear list. In a queue insertions and deletions take place from different ends of the linear list. Consequently, a queue is a first-in-first-out (FIFO) list. Another variety of queue—a priority queue—from which deletions are made in order of element priority is developed in Chapter 13.

Although queue classes may be easily derived from any of the linear list classes developed in Chapters 5 through 7, we do not do so in this chapter. For run-time efficiency reasons, the array-based and linked classes for a queue are developed as base classes.

In the applications section we develop four sample codes that use a queue. The first is for the railroad-switching problem considered initially in Section 9.5.3. In this chapter the problem has been modified so that the shunting tracks at the railroad yard are FIFO rather than LIFO. The second application is the classical Lee's algorithm to find the shortest path for a wire that is to connect two given points. This application may also be viewed as a variant of the rat-in-a-maze problem of Section 9.5.6. In this variant we must find the shortest path between the maze entrance and exit. Notice that the code developed in Section 9.5.6 does not guarantee to find a shortest path. That code simply guarantees to find a path (of unspecifed length) whenever the maze has at least one entrance-to-exit path. The third application, from the computer-vision field, labels the pixels of a binary image so that two pixels have the same label iff they are part of the same image component. The final application is a machine shop simulation. The machine shop has several machines, each capable of performing a different task. Each job in the shop requires one or more tasks to be performed. We provide a program to simulate the flow of jobs through the machine shop. Our program determines the total time each job spends waiting to be processed as well as the total wait at each machine. We can use this information to improve the machine shop. Although the machine shop simulator developed in this chapter uses FIFO queues, real-world machine shops may require some or all of these FIFO queues be replaced by priority queues. Additional queue applications appear in later chapters.

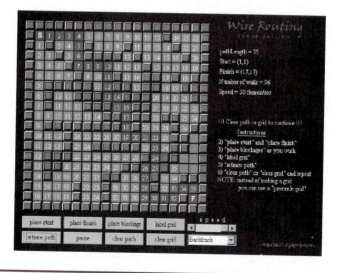

Wire routing—On the Web

10.1   DEFINITION AND APPLICATIONS

Definition 10.1 *A **queue** is a linear list in which insertions (also called additions and puts) and deletions (also called removals) take place at different ends. The end at which new elements are added is called the **rear**, and that from which old elements are deleted is called the **front**.* ■

A queue with three elements is shown in Figure 10.1(a). The first element we delete from the queue of Figure 10.1(a) is A. Following the deletion, the configuration of Figure 10.1(b) results. To add element D to the queue of Figure 10.1(b), we must place it after element C. The new configuration is shown in Figure 10.1(c).

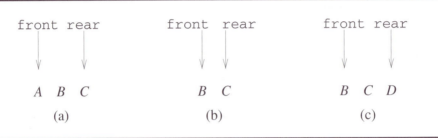

	front rear			front rear			front rear	
	↓ ↓			↓ ↓			↓ ↓	
A	B	C		B	C		B C	D
	(a)			(b)			(c)	

Figure 10.1 Sample queues

So a queue is a FIFO list, whereas a stack is a LIFO list.

Example 10.1 [Queues in the Real World]

- Although the stack of trays in a cafeteria works in a LIFO manner (see Example 9.1), the food line you stand in works in a FIFO manner. Customers exit at the checkout register in the order in which they entered the food line—the food line is a queue. Most other lines you find yourself in—the check-out line at a store, the line in front of a bank teller, the line of cars waiting at a car wash, the line at the postal center—also work in a FIFO manner.

- In a soda vending machine, you have a column of soda cans for each variety of soda dispensed. In each column cans are piled one on top of another. When you buy a can of soda, the can at the bottom of a column is given; when the stock is replenished, cans are added to the top of the column. The vending machine dispenses soda cans in a FIFO manner; the machine maintains a queue for each variety of soda dispensed.

- In a distributed system a single queue often feeds a bank of queues. A distributed system that has m servers has a bank of m server queues, one for each server. In addition, there is a queue called the broker or trader queue. Requests for service are first queued in the broker queue; a broker (or trader or dispatcher) examines the service requests in the broker queue in a FIFO order and sends each request to the queue for the most appropriate server; servers handle the service requests in their queues in a FIFO order. Two specific examples follow.

1. In a distributed file system, computer files are replicated across file servers so as to provide a better level of service. All requests for a file are first queued in a broker queue; a broker dispatches each request to the least loaded server that has a copy of the requested file; the dispatched request waits its turn in the queue for the file server to which it is dispatched.

2. Voter polling stations provide a rather interesting application of queues. When you arrive at the polling station, you join a broker queue. When you get to the front of the broker queue, a polling volunteer directs you to a server queue based on the first letter of your surname. At the head of each server queue is a volunteer who checks your ID, gets your signature, and issues a ballot card. Once you have a card, you get into another queue and wait for a booth where you can punch holes in the ballot card to select your desired candidates. ■

EXERCISES

1. The following sequence of operations is done on an initially empty queue: add X, add Y, remove, add D, add A, remove, add T, add A. Draw figures similar to those of Figure 10.1 to show the queue configuration after each operation.

2. Identify three additional real-world applications of a queue. Do not include applications that involve people in a single line or vending machines. Distributed systems that involve people are okay.

3. Identify three real-world applications in which a stack is used sometimes and a queue is used at other times. For example, if you examine napkin dispensers, you will notice that some work as a stack and others work as a queue.

4. Which applications from Section 9.5 can use a queue instead of a stack without affecting the correctness of the program?

10.2   THE ABSTRACT DATA TYPE

The ADT queue is specified in ADT 10.1.

Program 10.1 gives the Java interface that corresponds to ADT 10.1.

AbstractDataType *Queue*
{
    instances
        ordered list of elements; one end is called the `front`; the other is the `rear`;

    operations
        isEmpty() : Return `true` if the queue is empty, return `false` otherwise;

getFrontElement() : Return the front element of the queue;

getRearElement() : Return the rear element of the queue;

put(*x*) : Add element *x* at the rear of the queue;

remove() : Remove an element from the front of the queue and return it;

}

ADT 10.1 The abstract data type queue

```
public interface Queue
{
   public boolean isEmpty();
   public Object getFrontElement();
   public Object getRearElement();
   public void put(Object theObject);
   public Object remove();
}
```

Program 10.1 The interface `Queue`

10.3   ARRAY REPRESENTATION

10.3.1   The Representation

Suppose that the queue elements are mapped into an array `queue` using Equation 10.1.

$$location(i) = i \tag{10.1}$$

This equation worked well for the array-based representation of linear lists and stacks. Element *i* of the queue is stored in `queue[i]`, $i \geq 0$, `front` equals 0, `rear` is the location of the last element, and the queue size is `rear+1`. An empty queue has `rear = −1`. Using Equation 10.1, the queues of Figure 10.1 are represented as in Figure 10.2.

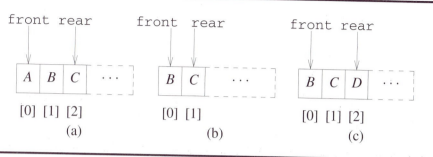

Figure 10.2 Queues of Figure 10.1 using Equation 10.1

To insert/add/put an element at the rear of a queue, we need to increase `rear` by 1 and place the new element at `queue[rear]`, which means that an insertion requires $\Theta(1)$ time. To delete/remove an element from the front, we must slide the elements in positions 1 through `rear` one position down the array. Sliding the elements takes $\Theta(n)$ time where n is the number of elements in the queue following the deletion.

We can remove elements from the front of a queue in $\Theta(1)$ time if we use Equation 10.2 instead of Equation 10.1. The index i for the front element is 0.

$$location(i) = location(\text{front element}) + i \qquad (10.2)$$

Equation 10.2 does not require us to shift the queue one position left each time an element is deleted from the queue. Instead, we simply increase $location$(front element) by 1. Figure 10.3 shows the representation of the queues of Figure 10.1 that results when Equation 10.2 is used. Notice that `front` = $location$(front element), `rear` = $location$(last element), and an empty queue has `rear < front`.

As Figure 10.3(b) shows, each deletion causes `front` to move right by 1. Hence there will be times when `rear` = `queue.length` and `front > 0`. At these times the number of elements in the queue is less than `queue.length`, and there is space for additional elements at the left end of the array. To continue inserting elements into the queue, we can shift all elements to the left end of the queue (as in Figure 10.4) and create space at the right end. This shifting increases the worst-case time for a `put` operation from $\Theta(1)$, when Equation 10.1 is used, to $\Theta(\texttt{queue.length})$. So the trade-off for improved efficiency of the `remove` operation is a loss of efficiency for the `put` operation.

The worst-case insert and delete times (assuming no array resizing is needed) become $\Theta(1)$ when we permit the queue to wrap around the end of the array. At

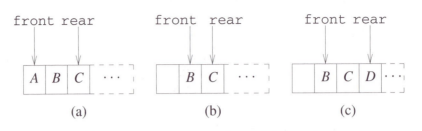

Figure 10.3 Queues of Figure 10.1 using Equation 10.2

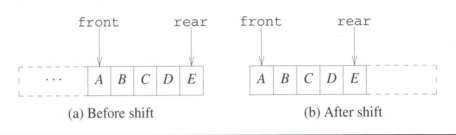

Figure 10.4 Shifting a queue

this time it is convenient to think of the array positions as arranged in a circle (Figure 10.5) rather than in a straight line (Figure 10.4).

When the array is viewed as a circle, each array position has a next and a previous position. The position next to position `queue.length` $- 1$ is 0, and the position that precedes 0 is `queue.length` $- 1$. When the queue rear is at `queue.length` $- 1$, the next element is put into position 0. The circular array representation of a queue uses the following mapping function:

$$location(i) = (location(\text{front element}) + i)\%\texttt{queue.length} \qquad (10.3)$$

In Figure 10.5 we have changed the convention for the variable `front`. This variable now points one position counterclockwise from the location of the front element in the queue. The convention for `rear` is unchanged. This change simplifies the codes.

Inserting an element at the end of the queue of Figure 10.5(a) results in the queue of Figure 10.5(b). Removing an element from the front of the queue of Figure 10.5(b) results in the queue of Figure 10.5(c).

A queue is empty iff `front = rear`. The initial condition `front = rear =` 0 defines an initially empty queue. If we insert elements into the queue of Fig-

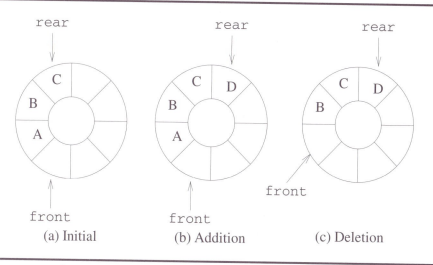

Figure 10.5 Circular queues

ure 10.5(b) until the number of elements in the array `queue` equals `queue.length` (i.e., the queue becomes full), we obtain the configuration of Figure 10.6. This configuration has `front = rear`, which is the same condition as when the queue is empty! Therefore, we cannot distinguish between an empty and a full queue. To avoid this difficulty, we will not permit a queue to get full. Before inserting an element into a queue, we verify whether this insertion will cause the queue to get full. If so, we double the length of the array `queue` and then proceed with the insertion. Using this strategy, the array `queue` can have at most `queue.length-1` elements in it.

10.3.2   The Class `ArrayQueue`

The class `ArrayQueue` uses Equation 10.3 to map a queue into a one-dimensional array `queue`. The data members of `ArrayQueue` are `front`, `rear`, and `queue`; the codes for all methods other than `put` and `remove` are similar to those for the corresponding methods of `ArrayStack`. These codes are available from the Web site. The method `put` (Program 10.2) uses customized code (Program 10.3) to double the array length.

To visualize array doubling when a circular queue is used, it is better to flatten out the array as in Figure 10.7(a). This figure shows a queue with seven elements in an array whose length is 8. Figure 10.7(b) shows the the flattened view of the same queue. Figure 10.7(c) shows the array after array doubling by `ChangeArray-Length.changeLength1D`.

To get a proper circular queue configuration, we must slide the elements in

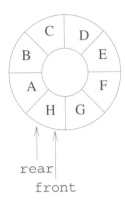

Figure 10.6 A circular queue with `queue.length` elements

```
/** insert theElement at the rear of the queue */
public void put(Object theElement)
{
   // increase array length if necessary
   if ((rear + 1) % queue.length == front)
   {// double array size
      // code to double array size comes here
   }

   // put theElement at the rear of the queue
   rear = (rear + 1) % queue.length;
   queue[rear] = theElement;
}
```

Program 10.2 Adding an element to a queue

the right segment (i.e., elements A and B) to the right end of the array as in Figure 10.7(d). The array doubling copies `queue.length` element references, and when the second segment is slid right, up to `queue.length-2` additional element references are copied. The number of references copied can be limited to `queue.length-1` by customizing the array doubling code. Figure 10.7(e) shows an alternative configuration for the array after doubling. This configuration may be obtained as follows:

- Create a new array `newQueue` of twice the length.

- Use `arraycopy` to copy the second segment (i.e., the `queue.length-front-1`

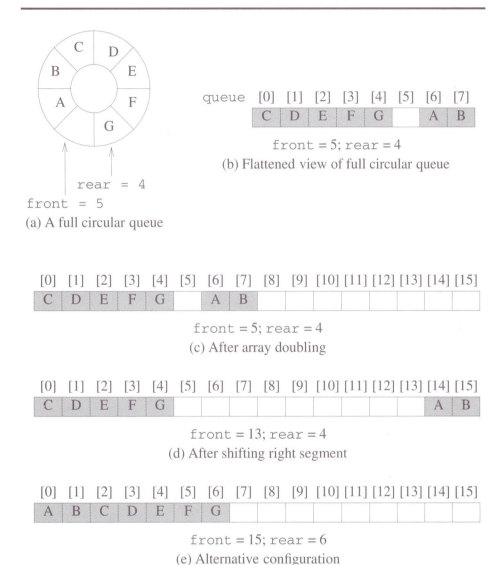

Figure 10.7 Doubling array length

elements beginning at `queue[front+1]`) to positions in `newQueue` beginning
at 0.

- Use `arraycopy` to copy the first segment (i.e., the `rear+1` elements beginning
  at `queue[0]`) to positions in `newQueue` beginning at `queue.length-front-1`.

The code of Program 10.3 obtains the configuration of Figure 10.7(e). Program 10.4 gives the code for the method that removes an element from a queue.

```java
// allocate a new array
Object [] newQueue = new Object [2 * queue.length];

// copy elements into new array
int start = (front + 1) % queue.length;
if (start < 2)
   // no wrap around
   System.arraycopy(queue, start, newQueue, 0,
                    queue.length - 1);
else
{  // queue wraps around
   System.arraycopy(queue, start, newQueue, 0,
                    queue.length - start);
   System.arraycopy(queue, 0, newQueue,
                    queue.length - start, rear + 1);
}

// switch to newQueue and set front and rear
front = newQueue.length - 1;
rear = queue.length - 2;   // queue size is queue.length - 1
queue = newQueue;
```

Program 10.3 Doubling the length of the array queue

```java
public Object remove()
{
   if (isEmpty())
      return null;
   front = (front + 1) % queue.length;
   Object frontElement = queue[front];
   queue[front] = null;   // enable garbage collection
   return frontElement;
}
```

Program 10.4 Removing an element from a queue

The complexity of the queue constructor is $O(\texttt{initialCapacity})$; the complexity of $\texttt{isEmpty}$, $\texttt{getFrontElement}$, $\texttt{getRearElement}$, and $\texttt{remove}$ is $\Theta(1)$; and the complexity of $\texttt{put}$ is $\Theta(1)$ when no array doubling is done and is $\Theta(\text{queue size})$ when array doubling is done. From the analysis used to establish Theorem 5.1, it follows that the complexity of m invocations of $\texttt{put}$ is $O(m)$.

EXERCISES

5. (a) Extend the queue ADT by adding functions to
     i. Determine the size (i.e., number of elements) of the queue.
     ii. Input a queue.
     iii. Output a queue.
     iv. Split a queue into two queues. The first of the resulting queues contains the first, third, fifth, $\cdots$ elements of the original queue; the second contains the remaining elements.
     v. Combine two queues by selecting elements alternately from the two queues beginning with queue 1. When a queue exhausts, append the remaining elements from the other queue to the combined queue. The relative order of elements from each queue is unchanged.
   (b) Define the interface $\texttt{ExtendedQueue}$ that extends the interface $\texttt{Queue}$ and includes methods that correspond to the functions of (a).
   (c) Develop code for the class $\texttt{ExtendedArrayQueue}$ that extends the class $\texttt{ArrayQueue}$ and implements the interface $\texttt{ExtendedQueue}$ of (b).
   (d) Test your code.

6. Modify the representation used in the class $\texttt{ArrayQueue}$ so that a queue can hold as many elements as the length of the array $\texttt{queue}$. For this modification introduce another data member $\texttt{lastOp}$ that keeps track of the last operation (from among the operations $\texttt{put}$ and $\texttt{remove}$) performed on the queue. Notice that if the last operation performed was $\texttt{put}$, the queue cannot be empty. Also, if the last operation was $\texttt{remove}$, the queue cannot be full. So $\texttt{lastOp}$ can be used to distinguish between an empty and full queue when $\texttt{front} = \texttt{rear}$. Test the correctness of your modifed code.

7. A **deque** (pronounced *deck*) is an ordered list to/from which we can make insertions and removals at/from either end. Therefore, we can call it a double-ended queue.

   (a) Define the ADT *Deque*. Include the operations *isEmpty, getLeftElement, getRightElement, putAtLeft, putAtRight, removeFromLeft*, and *removeFromRight*.
   (b) Define a Java inteface $\texttt{Deque}$ that includes methods for each function of the ADT *Deque*.

    (c) Use Equation 10.3 to represent a deque. Develop a Java class `ArrayDeque` that implements the interface `Deque`.

    (d) Test your code using suitable test data.

8. (a) Develop the class `DequeStack` that implements the interface `Stack` (Program 9.1) and whose superclass is `ArrayDeque` (see Exercise 7).

    (b) What is the time complexity of each method of `DequeStack`?

    (c) Comment on the expected performance of the methods of `DequeStack` relative to their counterparts in `ArrayStack`.

9. (a) Develop the class `DequeQueue` that implements the interface `Queue` (Program 10.1) and whose superclass is `ArrayDeque` (see Exercise 7).

    (b) What is the time complexity of each method of `DequeQueue`?

    (c) Comment on the expected performance of the methods of `DequeQueue` relative to their counterparts in `ArrayQueue`.

10.4   LINKED REPRESENTATION

A queue, like a stack, can be represented as a chain. We need two variables, `front` and `rear`, to keep track of the two ends of a queue. There are two possibilities for binding these two variables to the two ends of a chain. The nodes can be linked from front to rear (Figure 10.8(a)) or from rear to front (Figure 10.8(b)). The relative difficulty of performing inserts and removes determines the direction of linkage. Figures 10.9 and 10.10, respectively, illustrate the mechanics of an insert and a remove. We can see that both linkage directions are well suited for inserts, but the front-to-rear linkage is more efficient for removes. Hence we will link the nodes in a queue from front to rear.

    We can use the initial values `front = rear = null` and the boundary value `front = null` iff the queue is empty. The class `LinkedQueue` may be defined as a derived class of `ExtendedChain` (Program 6.10). Exercise 10 considers this way of developing `LinkedQueue`. In this section we develop the class `LinkedQueue` from scratch.

    Program 10.5 gives the `put` and `remove` methods of `LinkedQueue`. You should run through these codes by hand using an empty queue, a queue with one element, and a queue with many elements as examples. The complexity of each of the linked queue methods is $\Theta(1)$.

EXERCISES

10. Develop the class `LinkedQueueFromExtendedChain` to extend the class `ExtendedChain` (Section 6.1.5) and implement the interface `Queue`.

11. Do Exercise 5 using a linked queue.

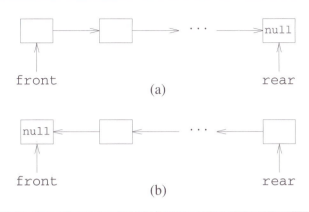

Figure 10.8 Linked queues

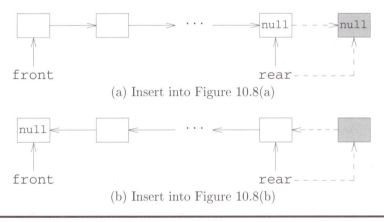

Figure 10.9 Insert into a linked queue

12. Compare the performance of `ArrayQueue` and `LinkedQueue` by performing a sequence of 500,000 `put` operations followed by 500,000 `remove` operations.

13. In some queue applications the elements to be put on a queue are already in nodes of type `ChainNode`. For these applications it is desirable to have the methods `putNode(ChainNode theNode)`, which adds `theNode` at the end of the queue (notice that no call to `new` is made), and `removeNode`, which removes and returns the front node of the queue.

    (a) Write code for these methods.

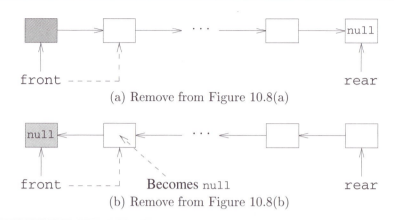

(a) Remove from Figure 10.8(a)

(b) Remove from Figure 10.8(b)

Figure 10.10 Remove from a linked queue

  (b) Test your code.

  (c) Compare the time required by a sequence of 500,000 `puts` followed by 500,000 `removes` with that required by 500,000 `putNodes` followed by 500,000 `removeNodes`.

14. See Exercise 7 or the definition of a deque.

  (a) Develop a Java class `DoublyLinkedDeque` that implements the interface `Deque` of Exercise 7 using a doubly linked list. Your class should not extend any other class.

  (b) What is the complexity of each method of your class?

  (c) Test your code using suitable test data.

15. Do Exercise 14 using a singly linked list (i.e., a chain) rather than a doubly linked list. Name your class `LinkedDeque`.

16. Do Exercise 14 using a singly linked circular list rather than a doubly linked list. Name your class `CircularDeque`.

```
/** insert theElement at the rear of the queue */
public void put(Object theElement)
{
   // create a node for theElement
   ChainNode p = new ChainNode(theElement, null);

   // append p to the chain
   if (front == null)
      front = p;                    // empty queue
   else
      rear.next = p;                // nonempty queue
   rear = p;
}


/** remove an element from the front of the queue
  * @return removed element
  * @return null if the queue is empty */
public Object remove()
{
   if (isEmpty())
      return null;
   Object frontElement = front.element;
   front = front.next;
   if (isEmpty())
      rear = null;  // enable garbage collection
   return frontElement;
}
```

Program 10.5 Adding to and removing from a linked queue

10.5   APPLICATIONS

10.5.1   Railroad Car Rearrangement

Problem Description and Solution Strategy

We will reconsider the railroad car rearrangement problem of Section 9.5.3. This time the holding tracks lie between the input and output track as in Figure 10.11. These tracks operate in a FIFO manner and so may be regarded as queues. As in the case of Section 9.5.3, moving a car from a holding track to the input track or from the output track to a holding track is forbidden. All car motion is in the direction indicated by the arrowheads of Figure 10.11.

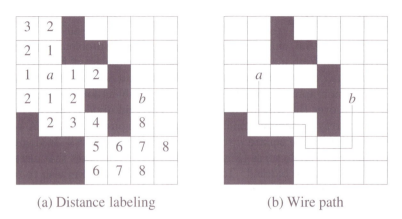

(a) Distance labeling   (b) Wire path

Figure 10.13 Wire routing

Once we have reached b, we can label it with its distance (9 in the case of Figure 10.13(a)). The distance-labeling pass is followed by the path-identification pass in which we begin at b and move to any one its neighbors labeled 1 less than b's label. Such a neighbor must exist as each grid's label is 1 more than that of at least one of its neighbors. In the case of Figure 10.13(a), we move from b to (5, 6). From here we move to one of its neighbors whose label is 1 less and so on until we reach a. In the example of Figure 10.13(a), from (5, 6) we move to (6, 6) and then to (6, 5), (6, 4), (5, 4), and so on. Figure 10.13(b) shows the constructed path, which is a shortest path between (3, 2) and (4, 6). Notice that the shortest path between (3, 2) and (4, 6) is not unique; (3, 2), (3, 3), (4, 3), (5, 3), (5, 4), (6, 4), (6, 5), (6, 6), (5, 6), (4, 6) is another shortest path.

Java Implementation

Now let us take the strategy outlined above and obtain Java code to find a shortest path in a grid. We will use many ideas from the rat-in-a-maze solution of Section 9.5.6. An $m \times m$ grid is represented as a two-dimensional array `grid` with a 0 representing an open position and a 1 a blocked position, The grid is surrounded by a "wall" of 1s; the array `offsets` helps us move from a position to its neighbors; and a queue keeps track of labeled grid positions whose neighbors have not been examined.

To implement the distance-labeling pass, we can either use an additional two-dimensional array for the distances or we can overload the use of the array `grid`. In practice, wire-routing grids do get large enough to tax the memory of even the most memory-rich computers. Therefore, the use of a second array is not recommended. When we overload the array `grid`, we have a conflict between our use of the label

1 to designate a blocked grid position and our use of the label 1 for a position that is a unit distance from the start position a. To resolve this conflict, we increase all distance labels by 2. So grid[i][j] = 1 for a blocked position; grid[i][j] > 1 for a position whose distance from the start position is grid[i][j] − 2; and grid[i][j] = 0 for an unblocked and unreached position.

Program 10.8 gives the code. This code is part of the class WireRouter, and the variables start (a) and finish (b) are static data members of this class.

Our code assumes that the positions start and finish are not blocked. The code begins with a check to see whether the start and finish positions are the same. In this case the path length is 0, and the code terminates. Otherwise, we set up a wall of blocked positions around the grid, initialize the offset array, and label the start position with a distance of 2. Using the queue q and beginning at position start, we move to reachable grid positions that are distance 1 from the start and then to those that are distance 2, and so on until we either reach the finish position or are unable to move to a new, unblocked position. In the latter case there is no path to the finish position. In the former case the finish position is labeled by its distance value.

If we reach the finish position, the path is reconstructed using the distance labels. The positions on the path (except for start) are stored in the array path.

Complexity

Since no grid position can get on the queue more than once, it takes $O(m^2)$ time (for an $m \times m$ grid) to complete the distance-labeling phase. The time needed for the path-construction phase is $O(\text{length of the shortest path})$.

10.5.3   Image-Component Labeling

Problem Description

A digitized image is an $m \times m$ matrix of pixels. In a binary image each pixel is either 0 or 1. A 0 pixel represents image background, while a 1 represents a point on an image component. We will refer to pixels whose value is 1 as component pixels. Two pixels are adjacent if one is to the left, above, right, or below the other. Two component pixels that are adjacent are pixels of the same image component. The objective of component labeling is to label the component pixels so that two pixels get the same label iff they are pixels of the same image component.

Consider Figure 10.14(a) that shows a 7×7 image. The blank squares represent background pixels, and the 1s represent component pixels. Pixels (1, 3) and (2, 3) are pixels of the same component because they are adjacent. Since component pixels (2, 3) and (2, 4) are adjacent, they are also of the same component. Hence the three pixels (1, 3), (2, 3), and (2, 4) are from the same component. Since no other image pixels are adjacent to these three pixels, these three define an image component. The image of Figure 10.14(a) has four components. The first component is defined by the pixel set (1, 3), (2, 3), (2, 4); the second is (3, 5), (4, 4), (4, 5), (5, 5); the

```
                    if (pixel[nbr.row][nbr.col] == 1)
                    {// pixel is part of current component
                       pixel[nbr.row][nbr.col] = id;
                       q.put(new Position(nbr.row, nbr.col));
                    }
                 }

                 // any unexplored pixels in component?
                 here = (Position) q.remove(); // a component pixel
            } while(here != null);

        } // end of if, for c, and for r
}
```

Program 10.9 Component labeling (concluded)

Program 10.9 begins by setting up a wall of background (0) pixels around the image and initializing the array of neighbor/adjacent pixel offsets. The next two `for` loops scan the image for a seed for the next component. The seed is an unmarked component pixel. For such a pixel, `pixel[r][c]` is 1. The seed is assigned a component label by changing `pixel[r][c]` from 1 to a component identifier/label (`id`). Then with the help of a queue (a stack can be used instead), the remaining pixels in this component are identified. By the time the method `labelComponents` terminates, all component pixels have been assigned a label.

Complexity

It takes $\Theta(m)$ time to initialize the wall of background pixels and $\Theta(1)$ time to initialize `offsets`. Although the condition `pixel[r][c] == 1` is checked m^2 times, it is true only as many times as the number of components in the image. For each component $O(\text{number of pixels in component})$ time is spent identifying and labeling its pixels (other than the component seed). Since no pixel is in two or more components, the total time spent identifying and labeling nonseed component pixels is $O(\text{number of component pixels in image})$. Since the number of component pixels equals the number of pixels with value 1 in the input image and since this number is at most m^2, the overall time complexity of method `labelComponents` is $O(m^2)$.

10.5.4   Machine Shop Simulation

Problem Description

A machine shop (or factory or plant) comprises m machines or workstations. The machine shop works on jobs, and each job comprises several tasks. Each machine can process one task of one job at any time, and different machines perform different tasks. Once a machine begins to process a task, it continues processing that task until the task completes.

Example 10.2 A sheet metal plant might have one machine (or station) for each of the following tasks: design; cut the sheet metal to size; drill holes; cut holes; trim edges; shape the metal; and seal seams. Each of these machines/stations can work on one task at a time.

Each job includes several tasks. For example, to fabricate the heating and air-conditioning ducts for a new house, we would need to spend some time in the design phase, and then some time cutting the sheet metal stock to the right size pieces. We need to drill or cut the holes (depending on their size), shape the cut pieces into ducts, seal the seams, and trim any rough edges.   ■

For each task of a job, there is a task time (i.e., how long does it take) and a machine on which it is to be performed. The tasks of a job are to be performed in a specified order. So a job goes first to the machine for its first task. When this first task is complete, the job goes to the machine for its second task, and so on until its last task completes. When a job arrives at a machine, the job may have to wait because the machine might be busy. In fact, several jobs may already be waiting for that machine.

Each machine in our machine shop can be in one of three states: active, idle, and change over. In the active state the machine is working on a task of some job; in the idle state it is doing nothing; and in the change-over state the machine has completed a task and is preparing for a new task. In the change-over state, the machine operator might, for example, clean the machine, put away tools used for the last task, and take a break. The time each machine must spend in its change-over state depends on the machine.

When a machine becomes available for a new job, it will need to pick one of the waiting jobs to work on. We assume that each machine serves its waiting jobs in a FIFO manner, and so the waiting jobs at each machine form a (FIFO) queue. Other assumptions for the selection of the next job are possible. For example, the next job may be selected by priority. Each job has a priority, and when a machine becomes free, the waiting job with highest priority is selected.

The time at which a job's last task completes is called its **finish time**. The **length** of a job is the sum of its task times. If a job of length l arrives at the machine shop at time 0 and completes at time f, then it must have spent exactly $f - l$ amount of time waiting in machine queues. To keep customers happy, it is desirable to minimize the time a job spends waiting in machine queues. Machine shop performance can be improved if we know how much time jobs spend waiting and which machines are contributing most to this wait.

How the Simulation Works

When simulating a machine shop, we follow the jobs from machine to machine without physically performing the tasks. We simulate time by using a simulated clock that is advanced each time a task completes or a new job enters the machine shop. As tasks complete, new tasks are scheduled. Each time a task completes or a new job enters the shop, we say that an **event** has occurred. In addition, a **start event** initiates the simulation. When two or more events occur at the same time, we arbitrarily order these events. Figure 10.15 describes how a simulation works.

```
// initialize
input the data;
create the job queues at each machine;
schedule first job in each machine queue;

// do the simulation
while (an unfinished job remains)
{
    determine the next event;
    if (the next event is the completion of a machine change over)
        schedule the next job (if any) from this machine's queue;
    else
      {// a job task has completed
       put the machine that finished the job task into its change-over state;
       move the job whose task has finished to the machine for its next task
       (if any);
      }
}
```

Figure 10.15 The mechanics of simulation

Example 10.3 Consider a machine shop that has $m = 3$ machines and $n = 4$ jobs. We assume that all four jobs are available at time 0 and that no new jobs become available during the simulation. The simulation will continue until all jobs have completed.

The three machines, $M1$, $M2$, and $M3$, have a change-over time of 2, 3, and 1, respectively. So when a task completes, machine 1 must wait two time units before starting another, machine 2 must wait three time units, and machine 3 must wait one time unit. Figure 10.16(a) gives the characteristics of the four jobs. Job 1, for example, has three tasks. Each task is specified as a pair of the form (machine, time). The first task of job 1 is to be done on $M1$ and takes two time units, the second is to be done on $M2$ and takes four time units, the third is to be done on $M1$ and takes one time unit. The job lengths (i.e., the sum of their task times) are 7, 6, 8, and 4, respectively.

Figure 10.16(b) shows the machine shop simulation. Initially, the four jobs are placed into queues corresponding to their first tasks. The first task for jobs 1 and 3 are to be done on $M1$, so these jobs are placed on the queue for $M1$. The first tasks for jobs 2 and 4 are to be done on $M3$. Consequently, these jobs begin on the queue for $M3$. The queue for $M2$ is empty. At the start all three machines are idle. We use the symbol I to indicate that the machines have no active job at this time. Since no machine is active, the time at which they will finish their current active task is undefined and denoted by the symbol L (large time).

The simulation begins at time 0. That is, the first event, the start event, occurs at time 0. At this time the first job in each machine queue is scheduled on the corresponding machine. Job 1's first task is scheduled on $M1$, and job 2's first task on $M3$. The queue for $M1$ now contains job 3 only, while that for $M3$ contains job 4 only. The queue for $M2$ remains empty. Job 1 becomes the active job on $M1$, and job 2 the active job on $M3$. $M2$ remains idle. The finish time for $M1$ becomes 2 (current time of 0 plus task time of 2), and the finish time for $M3$ becomes 4.

The next event occurs at time 2. This time is determined by finding the minimum of the machine finish times. At time 2 machine $M1$ completes its active task. This task is a job 1 task. Job 1 is moved to machine $M2$ for the next task. Since $M2$ is idle, the processing of job 1's second task begins immediately. This task will complete at time 6 (current time of 2 plus task time of 4). $M1$ goes into its change-over state and will remain in this state for two time units. Its active job is set to C (change over), and its finish time is set to 4.

At time 4 both $M1$ and $M3$ complete their active tasks. As machine $M1$ completes a change-over task, that machine begins a new job; selecting the first job, job 3, from its queue. Since the task length for job 3's next task is 4, the task will complete at time 8 and the finish time for $M1$ becomes 8. The next task for job 2, which just completed its first task on machine $M3$, needs to be done on $M1$. Since $M1$ is busy, job 2 is added to $M1$'s job queue. $M3$ moves into its change-over state and completes this change-over task at time 5. You should now be able to follow the remaining sequence of events.

Figure 10.16(c) gives the finish and wait times. Since the length of job 2 is 6 and its finish time 12, job 2 must have spent a total of $12 - 6 = 6$ time units waiting in machine queues. Similarly, job 4 must have spent $12 - 4 = 8$ time units waiting in queues.

We may determine the distribution of the 33 units of total wait time across the three machines. For example, job 4 joined the queue for $M3$ at time 0 and did not become active until time 5. So this job waited at $M3$ for five time units. No other job experienced a wait at $M3$. The total wait time at $M3$ was, therefore, five time

Job#	#Tasks	Tasks	Length
1	3	(1,2) (2,4) (1,1)	7
2	2	(3,4) (1,2)	6
3	2	(1,4) (2,4)	8
4	2	(3,1) (2,3)	4

(a) Job characteristics

Time	Machine Queues			Active Jobs			Finish Times		
	$M1$	$M2$	$M3$	$M1$	$M2$	$M3$	$M1$	$M2$	$M3$
Init	1,3	—	2,4	I	I	I	L	L	L
0	3	—	4	1	I	2	2	L	4
2	3	—	4	C	1	2	4	6	4
4	2	—	4	3	1	C	8	6	5
5	2	—	—	3	1	4	8	6	6
6	2,1	4	—	3	C	C	8	9	7
7	2,1	4	—	3	C	I	8	9	L
8	2,1	4,3	—	C	C	I	10	9	L
9	2,1	3	—	C	4	I	10	12	L
10	1	3	—	2	4	I	12	12	L
12	1	3	—	C	C	I	14	15	L
14	—	3	—	1	C	I	15	15	L
15	—	—	—	C	3	I	17	19	L
16	—	—	—	C	3	I	17	19	L
17	—	—	—	I	3	I	L	19	L

(b) Simulation

Job#	Finish Time	Wait Time
1	15	8
2	12	6
3	19	11
4	12	8
Total	58	33

(c) Finish and wait times

Figure 10.16 Machine shop simulation example

units. Going through Figure 10.16(b), we can compute the wait times for $M1$ and $M2$. The numbers are 18 and 10, respectively. As expected the sum of the job wait times (33) equals the sum of the machine wait times. ∎

Benefits of Simulating a Machine Shop

Why do we want to simulate a machine shop? Here are some reasons:

- By simulating the shop, we can identify bottleneck machines/stations. If we determine that the paint station is going to be a bottleneck for the current mix of jobs, we can increase the number of paint stations in operation for the next few shifts. Similarly, if our simulation determines that the wait time at the drill station will be excessive in the next shift, we can schedule more drill station operators and put more drilling machines to work. Therefore, the simulator can be used for short-term operator-scheduling decisions.

- Using a machine shop simulator, we can answer questions such as, How is average wait time affected if we replace a certain machine with a more expensive but more effective machine? So the simulator can be used to help make expansion/modernization decisions at the factory.

- When customers arrive at the plant, they would like a fairly accurate estimate of when their jobs will complete. Such an estimate may be obtained by using a machine shop simulator.

High-Level Simulator Design

In designing our simulator, we will assume that all jobs are available initially (i.e., no jobs enter the shop during the simulation). Further, we assume that the simulation is to be run until all jobs complete.

The simulator is implemented as the class `MachineShopSimulator`. Since the simulator is a fairly complex program, we break it into modules. The tasks to be performed by the simulator are input the data and put the jobs into the queues for their first tasks; perform the start event (i.e., do the initial loading of jobs onto the machines); run through all the events (i.e., perform the actual simulation); and output the machine wait times. We will have one Java method for each task. Program 10.10 gives the main method. The variable `largeTime` is a class data member of `MachineShopSimulator`. This variable denotes a time that is larger than any permissible simulated time; that is all tasks of all jobs must complete before the time `largeTime`.

The Class Task

Before we can develop the code for the four methods invoked by Program 10.10, we must develop representations for the data objects that are needed. These objects include tasks, jobs, machines, and an event list. We define a class for each of these data objects; each of the defined classes is a top-level nested class of `MachineShopSimulator`.

Each task has two components: `machine` (the machine on which it is to be performed) and `time` (the time needed to complete the task). Program 10.11 gives

```
public static void main(String [] args)
{
   largeTime = Integer.MAX_VALUE;
   inputData();          // get machine and job data
   startShop();          // initial machine loading
   simulate();           // run all jobs through shop
   outputStatistics();   // output machine wait times
}
```

Program 10.10 Main method for machine shop simulation

the class Task. Since machines are assumed to be have integer labels, machine is of type int. We will assume that all times are integral.

```
private static class Task
{
   // data members
   private int machine;
   private int time;

   // constructor
   private Task(int theMachine, int theTime)
   {
      machine = theMachine;
      time = theTime;
   }
}
```

Program 10.11 The class Task

The Class Job

Each job has a list of associated tasks that are performed in list order. Consequently, the task list may be represented as a queue taskQ. To determine the total wait time experienced by a job, we need to know its length and finish time. The finish time is determined by the event clock, while the job length is the sum of task times. To determine a job's length, we associate a data member length with it. Program 10.12 gives the class Job.

```
private static class Job
{
   // data members
   private LinkedQueue taskQ;    // this job's tasks
   private int length;           // sum of scheduled task times
   private int arrivalTime;      // arrival time at current queue
   private int id;               // job identifier

   // constructor
   private Job(int theId)
   {
      id = theId;
      taskQ = new LinkedQueue();
      // length and arrivalTime have default value 0
   }

   // other methods
   private void addTask(int theMachine, int theTime)
   {taskQ.put(new Task(theMachine, theTime));}

   /** remove next task of job and return its time
     * also update length */
   private int removeNextTask()
   {
      int theTime = ((Task) taskQ.remove()).time;
      length += theTime;
      return theTime;
   }
}
```

Program 10.12 The class Job

taskQ has been defined as a linked queue of tasks; we could have used an array-based queue instead. The data member arrivalTime records the time at which a job enters its current machine queue and determines the time the job waits in this queue. The job identifier is stored in id and is used only when outputting the total wait time encountered by this job.

The method addTask adds a task to the job's task queue. The task is to be performed on machine theMachine and takes theTime time. This method is used only during data input. The method removeNextTask is used when a job is moved from a machine queue to active status. At this time the job's first task is removed from the task queue (the task queue maintains a list of tasks yet to be scheduled on machines), the job length is incremented by the task time, and the task time is returned. The data member `length` becomes equal to the job length when we schedule the last task for the job.

The Class Machine

Each machine has a change-over time, an active job, and a queue of waiting jobs. Since each job can be in at most one machine queue at any time, the total space needed for all queues is bounded by the number of jobs. However, the distribution of jobs over the machine queues changes as the simulation proceeds. It is possible to have a few very long queues at one time. These queues might become very short later, and some other queues become long. By using linked queues, we limit the space required for the machine queues to that required for n nodes where n is the number of jobs.

Program 10.13 gives the class `Machine`. The data members `jobQ`, `changeTime`, `totalWait`, `numTasks`, and `activeJob`, respectively, denote the queue of waiting jobs, the change-over time for the machine, the total time jobs have spent waiting at this machine, the number of tasks processed by the machine, and the currently active job. The currently active job is `null` whenever the machine is idle or in its change-over state.

```
private static class Machine
{
    // data members
    LinkedQueue jobQ; // queue of waiting jobs for this machine
    int changeTime;   // machine change-over time
    int totalWait;    // total delay at this machine
    int numTasks;     // number of tasks processed on this machine
    Job activeJob;    // job currently active on this machine

    // constructor
    private Machine()
       {jobQ = new LinkedQueue();}
}
```

Program 10.13 The class Machine

The Class EventList

We store the finish times of all machines in an event list. To go from one event to the next, we need to determine the minimum of these finish times. Our simulator also needs an operation that sets the finish time of a particular machine. This operation has to be done each time a new job is scheduled on a machine. When a machine becomes idle, its finish time is set to the large number largeTime. Program 10.14 gives the class EventList that implements the event list as a one-dimensional array finishTime, with finishTime[p] being the finish time of machine p.

```java
private static class EventList
{
   int [] finishTime; // finish time array

   // constructor
   private EventList(int theNumMachines, int theLargeTime)
   {// initialize finish times for m machines
      if (theNumMachines < 1)
         throw new IllegalArgumentException
               ("number of machines must be >= 1");
      finishTime = new int [theNumMachines + 1];

      // all machines are idle, initialize with
      // large finish time
      for (int i = 1; i <= theNumMachines; i++)
         finishTime[i] = theLargeTime;
   }

   /** @return machine for next event */
   private int nextEventMachine()
   {
      // find first machine to finish, this is the
      // machine with smallest finish time
      int p = 1;
      int t = finishTime[1];
      for (int i = 2; i < finishTime.length; i++)
         if (finishTime[i] < t)
         {// i finishes earlier
            p = i;
            t = finishTime[i];
         }
      return p;
   }
}
```

Program 10.14 The class EventList (continues)

```
    private int nextEventTime(int theMachine)
    {return finishTime[theMachine];}

    private void setFinishTime(int theMachine, int theTime)
    {finishTime[theMachine] = theTime;}
}
```

Program 10.14 The class EventList (concluded)

The method `nextEventMachine` returns the machine that completes its active task first. The time at which machine `p` finishes its active task can be determined by invoking the method `nextEventTime(p)`. For a machine shop with m machines, it takes $\Theta(m)$ time to find the minimum of the finish times, so the complexity of `nextEventMachine` is $\Theta(m)$. The method to set the finish time of a machine, `setFinishTime`, runs in $\Theta(1)$ time. In Chapter 14 we will see two data structures—heaps and leftist trees—that may also represent an event list. When we use either of these data structures, the complexity of both `nextEventMachine` and `setFinishTime` becomes $O(\log m)$. If the total number of tasks across all jobs is $numTasks$, then, in a successful simulation run, our simulator will invoke `nextEventMachine` and `setFinishTime` $\Theta(numTasks)$ times each. Using the event list implementation of Program 10.14, these invocations take a total of $\Theta(numTasks * m)$ time; using one of the data structures of Chapter 14, the invocations take $O(numTasks * \log m)$ time. Even though the data structures of Chapter 14 are more complex, they result in a faster simulation when the number of machines m is suitably large.

Data Members of MachineShopSimulator

Program 10.15 gives the data members of the class `MachineShopSimulator`. The significance of most of these variables is self-evident. `timeNow` is the simulated clock and records the current time. Each time an event occurs, it is updated to the event time. `largeTime` is a time that exceeds the finish time of the last job and denotes the finish time of an idle machine.

The Method inputData

The code for the method `inputData` (Program 10.16) begins by inputting the number of machines and jobs in the shop. Next we create the initial event list `eList`, with finish times equal to `largeTime` for each machine, and the array `machine` of machines. Then we input the change-over times for the machines. Next we input the jobs one by one. For each job we first input the number of tasks it has, and then we input the tasks as pairs of the form (machine, time). The machine for the

```
// data members of MachineShopSimulator
private static int timeNow;         // current time
private static int numMachines;     // number of machines
private static int numJobs;         // number of jobs
private static EventList eList;     // pointer to event list
private static Machine [] machine;  // array of machines
private static int largeTime;       // all machines finish before this
```

Program 10.15 Data members of MachineShopSimulator

```
static void inputData()
{
    // define the input stream to be the standard input stream
    MyInputStream keyboard = new MyInputStream();

    System.out.println("Enter number of machines and jobs");
    numMachines = keyboard.readInteger();
    numJobs = keyboard.readInteger();
    if (numMachines < 1 || numJobs < 1)
        throw new MyInputException
                ("number of machines and jobs must be >= 1");

    // create event and machine queues
    eList = new EventList(numMachines, largeTime);
    machine = new Machine [numMachines + 1];
    for (int i = 1; i <= numMachines; i++)
        machine[i] = new Machine();

    // input the change-over times
    System.out.println("Enter change-over times for machines");
    for (int j = 1; j <= numMachines; j++)
    {
        int ct = keyboard.readInteger();
        if (ct < 0)
            throw new MyInputException
                    ("change-over time must be >= 0");
        machine[j].changeTime = ct;
    }
```

Program 10.16 Code to input machine shop data (continues)

```
   // input the jobs
   Job theJob;
   for (int i = 1; i <= numJobs; i++)
   {
      System.out.println("Enter number of tasks for job " + i);
      int tasks = keyboard.readInteger();  // number of tasks
      int firstMachine = 0;                // machine for first task
      if (tasks < 1)
         throw new MyInputException
               ("each job must have > 1 task");

      // create the job
      theJob = new Job(i);
      System.out.println("Enter the tasks (machine, time)"
            + " in process order");
      for (int j = 1; j <= tasks; j++)
      {// get tasks for job i
         int theMachine = keyboard.readInteger();
         int theTaskTime = keyboard.readInteger();
         if (theMachine < 1 || theMachine > numMachines
             || theTaskTime < 1)
         throw new MyInputException
               ("bad machine number or task time");
         if (j == 1)
            firstMachine = theMachine;    // job's first machine
         theJob.addTask(theMachine, theTaskTime);  // add to
      }                                             // task queue
      machine[firstMachine].jobQ.put(theJob);
   }
}
```

Program 10.16 Code to input machine shop data (concluded)

first task of the job is recorded in the variable **firstMachine**. When all tasks of a job have been input, the job is added to the queue for the first task's machine.

The Methods startShop and changeState

To start the simulation, we need to move the first job from each machine's job queue to the machine and commence processing. Since each machine is initialized in its idle state, we perform the initial loading in the same way as we change a machine from its idle state, which may happen during simulation, to an active state. The

```
/** load first jobs onto each machine */
static void startShop()
{
   for (int p = 1; p <= numMachines; p++)
      changeState(p);
}
```

Program 10.17 Initial loading of machines

method `changeState(i)` performs this change over for machine `i`. The method to start the shop, Program 10.17, needs merely invoke `changeState` for each machine.

Program 10.18 gives the code for `changeState`. If machine `theMachine` is idle or in its change-over state, `changeState` returns `null`. Otherwise, it returns the job that `theMachine` has been working on. Additionally, `changeState(theMachine)` changes the state of machine `theMachine`. If machine `theMachine` was previously idle or in its change-over state, then it begins to process the next job on its queue. If that queue is empty, the machine's new state is "idle." If machine `theMachine` was previously processing a job, machine `theMachine` moves into its change-over state.

If `machine[theMachine].activeJob` is `null`, then machine `theMachine` is either in its idle or change-over state; the job, `lastJob`, to return is `null`. If the job queue is empty, the machine moves into its idle state and its finish time is set to `largeTime`. If its job queue is not empty, the first job is removed from the queue and becomes machine `theMachine`'s active job. The time this job has spent waiting in machine `theMachine`'s queue is added to the total wait time for this machine, and the number of tasks processed by the machine incremented by 1. Next the task that this machine is going to work on is deleted from the job's task list, and the finish time of the machine is set to the time at which the new task will complete.

If `machine[p].activeJob` is not `null`, the machine has been working on a job whose task has just completed. Since this job is to be returned, we save it in `lastJob`. The machine should now move into its change-over state and remain in that state for `changeTime` time units.

The Methods `simulate` and `moveToNextMachine`

The method `simulate`, Program 10.19, cycles through all shop events until the last job completes. `numJobs` is the number of incomplete jobs, so the `while` loop of Program 10.19 terminates when no incomplete jobs remain. In each iteration of the `while` loop, the time for the next event is determined, and the clock time `timeNow` updated to this event time. A change-job operation is performed on the machine `nextToFinish` on which the event occurred. If this machine has just finished a

```
static Job changeState(int theMachine)
{// Task on theMachine has finished, schedule next one.
   Job lastJob;
   if (machine[theMachine].activeJob == null)
   {// in idle or change-over state
      lastJob = null;
      // wait over, ready for new job
      if (machine[theMachine].jobQ.isEmpty()) // no waiting job
           eList.setFinishTime(theMachine, largeTime);
      else
      {// take job off the queue and work on it
         machine[theMachine].activeJob =
             (Job) machine[theMachine].jobQ.remove();
         machine[theMachine].totalWait +=
             timeNow - machine[theMachine].activeJob.arrivalTime;
         machine[theMachine].numTasks++;
         int t = machine[theMachine].activeJob.removeNextTask();
         eList.setFinishTime(theMachine, timeNow + t);
      }
   }
   else
   {// task has just finished on machine[theMachine]
    // schedule change-over time
      lastJob = machine[theMachine].activeJob;
      machine[theMachine].activeJob = null;
      eList.setFinishTime(theMachine, timeNow +
                          machine[theMachine].changeTime);
   }

   return lastJob;
}
```

Program 10.18 Code to change the active job at a machine

task of a job (theJob is not null), job theJob moves to the machine on which its next task is to be performed. The method moveToNextMachine performs this move. If there is no next task for job theJob, the job has completed, method moveToNextMachine returns false, and numJobs is decremented by 1.

The method moveToNextMachine (Program 10.20) first checks to see whether any unprocessed tasks remain for the job theJob. If not, the job has completed and its finish time and wait time are output. The method returns false to indicate there was no next machine for this job.

```
static void simulate()
{
   while (numJobs > 0)
   {// at least one job left
      int nextToFinish = eList.nextEventMachine();
      timeNow = eList.nextEventTime(nextToFinish);
      // change job on machine nextToFinish
      Job theJob = changeState(nextToFinish);
      // move theJob to its next machine
      // decrement numJobs if theJob has finished
      if (theJob != null && !moveToNextMachine(theJob)) numJobs--;
   }
}
```

Program 10.19 Run all jobs through their machines

When the job theJob to be moved has a next task, the machine p for this task is determined and the job is added to this machine's queue of waiting jobs. In case machine p is idle, changeState is invoked to change the state of machine p so that machine p begins immediately to process the next task of theJob.

The Method outputStatistics

Since both the time at which a job finishes and the time a job spends waiting in machine queues are output by moveToNextMachine, outputStatistics needs to output only the time at which the machine shop completes all jobs (this time is also the time at which the last job completed and has been output by moveToNextMachine) and the statistics (total wait time and number of tasks processed) for each machine. Program 10.21 gives the code.

EXERCISES

17. Which applications from this section can use a stack instead of a queue without affecting the correctness of the program?

18. (a) You have a railroad shunting yard with three shunting tracks that operate as queues. The initial ordering of cars is 3, 1, 7, 6, 2, 8, 5, 4. Draw figures similar to Figures 10.11 to show the configuration of the shunting tracks, the input track, and the output track following each car move made by the solution of Section 10.5.1.

    (b) Do part (a) for the case when the number of shunting tracks is 2.

```
static boolean moveToNextMachine(Job theJob)
{
   if (theJob.taskQ.isEmpty())
   {// no next task
      System.out.println("Job " + theJob.id + " has completed at "
         + timeNow + " Total wait was " + (timeNow - theJob.length));
      return false;
   }
   else
   {// theJob has a next task
    // get machine for next task
      int p = ((Task) theJob.taskQ.getFrontElement()).machine;
      // put on machine p's wait queue
      machine[p].jobQ.put(theJob);
      theJob.arrivalTime = timeNow;
      // if p idle, schedule immediately
      if (eList.nextEventTime(p) == largeTime)
      {// machine is idle
         changeState(p);
      }
      return true;
   }
}
```

Program 10.20 Move a job to the machine for the next task

19. Does Program 10.6 successfully rearrange all input car permutations that can be rearranged using k holding tracks that operate as queues? Prove your answer.

20. Rewrite Program 10.6 under the assumption that at most s_i cars can be in holding track i at any time. Reserve the track with smallest s_i for direct input to output moves.

21. Can you eliminate the use of queues and, instead, use the strategy of the second implementation of the railroad car problem when you have to display the state of the holding tracks following each move of a railroad car? Justify your answer.

22. Is it possible to solve the problem of Section 9.5.3 without the use of a stack (see second implementation of Section 10.5.1)? If so, develop and test such a program.

```
/** output wait times at machines */
static void outputStatistics()
{
   System.out.println("Finish time = " + timeNow);
   for (int p = 1; p <= numMachines; p++)
   {
      System.out.println("Machine " + p + " completed "
            + machine[p].numTasks + " tasks");
      System.out.println("The total wait time was "
            + machine[p].totalWait);
      System.out.println();
   }
}
```

Program 10.21 Output the wait times at each machine

23. Consider the wire-routing grid of Figure 10.13(a). You are to route a wire between (1, 4) and (2, 2). Label all grid positions that are reached in the distance-labeling pass by their distance value. Now use the methodology of the path-identification pass to mark the shortest wire path.

24. Develop a complete Java program for wire routing. Your program should include a `welcome` method that displays the program name and functionality; a method to input the wire grid size, blocked and unblocked grid positions, and wire endpoints; the method `findPath` (Program 10.8); and a method to output the input grid with the wire path shown. Test your code.

25. In a typical wire-routing application, several wires are routed in sequence. After a path has been found for one wire, the grid positions used by this path are blocked and we proceed to find a path for the next wire. When the array `grid` is overloaded to designate both blocked and unblocked positions as well as distances, we must clean the grid (i.e., set all grid positions that are on the wire path to 1 and all remaining positions with a label > 1 to 0) before we can begin on the next wire. Write a method to clean the grid. Do so by first restoring the grid to its initial state, using a process similar to that used in the distance-labeling pass. The wirte code to block the positions on the wire path just found. This way the complexity of the cleanup pass is the same as that of the distance-labeling pass.

26. Develop a complete Java program for image-component labeling. Your program should include a `welcome` method that displays the program name and functionality; a method to input the image size and binary image; the method

labelComponents (Program 10.9); and a method to output the image using a different color for pixels that are in different components. Test your code.

27. Rewrite method labelComponents using a stack. What are the relative merits/demerits of using a stack rather than a queue for this method?

28. Can we replace the stack in Program 9.6 with a queue? Why?

29. Can we replace the stack in Program 9.13 with a queue? Why?

30. Can we replace the stack in Program 9.14 with a queue? Why?

31. Can we replace the stack in Program 9.15 with a queue? Why?

★ 32. Write an enhanced machine shop simulator that allows you to specify a minimum wait time between successive tasks of the same job. Your simulator must move a job into a wait state following the completion of each task (including the last one). Therefore, a job is placed on its next queue as soon as a task is complete. Upon arriving in this queue, the job enters its wait state. When a machine is ready to start a new task, it must bypass jobs at the front of the queue that are still in a wait state. The bypassed jobs could, for example, be moved to the end of the queue.

★ 33. Write an enhanced machine shop simulator that allows jobs to enter the shop during simulation. The simulation stops at a specified time. Jobs that have not been completed by this time remain incomplete.

10.6   REFERENCES AND SELECTED READINGS

The wire-routing algorithm of Section 10.5.2 is known as Lee's router. The book *Algorithms for VLSI Physical Design Automation*, 2nd edition, by N. Sherwani, Kluwer Academic Publishers, Boston, 1995, contains a detailed discussion of this and other routing algorithms.

CHAPTER 11

SKIP LISTS AND HASHING

BIRD'S-EYE VIEW

Although a sorted array of n elements can be searched in $O(\log n)$ time with the binary search method, the search (or get) operation on a sorted chain takes $O(n)$ time. We can improve the expected performance of a sorted chain by placing additional pointers in some or all of the chain nodes. These pointers permit us to skip over several nodes of the chain during a search. Thus it is no longer necessary to examine all chain nodes from left to right during a search.

Chains augmented with additional forward pointers are called **skip lists**. Skip lists employ a randomization technique to determine which chain nodes are to be augmented by additional forward pointers and how many additional pointers are to be placed in the node. Using this randomization technique, skip lists deliver an expected search, insert, and remove performance of $O(\log n)$. However, the worst-case performance is $\Theta(n)$.

Hashing is another randomization scheme that may be used to search, insert, and remove elements. It provides improved expected performance, $\Theta(1)$, over skip lists but has the same worst-case performance, $\Theta(n)$. Despite this performance, skip lists have an advantage over hashing in applications where we need to frequently output all elements in sorted order and/or search by element rank (e.g., find the 10th-smallest element). These latter two operations can be performed more efficiently with skip lists.

The asymptotic performance of sorted arrays, sorted chains, skip lists, and hash tables is summarized in the following table.

Method	Worst Case			Expected		
	Search	Insert	Remove	Search	Insert	Remove
sorted array	$\Theta(\log n)$	$\Theta(n)$	$\Theta(n)$	$\Theta(\log n)$	$\Theta(n)$	$\Theta(n)$
sorted chain	$\Theta(n)$	$\Theta(n)$	$\Theta(n)$	$\Theta(n)$	$\Theta(n)$	$\Theta(n)$
skip lists	$\Theta(n)$	$\Theta(n)$	$\Theta(n)$	$\Theta(\log n)$	$\Theta(\log n)$	$\Theta(\log n)$
hash tables	$\Theta(n)$	$\Theta(n)$	$\Theta(n)$	$\Theta(1)$	$\Theta(1)$	$\Theta(1)$

Java provides several implementations of a hash table—`java.util.HashTable`, `java.util.HashMap`, and `java.util.HashSet`.

One application of hashing is developed in this chapter. This application is text compression and decompression. The program we develop is based on the popular Lempel-Ziv-Welch algorithm.

11.1   DICTIONARIES

A **dictionary** is a collection of pairs of the form (k, e), where k is a **key** and e is the element associated with the key k (equivalently, e is the element whose key is k). No two pairs in a dictionary have the same key.

The following operations are performed on a dictionary:

- Get the element associated with a specified key from the dictionary.

- Insert or put an element with a specified key into the dictionary.

- Delete or remove an element with a specified key.

Example 11.1 The class list for the data structures course is a dictionary with as many elements as students registered for the course. When a new student registers, an element/record corresponding to this student is inserted into the dictionary; when a student drops the course, his/her record may be deleted. During the course the instructor may query the dictionary to determine the record corresponding to a particular student and make changes to the record (for example, add/change test or assignment scores). The student name may be used as the element key.   ∎

A **dictionary with duplicates** is similar to a dictionary as defined above. However, it permits two or more (key, element) pairs to have the same key.

Example 11.2 A word dictionary is a collection of elements; each element comprises a word, the meaning of the word, the pronunciation, etymologies, and so on. Webster's dictionary contains an element (or entry) for the word *date*. Part of this element reads "date, the point of time at which a transaction or event takes place." For this element *date* is the key. Webster's dictionary actually has two more elements with the key *date*. Abbreviated forms of these elements are "date, the oblong fruit of a palm" and "date, to assign a chronology record." The dictionary manufacturer puts new elements into the word dictionary as new words are created and as words take on new meanings; the manufacturer also removes elements that are no longer required. Users of a word dictionary, that is you and I, generally only search the dictionary for elements with a given key. Occasionally, we might jot down a new entry into our copy of a dictionary. In data structures terminology a word dictionary is a dictionary with duplicates—it is a collection of elements, each element has a key, the keys need not be distinct, and the operations you perform on the element collection are get, insert, and delete. Although the book form of a word dictionary lists the elements in alphabetical order of the keys, this arrangement is not required by an electronic dictionary. In a computer you can store the elements any way you like.

A telephone directory is another example of a dictionary with duplicates.   ∎

In a dictionary with duplicates, we need a rule to eliminate the ambiguity in the get and remove operations. That is, if we are to get (or remove) an element with a specified key, then which of the several elements with this key is to be returned (or removed)? Two possibilities for the get operation are (1) get any element that has the specified key and (2) get all elements that have the specified key. For the remove operation, we may require that the user be presented with all elements that have the specified key; the user must select which element(s) to remove. Alternatively, we may arbitrarily remove any one element that has the specified key.

In the case of both dictionaries and dictionaries with duplicates, some applications require a different form of the remove operation in which all elements inserted after a particular time are to be removed.

Example 11.3 A compiler uses a dictionary with duplicates, called the **symbol table**, of user-defined identifiers. When an identifier is defined, a record is created for it and inserted into the symbol table. This record includes the identifier as key as well as other information, such as identifier type (int, float, etc.) and (relative) memory address for its value. Since the same identifier name may be defined more than once (in different program blocks), the symbol table must be able to hold multiple records/elements with the same key. A search should return the most recently inserted element with the given key. Deletions are done only when the end of a program block is reached. All elements inserted after the start of that block are to be deleted. ■

The get operation allows you to retrieve dictionary elements **randomly**, by providing the key of the element you want. Some dictionary applications require an additional access mode—**sequential access**—in which elements are retrieved one by one in ascending order of keys. Sequential access requires an iterator that can sequence through the elements in the dictionary in ascending order of their keys. All dictionary implementations developed in this chapter (other than hash tables) are suitable for both random and sequential access.

EXERCISES

1. Look in a word dictionary and find a word (other than *date*) for which there are multiple entries. Try to find a word that has more than three entries.

2. Give three real-world applications of dictionaries and/or dictionaries with duplicates. Do not repeat the ones given in this section. Explain which dictionary operations are used in each of your applications.

3. Give an application of a dictionary or dictionary with duplicates in which sequential access is desired.

11.2   THE ABSTRACT DATA TYPE

The abstract data type *Dictionary* is specified in ADT 11.1. When the dictionary contains no element with key k, $put(k, x)$ inserts the pair (k, x) into the dictionary; when the dictionary already contains an element with key k, the old element associated with k is replaced by the new element x. This behavior of the *put* operation as well as the operation names agree with the behavior and names used in the interface `java.util.Map`.

AbstractDataType *Dictionary*
{

    instances
        collection of elements with distinct keys

    operations
            $get(k)$: return the element with key k;

        $put(k, x)$: put the element x whose key is k into the dictionary and return the old element (if any) associated with k;

     $remove(k)$: remove the element with key k and return it;

}

ADT 11.1 Dictionary abstract data type

Program 11.1 gives the Java interface that corresponds to ADT 11.1. We require that the methods `get`, `put`, and `remove` return `null` in case the dictionary does not contain an element with the given key. This behavior conforms to that of the corresponding methods of `java.util.Map`.

```
public interface Dictionary
{
   public Object get(Object key);
   public Object put(Object key, Object theElement);
   public Object remove(Object key);
}
```

Program 11.1 The interface `Dictionary`

In this chapter we do not explicitly develop representations for dictionaries with duplicates. However, the representations developed for dictionaries without duplicates may be adapted to the case when duplicate entries are permitted.

EXERCISE

4. List the methods included in the interface `java.util.Map` that are not included in our interface `Dictionary`? What does each new method do?

11.3   LINEAR LIST REPRESENTATION

A dictionary can be maintained as an ordered linear list $(e_0, e_1, \cdots)$ where the e_is are the dictionary pairs in ascending order of key. To facilitate this representation, we may define two classes `SortedArrayList` and `SortedChain`. The first uses an array-based representation of a linear list (see Section 5.3), while the latter uses a linked representation (see Section 6.1).

Exercise 5 asks you to develop the class `SortedArrayList`. We note that you can search a `SortedArrayList` using the binary search method. So the *get* operation takes $O(\log n)$ time for an n-element dictionary. To make an insertion, we need to verify that the dictionary doesn't already contain an element with the same key. This verification is done by performing a search. Following this search, the insertion may be done in $O(n)$ additional time, as $O(n)$ elements must be moved to make room for the new element. Each remove is done by first searching for the element to be removed and then removing it. Following the search, the removal takes $O(n)$ time as $O(n)$ elements must be moved to fill up the vacancy left by the deleted element.

Programs 11.2, 11.3, and 11.4 give the `get`, `put`, and `remove` methods of the class `SortedChain`. The nodes in `SortedChain` are instances of `SortedChainNode`, which is like `ChainNode` (Program 6.1) with an additional data member, `key`, whose data type implements the interface `Comparable`.

Using either the class `SortedArrayList` or `SortedChain` and the corresponding iterator methods, we can provide sequential access to the dictionary elements; elements can be examined in ascending order of keys at a cost of $\Theta(1)$ time per element.

EXERCISES

5. Develop the Java class `SortedArrayList` that uses an array-based representation. Provide the same member methods as provided in the class `SortedChain`. Write and test code for all methods.

6. Modify the class `SortedChain` to use a chain that has both a head node and a tail node. Use the tail node to simplify your code by placing the key being searched for, inserted, or removed into the tail node at the start of the operation.

```
public Object get(Object theKey)
{
   SortedChainNode currentNode = firstNode;

   // search for match with theKey
   while (currentNode != null &&
          currentNode.key.compareTo(theKey) < 0)
      currentNode = currentNode.next;

   // verify match
   if (currentNode != null && currentNode.key.equals(theKey))
      // yes, found match
      return currentNode.element;

   // no match
   return null;
}
```

Program 11.2 The method SortedChain.get

11.4   SKIP LIST REPRESENTATION (OPTIONAL)

11.4.1   The Ideal Case

A search in an n-element dictionary that is represented as a sorted chain requires up to n element comparisons. The number of comparisons can be reduced to $n/2 + 1$ if we keep a pointer to the middle element. Now to search for an element, we first compare with the middle one. If we are looking for a smaller element, we need search only the left half of the sorted chain. If we are looking for a larger element, we need compare only the right half of the chain.

Example 11.4 Consider the seven-element sorted chain of Figure 11.1(a). This sorted chain has been augmented by a head node and a tail node. The number inside a node is its value. A search of this chain may involve up to seven element comparisons. We can reduce this worst-case number of comparisons to 4 by keeping a pointer to the middle element as in Figure 11.1(b). Now to search for an element, we first compare with the middle element and then, depending on the outcome, compare with either the left or right half of the chain. If we are looking for an element with value 26, then we begin by comparing 26 with the middle value 40. Since $26 < 40$, we need not examine the elements to the right of 40. If we are searching for an element with value 75, then we can limit the search to the elements that follow 40. ■

```
public Object put(Object theKey, Object theElement)
{
   SortedChainNode p = firstNode,
                   tp = null; // tp trails p

   // move tp so that theElement can be inserted after tp
   while (p != null && p.key.compareTo(theKey) < 0)
   {
      tp = p;
      p = p.next;
   }

   // check if there is a matching element
   if (p != null && p.key.equals(theKey))
   {// replace old element
      Object elementToReturn = p.element;
      p.element = theElement;
      return elementToReturn;
   }

   // no match, set up node for theElement
   SortedChainNode q = new SortedChainNode(theKey, theElement, p);

   // insert node just after tp
   if (tp == null) firstNode = q;
   else tp.next = q;

   size++;
   return null;
}
```

Program 11.3 The method `SortedChain.put`

We can reduce the worst-case number of element comparisons by keeping point-ers to the middle elements of each half as in Figure 11.1(c). The level 0 chain is essentially that of Figure 11.1(a) and includes all seven elements of the dictionary. The level 1 chain includes the second, fourth, and sixth elements, while the level 2 chain includes only the fourth element. To search for an element with value 30, we begin with a comparison against the middle element. This element is found in $\Theta(1)$ time using the level 2 chain. Since $30 < 40$, the search continues by examining the middle element of the left half. This element is also found in $\Theta(1)$ time using the

```
public Object remove(Object theKey)
{
   SortedChainNode p = firstNode,
                   tp = null; // tp trails p

   // search for match with theKey
   while (p != null && p.key.compareTo(theKey) < 0)
   {
      tp = p;
      p = p.next;
   }

   // verify match
   if (p != null && p.key.equals(theKey))
   {// found a match
      Object e = p.element;  // the matching element

      // remove p from the chain
      if (tp == null) firstNode = p.next;  // p is first node
      else tp.next = p.next;

      size--;
      return e;
   }

   // no matching element to remove
   return null;
}
```

Program 11.4 The method SortedChain.remove

level 1 chain. Since $30 > 24$, we continue the search by dropping into the level 0 chain and comparing with the next element in this chain.

As another example, consider the search for an element with value 77. The first comparison is with 40. Since $77 > 40$, we drop into the level 1 chain and compare with the element (75) in this chain that comes just after 40. Since $77 > 75$, we drop into the level 0 chain and compare with the element (80) in this chain that comes just after 75. At this time we know that 77 is not in the dictionary. Using the three-chain structure of Figure 11.1(c), we can perform all searches using at most three comparisons. The three-chain structure allows us to perform a binary search in the sorted chain.

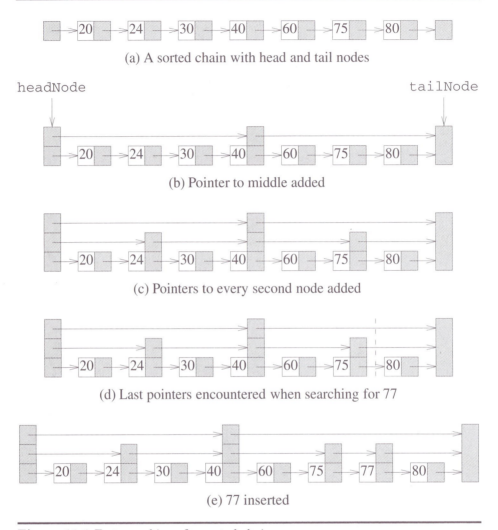

(a) A sorted chain with head and tail nodes

(b) Pointer to middle added

(c) Pointers to every second node added

(d) Last pointers encountered when searching for 77

(e) 77 inserted

Figure 11.1 Fast searching of a sorted chain

For general n the level 0 chain includes all elements; the level 1 chain includes every second element; the level 2 chain every fourth element; and the level i chain every 2^ith element. We will say that an element is a **level i element** iff it is in the chains for levels 0 through i and it is not on the level $i + 1$ chain (in case this chain exists). In Figure 11.1(c), 40 is the only level 2 element; 24 and 75 are the level 1 elements; and 20, 30, 60, and 80 are the level 0 elements.

We will use the term **skip list** to refer to a structure such as that of Figure 11.1(c). In such a structure we have a heirarchy of chains. The level 0 chain is a sorted chain of all elements. The level 1 chain is also a sorted chain that comprises some subset of the elements on the level 0 chain. In general, the level i chain comprises a subset of the elements in the level $i-1$ chain. The skip list of Figure 11.1(c) has a very regular structure in that the level i chain comprises every other element of the level $i-1$ chain.

11.4.2 Insertions and Deletions

When insertions and deletions occur, we cannot maintain the regular structure of Figure 11.1(c) without doing $O(n)$ work. We can attempt to approximate this structure in the face of insertions by noting that in the regular structure, $n/2^i$ elements are level i elements. When an insertion is made, the element level is i with probability $1/2^i$. We can actually allow for any probability to be used when making this determination. Therefore, we can assign the newly inserted element at level i with probability p^i. Figure 11.1(c) corresponds to the case $p = 0.5$. For general p the number of chain levels is $\lfloor \log_{1/p} n \rfloor + 1$. In this case a regular skip list structure has the property that the level i chain comprises every $1/p$th element of the level $i-1$ chain.

Suppose we are to insert an element with value 77. We first search to make sure that no element with this value is present. During this search the last level 2 pointer seen is associated with element 40, the last level 1 pointer seen is associated with element 75, and the last level 0 pointer seen is associated with element 75. These pointers are cut by the broken line of Figure 11.1(d). The new element is to be inserted between elements 75 and 80 at the position shown by the broken line of Figure 11.1(d). To make the insertion, we need to assign a level to the new element. This assignment can be made by using a random number generator as described later.

If the new element is a level i element, then only the level 0 through level i pointers cut by the broken line are affected. Figure 11.1(e) shows the list structure following the insertion of 77 as a level 1 element.

We have no control over the structure that is left following a deletion. To delete the 77 from the skip list structure of Figure 11.1(e), we first search for 77. The last pointers encountered in the chains are the level 2 pointer in the node with 40 and the level 1 and level 0 pointers in the node with 75. Of these pointers only the level 0 and level 1 pointers are to be changed, as 77 is a level 1 element. When these pointers are changed to point to the element after 77 in their respective chains, we get the structure of Figure 11.1(d).

11.4.3 Assigning Levels

The basis of level assignment is the observation that in a regular skip list structure, a fraction p of the elements on the level $i-1$ chain are also on the level i chain.

Therefore, the probablity that an element that is on the level $i - 1$ chain is also on the level i chain is p. Suppose we have a uniform random number generator that generates real numbers between 0 and 1. Then the probability that the next random number is $\leq p$ is p. Consequently, if the next random number is $\leq p$, then the new element should be on the level 1 chain. Now we need to decide whether it should also be on the level 2 chain. To make this decision, we simply generate another random number. If the new random number is $\leq p$, then the element is also on the level 2 chain. We can continue this process until a random number $> p$ is generated.

A potential shortcoming of this way of assigning levels is that some elements may be assigned a very large level, resulting in a number of chains far in excess of $\log_{1/p} N$ where N is the maximum number of elements expected in the dictionary. To prevent this possibility, we can set an upper limit to the assignable level number. In a regular skip list structure with N elements, the maximum level `maxLevel` is

$$\lceil \log_{1/p} N \rceil - 1 \tag{11.1}$$

We can use this value as the upper limit.

Another shortcoming is that even with the use of an upper limit as above, we may find ourselves in a situation where, for example, we have 3 chains just before the insertion and 10 just after. In this case the new element was assigned the level 9 even though there were no elements at levels 3 through 8 prior to the insertion. In other words, prior to and following the insertion, there are no level 3, 4, $\cdots$, 8 elements. Since there is no immediate benefit to having these empty levels, we may alter the level assignment of the element to 3.

Example 11.5 We are using a skip list to represent a dictionary that will have no more than 1024 elements. We have decided to use $p = 0.5$, so `maxLevel` is $\log_2 1024 - 1 = 9$.

Suppose we start with an empty dictionary that is represented by a skip list structure that has a head and a tail. The head has 10 pointers, one for each of the 10 chains we might have. Each pointer goes from the head to the tail.

When the first element is inserted, it is assigned a level. The permissible levels are 0 through 9 (`maxLevel`). If the level assigned is 9, then to insert the first element, we will need to change nine chain pointers. On the other hand, as we have no level 0, level 1, $\cdots$, level 8 elements, we may alter the level assignment to 0 and change only one chain pointer. ■

An alternative way to assign levels is to divide the range of values the random number generator outputs into segments. The first segment contains $1 - 1/p$ of the range, the second $1/p - 1/p^2$ of the range, and so on. If the random number generated falls in the ith segment, the element to be inserted is a level $i - 1$ element.

11.4.4   The Class `SkipNode`

The head node of a skip list structure needs sufficient pointer fields for the maximum number of level chains that might be constructed. The tail node needs no pointer field. Each node that contains an element needs an `element` field for the element, a `key` field for the element's key, and a number of pointer fields that is one more than its level number. The class `SkipNode` of Program 11.5 can meet the needs of all kinds of nodes.

```
protected static class SkipNode
{
   // data members
   protected Comparable key;
   protected Object element;
   protected SkipNode [] next;

   // constructor
   protected SkipNode(Object theKey, Object theElement, int size)
   {
      key = (Comparable) theKey;
      element = theElement;
      next = new SkipNode [size];
   }
}
```

Program 11.5 The class `SkipNode`

As in the case of the class `SortedChain`, we require that the `key` field of a node be of type `Comparable`. The pointer fields are represented by the array `next` with `next[i]` being the pointer for the level i chain. The constructor allocates space for the array of pointers. When invoked, the value of `size` should be `lev + 1` for a level `lev` element.

11.4.5   The Class `SkipList`

The Data Members of `SkipList`

Program 11.6 gives the data members of the class `SkipList`. The significance of each data member should be clear from its name and the attached comment.

The Constructor for `SkipList`

Program 11.7 gives the constructor. `largeKey` is a value larger than the key of any element to be kept in the dictionary. The value `largeKey` is used in the tail

```
protected float prob;          // probability used to decide level number
protected int maxLevel;        // max permissible chain level
protected int levels;          // max current nonempty chain
protected int size;            // current number of elements
protected Comparable tailKey;  // a large key
protected SkipNode headNode;   // head node
protected SkipNode tailNode;   // tail node
protected SkipNode [] last;    // last node seen on each level
protected Random r;            // needed for random numbers
```

Program 11.6 The data members of SkipList

```
public SkipList(Comparable largeKey, int maxElements, float theProb)
{
   prob = theProb;
   maxLevel = (int) Math.round(Math.log(maxElements) /
                               Math.log(1/prob)) - 1;

   // size and levels have default initial value 0
   tailKey = largeKey;

   // create head & tail nodes and last array
   headNode = new SkipNode (null, null, maxLevel + 1);
   tailNode = new SkipNode (tailKey, null, 0);
   last = new SkipNode [maxLevel + 1];

   // headNode points to tailNode at all levels initially
   for (int i = 0; i <= maxLevel; i++)
      headNode.next[i] = tailNode;

   r = new Random();  // initialize random number generator
}
```

Program 11.7 Constructor

node. maxElements is the maximum number of elements the dictionary is to hold. Although our codes permit more elements than maxElements, the expected performance is better if the number of elements does not exceed maxElements, as the number of chains is limited by substituting maxElements for N in Equation 11.1.

theProb is the probablity that an element in the level $i-1$ chain is also in the level i chain. The constructor initializes the data members of SkipList to the values stated earlier, and the data member r of type java.util.Random is initialized so that successive calls to Random.nextFloat will return the next random number, a number between 0 and 1. The constructor also allocates space for the head and tail nodes and the array last that is used to keep track of the last node encountered in each chain during the search phase that precedes a put and remove; the skip list is initialized to the empty configuration in which we have maxLevel+1 pointers from the head node to the tail node. The complexity of the constructor is $O(\texttt{maxLevel})$.

The Method SkipList.get

Program 11.8 gives the code for the method get. The method returns null in case no element with key theKey is in the dictionary. When the dictionary contains an element with key theKey, this element is returned.

```
public Object get(Object theKey)
{
    if (tailKey.compareTo(theKey) <= 0)
        return null;  // no matching element possible

    // position p just before possible node with theKey
    SkipNode p = headNode;
    for (int i = levels; i >= 0; i--)          // go down levels
        while (p.next[i].key.compareTo(theKey) < 0) // follow level i
            p = p.next[i];                          // pointers

    // check if next node has theKey
    if (p.next[0].key.equals(theKey))
        return p.next[0].element;
    return null;  // no matching element
}
```

Program 11.8 The method SkipList.get

get begins with the highest level chain—the level levels chain—that contains an element and works its way down to the level 0 chain. At each level we advance as close to the element being searched as possible without advancing to the right of the element. Although we can terminate the search at level i if we reach an element whose key equals theKey, the additional comparison needed to test for equality isn't justified because most elements are expected to be only in the level 0 chain. When we exit from the for loop, we are positioned just to the left of the element we seek. Comparing with the next element on the level 0 chain permits us to determine whether or not the element we seek is in the structure.

The Method SkipList.put

Before we can write code for the method to insert elements into a skip list, we must write methods to assign a level number to a new element and to search the skip list as is done by get but saving a pointer (reference) to the last node encountered at each level of the search. Programs 11.9 and 11.10 give these two methods.

```
int level()
{
   int lev = 0;
   while (r.nextFloat() <= prob)
      lev++;
   return (lev <= maxLevel) ? lev : maxLevel;
}
```

Program 11.9 Method to assign a level number

```
SkipNode search(Object theKey)
{
   // position p just before possible node with theKey
   SkipNode p = headNode;
   for (int i = levels; i >= 0; i--)
   {
      while (p.next[i].key.compareTo(theKey) < 0)
         p = p.next[i];
      last[i] = p;   // last level i node seen
   }
   return (p.next[0]);
}
```

Program 11.10 Method to search a skip list and save the last node encountered at each level

Program 11.11 gives the code to insert an element theElement with key theKey into a skip list. The element is not inserted if largeKey ≤ theKey. Also, if the skip list already has an element whose key is theKey, the element with this key is changed to theElement.

```
public Object put(Object theKey, Object theElement)
{
   if (tailKey.compareTo(theKey) <= 0) // key too large
      throw new IllegalArgumentException("key is too large");

   // see if element with theKey already present
   SkipNode p = search(theKey);
   if (p.key.equals(theKey))
   {// update p.element
      Object elementToReturn = p.element;
      p.element = theElement;
      return elementToReturn;
   }

   // not present, determine level for new node
   int lev = level(); // level of new node
   // fix lev to be <= levels + 1
   if (lev > levels)
   {
      lev = ++levels;
      last[lev] = headNode;
   }

   // get and insert new node just after p
   SkipNode y = new SkipNode (theKey, theElement, lev + 1);
   for (int i = 0; i <= lev; i++)
   {// insert into level i chain
      y.next[i] = last[i].next[i];
      last[i].next[i] = y;
   }
   size++;
   return null;
}
```

Program 11.11 Skip list insertion

The Method SkipList.remove

Program 11.12 gives the code to remove and return an element with key theKey. In case the skip list does not have an element whose key is theKey, null is returned. The while loop updates levels so that there is at least one level levels element unless the skip list is empty. In the latter case levels is set to 0.

```
public Object remove(Object theKey)
{
   if (tailKey.compareTo(theKey) <= 0) // too large
      return null;

   // see if matching element present
   SkipNode p = search(theKey);
   if (!p.key.equals(theKey)) // not present
      return null;

   // delete node from skip list
   for (int i = 0; i <= levels &&
                  last[i].next[i] == p; i++)
      last[i].next[i] = p.next[i];

   // update Levels
   while (levels > 0 && headNode.next[levels] == tailNode)
      levels--;

   size--;
   return p.element;
}
```

Program 11.12 Removing an element from a skip list

Other Methods

The codes for other member methods such as `size`, `isEmpty`, `elements`, and the iterator methods are similar to the codes for the corresponding methods of `Chain`. Recall that the elements in the chain for each level (excluding the head node, which has no value) are in ascending order from left to right. In particular, the level 0 chain contains all elements in the dictionary in ascending order of their key. Therefore the `SkipList` iterator is able to provide sequential access to the dictionary elements in sorted order in $\Theta(1)$ time per element accessed.

11.4.6 Complexity of `SkipList` Methods

The complexity of methods `get`, `put`, and `remove` is $O(n+\texttt{maxLevel})$ where n is the number of elements in the skip list. In the worst case there may be only one level `maxLevel` element, and the remaining elements may all be level 0 elements. Now $O(\texttt{maxLevel})$ time is spent on the level i chains for $i > 0$, and $O(n)$ time on the level 0 chain. Despite this poor worst-case performance, skip lists are a valuable representation method, as the expected complexity of methods `get`, `put`, and `remove` is $O(\log n)$.

As for the space complexity, we note that in the worst case each element might be a level `maxLevel` element requiring `maxLevel+1` pointers. Therefore, in addition to the space needed to store references to the n elements and to the n keys, we need space for $O(n*\text{MaxLevel})$ chain pointers. On the average, however, only $n*p$ of the elements are expected to be on the level 1 chain, $n*p^2$ on the level 2 chain, and $n*p^i$ on the level i chain. So the expected number of pointer fields (excluding those in the head and tail nodes) is $n \sum_i p^i = n/(1-p)$. So while the worst-case space requirements are large, the expected requirements are not. When $p = 0.5$, the expected space requirements (in addition to that for the element and key references) is that for approximately $2n$ pointers!

EXERCISES

7. Write a level allocation program that divides the range of random number values into segments as described in the text and then determines the level on the basis of which segment a random number falls into.

8. Modify the class `SkipList` to allow for the presence of elements that have the same value. Each chain is now in nondecreasing order of value from left to right. Test your code.

9. Extend the class `SkipList` by including methods to remove the element with smallest key and to remove the element with largest key. What is the expected complexity of each method?

11.5   HASH TABLE REPRESENTATION

11.5.1   Ideal Hashing

Another possibility for the representation of a dictionary is to use **hashing**. This method uses a **hash function** to map keys into positions in a table called the **hash table**. In the ideal situation, if element e has the key k and f is the hash function, then e is stored in position $f(k)$ of the table. To search for an element with key k, we compute $f(k)$ and see whether an element exists at position $f(k)$ of the table. If so, we have found the element. If not, the dictionary contains no element with this key. In the former case the element may be deleted (if desired) by making position $f(k)$ of the table empty. In the latter case the element may be inserted by placing it in position $f(k)$.

Example 11.6 Consider the student records dictionary of Example 11.1. Suppose that instead of using student names as the key, we use student ID numbers, which are six-digit integers. For our class assume we will have at most 100 students and their ID numbers will be in the range 951000 and 952000. The function $f(k) = k - 951,000$ maps student IDs into table positions 0 through 1000. We may use an array `table[1001]` to store pairs of the form (key, element). This array is initialized so that `table[i]` is `null` for $0 \le i \le 1000$. To search for an element with key k, we compute $f(k) = k - 951,000$. The element is at `table`$[f(k)]$ provided `table`$[f(k)]$ is not `null`. If `table`$[f(k)]$ is `null`, the dictionary contains no element with key k. In the latter case the element may be inserted at this position. In the former case the element may be removed by setting `table`$[f(k)]$ to `null`. ■

   In the ideal situation just described, it takes $O(b)$ time to initialize an empty dictionary (b is the number of positions in the hash table) and $\Theta(1)$ time to perform a `get`, `put`, or `remove` operation.

   Although the ideal hashing solution just described may be used in many applications of a dictionary, in many other applications the range in key values is so large that a table either doesn't make sense or is impractical (or both).

Example 11.7 Suppose that in the class list example (Example 11.1) the student IDs are in the range [100000, 999999] and we are to use the hash function $f(k) = k - 100,000$. Since the value of $f()$ is in the range [0, 899,999], we need a table whose length is 900,000. It doesn't make sense to use a table this large for a class with only 100 students. Besides being terribly wasteful of space, it takes quite a bit of time to initialize the 900,000 array entries to `null`. ■

Example 11.8 [Converting Strings to Unique Numbers] Imagine you are maintaining a dictionary in which the keys are exactly three characters long. For example, each key may be the initials in a name; the key for Mohandas Karamchand Gandhi would be MKG.

   Since each character in Java is 2 bytes long, we could convert a three-character string into a long integer using the code of Program 11.13.

   When `s = abc`, `s.charAt(0) = a`, `s.charAt(1) = b`, and `s.charAt(2) = c`. If each of the characters a, b, and c is typecast into an integer, you get the numbers 97, 98, and 99, respectively. The left shifts (in Program 11.13) by 16 are done so that the bits of one character do not interfere with the bits of another character. Because of this shifting, different three-character strings convert to different long integers and it is possible to reconstruct s from `threeToLong(s)` (see Exercise 12).

   Since a left shift by 16 is equivalent to multiplying by $2^{16} = 65,536$, the computation performed by Program 11.13 when `s = abc` is equivalent to computing $((97 * 65,536 + 98) * 65,536) + 99 = 416,618,250,339$.

   Although Program 11.13 converts each three-character key into a unique long integer, the range of these long integers is [0, $2^{48} - 1$]. Since 2^{48} is more than 280 trillion, it is infeasible for us to create the array `table` used in ideal hashing. ■

```
public static long threeToLong(String s)
{
   // leftmost char
   long answer = s.charAt(0);

   // shift left 16 bits and add in next char
   answer = (answer << 16) + s.charAt(1);

   // shift left 16 bits and add in next char
   return (answer << 16) + s.charAt(2);
}
```

Program 11.13 Converting a three-character string to a long integer

11.5.2   Hash Functions and Tables

Buckets, Home Buckets, and Slots

When the key range is too large to use the ideal method described above, we use a hash table whose length is smaller than the key range and a hash function $f(k)$ that maps several different keys into the same position of the hash table. Each position of the table is a **bucket**; $f(k)$ is the **home bucket** for the element whose key is k; and the number of buckets in a table equals the table length. Since a hash function may map several keys into the same bucket, we may consider designing buckets that can hold more than one element. The number of elements that a bucket may hold equals the number of **slots** in the bucket. Although hash tables that are kept in the main memory of a computer generally have either 0 (yes 0, we will see how this works in Section 11.5.4) or 1 slot per bucket, hash tables that are stored on disk may have 20 or more slots per bucket.

The Division Hash Function

Of the many hash functions that have been proposed, hashing by division is most common. In hashing by division, the hash function has the form

$$f(k) = k\%D \tag{11.2}$$

where k is the key, D is the length (i.e., number of buckets) of the hash table, and $\%$ is the modulo operator. The positions in the hash table are indexed 0 through $D - 1$. When $D = 11$, the home buckets for the keys 3, 22, 27, 40, 80, and 96 are $f(3) = 3$, $f(22) = 0$, $f(27) = 5$, 7, 3, and 8, respectively.

Other hash functions are described in this book's Web site.

Collisions and Overflows

Figure 11.2(a) shows a hash table with 11 buckets numbered 0 through 10, and each bucket has one slot. The divisor D that has been used is 11. The 80 is in position 3 because 80 % 11 = 3; the 40 is in position 40 % 11 = 7; and the 65 is in position 65 % 11 = 10. Each element is in its home bucket. The remaining buckets in the hash table are empty.

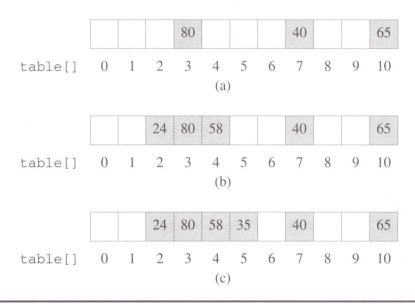

Figure 11.2 Hash tables

Now suppose we wish to enter the value 58 into the table. The home bucket is $f(58) = 58$ % 11 = 3. This bucket is already occupied by a different value. We say that a **collision** has occurred. A collision occurs whenever two different keys have the same home bucket. Since a bucket may contain space for more than one element, a collision may not be a problem. All elements that have the same home bucket can be stored in their home bucket provided enough slots are available. An **overflow** occurs when there isn't room in the home bucket for the new element.

In our example each bucket has just one slot. So collisions and overflows occur at the same time. If we cannot put 58 into its home bucket, where should we put it? This question is answered by the overflow-handling mechanism in use. The most popular overflow-handling mechanisms are linear probing (11.5.3) and chaining (11.5.4). Other mechanisms such as quadratic probing and double hashing are described in the Web site.

I Want a Good Hash Function

Although collisions may not give you a headache, they lead to overflows, which are guaranteed to cause a headache as far as the insertion operation is concerned. The expected occurrence of collisions and overflows is minimized when approximately the same number of keys from the key range hashes into any bucket of the table. A **uniform hash function** provides such a distribution of home buckets.

Example 11.9 [Uniform Hash Function] Assume that our hash table has $b > 1$ buckets numbered 0 through $b - 1$. The hash function $f(k) = 0$ for all k is not a uniform hash function because all keys hash into the same bucket, bucket 0. When this hash function is used, we get the maximum number of collisions and overflows that are possible. Suppose $b = 11$ and the key range is $[0, 98]$. A uniform hash function will hash approximately 9 of these keys into each bucket; when the key range is $[0, 999]$, approximately 91 keys are hashed into each bucket.

The function $f(k) = k\%b$ is a uniform hash function for every key range $[0, r]$ where r is a positive integer. When $r = 20$ and $b = 11$, for example, some buckets get two keys and others get one; and when $r = 50$ and $b = 11$, some buckets get five keys and others get four. No matter what r and $b > 1$ are, when division is used, some buckets get $\lfloor r/b \rfloor$ keys and the remaining buckets get $\lceil r/b \rceil$ keys. Division yields a uniform hash function. ∎

If people would select the set of keys in their dictionary uniformly from the key range, the use of a uniform hash function would result in a uniform assignment of dictionary keys to home buckets. Unfortunately, we haven't figured out how to make people select keys in this manner. In practice, dictionary applications have keys that show some degree of correlation. For example, when the keys are integers, you might have a preponderance of odd keys or even keys, rather than an equal number of odd and even keys; when the keys are alphanumeric, you may have clusters of keys that have the same prefix or the same suffix. Because keys in real-world applications are not selected uniformly from the key range, some uniform hash functions work better than others in providing an approximately equal distribution of keys to home buckets. These uniform hash functions that actually give a good distribution of keys in practice are called **good hash functions**.

Example 11.10 [Selecting the Hash Function Divisor D] When using the hash function $f(k) = k\%D$ ($D = b$), some choices of D result in a good hash function and other choices result in a bad hash function. As noted above, all choices of D, $D > 1$, result in a uniform hash function.

Suppose that D is an even integer. Now $f(k)$ is even whenever k is even, and $f(k)$ is odd whenever k is odd. For example, $k\%20$ is even whenever k is even and is odd whenever k is odd. If your application has a preponderance of even keys, then many more keys get even home buckets than get odd home buckets. We do not get a uniform assignment of home buckets. The same is true when your application has a preponderance of odd keys. This time many more keys get an odd home bucket than get an even home bucket. So choosing D to be even gives us a bad hash function.

When D is divisible by small odd numbers such as 3, 5, and 7, hashing by division does not distribute the use of home buckets uniformly in real-world dictionaries. Therefore, for division by hashing to be a good hash function, we must choose a divisor D that is neither even nor divisible by small odd numbers. *The ideal choice for D is a prime number. When you cannot find a prime number close to the table length you have in mind, you should choose D so that it is not divisible by any number between 2 and 19.* Other considerations for the choice of D are discussed in Sections 11.5.3 and 11.5.4. ■

Because of the correlation among keys in a dictionary application, you should choose uniform hash functions whose value depends on all bits of the key (as opposed to just the first few, last few, or middle few). The hash functions described in this book's Web site have this property. Therefore, these hash functions are good hash functions. When using the division hash function, dependence on all bits is obtained by using an odd value for D. Best results are obtained when D (and therefore the number of buckets b) is either a prime number or has *no prime factors less than* 20.

Division and Nonintegral Keys

To use the division hash function, keys that are not of an integral type (e.g., `int`, `long`, `char`) will need to be converted to nonnegative integers before $f(k)$ can be computed. Since all hash functions hash several keys into the same home bucket, it is not necessary for us to convert nonintegral keys into unique integers. It is ok for us to convert the strings *data*, *structures*, and *algorithms* into the same integer (say, 199).

Example 11.11 [Converting Strings to Integers] Program 11.13 cannot be extended to convert strings with more than four characters into a number because a long integer has only 64 bits. Since it is not necessary to convert strings into unique integers, we can map every string, no matter how long, into a 32-bit integer. Program 11.14 shows you one way to do this.

Program 11.14 converts pairs of characters into a unique integer, using the technique of Program 11.13, and then sums these unique integers. Since overflows may occur in the additions, a negative result is possible. Negative results are converted to positive ones. Although it would have been easier to simply add all the characters together (rather than shift every other one by 16 bits), doing so would give us integers that are not much more than 16 bits long; strings that are eight characters long would produce integers up to 19 bits long. Shifting by 16 bits allows us to cover the range of positive integers even with strings that are two characters long.

If you expect your strings to be made up essentially of ASCII characters, then you can better cover the range of positive integers by first converting each character from 16 bits to 8 bits by adding the two 8-bit components and then adding together

```
public static int integer(String s)
{
   int length = s.length();    // number of characters in s
   int answer = 0;
   if (length % 2 == 1)
   {// length is odd
      answer = s.charAt(length - 1);
      length--;
   }

   // length is now even
   for (int i = 0; i < length; i += 2)
   {// do two characters at a time
      answer += s.charAt(i);
      answer += ((int) s.charAt(i + 1)) << 16;
   }

   return (answer < 0) ? -answer : answer;
}
```

Program 11.14 Converting a string into a nonunique integer

the 8-bit numbers in groups of four (shifting each number in a group by either 0, 8, 16, or 24 bits). ∎

Java provides a method `Object.hashCode` that returns an integer suitable for use by a division hash function. Unless you override `Object.hashCode`, the integer that is returned by `s.hashCode` is based on the reference in `s`. This method overriding has been done, in Java, for its wrapper classes `Integer`, `Double`, `String`, and so on. The invocation `s.hashCode()`, where `s` may be a `String`, `Double`, and so on, gives you an integer that is based on the value of the object `s` rather than on the reference to this object. You can use Java's class `HashTable` with keys of any data type you define provided you write the instance method `hashCode` for your data type.

11.5.3   Linear Probing

The Method

The easiest way to find a place to put 58 into the table of Figure 11.2(a) is to search the table for the next available bucket and then put 58 into it. This method of handling overflows is called **linear probing** (also referred to as linear open addressing).

The 58 gets inserted into position 4. Suppose that the next value to be inserted is 24. 24 % 11 is 2. This bucket is empty, and so the 24 is placed there. Our hash table now has the form shown in Figure 11.2(b). Let us attempt to insert the value 35 into this table. Its home bucket (2) is full. Using linear probing, this value is placed in the next available bucket, and the table of Figure 11.2(c) results. As a final example, consider inserting 98 into the table. Its home bucket (10) is full. The next available bucket is 0, and the insertion is made into this bucket. So the search for the next available bucket is made by regarding the table as circular!

Having seen how insertions are made when linear probing is used, we can devise a method to search such a table. The search begins at the home bucket $f(k)$ of the key k we are searching for and continues by examining successive buckets in the table (regarding the table as circular) until one of the following happens: (1) a bucket containing an element with key k is reached, in which case we have found the element we were searching for; (2) an empty bucket is reached; and (3) we return to the home bucket. In the latter two cases, the table contains no element with key k.

The removal of an element must leave behind a table on which the search method just described works correctly. If we are to remove the element with key 58 from the table of Figure 11.2(c), we cannot simply make position 4 of the table null. Doing so will result in the search method failing to find the element with key 35. A removal may require us to move several elements. The search for elements to move begins just after the bucket vacated by the removed element and proceeds to successive buckets until we either reach an empty bucket or we return to the bucket from which the deletion took place. When elements are moved up the table following the removal of an element, we must take care not to move an element to a position before its home bucket because making such an element move would cause the search for this element to fail.

An alternative to this rather cumbersome deletion strategy is to introduce the field neverUsed in each bucket. When the table is initialized, this field is set to true for all buckets. When an element is placed into a bucket, its neverUsed field is set to false. Now condition (2) for search termination is replaced by: a bucket with its neverUsed field equal to true is reached. We accomplish a removal by setting the table position occupied by the removed element to null. A new element may be inserted into the first empty bucket encountered during a search that begins at the element's home bucket. Notice that in this alternative scheme, neverUsed is never reset to true. After a while all (or almost all) buckets have this field equal to false, and unsuccessful searches examine all buckets. To improve performance, we must reorganize the table when many empty buckets have their neverUsed field equal to false. This reorganization could, for example, involve reinserting all remaining elements into an empty hash table.

Java Implementation of Linear Probing

Since each dictionary entry is a (key, element) pair, we define a class HashEntry for the pairs stored in a bucket. The data members of this class are key and element; both data members are of type Object. When we use buckets that have just one slot, the hash table may be defined as a one-dimensional array table[b] of type HashEntry; b is the number of buckets.

When the number of slots per bucket exceeds 1, we may use a two-dimensional array table[b][s] of type HashEntry. Here s is the number of slots per bucket. Alternatively, we can define a data type bucket that can accommodate s (key, element) pairs and then define the hash table as a one-dimensional array whose data type is bucket.

Program 11.15 gives the data members and the constructor for a hash table class HashTable that uses linear probing. This class uses a hash table that has one slot per bucket.

```
// data members of HashTable
protected int divisor;          // hash function divisor
protected HashEntry [] table;   // hash table array
protected int size;             // number of elements in table

// constructor
public HashTable(int theDivisor)
{
   divisor = theDivisor;

   // allocate hash table array
   table = new HashEntry [divisor];
}
```

Program 11.15 Data members and constructor for HashTable

Program 11.16 gives the member method search of HashTable. This method returns a bucket b in the table that satisfies exactly one of the following: (1) table[b] has the key theKey; (2) no element in the table has the key theKey, table[b] is null, and the element with key theKey may be inserted into bucket b if desired; and (3) no element in the table has the key theKey, table[b] has a key other than theKey, and the table is full.

Program 11.17 implements the method HashTable.get.

Program 11.18 gives the implementation of function put. This code begins by invoking the method search. From the specification of search, if the returned bucket i is empty, then there is no element in the table with key theKey and

```
private int search(Object theKey)
{
   int i = Math.abs(theKey.hashCode()) % divisor;  // home bucket
   int j = i;                                       // start at home bucket
   do
   {
      if (table[j] == null || table[j].key.equals(theKey))
         return j;
      j = (j + 1) % divisor;  // next bucket
   } while (j != i);          // returned to home bucket?

   return j;  // table full
}
```

Program 11.16 The method HashTable.search

```
public Object get(Object theKey)
{
   // search the table
   int b = search(theKey);

   // see if a match was found at table[b]
   if (table[b] == null || !table[b].key.equals(theKey))
      return null;              // no match

   return table[b].element;  // matching element
}
```

Program 11.17 The method HashTable.get

element theElement may be inserted into this bucket. If the returned bucket is not empty, then it either contains an element with key theKey or the table is full. In the former case we change the element stored in the bucket to theElement; in the latter, we throw an exception (increasing the table size is an alternative to throwing an exception; this alternative is considered in Exercise 25). Exercise 26 asks you to write code for the method remove.

```
public Object put(Object theKey, Object theElement)
{
   // search the table for a matching element
   int b = search(theKey);

   // check if matching element found
   if (table[b] == null)
   {
      // no matching element and table not full
      table[b] = new HashEntry(theKey, theElement);
      size++;
      return null;
   }
   else
   {// check if duplicate or table full
      if (table[b].key.equals(theKey))
      {// duplicate, change table[b].element
         Object elementToReturn = table[b].element;
         table[b].element = theElement;
         return elementToReturn;
      }
      else // table is full
         throw new IllegalArgumentException("table is full");
   }
}
```

Program 11.18 The method HashTable.put

Performance Analysis

We will analyze the time complexity only. Let b be the number of buckets in the hash table. When division with divisor D is used as the hash function, $b = D$. The time needed to initialize the table is $O(b)$. The worst-case insert and search time is $\Theta(n)$ when n elements are present in the table. The worst case happens, for instance, when all n key values have the same home bucket. Comparing the worst-case complexity of hashing to that of the linear list method to maintain a dictionary, we see that both have the same worst-case complexity.

For average performance, however, hashing is considerably superior. Let U_n and S_n, respectively, denote the average number of buckets examined during an unsuccessful and a successful search when n is large. This average is defined over all possible sequences of n key values being inserted into the table. For linear probing, it can be shown that

$$U_n \approx \frac{1}{2}\left(1 + \frac{1}{(1-\alpha)^2}\right) \qquad (11.3)$$

$$S_n \approx \frac{1}{2}\left(1 + \frac{1}{1-\alpha}\right) \qquad (11.4)$$

where $\alpha = n/b$ is the **loading factor**. Although Equation 11.3 is rather difficult to derive, Equation 11.4 can be derived from Equation 11.3 with modest effort (Exercise 21a).

From Equations 11.3 and 11.4, it follows that when $\alpha = 0.5$, an unsuccessful search will examine 2.5 buckets on the average and an average successful search will examine 1.5 buckets. When $\alpha = 0.9$, these figures are 50.5 and 5.5. These figures, of course, assume that n is much larger than 51. When it is possible to work with small loading factors, the average performance of hashing with linear probing is significantly superior to that of the linear list method. Generally, when linear probing is used, we try to keep $\alpha \leq 0.75$ (the default maximum loading factor for Java's hash table classes is 0.75).

Analysis of Random Probing

To give you a taste of what is involved in determining U_n and S_n, we derive U_n and S_n formulas for the random probing method to handle overflows. In random probing, when an overflow occurs, the search for a free bucket in which the new key is inserted is done in a random manner (in practice, a pseudorandom number generator is used so we can reproduce the bucket search sequence and use this sequence in subsequent searches for the inserted element).

Our derivation of the formula for U_n makes use of the following result from probability theory.

Theorem 11.1 *Let p be the probability that a certain event occurs. The expected number of independent trials needed for that event to occur is $1/\alpha$.*

To get a feel for the validity of Theorem 11.1, suppose that you flip a coin. The probability that the coin lands heads up is $p = 1/2$. The number of times you expect to flip the coin before it lands heads up is $1/p = 2$. A die has six sides labeled 1 through 6. When you throw a die, the probability of drawing an odd number is $p = 1/2$. You expect to throw the die $1/p = 2$ times before drawing an odd number. The probability that a die throw draws a 6 is $p = 1/6$, so you expect to throw the die $1/p = 6$ times before drawing a 6.

The formula for U_n is derived as follows. When the loading density is α, the probability that any bucket is occupied is also α. Therefore, the probability that a bucket is empty is $p = 1 - \alpha$. In random probing an unsuccessful search looks for an empty bucket, using a sequence of independent trials. Therefore, the expected number of buckets examined is

$$U_n \approx \frac{1}{p} = \frac{1}{1-\alpha} \tag{11.5}$$

The equation for S_n may be derived from that for U_n. Number the n elements in the table 1, 2, $\cdots$, n in the order they were inserted. When the ith element is inserted, an unsuccesful search is done and the item is inserted into the empty bucket where the unsuccessful search terminates. At the time the ith element is inserted, the loading factor is $(i-1)/b$ where b is the number of buckets. From Equation 11.5 it follows that the expected number of buckets that are to be examined when searching for the ith element is

$$\frac{1}{1 - \frac{i-1}{b}}$$

Assuming that each element in the table is searched for with equal probability, we get

$$
\begin{aligned}
S_n &\approx \frac{1}{n} \sum_{i=1}^{n} \frac{1}{1 - \frac{i-1}{b}} \\
&= \frac{1}{n} \sum_{i=0}^{n-1} \frac{1}{1 - \frac{i}{b}} \\
&\approx \frac{1}{n} \int_{i=0}^{n-1} \frac{1}{1 - \frac{i}{b}} di \\
&\approx \frac{1}{n} \int_{i=0}^{n} \frac{1}{1 - \frac{i}{b}} di \\
&= -\frac{b}{n} \log_e (1 - i/b) \Big]_0^n \\
&= -\frac{1}{\alpha} \log_e (1 - \alpha) \tag{11.6}
\end{aligned}
$$

Linear probing incurs a preformance penalty relative to random probing as far as the number of examined buckets is concerned. For example, when $\alpha = 0.9$, an unsuccesful search using linear probing is expected to examine 50.5 buckets; when random probing is used, this expected number drops to 10. So why do we not use random probing? Here are two reasons:

- Our real interest is run time, not number of buckets examined. It takes more time to compute the next random number than it does to examine several buckets.

- Since random probing searches the table in a random fashion, it pays a run-time penalty because of the cache effect (Section 4.5). Therefore, even though random probing examines a smaller number of buckets than does linear probing, examining this smaller number of buckets actually takes more time except when the loading factor is close to 1.

In Section 11.5.4 we will see an even more effective way to reduce the expected number of buckets examined.

Choosing a Divisor D

To determine D, we first determine what constitutes acceptable performance for unsuccessful and successful searches. Using the formulas for U_n and S_n, we can determine the largest α that can be used. From the value of n (or an estimate) and the computed value of α, we obtain the smallest permissible value for b. Next we find the smallest integer that is at least as large as this value of b and that either is a prime or has no factors smaller than 20. This integer is the value of D and b to use.

Example 11.12 We are to design a hash table for up to 1000 elements. Successful searches should require no more than four bucket examinations on average, and unsuccessful searches should examine no more than 50.5 buckets on average. From the formula for U_n, we obtain $\alpha \leq 0.9$, and from that for S_n, we obtain $4 \geq 0.5 + 1/(2(1-\alpha))$ or $\alpha \leq 6/7$. Therefore, we require $\alpha \leq \min\{0.9, 6/7\} = 6/7$. Hence b should be at least $\lceil 7n/6 \rceil = 1167$. $b = D = 1171$ is a suitable choice.   ∎

Another way to compute D is to begin with a knowledge of the largest possible value for b as determined by the maximum amount of space available for the hash table. Now we find the largest D no larger than this largest value that is either a prime or has no factors smaller than 20. For instance, if we can allot at most 530 buckets to the table, then $23 * 23 = 529$ is the right choice for D and b.

11.5.4   Hashing with Chains

The Method

Chains provide a good solution to the overflow problem that arises when hashing is used. Rather than place an element into a bucket other than its home bucket, we maintain chains of elements that have the same home bucket. Figure 11.3 shows a hash table in which overflows are handled by **chaining**. As in our earlier example, the hash function divisor is 11. In this hash table organization, each bucket has

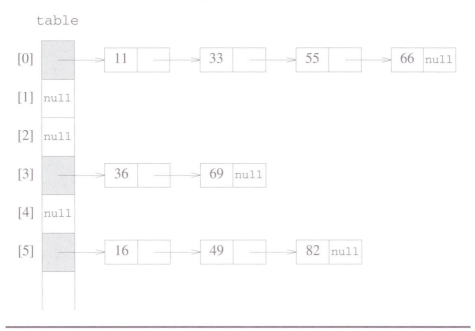

Figure 11.3 A chained hash table

space for just a pointer. Since no element is kept in a bucket, the number of slots per bucket is 0. All elements are kept on chains.

To search for an element with key k, we first compute the home bucket, $k\%D$, for the key and then search the chain this bucket points to. To insert an element, we need to first verify that the table does not already have an element with the same key. This search can, of course, be limited to the chain for the home bucket of the new element. As each insert is preceded by a search, it is easy to maintain the chains in ascending order of the key values (as in Figure 11.3). Finally, to delete an element with key k, we access the home bucket chain, search this chain for an element with the given key, and then delete the element.

Java Implementation of Chained Hash Tables

The class **HashChains** implements a dictionary using a one-dimensional array **table-[0:divisor-1]** of sorted chains. Each sorted chain is of type **SortedChain** (see Section 11.3). Program 11.19 gives the important methods of **HashChains**.

```
public Object get(Object theKey)
   {return table[Math.abs(theKey.hashCode()) % divisor].get(theKey);}

public Object put(Object theKey, Object theElement)
{
   int b = Math.abs(theKey.hashCode()) % divisor;   // home bucket
   Object elementToReturn = table[b].put(theKey, theElement);
   if (elementToReturn == null) size++;             // new key
   return elementToReturn;
}

public Object remove(Object theKey)
{
   Object x = table[Math.abs(theKey.hashCode()) % divisor]
            .remove(theKey);
   if (x != null) size--;
   return x;
}
```

Program 11.19 get, put and remove methods for a chained hash table

An Improved Implementation

We can get slightly improved performance by adding a tail node to the end of each chain as in Figure 11.4. The tail node has a key that is at least as large as that of any element to be inserted into the table. In Figure 11.4 this large key is denoted by the symbol ∞. In practice, when the keys are integer, we can use the constant Integer.MAX_VALUE. With the use of a tail node, we can eliminate most of the checks against null that are used in the codes for the methods of SortedChain. Also, notice that although Figure 11.4 has been drawn so as to use a separate tail for each chain, in practice, we may use the same tail node for all chains.

Comparison with Linear Probing

We will explicitly compare linear probing with chaining for the case where the chains do not have a tail node. The space requirements for linear probing are less than those for chaining because when chaining is used, each element has the additional field next associated with it.

As far as the worst-case time complexities are concerned, a search can require the examination of all n elements in both cases. The average performance of a search when chaining is used can be derived in the following way. An unsuccessful search of an ordered chain with i nodes on it will examine either one, two, three,

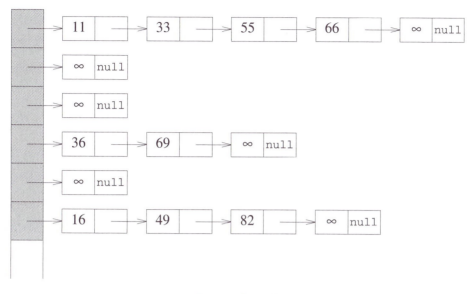

∞ denotes large key

Figure 11.4 Hash table with tail nodes

···, or i nodes, for $i \geq 1$. Consider the chain `table[3]` of Figure 11.3. A search for a key that is less than 36 examines one node; a search for a key greater than 36 and less than 69 examines two nodes; and a search for a key greater than 69 examines 2 nodes. For an i-node chain, there are $i+1$ possibilities for the range in which the search key falls. If each of these possibilities happens with equal probability, then the average number of nodes that get examined in an unsuccessful search is

$$\frac{1}{i+1}(i + \sum_{j=1}^{i} j) = \frac{1}{i+1}(i + \frac{i(i+1)}{2}) = \frac{i(i+3)}{2(i+1)}$$

when $i \geq 1$. When $i = 0$, the average number of nodes examined is 0. For chained hash tables we expect the length of a chain to be $n/b = \alpha$ on average. When $\alpha \geq 1$, we may substitute α for i in the above expression to get

$$U_n \approx \frac{\alpha(\alpha+3)}{2(\alpha+1)}, \ \alpha \geq 1 \tag{11.7}$$

When $\alpha < 1$, $U_n \leq \alpha$ because the average chain length is α and no search requires us to examine more nodes than on a chain.

For S_n we need to know the expected distance of each of the n identifiers from the head of its chain. To determine this distance, assume that the identifiers are inserted in increasing order. This assumption does not affect the positioning of identifiers on their respective chains. When the ith identifier is inserted, its chain is expected to have a length of $(i-1)/b$. The ith identifier gets added to the end of the chain as identifiers are inserted in increasing order. Hence a search for this identifier will require us to examine $1 + (i - 1)/b$ nodes. Note also that when identifiers are inserted in increasing order, their distance from the chain head does not change as a result of further insertions. Assuming that each of the n identifiers is searched for with equal probability, we get

$$S_n = \frac{1}{n} \sum_{i=1}^{n} \{1 + (i - 1)/b\} = 1 + \frac{n - 1}{2b} \approx 1 + \frac{\alpha}{2} \qquad (11.8)$$

Comparing the formulas for chaining with those for linear and random probing, we see that, on average, chaining examines a smaller number of buckets. For instance, when $\alpha = 0.9$, an unsuccessful search in a chained hash table is expected to examine 0.9 bucket and a successful search, 1.45 buckets. On the other hand, when linear probing is used, 50.5 buckets are expected to be examined if the search is unsuccessful and 5.5 if it is successful!

Comparison with Skip Lists

Both skip lists and hashing utilize a randomization process to improve the expected performance of the dictionary operations. In the case of skip lists, randomization is used to assign a level to an element at the time of insertion. This level assignment is done without examining the value of the element being inserted. In the case of hashing, the hash function assigns a bucket so as to randomly distribute the bucket assignments for the different elements being inserted. The hash function does utilize the element value.

By using randomization, skip lists and hashing, respectively, obtain logarithmic and constant time expected performance. However, the worst-case complexity of the skip list method is $\Theta(n+\texttt{maxLevel})$, while that of hashing is $\Theta(n)$. When skip lists are used, the expected space required for the pointers is approximately $\texttt{maxLevel}+n/(1 - p)$; in the worst case, space for $\texttt{maxLevel}*(n + 1)$ pointers is required. The worst-case space requirements are considerably larger for skip lists than for a chained hash table; a chained hash table requires $D + n$ space for pointers.

The skip list structure is, however, more versatile than a hash table. For example, we can output the elements in ascending order of value in linear time by simply going down the level 0 chain. When a chained hash table is used, it takes $\Theta(D)$ time to collect, at most, D nonempty chains and an additional $O(n \log D)$ to combine the sorted chains in ascending order of key. The combining process is done as follows: (1) put the chains on a queue; (2) extract a pair of chains from the queue, merge the pair of chains into a single sorted chain, and put the resulting chain into the queue; and (3) repeat (2) until only one chain remains. Other operations, such as find or remove the element with largest or smallest value, are also more expensive (in terms of expected complexity) when a hash table is used.

EXERCISES

10. Use ideal hashing to implement a Java class for dictionaries. Assume that element keys are integers in the range 0 through maxKey where maxKey is specified by the user at the time the dictionary is created. Test your code.

11. Let u and v be two different three-character strings. Prove that Program 11.13 converts u and v into different numbers.

12. Write a method to take the value returned by Program 11.13 and convert it into the three-character string from which it came.

13. In which of the following cases is the specified hash function a uniform hash function (b is the number of buckets in the hash table)? Explain.

   (a) The keys are integers in the range [0, 999], $b = 50$, and $f(k) = k\%47$.

   (b) The keys are even numbers in the range [0, 999], $b = 70$, and $f(k) = k\%70$.

   (c) The keys are odd numbers in the range [0, 999], $b = 70$, and $f(k) = k\%70$.

   (d) The keys are three lowercase letters from the English alphabet, $b = 70$, and $f(k) = $ first letter in the key k.

14. You have a hash table with b buckets; the hash function is $f(k) = k\%b$. Which of the following b values satisifes the recommendation made for the hash function divisor is Example 11.10? That is, which of the following values gives a good hash function?

   (a) $b = 93$

   (b) $b = 37$

   (c) $b = 1024$

   (d) $b = 529$

15. Use the recommendation made at the end of Example 11.11 and write a method to convert a string into an integer. Your method should cover the range of positive integers even when most string characters are ASCII and the string length is small.

16. Write a method to convert a double into an integer suitable for use by the division hash function.

17. Use linear probing, a hash table with $b = 13$ buckets, and the hash function $f(k) = k\%b$. Start with an empty hash table and insert elements whose keys are 7, 42, 25, 70, 14, 38, 8, 21, 34, 11. The elements are inserted in this order.

    (a) Draw the hash table following each insert.

    (b) What is the loading factor of your table after the last insert?

    (c) What is the maximum and average number of buckets examined in an unsuccessful search of your table?

    (d) What is the maximum and average number of buckets examined in a successful search?

    (e) Compute U_n and S_n using your loading factor and the formulas for linear probing (Equations 11.3 and 11.4). How do these numbers compare with the numbers you computed in parts (c) and (d). Explain any discrepancy.

18. Do Exercise 17 for the case when $b = 17$.

19. Do Exercise 17 for the case when $b = 27$.

20. Design an experiment to determine the accuracy of the formulas for U_n and S_n for linear probing. Conduct the experiment and present your results as a table in which you give both the measured and computed values.

21. (a) Derive Equation 11.4 from Equation 11.3. Use the same approach as used to derive Equation 11.6 from Equation 11.5.

    (b) Can this approach be used to derive Equation 11.8 from Equation 11.7? Why?

22. Develop a table of U_n and S_n values for $\alpha = 0.1, 0.2, 0.3, \cdots, 0.9$ for both linear probing and random probing.

23. Determine a suitable value for the hash function divisor D when linear probing is used. Do this for each of the following situations:

    (a) $n = 50$, $S_n \leq 3$, $U_n \leq 20$.

    (b) $n = 500$, $S_n \leq 5$, $U_n \leq 60$.

    (c) $n = 10$, $S_n \leq 2$, $U_n \leq 10$.

24. For each of the following conditions, obtain a suitable value for the hash function divisor D. For this value of D determine S_n and U_n as a function of n. Assume that linear probing is used.

    (a) $MaxElements \leq 530$.

    (b) $MaxElements \leq 130$.

    (c) $MaxElements \leq 150$.

25. Write a version of the method `HashTable.put` (Program 11.18) in which the table size is approximately doubled whenever the loading density exceeds a user-specified amount. This loading density is specified along with the initial capacity when the hash table is constructed. Specifically, we limit ourselves to odd table sizes (and so to odd divisors); and each time the loading density is exceeded, the new table size is $2 * (\text{oldtablesize}) + 1$. Although this method does not pick divisors according to the rule we have specified, this approach is consistent with the choice of table sizes (and hence divisors) used by the hash table implementations in `java.util`.

★ 26. Write code for the method `remove`, which is a public member of the class `HashTable`. Do not change any other members of this class. What is the worst-case time complexity of your code to delete an element? Use suitable data to test its correctness.

27. Develop a class for hash tables using linear probing and the `neverUsed` concept to handle a delete operation. Write complete Java code for all methods. Include a method to reorganize the table when (say) 60 percent of the empty buckets have `neverUsed` equal to `false`. The reorganization should move elements around as necessary and leave a properly configured hash table in which `neverUsed` is `true` for every empty bucket. Test the correctness of your code.

28. Comment on the difficulty of providing sequential access when (a) linear probing is used and (b) when a chained hash table is used.

29. Do Exercise 17 for a chained hash table.

30. Do Exercise 20 for a chained hash table.

31. Develop a new class `SortedChainWithTail` in which the sorted chain has a tail node. Use the tail node to simplify your code by placing the element or key being searched for, inserted, or deleted into the tail at the start of the operation. Compare the run-time performance of sorted chains with and without tail nodes.

32. Develop the class `ChainedHashTable` that implements all methods of `Hash-Chains`. The class should be developed from scratch and should make insertions and removals from its chains without invoking any method of any chain class. Test your code.

33. Develop a chained hash table class `HashChainsWithTails` in which the chains are instances of the class `SortedChainWithTail` (see Exercise 31). Compare the run-time performance of hash tables that are instances of `HashChains` and those that are instances of `HashChainsWithTails`.

34. Develop a class `HashChainsWithTail` in which each hash table chain is a sorted chain with a tail node. The tail node for all chains is the same physical node. The class should be developed from scratch and should make insertions and removals from its chains without invoking any method of any chain class. Compare the run-time performance of this class with that of `HashChains` (Program 11.19).

35. In an effort to simplify the insert and delete codes for chained hash tables, we might consider adding a head node to each chain. The head node is in addition to a tail node as discussed in the text. All insertions and removals now take place between the head and tail of a chain. As a result, the case of insertion and removal at/from the front of a chain is eliminated.

    (a) Is it possible to use the same head node for all chains? Why?

    (b) Is it desirable to set the key field(s) of the head node(s) to a particular value? Why?

    (c) Develop and test the class `HashChainsWithHeadsAndTail` in which each chain has a head node and a tail node. The class should be developed from scratch and should make insertions and removals from its chains without invoking any method of any chain class. Include all methods included in `HashChains`.

    (d) State the merits and demerits of using head and tail nodes versus using only tail nodes versus using neither head nor tail nodes. Of these options which do you recommend? Why?

36. (a) Implement a hash table class that uses quadratic probing instead of linear probing. You need not implement a method to remove elements. See the Web site for a description of quadratic probing.

    (b) Compare the performance of your class with that of the class `Hash-Table` that was developed in Section 11.5.3. Do this comparison by experimentally measuring the average number of key comparisons made in successful and unsuccessful searches as well as by measuring the actual run time.

37. Do Exercise 36 using double hashing rather than quadratic probing. See the Web site for a description of double hashing.

38. (a) Design an experiment to compare the expected run-time performance of `SortedChain`, `SkipList`, `HashTable`, `HashChains`, and `java.util.-HashTable`. Since we have not implemented `Hash.Table.remove` in the text, your experiment should include only the `get` and `put` methods.

    (b) Perform your experiment of part (a) and measure the run times. Present your times both as a table and as a bar chart.

    (c) Which class do you recommend for dictionary applications?

39. Derive formulas for U_n and S_n for a chained hash table in which the chains are not sorted; whenever an element is inserted into a chain, it is appended to the right end of the chain.

11.6   AN APPLICATION—TEXT COMPRESSION

In this section we use the term *character* to refer to a one of the standard 256 ASCII characters which take 1 byte (or 8 bits) each. Note that Java unicode characters take 2 bytes each. So do not confuse the use of the word *character* in this section with the Java data type `char`.

We can often reduce the disk storage needed to store a text file by storing a coded version of the file. For example, a text file that is a string of 1000 *x*s followed by a string of 2000 *y*s will take 3002 bytes of space (1 byte for each *x* and *y* and 2 bytes to denote the string end) when stored as an uncoded text file. The same file can be coded, using *run-length coding*, as the string $1000x2000y$, which is 10 characters long and can be stored in 12 bytes of space. The space can be further reduced by storing the run lengths (1000 and 2000) in their binary representation. With 2 bytes per run length, the maximum run length is 2^{16}. Our example string can now be stored using 8 bytes. When the coded file is read back from storage, it needs to be decoded into the original file. File coding is done by a **compressor** and decoding by a **decompressor**.

In this section we will develop Java code to compress and decompress text files using a technique developed by Lempel, Ziv, and Welch. Hence we will refer to the technique as the LZW method. The method is relatively simple and employs both ideal hashing and chained hashing.

11.6.1   LZW Compression

The LZW compression method maps strings of text characters into numeric codes. To begin with, all characters that may occur in the string are assigned a code. For example, suppose that the string $S =$ aaabbbbbbaabaaba is to be compressed. This string is composed of the characters a and b. a is assigned the code 0, and b the code 1.

The mapping between character strings and their codes is stored in a dictionary. Each dictionary entry has two fields: `key` and `code`. The character string represented by `code` is stored in the field `key`. Figure 11.5(a) gives the initial dictionary for our example.

Beginning with the configuration of Figure 11.5, the LZW compressor repeatedly finds the longest prefix, p, of the unencoded part of S (the unencoded part of S is shaded in Figure 11.5) that is in the dictionary and outputs its code. If there is a next character c in S, then pc (pc is the prefix string p followed by the character c) is assigned the next code and inserted into the dictionary. This strategy is called the **LZW rule**.

code	0	1
key	a	b

a a a b b b b b b a a b a a b a

Compressed string = null

(a) Initial configuration

0	1	2
a	b	aa

a a a b b b b b b a a b a a b a

Compressed string = 0

(b) a has been compressed

0	1	2	3
a	b	aa	aab

a a a b b b b b b a a b a a b a

Compressed string = 02

(c) aaa has been compressed

0	1	2	3	4
a	b	aa	aab	bb

a a a b b b b b b a a b a a b a

Compressed string = 021

(d) aaab has been compressed

0	1	2	3	4	5
a	b	aa	aab	bb	bbb

a a a b b b b b b a a b a a b a

Compressed string = 0214

(e) aaabbb has been compressed

0	1	2	3	4	5	6
a	b	aa	aab	bb	bbb	bbba

a a a b b b b b b a a b a a b a

Compressed string = 02145

(f) aaabbbbbb has been compressed

0	1	2	3	4	5	6	7
a	b	aa	aab	bb	bbb	bbba	aaba

a a a b b b b b b a a b a a b a

Compressed string = 021453

(g) aaabbbbbbaab has been compressed

Figure 11.5 LZW compression

Let us try the LZW method on our sample string. The longest prefix of the input that is in the initial dictionary is a. Its code, 0, is output, and the string aa is assigned the code 2 and entered into the dictionary. Figure 11.5(b) shows the new configuration for the dictionary and string S. aa is the longest prefix of the remaining string that is in the dictionary. Its code, 2, is output; the string aab is assigned the code 3 and entered into the dictionary (Figure 11.5(c)). *Notice that even though aab has the code 3 assigned to it, only the code 2 for aa is output. The suffix b will be part of the next code output. The reason for not outputting 3 is that the code table is not part of the compressed file. Instead, the code table is reconstructed during decompression using the compressed file. This reconstruction is possible only if we adhere strictly to the LZW rule.*

Following the output of code 2, the code for b is output; bb is assigned code 4 and entered into the code dictionary (Figure 11.5(d)). Then the code for bb is output, and bbb is entered into the table with code 5 (Figure 11.5(e)). Next code 5 is output, and bbba is entered with code 6 (Figure 11.5(f)). Then code 3 is output for aab, and aaba is entered into the dictionary with code 7 (Figure 11.5(g)). Finally, code 7 is output for the remaining string aaba. Our 16-character sample string S is encoded as the string 0214537.

11.6.2   Implementation of LZW Compression

The LZW compression program is developed as the class Compress. This class includes methods to open the input and output files (setFiles), output a byte of the compressed file (output), read bytes of the input file and determine their output code (compress), and a main method (main).

Establish Input and Output Streams

The input to the compressor is a text file, and the output is a binary file. If the input file name is inputFile, then the output file name is to be inputFile.zzz. We further assume that the user is to have the option of providing the input file name on the command line. So if the compression program is called Compress, then the command line

```
java Compress text
```

should result in the compressed version of the file text being saved as the file text.zzz. If the user does not specify the file name on the command line, then we are to prompt the user for this name.

Method setFiles (Program 11.20) establishes the input and output streams in and out, which are class data members. This method uses four classes Buffered-InputStream, BufferedOutputStream, FileInputStream, and FileOutputStream that are in the package java.io. FileInputStream reads bytes from a file and returns −1 when the end of file is reached. Reading from a file is usually done with a BufferedInputStream object to provide input buffering. With input buffering each disk access brings in a buffer load of data rather than a single byte. Therefore, several requests to read a byte from the input file are satisfied by a single disk access and so input is faster. `FileOutputStream` and `BufferedOutputStream` are the output counterparts of `FileInputStream` and `BufferedInputStream`. The constructor of `FileInputStream` throws an exception of type `FileNotFoundException` (a subclass of `IOException`) if a file with the specified name does not exist; and the constructor for `FileOutputStream` throws an exception of type `IOException` if a file with the specified name cannot be opened for output. The variables `in` and `out` are class data members of `Compress`, and their data types are, respectively, `BufferedInputStream` and `BufferedOutputStream`.

```
private static void setFiles(String [] args) throws IOException
{
   String inputFile, outputFile;
   // see if file name provided
   if (args.length >= 2)
      inputFile = args[1];
   else
   {// input file name not provided, ask for it
      System.out.println("Enter name of file to compress");
      MyInputStream keyboard = new MyInputStream();
      inputFile = keyboard.readString();
   }

   // establish input and output streams
   in = new BufferedInputStream(new FileInputStream(inputFile));
   outputFile = inputFile + ".zzz";
   out = new BufferedOutputStream(new FileOutputStream(outputFile));
}
```

Program 11.20 Establish input and output streams

Dictionary Organization

Each element of the dictionary is to have the two fields: **code** and **key**. Although **code** is an integer, **key** is a potentially long sequence of characters. However, each **key** of length $l > 1$ has the property that its first $l - 1$ characters (called the key prefix) are the key of some other entry in the dictionary. Since each dictionary entry has a unique code (in addition to having a unique key), we may replace the key prefix by its code. So in the example of Figure 11.5, the key aa may be represented as 0a and aaba as 3a. The dictionary now takes the form given in Figure 11.6.

code	0	1	2	3	4	5	6	7
key	a	b	0a	2b	1b	4b	5a	3a

Figure 11.6 Modified LZW compression dictionary for aaabbbbbbaabaaba

To simplify decoding the compressed file, we will write each code using a fixed number of bits. In further development we will assume that each code is 12 bits long. Hence we can assign at most $2^{12} = 4096$ codes. Under this assumption, the encoding 0214537 for our 16-character sample string S is written out as $12 * 7 = 84$ bits, which rounds to 11 bytes.

Since each character is 8 bits long (we are assuming each character is one of the 256 ASCII characters), a key is 20 bits long (12 bits for the code of the prefix and 8 bits for the last character in the key) and can be represented using an integer (32 bits). The least significant 8 bits are used for the last character in the key, and the next 12 bits for the code of its prefix. The dictionary itself may be represented as a chained hash table. If the prime number D = 4099 is used as the hash function divisor, the loading density will be less than 1, as we can have at most 4096 entries in the dictionary. The declaration

```
HashChains h = new HashChains(D);
```

suffices to create the table. Our application will not use the method `HashChains.remove`.

Output of Codes

Since each code is 12 bits long and each byte is 8 bits, we can output only part of a code as a byte. Eight bits of the first code are output, and the remaining four are saved for later output. When the next code is to be output, we have 4 bits from before, resulting in a total of 16 bits. These 16 bits can be output as 2 bytes. Program 11.21 gives the Java code for the output method. MASK1 is 255, MASK2 is 15, EXCESS is 4, and BYTE_SIZE is 8. `bitsLeftOver` is true iff 4 bits of the previous code remain to be ouput. When `bitsLeftOver` is true, the 4 bits that remain to be output are in the variable `leftOver`.

Compression

Program 11.22 gives the code for the LZW compression algorithm. We begin by initializing the dictionary with all 256 (ALPHA = 256) 8-bit bytes (these correspond to the 256 ASCII characters) and their codes. The variable `codesUsed` keeps track of the number of codes used so far. With 12 bits per code, at most MAX_CODES = 4096 codes may be assigned. To find the longest prefix that is in the dictionary, we

```
/** output 1 byte and save remaining half byte */
private static void output(int pcode) throws IOException
{
    int c, d;
    if (bitsLeftOver)
    {// half byte remains from before
        d = pcode & MASK1; // right BYTE_SIZE bits
        c = (leftOver << EXCESS) + (pcode >> BYTE_SIZE);
        out.write(c);
        out.write(d);
        bitsLeftOver = false;
    }
    else
    {// no bits remain from before
        leftOver = pcode & MASK2; // right EXCESS bits
        c = pcode >> EXCESS;
        out.write(c);
        bitsLeftOver = true;
    }
}
```

Program 11.21 Output a code

examine prefixes of length 1, 2, 3, $\cdots$, in this order until we reach the first one that is not in the table. At this time a code is output, and a new code is created (unless we have used all 4096 codes).

Data Members and the Method `Compress.main`

Program 11.23 gives the data members of `Compress` as well as the `main` method.

11.6.3   LZW Decompression

For decompression we input the codes one at a time and replace them by the texts they denote. The code-to-text mapping can be reconstructed in the following way. The codes assigned for single-character texts are entered into the dictionary. As before, the dictionary entries are code-text pairs. This time, however, the dictionary is searched for an entry with a given code (rather than with a given text). The first code in the compressed file corresponds to a single character and so may be replaced by the corresponding character. For all other codes p in the compressed file, we have two cases to consider: (1) the code p is in the dictionary, and (2) it is not.

```
private static void compress() throws IOException
{
   // define and initialize the code dictionary
   HashChains h = new HashChains(D);
   for (int i = 0; i < ALPHA; i++)
      // initialize code table
      h.put(new MyInteger(i), new MyInteger(i));

   int codesUsed = ALPHA;

   // input and compress
   int c = in.read();           // first byte of input
   if (c != -1)
   {// input file is not empty
      int pcode = c;
      c = in.read();         // second byte
      while (c != -1)        // not at end of file
      {// process byte c
         int k = (pcode << BYTE_SIZE) + c;
         // see if code for k is in the dictionary
         MyInteger e = (MyInteger) h.get(new MyInteger(k));
         if (e == null)
         {// k is not in the table
            output(pcode);
            if (codesUsed < MAX_CODES) // create new code
               h.put(new MyInteger((pcode << BYTE_SIZE) + c),
                     new MyInteger(codesUsed++));
            pcode = c;
         }
         else pcode = e.intValue();
         c = in.read();
      }

      // output last code(s)
      output(pcode);
      if (bitsLeftOver)
         out.write(leftOver << EXCESS);
   }
   in.close();
   out.close();
}
```

Program 11.22 LZW compressor

```
public class Compress
{
    // class data members
    // constants
    final static int D = 4099;          // hash function divisor
    final static int MAX_CODES = 4096;  // 2^12
    final static int BYTE_SIZE = 8;
    final static int EXCESS = 4;        // 12 - ByteSize
    final static int ALPHA = 256;       // 2^ByteSize
    final static int MASK1 = 255;       // ALPHA - 1
    final static int MASK2 = 15;        // 2^EXCESS - 1
    // variables
    static int leftOver;                // code bits yet to be output
    static boolean bitsLeftOver;
    static BufferedInputStream in;
    static BufferedOutputStream out;

    // other methods come here

    public static void main(String [] args) throws IOException
    {
        setFiles(args);
        compress();
    }
}
```

Program 11.23 Data members and main method of Compress

Case When Code p Is in the Dictionary

When p is in the dictionary, the text $text(p)$ to which it corresponds is extracted from the dictionary and output. Also, from the working of the compressor, we know that if the code that precedes p in the compressed file is q and $text(q)$ is the corresponding text, then the compressor would have created a new code for the text $text(q)$ followed by the first character $fc(p)$ of $text(p)$. So we enter the pair (next code, $text(q)fc(p)$) into the directory. Case (2) arises only when the current text segment has the form $text(q)text(q)fc(q)$ and $text(p) = text(q)fc(q)$. The corresponding compressed file segment is qp. During compression, $text(q)fc(q)$ is assigned the code p, and the code p is output for the text $text(q)fc(q)$. During decompression, after q is replaced by $text(q)$, we encounter the code p. However, there is no code-to-text mapping for p in our table. We are able to decode p by knowing that this situation arises only when the decompressed text segment is $text(q)text(q)fc(q)$.

Case When Code p Is Not in the Dictionary

When we encounter a code p for which the code-to-text mapping is undefined, the code-to-text mapping for p is $text(q)fc(q)$ where q is the code that precedes p.

An Example

Let us try this decompression scheme on our earlier sample string

aaabbbbbbaabaaba

which was compressed into the coded string 0214537. To begin, we initialize the dictionary with the pairs (0, a) and (1, b) and obtain the first two entries in the dictionary of Figure 11.5. The first code in the compressed file is 0. It is replaced by the text a. The next code 2 is undefined. Since the previous code, 0, has $text(0)$ = a, $fc(0)$ = a and $text(2) = text(0)fc(0)$ = aa. So the code 2 is replaced by aa, and (2, aa) is entered into the dictionary. The next code, 1, is replaced by $text(1)$ = b, and $(3, text(2)fc(1))$ = (3, aab) is entered into the dictionary. The next code, 4, is not in the dictionary. The code preceding it is 1, and so $text(4)$ = $text(1)fc(1)$ = bb. The pair (4, bb) is entered into the dictionary, and bb is output to the decompressed file. When the next code, 5, is encountered, (5, bbb) is entered into the directory; bbb is output to the decompressed file. The next code is 3. $text(3)$ = aab is output to the decompressed file, and the pair $(6, text(5)fc(3))$ = (6, bbba) is entered into the dictionary. Finally, when the code 7 is encountered, $(7, text(3)fc(3))$ = (7, aaba) is entered into the dictionary and aaba output.

11.6.4   Implementation of LZW Decompression

The LZW decompression method is implemented as the Java class `Decompress`. As was the case for the implementation of the compression algorithm, the decompression task is decomposed into several subtasks, and each is implemented by a member method of `Decompress`. Since the method `Decompress.setFiles`, which establishes the input and output streams, is very similar to `Compress.setFiles`, we do not discuss this method further.

Dictionary Organization

Because we will be querying the dictionary by providing a code and since the number of codes is 4096, we can use an array `h[4096]` and store $text(p)$ in $h[p]$. Using array h in this way corresponds to ideal hashing with $f(k) = k$. $text(p)$ may be compactly stored by using the code for the prefix of $text(p)$ and the last character (suffix) of $text(p)$ as in Figure 11.6. For our decompression application it is convenient to store the prefix code and suffix separately as two integers. The class `Element` is used for this purpose. Each instance of `Element` has the two data members `prefix` and `suffix`, and both are of type `int`. So if $text(p) = text(q)c$, then the least significant 8 bits of `h[p].suffix` give the byte code for the character c and `h[p].prefix` equals q.

When this dictionary organization is used, $text(p)$ may be constructed from right to left beginning with the last character `h[p].suffix`, as is shown in Program 11.24. This code obtains suffix values of codes $\geq$ `ALPHA` from the table `h`, and for codes $<$ `ALPHA` it uses the knowledge that the code is just the integer representation of the corresponding character. $text(p)$ is assembled into the array `s[]` and then output. Since $text(p)$ is assembled from right to left, the first character of $text(p)$ is in `s[size]`.

```
/** output the byte sequence that corresponds to code */
private static void output(int code) throws IOException
{
   size = -1;
   while (code >= ALPHA)
   {// suffix is in the dictionary
      s[++size] = h[code].suffix;
      code = h[code].prefix;
   }
   s[++size] = code;   // code < ALPHA

   // decompressed string is s[size] ... s[0]
   for (int i = size; i >= 0; i--)
      out.write(s[i]);
}
```

Program 11.24 Compute $text(\texttt{code})$

Input of Codes

Since the sequence of 12-bit codes is represented as a sequence of 8-bit bytes in the compressed file, we need to reverse the process employed by the method `Compress.-output` (Program 11.21). This reversal is done by the method `Decompress.getCode` (Program 11.25). The only new constant here is `MASK`. Its value, 15, enables us to extract the low-order 4 bits of a byte.

```
/** @return next code from compressed file
  * @return -1 if there is no next code */
private static int getCode() throws IOException
{
   int c = in.read();
   if (c == -1) return -1;  // no more codes

   // see if any leftover bits from before
   // if yes, concatenate with leftover bits
   int code;
   if (bitsLeftOver)
      code = (leftOver << BYTE_SIZE) + c;
   else
   {// no leftover bits, need more bits to complete code
      int d = in.read();  // another byte
      code = (c << EXCESS) + (d >> EXCESS);
      leftOver = d & MASK;  // save unused bits
   }
   bitsLeftOver = !bitsLeftOver;
   return code;
}
```

Program 11.25 Extracting codes from a compressed file

Decompression

Program 11.26 gives the LZW decompressor. The first code in the compressed file is decoded outside the `while` loop by doing a type conversion to the type `unsigned char`, and the remaining codes are decoded inside this loop. *At the start of each iteration of the `do-while` loop, `s[size]` contains the first character of the last decoded text that was output.* To establish this condition for the first iteration, we set `size` to 0 and `s[0]` to the first and only character corresponding to the first code in the compressed file.

The `do-while` loop repeatedly obtains a code `ccode` from the compressed file and decodes it. There are two cases for `ccode`—(1) `ccode` is in the dictionary, and (2) it is not. `ccode` is in the dictionary iff `ccode < codesUsed` where `h[0:codesUsed-1]` is the defined part of table `h`. In this case the code is decoded using the method `Decompress.output`, and following the LZW rule, a new code is created with suffix being the first character of the text just output for `ccode`. When `ccode` is not defined, we are in the special case discussed at the beginning of this section and `ccode` is *text*(pcode)s[size]. This information is used to create a table entry for `code` and to output the decoded text to which it corresponds.

```
private static void decompress() throws IOException
{
   int codesUsed = ALPHA; // codes used so far
   s = new int [MAX_CODES];
   h = new Element [MAX_CODES];

   // input and decompress
   int pcode = getCode(),  // previous code
       ccode;              // current code

   if (pcode >= 0)
   {// input file is not empty
      s[0] = pcode;       // byte for pcode
      out.write(s[0]);
      size = 0; // s[size] is first character of
                // last string output

      do
      {// get another code
         ccode = getCode();
         if (ccode < 0) break;  // no more codes
         if (ccode < codesUsed)
         {// ccode is defined
            output(ccode);
            if (codesUsed < MAX_CODES)
               // create new code
               h[codesUsed++] = new Element(pcode, s[size]);
         }
         else
         {// special case, undefined code
            h[codesUsed++] = new Element(pcode, s[size]);
            output(ccode);
         }
         pcode = ccode;
      } while(true);
   }
   out.close();
   in.close();
}
```

Program 11.26 LZW decompressor

Data Members and the Method Decompress.main

Program 11.27 gives the data members and the **main** method for LZW decompression.

```
public class Decompress
{
   // top-level member class Element defined here

   // class data members
   // constants
   final static int MAX_CODES = 4096;   // 2^12
   final static int BYTE_SIZE = 8;
   final static int EXCESS = 4;      // 12 - ByteSize
   final static int ALPHA = 256;     // 2^ByteSize
   final static int MASK = 15;       // 2^EXCESS - 1
   // variables
   static int [] s;                  // used to reconstruct text
   static int size;                  // size of reconstructed text
   static Element [] h;              // dictionary
   static int leftOver;              // input bits yet to be output
   static boolean bitsLeftOver;
   static BufferedInputStream in;
   static BufferedOutputStream out;

   // other methods defined here

   public static void main(String [] args) throws IOException
   {
      setFiles(args);
      decompress();
   }
}
```

Program 11.27 Data members and method main of Decompress

11.6.5   Performance Evaluation

Well, how good is our compressor compared to, say, the popular compression program **zip**? Our program compressed a 33,772-byte ASCII file to 18,765 bytes, achieving a compression ratio of 33,772/18,765 = 1.8; **zip** did much better—it compressed the same file to 11,041 bytes, achieving a compression ratio of 3.1. This disappointing showing by our compression program should not be a cause for concern, since commercial compression programs such as `zip` couple methods such as LZW compression with good coding techniques such as Huffman coding (see Section 13.6.3) to obtain a higher compression ratio. So we should not expect a raw LZW compressor to match the performance of a commercial compressor.

EXERCISES

40. Start with an LZW compression dictionary that has the entries (a, 0) and (b, 1).

    (a) Draw figures similar to Figure 11.5 for the LZW compression dictionary following the processing of each character of the string babababbbabba.

    (b) Give the code sequence for the compressed form of babababbbabba.

    (c) Now decompress the code sequence of part (b). For each code encountered, explaining how it is decoded. Draw the decode table following the decoding of each code.

41. Do Exercise 40 for the string $A(10) = $ aaaaaaaaaa whose length is 10. This time start with a dictionary that has the single entry (a, 0). Can you predict the code sequence for the string $A(100)$ whose length is 100 and all of whose characters are the letter a?

42. Our LZW compressor code uses the class `HashChains`. Determine the effect of changing the hash table class to each of the classes `SortedChain`, `HashTable`, and `java.util.HashTable`. Do this exercise by measuring the time needed to compress the sample input file `Compress.input` that is given in the Web site. Based on your experiment, which hash table class do you recommend for LZW compression? Why?

43. Is is possible for the compressed file generated by our LZW compressor to be longer than the original file? If so, by how much?

44. Write an LZW compressor and decompressor for files composed of the characters {a, b, $\cdots$, z, 0, 1, $\cdots$, 9, '.', ',', ';', ':'} and the end-of-line character. Use 8 bits per code. Test the correctness of your program. Is it possible for the compressed file to be longer than the original file?

45. Modify the LZW compress and decompress programs so that the code table is reinitialized after every x kilobytes of the text file have been compressed / decompressed. Experiment with the modified compression code using text files that are 100K to 200K bytes long and $x = 10, 20, 30, 40,$ and 50. Which value of x gives the best compression?

46. A **concordance** is an alphabetized list of all the words in a text. Together with each word is a sorted list of all the lines of the text that contain this word. That is, each entry of a concordance is a pair of the form (word, sorted list of all line numbers where this word occurs). Notice that a concordance is similar to a book index; however, unlike a book index, which lists the page numbers on which only some of the words in the book occur, a concordance includes every word and lists line numbers rather than page numbers. The objective of this exercise is to write a program that uses a hash table to create a concordance. Each hash table entry is a pair (`key`, `list`) = (word, sorted list of line numbers where this word occurs).

   (a) Develop a Java class for the hash table pairs. Justify your selection of data types for the data members `key` and `list`. When selecting a data type for `list`, consider the types `java.util.Vector`, `ArrayLinearList`, `Chain`, `ArrayQueue`, `LinkedQueue`, and any customized type(s) that may be appropriate.

   (b) Develop two Java programs to input text and output its concordance. The first program should use the Java class `java.util.HashTable` to construct the concordance entries and then use a suitable sort method to sort these entries by their `key` fields. The second program should use the class `HashChains` to construct the concordance entries and then should merge the hash table chains to obtain a sorted list of concordance entries.

   (c) Compare the run-time performance of the two programs you have developed.

11.7   REFERENCES AND SELECTED READINGS

Skip lists were proposed by William Pugh. An analysis of their expected complexity can be found in the paper "Skip Lists: A Probabilistic Alternative to Balanced Trees" by W. Pugh, *Communications of the ACM*, 33, 6, 1990, 668–676.

Visit this book's Web site to learn more about hash functions and overflow-handling mechanisms. To find out everything you ever wanted to know about hashing, see the book *The Art of Computer Programming: Sorting and Searching*, Volume 3, Second Edition, by D. Knuth, Addison-Wesley, Menlo Park, CA, 1998.

Our description of the Lempel-Ziv-Welch compression method is based on the paper "A Technique for High-Performance Data Compression" by T. Welch, *IEEE Computer*, June 1994, 8–19. For more on data compression, see the survey article "Data Compression" by D. Lelewer and D. Hirschberg, *ACM Computing Surveys*, 19, 3, 1987, 261–296.

CHAPTER **12**

BINARY AND OTHER TREES

BIRD'S-EYE VIEW

Yes, it's a jungle out there. The jungle is populated with many varieties of trees, plants, and animals. The world of data structures also has a wide variety of trees, too many for us to discuss in this book. In the present chapter we study two basic varieties: general trees (or simply trees) and binary trees. Chapters 13 through 16 consider the more popular of the remaining varieties—heaps, leftist trees, tournament trees, binary search trees, AVL trees, red-black trees, splay trees, and B-trees. Chapters 13 through 15 are fairly independent and may be read in any order. However, Chapter 16 should be read only after you have assimilated Chapter 15. If you are still hungry for trees when you are done with these chapters, you can find additional tree varieties—pairing heaps, interval heaps, tree structures for double-ended priority queues, tries, and suffix trees—on the Web site for this book.

Two applications of trees are developed in the applications section. The first concerns the placement of signal boosters in a tree distribution network. The second revisits the online equivalence problem introduced in Section 7.7. This problem is also known as the union/find problem. By using trees to represent the sets, we can obtain improved run-time performance over the chain representation developed in Section 7.7.

In addition, this chapter covers the following topics:

- Tree and binary tree terminology such as height, depth, level, root, leaf, child, parent, and sibling.

- Array-based and linked representations of binary trees.

- The four common ways to traverse a binary tree: preorder, inorder, postorder, and level order.

12.1   TREES

So far in this text we have seen data structures for linear and tabular data. These data structures are generally not suitable for the representation of hierarchical data. In hierarchical data we have an ancestor-descendant, superior-subordinate, whole-part, or similar relationship among the data elements. The Java class hierarchy (Figure 1.1) is an example of hierarchical data

Example 12.1 [Joe's Descendants] Figure 12.1 shows Joe and his descendants arranged in a hierarchical manner, beginning with Joe at the top of the hierarchy. Joe's children (Ann, Mary, and John) are listed next in the hierarchy, and a line or edge joins Joe and his children. Ann has no children, while Mary has two and John has one. Mary's children are listed below her, and John's child is listed below him. There is an edge between each parent and his/her children. From this hierarchical representation, it is easy to identify Ann's siblings, Joe's descendants, Chris's ancestors, and so on.   ■

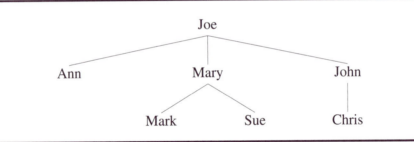

Figure 12.1 Descendants of Joe

Example 12.2 [Corporate Structure] As an example of hierarchical data, consider the administrative structure of the corporation of Figure 12.2. The person (in this case the president) highest in the hierarchy appears at the top of the diagram. Those who are next in the hierarchy (i.e., the vice presidents) are shown below the president and so on. The vice presidents are the president's subordinates, and the president is their superior. Each vice president, in turn, has his/her subordinates who may themselves have subordinates. In the diagram we have drawn a line or edge between each person and his/her direct subordinates or superior.   ■

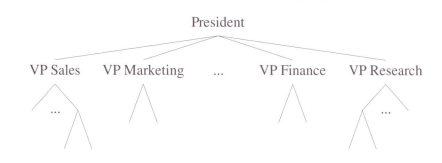

Figure 12.2 Hierarchical administrative structure of a corporation

Example 12.3 [Governmental Subdivisions] Figure 12.3 is a hierarchical drawing of the branches of the federal government. At the top of the hierarchy, we have the entire federal government. At the next level of the hierarchy, we have drawn its major subdivisions (i.e., the different departments). Each department may be further subdivided. These subdivisions are drawn at the next level of the hierarchy. For example, the Department of Defense has been subdivided into the Army, Navy, Air Force, and Marines. A line runs between each element and its components. The data of Figure 12.3 are an example of whole-part relationships. ∎

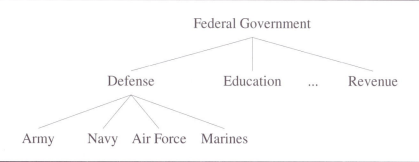

Figure 12.3 Modules of the federal government

Example 12.4 [Software Engineering] For another example of hierarchical data, consider the software-engineering technique referred to as modularization. In modularization we decompose a large and complex task into a collection of smaller, less complex tasks. The objective is to divide the software system into many functionally independent parts or **modules** so that each can be developed relatively independently. This decision reduces the overall software development time, as it is much

easier to solve several small problems than one large one. Additionally, different programmers can develop different modules at the same time. If necessary, each module may be further decomposed so as to obtain a hierarchy of modules as shown by the tree of Figure 12.4. This tree represents a possible modular decomposition of a text processor.

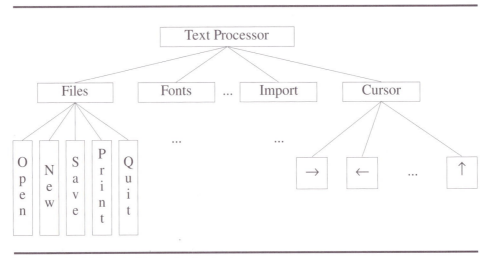

Figure 12.4 Module hierarchy for text processor

At the top level the text processor has been split into several modules. Only four are shown in the figure. The Files module performs functions related to text files such as opening an existing file, opening a new file, saving a file, printing a file, and exiting from the text processor (exiting requires saving files if the user so desires). Each function is represented by a module at the next level of the hierarchy. The Fonts module handles all functions related to the font in use. These functions include changing the font, its size, color, and so on. If modules for these functions were shown in the figure, they would appear below the module Fonts. The Import module handles functions associated with the import of material such as graphics, tables, and text in a format not native to this text processor. The Cursor module handles the movement of the cursor on the screen. Its subordinate modules correspond to various cursor motions. Programmers can carry out the specification, design, and development of each module in a relatively independent manner after the interfaces are fully specified.

When the software system is specified and designed in a modular fashion, it is natural to develop the system itself in this way. The resulting software system will have as many modules as there are nodes in the module hierarchy. Modularization improves the intellectual manageability of a problem. By systematically dividing a large problem into smaller relatively independent problems, we can solve the large problem with much less effort. The independent problems can be assigned to different persons for parallel solution. It is harder to share labor on a single module. Another advantage of developing modular software is that it is much easier to test and verify many small modules independently before testing them as a unit than to do so for one large module. The hierarchical organization clearly shows the relationship among the modules.   ■

Definition 12.1 *A* **tree** *t is a finite nonempty set of elements. One of these elements is called the* **root***, and the remaining elements (if any) are partitioned into trees, which are called the* **subtrees** *of t.*   ■

Let us see how this definition relates to our examples of hierarchical data. The element at the highest level of the hierarchy is the root. The elements at the next level are the roots of the subtrees formed by a partitioning of the remaining elements.

Example 12.5 In the descendants-of-Joe example (Example 12.1), the data set is {Joe, Ann, Mary, Mark, Sue, John, Chris}. So $n = 7$. The root of the collection is Joe. The remaining elements are partitioned into the three disjoint sets {Ann}; {Mary, Mark, Sue}; and {John, Chris}. {Ann} is a tree with a single element; its root is Ann. The root of {Mary, Mark, Sue} is Mary, and that of {John, Chris} is John. The remaining elements of {Mary, Mark, Sue} are partitioned into the disjoint sets {Mark} and {Sue}, which are both single-element (sub)trees, and the remaining element of {John, Chris} is also a single-element subtree.   ■

When drawing a tree, each element is represented as a node. The tree root is drawn at the top, and its subtrees are drawn below. There is a line or edge from the tree root to the roots of its subtrees (if any). Each subtree is drawn similarly with its root at the top and its subtrees below. The edges in a tree connect an element node and its **children** nodes. In Figure 12.1, for example, Ann, Mary, and John are the children of Joe, and Joe is their **parent**. Children of the same parent are called **siblings**. Ann, Mary, and John are siblings in the tree of Figure 12.1, but Mark and Chris are not. The extension of this terminology to include the terms **grandchild**, **grandparent**, **ancestor**, **descendent**, and so forth is straightforward. In a tree, elements with no children are called **leaves**. So Ann, Mark, Sue, and Chris are the leaves of the tree of Figure 12.1. The tree root is the only tree element that has no parent.

Example 12.6 In the corporate-structure example (Example 12.2), the company employees are the tree elements. The president is the tree root. The remaining employees are partitioned into disjoint sets, which represent different divisions of the company. Each division has a vice president, who is the root of the subtree that represents the division. The remaining employees of a division are partitioned into disjoint sets representing departments. The department head will be the root of the department subtree. The remaining employees of a department could be partitioned into projects and so on.

The vice presidents are children of the president; department heads are children of their vice president, and so on. The president is the parent of the vice presidents, and each vice president is the parent of the department heads in his/her division.

In Figure 12.3 the root is the element Federal Government. Its subtrees have the roots Defense, Education, · · ·, and Revenue, which are the children of Federal Government. Federal Government is the parent of its children. Defense has the children Army, Navy, Air Force, and Marines. The children of Defense are siblings and are also leaves. ■

Another commonly used tree term is **level**. By definition the tree root is at level 1; its children (if any) are at level 2; their children (if any) are at level 3; and so on.[1] In the tree of Figure 12.3, Federal Government is at level 1; Defense, Education, and Revenue are at level 2; and Army, Navy, Air Force, and Marines are at level 3.

The **height** (or **depth**) of a tree is the number of levels in it. The trees of Figures 12.1, 12.3, and 12.4 have a height of 3.

The **degree of an element** is the number of children it has. The degree of a leaf is 0. The degree of Files in Figure 12.4 is 5. The **degree of a tree** is the maximum of its element degrees.

EXERCISES

1. Explain why the Java class hierachy of Figure 1.1 is a tree. Label the root node and mark each node with its level number and degree. What is the depth of this tree.

2. Do Exercise 1 for the recursion diagram of Figure 1.11.

3. Develop a tree representation for the major elements (whole book, chapters, sections, and subsections) of this text.

   (a) What is the total number of elements in your tree?

   (b) Identify the leaf elements.

   (c) Identify the elements on level 3.

   (d) List the degree of each element.

4. Access the World Wide Web home page for your department. (Alternatively, access http://www.cise.ufl.edu.)

   (a) Follow some of the links to lower-level pages and draw the resulting structure. In your drawing the Web pages should be represented by nodes, and the links by edges that join pairs of nodes.

---

[1] Some authors number tree levels beginning at 0 rather than 1. In this case the root of a tree is at level 0.

(b) Is it necessary for the structure to be a tree? Why?

(c) In case your structure is a tree, identify the root and the leaves.

12.2 BINARY TREES

Definition 12.2 *A **binary tree** t is a finite (possibly empty) collection of elements. When the binary tree is not empty, it has a **root** element and the remaining elements (if any) are partitioned into two binary trees, which are called the left and right subtrees of t.* ∎

The essential differences between a binary tree and a tree are

- Each element in a binary tree has exactly two subtrees (one or both of these subtrees may be empty). Each element in a tree can have any number of subtrees.

- The subtrees of each element in a binary tree are ordered. That is, we distinguish between the left and the right subtrees. The subtrees in a tree are unordered.

Another difference between a tree and a binary tree—a binary tree can be empty, whereas a tree cannot—is largely a matter of definition. Some authors relax the definition of a tree to allow for an empty tree.

Like a tree, a binary tree is drawn with its root at the top. The elements in the left (right) subtree of the root are drawn below and to the left (right) of the root. Between each element and its children is a line or edge.

Figure 12.5 shows some binary trees that represent arithmetic expressions. Each operator (+, −, ∗, /) may have one or two operands. The left operand (if any) is the left subtree of the operator. The right operand is its right subtree. The leaf elements in an expression tree are either constants or variables. Note that an expression tree contains no parentheses.

One application of expression trees is in the generation of optimal computer code to evaluate an expression. Although we do not study algorithms to generate optimal code from an expression tree, we will use these trees to illustrate some of the operations that are commonly performed on binary trees.

EXERCISES

5. (a) Identify the leaves of the binary trees of Figure 12.5.

(b) Identify all level 3 nodes in Figure 12.5(b).

(c) How many level 4 nodes are in Figure 12.5(c)?

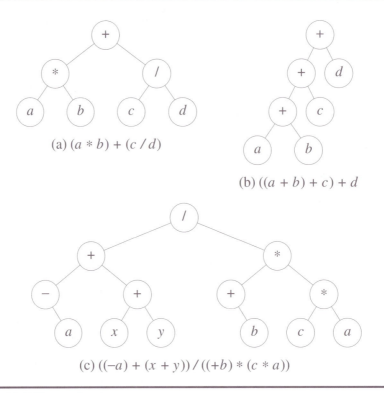

Figure 12.5 Expression trees

6. Draw the binary expression trees corresponding to each of the following expressions:

   (a) $(a + b)/(c - d) + e + g * h/a$

   (b) $-x - y * z + (a + b + c/d * e)$

   (c) $((a + b) > (c - e))||a < b\&\&(x < y||y > z)$

12.3 PROPERTIES OF BINARY TREES

Property 12.1 *The drawing of every binary tree with n elements, n > 0, has exactly n − 1 edges.*

Proof Every element in a binary tree (except the root) has exactly one parent. There is exactly one edge between each child and its parent. So the number of edges is $n - 1$. ∎

Property 12.2 *A binary tree of height h, $h \geq 0$, has at least h and at most $2^h - 1$ elements in it.*

Proof Since each level has at least one element, the number of elements is at least h. As each element can have at most two children, the number of elements at level i is at most 2^{i-1}, $i > 0$. For $h = 0$, the total number of elements is 0, which equals $2^0 - 1$. For $h > 0$, the number of elements cannot exceed $\sum_{i=1}^{h} 2^{i-1} = 2^h - 1$. ∎

Property 12.3 *The height of a binary tree that contains n, $n \geq 0$, elements is at most n and at least $\lceil \log_2(n+1) \rceil$.*

Proof Since there must be at least one element at each level, the height cannot exceed n. From Property 12.2 we know that a binary tree of height h can have no more than $2^h - 1$ elements. So $n \leq 2^h - 1$. Hence $h \geq \log_2(n+1)$. Since h is an integer, we get $h \geq \lceil \log_2(n+1) \rceil$. ∎

A binary tree of height h that contains exactly $2^h - 1$ elements is called a **full binary tree**. The binary tree of Figure 12.5(a) is a full binary tree of height 3. The binary trees of Figures 12.5(b) and (c) are not full binary trees. Figure 12.6 shows a full binary tree of height 4.

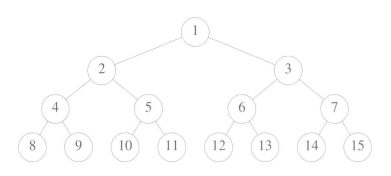

Figure 12.6 Full binary tree of height 4

Suppose we number the elements in a full binary tree of height h using the numbers 1 through $2^h - 1$. We begin at level 1 and go down to level h. Within levels the elements are numbered left to right. The elements of the full binary tree of Figure 12.6 have been numbered in this way. Now suppose we delete the k elements numbered $2^h - i$, $1 \leq i \leq k < 2^h$. The resulting binary tree is called a **complete binary tree**. Figure 12.7 gives some examples. Note that a full binary tree is a special case of a complete binary tree. Also, note that the height of a complete binary tree that contains n elements is $\lceil \log_2(n+1) \rceil$.

There is a very nice relationship among the numbers assigned to an element and its children in a complete binary tree, as given by Property 12.4.

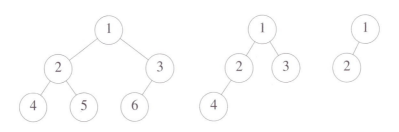

Figure 12.7 Complete binary trees

Property 12.4 *Let i, $1 \le i \le n$, be the number assigned to an element of a complete binary tree. The following are true:*

1. *If $i = 1$, then this element is the root of the binary tree. If $i > 1$, then the parent of this element has been assigned the number $\lfloor i/2 \rfloor$.*

2. *If $2i > n$, then this element has no left child. Otherwise, its left child has been assigned the number $2i$.*

3. *If $2i + 1 > n$, then this element has no right child. Otherwise, its right child has been assigned the number $2i + 1$.*

Proof Can be established by induction on i.   ■

EXERCISES

7. Prove Property 12.4.

8. In a k-ary tree, $k > 1$, each node may have up to k children. These children are called, respectively, the first, second, $\cdots$, kth child of the node. A 2-ary tree is a binary tree.

   (a) Determine the analogue of Property 12.1 for k-ary trees.

   (b) Determine the analogue of Property 12.2 for k-ary trees.

   (c) Determine the analogue of Property 12.3 for k-ary trees.

   (d) Determine the analogue of Property 12.4 for k-ary trees.

9. What is the maximum number of nodes in a binary tree that has m leaves?

12.4   REPRESENTATION OF BINARY TREES

12.4.1   Array-Based Representation

The array-based representation of a binary tree utilizes Property 12.4. The binary tree to be represented is regarded as a complete binary tree with some missing elements. Figure 12.8 shows two sample binary trees. The first binary tree has three elements (A, B, and C), and the second has five elements (A, B, C, D, and E). Neither is complete. Unshaded circles represent missing elements. All elements (including the missing ones) are numbered as described in the previous section.

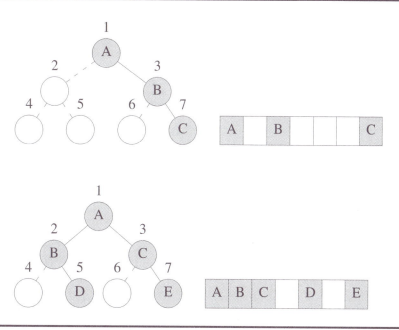

Figure 12.8 Incomplete binary trees

In an array-based representation, the binary tree is represented in an array by storing each element at the array position corresponding to the number assigned to it. Figure 12.8 also shows the array-based representations for its binary trees. Missing elements are represented by white boxes. As can be seen, this representation scheme is quite wasteful of space when many elements are missing. In fact, a binary tree that has n elements may require an array of size up to $2^n - 1$ for its representation. This maximum size is needed when each element (except the root) of the n-element binary tree is the right child of its parent. Figure 12.9 shows such a binary tree with four elements. Binary trees of this type are called **right-skewed** binary trees.

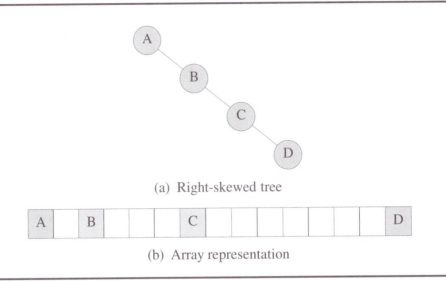

(a) Right-skewed tree

A	B			C						D

(b) Array representation

Figure 12.9 Right-skewed binary tree

The array-based representation is useful only when the number of missing elements is small.

12.4.2 Linked Representation

The most popular way to represent a binary tree is by using links or pointers. A node that has exactly two link fields represents each element. Let us call these link fields `leftChild` and `rightChild`. In addition to these two link fields, each node has a field named `element`. This node structure is implemented by the Java class `BinaryTreeNode` (Program 12.1). We have provided three constructors for a binary tree node. The first takes no parameters and leaves the data members with their default value of `null`; the second takes one parameter and uses it to initialize `element`, and the child fields have their default value of `null`; the third takes three parameters and uses these to initialize all three fields of the node. Though not shown in Program 12.1, the class `BinaryTreeNode` also has accessor methods (e.g., `getLeftChild`) to get the fields of a node, mutator methods (e.g., `setLeftChild`) to set the fields of a node, and a `toString` method that returns `element.toString()`.

A pointer from the parent node to the child node represents each edge in the drawing of a binary tree. This pointer is placed in the appropriate link field of the parent node. Since an n-element binary tree has exactly $n-1$ edges, we are left with $2n - (n-1) = n+1$ link fields that have no value. These link fields are set to `null`. Figure 12.10 shows the linked representations of the binary trees of Figure 12.8.

```java
public class BinaryTreeNode
{
   // package visible data members
   Object element;
   BinaryTreeNode leftChild;    // left subtree
   BinaryTreeNode rightChild;   // right subtree

   // constructors
   public BinaryTreeNode() {}

   public BinaryTreeNode(Object theElement)
      {element = theElement;}

   public BinaryTreeNode(Object theElement,
                         BinaryTreeNode theleftChild,
                         BinaryTreeNode therightChild)
   {
       element = theElement;
       leftChild = theleftChild;
       rightChild = therightChild;
   }
}
```

Program 12.1 Node class for linked binary trees

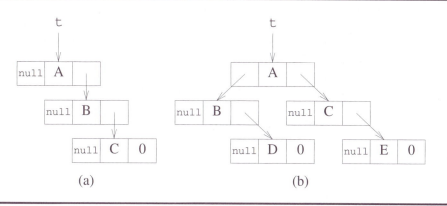

(a)   (b)

Figure 12.10 Linked representations

We can access all nodes in a binary tree by starting at the root and following `leftChild` and `rightChild` links. The absence of a parent link from the linked representation of a binary tree generally causes no difficulties, as most of the functions we perform on a binary tree do not require this link. If some application needs this link, we can add another link field to each node.

EXERCISES

10. Draw the array-based representation of the binary trees that correspond to the expressions of Exercise 6.

11. Do Exercise 10 for the binary trees of Figure 12.5.

12.5   COMMON BINARY TREE OPERATIONS

Some of the operations that are commonly performed on binary trees are

- Determine its height.

- Determine the number of elements in it.

- Make a copy.

- Display the binary tree on a screen or on paper.

- Determine whether two binary trees are identical.

- Make the tree empty.

These operations can be performed by traversing the binary tree in a systematic manner. In a binary tree **traversal**, each element is **visited** exactly once. During this visit all action with respect to this element is taken. This action can include writing the element on a screen or on paper, evaluating the expression represented by the subtree of which this element is the root, and adding one to a running count of the number of elements in the binary tree.

12.6   BINARY TREE TRAVERSAL

There are four common ways to traverse a binary tree:

1. Preorder

2. Inorder

3. Postorder

4. Level order

The first three traversal methods are best described recursively as in Programs 12.2, 12.3, and 12.4. These codes assume that the binary tree being traversed is represented with the linked scheme of the previous section.

```java
public static void preOrder(BinaryTreeNode t)
{
   if (t != null)
   {
      visit(t);                   // visit tree root
      preOrder(t.leftChild);   // do left subtree
      preOrder(t.rightChild);  // do right subtree
   }
}
```

Program 12.2 Preorder traversal

```java
public static void inOrder(BinaryTreeNode t)
{
   if (t != null)
   {
      inOrder(t.leftChild);    // do left subtree
      visit(t);                   // visit tree root
      inOrder(t.rightChild);   // do right subtree
   }
}
```

Program 12.3 Inorder traversal

In the first three traversal methods, the left subtree of a node is traversed before the right subtree. The difference among the three orders comes from the difference in the time at which a node is visited. In the case of a preorder traversal, each node is visited before its left and right subtrees are traversed. In an inorder traversal, the root of each subtree is visited after its left subtree has been traversed but before the traversal of its right subtree begins. In a postorder traversal, each root is visited after its left and right subtrees have been traversed.

Figure 12.11 shows the output generated by Programs 12.2—12.4 when visit(t) is as shown in Program 12.5. The input binary trees are those of Figure 12.5.

When an expression tree is output in pre-, in-, or postorder, we get the prefix, infix, and postfix forms of the expression, respectively. The **infix** form of an expression is the form in which we normally write an expression. In this form each

```
public static void postOrder(BinaryTreeNode t)
{
   if (t != null)
   {
      postOrder(t.leftChild);   // do left subtree
      postOrder(t.rightChild);  // do right subtree
      visit(t);                 // visit tree root
   }
}
```

Program 12.4 Postorder traversal

```
public static void visit(BinaryTreeNode t)
   {System.out.print(t.element + " ");}
```

Program 12.5 A visit method

Preorder	$+*ab/cd$	$+++abcd$	$/+-a+xy*+b*ca$
Inorder	$a*b+c/d$	$a+b+c+d$	$-a+x+y/+b*c*a$
Postorder	$ab*cd/+$	$ab+c+d+$	$a-xy++b+ca**/$
	(a)	(b)	(c)

Figure 12.11 Elements of a binary tree listed in pre-, in-, and postorder

binary operator (i.e., operator with two operands) appears just after the infix form of its left operand and just before the infix form of its right operand. An expression presented as a binary tree is unambiguous in the sense that the association between operators and operands is uniquely determined by the representation. This association is not uniquely determined by the representation when the infix form is used. For example, is $x + y * z$ to be interpreted as $(x + y) * z$ or $x + (y * z)$. To resolve this ambiguity, one assigns priorities to operators and employs priority rules. Further, delimiters such as parentheses are used to override these rules if necessary. In a *fully parenthesized* infix representation, each operator and its operands are enclosed in a pair of parentheses. Furthermore, each of the operands of the operator are in fully parenthesized form. Some representations of this type are $((x) + (y))$, $((x) + ((y) * (z)))$, and $((((x) + (y)) * ((y) + (z))) * (w))$. This form of the expression is obtained by modifying inorder traversal as in Program 12.6. Program 12.6 uses the accessor methods of `BinaryTreeNode` to obtain the fields of a node because the method `infix` is in the package `applications`, whereas the class `BinaryTreeNode` is in the package `dataStructures` and the data members of `BinaryTreeNode` have package visibility. Therefore, the data members of `BinaryTreeNode` are not visible outside the package `dataStructures`.

```
public static void infix(BinaryTreeNode t)
{
   if (t != null)
   {
      System.out.print("(");
      infix(t.getLeftChild());    // output left operand
      System.out.print(t);        // output operator
      infix(t.getRightChild());   // output right operand
      System.out.print(")");
   }
}
```

Program 12.6 Output fully parenthesized infix form

In the **postfix form** each operator comes immediately after the postfix form of its operands. The operands themselves appear in left-to-right order. In the **prefix form** each operator comes immediately before the prefix form of its operands. The operands themselves appear in left-to-right order. Like the binary tree representation, the prefix and postfix representations are unambiguous. As a result, neither the prefix nor the postfix representation employs parentheses or operator priorities. The association between operators and operands is easily determined by scanning the expression from right to left or from left to right and by employing a stack of operands. If an operand is encountered during this scan, it is stacked. If an operator is encountered, it is associated with the correct number of operands from the top of the stack. These operands are deleted from the stack and replaced by an operand that represents the result produced by the operator.

In a level-order traversal, elements are visited by level from top to bottom. Within levels, elements are visited from left to right. It is quite difficult to write a recursive function for level-order traversal, as the correct data structure to use here is a queue and not a stack. Program 12.7 traverses a binary tree in level order.

Program 12.7 enters the `while` loop only if the tree is not empty. The root is visited, and its children, if any, are added to the queue. Following the addition of the children of `t` to the queue, we attempt to remove an element from the queue. When the queue is empty, `remove` returns the value `null`; and when the queue is not empty, `remove` returns the removed element. This removed element is a reference/pointer to the next node that is to be visited.

```
public static void levelOrder(BinaryTreeNode t)
{
   ArrayQueue q = new ArrayQueue();
   while (t != null)
   {
      visit(t);  // visit t

      // put t's children on queue
      if (t.leftChild != null)
         q.put(t.leftChild);
      if (t.rightChild != null)
         q.put(t.rightChild);

      // get next node to visit
      t = (BinaryTreeNode) q.remove();
   }
}
```

Program 12.7 Level-order traversal

Let n be the number of elements in a binary tree. The space and time complexity of each of the four traversal programs is $O(n)$. To verify this claim, observe that the recursion stack space needed by pre-, in-, and postorder traversal is $\Theta(n)$ when the tree height is n (as is the case for a right-skewed binary tree (Figure 12.9)); the queue space needed by level-order traversal is $\Theta(n)$ when the tree is a full binary tree. For the time complexity observe that each of the traversal methods spends $\Theta(1)$ time at each node of the tree (assuming the time needed to visit a node is $\Theta(1)$).

EXERCISES

12. List the nodes of the binary trees of Figure 12.10 in pre-, in-, post-, and level order.

13. Do Exercise 12 for the full binary tree of Figure 12.6.

14. List the nodes of the binary trees for the expressions of Exercise 6 in pre-, in-, post-, and level order.

15. The nodes of a binary tree are labeled $a - h$. The preorder listing is *abcdefgh*, and the inorder listing is *cdbagfeh*. Draw the binary tree. Also, list the nodes of your binary tree in postorder and level order.

16. Do Exercise 15 for a binary tree with node labels $a - l$, preorder listing *abcde-fghijkl*, and inorder listing *aefdcgihjklb*.

17. The nodes of a binary tree are labeled $a - h$. The postorder listing is *abcdefgh*, and the inorder listing is *aedbchgf*. Draw the binary tree. Also, list the nodes of your binary tree in preorder and level order.

18. Do Exercise 17 for a binary tree with node labels $a - l$, postorder listing *abcdefghijkl*, and inorder listing *backdejifghl*.

19. Draw two binary trees whose preorder listing is *abcdefgh* and whose postorder listing is *dcbgfhea*. Also, list the nodes of your binary trees in inorder and level order.

20. Write a method to perform a preorder traversal on a binary tree represented with the array-based scheme. Assume that the elements of the binary tree are stored in array a and that `last` is the position of the last element of the tree. a[i] = `null` iff there is no element at position i. What is the time complexity of your procedure?

21. Do Exercise 20 for inorder.

22. Do Exercise 20 for postorder.

23. Do Exercise 20 for level order.

24. Write a Java method to make a clone of a binary tree represented with the array-based scheme.

25. Write two Java methods to clone a binary tree that is represented with the class `BinaryTreeNode`. The first method should traverse the tree in postorder, and the second in preorder. What is the difference (if any) in the recursion stack space needed by these two methods?

26. Write a method to evaluate an expression tree that is represented with the class `BinaryTreeNode`. Develop a suitable data type for the elements in the tree.

27. Write a method to determine the height of a linked binary tree. What is the time complexity of your method?

28. Write a method to determine the number of nodes in a linked binary tree. What is the time complexity of your method?

29. Write a method to determine the level of a linked binary tree that has the maximum number of nodes (*Hint:* perform a level-order traversal). What is the time complexity of your method?

30. Write an iterative method to traverse a linked binary tree in inorder. Your procedure can use an array-based stack. Make your procedure as elegant as possible. How much stack space does the traversal need? Give this stack space as a function of the height of the binary tree.

31. Do Exercise 30 for preorder.

32. Do Exercise 30 for postorder.

★ 33. Suppose you have a binary tree whose nodes have distinct data. Do the pre- and inorder listings of the data fields uniquely define the binary tree? If so, write a method to construct the binary tree. What is the time complexity of your method?

34. Do Exercise 33 for pre- and postorder.

★ 35. Do Exercise 33 for post- and inorder.

★ 36. Write a Java method to accept an expression in postfix form and construct its binary tree representation. Assume that each operator may have either one or two operands.

★ 37. Do Exercise 36 beginning with the prefix form.

★ 38. Write a Java method to transform a postfix expression into its fully parenthesized infix form.

★ 39. Do Exercise 38 beginning with a prefix expression.

★ 40. Begin with an infix expression (not necessarily fully parenthesized) and obtain its postfix form. For this exercise assume that the permissible operators are binary $+$, $-$, $*$, $/$ and the permissible delimiters are (and). Notice that since the order of operands is the same in infix, prefix, and postfix, the translation from infix to prefix or postfix can be done by scanning the infix form from left to right and outputting operands as they are encountered. Operators are held in a stack until the right time to output them, which is determined by assigning priorities to the operators and to (. Use the priorities 1 (for $+$ and $-$) and 2 (for $*$ and $/$). Use priority 3 for a (that is outside the stack and 0 for a (that is in the stack.

★ 41. Do Exercise 40 but this time generate the prefix form.

★ 42. Do Exercise 40 but this time generate the binary tree form.

43. Write a method to evaluate an expression that is in its postfix form. Assume a suitable array representation for the expression.

12.7 THE ADT *BinaryTree*

Now that we have some understanding of what a binary tree is, we can specify it as an abstract data type (ADT 12.1). Since the number of operations we may wish to perform on a binary tree is quite large, we list only some of the commonly performed ones.

AbstractDataType *BinaryTree*
{

   instances

   collection of elements; if not empty, the collection is partitioned into a root, left subtree, and right subtree; each subtree is also a binary tree;

   operations

   isEmpty : return **true** if empty, return **false** otherwise;

   root() : return the root element;
   return **null** if the tree is empty;

   makeTree(*root, left, right*) : create a binary tree with *root* as the root element, *left* (*right*) as the left (right) subtree.

   removeLeftSubtree() : remove the left subtree and return it;

   removeRightSubtree() : remove the right subtree and return it;

   preOrder : preorder traversal of binary tree

   inOrder : inorder traversal of binary tree

   postOrder : postorder traversal of binary tree

   levelOrder : level-order traversal of binary tree

}

ADT 12.1 The abstract data type binary tree

Before we can write a Java interface that corresponds to the ADT *BinaryTree*, we must decide how the traversal methods determine the visit method that is to be used. Since a user may wish to traverse a binary tree several times using different visit methods in each traversal, the visit method must be a parameter to the traversal method. Program 12.8 gives the interface `BinaryTree`. The class `Method` referred to in this interface is `java.lang.reflect.Method`.

```
public interface BinaryTree
{
   public boolean isEmpty();
   public Object root();
   public void makeTree(Object root, Object left, Object right);
   public BinaryTree removeLeftSubtree();
   public BinaryTree removeRightSubtree();
   public void preOrder(Method visit);
   public void inOrder(Method visit);
   public void postOrder(Method visit);
   public void levelOrder(Method visit);
}
```

Program 12.8 Binary tree interface

12.8   THE CLASS LinkedBinaryTree

The class LinkedBinaryTree implements the interface BinaryTree using nodes of the type BinaryTreeNode (Program 12.1). Program 12.9 gives the data members as well as two visit methods (output and add1) of LinkedBinaryTree.

LinkedBinaryTree has only one instance data member root; this is a pointer to the root node of the binary tree. The class data members theOutput and theAdd1 are of type Method. These data members are initialized inside a static initializer block because the initialization of these data members requires us to invoke the method Class.getMethod, which throws exceptions of types NoSuchMethodException and SecurityException. Since NoSuchMethodException is not a subclass of RuntimeException, we must either catch exceptions of this type or declare that the method that encloses the Class.getMethod invocation throws an exception of type NoSuchMethodException. Therefore, theOutput and theAdd1 cannot be initialized by using a simple assignment as is used to initialize paramType; an assignment statement cannot throw an exception.

Program 12.10 gives the code for the methods makeTree and removeLeftSubtree. The code for makeTree is rather simplistic and prone to generate undesired effects unless the user is very careful. For example, the invocation y.makeTree(e, x, x) results in a binary tree whose left and right subtrees share the same nodes. This sharing is correct only when x is the empty binary tree. If we make changes in the left subtree of y, these changes automatically become changes in the right subtree of y as well as in the binary tree x. Exercise 44 asks you to write a version of makeTree that avoids these pitfalls.

```
// instance data member
BinaryTreeNode root;  // root node

// class data members
static Method visit;       // visit method to use during a traversal
static Object [] visitArgs = new Object [1];
                           // parameters of visit method
static int count;          // counter
static Class [] paramType = {BinaryTreeNode.class};
                           // type of parameter for visit
static Method theAdd1;     // method to increment count by 1
static Method theOutput;   // method to output node element

// method to initialize class data members
static
{
   try
   {
      Class lbt = LinkedBinaryTree.class;
      theAdd1 = lbt.getMethod("add1", paramType);
      theOutput = lbt.getMethod("output", paramType);
   }
   catch (Exception e) {}
      // exception not possible
}

// only default constructor available

// class methods
/** visit method that outputs element */
public static void output(BinaryTreeNode t)
   {System.out.print(t.element + " ");}

/** visit method to count nodes */
public static void add1(BinaryTreeNode t)
   {count++;}
```

Program 12.9 Data members and visit methods of LinkedBinaryTree

```java
/** set this to the tree with the given root and subtrees
  * CAUTION: does not clone left and right */
public void makeTree(Object root, Object left, Object right)
{
   this.root = new BinaryTreeNode(root,
                    ((LinkedBinaryTree) left).root,
                    ((LinkedBinaryTree) right).root);
}

/** remove the left subtree
  * @throws IllegalArgumentException when tree is empty
  * @return removed subtree */
public BinaryTree removeLeftSubtree()
{
   if (root == null)
      throw new IllegalArgumentException("tree is empty");

   // detach left subtree and save in leftSubtree
   LinkedBinaryTree leftSubtree = new LinkedBinaryTree();
   leftSubtree.root = root.leftChild;
   root.leftChild = null;

   return (BinaryTree) leftSubtree;
}

// code for removeRightSubtree is similar
```

Program 12.10 The make and remove methods of LinkedBinaryTree

Program 12.11 gives the code for the preorder traversal and output methods. The public method preOrder sets the class data member visit so that the desired method is used during the visit step. Following this step, preOrder invokes the recursive method thePreOrder, which does the actual preorder traversal. The public method preOrderOutput prints the elements in a binary tree in preorder. This task is accomplished by simply invoking the preorder traversal method preOrder with the visit method output, which prints the element in the node being visited. The corresponding inorder and postorder methods are similar.

The code for level-order traversal is quite similar to that given in Program 12.7.

Program 12.12 gives two additional public member methods of LinkedBinary-Tree. The first of these, size, determines the number of nodes in a binary tree by traversing the tree in preorder. Since each node is visited exactly once during a

```
/** preorder traversal */
public void preOrder(Method visit)
{
   this.visit = visit;
   thePreOrder(root);
}

/** actual preorder traversal method */
static void thePreOrder(BinaryTreeNode t)
{
   if (t != null)
   {
     visitArgs[0] = t;
     try {visit.invoke(null, visitArgs);}  // visit tree root
     catch (Exception e)
        {System.out.println(e);}
     thePreOrder(t.leftChild);             // do left subtree
     thePreOrder(t.rightChild);            // do right subtree
   }
}

/** output elements in preorder */
public void preOrderOutput()
   {preOrder(theOutput);}
```

Program 12.11 Preorder methods of LinkedBinaryTree

traversal, the number of nodes can be determined by initializing a counter count to 0 and then incrementing the counter by 1 each time a node is visited. Incrementing the counter is done by using the visit method add1.

The second public method of Program 12.12 is height. This method invokes the recursive method theHeight that does the actual computation of the height of the tree. The method theHeight determines the height of a binary tree by performing a postorder traversal of the binary tree. The method first determines the height of the left subtree, then determines the height of the right subtree, and finally (in the visit step) determines the tree height by adding 1 to the larger of the left and right subtree heights.

```
/** count number of nodes in tree */
public int size()
{
   count = 0;
   preOrder(theAdd1);
   return count;
}

/** @return tree height */
public int height()
   {return theHeight(root);}

/** @return height of subtree rooted at t */
static int theHeight(BinaryTreeNode t)
{
   if (t == null) return 0;
   int hl = theHeight(t.leftChild);  // height of left subtree
   int hr = theHeight(t.rightChild); // height of right subtree
   if (hl > hr) return ++hl;
   else return ++hr;
}
```

Program 12.12 Determining the size and height of a binary tree

EXERCISES

44. Write a new version of the binary tree method `makeTree` that makes a clone of the given left and right subtrees before creating the resulting tree.

45. (a) Extend the ADT *BinaryTree* to include these operations:

     i. *compare(x)*, which compares a binary tree with the binary tree *x*. It returns **true** iff the two binary trees are identical.

     ii. *clone()*, which creates a clone of a binary tree.

     iii. *swapSubtrees()*, which swaps the left and right subtrees of every node.

   (b) Define the Java interface `ExtendedBinaryTree` that extends `BinaryTree` and includes methods corresponding to the ADT operations *compare*, *clone* and *swapSubtrees*.

   (c) Develop the class `ExtendedLinkedBinaryTree` that implements the interface `ExtendedBinaryTree`. Your class should extend the class `LinkedBinaryTree`. Test your code.

46. Develop an inorder iterator for the class `LinkedBinaryTree` (the solution to Exercise 30 should help you with this exercise). The time taken to enumerate all elements of an n-element binary tree should be $O(n)$. The complexity of no method should exceed $O(h)$, where h is the tree height, and the space requirements should be $O(h)$. Test your code.

47. Develop a preorder iterator for the class `LinkedBinaryTree`. Excluding the time needed to double the stack size (in case you use `ArrayStack`), the complexity of each method should be $O(1)$, and the space requirements should be $O(h)$. Test your code.

48. Develop a postorder iterator for the class `LinkedBinaryTree` (the solution to Exercise 32 should help you with this exercise). The time taken to enumerate all elements of an n-element binary tree should be $O(n)$. The complexity of no method should exceed $O(h)$, where h is the tree height, and the space requirements should be $O(h)$. Test your code.

49. Develop a level-order iterator for the class `LinkedBinaryTree`. Excluding the time needed to double the queue size (in case you use `ArrayQueue`), the complexity of each method should be $O(1)$. Test your code.

50. Develop the class `Expression` as a derived class of `LinkedBinaryTree`. This class should permit the following operations:

    (a) Output the fully parenthesized infix form of the expression.

    (b) Output the prefix and postfix forms.

    (c) Convert from prefix to expression tree.

    (d) Convert from postfix to expression tree.

    (e) Convert from infix to expression tree.

    (f) Evaluate an expression tree.

    Test your code.

12.9   APPLICATIONS

12.9.1   Placement of Signal Boosters

Problem Descripton

In a distribution network a resource is distributed from its origin to several other sites. For example, petroleum or natural gas can be distributed through a network of pipes from the source of the petroleum/natural gas to the consumption sites. Similarly, electrical power may be distributed through a network of wires from the power plant to the points of consumption. We will use the term **signal** to refer to the resource (petroleum, natural gas, power, etc.) that is to be distributed. While the signal is being transported through the distribution network, it may experience a loss in or degradation of one or more of its characteristics. For example, there may be a pressure drop along a natural gas pipeline or a voltage drop along an electrical transmission line. In other situations noise may enter the signal as it moves along the network. Between the signal source and point of consumption, we can tolerate only a certain amount, *tolerance*, of signal degradation. To guarantee a degradation that does not exceed this amount, **signal boosters** are placed at strategic places in the network. A signal booster might, for example, increase the signal pressure or voltage so that it equals that at the source or may enhance the signal so that the signal-to-noise ratio is the same as that at the source. In this section we develop an algorithm to determine where to place signal boosters. Our objective is to minimize the number of boosters in use while ensuring that the degradation in signal (relative to that at the source) does not exceed the given tolerance.

To simplify the problem, we assume that the distribution network is a tree with the source as the root. Each node in the tree (other than the root) represents a substation where we can place a booster. Some of these nodes also represent points of consumption. The signal flows from a node to its children. Figure 12.12 shows a distribution network that is a tree. Each edge is labeled by the amount of signal degradation that takes place when a signal flows between the corresponding parent and child. The units of degradation are assumed to be additive. That is, when a signal flows from node p to node v in Figure 12.12, the degradation is 5; the degradation from node q to node x is 3. When a signal booster is placed at node r, the strength of the signal that arrives at r is three units less than that of the signal that leaves source p; however, the signal that leaves r has the same strength as the signal that left p. Therefore, the signal that arrives at v has degraded by two units relative to the signal at the source; and the signal that arrives at z is four units weaker than the signal that left p. Without the booster at r, the arriving signal at z will be seven units weaker than the signal that left p.

Solution Strategy

Let $degradeFromParent(i)$ denote the degradation between node i and its parent. Therefore, in Figure 12.12, $degradeFromParent(w) = 2$, $degradeFromParent(p) = 0$, and $degradeFromParent(r) = 3$. Since signal boosters can be placed only at nodes of the distribution tree, the presence of a node i with $degradeFromParent(i) >$ *tolerance* implies that no placement of boosters can prevent signal degradation from exceeding *tolerance*. For example, if *tolerance* $= 2$, then there is no way to place signal boosters so that the degradation between p and r is $\leq$ *tolerance* $= 2$ in Figure 12.12.

For any node i let $degradeToLeaf(i)$ denote the maximum signal degradation from node i to any leaf in the subtree rooted at i. If i is a leaf node, then $degradeToLeaf(i) = 0$. For the example of Figure 12.12, $degradeToLeaf(i) = 0$ for $i \in \{w, x, t, y, z\}$. For the remaining nodes $degradeToLeaf(i)$ may be computed using the following equality:

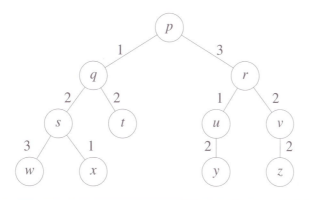

Figure 12.12 Tree distribution network

$$degrade\,ToLeaf(i) = \max_{j \text{ is a child of } i} \{degrade\,ToLeaf(j) + degradeFromParent(j)\}$$

So $degrade\,ToLeaf(s) = 3$. To use this equation, we must compute the $degrade\,ToLeaf$ value of a node after computing that of its children. Therefore, we must traverse the tree so that we visit a node after we visit its children. We can compute the $degrade\,ToLeaf$ value of a node when we visit it. This traversal order is a natural extension of postorder traversal to trees of degree (possibly) more than 2.

Suppose that during the computation of $degrade\,ToLeaf$ as described above, we encounter a node i with a child j such that

$$degrade\,ToLeaf(j) + degradeFromParent(j) > tolerance$$

If we do not place a booster at j, then the signal degradation from i to a leaf will exceed *tolerance* even if a booster is placed at i. For example, in Figure 12.12, when computing $degrade\,ToLeaf(q)$, we compute

$$degrade\,ToLeaf(s) + degradeFromParent(s) = 5$$

If *tolerance* $= 3$, then placing a booster at q or at any of q's ancestors doesn't reduce signal degradation between q and its descendents. We need to place a booster at s. If a booster is placed at s, then $degrade\,ToLeaf(q) = 3$.

Figure 12.13 gives the pseudocode to place boosters and compute $degrade\,ToLeaf$.

```
degradeToLeaf(i) = 0;
for (each child j of i)
```
$\quad$ if $(degradeToLeaf(j) + degradeFromParent(j)) > tolerance)$
$\quad$ {

$\qquad$ place a booster at j;
$\qquad degradeToLeaf(i) = \max\{degradeToLeaf(i),$
$\qquad\qquad\qquad\qquad\qquad degradeFromParent(j)\};$

$\quad$ }
$\quad$ else
$\qquad degradeToLeaf(i) = \max\{degradeToLeaf(i),$
$\qquad\qquad\qquad\qquad degradeToLeaf(j) + degradeFromParent(j)\};$

Figure 12.13 Pseudocode to place boosters and compute *degradeToLeaf*

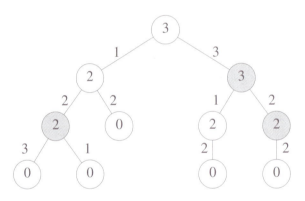

Signal boosters are at shaded nodes
Numbers inside nodes are *degradeToLeaf* values

Figure 12.14 Distribution network with signal boosters

Applying this computation method to the distribution tree of Figure 12.12 results in the placement of boosters at nodes r, s, and v (see Figure 12.14). The *degradeToLeaf* values for nodes are given inside the node.

Theorem 12.1 *The procedure outlined above uses the minimum number of boosters.*

Proof The proof is by induction on the number n of nodes in the distribution tree. If $n = 1$, the theorem is trivially valid. Assume that the theorem is valid for

$n \leq m$ where m is an arbitrary natural number. Let t be a tree with $n + 1$ nodes. Let X be the set of vertices at which the outlined procedure places boosters and let W be a minimum cardinality placement of boosters that satisfies the tolerance requirements. We need to show that $|X| = |W|$.

If $|X| = 0$, then $|X| = |W|$. If $|X| > 0$, then let z be the first vertex at which a booster is placed by the outlined procedure. Let t_z be the subtree of t rooted at z. Since $degradeToLeaf(z) + degradeFromParent(z) > tolerance$, W must contain at least one vertex u that is in t_z. If W contains more than one such u, then W cannot be of minimum cardinality because by placing boosters at $W - \{$all such $u\} + \{z\}$, we can satisfy the tolerance requirement. Hence W contains exactly one such u. Let $W' = W - \{u\}$. Let t' be the tree that results from the removal of t_z from t except z. We see that W' is a minimum cardinality booster placement for t' that satisfies the tolerance requirement. Also, $X' = X - \{z\}$ satisfies the tolerance requirement for t' and is the booster placement generated by our outlined procedure on the tree t'. Since the number of vertices in t' is less than $m + 1$, $|X'| = |W'|$. Hence $|X| = |X'| + 1 = |W'| + 1 = |W|$. ∎

Java Implementation

When no node of the distribution tree has more than two children, it may be represented as a binary tree by using the classes LinkedBinaryTree (Program 12.9) and Booster (Program 12.13). The field boosterHere is used to differentiate between nodes at which a booster is placed and those where it is not. The element fields of our binary tree will be of type Booster.

We can compute the $degradeToLeaf$ values for the nodes and the location of a minimum set of boosters by performing a postorder traversal of the binary distribution tree. During the visit step, we execute the code of Program 12.14. The code for PlaceBoosters.placeBoosters assumes that tolerance is a class (i.e., static) data member of PlaceBoosters.

If t is a LinkedBinaryTree whose degradeFromParent fields have been set to the degradation values and whose boosterHere fields have been set to false, then the invocation t.postOrder(thePlaceMethod), where thePlaceMethod is of type Method and is a reference to the method PlaceBoosters.placeBoosters, will reset the degradeToLeaf and boosterHere fields correctly. The values computed by placeBoosters can be output using the invocation t.postOrderOutput(). Since the complexity of placeBoosters is $\Theta(1)$, the invocation t.PostOrder(thePlace-Method) takes $O(n)$ time where n is the number of nodes in the distribution tree.

Binary Tree Representation of a Tree

When the distribution tree t contains nodes that have more than two children, we can still represent the tree as a binary tree. This time, for each node x of the tree t, we link its children into a chain using the rightChild fields of the children nodes. The leftChild field of x points to the first node in this chain. The rightChild

```
private static class Booster
{
   // data members
   int degradeToLeaf,       // degradation to leaf
       degradeFromParent;   // degradation from parent
   boolean boosterHere;     // true iff booster placed here

   // methods
   public Booster(int fromParent)
      {degradeFromParent = fromParent;}

   public String toString()
      {return boosterHere + " " + degradeToLeaf + " "
             + degradeFromParent;}
}
```

Program 12.13 The class Booster

field of x is used for the chain of x's siblings. Figure 12.15 shows a tree and its binary tree representation. Solid lines represent left-child pointers, and right-child pointers are shown as dotted lines.

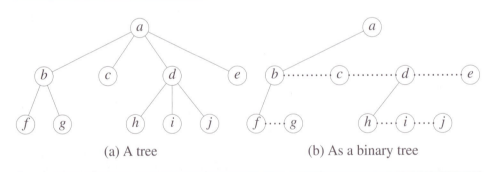

(a) A tree   (b) As a binary tree

Figure 12.15 A tree and its binary tree representation

When the binary tree representation of a tree is used, the invocation t.postOrder-(thePlaceMethod) does not have the desired effect. The development of the new method to compute degradeToLeaf and boosterHere is considered in Exercise 55.

```
public static void placeBoosters(BinaryTreeNode x)
{// Compute degradation at x.  Place booster
 // here if degradation exceeds tolerance.

   // initialize degradation at x
   Booster elementX = (Booster) x.getElement();
   elementX.degradeToLeaf = 0;

   // compute degradation from left subtree of x and
   // place a booster at the left child of x if needed
   BinaryTreeNode y = x.getLeftChild();
   if (y != null)
   {// x has a nonempty left subtree
      Booster elementY = (Booster) y.getElement();
      int degradation = elementY.degradeToLeaf +
                        elementY.degradeFromParent;
      if (degradation > tolerance)
      {// place booster at y
         elementY.boosterHere = true;
         elementX.degradeToLeaf = elementY.degradeFromParent;
      }
      else // no booster needed at y
         elementX.degradeToLeaf = degradation;
   }

   // compute degradation from right subtree of x and
   // place a booster at the right child of x if needed
   y = x.getRightChild();
   if (y != null)
   {// x has a nonempty right subtree
      Booster elementY = (Booster) y.getElement();
      int degradation = elementY.degradeToLeaf +
                        elementY.degradeFromParent;
      if (degradation > tolerance)
      {// place booster at y
         elementY.boosterHere = true;
         degradation = elementY.degradeFromParent;
      }
      elementX.degradeToLeaf = Math.max(elementX.degradeToLeaf,
                                        degradation);
   }
}
```

Program 12.14 Place boosters and determine degradeToLeaf for binary distribution trees

12.9.2   Union-Find Problem

Problem Description

The union-find problem was introduced in Section 7.7. Basically, we begin with n elements numbered 1 through n; initially, each is in a class of its own, and we perform a sequence of find and combine operations. The operation `find(the-Element)` returns a unique characteristic of the class that `theElement` is in, and `combine(a,b)` combines the classes that contain the elements a and b. In Section 7.7 we saw that `combine(a,b)` is usually implemented by using the union operation `union(classA,classB)` where `classA = find(a)`, `classB = find(b)`, and `classA ≠ classB`. The solution provided in Section 7.7 used chains and had a complexity $O(n + u \log u + f)$ where u is the number of union operations and f is the number of find operations performed. In this section we explore an alternative solution in which each set (or class) is represented as a tree.

Representing a Set as a Tree

Any set S may be represented as a tree with $|S|$ nodes, one node per element. Any element of S may be selected as the root element; any subset of the remaining elements could be the children of the root; any subset of the elements that remain could be the grandchildren of the root; and so on.

   Figure 12.16 shows some sets represented as trees. Notice that each node that is not a root has a pointer to its parent in the tree. Our pointers go from a node to its parent because the find operation will require us to move up a tree. Neither the find nor union operations requires us to move down a tree.

   We say that the elements 1, 2, 20, 30, and so on are in the set with root 20; the elements 11, 16, 25, and 28 are in the set with root 16; the element 15 is in the set with root 15; and the elements 26 and 32 are in the set with root 26 (or simply the set 26).

Solution Strategy

Our strategy to solve the union-find problem is to represent each set as a tree. For the find operation we use the element in the root as the set identifier. So `find(3)` returns the value 20 (see Figure 12.16); `find(1)` returns 20; and `find(26)` returns 26. Since each tree has a unique root, `find(i) = find(j)` iff i and j are in the same set. To find the set that contains `theElement`, we begin at the node for element `theElement` and move up the tree until we reach the root.

   For the union operation we assume that the invocation `union(classA, classB)` is done with `classA` and `classB` being the elements in the roots of two different trees (i.e., `classA ≠ classB`). To unite the two trees (or sets) of elements, we make one tree a subtree of the other. For instance, if `classA = 16` and `classB = 26` (Figure 12.16), the tree of Figure 12.17(a) results if `classA` is made a subtree of `classB`, whereas the result is Figure 12.17(b) if `classB` is made a subtree of `classA`.

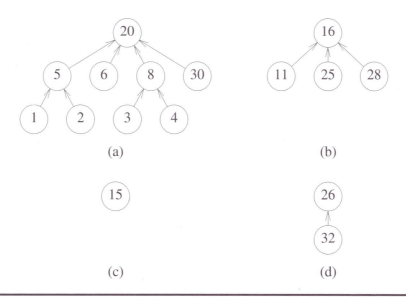

Figure 12.16 Tree representation of disjoint sets

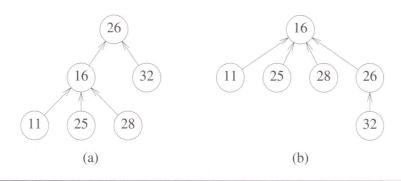

Figure 12.17 Union

Java Implementation

The solution to the union-find problem is a good example of the use of simulated pointers. A linked representation of the trees is needed. Each node must have a **parent** field. Children fields are, however, not needed. We also have a need to make direct access to nodes. To find the set containing element 10, we need to determine which node represents the element 10 and then follow a sequence of **parent** pointers to the root. This direct access is best obtained if the nodes are indexed 1 through n (the number of elements) and if node e represents element e. Each `parent` field gives the index of the parent node. Hence the `parent` fields are of type `int`.

Figure 12.18 represents the trees of Figure 12.16 using this representation. The number inside a node is the value of its parent field. The number outside a node is its index. This index is also the element it represents. The parent field for a root node is set to 0. Since there is no node with index 0, a parent field of 0 is detected as a link to no node (or a null link).

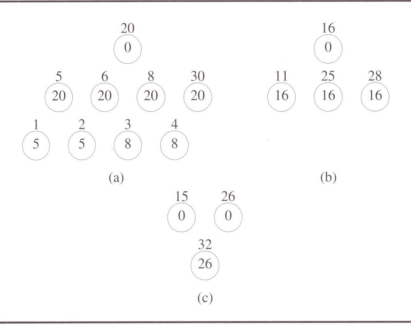

Figure 12.18 Representation of trees of Figure 12.16

The tree-based solution to the union-find problem is implemented as the class `UnionFindWithTrees`. To create the initial configuration in which each element is in a set of its own, we need to allocate space for the array `parent` and set `parent[1:n]` to 0. This initialization is done by the constructor for the class `UnionFindWithTrees` (Program 12.15).

To find the set that contains `theElement`, we begin at node `theElement` and follow `parent` pointers until we reach the root. For instance, if `theElement = 4` and the status of the sets is as in Figure 12.16(a), we begin at 4. Following the pointer `parent[4]` gets us to node 8, and `parent[8]` gets us to node 20 whose `parent` is 0. Hence 20 is the root of the tree that contains element 4. The method `find` of Program 12.15 implements this strategy. This method assumes that the test $1 \leq e \leq n$ (i.e., `theElement` is a valid element) is performed externally.

```
public class UnionFindWithTrees
{
   int [] parent;    // pointer to parent in tree

   /** initialize n trees, one element per tree/class/set */
   public UnionFindWithTrees(int n)
   {
      parent = new int [n + 1];
      for (int e = 1; e <= n; e++)
         parent[e] = 0;
   }

   /** @return root of the tree that contains theElement */
   public int find(int theElement)
   {
      while (parent[theElement] != 0)
         theElement = parent[theElement];  // move up one level
      return theElement;
   }

   /** combine trees with distinct roots rootA and rootB */
   void union(int rootA, int rootB)
      {parent[rootB] = rootA;}
}
```

Program 12.15 Simple tree solution to the union-find problem

The method **union** of Program 12.15 performs a union. It assumes that the check **rootA** $\neq$ **rootB** is performed before it is invoked. **rootB** is always made a subtree of **rootA**.

Performance Analysis

Let n be the number of elements. The time complexity of the constructor is $O(n)$; the complexity of **find(theElement)** is $O(h)$ where h is the height of the tree that contains element **theElement**; and the complexity of **union(rootA, rootB)** is $\Theta(1)$.

In a typical application of the union-find problem, many union and find operations are performed. Furthermore, in typical applications we do not care how much time an individual operation takes; we are concerned with the time taken for all operations collectively. Assume that u unions and f finds are to be performed. Since each union is necessarily preceded by two finds (these finds determine the roots of the trees to be united), we may assume that $f > u$. Each union takes $\Theta(1)$ time. The time for each find depends on the height of the trees that get created. In the worst case a tree with m elements can have a height of m. This worst case happens, for example, when the following sequence of unions is performed:

$$union(2, 1), union(3, 2), union(4, 3), union(5, 4), \cdots$$

Hence each find can take as much as $\Theta(q)$ time where q is the number of unions that have been performed before the find. Therefore, the time for a sequence of operations becomes $O(fu)$. The worst-case time needed for a sequence of operations can be reduced to almost $O(f + u) = O(f)$ by enhancing the union and find methods as described next.

Enhancing the Union Method

We can enhance the performance of the union-find algorithms by using either the **weight** or the **height** rule when performing a union of the trees with roots i and j.

Definition 12.3 [Weight rule] *If the number of nodes in the tree with root i is less than the number in the tree with root j, then make i a child of j; otherwise, make j a child of i.* ∎

Definition 12.4 [Height rule] *If the height of tree i is less than that of tree j, then make j the parent of i; otherwise, make i the parent of j.* ∎

If we perform a union on the trees of Figure 12.16 (a) and (b), then the tree with root 16 becomes a subtree of the tree with root 20 regardless of whether the weight or the height rule is used. When we perform a union on the trees of Figure 12.19 (a) and (b), the tree with root 16 becomes a subtree of the tree with root 20 in case the weight rule is used. However, when the height rule is used, the tree with root 20 becomes a subtree of the one with root 16.

To incorporate the weight rule into the procedure for a union, we add a Boolean field `root` to each node. The `root` field of a node is `true` iff the node is currently a root node. The `parent` field of each root node keeps a count of the total number of nodes in the tree. For the trees of Figure 12.16, we have `node[i].root = true` iff i = 20, 16, 15, or 26. Also, `node[i].parent` = 9, 4, 1, and 2 for i = 20, 16, 15, and 26, respectively. The remaining `parent` fields are unchanged.

To implement the weighting rule, we define the class `Node` that defines the data type of the nodes in a tree. Program 12.16 gives the code for this class.

The class `FastUnionFind` implements the weighting rule, and the class `Node` is a top-level nested class of `FastUnionFind`. The lone data member, constructor, and `union` method now take the form given in Program 12.17.

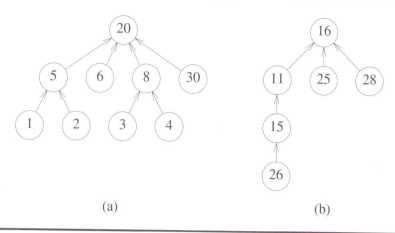

(a)   (b)

Figure 12.19 Two sample trees

```
private static class Node
{
    // data members
    int parent;      // pointer to parent in tree
    boolean root;    // true iff node is a root

    // constructor
    private Node()
    {
        parent = 1;    // one node in tree
        root = true;   // this node is a root
    }
}
```

Program 12.16 Node class used when implementing the weighting rule

The time required to perform a union has increased somewhat but is still bounded by a constant; it is $\Theta(1)$. Lemma 12.1 determines the maximum time to perform a find.

Lemma 12.1 [Weight rule lemma] *Assume that we start with singleton sets and perform unions, using the weight rule (as in Program 12.17). Let t be a tree with p nodes created in this way. The height of t is at most $\lfloor \log_2 p \rfloor + 1$.*

```java
// data member of FastUnionFind
Node [] node;

/** initialize n trees, one element per tree/class/set */
public FastUnionFind(int n)
{
   // allocate an array for the nodes
   node = new Node [n + 1];

   // now allocate the nodes
   for (int e = 1; e <= n; e++)
      node[e] = new Node();
}

/** combine trees with distinct roots rootA and rootB */
public void union(int rootA, int rootB)
{// use the weighting rule
   if (node[rootA].parent < node[rootB].parent)
   {
      // rootA becomes subtree of rootB
      node[rootB].parent += node[rootA].parent;
      node[rootA].root = false;
      node[rootA].parent = rootB;
   }
   else
   {// rootB becomes subtree of rootA
      node[rootA].parent += node[rootB].parent;
      node[rootB].root = false;
      node[rootB].parent = rootA;
   }
}
```

Program 12.17 Data member, constructor, and union method of FastUnionFind

Proof The lemma is clearly true for $p = 1$. Assume it is true for all trees with i nodes, $i \leq p - 1$. We will show that it is also true for $i = p$. Consider the last union operation, $union(k, j)$, performed to create tree t. Let m be the number of nodes in tree j and let $p - m$ be the number of nodes in k. Without loss of generality, we may assume $1 \leq m \leq p/2$. So j is made a subtree of tree k. Therefore, the height of t either is the same as that of k or is one more than that of j. If the former is the case, then the height of t is $\leq \lfloor \log_2(p-m) \rfloor + 1 \leq \lfloor \log_2 p \rfloor + 1$. If the latter is the case then the height of t is $\leq \lfloor \log_2 m \rfloor + 2 \leq \lfloor \log_2 p/2 \rfloor + 2 \leq \lfloor \log_2 p \rfloor + 1$.   ■

If we start with singleton sets and perform an intermixed sequence of u unions and f finds, no set will have more than $u + 1$ elements in it. From Lemma 12.1 it follows that when the weight rule is used, the cost of the sequence of union and find operations (excluding the initialization time) is $O(u + f \log u) = O(f \log u)$ (since we assume $f > u$).

When the weight rule is replaced by the height rule in Program 12.17, the bound of Lemma 12.1 still governs the height of the resulting trees. Exercises 58, 59, and 60 explore the use of the height rule.

Enhancing the Find Method

Further improvement in the worst-case performance is possible by modifying the find method of Program 12.15 so as to reduce the length of the path from the find element e to the root. This reduction in path length is obtained by using a process called **path compression**, which we can do in at least three different ways—path compaction, path splitting, and path halving.

In **path compaction** we change the pointers in all nodes on the path from the element being searched to the root so that these nodes point directly to the root. As an example, consider the tree of Figure 12.20. When we perform a `find(10)`, the nodes 10, 15, and 3 are determined to be on the path from 10 to the root. Their parent fields are changed to 2, and the tree of Figure 12.21 is obtained. (Since node 3 already points to 2, its field doesn't have to be changed; when writing the program, it turns out to be easier to include this node in the set of nodes whose parent field is to be changed.)

Although path compaction increases the time needed for an individual find, it reduces the cost of future finds. For instance, finding the elements in the subtrees of 10 and 15 is quicker in the compacted tree of Figure 12.21. Program 12.18 implements the compaction rule.

In **path splitting** we change the parent pointer in each node (except the root and its child) on the path from e to the root to point to the node's original grandparent. In the tree of Figure 12.20, path splitting beginning at node 13 results in the tree of Figure 12.22. Note that when we use path splitting, a single pass from e to the root suffices.

In **path halving** we change the parent pointer of every other node (except the root and its child) on the path from e to the root to point to the node's grandparent. As a result, in path halving only half as many pointers are changed as in path splitting. As in the case of path splitting, a single pass from e to the root suffices. Figure 12.23 shows the result of path halving beginning at node 13 of Figure 12.20.

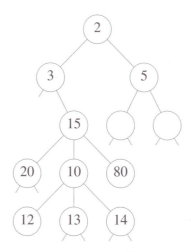

Figure 12.20 Sample tree

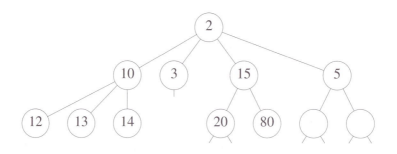

Figure 12.21 Path compaction

Enhancing Both the Union and the Find Methods

Path compression may change the height of a tree, but not its weight. Determining the new tree height following path compression requires considerable effort. So while it is relatively easy to use any of the path-compression schemes in conjunction with the weight rule, using path compression in conjunction with the height rule is difficult. We can, however, modify the height rule so as to use the tree height under the assumption that no path compression is done. With this modification the *modified tree height* changes only when two trees of equal modified height are united.

```
public int find(int theElement)
{
   // theRoot will eventually be the root
   int theRoot = theElement;
   while (!node[theRoot].root)
      theRoot = node[theRoot].parent;

   // compact path from theElement to theRoot
   int currentNode = theElement;                // start at theElement
   while (currentNode != theRoot)
   {
      int parentNode = node[currentNode].parent;
      node[currentNode].parent = theRoot;   // move to level 2
      currentNode = parentNode;                 // move to old parent
   }

   return theRoot;
}
```

Program 12.18 Path compaction. The method FastUnionFind.find

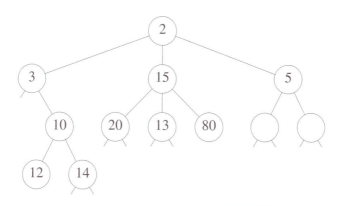

Figure 12.22 Path splitting

Worst-Case Complexity of Enhanced Union-Find Solution

When unions are done with either the weight or the modified height rule and finds are done with any of the three path-compression methods, the time needed to

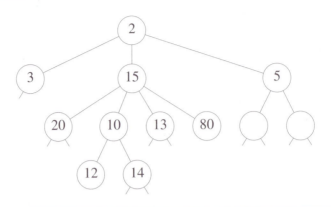

Figure 12.23 Path halving

process an intermixed sequence of unions and finds is almost linear in the number of unions and finds. Not only is the complexity analysis exceptionally difficult, but stating the result is also quite difficult.

We first define the explosively growing Ackermann's function $A(i,j)$ and its inverse $\alpha(p,q)$ (which grows at a snail's pace) as follows:

$$A(i,j) = \begin{cases} 2^j & i = 1 \text{ and } j \geq 1 \\ A(i-1,2) & i \geq 2 \text{ and } j = 1 \\ A(i-1, A(i,j-1)) & i,j \geq 2 \end{cases}$$

$$\alpha(p,q) = \min\{z \geq 1 | A(z, \lfloor p/q \rfloor) > \log_2 q\}, \ p \geq q \geq 1$$

Exrecise 65 shows that $A(i,j)$ is an increasing function of i and j; that is, $A(i,j) > A(i-1,j)$, and $A(i,j) > A(i,j-1)$. Actually, $A(i,j)$ is a very rapidly growing function of i and j. Consequently, its inverse α grows very slowly as p and q are increased.

Example 12.7 To get a feel for how fast Ackermann's function grows, let us evaluate $A(i,j)$ for a few small values of i and j. From the definition we get $A(2,1) = A(1,2) = 2^2 = 4$. Further, for $j \geq 2$, $A(2,j) = A(1, A(2,j-1)) = 2^{A(2,j-1)}$. So $A(2,2) = 2^{A(2,1)} = 2^4 = 16$; $A(2,3) = 2^{A(2,2)} = 2^{16} = 65{,}536$; $A(2,4) = 2^{A(2,3)} = 2^{65{,}536}$ (which is toooooooo big to write here); and

$$A(2,j) = 2^{2^{2^{2^{2^{-^-}}}}}$$

where the stack of twos on the right side is made up of $j + 1$ twos. $A(2, j)$ is quite a frightening number for $j > 3$.

$A(3, 1) = A(2, 2) = 16$ is not a number to be frightened by. But $A(4, 1) = A(3, 2)$ $= A(2, A(3, 1)) = A(2, 16)$. If $A(2, 4)$ is tooooooooo big, then how big is $A(4, 1) = A(2, 16)$?

The intent of this example is not to impress you with how fast $A(i, j)$ grows, but with how slow $\alpha(p, q)$ grows. When $q = 65,535 = 2^{16} - 1$, $\log q < 16$. Since $A(3, 1) = 16$, $\alpha(65,535, 65,535) = 3$ and $\alpha(p, 65,535) \leq 3$ for $p \geq 65,535$. $\alpha(65,536, 65,536) = 4$ and $\alpha(p, 65,536) \leq 4$ for $p \geq 65,536$. $\alpha(q, q)$ does not become 5 until $q = 2^{A(4,1)}$, an amazingly large number. Therefore, $\alpha(p, q)$, $p \geq q$, does not become 5 until $q = 2^{A(4,1)}$.

In the complexity analysis of the enhanced union-find algorithms, q is the number of elements, and p is the sum of the number of finds and the number of elements. Therefore, for all practical purposes, we can assume that $\alpha(p, q) \leq 4$.   ■

Theorem 12.2 [Tarjan and Van Leeuwen] *Let $T(f, u)$ be the maximum time required to process any intermixed sequence of f finds and u unions. Assume that $u \geq n/2$. Then*

$$k_1(n + f\alpha(f + n, n)) \leq T(f, u) \leq k_2(n + f\alpha(f + n, n))$$

for some positive constants k_1 and k_2. These bounds apply when we start with singleton sets and use either the weight or height rule for unions and any one of the three path-compression methods for a find.

The requirement that $u \geq n/2$ in Theorem 12.2 is really not significant because when $u < n/2$, some elements are not involved in union operations. These elements remain in singleton sets throughout the sequence of union and find operations, and we can eliminate them from consideration because find operations that involve these elements can be done in $O(1)$ time each. Even though the function $\alpha(f + n, n)$ is ≤ 4 for all practical purposes, the function remains a very slowly growing function and the complexity of a sequence of union and find operations is not linear in the number of elements and operations.

We have two choices for enhancing the union operation, and three for enhancing the union operation. In all, we have six possibilities for an implementation of a program to solve the union-find problem in the time bound given in Theorem 12.2. We can determine which of these six possibilities works best by experiment.

EXERCISES

51. You have a distribution network that is a full binary tree whose height is 4. The nodes are numbered 1–15 as in Figure 12.6 and $degradeFromParent(2 : 15) = [4, 3, 6, 2, 5, 2, 2, 4, 6, 4, 5, 3, 6, 2]$.

(a) Draw the distribution network with each edge labeled by its *degrade-FromParent* value (see Figure 12.12).

(b) Label each node of your distribution tree by its *degrateToLeaf* value.

(c) Use the method of Section 12.9.1 to determine the minimum number of signal boosters needed when *tolerance* = 8. Label each node and edge as in Figure 12.14.

52. Do Exercise 51 with *degradeFromParent*(2 : 15) = [2, 4, 5, 6, 3, 4, 2, 6, 3, 1, 3, 2, 6, 3] and *tolerance* = 11.

53. (a) Draw the binary tree representations of the trees of Figures 12.16(a) and (b), Figures 12.17(a) and (b), and Figures 12.19(a) and (b).

(b) Draw the binary tree representation of the tree of Figure 12.12. (Note that the binary tree representation of this tree is different from that obtained by using the left-child pointer of a node to point to one child and the right-child pointer to point to the other.)

54. A **forest** is a collection of zero or more trees. In the binary tree representation of a tree, the root has no right child. We may use this observation to arrive at a binary tree representation for a forest with m trees. First we obtain the binary tree representation of each tree in the forest. Next the ith tree is made the right subtree of the $(i - 1)$th, $2 \leq i \leq m$. Draw the binary tree representation of the four-tree forest of Figure 12.16, the two-tree forest of Figure 12.17, and the two-tree forest of Figure 12.19.

55. Let t be an instance of `LinkedBinaryTree`. Assume that t is the binary tree representation of a distribution tree (see Figure 12.15). Develop a program to compute the `degradeToLeaf` and `boosterHere` values of each node in t. Your program should also output these values by invoking `t.postOrderOutput()`. Use suitable distribution trees to test your program.

56. Suppose we start with n sets, each containing a distinct element.

(a) Show that if u unions are peformed, then no set contains more than $u + 1$ elements.

(b) Show that at most $n - 1$ unions can be performed before the number of sets becomes 1.

(c) Show that if fewer than $\lceil n/2 \rceil$ unions are performed, then at least one set with a single element in it remains.

(d) Show that if u unions are performed, then at least max$\{n - 2u, 0\}$ singleton sets remain.

57. Give an example of a sequence of unions that start with singleton sets and create trees whose height equals the upper bound given in Lemma 12.1. Assume that each union is performed with the weight rule.

58. Write a version of the method `union` (Program 12.15) that uses the height rule instead of the weight rule.

59. Prove Lemma 12.1 for the case when the height rule is used instead of the weight rule.

60. Give an example of a sequence of unions that start with singleton sets and create trees whose height equals the upper bound given in Lemma 12.1. Assume that each union is performed with the height rule.

61. Compare the average performance of the class `UnionFindWithTrees` (Program 12.15) with that of the class `FastUnionFind` (Programs 12.17 and 12.18). Do this comparison for different values of n. For each value of n, generate a random sequence of pairs (i, j). Replace each pair by two finds (one for i and the other for j). If the two are in different sets, then a union is to be performed. Repeat the experiment with many different random sequences. Measure the total time taken over these sequences. It is left to you to take this basic description of the experiment and plan a meaningful experiment to compare the average performance of the two sets of programs. Write a report that describes your experiment and your conclusions. Include program listings, a table of average times, and graphs in your report.

62. Write a method for the find operation that uses path halving instead of path compaction (as used in Program 12.18).

63. Write a method for the find operation that uses path splitting instead of path compaction (as used in Program 12.18).

64. Program the six ways in which you can achieve the performance stated in Theorem 12.2. Conduct experiments to evaluate these six solutions to determine which performs best.

65. Show that

    (a) $A(i, j) > A(i - 1, j)$ for $i > 1$ and $j \geq 1$.
    (b) $A(i, j) > A(i, j - 1)$ for $i \geq 1$ and $j > 1$.
    (c) $\alpha(r, q) \geq \alpha(p, q)$ for $r > p \geq q \geq 1$.

12.10   REFERENCES AND SELECTED READINGS

The book *The Art of Computer Programming: Fundamental Algorithms*, Volume 1, Third Edition, by D. Knuth, Addison-Wesley, Reading, MA, 1997, is a good reference for material on binary trees. The problem of placing boosters is studied in the following papers: "Deleting Vertices in Dags to Bound Path Lengths" by D. Paik,, S. Reddy, and S. Sahni, *IEEE Transactions on Computers*, 43, 9, 1994,

1091–1096, and "Heuristics for the Placement of Flip-Flops in Partial Scan Designs and for the Placement of Signal Boosters in Lossy Circuits" by D. Paik, S. Reddy, and S. Sahni, *Sixth International Conference on VLSI Design*, 1993, 45–50.

A complete analysis of the tree representations for the inline equivalence problem appears in the paper "Worst Case Analysis of Set Union Algorithms" by R. Tarjan and J. Leeuwen, *Journal of the ACM*, 31, 2, 1984, 245–281.

The Web site for this book develops some tree varieties not covered in the text—pairing heaps, interval heaps, tree structures for double-ended priority queues, tries, and suffix trees. You should look at these only after you have read Chapters 13 through 16.

CHAPTER 13

PRIORITY QUEUES

BIRD'S-EYE VIEW

Unlike the queues of Chapter 10, which are FIFO structures, the order of deletion from a priority queue is determined by the element priority. Elements are removed/deleted either in increasing or decreasing order of priority rather than in the order in which they arrived in the queue.

A priority queue is efficiently implemented with the heap data structure, which is a complete binary tree that is most efficiently stored by using the array-based representation described in Section 12.4.1. Linked data structures suitable for the implementation of a priority queue include height- and weight-biased leftist trees. This chapter covers both heaps and leftist trees. An additional priority queue data structure—pairing heaps—is developed in the Web site. The Web site also includes data structures for double-ended priority queues that allow you to delete both in increasing and in decreasing order of priority.

In the applications section at the end of the chapter, we use heaps to develop an $O(n \log n)$ sorting method called heap sort. The sort methods of Chapter 2 take $O(n^2)$ to sort n elements. Even though the bin sort and radix sort methods of Chapter 6 run in $O(n)$ time, they are limited to elements with keys in an appropriate range. So heap sort is the first general-purpose sort we are seeing that has a complexity better than $O(n^2)$. Chapter 19 discusses other sort methods with this complexity. From the asymptotic-complexity point of view, heap sort is an optimal sorting method because we can show that every general-purpose sorting method that relies on comparing pairs of elements has a complexity that is $\Omega(n \log n)$ (Section 19.4.2).

The other applications considered in this chapter are machine scheduling and the generation of Huffman codes. The machine-scheduling application allows us to introduce the NP-hard class of problems. This class includes problems for which no polynomial-time algorithms are known. As noted in Chapter 3, for large instances only polynomial-time algorithms are practical. As a result, NP-hard problems are often solved by approximation algorithms or heuristics that complete in a reasonable amount of computer time, but do not guarantee to find the best answer. For the machine-scheduling application, we use the heap data structure to obtain an efficient implementation of a much-studied machine-scheduling approximation algorithm.

13.1 DEFINITION AND APPLICATIONS

A **priority queue** is a collection of zero or more elements. Each element has a priority or value. The operations performed on a priority queue are (1) find an element, (2) insert a new element, and (3) remove (or delete) an element. In a **min priority queue**, the find operation finds the element with minimum priority, and the remove operation removes this element. In a **max priority queue**, the find operation finds the element with maximum priority, and the remove operation removes this element. The elements in a priority queue need not have distinct priorities. The find and remove operations may break ties in any manner.

Example 13.1 Suppose that we are selling the services of a machine over a fixed period of time (say, a day or a month). Although each user pays a fixed amount per use, the time needed by each user is different. To maximize the earning from this machine (under the assumption that the machine is not to be kept idle unless no user is available), we maintain a min priority queue of all users waiting for the machine. The priority of a user is the amount of time he/she needs. When a new user requests the machine, his/her request is put into the priority queue. Whenever the machine becomes available, the user with the smallest time requirement (i.e., priority) is selected.

   If each user needs the same amount of time on the machine but users are willing to pay different amounts for the service, then we can use a priority queue in which the element priorities are the amount of payment. Whenever the machine becomes available, the user paying the most is selected. This selection requires a max priority queue. ∎

Example 13.2 [Event List] The machine shop simulation problem was introduced in Section 10.5.4. The operations performed on the event queue are (1) find the machine with minimum finish time and (2) change the finish time of this machine. Suppose we set up a min priority queue in which each element represents a machine, and an element's priority is the finish time of the machine it represents. The *getMin* operation of a min priority queue gives us the machine with the smallest finish time. To change a machine's finish time, we may first do a *removeMin* and then reinsert the removed element with its priority changed to the new finish time. Actually, for event list applications we may extend the ADT min priority queue to include an operation to change the priority of the min element to a new value.

   Max priority queues may also be used in the machine shop simulation problem. In the simulation programs of Section 10.5.4, each machine served its set of waiting jobs in a first-come-first-served manner. Therefore, we used a FIFO queue at each machine. If the service discipline is changed to "when a machine is ready for a new job, it selects the waiting job with maximum priority," we need a max priority queue at each machine. The operations that are to be performed at each machine are (1) when a new job arrives at the machine, it is inserted into the max priority queue for that machine, and (2) when a machine is ready to work on a new job, a job with maximum priority is removed from its queue and made active.

When the service discipline at each machine is changed as above, the simulation problem of Section 10.5.4 requires a min priority queue for the event list and a max priority queue at each machine. ■

In this chapter we develop efficient representations for priority queues. Since the implementations for min and max priority queues are very similar, we explicitly develop only those for max priority queues.

13.2   THE ABSTRACT DATA TYPE

The abstract data type specification for a max priority queue is given in ADT 13.1. The specification for a min priority queue is the same except that $getMin$ and $removeMin$ operations replace the $getMax$ and $removeMax$ operations of a max priority queue.

AbstractDataType *MaxPriorityQueue*
{

    instances
        finite collection of elements, each has a priority

    operations
            $isEmpty()$: return `true` iff the queue is empty

                 $size()$: return number of elements in the queue

             $getMax()$: return element with maximum priority

                $put(x)$: insert the element x into the queue

        $removeMax()$: remove the element with largest priority from the queue
                      and return this element;

}

ADT 13.1 Abstract data type specification of a max priority queue

Program 13.1 gives the Java interface that corresponds to the ADT *MaxPriority-Queue*. This interface specification requires that the max priority queue elements be of type `Comparable` and that the `Comparable` interface methods are implemented to compare the priorities of two elements. Exercise 11 considers an alternative specification in which the priority is specified external to the element. In this case the `put` method has two parameters, `thePriority` and `theElement`, much like the `put` method for a dictionary (Program 11.1).

```
public interface MaxPriorityQueue
{
    public boolean isEmpty();
    public int size();
    public Comparable getMax();
    public void put(Comparable theObject);
    public Comparable removeMax();
}
```

Program 13.1 The interface `MaxPriorityQueue`

13.3   LINEAR LISTS

The simplest way to represent a max priority queue is as an unordered linear list. Suppose that we have a priority queue with n elements. If Equation 5.1 is used, new elements are most easily inserted at the right end of this list. Hence the insert or *put* time is $\Theta(1)$. A *removeMax* operation requires a search for the element with largest priority followed by the removal of this element. Since it takes $\Theta(n)$ time to find the largest element in an n-element unordered list, the removal time is $\Theta(n)$. If a chain is used, *puts* can be performed at the front of the chain in $\Theta(1)$ time. Each *removeMax* takes $\Theta(n)$ time.

An alternative is to use an ordered linear list. The elements are in nondecreasing order when we use Equation 5.1 and in nonincreasing order when we use an ordered chain. The *removeMax* time for each representation is $\Theta(1)$, and the *put* time is $O(n)$.

EXERCISES

1. Develop a Java class for the ADT *MaxPriorityQueue*, using an array-based linear list (i.e., use one of the classes developed in Section 5.3). The *put* time should be $\Theta(1)$, and the *getMax* and *removeMax* times should be $O(n)$, where n is the number of elements in the priority queue.

2. Do Exercise 1 using a chain (i.e., use the class `Chain` of Section 6.1).

3. Do Exercise 1 using a sorted array-based linear list. This time the *put* time should be $O(n)$, and the *removeMax* time should be $\Theta(1)$.

4. Do Exercise 1 using a modified version of the class `SortedChain` of Program 11.2. In the modifed version there is no explicit `key` field. Rather, elements are assumed to be of type `Comparable` and so may be compared against one another. Also, elements are in decreasing order rather than in

increasing order, and the chain may have several elements that have the same value.

5. Suppose that the priorities are integers in the range 1 through `maxPriority` where `maxPriority` is a small constant such as 3 or 4. Write a Java class that uses an array `priority[]` of queues; the queue `priority[i]` holds all elements whose priority is i. Include methods equivalent to the max priority queue operations. The *put* operation will have an additional parameter—the priority of the element being inserted. The class constructor should require that the value of `maxPriority` be specified, and the complexity of each ADT operation should be $\Theta(1)$ (exclusive of the time spent resizing arrays). Test your code.

13.4   HEAPS

13.4.1   Definitions

Definition 13.1 *A* **max tree** *(***min tree***) is a tree in which the value in each node is greater (less) than or equal to those in its children (if any).*   ■

Some max trees appear in Figure 13.1, and some min trees appear in Figure 13.2. Although these examples are all binary trees, it is not necessary for a max tree to be binary. Nodes of a max or min tree may have an arbitrary number of children.

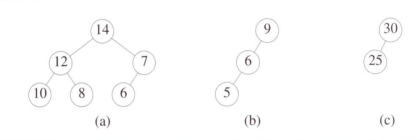

(a)   (b)   (c)

Figure 13.1 Max trees

Definition 13.2 *A* **max heap** *(***min heap***) is a max (min) tree that is also a complete binary tree.*   ■

The max tree of Figure 13.1(b) is not a max heap because it is not a complete binary tree. The other two max trees of Figure 13.1 are complete binary trees, so they are max heaps. The min tree of Figure 13.2(b) is not a min heap because it is not a complete binary tree. The other two min trees of Figure 13.2 are complete binary trees; therefore, these two min trees are min heaps.

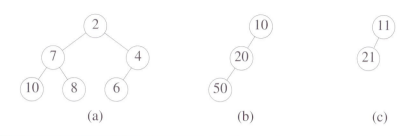

Figure 13.2 Min trees

Since a heap is a complete binary tree, a heap can be efficiently represented in a one-dimensional array by using the array-based scheme described in Section 12.4.1. We can use Property 12.4 to move from a node in the heap to its parent or to one of its children. Our subsequent discussion of heaps will refer to nodes in a heap by their position in the array representation. The position of the root is 1, that of its left child is 2, the root's right child is at 3, and so on. Also, note that since a heap is a complete binary tree, a heap with n elements has height $\lceil \log_2(n + 1) \rceil$. Consequently, if we can do the *put* and *removeMax* operations in time $O(height)$, then these operations will have complexity $O(\log n)$.

13.4.2 Insertion into a Max Heap

Figure 13.3(a) shows a max heap with five elements. When an element is added to this heap, the resulting six-element heap must have the structure shown in Figure 13.3(b) because a heap is a complete binary tree. The insertion can be completed by placing the new element into the new node and then bubbling the new element up the tree (along the path from the new node to the root) until the new element has a parent whose priority is $\geq$ that of the new element.

If the element to be inserted has value 1, it may be inserted as the left child of 2. If instead the value of the new element is 5, the element cannot be inserted as the left child of 2 (as otherwise, we will violate the max tree property). Therefore, the 2 is moved down to its left child (Figure 13.3(c)) (equivalently, 5 is bubbled up one node), and we determine whether placing the 5 at the old position of 2 results in a max heap. Since the parent element 20 is at least as large as the element 5 being inserted, we can insert the new element at the position shown in Figure 13.3(c). Next suppose that the new element has value 21, rather than 5. In this case the 2 moves down to its left child as in Figure 13.3(c). The 21 cannot be inserted into the old position occupied by the 2, as the parent 20 of this position is smaller than 21. Hence the 20 is moved down to its right child, and the 21 is inserted in the root of the heap (Figure 13.3(d)).

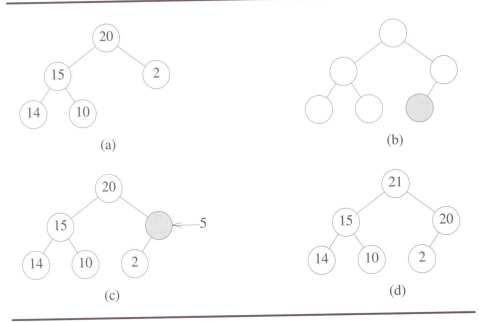

Figure 13.3 Insertion into a max heap

The insertion strategy just outlined makes a single bubbling pass from a leaf toward the root. At each level we do $\Theta(1)$ work, so we should be able to implement the strategy to have complexity $O(height) = O(\log n)$.

13.4.3 Deletion from a Max Heap

When an element is to be removed from a max heap, it is taken from the root of the heap. For instance, a removal from the max heap of Figure 13.3(d) results in the deletion of the element 21. Since the resulting max heap has only five elements, the binary tree of Figure 13.3(d) needs to be *reheapified* (i.e., restructured to correspond to a complete binary tree, which is a min tree with five elements). To do this reheapification, we remove the element in position 6, that is, the element 2. Now we have the right structure (Figure 13.4(a)), but the root is vacant, and the element 2 is not in the heap. If the 2 is put into the root, the resulting binary tree is not a max tree. The larger of the two children of the root (i.e., the element 20) is moved into the root, thereby creating a vacancy in position 3. Since this position has no children, the 2 may be put here. Figure 13.3(a) shows the resulting max heap.

Now suppose we wish to remove 20. Following this removal the heap has the binary tree structure shown in Figure 13.4(b). To get this structure, the 10 is removed from position 5. If we put the 10 into the root, the result is not a max

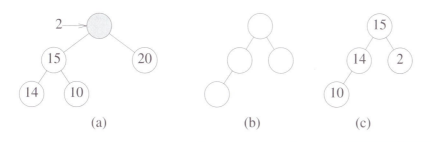

Figure 13.4 Removing the max element from a max heap

heap. The larger of the two children of the root (15 and 2) is moved to the root, and we attempt to insert the 10 into position 2. If the 10 is put here, the result is, again, not a max heap. So the 14 is moved up, and the 10 is put into position 4. The resulting heap is shown in Figure 13.4(c).

The *removeMax* strategy just outlined makes a single pass from the heap root down toward a leaf. At each level $\Theta(1)$ work is done, so we should be able to implement the strategy to have complexity $O(height) = O(\log n)$.

13.4.4   Max Heap Initialization

In several max heap applications, including the event list of the machine shop scheduling problem of Example 13.2, we begin with a heap that contains $n > 0$ elements. We can construct this initial nonempty heap by performing n *puts* into an initially empty heap. The total time taken by these n puts is $O(n \log n)$. We may initialize the heap in $\Theta(n)$ time by using a different strategy.

Suppose we begin with an array a of n elements. Assume that $n = 10$ and the priority of the elements in a[1:10] is [20, 12, 35, 15, 10, 80, 30, 17, 2, 1]. This array may be interpreted as representing a complete binary tree as shown in Figure 13.5(a). This complete binary tree is not a max heap.

To *heapify* (i.e., make into a max heap) the complete binary tree of Figure 13.5(a), we begin with the last element that has a child (i.e., 10). This element is at position $i = \lfloor n/2 \rfloor$ of the array. If the subtree that rooted at this position is a max heap, then no work is done here. If this subtree is not a max heap, then we adjust the subtree so that it is a heap. Following this adjustment, we examine the subtree whose root is at $i - 1$, then $i - 2$, and so on until we have examined the root of the entire binary tree, which is at position 1.

Let us try this process on the binary tree of Figure 13.5(a). Initially, $i = 5$. The subtree with root at i is a max heap, as $10 > 1$. Next we examine the subtree rooted at position 4. This subtree is not a max heap, as $15 < 17$. To convert this subtree into a max heap, the 15 and 17 are interchanged to get the tree of Figure 13.5(b). The next subtree examined has its root at position 3. To make this subtree into

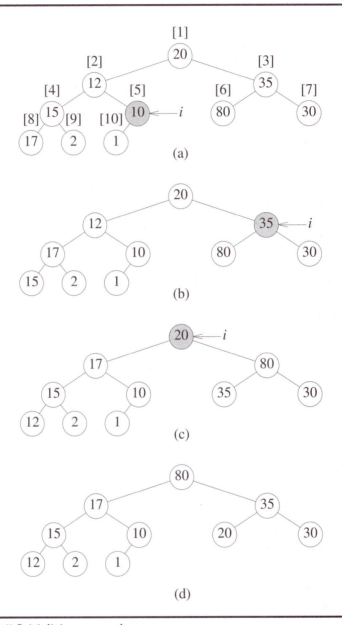

Figure 13.5 Initializing a max heap

a max heap, we interchange the 80 and 35. Next we examine the subtree with its root at position 2. From the way the restructuring progresses, the subtrees of this element are guaranteed to be max heaps. So restructuring this subtree into a max heap involves determining the larger of its two children, 17. As $12 < 17$, the 17 should be the root of the restructured subtree. Next we compare 12 with the larger of the two children of position 4. As $12 < 15$, the 15 is moved to position 4. The vacant position 8 has no children, and the 12 is inserted here. The resulting binary tree appears in Figure 13.5(c). Finally, we examine position 1. The subtrees with roots at positions 2 and 3 are max heaps at this time. However, $20 < \max\{17, 80\}$. So the 80 should be in the root of the max heap. When the 80 is moved there, it leaves a vacancy at position 3. Since $20 < \max\{35, 30\}$, position 3 is to be occupied by the 35. The 20 can now occupy position 6. Figure 13.5(d) shows the resulting max heap.

13.4.5   The Class MaxHeap

The class MaxHeap implements the interface MaxPriorityQueue. Its data members are heap (a one-dimensional array of type Comparable) and size (the number of elements in the heap). The getMax method returns null if the max heap is empty; otherwise, it returns the element heap[1]. The code for this method is omitted. The codes for put (Program 13.2) and removeMax (Program 13.3) mirror the discussion of Sections 13.4.2 and 13.4.3.

In the code to put an element into the max heap, we start currentNode at the newly created leaf position size of the heap and traverse the path from here to the root. We essentially bubble theElement up the tree until it reaches its proper place. At each positioning of currentNode, we check to see whether we are at the root (currentNode $= 1$) or whether the insertion of the new element theElement at currentNode does not violate the max tree property (theElement $\leq$ heap[currentNode/2]). If either of these conditions holds, we can put theElement at position currentNode. Otherwise, we enter the body of the while loop, move the element at currentNode/2 down to currentNode, and advance currentNode up to its parent (currentNode/2). For a max heap with n elements (i.e., size $= n$), the number of iterations of the while loop is $O(height) = O(\log n)$, and each iteration takes $\Theta(1)$ time. Therefore, the complexity of put is $O(\log n)$.

For a removeMax operation the maximum element, which is in the root (heap[1]), is saved in maxElement; the element in the last heap position (heap[size]) is saved in lastElement; and the heap size (size) is reduced by 1. In the while loop we reheapify the array. The reheapification process requires us to find the proper place to reinsert lastElement. The search for this proper place begins at the root and proceeds down the heap. For an n-element heap, the number of iterations of the while loop is $O(\log n)$, and each iteration takes $\Theta(1)$ time. Therefore, the overall complexity of removeMax is $O(\log n)$. Notice that the code works correctly even when the size of the heap following the deletion is 0. In this case the while loop is not entered, and a redundant assignment to position 1 of the heap is made.

```
public void put(Comparable theElement)
{
    // increase array size if necessary
    if (size == heap.length - 1)
        heap = (Comparable []) ChangeArrayLength.changeLength1D
                                (heap, 2 * heap.length);

    // find place for theElement
    // currentNode starts at new leaf and moves up tree
    int currentNode = ++size;
    while (currentNode != 1 &&
           heap[currentNode / 2].compareTo(theElement) < 0)
    {
        // cannot put theElement in heap[currentNode]
        heap[currentNode] = heap[currentNode / 2]; // move element down
        currentNode /= 2;                          // move to parent
    }

    heap[currentNode] = theElement;
}
```

Program 13.2 Putting an element into a max heap

The method `initialize` (Program 13.4) heapifies the array `theHeap` by first assigning `theHeap` to `heap`. `theSize` is the number of elements in `theHeap`. In the `for` loop of Program 13.4, we begin at the last node in the binary tree interpretation of the array `heap` (now equivalent to the array `theHeap`) that has a child and work our way to the root. At each positioning of the variable `root`, the embedded `while` loop ensures that the subtree rooted at `root` is a max heap. Notice the similarity between the body of the `for` loop and the code for `removeMax` (Program 13.3).

Complexity of initialize

If the number of elements is n (i.e., `theSize` $= n$), each iteration of the `for` loop of `initialize` (Program 13.4) takes $O(\log n)$ time and the number of iterations is $n/2$. So the complexity of `initialize` is $O(n \log n)$. Recall that the big oh notation provides only an upper bound on the complexity of an algorithm. Consequently, the complexity of `initialize` could be better. A more careful analysis allows us to conclude that its complexity is actually $\Theta(n)$.

Each iteration of the `while` loop of `initialize` takes $O(h_i)$ time where h_i is the height of the subtree with root i. The complete binary tree `theHeap`$[1 : n]$ has

```
public Comparable removeMax()
{
   // if heap is empty return null
   if (size == 0) return null;        // heap empty

   Comparable maxElement = heap[1];  // max element

   // reheapify
   Comparable lastElement = heap[size--];

   // find place for lastElement starting at root
   int currentNode = 1,
       child = 2;       // child of currentNode
   while (child <= size)
   {
      // heap[child] should be larger child of currentNode
      if (child < size &&
          heap[child].compareTo(heap[child + 1]) < 0) child++;

      // can we put lastElement in heap[currentNode]?
      if (lastElement.compareTo(heap[child]) >= 0)
         break;    // yes

      // no
      heap[currentNode] = heap[child]; // move child up
      currentNode = child;             // move down a level
      child *= 2;
   }
   heap[currentNode] = lastElement;

   return maxElement;
}
```

Program 13.3 Removing the max element from a max heap

height $h = \lceil \log_2(n+1) \rceil$. It has at most 2^{j-1} nodes at level j. Hence at most 2^{j-1} of the is have $h_i = h - j + 1$. The time to initialize the max heap is therefore:

$$O(\sum_{j=1}^{h-1} 2^{j-1}(h-j+1)) = O(\sum_{k=2}^{h} k2^{h-k}) = O(2^h \sum_{k=2}^{h} (k/2^k)) = O(2^h) = O(n)$$

```java
public void initialize(Comparable [] theHeap, int theSize)
{
   heap = theHeap;
   size = theSize;

   // heapify
   for (int root = size / 2; root >= 1; root--)
   {
      Comparable rootElement = heap[root];

      // find place to put rootElement
      int child = 2 * root; // parent of child is target
                            // location for rootElement
      while (child <= size)
      {
         // heap[child] should be larger sibling
         if (child < size &&
             heap[child].compareTo(heap[child + 1]) < 0) child++;

         // can we put rootElement in heap[child/2]?
         if (rootElement.compareTo(heap[child]) >= 0)
            break;  // yes

         // no
         heap[child / 2] = heap[child]; // move child up
         child *= 2;                    // move down a level
      }
      heap[child / 2] = rootElement;
   }
}
```

Program 13.4 Initialize a nonempty max heap

This derivation uses the identity (Exercise 10)

$$\sum_{k=1}^{m} \frac{k}{2^k} = 2 - \frac{m+2}{2^m} \tag{13.1}$$

Since the for loop goes through $n/2$ iterations, the complexity is also $\Omega(n)$. Combining these two bounds, we get $\Theta(n)$ as the complexity of initialize.

EXERCISES

6. Consider the array theHeap = [3, 5, 6, 7, 20, 8, 2, 9, 12, 15, 30, 17].

   (a) Draw the corresponding complete binary tree.

   (b) Heapify the tree by using the method of Program 13.4. Show the result in both tree and array format.

   (c) Now insert the elements 15, 20, and 45 (in this order) using the bubbling up process of Program 13.2. Show the max heap following each insert.

   (d) Perform four remove max operations on the max heap of part (c). Use the remove method of Program 13.3. Show the max heap following each remove.

7. Do Exercise 6 beginning with the array [10, 2, 7, 6, 5, 9, 12, 35, 22, 15, 1, 3, 4].

8. Do Exercise 6 beginning with the array [1, 2, 3, 4, 5, 6, 7, 8, 9, 10, 12, 15, 22, 35].

9. Do Exercise 6 under the assumption that you are to have a min heap. The initial array is [30, 17, 20, 15, 10, 12, 5, 7, 8, 5, 2, 9]. For part (b) insert 1, 10, 6, and 4. For part (d) perform three remove min operations.

10. Use induction on m to prove Equation 13.1.

11. (a) Rewrite the ADT *MaxPriorityQueue* so that the form of the *put* operation is $put(p, x)$ where p is the priority (or key) of the element x that is to be inserted into the max heap.

    (b) Develop a Java interface that corresponds to the ADT specification of (a). Heap elements and priorities are of type Object.

    (c) Develop a max heap class that implements the interface of (b). Each element in the heap array will be of type HeapElement, which has data members key (of type Comparable) and element (of type Object).

    (d) Test the correctness of your code.

12. Extend the class MaxHeap by adding a public member changeMax(newElement) that changes the current maximum element to newElement. newElement may have a value that is either smaller or larger than the current priority of the element in heap[1]. Your code should follow a downward path from the root, as is done in the removeMax method. In case the max heap is currently empty, you should throw an IllegalArgumentException. The complexity of your code should be $O(\log n)$ where n is the number of elements in the max heap. Show that this is the case. Test the correctness of your code.

13. Extend the class `MaxHeap` by adding a public member `remove(i)` that removes and returns the element in `heap[i]`. The complexity of your code should be $O(\log n)$ where n is the number of elements in the max heap. Show that this is the case. Test the correctness of your code.

14. Develop an iterator for the class `MaxHeap`. You may enumerate the elements in any order. The time taken to enumerate the elements of an n-element max heap should be $O(n)$. Show that this is the case. Test the correctness of your code.

15. Since the element `y` that is reinserted into the max heap during a `removeMax` (see Program 13.3) was removed from the bottom of the heap, we expect to reinsert it near the bottom. Write a new version of `removeMax` in which the vacancy in the root is first moved down to a leaf, and then the place for `y` is determined making an upward pass from this leaf. Experiment with the new code to see whether it works faster than the old one.

16. Rewrite the methods of `MaxHeap` under the following assumptions:

    (a) When a heap is created, the creator provides two elements `maxElement` and `minElement`; no element in the heap is larger than `maxElement` or smaller than `minElement`.

    (b) A heap with n elements requires an array `heap[0:2n+1]`.

    (c) The n elements are stored in `heap[1:n]` as described in this section.

    (d) `maxElement` is stored in `heap[0]`.

    (e) `minElement` is stored in `heap[n+1:2n+1]`.

    These assumptions should simplify the codes for `put` and `removeMax`. Conduct experiments to compare the implementation of this section with the one of this exercise.

17. A d-heap is a complete tree whose degree is d. Develop the class `MaxDHeap` which implements the interface `MaxPriorityQueue` using a d-heap. Compare the performance of your implementation with that of `MaxHeap` for $d = 2$, 3, and 4.

18. Do Exercise 12 for the class `MaxDHeap` (see Exercise 17).

13.5   LEFTIST TREES

13.5.1   Height- and Weight-Biased Min and Max Leftist Trees

The heap structure of Section 13.4 is an example of an **implicit data structure**. The complete binary tree representing the heap is stored implicitly (i.e., there are no explicit pointers or other explicit data from which the structure may be deduced) in an array. Since no explicit structural information is stored, the representation is very space efficient; in fact, there is no space overhead. Despite the heap structure being both space and time efficient, it is not suitable for all applications of priority queues. In particular, applications in which we wish to meld (i.e., combine or blend) pairs of priority queues, as well as those in which we have multiple queues of varying size, require a different data structure. Leftist tree structures are suitable for these applications.

Consider a binary tree in which a special node called an **external node** replaces each empty subtree. The remaining nodes are called **internal nodes**. A binary tree with external nodes added is called an **extended binary tree**. Figure 13.6(a) shows a binary tree. Its corresponding extended binary tree is shown in Figure 13.6(b). The external nodes appear as shaded boxes. These nodes have been labeled a through f for convenience.

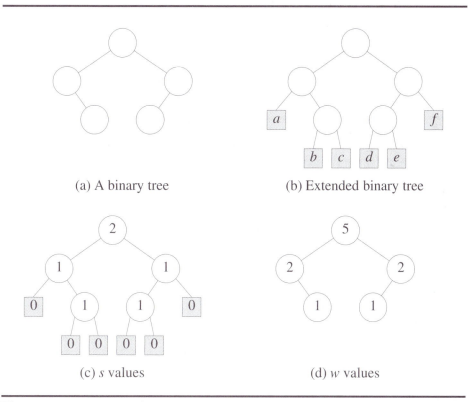

(a) A binary tree   (b) Extended binary tree

(c) s values   (d) w values

Figure 13.6 s and w values

Let $s(x)$ be the length of a shortest path from node x to an external node in its subtree. From the definition of $s(x)$, it follows that if x is an external node, its s value is 0. Furthermore, if x is an internal node, its s value is

$$\min\{s(L), s(R)\} + 1$$

where L and R are, respectively, the left and right children of x. The s values for the nodes of the extended binary tree of Figure 13.6(b) appear in Figure 13.6(c).

Definition 13.3 *A binary tree is a* **height-biased leftist tree (HBLT)** *iff at every internal node, the s value of the left child is greater than or equal to the s value of the right child.* ■

The binary tree of Figure 13.6(a) is not an HBLT. To see this, consider the parent of the external node a. The s value of its left child is 0, while that of its right is 1. All other internal nodes satisfy the requirements of the HBLT definition. By swapping the left and right subtrees of the parent of a, the binary tree of Figure 13.6(a) becomes an HBLT.

Theorem 13.1 *Let x be any internal node of an HBLT.*

(a) The number of nodes in the subtree with root x is at least $2^{s(x)} - 1$.

(b) If the subtree with root x has m nodes, $s(x)$ is at most $\log_2(m + 1)$.

(c) The length of the right-most path from x to an external node (i.e., the path obtained by beginning at x and making a sequence of right-child moves) is $s(x)$.

Proof From the definition of $s(x)$, it follows that there are no external nodes on the $s(x) - 1$ levels immediately below node x (as otherwise the s value of x would be less). The subtree with root x has exactly one node on the level at which x is, two on the next level, four on the next, $\cdots$, and $2^{s(x)-1}$ nodes $s(x) - 1$ levels below x. The subtree may have additional nodes at levels more than $s(x) - 1$ below x. Hence the number of nodes in the subtree x is at least $\sum_{i=0}^{s(x)-1} 2^i = 2^{s(x)} - 1$. Part (b) follows from (a). Part (c) follows from the definition of s and the fact that, in an HBLT, the s value of the left child of a node is always greater than or equal to that of the right child. ■

Definition 13.4 *A* **max HBLT** *is an HBLT that is also a max tree. A* **min HBLT** *is an HBLT that is also a min tree.* ■

The max trees of Figure 13.1 as well as the min trees of Figure 13.2 are also HBLTs; therefore, the trees of Figure 13.1 are max HBLTs, and those of Figure 13.2 are min HBLTs. A max priority queue may be represented as a max HBLT, and a min priority queue may be represented as a min HBLT.

We arrive at another variety of leftist tree by considering the number of nodes in a subtree, rather than the length of a shortest root to external node path. Define the weight $w(x)$ of node x to be the number of internal nodes in the subtree with root x. Notice that if x is an external node, its weight is 0. If x is an internal node, its weight is 1 more than the sum of the weights of its children. The weights of the nodes of the binary tree of Figure 13.6(a) appear in Figure 13.6(d)

Definition 13.5 *A binary tree is a* **weight-biased leftist tree (WBLT)** *iff at every internal node the w value of the left child is greater than or equal to the w value of the right child. A max (min) WBLT is a max (min) tree that is also a WBLT.* ∎

As was the case for HBLTs, the length of the right-most path in a WBLT that has m nodes is at most $\log_2(m+1)$. Using either WBLTs or HBLTs, we can perform the priority queue operations find, insert, and delete in the same asymptotic time as heaps take. Like heaps, WBLTs and HBLTs may be initialized in linear time. Two priority queues represented as WBLTs or HBLTs can be melded into one in logarithmic time. When priority queues are represented as heaps, they cannot be melded in logarithmic time.

The way in which finds, inserts, deletes, melds, and initializations are done in WBLTs and HBLTs is similar. Consequently, we describe these operations for HBLTs only and leave the adaptation of these methods to WBLTs as an exercise (Exercise 24).

13.5.2 Insertion into a Max HBLT

The insertion operation for max HBLTs may be performed by using the max HBLT meld operation. Suppose we are to insert an element x into the max HBLT H. If we create a max HBLT with the single element x and then meld this max HBLT and H, the resulting max HBLT will include all elements in H as well as the element x. Hence an insertion may be performed by creating a new max HBLT with just the element that is to be inserted and then melding this max HBLT and the original.

13.5.3 Deletion from a Max HBLT

The max element is in the root. If the root is deleted, two max HBLTs, the left and right subtrees of the root, remain. By melding together these two max HBLTs, we obtain a max HBLT that contains all elements in the original max HBLT other than the deleted max element. So the delete max operation may be performed by deleting the root and then melding its two subtrees.

13.5.4 Melding Two Max HBLTs

Since the length of the right-most path of an HBLT with n elements is $O(\log n)$, a meld algorithm that traverses only the right-most paths of the HBLTs being melded, spending $O(1)$ time at each node on these two paths, will have complexity logarithmic in the number of elements in the resulting HBLT. With this observation in mind, we develop a meld algorithm that begins at the roots of the two HBLTs and makes right-child moves only.

The meld strategy is best described using recursion. Let A and B be the two max HBLTs that are to be melded. If one is empty, then we may use the other as the result. So assume that neither is empty. To perform the meld, we compare the elements in the two roots. The root with the larger element becomes the root of the melded HBLT. Ties may be broken arbitrarily. Suppose that A has the larger root and that its left subtree is L. Let C be the max HBLT that results from melding the right subtree of A and the max HBLT B. The result of melding A and B is the max HBLT that has A as its root and L and C as its subtrees. If the s value of L is smaller than that of C, then C is the left subtree. Otherwise, L is.

Example 13.3 Consider the two max HBLTs of Figure 13.7(a). The s value of a node is shown outside the node, while the element value is shown inside. When drawing two max HBLTs that are to be melded, we will always draw the one with larger root value on the left. Ties are broken arbitrarily. Because of this convention, the root of the left HBLT always becomes the root of the final HBLT. Also, we will shade the nodes of the HBLT on the right.

Since the right subtree of 9 is empty, the result of melding this subtree of 9 and the tree with root 7 is just the tree with root 7. We make the tree with root 7 the right subtree of 9 temporarily to get the max tree of Figure 13.7(b). Since the s value of the left subtree of 9 is 0 while that of its right subtree is 1, the left and right subtrees are swapped to get the max HBLT of Figure 13.7(c).

Next consider melding the two max HBLTs of Figure 13.7(d). The root of the left subtree becomes the root of the result. When the right subtree of 10 is melded with the HBLT with root 7, the result is just this latter HBLT. If this HBLT is made the right subtree of 10, we get the max tree of Figure 13.7(e). Comparing the s values of the left and right children of 10, we see that a swap is not neccessary.

Now consider melding the two max HBLTs of Figure 13.7(f). The root of the left subtree is the root of the result. We proceed to meld the right subtree of 18 and the max HBLT with root 10. The two max HBLTs being melded are the same as those melded in Figure 13.7(d). The resultant max HBLT (Figure 13.7(e)) becomes the right subtree of 18, and the max tree of Figure 13.7(g) results. Comparing the s values of the left and right subtrees of 18, we see that these subtrees must be swapped. Swapping results in the max HBLT of Figure 13.7(h).

As a final example, consider melding the two max HBLTs of Figure 13.7(i). The root of the left max HBLT becomes the root of the result. We proceed to meld the right subtree of 40 and the max HBLT with root 18. These max HBLTs were melded in Figure 13.7(f). The resultant max HBLT (Figure 13.7(g)) becomes the right subtree of 40. Since the left subtree of 40 has a smaller s value than the right has, the two subtrees are swapped to get the max HBLT of Figure 13.7(k). Notice that when melding the max HBLTs of Figure 13.7(i), we first move to the right

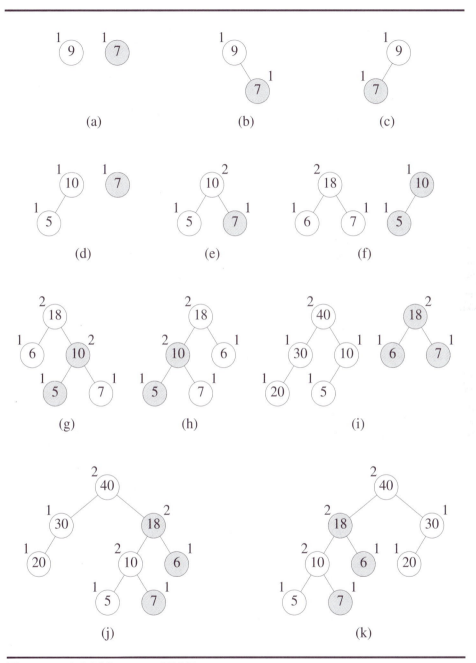

Figure 13.7 Melding max HBLTs

child of 40, then to the right child of 18, and finally to the right child of 10. All moves follow the right-most paths of the initial max HBLTs.   ■

13.5.5   Initialization

It takes $O(n \log n)$ time to initialize a max HBLT with n elements by inserting these elements into an initially empty max HBLT one at a time. To get a linear time initialization algorithm, we begin by creating n max HBLTs with each containing one of the n elements. These n max HBLTs are placed on a FIFO queue. Then max HBLTs are deleted from this queue in pairs, melded, and added to the end of the queue until only one max HBLT remains.

Example 13.4 We wish to create a max HBLT with the five elements 7, 1, 9, 11, and 2. Five single-element max HBLTs are created and placed in a FIFO queue. The first two, 7 and 1, are deleted from the queue and melded. The result (Figure 13.8(a)) is added to the queue. Next the max HBLTs 9 and 11 are deleted from the queue and melded. The result appears in Figure 13.8(b). This max HBLT is added to the queue. Now the max HBLT 2 and that of Figure 13.8(a) are deleted from the queue and melded. The resulting max HBLT (Figure 13.8(c)) is added to the queue. The next pair to be deleted from the queue consists of the max HBLTs of Figures Figure 13.8 (b) and (c). These HBLTs are melded to get the max HBLT of Figure 13.8(d). This max HBLT is added to the queue. The queue now has just one max HBLT, and we are done with the initialization.   ■

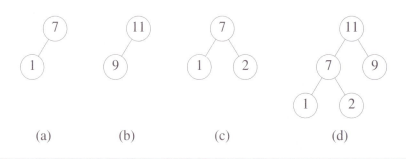

(a)   (b)   (c)   (d)

Figure 13.8 Initializing a max HBLT

13.5.6   The Class `MaxHBLT`

The data type of each node of a max HBLT is `HbltNode`; and each node has the fields `element`, `leftChild`, `rightChild`, and `s`. Max HBLTs may be implemented as the class `MaxHblt` whose data members are `root`, which is of type `HbltNode`, and size, which is of type `int`. `root` points to the root of the max HBLT, and `size` gives the number of elements in the max HBLT.

The class `MaxHblt` has only the default constructor, which takes no parameters. Therefore, when a max HBLT is created, the values of `root` and `size` are, respectively, `null` and 0. For compatibility with the class `MaxHeap`, we can provide a constructor with a single integer parameter and an empty body. Providing such a constructor would make the two max priority queue classes interchangeable. The code for the elementary methods `isEmpty`, `size`, and `getMax` of `MaxHblt` is very similar to the code for the corresponding methods of `MaxHeap`.

Since the `put`, `removeMax`, and `intialize` methods of `MaxHblt` use the meld operation, let us examine the meld operation first. The public method `meld(MaxHblt x)` melds the two max HBLTs `this` and `x` and returns the resulting max HBLT. This method accomplishes its task by invoking a private method `meld(HbltNode x, HbltNode y)` (Program 13.5) that recursively melds the max HBLTs whose roots are `x` and `y` and returns the root of the resulting max HBLT.

The private meld method given in Program 13.5 begins by handling the special case when at least one of the trees being melded is empty. When neither tree is empty, we make sure that node `x` has the larger element (i.e., the tree with larger root is on the left). If the element in `x` is not larger than that in `y`, the `x` and `y` values are swapped. Next the right subtree of `x` and the max HBLT with root `y` are melded recursively. Following this meld, `x` is the root of a max tree whose left and right subtrees may need to be swapped so as to ensure that the entire tree is, in fact, a max HBLT. This swapping is done, if necessary, and the `s` value of `x` is computed.

To put an element `x` into a max HBLT, the code of Program 13.6 creates a max HBLT with the single element `x` and then uses the private method `meld` to meld this tree and the original one. A reference to the resulting max HBLT is returned.

The code for `removeMax` (Program 13.6) returns `null` in case the max HBLT is empty. When the max HBLT is not empty, the element in the root is saved, the left and right subtrees of the root are melded to get the max HBLT that reults from the removal of the root element, and the saved element originally in the root is returned.

The max HBLT initialization code is given in Program 13.7. An array-based FIFO queue holds the intermediate max HBLTs created by the initialization algorithm. In the first `for` loop, `size` single-element max HBLTs are created and added to an initially empty queue. In the next `for` loop, pairs of max HBLTs are deleted from the queue, melded, and the result added to the queue. When this `for` loop terminates, the queue contains a single max HBLT (provided `size > 0`), which includes all `size` elements.

Complexity Analysis

The complexity of the `getMax` method is $\Theta(1)$. The complexity of `put`, `removeMax`, and the public method `meld` is the same as that of the private method `meld`. Since

```
public void initialize(Comparable [] theElements, int theSize)
{
   size = theSize;
   ArrayQueue q = new ArrayQueue(size);
   // initialize queue of trees
   for (int i = 1; i <= size; i++)
      // create trees with one node each
      q.put(new HbltNode(theElements[i], 1));

   // repeatedly meld from queue q
   for (int i = 1; i <= size - 1; i++)
   {  // remove and meld two trees from the queue
      HbltNode b = (HbltNode) q.remove();
      HbltNode c = (HbltNode) q.remove();
      b = meld(b, c);
      // put melded tree on queue
      q.put(b);
   }

   if (size > 0)
      root = (HbltNode) q.remove();
}
```

Program 13.7 Initializing a max HBLT

For the complexity analysis of `initialize`, assume, for simplicity, that $n =$ `size` is a power of 2. The first $n/2$ melds involve max HBLTs with one element each, the next $n/4$ melds involve max HBLTs with two elements each; the next $n/8$ melds are with trees that have four elements each; and so on. The time needed to meld two trees with 2^i elements each is $O(i + 1)$, and so the total time taken by `initialize` is

$$O(n/2 + 2 * (n/4) + 3 * (n/8) + \cdots) = O(n \sum \frac{i}{2^i}) = O(n)$$

EXERCISES

19. Consider the array `theElements` = [3, 5, 6, 7, 20, 8, 2, 9, 12, 15, 30, 17].

    (a) Draw the max leftist tree created by Program 13.7.

(b) Now insert the elements 10, 18, 11, and 4 (in this order) using the insert method of Program 13.6. Show the max leftist tree following each insert.

(c) Perform three remove max operations on the max leftist tree of part (c). Use the remove method of Program 13.6. Show the max leftist tree following each remove.

20. Do Exercise 19 beginning with the element array [10, 2, 7, 6, 5, 9, 12, 35, 22, 15, 1, 3, 4].

21. Write the code for the class `MinHblt`. This class differs from the class `MaxHblt` only in that class members are now min HBLTs rather than max HBLTs. The operations `getMin` and `removeMin` replace the operations `getMax` and `removeMax`.

22. Develop an iterator for the class `MaxHblt`. You may enumerate the elements in any order. The complexity of each of your iterator methods should be $O(1)$. Show that this is the case. Test the correctness of your code.

23. Develop the class `MaxHbltWithRemoveNode` that implements the interface `MaxPriorityQueue` and includes the additional public methods `putAndReturnNode` and `removeElementInNode`. The method `putAndReturnNode(theElement)` puts `theElement` into the leftist tree and returns the node into which the element was put; the method `removeElementInNode(theNode)` removes and returns the element in `theNode`; the node `theNode` is also removed from the tree. *Hint:* add a parent field to each node. The complexity of the methods that are common to `MaxHblt` should be the same as that of the corresponding methods of `MaxHblt`, and the complexity of the new methods should be $O(\log n)$ where n is the number of elements in the leftist tree. Show that this is the case. Test the correctness of your code.

24. [Max WBLTs]

(a) Which (if any) of the binary trees of Figure 13.1 are WBLTs?

(b) Let x be a node in a WBLT. Use induction on $w(x)$ to show that the length of the right-most path from x to an external node is at most $\log_2(w(x) + 1)$.

(c) Develop the class `WbltNode` to represent the nodes of a weight-biased leftist tree. Each class member has the fields `w` (weight), `element`, `leftChild`, and `rightChild`.

(d) Develop the class `MaxWblt` as one whose objects are max WBLTs. Your class should include all the methods of `MaxHblt`. Your code for these methods should have the same asymptotic complexity as the corresponding codes for `MaxHblt`. Write the code for the private method `meld` without using recursion. Note that since the `w` value of a node can be

13.6.2   Machine Scheduling

Consider a machine shop that has m identical machines. We have n jobs that need to be processed. The processing time required by job i is t_i. This time includes the time needed to set up and remove the job on/from a machine. A **schedule** is an assignment of jobs to time intervals on machines such that

- No machine processes more than one job at any time.

- No job is processed by more than one machine at any time.

- Each job i is assigned for a total of t_i units of processing.

Each machine is assumed to be available at time 0. The **finish time** or **length** of a schedule is the time at which all jobs have completed. In a nonpreemptive schedule, each job i is processed by a single machine from some start time s_i to its completion time $s_i + t_i$. We will concern ourselves only with nonpreemptive schedules.

Figure 13.10 shows a three-machine schedule for seven jobs with processing requirements (2, 14, 4, 16, 6, 5, 3). The machines are labeled M1, M2, and M3. Each shaded area represents the duration for which a job is scheduled. The number inside the area is the job index. Job 4 is scheduled on machine 1 (M1) from time 0 to time 16. In these 16 units of time, machine 1 completes the processing of job 4. The schedule for machine 2 is do job 2 from time 0 to time 14 and then do job 7 from time 14 to 17. On machine 3 job 5 is done from 0 to 6, job 6 from 6 to 11, job 3 from 11 to 15, and job 1 from 15 to 17. Notice that each job i is processed on a single machine from a start time s_i to a finish time $s_i + t_i$ and that no machine works on more than one job at any time. The time at which all jobs have completed is 17. So the schedule finish time or length is 17.

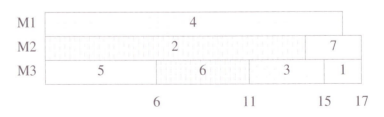

Figure 13.10 A three-machine schedule

The schedule of Figure 13.10 is a minimum-finish-time schedule for the given processing requirements. To see this, note the sum of the processing times is 50. Therefore, every three-machine schedule will take at least $\lceil 50/3 \rceil = 17$ time units to complete the jobs.

Our task is to write a program that constructs a minimum-finish-time m-machine schedule for a given set of n jobs. Constructing such a schedule is very hard. In fact, no one has ever developed a polynomial time algorithm (i.e., an algorithm whose complexity is $O(n^k m^l)$ for any constants k and l) to construct a minimum-finish-time schedule.

The scheduling problem we have just defined is a member of the infamous class of NP-hard (NP stands for **nondeterministic polynomial**) problems. The NP-hard and NP-complete problem classes contain problems for which no one has developed a polynomial-time algorithm. The problems in the class NP-complete are decision problems. That is, for each problem instance the answer is either yes or no. Our machine-scheduling problem is not a decision problem, as the answer for each instance is an assignment of jobs to machines such that the finish time is minimum. We may formulate a related machine-scheduling problem in which, in addition to the tasks and machines, we are given a time $TMin$ and are asked to determine whether or not there is a schedule with finish time $TMin$ or less. For this related problem, the answer to each instance is either yes or no. This related problem is a decision problem that is NP-complete. NP-hard problems may or may not be decision problems.

Thousands of problems of practical interest are NP-hard or NP-complete. If anyone discovers a polynomial-time algorithm for an NP-hard or NP-complete problem, then he/she would have simultaneously discovered a way to solve all NP-complete problems in polynomial time. Although we are unable to prove that NP-complete problems cannot be solved in polynomial time, common wisdom very strongly suggests that this is the case. As a result, optimization problems that are NP-hard are often solved by **approximation algorithms**. Although approximation algorithms do not guarantee to obtain optimal solutions, they guarantee solutions "close" to optimal.

In the case of our scheduling problem, we can generate schedules whose lengths are at most $4/3 - 1/(3m)$ of optimal by employing a simple scheduling strategy called **longest processing time** (LPT). In LPT, jobs are assigned to machines in descending order of their processing time requirements t_i. When a job is being assigned to a machine, it is assigned to the machine that becomes idle first. Ties are broken arbitrarily.

For the job set example in Figure 13.10, we may construct an LPT schedule by first sorting the jobs into descending order of processing times. The job order is $(4, 2, 5, 6, 3, 7, 1)$. First, job 4 is assigned to a machine. Since all three machines become available at time 0, job 4 may be assigned to any machine. Suppose we assign it to machine 1. Now machine 1 is unavailable until time 16. Job 2 is next assigned; we can assign it to either machine 2 or 3, as both become available at the same time (i.e., time 0). Assume that we assign job 2 to machine 2. Now machine 2 is unavailable until time 14. Next we assign job 5 to machine 3 from time 0 to time 6. Job 6 is to be assigned next. The first available machine is machine 3. It becomes available at time 6. Following the assignment of job 6 from time 6 to time

11 on this machine, the availability time of machine 3 becomes 11. Job 3 is next considered for scheduling. The first machine to become available is machine 3 at time 11; we assign job 3 to this machine. Continuing in this way, we obtain the schedule of Figure 13.10.

Theorem 13.2 [Graham] *Let $F^*(I)$ be the finish time of an optimal m-machine schedule for a job set I and let $F(I)$ be the finish time of the LPT schedule for this job set. Then*

$$\frac{F(I)}{F^*(I)} \leq \frac{4}{3} - \frac{1}{3m}$$

In practice, LPT schedules are often much closer to optimal than suggested by the bound of Theorem 13.2. In fact, as noted above, the LPT schedule of Figure 13.10 is optimal.

LPT schedules can be constructed in $O(n \log n)$ time by using heaps. First we notice that when $n \leq m$, we need merely assign job i to machine i from time 0 to t_i. When $n > m$, we begin by sorting the jobs into ascending order of processing times using `heapSort` (Program 13.8). To construct the LPT schedule, the jobs are assigned in reverse order. To determine which machine a job is to be assigned to, we need to determine which machine becomes available first. To make this determination, we maintain a min heap of the m machines. Each element on this min heap is of type `MachineNode`, which has the data members `avail` (the time at which the machine becomes available) and `id` (the machine identifier). Since machine nodes are to be put into a min heap, `MachineNode` must implement the interface `Comparable`. This implementation of `Comparable` is done by using the `avail` field.

A `removeMin` is used to extract the machine that becomes available first. The machine's availability time is increased, and the machine is inserted back into the min heap. This min heap is initialized by inserting a node for each machine. Since all machines are initially available at time 0, the `avail` value for each of these machines is 0.

The jobs are represented using the class `JobNode`, which has the data member `id` (the job's unique identifier) and `time` (the processing requirements of the job). Since we will be sorting jobs using `heapSort` and since `heapSort` uses a max heap, `JobNode` must implement the interface `Comparable`. This implementation of `Comparable` uses the `time` field.

Program 13.9 gives the code to sort jobs by their processing times and then schedule them on `m` machines using the LPT method.

Complexity Analysis of `makeSchedule`

Let $n = $ `a.length` - 1 denote the number of jobs to be scheduled. When $n \leq$ `m`, `makeSchedule` takes $\Theta(1)$ time. When $n >$ `m`, the heap sort takes $O(n \log n)$ time.

```
public static void makeSchedule(JobNode [] a, int m)
{
   if (a.length <= m)
   {
      System.out.println("Schedule each job on a different machine.");
      return;
   }

   HeapSort.heapSort(a); // in ascending order

   // initialize m machines and the min heap
   MinHeap machineHeap = new MinHeap(m);
   for (int i = 1; i <= m; i++)
   {
      MachineNode x = new MachineNode(i, (Operable) a[1].time.zero());
      machineHeap.put(x);
   }

   // construct schedule
   for (int i = a.length - 1; i >= 1; i--)
   {// schedule job i on first free machine
      MachineNode x = (MachineNode) machineHeap.removeMin();
      System.out.println("Schedule job " + a[i].id
            + " on machine " + x.id + " from " + x.avail
            + " to " + x.avail.add(a[i].time));
      x.avail.increment(a[i].time);  // new available time
      machineHeap.put(x);
   }
}
```

Program 13.9 Output an LPT schedule for a[1:a.length-1]

The heap initialization takes $O(m)$ time, even though we are doing m inserts, because all elements have the same value; therefore, each insert actually takes only $\Theta(1)$ time. In the second **for** loop, n removeMin and n put operations are performed. Each takes $O(\log m)$ time. So the second **for** loop takes $O(n \log m)$ time. The total time is therefore $O(n \log n + n \log m) = O(n \log n)$ (as $n > m$).

13.6.3 Huffman Codes

In Section 11.6 we developed a text compressor based on the LZW method. This method relies on the recurrence of substrings in a text. Another approach to text compression, **Huffman codes**, relies on the relative frequency with which different symbols appear in a piece of text. Suppose our text is a string that comprises the characters a, u, x, and z. If the length of this string is 1000, then storing it as 1000 one-byte characters will take 1000 bytes (or 8000 bits) of space. If we encode the symbols in the string using 2 bits per symbol ($00 = a$, $01 = x$, $10 = u$, $11 = z$), then the 1000 symbols can be represented with 2000 bits of space. We also need space for the code table, which may be stored in following format:

Eight bits are adequate for the number of entries and for each of the symbols. Each code is of size $\lceil \log_2 (\text{number of table entries}) \rceil$ bits. For our example the code table may be saved in $5 * 8 + 4 * 2 = 48$ bits. The compression ratio is $8000/2048 = 3.9$.

Using the above 2 bits per symbol encoding, the string $aaxuaxz$ is encoded as 00000110000111. The code for each symbol has the same number of bits (i.e., 2). By picking off pairs of bits from the coded string from left to right and using the code table, we can obtain the original string.

In the string $aaxuaxz$, the symbol a occurs three times. The number of occurrences of a symbol is called its **frequency**. The frequencies of the symbols a, x, u, and z in the sample string are 3, 2, 1, and 1, respectively. When there is significant variation in the frequencies of different symbols, we can reduce the size of the coded string by using variable-length codes. If we use the codes ($0 = a$, $10 = x$, $110 = u$, $111 = z$), the encoded version of $aaxuaxz$ is 0010110010111. The length of this encoded version is 13 bits compared to 14 bits using the 2 bits per symbol code! The difference is more dramatic when the spread in frequencies is greater. If the frequencies of the four symbols are (996, 2, 1, 1), then the 2 bits per symbol code results in an encoding that is 2000 bits long, whereas the variable-length code results in an encoding that is 1006 bits.

But how do we decode the encoded string? When each code is 2 bits long, decoding is easy—just pick off every pair of bits and use the code table to determine what these 2 bits stand for. With variable-length codes, we do not know how many bits to pick off. The string $aaxuaxz$ was coded as 0010110010111. When decoding this code from left to right, we need to know whether the code for the first symbol is 0, 00, or 001. Since we have no codes that begin with 00, the first code must be 0. This code is decoded using the code table to get a. The next code is 0, 01, or 010. Again, because no codes begin with 01, the code must be 0. Continuing in this way, we are able to decode the encoded bit string.

What makes this decoding method work? If we examine the four codes in use (0, 10, 110, 111), we observe that no code is a prefix of another. Consequently, when examining the coded bit string from left to right, we can get a match with exactly one code.

We may use extended binary trees (see Section 13.5.1 for a definition) to derive a special class of variable-length codes that satisfy this prefix property. This class of codes is called **Huffman codes**.

The root to external node paths in an extended binary tree may be coded by using 0 to represent a move to a left subtree and 1 to represent a move to a right subtree. In Figure 13.6(b) the path from the root to the external node b gets the code 010. The codes for the paths to the nodes (a, b, c, d, e, f) are (00, 010, 011, 100, 101, 11). Notice that since no root-to-external-node path is a prefix of another such path, no path code is a prefix of another path code. Therefore, these codes may be used to encode the symbols a, b, $\cdots$, f, respectively. Let S be a string made up of these symbols and let $F(x)$ be the frequency of the symbol $x \in \{a, b, c, d, e, f\}$. If S is encoded using these codes, the encoded string has a length

$$2 * F(a) + 3 * F(b) + 3 * F(c) + 3 * F(d) + 3 * F(e) + 2 * F(f)$$

For an extended binary tree with external nodes labeled $1, \cdots, n$, the length of the encoded string is

$$WEP = \sum_{i=1}^{n} L(i) * F(i)$$

where $L(i)$ is the length of the path (i.e., number of edges on the path) from the root to the external node labeled i. WEP is called the **weighted external path length** of the binary tree. To minimize the length of the coded string, we must use codes from a binary tree whose external nodes correspond to the symbols in the string being encoded and whose WEP is minimum. A binary tree with minimum WEP for a given set of frequencies (weights) is called a **Huffman tree**.

To encode a string (or piece of text) using Huffman codes, we need to

1. Determine the different symbols in the string and their frequencies.

2. Construct a binary tree with minimum WEP (i.e., a Huffman tree). The external nodes of this tree are labeled by the symbols in the string, and the weight of each external node is the frequency of the symbol that is its label.

3. Traverse the root-to-external-node paths and obtain the codes.

4. Replace the symbols in the string by their codes.

To facilitate decoding, we need to save a table that contains the symbol to code mapping or a table that contains the frequency of each symbol. In the latter case the Huffman codes can be reconstructed using the method for (2). We will elaborate on step (2) only.

A Huffman tree can be constructed by beginning with a collection of binary trees, each having just an external node. Each external node represents a different string symbol and has a **weight** equal to the frequency of this symbol. Then we repeatedly select two binary trees of lowest weight (ties are broken arbitrarily) from the collection and combine them into one by making them subtrees of a new root node. The weight of the newly formed tree is the sum of the weights of the constituent subtrees. The process terminates when only one tree remains.

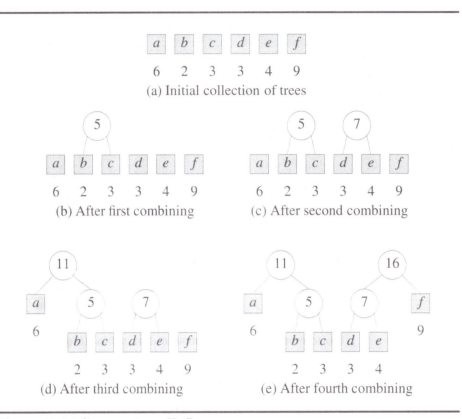

Figure 13.11 Constructing a Huffman tree

Let us try this construction method on a six-symbol (a, b, c, d, e, f) example with frequencies $(6, 2, 3, 3, 4, 9)$. The initial binary trees are shown in Figure 13.11(a). The numbers outside the boxes are the tree weights. The tree with the lowest weight is b. We have a tie for the tree with the second-lowest weight. Suppose that we select tree c. Combining trees b and c yields the configuration of Figure 13.11(b). The root node is labeled with the weight 5. From the five trees of Figure 13.11(b), we select two of lowest weight. Trees d and e are selected and combined to get a tree of weight 7 (Figure 13.11(c)). From the four trees of Figure 13.11(c), we select two of lowest weight to combine. Tree a and the one with weight 5 are selected. Combining these trees results in a tree of weight 11. From the remaining three trees

(Figure 13.11(d)), the tree with weight 7 and the tree f are selected for combining. When these two trees are combined, the two trees of Figure 13.11(e) remain. These trees are next combined to get the single tree of Figure 13.6(b), whose weight is 27.

Theorem 13.3 *The procedure outlined above constructs binary trees with minimum WEP.*

Proof Left as an exercise (Exercise 41). ■

The Huffman tree construction procedure can be implemented using a min heap to store the collection of binary trees. Each element of the min heap consists of a binary tree and a value that is the weight of this binary tree. The binary tree itself is an instance of the class `LinkedBinaryTree` defined in Section 12.8. For an external node the `element` field is set to the symbol it represents, and for an internal node this field is set to `null`. We may assume, for convenience, that the symbols are of type `MyInteger` and are numbered 0 through $n-1$. Method `huffmanTree` (Program 13.10) assumes that the class `HuffmanNode` has the data members `tree`, which is of type `LinkedBinaryTree`, and `weight`, which is of type `Operable`. `HuffmanNode` implements the interface `Comparable`, using the `weight` field.

The method `huffmanTree` inputs a collection of $n =$ `w.length` frequencies (or weights) in the array `w` and returns a Huffman tree. The method begins by constructing n binary trees, each with just an external node. These trees are saved in the array `hNode`, which is later initialized to be a min heap. Each iteration of the second `for` loop removes two binary trees of minimum weight from the min heap and combines them into a single binary tree, which is then put into the min heap.

Complexity of `huffmanTree`

The time needed to create the array `hNode` is $O(n)$. The first `for` loop and the heap initialization also take $O(n)$ time. In the second `for` loop, a total of $2(n-1)$ remove and $n-1$ put operations are performed, taking $O(n \log n)$ time. The remainder of `huffmanTree` takes $\Theta(1)$ time. So the overall time complexity is $O(n \log n)$.

EXERCISES

26. Show how the array [5, 7, 2, 9, 3, 8, 6, 1] is sorted using heap sort. First draw the corresponding complete binary tree, then draw the heapified tree, and then draw figures similar to those in Figure 13.9 to show the state of the tree following each removal from the max heap.

27. Do Exercise 26 using the array [11, 10, 9, 8, 7, 6, 5, 4, 3, 2, 1].

28. Write a heap sort method that uses d-heaps (see Exercise 17). Compare the worst-case run times of heap sort using d-heaps for different d values. What value of d gives best performance?

```
/** @return Huffman tree with weights w[0:a.length-1] */
public static LinkedBinaryTree huffmanTree(Operable [] w)
{
   // create an array of single-node trees
   HuffmanNode [] hNode = new HuffmanNode [w.length + 1];
   LinkedBinaryTree emptyTree = new LinkedBinaryTree();
   for (int i = 0; i < w.length; i++)
   {
      LinkedBinaryTree x = new LinkedBinaryTree();
      x.makeTree(new MyInteger(i), emptyTree, emptyTree);
      hNode[i + 1] = new HuffmanNode(x, w[i]);
   }

   // make node array into a min heap
   MinHeap h = new MinHeap();
   h.initialize(hNode, w.length);

   // repeatedly combine pairs of trees from min heap
   // until only one tree remains
   for (int i = 1; i < w.length; i++)
   {
      // remove two lightest trees from the min heap
      HuffmanNode x = (HuffmanNode) h.removeMin();
      HuffmanNode y = (HuffmanNode) h.removeMin();

      // combine them into a single tree t
      LinkedBinaryTree z = new LinkedBinaryTree();
      z.makeTree(null, x.tree, y.tree);
      HuffmanNode t = new HuffmanNode(z,
                         (Operable) x.weight.add(y.weight));

      // put new tree into the min heap
      h.put(t);
   }

   return ((HuffmanNode) h.removeMin()).tree;  // final tree
}
```

Program 13.10 Construct a Huffman tree

29. Use the ideas of Exercises 15 and 16 to arrive at an implementation of heap sort that is faster than Program 13.8. Experiment with random data and compare the run times of the two implementations.

30. A sort method is said to be **stable** if the relative order of records with equal keys is the same after the sort as it was before the sort. Suppose that records 3 and 10 have the same key. In a stable sort record 3 will precede record 10 following the sort. Is heap sort a stable sort? How about insertion sort?

31. Draw the three-machine LPT schedule for the processing times [6, 5, 3, 2, 9, 7, 1, 4, 8]. What is the finish time for your schedule. Can you find a schedule with a smaller finish time or is your schedule optimal?

32. Do Exercise 31 using the processing times [20, 15, 10, 8, 8, 8].

33. Each iteration of the second `for` loop of Program 13.9 performs one `removeMin` and one `put`. The two operations together essentially increase the value of the minimum key by an amount equal to the processing time of the job just scheduled. We can speed up Program 13.9 by a constant factor by using an extended min priority queue. The extension includes the methods normally supported by a min priority queue plus the method `changeMin(x)` that changes the minimum element to `x`. This method moves down the heap (as in a remove min operation), moving elements up the heap until it finds an appropriate place for the changed element.

    (a) Develop a new class `ExtendedMinHeap` that provides all the methods provided by the class `MinHeap` plus the method `changeMin`. The class `ExtendedMinHeap` should be derived from the class `MinHeap`.

    (b) Rewrite Program 13.9 using the method `changeMin`.

    (c) Conduct experiments to determine the improvement in run time of your new code versus that of Program 13.9.

34. Construct a machine-scheduling instance for which the two-machine LPT schedule achieves the upper bound given in Theorem 13.2.

35. Do Exercise 34 for a three-machine LPT schedule.

36. n items are to be packed into containers. Item i uses s_i units of space, and each container has a capacity c. The packing is to be done using the **worst-fit** rule in which the items are assigned to containers one at a time. When an item is being assigned, we look for the container with maximum available capacity. If the item fits in this container, the assignment is made; otherwise, this item starts a new container.

    (a) Develop a program to input n, the s_is, and c and to output the assignment of items to containers. Use a max heap to keep track of the available space in the containers.

(b) What is the time complexity of your program (as a function of n and the number m of containers used)?

37. Draw the Huffman tree for the weights (frequencies) [3, 7, 9, 12, 15, 20, 25].

38. Do Exercise 37 using the weights (frequencies) [2, 4, 5, 7, 9, 10, 14, 17, 18, 50].

39. A **run** is a sorted sequence of elements. Assume that two runs can be merged into a single run in time $O(r+s)$ where r and s are, respectively, the lengths of the two runs being merged. n runs of different lengths are to be merged into a single run by repeatedly merging pairs of runs until only one run remains. Explain how to use Huffman trees to determine a minimum-cost way to merge the n runs.

40. Suppose you are to code text that uses n symbols. A simple way to assign codes that satisfy the prefix property is to start with a right-skewed extended binary tree that has n external nodes, sort the n symbols in decreasing order of frequency $F()$, and assign symbols to external nodes so that an inorder listing of external nodes gives the symbols in decreasing order of their frequency. The sort step takes $O(n \log n)$ time, and the remaining steps take $O(n)$ time. So this method has the same asymptotic complexity as the optimal method described in Section 13.6.3.

    (a) Draw the Huffman tree and the right-skewed tree for the case when you have $n = 5$ symbols a–e with frequencies [4, 6, 7, 9, 10]. Label each external node with the symbol it represents, list the code for each symbol, and give the WEP of each tree.

    (b) Suppose that the n symbols have the same frequency. What is the ratio of the WEPs of the Huffman tree and the right-skewed tree? Assume that n is a power of 2.

    (c) Write a method to construct the right-skewed extended binary tree as described above.

    (d) Compare the actual run time of your method of part (c) and that of Program 13.10.

    (e) Generate random instances and measure the difference in the WEPs of the trees generated by the two methods.

    (f) Based on your results for parts (b), (d), and (e), can you recommend the use of the method of this exercise over the method of Program 13.10? Why?

⋆ 41. Prove Theorem 13.3 by using induction on the number of external nodes. The induction step should establish the existence of a binary tree with minimum WEP that has a subtree with one internal node and two external nodes corresponding to the two lowest frequencies.

42. Write a method to convert a Huffman tree as created by `huffmanTree` (Program 13.10) and to output the code table. What is the time complexity of your method?

★ 43. Develop a complete compression-decompression package based on Huffman codes. Test your code.

★ 44. A collection of n integers in the range 0 through 511 is to be stored. Develop a compression-decompression package for this application. Use Huffman codes.

13.7 REFERENCES AND SELECTED READINGS

A more detailed study of data structures for priority queues and priority-queue variants can be found in the text *Fundamentals of Data Structures in C++* by E. Horowitz, S. Sahni, and D. Mehta, W. H. Freeman, New York, NY, 1994.

Height-biased leftist trees are described in the monograph *Data Structures and Network Algorithms* by R. Tarjan, SIAM, Philadelphia, PA, 1983, while weight-biased leftist trees are developed in the paper "Weight Biased Leftist Trees and Modified Skip Lists" by S. Cho and S. Sahni in *Proceedings, Second International Conference, COCOON'96*, Lecture Notes in Computer Science, Springer Verlag, 1090, 1996, 361–370.

You can find out more about NP-hard problems from the books *Computers and Intractability: A Guide to the Theory of NP-Completeness* by M. Garey and D. Johnson, W. H. Freeman, New York, NY, 1979, and *Computer Algorithms* by E. Horowitz, S. Sahni, and S. Rajasekeran, Computer Science Press, New York, NY, 1998. Chapter 12 of *Computer Algorithms* proves Theorem 13.2.

CHAPTER 14

TOURNAMENT TREES

BIRD'S-EYE VIEW

We have reached the halfway point in our journey through the forest of trees. The new tree variety we encounter in this chapter is the tournament tree. Like the heap of Section 13.4, a tournament tree is a complete binary tree that is most efficiently stored by using the array-based binary tree representation of Section 12.4.1. The basic operation that a tournament tree supports is replacing the maximum (or minimum) element. If we have n elements, this operation takes $\Theta(\log n)$ time. Although this operation can be done with the same asymptotic complexity—in fact, $O(\log n)$—using either a heap or a leftist tree, neither of these structures can implement a predictable tie breaker easily. The tournament tree becomes the data structure of choice when we need to break ties in a prescribed manner, such as to select the element that was inserted first or to select the element on the left (all elements are assumed to have a left-to-right ordering).

We study two varieties of tournament trees: winner and loser trees. Although winner trees are more intuitive and model real-world tournament trees, loser trees can be implemented more efficiently. The applications section at the end of the chapter considers another NP-hard problem, bin packing. Tournament trees are used to obtain efficient implementations of two approximation algorithms for the bin-packing problem. You will find it instructive to see whether you can implement these algorithms in the same time bounds with any of the other data structures developed so far in this text.

14.1   WINNER TREES AND APPLICATIONS

Suppose that n players enter a tennis tournament. The tournament is to be played in the *sudden-death* mode in which a player is eliminated upon losing a match. Pairs of players play matches until only one player remains undefeated. This surviving player is declared the tournament winner. Figure 14.1(a) shows a possible tennis tournament involving eight players a through h. The tournament is described by a binary tree in which each external node represents a player and each internal node represents a match played between players designated by the children of the node. Each level of internal nodes defines a *round* of matches that can be played in parallel. In the first round players a and b, c and d, e and f, and g and h play. The winner of each match is recorded at the internal node that represents the match. In the case of Figure 14.1(a), the four winners are b, d, e, and h. The remaining four players (i.e., the losers) are eliminated. In the next round of matches, b and d play against each other as do e and h. The winners are b and e, who play the final match. The overall winner is e. Figure 14.1(b) shows a possible tournament that involves five players a through e. The winner in this case is c.

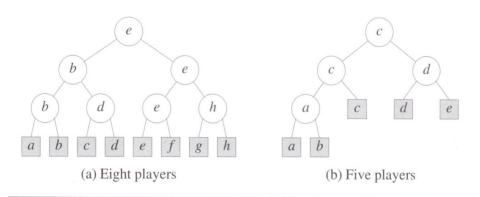

(a) Eight players   (b) Five players

Figure 14.1 Tournament trees

   Although both trees of Figure 14.1 are complete binary trees (actually, tree (a) is also a full binary tree), trees that correspond to real-world tournaments do not have to be complete binary trees. However, using complete binary trees minimizes the number of rounds of matches that have to be played. For an n-player tournament, this number is $\lceil \log_2 n \rceil$. The tournament tree depicted in Figure 14.1 is called a **winner tree** because at each internal node, we record the winner of the match played at that node. Section 14.4 considers another variety, called a **loser tree**, in which we record the loser at each internal node. Tournament trees are also known as **selection trees**.

Winner trees may be adapted for computer use. In this adaptation we restrict ourselves to complete binary trees.

Definition 14.1 *A **winner tree** for n players is a complete binary tree with n external and n − 1 internal nodes. Each internal node records the winner of the match played there.* ■

To determine the winner of a match, we assume that each player has a *value* and that there is a rule to determine the winner based on a comparison of the two players' values. In a **min winner tree**, the player with the smaller value wins, while in a **max winner tree**, the player with the larger value wins. In case of a tie, the player represented by the left child of the node wins. Figure 14.2(a) shows an eight-player min winner tree, while Figure 14.2(b) shows a five-player max winner tree. The number below each external node is the player's value.

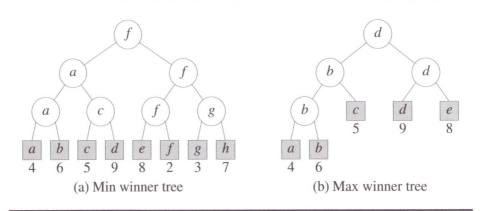

(a) Min winner tree   (b) Max winner tree

Figure 14.2 Winner trees

One of the nice things about a winner tree is that we can easily modify the tree to accommodate a change in one of the players. For example, if the value of player *d* changes from 9 to 1, then we need only replay matches on the path from *d* to the root. The change in this value does not affect the outcome of the remaining matches. In some situations we can avoid replaying some of the matches on the path to the root. For example, if in the min winner tree of Figure 14.2(a), the value of player *b* changes from 6 to 5, we play at its parent and *b* loses. There is no need to replay the matches at the grandparent and great-grandparent of *b*, as these matches will have the same outcome as they had before.

Since the number of matches needed to restructure an *n*-player winner tree following a change in one value ranges from a low of 1 to a high of $\lceil \log_2 n \rceil$, the time needed for restructuring is $O(\log n)$. Also, an *n*-player winner tree can be initialized in $\Theta(n)$ time by playing the $n - 1$ matches at the internal nodes by beginning with the matches at the lowest level and working up to the root. Alternatively, the tree can be initialized by performing a postorder traversal. During the visit step, a match is played.

Example 14.1 [Sorting] We may use a min winner tree to sort n elements in $\Theta(n \log n)$ time. First, the winner tree is initialized with the n elements as the players. The sort key is used to decide the outcome of each match. The overall winner is the element with the smallest key. This player's key is now changed to a very large number (say ∞) so that it cannot win against any of the remaining players. We restructure the tree to reflect the change in this player's key. The new overall winner is the element that comes next in sorted order. Its key is changed to ∞, and the tree is restructured. Now the overall winner is the element that is third in sorted order. Continuing in this way, we can sort the n elements. It takes $\Theta(n)$ time to initialize the winner tree. Each key change and restructure operation takes $\Theta(\log n)$ time because when the key of the tournament winner changes, we need to replay all matches on the path to the root. The restructuring needs to be done $n-1$ times, so the overall restructuring time is $\Theta(n \log n)$. Adding in the time needed to initialize the winner tree, the complexity of the sort method becomes $\Theta(n + n \log n) = \Theta(n \log n)$. ∎

Example 14.2 [Run Generation] The sorting methods (insertion sort, heap sort, etc.) we have discussed so far are all **internal sorting methods**. These methods require that the elements to be sorted fit in the memory of our computer. When the element collection does not fit in memory, internal sort methods do not work well because they require too many accesses to the external storage media (say a disk) on which all or part of the collection resides. In this case sorting is accomplished with an **external sorting method**. A popular approach to external sorting involves (1) generating sorted sequences called **runs** and (2) merging these runs together to create a single run.

Suppose we wish to sort a collection of 16,000 records and we are able to sort up to 1000 records at a time using an internal sort. Then in step 1, we do the following 16 times to create 16 runs:

> Input 1000 records.
> Sort these records using an internal sort.
> Output the sorted sequence (or run).

Following this run-generation step, we initiate the run-merging step, step 2. In this step we make several merge passes over the runs. In each merge pass we merge up to k runs, creating a single sorted run. So each merge pass reduces the number of runs by a factor of $1/k$. Merge passes are continued until the number of runs becomes 1.

In our example of 16 runs, we could perform two passes of four-way merges, as in Figure 14.3. The initial 16 runs are labeled R1 $\cdots$ R16. First, runs R1 $\cdots$ R4 merge to obtain the run $S1$, which is 4000 records long. Then R5 $\cdots$ R8 merge, and so on. At the second merge pass, $S1 \cdots S4$ are merged to create the single run T1, which is the desired output from the external sort.

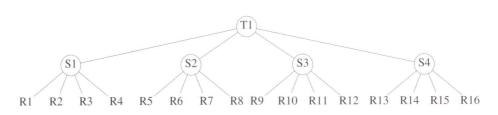

Figure 14.3 Four-way merging of 16 runs

A simple way to merge k runs is to repeatedly remove the element with smallest key from the front of these k runs. This element is moved to the output run being generated. The process is complete when all elements have been moved from the input k runs to the output run. Notice that to determine the next element in the output run all we need in memory is the key of the front element of each input run. We can merge k runs of arbitrary length as long as we have enough memory to hold k keys. In practice, we will want to input and output many elements at a time so as to reduce the input/output time.

In our 16,000-record example, each run is 1000 records long, and our memory capacity is also 1000 records. To merge the first four runs, we could partition memory into five buffers, each large enough to hold 200 records. Four of these buffers are designated input buffers, and the fifth is an output buffer. Two hundred records from each of the first four runs are input into the four input buffers. The output buffer is used to collect the merged records. Records are merged from the input buffers into the output buffer until one of the following conditions occurs:

- The output buffer becomes full.

- An input buffer becomes empty.

When the first condition occurs, we write the output buffer to disk and resume merging when this write has completed. When the second condition occurs, we read in the next buffer load (if any) for the run that corresponds to the empty input buffer and resume merging when this input has completed. The merge of the four runs is complete when all 4000 records from these runs have been written out as the single run $S1$. (A more sophisticated run-merging scheme is described in *Fundamentals of Data Structures in C++* by E. Horowitz, S. Sahni, and D. Mehta, Computer Science Press, New York, NY, 1995.)

One of the factors that determines the amount of time spent in the run-merging step is the number of runs generated in step 1. By using a winner tree, we can often reduce the number of runs generated. We begin with a winner tree for p players where each player is an element of the input collection. Each player has an associated key and run number. The first p elements are assigned run number 1. When a match is played between two players, the element with the smaller run number wins. In case of a tie, the keys are compared, and the element with the smaller key wins. If a tie remains, it may be broken arbitrarily. To generate runs, we repeatedly move the overall winner W into the run corresponding to its run-number field and replace the moved element by the next input element N. If the key of N is $\geq$ the key of W, then element N can be output as part of the same run. It is assigned a run number equal to that of W. If the key of N is less than that of W, outputting N after W in the same run violates the sorting constraint on a run. N is assigned a run number that is 1 more than that of W.

When using this method to generate runs, the average run length is $\approx 2p$. When $2p$ is larger than the memory capacity, we expect to get fewer runs than we do by using the simple scheme proposed earlier. In fact, if our input collection is already sorted (or nearly sorted), only one run is generated and we can skip the run-merging step, step 2. ■

Example 14.3 [k-Way Merging] In a k-way merge (see Example 14.2), k runs are merged to generate a single sorted run. The simple scheme, described in Example 14.2, to perform a k-way merge requires $O(k)$ time per element merged to the output run because in each iteration we need to find the smallest of k keys. The total time to generate a run of size n is, therefore, $O(kn)$. We can reduce this time to $\Theta(k + n \log k)$ using a winner tree. First we spend $\Theta(k)$ time to initialize a winner tree for k players. The k players are the first elements of the k runs to be merged. Then the winner is moved to the output run and replaced by the next element from the corresponding input run. If there is no next element in this run, it is replaced by an element with very large key (say ∞). We remove and replace the winner a total of n times at a cost of $\Theta(\log k)$ each time. The total time needed to perform the k-way merge is $\Theta(k + n \log k)$. ■

EXERCISES

1. Draw the max and min winner trees for players [3, 5, 6, 7, 20, 8, 2, 9]. Now draw the trees that result when 20 is changed to 1. Obtain the new trees by replaying only the matches on the path from 1 to the root.

2. Draw the max and min winner trees for players [20, 10, 12, 18, 30, 16, 35, 33, 45, 7, 15, 19, 33, 11, 17, 25]. Now draw the trees that result when 17 is changed to 42. Obtain the new trees by replaying only the matches on the path from 42 to the root.

3. Draw the max and min winner trees for players [3, 5, 6, 7, 20, 8, 2, 9, 12, 15, 30, 17]. Now draw the trees that result when 2 is changed to 11. Obtain the new trees by replaying only the matches on the path from 11 to the root.

4. Draw the max and min winner trees for players [10, 2, 7, 6, 5, 9, 12, 35, 22, 15, 1, 3, 4]. Now draw the trees that result when 9 is changed to 0. Obtain the new trees by replaying only the matches on the path from 0 to the root.

5. (a) Describe how a min heap can be used in place of a min winner tree to generate runs (see Example 14.2). How much time does it take to generate each element of a run?

   (b) What are the advantages/disadvantages of using a min winner tree rather than a heap in this application?

6. (a) Describe how a min heap can be used in place of a min winner tree when performing a k-way merge (see Example 14.3).

   (b) What are the advantages/disadvantages of using a min winner tree rather than a heap in this application?

14.2   THE ADT *WinnerTree*

In specifying the abstract data type *WinnerTree*, we make the assumption that the number of players is static. That is, after the tree is initialized for some number n of players, we do not increase or decrease the number of players. The players themselves are not part of the winner tree. So only the internal nodes of Figure 14.1 make up the winner tree. As a result, the operations that a winner tree needs to support are initialize a winner tree for n players, return the winner, and replay the matches on the path from player i to the root. The specification of these operations is provided in ADT 14.1.

Program 14.1 gives the interface `WinnerTree`. The specification of this interface makes use of another interface, `Playable`, that includes the single method `winnerOf`. Player data types must implement the method `winnerOf` such that `this.winnerOf(x)` is true iff `this` wins the match between the players `this` and `x`. By suitably defining the method `winnerOf`, we can construct min winner trees, max winner trees, and so forth.

14.3   WINNER TREE IMPLEMENTATION

14.3.1   Representation

We will represent a winner tree using the array-based representation of a complete binary tree. A winner tree for n players requires n-1 internal nodes `tree[1:n-1]`. The players (or external nodes) are represented as an array `player[1:n]`, so `tree[i]` is an index into the array `player` and hence is of type `int`. `tree[i]` gives the winner

---

AbstractDataType *WinnerTree*
{

    instances

        complete binary trees with each node pointing to the winner of the match
        played there; the external nodes represent the players

    operations

        initialize(a) : initialize a winner tree for the players in the array *a*

        getWinner() : return the tournament winner

          rePlay(i) : replay matches following a change in player *i*

}

ADT 14.1 Abstract data type specification of a winner tree

```
public interface WinnerTree
{
    public void initialize(Playable [] thePlayer);
    public int getWinner();
    public void rePlay(int i);
}
```

Program 14.1 The interface `WinnerTree`

of the match played at node `i` of the winner tree. Figure 14.4 gives the correspondence between the nodes of a winner tree and the arrays `tree` and `player` for the case of a five-player tree.

To implement the interface methods, we must be able to determine the parent `tree[p]` of an external node `player[i]`. When the number of external nodes is n, the number of internal nodes is $n - 1$. The left-most internal node at the lowest level is numbered s where $s = 2^{\lfloor \log_2(n-1) \rfloor}$. Therefore, the number of internal nodes at the lowest level is $n - s$, and the number *lowExt* of external nodes at the lowest level is twice this number. For example, in the tree of Figure 14.4, $n = 5$ and $s = 4$. The left-most internal node at the lowest level is `tree[4]`, and the total number of internal nodes at this level is $n - 4 = 1$. The number of lowest-level external nodes is 2. The left-most external node at the second-lowest level is numbered *lowExt*+1. Let *offset* $= 2 * s - 1$. Then we see that for any external node `player[i]`, its parent `tree[p]` is given by

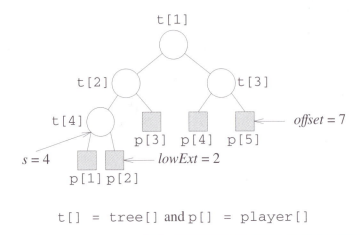

$$t[] = tree[] \text{ and } p[] = player[]$$

Figure 14.4 Tree-to-array correspondence

$$p = \begin{cases} (i + offset)/2 & i \leq lowExt \\ (i - lowExt + n - 1)/2 & i > lowExt \end{cases} \tag{14.1}$$

14.3.2   Initializing a Winner Tree

To initialize a winner tree, we play matches beginning at players that are right children and going up the tree whenever a match is played at a right child. For this purpose right-child players are considered from left to right. So in the tree of Figure 14.4, we first play matches beginning at player 2, then we begin at player 3, and finally, we begin at player 5. When we start at player 2, we play the match at `tree[4]`. The match at the next level, that is, at `tree[2]`, is not played because `tree[4]` is a left child. We now start playing at `player[3]`. The match at `tree[2]` is played, but the one at `tree[1]` is not (because `tree[2]` is a left child). Finally, we start at `player[5]` and play the matches at `tree[3]` and `tree[1]`. Notice that when a match is played at `tree[i]`, the players for this match have already been determined and recorded in the children of `tree[i]`.

14.3.3   Replaying Matches

When the value of player `thePlayer` is changed, it is necessary to replay some or all of the matches on the path from external node `player[thePlayer]` to the root `tree[1]`. For simplicity we replay all matches on this path. Actually, in the applications of Examples 14.1, 14.2, and 14.3, only the value of the winner is changed. Changing the value of the winner requires a replay of all matches on the path from the winner's external node to the root.

14.3.4   The Class `CompleteWinnerTree`

The winner tree data structure is implemented as the class `CompleteWinnerTree` (the code is available from the Web site for this book). The complexity of `get-Winner` is $O(1)$, that of `initialize` is $O(n)$, and that of `rePlay` is $O(\log n)$ where n is the number of players.

Exercises 9, 10, and 11 consider ways to simplify the implementation of a winner tree by using a larger array `tree` than is used in the class `CompleteWinnerTree`.

EXERCISES

7. Modify the method `CompleteWinnerTree.rePlay` to play only those matches that are necessary. In particular, we can stop playing when the winner of a match is the same as the previous winner of that match provided this previous winner is not the changed player `thePlayer`.

8. Write a sort program that uses a winner tree to repeatedly extract elements in sorted order (see Example 14.1).

9. Let n be the number of players and let m be the smallest integer that is a power of 2 and is $\geq n$. For example, if $n = 14$, then $m = 16$. We can simplify the implementation of `WinnerTree` by setting up a winner tree for m rather than n players. The parent of the external node `player[thePlayer]` is `tree[m+thePlayer-1]/2`. Note that `player[n+1:m]` is undefined.

   (a) What is the maximum additional space this scheme takes over that taken by the scheme of the text?

   (b) Implement a winner tree class using this scheme.

   (c) Test the correctness of your code.

   (d) Do you expect any significant difference in the run time between your new implementation and that of the text?

10. The winner tree code of the text is complex because the way we find the players for matches at the leaves of the tree `tree` is different from the way we find these players for the remaining matches. We can eliminate this difference (and hence simplify the code) by increasing the size of `tree` by n and placing the additional nodes between the external/player nodes and the nodes at which matches are played. Now the parent of `player[i]` is `tree[i + offset]` when i $\leq$ lowExt and is `tree[i - lowExt + n - 1]` when i $>$ lowExt. The parent of `player[i]` is initialized with the index i. With this modification, the match at `tree[i]` is always played between `player[tree[2*i]]` and `player[tree[2*i+1]]`, $1 \leq$ i $<$ n.

(a) Implement a winner tree class using this scheme.

(b) Test the correctness of your code.

(c) Do you expect any significant difference in the run time between your new implementation and that of the text?

11. In the implementation of `WinnerTree`, the special case when n is odd can be eliminated by setting up a tree for m = n players when n is even and for m = n+1 players when n is odd. This method requires us to use $O(1)$ additional space compared to the text's implementation of `WinnerTree`. When n is odd, `player[m]` is undefined.

(a) Implement a winner tree class using this scheme.

(b) Test the correctness of your code.

(c) Compare the relative advantages/disadvantages of the winner tree implementations of the text, Exercise 9, and this exercise.

14.4 LOSER TREES

Let us examine the `rePlay` operation on a winner tree. In many applications (see Examples 14.1, 14.2, and 14.3) this operation is performed only after a new player replaces the previous winner. In these applications all matches on the path from the external node that represents the winner up to the root have to be replayed. Consider the min winner tree of Figure 14.2(a). When a player (f') with key 5 replaces the winner f, the first match is played between e and f'. e is the player who lost the match previously played at this node against f. The winner, f', plays the next match at internal node `tree[3]` with g. Notice that g is the player who lost the match previously played at `tree[3]` between g and f. The winner at `tree[3]` is g. Next g plays at the root against a. Again a is the player who lost the match previously played at the root.

We can reduce the work needed to determine the players of each match on the path from the changed winner `player[i]` to the root if we record in each internal node the loser of the match played at that node, rather than the winner. The overall winner may be recorded in `tree[0]`. Figure 14.5(a) shows the loser tree for the eight players of Figure 14.2(a). Now when the winner f is changed to have key 5, we move to its parent `tree[6]`. The match is to be played between $player[tree[6]]$ and `player[6]`. To determine the opponent for f' = `player[6]`, we simply look at `tree[6]`. In a winner tree we would need to determine the other child of `tree[6]`. After playing the match at `tree[6]`, the loser e is recorded here, and f' advances to play at `tree[3]` with the previous loser of this match. This loser, g, is available from `tree[3]`. f' loses, and this fact is recorded in `tree[3]`. The winner g plays with the previous loser of the match at `tree[1]`. This loser, a, is available from `tree[1]`. The new loser tree appears in Figure 14.5(b).

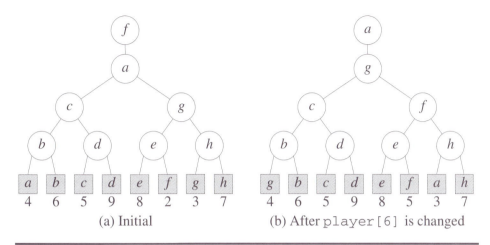

(a) Initial

(b) After player[6] is changed

Figure 14.5 Eight-player min loser trees

Although a loser tree simplifies the replaying of matches following a change in the previous winner, it does not result in a similar simplification when a change is made in other players. For example, suppose that the key of player d is changed from 9 to 3. Matches are to be replayed at tree[5], tree[2], and tree[1]. At tree[5] d has to play c, but c is not the previous loser of this match. At tree[2] d has to play a, but a did not lose the match previously played here. At tree[1] d has to play f, not the player who previously lost at tree[1]. To replay these matches easily, a winner tree is needed. Therefore, we expect a loser tree to give better performance than a winner tree only when the rePlay(i) method is restricted to the case when player[i] is the previous tournament winner.

EXERCISES

12. Draw the max and min loser trees for players [3, 5, 6, 7, 20, 8, 2, 9]. Now draw the trees that result when 20 is changed to 10 in the max loser tree and 2 is changed to 4 in the min loser tree. Obtain the new trees by replaying only the matches on the path from the changed element to the root.

13. Draw the max and min loser trees for players [20, 10, 12, 18, 30, 16, 35, 33, 45, 7, 15, 19, 33, 11, 17, 25]. Now draw the trees that result when 45 is changed to 34 in the max loser tree and 7 is changed to 12 in the min loser tree. Obtain the new trees by replaying only the matches on the path from the changed element to the root.

14. Draw the max and min loser trees for players [20, 10, 12, 14, 9, 11, 30, 33, 25, 7, 15]. Now draw the trees that result when 33 is changed to 5 in the max loser tree and 7 is changed to 16 in the min loser tree. Obtain the new trees by replaying only the matches on the path from the changed element to the root.

15. Draw the max and min loser trees for players [3, 5, 6, 7, 20, 8, 2, 9, 12, 15, 30, 17]. Now draw the trees that result when 30 is changed to 19 in the max loser tree and 2 is changed to 14 in the min loser tree. Obtain the new trees by replaying only the matches on the path from the changed element to the root.

16. Draw the max and min loser trees for players [10, 2, 7, 6, 5, 9, 12, 35, 22, 15, 1, 3, 4]. Now draw the trees that result when 35 is changed to 8 in the max loser tree and 1 is changed to 11 in the min loser tree. Obtain the new trees by replaying only the matches on the path from the changed element to the root.

17. (a) Develop a Java class `CompleteLoserTree` using a representation similar to that used for winner trees (Section 14.3). The tournament winner should be recorded in `tree[0]`. In place of the public method `rePlay(i)`, define the public method `rePlay()` to replay matches beginning at the winner of the previous tournament.

    (b) A simple way to initialize a loser tree is to first construct a winner tree and then make a level-order traversal, replacing the entry at each internal node with the loser. The traversal is done from top to bottom. When at `tree[i]`, its children tell us who played at `tree[i]`, and from this information we can determine who lost. Write code for `initialize` using this strategy. Show that your code takes $O(n)$ time to initialize a loser tree with n players.

    (c) Write a version of `initialize` that uses only the strategy used in `CompleteWinnerTree.initialize`. Play matches as far as you can, recording losers. When a match cannot be played, record the single player determined for that match. Show that your code takes $O(n)$ time to initialize a loser tree with n players.

18. Develop the Java class `FullLoserTree` that implements a loser tree as a full binary tree as described in Exercise 9. See Exercise 17 for initialization strategies. Test the correctness of your code.

19. Develop the Java class `CompleteLoserTree2` that implements a loser tree using the strategy described in Exercise 10. See Exercise 17 for initialization strategies. Test the correctness of your code.

20. Write a sort program that uses a loser tree to repeatedly extract elements in sorted order. What is the complexity of your program?

14.5   APPLICATIONS

14.5.1   Bin Packing Using First Fit

Problem Description

In the bin-packing problem, we have an unlimited supply of bins that have a capacity `binCapacity` each and n objects that need to be packed into these bins. Object i requires `objectSize[i]`, $0 < $ `objectSize[i]` $\leq$ `binCapacity`, units of capacity. A **feasible** packing is an assignment of objects to bins so that no bin's capacity is exceeded. A feasible packing that uses the fewest number of bins is an **optimal packing**.

Example 14.4 [Truck Loading] A freight company needs to pack parcels into trucks. Each parcel has a weight, and each truck has a load limit (assumed to be the same for all trucks). In the truck-loading problem, we are to pack the parcels into trucks using the fewest number of trucks. This problem may be modeled as a bin-packing problem with each truck being a bin and each parcel an object that needs to be packed. ∎

Example 14.5 [Chip Placement] A collection of electronic chips is to be placed in rows on a circuit board of a given width. The chips have the same height but different widths. The height, and hence area, of the circuit board is minimized by minimizing the number of rows used. The chip-placement problem may also be modeled as a bin-packing problem with each row being a bin and each chip an object that needs to be packed. The board's width is the bin capacity, and the chip's length, the capacity needed by the corresponding object. ∎

Approximation Algorithms

The bin-packing problem, like the machine-scheduling problem of Section 13.6.2, is an NP-hard problem. As a result, it is often solved using an approximation algorithm. In the case of bin packing, such an algorithm generates solutions that use a number of bins that is close to minimum. Four popular approximation algorithms for this problem are

1. *First Fit (FF)*
   Objects are considered for packing in the order 1, 2, ···, n. We assume a large number of bins arranged from left to right. Object i is packed into the left-most bin into which it fits.

2. *Best Fit (BF)*
   Let `bin[j].unusedCapacity` denote the capacity available in bin j. Initially, the unused capacity is `binCapacity` for all bins. Object i is packed into the bin with the least `unusedCapacity` that is at least `objectSize[i]`.

3. *First Fit Decreasing (FFD)*
   This method is the same as FF except that the objects are first reordered so that `objectSize[i]` $\geq$ `objectSize[i+1]`, $1 \leq i < n$.

4. *Best Fit Decreasing (BFD)*
   This method is the same as BF except that the objects are reordered as for FFD.

You should be able to show that none of these methods guarantee optimal packings. All four are intuitively appealing and can be expected to perform well in practice. A worst-fit packing strategy was considered in Exercise 36 of Chapter 13. We may also consider last fit, last-fit decreasing, and worst-fit decreasing strategies.

Theorem 14.1 *Let I be any instance of the bin-packing problem. Let $b(I)$ be the number of bins used by an optimal packing. The number of bins used by FF and BF never exceeds $(17/10)b(I) + 2$, while that used by FFD and BFD does not exceed $(11/9)b(I) + 4$.*

Example 14.6 Four objects with `objectSize[1:4]` $= [3, 5, 2, 4]$ are to be packed in bins of size 7. When FF is used, object 1 goes into bin 1 and object 2 into bin 2. Object 3 fits into the first bin and is placed there. Object 4 does not fit into either of the two bins used so far, and a new bin is used. The solution produced utilizes three bins and has objects 1 and 3 in bin 1, object 2 in bin 2, and object 4 in bin 3.

When BF is used, objects 1 and 2 get into bins 1 and 2, respectively. Object 3 gets into bin 2, as this bin provides a better fit than does bin 1. Object 4 now fits into bin 1. The packing obtained uses only two bins and has objects 1 and 4 in bin 1 and objects 2 and 3 in bin 2.

For FFD and BFD the objects are packed in the order 2, 4, 1, 3. In both cases a two-bin packing is obtained. Objects 2 and 3 are in bin 1, and objects 1 and 4 are in bin 2. ∎

First Fit and Winner Trees

The FF and FFD methods can be implemented so as to run in $O(n \log n)$ time using a winner tree. Since the maximum number of bins ever needed is n, we can begin with n empty bins. Initially, `bin[j].unusedCapacity = binCapacity` for all n bins. Next a max winner tree with the `bin[j]`'s as players is initialized. Figure 14.6(a) shows the max winner tree for the case n = 8 and `binCapacity = 10`. The external nodes represent bins 1 through 8 from left to right. The number below an external node is the space available in that bin. Suppose that `objectSize[1]` = 8. To find the left-most bin for this object, we begin at the root `tree[1]`. By definition, `bin[tree[1]].unusedCapacity` $\geq$ `objectSize[1]`. This relationship simply means that there is at least one bin into which the object fits. To find the

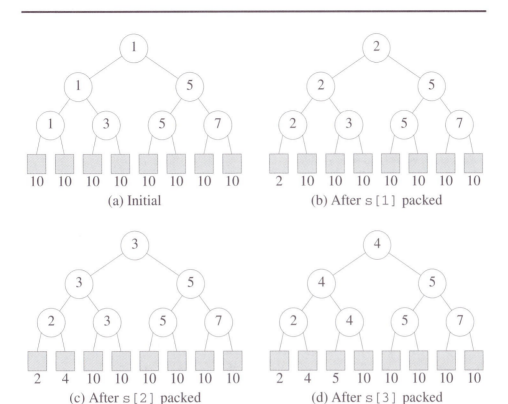

(a) Initial

(b) After s[1] packed

(c) After s[2] packed

(d) After s[3] packed

Figure 14.6 First-fit max winner trees

left-most bin, we determine whether there is enough space in one of the bins 1 through 4. One of these bins has enough space iff `bin[tree[2]].unusedCapacity` $\geq$ `objectSize[1]`. In our example this relationship holds, and so we can continue the search for a bin in the subtree with root 2. Now we determine whether there is adequate space in any bin covered by the left subtree of 2 (i.e., the subtree with root 4). If so, we are not interested in bins in the right subtree. In our example we move into the left subtree as `bin[tree[4]].unusedCapacity` $\geq$ `objectSize[1]`. Since the left subtree of 4 is an external node, we know that `objectSize[1]` is to be placed in one of node 4's two children. It goes in the left child provided this child has enough space. When object 1 is placed in bin 1, `bin[1].unused-Capacity` reduces to 2 and we must replay matches beginning at `bin[2]`. The new winner tree appears in Figure 14.6(b). Now suppose that `objectSize[2]` = 6. Since `bin[tree[2]].unusedCapacity` $\geq$ 6, we know that there is a bin with adequate space in the left subtree. So we move here. Then we move into the left subtree `tree[4]` and place object 2 in bin 2. The new configuration appears in Figure 14.6(c). When `objectSize[3]` = 5, the search for a bin leads us into the subtree with root 2. For its left subtree, `bin[tree[4]].unusedCapacity` < `objectSize[3]`, so no bin in the subtree with root 4 has enough space. As a result, we move into the right subtree 5 and place the object in bin 3. This placement results in the configuration of Figure 14.6(d). Next, suppose `objectSize[4]` = 3. Our search gets us to the subtree with root 4, as `bin[tree[4]].unusedCapacity` ≥ `objectSize[3]`, and we add object 3 to bin 2.

Java Implementation of First Fit

First we extend the class `CompleteWinnerTree` as shown in Program 14.2. The new public method `getWinner` returns the winner of the match played at internal node `i`.

```
public class ExtendedCWTree extends CompleteWinnerTree
{
   /** @return the winner recorded in tree[i]
     * @return 0 if i >= number of players */
   public int getWinner(int i)
      {return (i < tree.length) ? tree[i] : 0;}
}
```

Program 14.2 An extension of the class `CompleteWinnerTree`

The static method `FirstFit.firstFitPack` (Program 14.3) implements the first-fit strategy. This method assumes that the number of objects is at least 2 and that the size of each object is ≤ `binCapacity`. These assumptions are enforced by `FirstFit.main`, which inputs the bin capacity and object sizes and then invokes `firstFitPack`.

The method `firstFitPack` employs the data type `Bin` that has the lone instance data member `unusedCapacity`. The data type `Bin` implements the interface `Playable` so that `x.winnerOf(y)` returns `true` iff `x.unusedCapacity` ≥ `y.unused-Capacity`.

The method `firstFitPack` begins by initializing a max winner tree for `n` players, where `n` is the number of bins. Player `i` represents the current available capacity of bin `i`. This capacity is initially `binCapacity` for all bins. The method assumes that when a match is played, the left player is the winner unless the right one is larger.

In the second `for` loop, objects are assigned to bins one by one. When object `i` is being assigned, we follow a path beginning at the root and leading to the left-most bin with adequate space to accommodate the object. From our current position

```
public static void firstFitPack(int [] objectSize, int binCapacity)
{
   int n = objectSize.length - 1;        // number of objects
   Bin [] bin = new Bin [n + 1];         // bins
   ExtendedCWTree winTree = new ExtendedCWTree();

   // initialize n bins and winner tree
   for (int i = 1; i <= n; i++)
      bin[i] = new Bin(binCapacity);  // initial unused capacity
   winTree.initialize(bin);

   // put objects in bins
   for (int i = 1; i <= n; i++)
   {// put object i into a bin
      // find first bin with enough capacity
      int child = 2;  // start search at left child of root
      while (child < n)
      {
         int winner = winTree.getWinner(child);
         if (bin[winner].unusedCapacity < objectSize[i])
            child++ ;  // first bin is in right subtree
         child *= 2;   // move to left child
      }
      int binToUse;           // will be set to bin to use
      child /= 2;             // undo last left-child move
      if (child < n)
      {// at a tree node
         binToUse = winTree.getWinner(child);
         // if binToUse is right child, need to check
         // bin binToUse-1.  No harm done by checking
         // bin binToUse-1 even if binToUse is left child.
         if (binToUse > 1 &&
             bin[binToUse - 1].unusedCapacity >= objectSize[i])
            binToUse--;
       }
      else  // arises when n is odd
         binToUse = winTree.getWinner(child / 2);

      System.out.println("Pack object " + i + " in bin " + binToUse);
      bin[binToUse].unusedCapacity -= objectSize[i];
      winTree.rePlay(binToUse);
   }
}
```

Program 14.3 The method `firstFitPack`

we see whether the left subtree (the root of this subtree is `child`) has a bin with enough capacity. If not, the right subtree (whose root is `child+1`) is guaranteed to have such a bin. A bin in the left subtree is preferred over one in the right. The `while` loop is exited when the left subtree of the current node is an external node (i.e., `child` $\geq$ `n`). Notice that our code does not explicitly record the current position. However, we can always compute the current position by dividing `child` by 2 upon exiting the `while` loop. When `n` is odd, the current position can be an external node. At this time `child` equals `n`. In all other cases `child` is an internal node. When `child` is at an external node, the bin represented by this node is the winner of the match played at its parent. That is, it is bin `tree[child/2]`. When `child` is at an internal node, we are assured that bin `tree[child]` has enough capacity. However, if this bin is not the left child of its parent, it may not be the left-most such bin. So we check with the bin on its left. Once the bin (`binToUse`) to assign object `i` to has been determined, the unused capacity of this bin is reduced by `objectSize[i]` and the winner tree is restructured by replaying the matches on the path from this bin to the root.

Each iteration of the second `for` loop of Program 14.3 takes $\Theta(\log n)$ time. Therefore, the total time spent in the second `for` loop is $O(n \log n)$ time (note that we may not get as far as the second `for` loop for lack of memory to create the bin array and bin objects). The remainder of the method takes $O(n)$ time, and the total time needed to assign the objects to bins is $O(n \log n)$.

Commentary

The method `firstFitPack` uses intimate details of the implementation of a winner tree. For example, it uses the fact that a winner tree is a complete binary tree represented as an array. As a result, the method is able to move down the tree by multiplying by 2 and possibly by adding 1. Moving down the tree in this way defeats one of the objectives of using a class—information hiding. We wish to keep the implementation details of the class away from the user. When the user and class are so separated, we can change the implementation while keeping the public aspects of the class unchanged. Such changes do not affect the correctness of the applications. In the interests of information hiding, we may add methods to the class `CompleteWinnerTree` to enable the user to move to the left and right children of an internal node, and then we can use these methods in `firstFitPack`.

14.5.2   Bin Packing Using Next Fit

What Is Next Fit?

Next fit is a bin-packing strategy in which objects are packed into bins one at a time. We begin by packing object 1 in bin 1. For the remaining objects, we determine the next nonempty bin that can accommodate the object by polling the bins in a round-robin fashion, begining at the bin next to the one last used. In such a polling process, if bins 1 through `b` are in use, then these bins are viewed as arranged in a circle. The bin next to (or after) bin i is i+1 except when i = b; in this case the next bin is bin 1. If the last object placed went into bin j, then the search for a bin for the current object begins at the bin next to bin j. We examine successive bins until we either encounter a bin with enough space or return to bin j. If no bin with sufficient capacity is found, a new bin is started and the object placed into it.

Example 14.7 Six objects with objectSize[1:6] = [3, 5, 3, 4, 2, 1] are to be packed in bins of size 7. When next fit is used, object 1 goes into bin 1. Object 2 doesn't fit into a nonempty bin. So a new bin, bin 2, is started with this object in it. For object 3, we begin by examining the nonempty bin next to the last bin used. The last bin used was bin 2, and the bin next to it is bin 1. Bin 1 has enough space, and object 3 goes in it. For object 4, the search begins at bin 2, as bin 1 was the last one used. This bin doesn't have enough space. The bin next to bin 2 (i.e., bin 1) doesn't have enough space either. So a new bin, bin 3, is started with object 4 in it. The search for a bin for object 5 begins at the bin next to bin 3. This bin is bin 1. From here the search moves to bin 2 where the object is actually packed. For the last object we begin by examining bin 3. Since this bin has enough space, the object is placed here. ∎

The next-fit strategy described above is modeled after a dynamic memory allocation strategy that has the same name. In the context of bin packing, there is another next-fit strategy in which objects are packed one at a time. If an object does not fit into the current bin, then the current bin is closed and a new bin is started. We do not consider this variant of the next-fit strategy in this section.

Next Fit and Winner Trees

A max winner tree may be used to obtain an efficient implementation of the next-fit strategy. As in the case of first fit, the external nodes represent the bins, and matches are played by comparing the available space in the bins. For an n-object problem, we begin with n bins/external nodes. Consider the max winner tree of Figure 14.7, in which six of eight bins are in use. The labeling convention is the same as that used in Figure 14.6. Although the situation shown in Figure 14.7 cannot arise when n = 8, it illustrates how to determine the bin in which to pack the next object. If the last object was placed in bin lastBinUsed and b bins are currently in use, the search for the next bin to use can be broken into two searches as follows:

Step 1: Find the first bin j, j > lastBinUsed into which the object fits. Such a j always exists as the number of bins is n. If this bin is not empty (i.e., j ≤ b), this bin is the bin to use.

Step 2: If step 1 does not find a nonempty bin, find the left-most bin into which the object fits. This bin is now the bin to use.

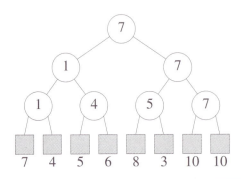

Figure 14.7 A next-fit max winner tree

Consider the situation depicted in Figure 14.7 and suppose that the next object to be placed needs seven units of space. If `lastBinUsed = 3`, then in step 1 we determine that bin 5 has adequate space. Since bin 5 is not an empty bin, the object is placed into it. On the other hand, if `lastBinUsed = 5`, then in step 1 bin 7 is identified as the bin with enough space. Since bin 7 is empty, we move to step 1 and look for the left-most bin with enough capacity. This left-most bin is bin 1, and the object is placed into it.

To implement step 1, we begin at bin `j = lastBinUsed+1`. Notice that if `lastBinUsed = n`, then all n objects must have been packed, as the only way to utilize n bins when the number of objects is n is to pack one object in each bin. So j $\leq$ n. The pseudocode of Figure 14.8 describes the search process adopted from bin j. Basically, we traverse the path from bin j to the root, examining right subtrees until we find the first one that contains a bin with sufficient available capacity. When we find such a subtree, the bin we seek is the left-most bin in this subtree that has sufficient available capacity.

Consider the winner tree of Figure 14.7. Suppose that `lastBinUsed = 1` and `objectSize[i] = 7`. We begin with j = 2. First we determine that bin 2 does not have enough capacity. Next we check bin j+1 = 3. It doesn't have enough capacity either. So we move to bin j's parent and set p equal to 4. Since p $\neq$ n-1, we reach the `while` loop and determine that the subtree with root 5 does not have a suitable bin. Next we move to node 2 and determine that the subtree with root 3 has a suitable bin. The required bin is the left-most bin in this subtree that has seven or more units of space available. This bin, bin 5, can be found following the strategy of Program 14.3. Suppose, instead, that `lastBinUsed = 3` and `objectSize[i] = 9`. We begin by checking bin 4. Since neither bin 4 nor bin 5 has enough capacity, p is set to 5 and we reach the `while` loop. The first iteration checks `bin[tree[6]].unusedCapacity` and determines that the subtree with root 6 has no suitable bin. p is then moved to node 2, and we determine that

```
// Find nearest bin to right of
// lastBinUsed into which object i fits.
j = lastBinUsed + 1;
if (bin[j].unusedCapacity >= objectSize[i])
   return j;
if (bin[j+1].unusedCapacity >= objectSize[i])
   return j + 1;

p = parent of bin[j];
if (p == n - 1)
{// special case
   let q be the external node to the right of tree[p];
   if (bin[q].unusedCapacity >= objectSize[i])
      return q;
}


// move toward root looking for first right
// subtree that has a bin with enough capacity
// subtree to right of p is p+1

p /= 2; // move to parent
while (bin[tree[p+1]].unusedCapacity < objectSize[i])
   p /= 2;


return first bin in subtree p+1 into which object i fits;
```

Figure 14.8 Pseudocode for step 1

the subtree with root 3 has a suitable bin. The left-most suitable bin in this subtree is identified, using a process similar to that of Program 14.3. This left-most bin is bin 7. Since this bin is an empty bin, we move to step 2 and determine that bin 7 is, in fact, the bin to use.

Step 1 requires us to follow a path up the tree and then make a downward pass to identify the left-most suitable bin. This step can be done in $O(\log n)$ time. Step 2 may be done in $O(\log n)$ by following the strategy of Program 14.3, so the overall complexity of the proposed next-fit implementation is $O(n \log n)$.

EXERCISES

21. Suppose that $binCapacity = 10$, $n = 5$, and $objectSize[0:4] = [6, 1, 4, 4, 5]$.

    (a) Determine an optimal packing for these objects.

    (b) Give the assignment of objects to bins obtained by using each of these methods: FF, BF, FFD, and BFD.

    (c) For the packings of part (b), determine the ratio (number of bins used) / (minimum number of bins needed).

22. Do Exercise 21 for the case when $binCapacity = 11$, $n = 30$, $objectSize[0:9] = 2$, $objectSize[10:19] = 3$, and $objectSize[20:29] = 6$.

23. The method `firstFitPack` (Program 14.3) takes $\Theta(\log n)$ time to assign an object to a bin, even when the number of bins used so far is much less than n. We can reduce this time by beginning the search for a bin at the root of the smallest subtree that includes both bin 1 and bin b where b is the right-most bin currently in use; that is, we begin at the nearest ancestor of external nodes 1 and b. So when b is 3, we begin at internal node 2. If none of the bins 1 through b has enough space, b is increased by 1. Also, during a replay, matches are played only as far as the nearest common ancestor of 1 and b. Rewrite Program 14.3 using these suggestions and then compare the run times of the two versions using randomly generated instances with n = 1000; 5000; 50,000; and 100,000.

24. (a) Add the public methods `root()`, `leftChild(i)`, and `rightChild(i)` to the class `CompleteWinnerTree`. These methods, respectively, return the root of the winner tree (i.e., 1) and the left and right children of the internal node i. The last two methods should return 0 in case the respective child is an external node.

    (b) Now rewrite `firstFitPack` (Program 14.3) so as to conform to the principles of information hiding described in the commentary of Section 14.5.1.

25. Although it is quite difficult to prove that the number of bins used by first fit and best fit never exceeds $\lceil (17/10)b(I) \rceil$, where $b(I)$ is the minimum number of bins needed by instance I, you should be able to prove that the number of bins never exceeds $2b(I)$ with modest effort. Prove this weaker bound.

26. Compare the number of bins required using worst fit (see Exercise 36 of Chapter 13), first fit, first-fit decreasing, and next fit. Do this comparison by generating random instances with $n = 500, 1000, 2000$, and 5000.

27. (a) Write a Java program for the next-fit strategy to pack bins. Use the two-step approach outlined in Section 14.5.2 and base the implementation of step 1 on the pseudocode of Figure 14.8.

    (b) Compare the number of bins used by next fit and first fit on randomly generated bin-packing instances.

28. Write a Java program to implement the last-fit bin-packing strategy that puts each object into the right-most bin into which it fits. If an object fits in no bin, a new bin is started. Test your code. What is its time complexity?

14.6   REFERENCES AND SELECTED READINGS

You can learn more about tournament trees from the book *The Art of Computer Programming: Sorting and Searching*, Volume 3, Second Edition, by D. Knuth, Addison-Wesley, Reading, MA, 1998.

The proof of Theorem 14.1 is rather laborious and can be found in the papers "Resource Constrained Scheduling as Generalized Bin-Packing" by M. Garey, R. Graham, D. Johnson, and A. Yao, *Journal of Combinatorial Theory*, Series A, 1976, 257–298 and "Worst-Case Performance Bounds for Simple One-Dimensional Packing Algorithms" by D. Johnson, A. Demers, J. Ullman, M. Garey, and R. Graham, *SIAM Journal on Computing*, 1974, 299–325.

CHAPTER 15

BINARY SEARCH TREES

BIRD'S-EYE VIEW

This chapter and the next develop tree structures suitable for the representation of a dictionary. Although we have already seen data structures such as skip lists and hash tables that can be used to represent a dictionary, the binary search tree data structures developed in this chapter and the balanced search tree structures developed in Chapter 16 provide additional flexibility and/or better worst-case performance guarantees.

This chapter examines binary search trees and indexed binary search trees. Binary search trees provide an asymptotic performance that is comparable to that of skip lists—the expected complexity of a search, insert, or delete operation is $\Theta(\log n)$, while the worst-case complexity is $\Theta(n)$; and elements may be output in ascending order in $\Theta(n)$ time. Although the worst-case complexities of the search, insert, and delete operations are the same for binary search trees and hash tables, hash tables have a superior expected complexity—$\Theta(1)$—for these operations. Binary search trees, however, allow you to search efficiently for keys that are close to a specified key. For example, you can find the key nearest to the key k (i.e., either largest key $\leq k$ or smallest key $\geq k$) in expected time $\Theta(n)$. The expected time for this operation is $\Theta(n + D)$ for hash tables and $\Theta(\log n)$ for skip lists.

Indexed binary search trees allow you to perform dictionary operations both by key value and by rank—get the element with the 10th smallest key and remove the element wth the 100th smallest key. The expected time for by-rank operations

566

is the same as for by-key operations. Indexed binary search trees may be used to represent linear lists (defined in Chapter 5); the elements have a rank (i.e., index) but no key. The result is a linear list representation in which the expected complexity of the *get*, *remove*, and *add* operations is $O(\log n)$. Recall that the array-based and linked representations of linear lists developed in Chapters 5 and 6 perform these operations with expected complexity $\Theta(n)$. The *get* operation for array-based representations is an exception; it takes $\Theta(1)$ time. Hash tables cannot be extended to support by-rank operations efficiently. Skip lists may be extended to permit by-rank operations with expected time complexity $\Theta(\log n)$.

Although the asymptotic complexity (both expected and worst case) for all tasks stated above is the same for binary search trees and skip lists, we can impose a balancing constraint on binary search trees so that the worst-case complexity for each of the stated tasks is $\Theta(\log n)$. Balanced search trees are the subject of Chapter 16.

Three applications of binary search trees are developed in the applications section. The first is the computation of a histogram. The second application is the implementation of the best-fit approximation method for the NP-hard bin-packing problem of Section 14.5.1. The final application is the crossing-distribution problem that arises when we route wires in a routing channel. We can improve the expected performance of the histogram application by using hashing in place of the search tree. In the best-fit application, the searches are not done by an exact match (i.e., we do a nearest key search), and so hashing cannot be used. In the crossing-distribution problem, the operations are done by rank, and so hashing cannot be used here either. The worst-case performance of each of these applications can be improved by using any of the balanced binary search tree structures developed in Chapter 16 in place of the unbalanced binary search tree developed in this chapter.

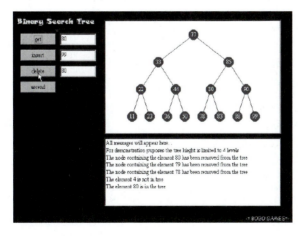

Experience binary search trees—On the Web

15.1 DEFINITIONS

15.1.1 Binary Search Trees

The abstract data type *Dictionary* was introduced in Section 11.1, and in Section 11.5 we saw that when a hash table represents a dictionary, the dictionary operations (get, put, and remove) take $\Theta(1)$ expected time. However, the worst-case time for these operations is linear in the number n of dictionary entries. A hash table no longer provides good expected performance when we extend the ADT *Dictionary* to include operations such as

1. Output in ascending order of keys.

2. Get the kth element in ascending order.

3. Remove the kth element.

To perform operation (1), we need to gather the elements from the table, sort them, and then output them. If a divisor D chained table is used, the elements can be gathered in $O(D + n)$ time, sorted in $O(n \log n)$ time, and output in $O(n)$ time. The total time for operation (1) is therefore $O(D + n \log n)$. If linear open addressing is used for the hash table, the gathering step takes $O(b)$ time where b is the number of buckets. The total time for operation (1) is then $O(b + n \log n)$. Operations (2) and (3) can be done in $O(D + n)$ time when a chained table is used and in $O(b)$ time when linear open addressing is used. To achieve these complexities for operations (2) and (3), we must use a linear-time algorithm to determine the kth element of a collection of n elements (explained in Section 19.2.4).

The basic dictionary operations (get, put, remove) can be performed in $O(\log n)$ time when a balanced search tree is used. Operation (1) can then be performed in $\Theta(n)$ time. By using an indexed balanced search tree, we can also perform operations (2) and (3) in $O(\log n)$ time. Section 15.6 examines other applications where a balanced tree results in an efficient solution, while a hash table does not.

Rather than jump straight into the study of balanced trees, we first develop a simpler structure called a binary search tree.

Definition 15.1 *A* **binary search tree** *is a binary tree that may be empty. A nonempty binary search tree satisfies the following properties:*

1. *Every element has a key (or value), and no two elements have the same key; therefore, all keys are distinct.*

2. *The keys (if any) in the left subtree of the root are smaller than the key in the root.*

3. *The keys (if any) in the right subtree of the root are larger than the key in the root.*

4. *The left and right subtrees of the root are also binary search trees.* ∎

There is some redundancy in this definition. Properties 2, 3, and 4 together imply that the keys must be distinct. Therefore, property 1 can be replaced by the following property: The root has a key. The preceding definition is, however, clearer than the nonredundant version.

Some binary trees in which the elements have distinct keys appear in Figure 15.1. The number inside a node is the element key. The tree of Figure 15.1(a) is not a binary search tree despite the fact that it satisfies properties 1, 2, and 3. The right subtree fails to satisfy property 4. This subtree is not a binary search tree, as its right subtree has a key value (22) that is smaller than the key value in the right subtrees' root (25). The binary trees of Figures 15.1(b) and (c) are binary search trees.

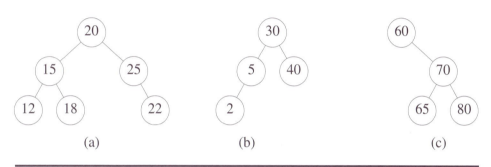

Figure 15.1 Binary trees

We can remove the requirement that all elements in a binary search tree need distinct keys. Now we replace smaller in property 2 by smaller or equal and larger in property 3 by larger or equal; the resulting tree is called a **binary search tree with duplicates**.

15.1.2   Indexed Binary Search Trees

An **indexed binary search tree** is derived from an ordinary binary search tree by adding the field `leftSize` to each tree node. This field gives the number of elements in the node's left subtree. Figure 15.2 shows two indexed binary search trees. The number inside a node is the element key, while that outside is the value of `leftSize`. Notice that `leftSize` also gives the index of an element with respect to the elements in its subtree (this condition is a consequence of the fact that all elements in the left subtree of x precede x). For example, in the tree of Figure 15.2 (a), the elements (in sorted order) in the subtree with root 20 are 12, 15, 18, 20, 25, and 30. Viewed as a linear list $(e_0, e_1, \cdots, e_4)$, the index of the root is 3, which equals its `leftSize` value. In the subtree with root 25, the elements (in sorted order) are 25 and 30, so the index of the root element 25 is 0 and its `leftSize` value is also 0.

(a)   (b)

Figure 15.2 Indexed binary search trees

EXERCISES

1. Start with a complete binary tree that has 10 nodes. Place the keys [1, 2, 3, 4, 5, 6, 7, 8, 9, 10], one key per node, so that the result is a binary search tree. Label each node with its `leftSize` value.

2. Start with a complete binary tree that has 13 nodes. Place the keys [1, 2, 3, 4, 5, 6, 7, 8, 9, 10, 11, 12, 13], one key per node, so that the result is a binary search tree. Label each node with its `leftSize` value.

15.2   ABSTRACT DATA TYPES

ADT 15.1 gives the abstract data type specification for a binary search tree. An indexed binary search tree supports all the binary search tree operations. In addition, it supports search and deletion by rank. Its abstract data type specification is given in ADT 15.2. The abstract data types *DBSTree* (binary search trees with duplicates) and *DIndexedBSTree* may be specified in a similar way.

Programs 15.1 and 15.2 give Java interfaces for the ADTs *BSTree* and *Indexed-BSTree*, respectively.

```
public interface BSTree extends Dictionary
   {public void ascend();}
```

Program 15.1 The Java interface BSTree

AbstractDataType *BSTree*
{

> **instances**
>> binary trees, each node has an element with a key field; all keys are distinct; keys in the left subtree of any node are smaller than the key in the node; those in the right subtree are larger

> **operations**
>> $get(k)$: return the element with key k
>>
>> $put(k, x)$: put element x with key k into the search tree
>>
>> $remove(k)$: remove the element with key k and return it
>>
>> $ascend()$: output all elements in ascending order of key

}

ADT 15.1 Abstract data type specification of a binary search tree

---

AbstractDataType *IndexedBSTree*
{

> **instances**
>> same as for `BSTree` except that each node has a `leftSize` field

> **operations**
>> $get(k)$: return the element with key k
>>
>> $get(index)$: return the *index*th element
>>
>> $put(k, x)$: put element x with key k into the search tree
>>
>> $remove(k)$: remove the element with key k and return it
>>
>> $remove(index)$: remove the *index*th element and return it
>>
>> $ascend()$: output all elements in ascending order of key

}

ADT 15.2 Abstract data type specification of an indexed binary search tree

```
public interface IndexedBSTree extends BSTree
{
    public Object get(int index);
    public Object remove(int index);
}
```

Program 15.2 The Java interface `IndexedBSTree`

EXERCISES

3. How much (expected) time does it take to do the *BSTree* operations of ADT 15.1 using skip lists?

4. Provide a specification for the abstract data type *DBSTree* (binary search tree with duplicates). Define a Java interface that corresponds to this ADT.

5. Provide a specification for the abstract data type *DIndexedBSTree*. Define a Java interface that corresponds to this ADT.

15.3   BINARY SEARCH TREE OPERATIONS AND IMPLEMENTATION

15.3.1   The Class `BinarySearchTree`

Since the number of elements in a binary search tree as well as its shape change as operations are performed, a binary search tree is represented by using the linked representation of Section 12.4.2. We can greatly simplify the task of developing the class `BinarySearchTree` if we define this class as a derived class of `LinkedBinaryTree` (Section 12.8). Each element in the linked binary tree is of type `Data`. The data members of `Data` are `element` and `key`, and their data types are `Object` and Comparable, respectively.

Since `BinarySearchTree` is derived from `LinkedBinaryTree`, the method `ascend` of the interface `BSTree` can be implemented as a call to the method `LinkedBinaryTree.inOrderOutput` as is done in Program 15.3. The method `inOrderOutput` first outputs the elements in the left subtree (i.e., smaller elements), then the root element, and finally those in the right subtree (i.e., larger elements). The time complexity is $O(n)$ for an n-element tree.

15.3.2   Searching

Suppose we wish to search for an element with key `theKey`. We begin at the root. If the root is `null`, the search tree contains no elements and the search is unsuccessful.

```
/** output elements in ascending order of key */
public void ascend()
   {inOrderOutput();}
```

Program 15.3 The method `BinarySearchTree.ascend`

Otherwise, we compare **theKey** with the key in the root. If **theKey** is less than the key in the root, then no element in the right subtree can have key value **theKey** and only the left subtree is to be searched. If **theKey** is larger than the key in the root, only the right subtree needs to be searched. If **theKey** equals the key in the root, then the search terminates successfully. The subtrees may be searched similarly. Program 15.4 gives the code. The time complexity is $O(h)$ where h is the height of the tree being searched.

```
public Object get(Object theKey)
{
   // pointer p starts at the root and moves through
   // the tree looking for an element with key theKey
   BinaryTreeNode p = root;
   Comparable searchKey = (Comparable) theKey;
   while (p != null)
      // examine p.element.key
      if (searchKey.compareTo(((Data) p.element).key) < 0)
         p = p.leftChild;
      else
         if (searchKey.compareTo(((Data) p.element).key) > 0)
            p = p.rightChild;
         else // found matching element
            return ((Data) p.element).element;

   // no matching element
   return null;
}
```

Program 15.4 Search a binary search tree

15.3.3   Inserting an Element

To put a new element `theElement` into a binary search tree, we must first determine whether its key `theKey` is different from those of existing elements by performing a search for `theKey`. If the search is successful, we must replace the old element associated with `theKey` with the element `theElement`. If the search is unsuccessful, then the new element is inserted as a child of the last node examined during the search. For instance, to put an element with key 80 into the tree of Figure 15.1(b), we first search for 80. This search terminates unsuccessfully, and the last node examined is the one with key 40. The new element is inserted as the right child of this node. The resulting search tree appears in Figure 15.3(a). Figure 15.3(b) shows the result of putting an element with key 35 into the search tree of Figure 15.3(a). Program 15.5 implements this strategy to put an element into a binary search tree.

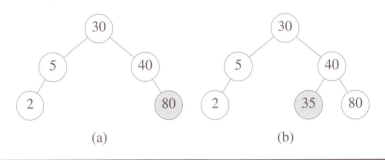

(a)   (b)

Figure 15.3 Inserting elements into a binary search tree

15.3.4   Deleting an Element

For element removal we consider the three possibilities for the node **p** that contains the element to be removed: (1) **p** is a leaf, (2) **p** has exactly one nonempty subtree, and (3) **p** has exactly two nonempty subtrees.

Case (1) is handled by discarding the leaf node, and if the discarded leaf was also the tree root, the root is set to `null`. To remove 35 from the tree of Figure 15.3(b), the left-child field of its parent is set to `null`, and the node discarded. The resulting tree appears in Figure 15.3(a). To remove the 80 from this tree, the right-child field of 40 is set to `null`, obtaining the tree of Figure 15.1(b), and the node containing 80 is discarded.

Next consider the case when the element to be removed is in a node **p** that has only one nonempty subtree. If **p** has no parent (i.e., it is the root), the root of its single subtree becomes the new search tree root. If **p** has a parent **pp**, then we change the pointer from **pp** so that it points to **p**'s only child. For instance, if we wish to remove the element with key 5 from the tree of Figure 15.3(b), we change

```
public Object put(Object theKey, Object theElement)
{
   BinaryTreeNode p = root,      // search pointer
                  pp = null;     // parent of p
   Comparable elementKey = (Comparable) theKey;
   // find place to insert theElement
   while (p != null)
   {// examine p.element.key
      pp = p;
      // move p to a child
      if (elementKey.compareTo(((Data) p.element).key) < 0)
         p = p.leftChild;
      else if (elementKey.compareTo(((Data) p.element).key) > 0)
            p = p.rightChild;
         else
         {// overwrite element with same key
            Object elementToReturn = ((Data) p.element).element;
            ((Data) p.element).element = theElement;
            return elementToReturn;
         }
   }

   // get a node for theElement and attach to pp
   BinaryTreeNode r = new BinaryTreeNode
                        (new Data(elementKey, theElement));
   if (root != null)
      // the tree is not empty
      if (elementKey.compareTo(((Data) pp.element).key) < 0)
         pp.leftChild = r;
      else
         pp.rightChild = r;
   else // insertion into empty tree
      root = r;
   return null;
}
```

Program 15.5 Insert an element into a binary search tree

the left-child field of its parent (i.e., the node containing 30) to point to the node containing the 2.

Finally, to remove an element in a node that has two nonempty subtrees, we replace this element with either the largest element in its left subtree or the smallest element in its right subtree. Following this replacement, the replacing element is removed from its original node. Suppose we wish to remove the element with key 40 from the tree of Figure 15.4(a). Either the largest element (35) from its left subtree or the smallest (60) from its right subtree can replace this element. If we opt for the smallest element in the right subtree, we move the element with key 60 to the node from which the 40 was removed; in addition, the leaf from which the 60 is moved is removed. The resulting tree appears in Figure 15.4(b).

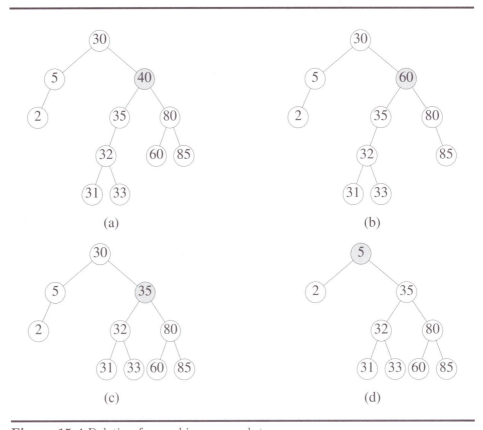

Figure 15.4 Deletion from a binary search tree

Suppose, instead, that when removing 40 from the search tree of Figure 15.4(a), we had opted for the largest element in the left subtree of 40. This element has key 35 and is in a node of degree 1. We move the element into the node that currently contains 40, and the left-child pointer of this node changes to point to the lone child of the node from which the 35 was moved. The result is shown in Figure 15.4(c).

As another example, consider the removal of 30 from the tree of Figure 15.4(c). We may replace this element with either the 5 or the 31. If we opt for the 5, then since 5 is currently in a node with degree 1, we change the left-child pointer of the parent node to point to the lone child. The result is the tree of Figure 15.4(d). If we had opted to replace 30 with 31, then since 31 is in a leaf, we need merely remove this leaf.

Notice that the element with smallest key in the right subtree (as well as that with largest key in the right subtree) is guaranteed to be in a node with either zero or one nonempty subtree. Note also that we can find the largest element in the left subtree of a node by moving to the root of that subtree and then following a sequence of right-child pointers until we reach a node whose right-child pointer is `null`. Similarly, we can find the smallest element in the right subtree of a node by moving to the root of the right subtree and then following a sequence of left-child pointers until we reach a node whose left-child pointer is `null`. Notice that our strategy to remove an element from a node with two nonempty subtrees may be viewed as a replacement followed by a removal from a leaf or a node with one nonempty subtree.

Program 15.6 implements the element removal strategy outlined above. When removing from a node with two nonempty subtrees, this code always uses the largest element in the left subtree as a replacement. The complexity of this code is $O(h)$.

15.3.5   Height of a Binary Search Tree

Unless care is taken, the height of a binary search tree with n elements can become as large as n. The tree height becomes this large, for instance, when Program 15.5 is used to put elements with keys $[1, 2, 3, \cdots, n]$, in this order, into an initially empty binary search tree. As a result, a get, put, or remove operation on a binary search tree takes $O(n)$ time. This time is no better than the times for these operations using an unordered chain. However, we can show that when puts and removals are made at random using Programs 15.5 and 15.6, the height of the binary search tree is $O(\log n)$ on the average. As a result, the expected time for each of the search tree operations is $O(\log n)$.

EXERCISES

6. Start with an empty binary search tree.

    (a) Insert the keys 4, 12, 8, 16, 6, 18, 24, 2, 14, 3 in this order. Draw the tree following each insert. Use the insert method described in this section.

    (b) From the tree of (a) remove the keys 6, 14, 16, and 4 in this order. Draw the search tree following each deletion. Use the deletion method of this section.

7. Do Exercise 6 using the key sequence 10, 5, 20, 14, 30, 8, 6, 9, 35, 25, 3, 12, 17 for part (a). For part (b) delete 35, 30, 20, and 10 in this order.

```
public Object remove(Object theKey)
{
   Comparable searchKey = (Comparable) theKey;

   // set p to point to node with key searchKey
   BinaryTreeNode p = root,     // search pointer
                 pp = null;   // parent of p
   while (p != null && !((Data) p.element).key.equals(searchKey))
   {// move to a child of p
      pp = p;
      if (searchKey.compareTo(((Data) p.element).key) < 0)
         p = p.leftChild;
      else
         p = p.rightChild;
   }

   if (p == null) // no element with key searchKey
      return null;

   // save element to be removed
   Object theElement = ((Data) p.element).element;

   // restructure tree
   // handle case when p has two children
   if (p.leftChild != null && p.rightChild != null)
   {// two children
      // convert to zero or one child case
      // find element with largest key in left subtree of p
      BinaryTreeNode s = p.leftChild,
                     ps = p;  // parent of s
      while (s.rightChild != null)
      {// move to larger element
         ps = s;
         s = s.rightChild;
      }

      // move largest element from s to p
      p.element = s.element;
      p = s;
      pp = ps;
   }
```

Program 15.6 Removing an element from a binary search tree (continues)

```
   // p has at most one child, save this child in c
   BinaryTreeNode c;
   if (p.leftChild == null)
      c = p.rightChild;
   else
      c = p.leftChild;

   // remove node p
   if (p == root) root = c;
   else
   {// is p left or right child of pp?
      if (p == pp.leftChild)
         pp.leftChild = c;
      else
         pp.rightChild = c;
   }

   return theElement;
}
```

Program 15.6 Removing an element from a binary search tree (concluded)

8. Extend the class `BinarySearchTree` by adding a public method `outputIn-Range(theLow, theHigh)` that outputs, in ascending order of key, all elements in a binary search tree whose key lies between `theLow` and `theHigh`. Use recursion and avoid entering subtrees that cannot possibly contain any elements with keys in the desired range. Test the correctness of your code.

9. Develop a modified version of Program 15.4 in which the first comparison in the `while` loop is `searchKey.compareTo(((Data) p.element).key) == 0`. Measure the time it takes to search for all elements in a binary search tree using Program 15.4 as well as the modified version just described. What conclusion can you draw?

10. A binary search tree can be used to sort n elements. Write a sort procedure that puts the n elements `a[0:n-1]` into an initially empty binary search tree and then performs an inorder traversal putting the elements into `a` in sorted order. For simplicity, assume that the objects in `a` are distinct. Compare the average run time of the resulting sort procedure with that for insertion sort and heap sort.

11. In Section 13.5 we saw how to initialize an n-element leftist tree in linear time and also how to meld/combine two leftist trees into one in logarithmic time. This exercise establishes that the asymptotic time complexity of the initialize and combine operations for binary search trees is larger than that for the corresponding operations for leftist trees. To establish this result, we will use the known lower bound on the asymptotic complexity of sorting. In Section 19.4.2 we will see that every algorithm that sorts n elements has a complexity that is at least $O(n \log n)$.

   (a) Use this result to prove that it is not possible to initialize/create an n-element binary search tree in less than $O(n \log n)$ time.

   (b) Use the above lower bound on the complexity of sorting to show that it is not possible to combine two binary search trees into a single binary search tree in less than $O(n + m)$ time, where n and m are, respectively, the number of elements in the two trees that are to be combined.

12. Extend the class `BinarySearchTree` by adding a method `split(theKey, lessThan, greaterThan)` that splits the binary search tree `this` into two binary search trees—`lessThan` contains all elements of `this` whose keys are less than `theKey`, and `greaterThan` contains all elements of `this` whose keys are greater than `theKey`. If the binary search tree `this` has an element whose key equals `theKey`, this element is returned as the value of the method invocation; otherwise, `null` is returned. Following the operation, `this` is an empty binary search tree. The complexity of your method should be $O(h)$, where h is the height of the tree being split. Test the correctness of your code.

13. Generate a random permutation of the integers 1 through n. Put the keys 1 through n into an initially empty binary search tree. Perform the put operations in the order specified by the random permutation. Measure the height of the resulting search tree. Repeat this experiment for several random permutations and compute the average of the measured heights. Compare this figure with $2\lceil \log_2(n + 1) \rceil$. For n use the values 100; 500; 1000; 10,000; 20,000; and 50,000.

★ 14. Extend the class `BinarySearchTree` by including an iterator that allows you to examine the elements in ascending order of the key. The time taken to enumerate all elements of an n-element binary tree should be $O(n)$, the complexity of no method should exceed $O(h)$ where h is the tree height, and the space requirements should be $O(h)$. Show that this is the case. Test your code.

15. Write a method to remove the max element from a binary search tree. Your method must have time complexity $O(h)$ where h is the height of the binary search tree. Show that your code has this complexity.

(a) Use suitable test data to test the correctness of your remove max procedure.

(b) Create a random list of n elements and a random sequence of put and remove max operations of length m. Create the latter sequence so that the probability of a put operation is approximately 0.5 (therefore, the probability of a remove max operation is also 0.5). Initialize a max heap and a binary search tree with duplicates to contain the n elements in the first random list. Now measure the time to perform the m operations, using the max heap as well as the binary search tree. Divide this time by m to get the average time per operation. Do this experiment for n = 100, 500, 1000, 2000, $\cdots$, and 5000. Let m be 5000. Tabulate your computing times.

(c) Based on your experiments, what can you say about the relative merits of the two priority queue schemes?

15.4   BINARY SEARCH TREES WITH DUPLICATES

The class for the case when the binary search tree is permitted to contain two or more elements that have the same key is called DBinarySearchTree. We can implement this class by changing the while loop of BinarySearchTree::put (Program 15.5) to that shown in Program 15.7 and by changing the second occurrence of the line

```
if (elementKey.compareTo(((Data) pp.element).key) < 0)
```

to

```
if (elementKey.compareTo(((Data) pp.element).key) <= 0)
```

If we insert n elements, all of which have the same key, into an an initially empty binary search tree, the result is a left-skewed tree whose height is n. An alternative approach that uses random numbers and results in trees with better height properties is considered in Exercise 17.

EXERCISES

16. Start with an empty binary search tree with duplicates and insert the keys 2, 2, 2, and 2 using the put method described in this section. Draw your tree following each insert. What is the tree height following the insertion of n 2s?

17. Develop a new implementation of the Java class DBinarySearchTree. During an insert, instead of consistently moving to the left subtree of a node that

```
// find place to insert theElement
while (p != null)
{// examine p.element.key
   pp = p;
   // move p to a child
   if (elementKey.compareTo(((Data) p.element).key) <= 0)
      p = p.leftChild;
   else
      p = p.rightChild;
}
```

Program 15.7 New while loop for Program 15.5 to permit duplicates

contains a key equal to `elementKey` (see Program 15.7), use a random number generator to move to the left or right subtree with equal probability. Test the correctness of your implementation.

15.5   INDEXED BINARY SEARCH TREES

The class `IndexedBinarySearchTree` may also be defined as a derived class of `LinkedBinaryTree` (see Exercise 19). For the class `IndexedBinarySearchTree`, the elements have the three fields `leftSize`, `key`, and `element`.

We can perform an indexed search in a manner similar to that used to search an element by key. Consider the tree of Figure 15.2(a). Suppose we are looking for the element whose index is 2. The `leftSize` field (and hence index) of the root is 3. So the element we desire is in the left subtree. Furthermore, the element we desire has index 2 in the left subtree. The root, 15, of the left subtree has `leftSize` = 1. So the element we desire is in the right subtree of 15. However, the index, in the right subtree of 15, of the element we desire is no longer 2 because all elements in the right subtree of 15 follow the elements in the left subtree of 15 as well as the element 15. To determine the index of the desired element in the right subtree, we subtract `leftSize + 1`. Since the `leftSize` value of 15 is 1, the index of the desired element in its right subtree is $2 - (1 + 1) = 0$. Since `leftSize` = 0 (which equals the index of the element we seek) for the root of the right subtree of 15, we have found the desired element 18.

When putting an element into an indexed binary search tree, we use a procedure similar to Program 15.5. This time, though, we also need to update `leftSize` fields on the path from the root to the newly inserted node.

A remove by index is done by first performing an indexed search to locate the element to be removed. Next we remove the element as outlined in Section 15.3.4

and update `leftSize` fields on the path from the root to the physically deleted node as necessary.

The time required to search, insert, and remove is $O(h)$ time where h is the height of the indexed search tree.

EXERCISES

18. Start with an empty indexed binary search tree.

    (a) Insert the keys 4, 12, 8, 16, 6, 18, 24, 2, 14, 3 in this order. Draw the tree following each insert. Show `leftSize` values. Use the insert method described in this section.

    (b) Use the method of this section to find the keys with index 3, 6, and 8. Describe the search process used in each case.

    (c) Start with the tree of (a) and remove the keys whose index is 7, 5, and 0 in this order. Draw the search tree following each deletion. Use the deletion method of this section.

19. Develop the Java class `IndexedBinarySearchTree` as a derived class of `BinarySearchTree`. You should make `leftSize` a subfield of `Data.element`. Test the correctness of all your code. Express the time complexity of each method in terms of the number of elements and/or the height of the tree.

20. Do Exercise 19 for the class `DIndexedBinarySearchTree`. This time derive from the class `DBinarySearchTree`.

21. You are to represent a linear list as an indexed binary tree which is like an indexed binary search tree except that no node has a key value. Each node of the indexed binary tree contains exactly one element of the linear list. When an indexed binary tree is traversed in inorder, we visit the elements in linear list order from left to right.

    (a) Start with a complete binary tree that has 11 nodes. Label each node with its `leftSize` value. Place the elements of the linear list $A = $ [a, b, c, d, e, f, g, h, i, j, k] into this indexed binary tree. Note that when you traverse the binary tree in inorder, you must visit the elements in linear list order.

    (b) Perform the following linear list insert operations on the tree of part (a): `add(4, m)`, `add(9, n)`, `add(0, p)`, and `add(14, q)`. Do these in the given order using a method similar to that used to insert into a binary search tree. Search for the proper place to add the new node using `leftSize` values.

    (c) Perform the following linear list delete operations on the tree of part (b): `remove(0)`, `remove(3)`, `remove(8)`, and `remove(7)`. Do these in the given order using a method similar to that used to delete from an indexed binary search tree.

★   22. Develop a class `LinearListAsBinaryTree` that represents a linear list as an indexed binary tree (see Exercise 21). Your implementation should support all the linear list operations defined in Program 5.1.

A simple way to implement the `add(index, theElement)` operation is to first find the `index` - 1th node p, make the new element the right child of p, and finally make the original right subtree of the p the right subtree of the newly inserted element. However, since this insertion method never makes an element a left child of another, the trees that are constructed are right skewed (i.e., all left-child fields are 0) and have height equal to the number of elements in the tree.

To construct binary trees with expected height logarithmic in the number of elements, we must create both left and right subtrees. When the `index` - 1th node p is found, we can (1) make the new element the right child of p and make the former right subtree of p the right subtree of the new element or (2) make the new element the left or right child of the parent of p (depending on which child p is of its parent), make p the left child of the new element, and make the original right subtree of p the right subtree of the new element or (3) insert the new element as the left-most node in the right subtree of p. By making this decision randomly, we can obtain better balanced trees. Your insert code should select from the available options randomly.

Other than the method `indexOf`, all methods should run in logarithmic or less expected time. Show that this is the case. You may assume that the expected height of the binary tree constructed is logarithmic in the number of elements.

15.6   APPLICATIONS

15.6.1   Histogramming

What Is Histogramming?

In the histogramming problem we start with a collection of n keys and must output a list of the distinct keys and the number of times (i.e., frequency) each occurs in the collection. Figure 15.5 gives an example with 10 keys. The problem input appears in Figure 15.5(a), and the histogram is presented in Figure 15.5(b) as a table and as a bar chart in Figure 15.5(c). Histogramming is commonly performed to determine the distribution of data. For example, we may histogram the scores on a test, the grayscale values in an image, the cars registered in Gainesville (the key being the manufacturer), and the highest degree earned by persons living in Los Angeles.

$$n = 10; keys = [2, 4, 2, 2, 3, 4, 2, 6, 4, 2]$$
(a) Input

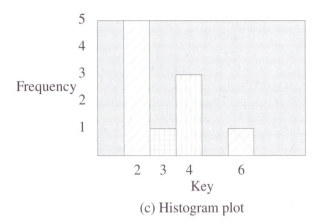

Key	Frequency
2	5
3	1
4	3
6	1

(b) Output histogram table

(c) Histogram plot

Figure 15.5 Histogramming example

Simple Histogramming Program

When the key values are integers in the range 0 through r and r is reasonably small, the histogram can be computed in linear time by a rather simple procedure (Program 15.8) that uses the array element $h[i]$ to determine the frequency of the key i. Other integral key types may be mapped into this range to use Program 15.8. For example, if the keys are lowercase letters, we may use the mapping [a, b, $\cdots$, z] = [0, 1, $\cdots$, 25].

Histogramming with a Binary Search Tree

Program 15.8 becomes infeasible when the key range is very large as well as when the key type is not integral (for example, when the keys are real numbers). Suppose we are determining the frequency with which different words occur in a text. The number of possible different words is very large compared to the number that might actually appear in the text. In such a situation we can use hashing to arrive at a solution whose expected complexity is $O(n)$ (Exercise 24). Alternatively, we may sort the keys and then use a simple left-to-right scan to determine the number of keys for each distinct key value. The sort can be accomplished in $O(n \log n)$ time (using heapSort (Program 13.8), for example), and the ensuing left-to-right scan takes $\Theta(n)$ time; the overall complexity is $O(n \log n)$.

```
public class SimpleHistogramming
{
    public static void main(String [] args)
    {
        // define keyboard to be the standard input stream
        MyInputStream keyboard = new MyInputStream();

        System.out.println("Enter number of elements and range");
        int n = keyboard.readInteger();    // number of elements
        int r = keyboard.readInteger();    // elements must be between
                                           // 0 and r

        // create histogram array h, initial values are 0
        int [] h = new int [r + 1];

        // input data and compute histogram
        for (int i = 1; i <= n; i++)
        {
            System.out.println("Enter element " + i);
            h[keyboard.readInteger()]++;
        }

        // output histogram
        System.out.println("Distinct elements and frequencies are");
        for (int i = 0; i <= r; i++)
            if (h[i] != 0)
                System.out.println(i + "    " + h[i]);
    }
}
```

Program 15.8 Simple histogramming program

The histogramming-by-sorting solution can be improved when the number m of distinct keys is small compared to n. By using balanced search trees such as AVL and red-black trees (see Chapter 16), we can solve the histogramming problem in $O(n \log m)$ time. Furthermore, the balanced search tree solution requires only the distinct keys to be stored in memory. Therefore, this solution is appropriate even in situations when n is so large that we do not have enough memory to accommodate all keys (provided, of course, there is enough memory for the distinct keys).

The solution we describe in this section uses a binary search tree that may not be balanced. Therefore, this solution has expected complexity $O(n \log m)$.

The Class `BinarySearchTreeWithVisit`

For our binary search tree solution, we first define the class `BinarySearchTreeWithVisit` that extends the class `BinarySearchTree` by adding the public member

```
public void put(Object theKey, Object theElement, Method theVisit)
```

This public member puts `theElement` into the search tree provided no element with key equal to `theKey` exists. If the tree already contains an element u that has the key `theKey`, the method `theVisit(e)` is invoked.

The Class `TreeHistogramming`

Program 15.9 gives the class `TreeHistogramming` that includes the top-level nested class `ElementType` and a static method to increase the `count` field of an object of type `ElementType` by 1.

Program 15.10 gives the `main` method of `TreeHistogramming`. This method inputs the data, enters it into an object of type `BinarySearchTreeWithVisit`, and finally outputs the histogram by invoking the `ascend` method of `BinarySearchTree`. During an element visit, its frequency count is incremented by 1.

15.6.2   Best-Fit Bin Packing

Using a Binary Search Tree with Duplicates

The best-fit method to pack n objects into bins of capacity c was described in Section 14.5.1. By using a binary search tree with duplicates, we can implement the method to run in $O(n \log n)$ expected time. The worst-case complexity becomes $\Theta(n \log n)$ when a balanced search tree is used.

In our implementation of the best-fit method, the binary search tree (with duplicates) will contain one element for each bin that is currently in use and has nonzero unused capacity. Suppose that when object i is to be packed, there are nine bins (a through i) in use that still have some space left. Let the unused capacity of these bins be 1, 3, 12, 6, 8, 1, 20, 6, and 5, respectively. Notice that it is possible for two or more bins to have the same unused capacity. The nine bins may be stored in a binary search tree with duplicates (i.e., an instance of `DBinarySearchTree`) using as key the unused capacity of a bin.

Figure 15.6 shows a possible binary search tree for the nine bins. For each bin the unused capacity is shown inside a node, and the bin name is shown outside. If the object i that is to be packed requires `objectSize[i]` = 4 units, we can find the bin that provides the best fit by starting at the root of the tree of Figure 15.6. The root tells us bin h has an unused capacity of 6. Since object i fits into this bin, bin h becomes the candidate for the best bin. Also, since the capacity of all bins in the right subtree is at least 6, we need not look at the bins in this subtree in our quest for the best bin. The search proceeds to the left subtree. The capacity of bin b isn't adequate to accommodate our object, so the search for the best bin

```java
public class TreeHistogramming
{
   // top-level member class
   public static class ElementType
   {
      // data members
      int key,     // element value
          count;   // frequency

      // constructor
      public ElementType(int theKey)
      {
         key = theKey;
         count = 1;
      }
      // output method
      public String toString()
         {return "[" + String.valueOf(key) + " " +
                  String.valueOf(count) + "]";}
   }
   // static data member
   static Method theAdd1;   // method to increase count by 1

   // static initializer
   static
   {
      try
      {
         Class histo = TreeHistogramming.class;
         Class [] paramType = {Object.class};
         theAdd1 = histo.getMethod("add1", paramType);
      }
      catch (Exception e) {}
         // exception not possible
   }
   /** increment the count of e by 1 */
   public static void add1(Object e)
      {((ElementType) e).count++;}
}
```

Program 15.9 The class `TreeHistogramming`

```
public static void main(String [] args)
{
   // define keyboard to be the standard input stream
   MyInputStream keyboard = new MyInputStream();

   System.out.println("Enter number of elements");
   int n = keyboard.readInteger();

   // input elements and enter into theTree
   BinarySearchTreeWithVisit theTree = new BinarySearchTreeWithVisit();
   for (int i = 1; i <= n; i++)
   {
      System.out.println("Enter element " + i);
      ElementType e = new ElementType(keyboard.readInteger());
      // put e in tree unless match already there
      // in latter case increase count by 1
      theTree.put(new MyInteger(e.key), e, theAdd1);
   }

   // output distinct elements and their counts
   System.out.println("Distinct elements and frequencies are");
   theTree.ascend();
   System.out.println();
}
```

Program 15.10 Histogramming with a search tree

moves into the right subtree of bin b. The bin, bin i, at the root of this subtree has enough capacity, and it becomes the new candidate for the best bin. From here the search moves into the left subtree of bin i. Since this subtree is empty, there are no better candidate bins and bin i is selected.

As another example of the search for the best bin, suppose objectSize[i] = 7. The search again starts at the root. The root bin, bin h, does not have enough capacity for this object, so our quest for a bin moves into the right subtree. Bin c has enough capacity and becomes the new candidate bin. From here we move into c's left subtree and examine bin d. It does not have enough capacity to accommodate the object, so we continue with the right subtree of d. Bin e has enough capacity and becomes the new candidate bin. We then move into its left subtree, which is empty. The search terminates.

When we find the best bin, we can delete it from the search tree, reduce its capacity by objectSize[i], and reinsert it (unless its remaining capacity is 0). If we do not find a bin with enough capacity, we can start a new bin.

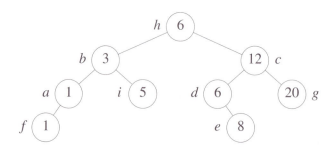

Figure 15.6 Binary search tree with duplicates

Java Implementation

To implement this scheme, we can use the class `DBinarySearchTree` to obtain $O(n \log n)$ expected performance or the class `DAVLtree` (Section 16.1) for $O(n \log n)$ performance in all instances. In either case we must first extend the class to include the public method `findGE(k)` that returns the smallest bin capacity that is $\geq$ `k`. This member takes the form given in Program 15.11. Its complexity is $O(height)$. The code for the method is unchanged if the class `DAVLTree` is extended instead of `DBinarySearchTree`.

The method `bestFitPack` (Program 15.12), which implements the best-fit packing strategy, uses the class `BinNode` that has the integer data members `id` and `unusedCapacity`.

15.6.3   Crossing Distribution

Channel Routing and Crossings

In the crossing-distribution problem, we start with a routing channel with n pins on both the top and bottom of the channel. Figure 15.7 shows an instance with $n = 10$. The routing region is the shaded rectangular region. The pins are numbered 1 through n, left to right, on both the top and bottom of the channel. In addition, we have a permutation C of the numbers $[1, 2, 3, \cdots, n]$. We must use a wire to connect pin i on the top side of the channel to pin C_i on the bottom side. The example in Figure 15.7 is for the case $C = [8, 7, 4, 2, 5, 1, 9, 3, 10, 6]$. The n wires needed to make these connections are numbered 1 through n. Wire i connects top pin i to bottom pin C_i. Wire i is to the left of wire j iff $i < j$.

No matter how we route wires 9 and 10 in the given routing region, these wires must cross at some point. Crossings are undesirable as special care must be taken at the crossing point to avoid a short circuit. This special care, for instance, might involve placing an insulator at the point of crossing or routing one wire onto another layer at this point and then bringing it back after the crossover point. Therefore, we

```
public class DBinarySearchTreeWithGE extends DBinarySearchTree
{
   /** @return element with smallest key >= theKey
     * @return null if no element has key >= theKey */
   public Object getGreaterThanOrEqual(Object theKey)
   {
      BinaryTreeNode currentNode = root;
      Object bestElement = null; // element with smallest key
                                 // >= theKey found so far
      // search the tree
      while (currentNode != null)
         // is currentNode.element.key a candidate
         if (((Data) currentNode.element).key.compareTo(theKey) >= 0)
         {// yes, currentNode.element.element is
          // a better candidate than bestElement
            bestElement = ((Data) currentNode.element).element;
            // smaller keys in left subtree only
            currentNode = currentNode.leftChild;
         }
         else
            // no, currentNode.element.key is too small
            // try right subtree
            currentNode = currentNode.rightChild;

      return bestElement;
   }
}
```

Program 15.11 Finding the smallest key $\geq$ theKey

seek to minimize the number of crossings. You may verify that the minimum number of crossings is made when the wires are run as straight lines as in Figure 15.7.

Each crossing is given by a pair (i, j) where i and j are the two wires that cross. To avoid listing the same pair of crossing wires twice, we require $i < j$ (note that the crossings $(9, 10)$ and $(10, 9)$ are the same). Note that wires i and j, $i < j$, cross iff $C_i > C_j$. Let k_i be the number of pairs (i, j), $i < j$, such that wires i and j cross. For the example of Figure 15.7, $k_9 = 1$ and $k_{10} = 0$. In Figure 15.8 we list all crossings and k_i values for the example of Figure 15.7. Row i of this table first gives the value of k_i and then the values of j, $i < j$, such that wires i and j cross. The total number of crossings K may be determined by adding together all k_is. For our example $K = 22$. Since k_i counts the crossings of wire i only with wires to its right (i.e., $i < j$), k_i gives the number of right-side crossings of wire i.

```
/** output best-fit packing into bins of size binCapacity
 * @param objectSize[1:objectSize.length-1] are the object sizes */
public static void bestFitPack(int [] objectSize, int binCapacity)
{
    int n = objectSize.length - 1;      // number of objects
    int binsUsed = 0;
    DBinarySearchTreeWithGE theTree;   // tree of bin capacities
    theTree = new DBinarySearchTreeWithGE();

    // pack objects one by one
    for (int i = 1; i <= n; i++)
    {// pack object i
        // find best bin
        BinNode bestBin = (BinNode) theTree.getGreaterThanOrEqual
                                (new Integer(objectSize[i]));
        if (bestBin == null)
            // no bin large enough, start a new bin
            bestBin = new BinNode(++binsUsed, binCapacity);
        else
            // remove best bin from theTree
            bestBin = (BinNode) theTree.remove
                        (new Integer(bestBin.unusedCapacity));

        System.out.println("Pack object " + i + " in bin " + bestBin.id);

        // update unused capacity and put bin
        // in tree unless unused capacity is 0
        bestBin.unusedCapacity -= objectSize[i];
        if (bestBin.unusedCapacity > 0)
            theTree.put(new Integer(bestBin.unusedCapacity), bestBin);
    }
}
```

Program 15.12 Bin packing using best fit

Distributing the Crossings

To balance the routing complexity in the top and lower halves of the channel, we require that each half have approximately the same number of crossings. (The top half should have $\lfloor K/2 \rfloor$ crossings, and the bottom should have $\lceil K/2 \rceil$ crossings.) Figure 15.9 shows a routing of Figure 15.7 in which we have exactly 11 crossings in each half of the channel.

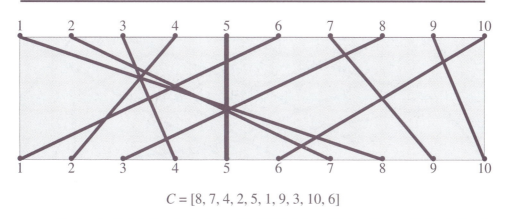

$$C = [8, 7, 4, 2, 5, 1, 9, 3, 10, 6]$$

Figure 15.7 A wiring instance

i	k_i	Crossings						
1	7	2	3	4	5	6	8	10
2	6	3	4	5	6	8	10	
3	3	4	6	8				
4	1	6						
5	2	6	7					
6	0							
7	2	8	10					
8	0							
9	1	10						
10	0							

Figure 15.8 Crossing table

The connections in the top half are given by the permutation $A = [1, 4, 6, 3, 7, 2, 9, 5, 10, 8]$. That is, top pin i is connected to center pin A_i. The connections in the bottom half are given by the permutation $B = [8, 1, 2, 7, 3, 4, 5, 6, 9, 10]$. That is, center pin i is connected to bottom pin B_i. Observe that $C_i = B_{A_i}$, $1 \le i \le n$. This equality is essential if we are to accomplish the connections given by C.

In this section we develop algorithms to compute the permutations A and B so that the top half of the channel has $\lfloor K/2 \rfloor$ crossings where K is the total number of crossings.

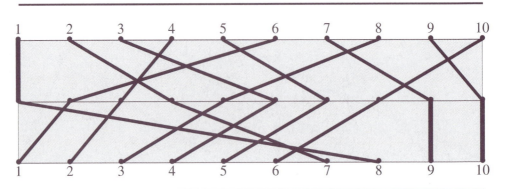

Figure 15.9 Splitting the crossings

Crossing Distribution Using a Linear List

The crossing numbers k_i and the total number of crossings K can be computed in $\Theta(n^2)$ time by examining each wire pair (i, j). The partitioning of C into A and B can then be computed by using an `ArrayLinearList` (or any of the other array-based data structures developed in Chapter 5 for a linear list) as in Program 15.13.

In the `while` loop, we scan the wires from right to left, determining their relative order at the center of the routing channel. The objective is to have a routing order at the center that requires exactly `crossingsNeeded = theK/2` crossings in the top half of the routing channel.

The linear list `list` keeps track of the current ordering, at the center, of the wires so far considered. When wire `currentWire` is considered, we can allocate up to `k[currentWire]` of its crossings with right-side wires to the upper half. The first crossing is with the zeroth wire in `list`, the second with the next wire in `list`, and so on. If c of the `k[currentWire]` right-side crossings of wire `currentWire` are allocated to the upper half, then this wire must cross the first c wires in `list`. In addition, the ordering of wires `currentWire` through `n` is obtained by inserting `currentWire` after the cth wire in `list`. Notice that when wire `currentWire` is considered in the `while` loop of Program 15.13, wires `currentWire+1` through `n` have already been considered and so are in `list`. Further, since `k[currentWire]` cannot exceed the number of wires to the right of `currentWire`, `list` has at least `k[w]` wires in it when `currentWire` is considered.

When `currentWire` is considered in the `while` loop of Program 15.13, all of its right-side crossings are allocated to the top half unless the remaining number `crossingsNeeded` of crossings needed in the top half is less than `k[currentWire]`. Then `crossingsNeeded` of the possible `k[currentWire]` right-side crossings are allocated to the upper half.

When the `while` loop terminates, the wire ordering `theX` at the center of the routing channel may be constructed by noting that wires 1 through `w` have no

```
// create data structures
ArrayLinearList list = new ArrayLinearList(n);
int [] theA = new int [n + 1];   // top-half permutation
int [] theB = new int [n + 1];   // bottom-half permutation
int [] theX = new int [n + 1];   // center connections

int crossingsNeeded = theK / 2;  // remaining number of crossings
                                 // needed in top half

// scan wires right to left
int currentWire = n;
while (crossingsNeeded > 0)
{// need more crossings in top half
   if (k[currentWire] < crossingsNeeded)
   {// use all crossings from currentWire
      list.add(k[currentWire], new Integer(currentWire));
      crossingsNeeded -= k[currentWire];
   }
   else
   {// use only crossingsNeeded crossings from currentWire
      list.add(crossingsNeeded, new Integer(currentWire));
      crossingsNeeded = 0;
   }
   currentWire--;
}

// determine wire permutation at center
// first currentWire wires have same ordering
for (int i = 1; i <= currentWire; i++)
   theX[i] = i;

// ordering of remaining wires is from list
for (int i = currentWire + 1; i <= n; i++)
   theX[i] = ((Integer) list.get(i - currentWire - 1)).intValue();

// compute top-half permutation
for (int i = 1; i <= n; i++)
   theA[theX[i]] = i;
```

Program 15.13 Crossing distribution using a linear list (continues)

```
// compute bottom-half permutation
for (int i = 1; i <= n; i++)
   theB[i] = theC[theX[i]];
```

Program 15.13 Crossing distribution using a linear list (concluded)

crossings in the upper half and so do not change their relative order in this half. Therefore, theX[1:currentWire] = $[1, 2, \cdots,$ currentWire]. The ordering of the remaining wires is given by the list list. The first two for loops of Program 15.13 construct theX.

An Example

Let us go through the construction of theX using our example of Figure 15.7. We begin by inserting wire 10 into list to get list = (10). No crossings are generated. Next we insert wire 9 to get list = (10, 9). The insertion of this wire generates one upper-half crossing. Then we insert wire 8 after the k_8th element to get list = (8, 10, 9). The total number of right-side crossings in the upper half remains 1. Next we insert wire 7 after the second element of list, generating two upper-half crossings. list becomes (8, 10, 7, 9), and the additional crossings needed r drops to 8. When wire 6 is inserted, we get list = (6, 8, 10, 7, 9); r = 8. The insertion of wire 5 generates two crossings and results in list = (6, 8, 5, 10, 7, 9); r = 6. When wire 4 is inserted after the first element of list, one crossing is generated and we get list = (6, 4, 8, 5, 10, 7, 9); r = 5. Next we add wire 3 to get list = (6, 4, 8, 3, 5, 10, 7, 9); r = 2. Finally, when wire 2 is considered, we see that although it is capable of generating $k_2 = 6$ crossings, only two of these crossings can be assigned to the top half of the channel. So it is inserted after the second element of the list to get list = (6, 4, 2, 8, 3, 5, 10, 7, 9). The remaining wires retain their current relative order.

Now we compute the wire permutation following the routing of the top half by appending list to the ordering $(1, 2, \cdots,$ w) to obtain theX = $[1, 6, 4, 2, 8, 3, 5, 10, 7, 9]$.

The permutation theA = A is closely related to theX. theA[j] tells us which center pin wire j should go to, while theX[i] tells us which wire comes to center pin j. The third for loop of Program 15.13 uses this information to compute theA. From theX and theC, theB = B may be computed, as in the fourth for loop.

Complexity Analysis

Since the time needed to insert an element into a linear list of size s is $O(s)$, the while loop of Program 15.13 takes $O(n^2)$ time. The remainder of the code takes $O(n)$ time, so the overall complexity of Program 15.13 is $O(n^2)$. Combining the time requirements of Program 15.13 with the time needed to compute theK and the k[i]s, we see that the overall time needed to solve the crossing-distribution problem is $O(n^2)$ when a linear list is used.

We can reduce the complexity of our solution to $O(n \log n)$ by using a balanced search tree rather than a linear list. To obtain a solution with expected complexity $O(n \log n)$, we may use an indexed binary search tree rather than an indexed balanced search tree. The technique is the same in both cases. We will use an indexed binary search tree to illustrate this technique.

Using an Indexed Binary Search Tree

First let us see how to compute the crossing numbers k_i, $1 \leq i \leq n$. Suppose we examine the wires in the order n, $n-1$, $\cdots$, 1 and put C_i into an indexed search tree when wire i is examined. For the example of Figure 15.7, we start with an empty tree. We examine wire 10 and insert $C_{10} = 6$ into an empty tree to get the tree of Figure 15.10(a). The number outside the node is its leftSize value, and that inside the node is its key (or C value). Note that k_n is always 0, so we set k_n = 0. Next we examine wire 9 and insert $C_9 = 10$ into the tree to get the tree of Figure 15.10(b). To make the insertion, we pass over the root that has leftSize = 1. From this leftSize value, we know that wire 9's bottom endpoint is to the right of exactly one of the wires seen so far, so $k_9 = 1$. We examine wire 8 and insert $C_8 = 3$ to get the tree of Figure 15.10(c). Since C_8 is the smallest entry in the tree, no wires are crossed and $k_8 = 0$. For wire 7, $C_7 = 9$ is inserted to obtain tree (d). C_7 becomes the third-smallest entry in the tree. We can determine that C_7 is the third-smallest entry by keeping a running sum of the leftSize values of the nodes whose right subtree we enter. When C_7 is inserted, this sum is 2. So the new element is currently the third smallest. From this information we conclude that its bottom endpoint is to the right of two others in the tree. As a result, $k_7 = 2$. Proceeding in this way, the trees of Figures 15.10(e) through 15.10(i) are generated when we examine wires 6 through 2. Finally, when we examine wire 1, we insert C_1 = 8 as the right child of the node with key 7. The sum of the leftSize values of the nodes whose right subtrees we enter is $6 + 1 = 7$. Wire 1 has a bottom endpoint that is to the right of seven of the wires in the tree, and so $k_1 = 7$.

The time needed to examine wire i and compute k_i is $O(h)$ where h is the current height of the indexed search tree. So all k_is can be computed in expected time $O(n \log n)$ by using an indexed binary search tree or in time $O(n \log n)$ by using an indexed balanced search tree.

To compute A, we can implement the code of Program 15.13, using an indexed binary tree representation of a linear list. To list the elements in order of rank, we can do an inorder traversal. The expected time needed by this implementation of Program 15.13 is $O(n \log n)$ when the linear list implementation of Exercise 22 is used; the worst-case time is $O(n \log n)$ when an indexed balanced tree implementation (see Exercise 20 in Chapter 16) is used.

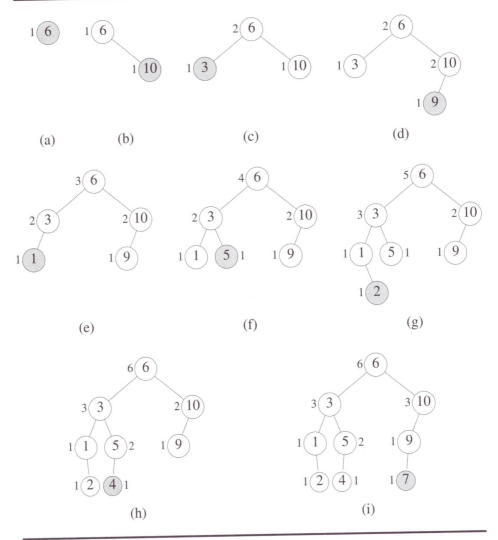

Figure 15.10 Computing the number of crossings

Another way to obtain the permutation A is to first compute $r = \sum_{i=1}^{n} k_i/2$ and $s = $ smallest i such that $\sum_{l=i}^{n} k_l \leq r$. For our example, $r = 11$ and $s = 3$. We see that Program 15.13 does all crossings (i.e., with wires whose top point is to the right) for wires n, $n - 1$, $\cdots$, s and $r - \sum_{l=s}^{n} k_l$ of the crossings for wire $s - 1$ in the top half. The remaining crossings are done in the bottom half. To get these top-half crossings, we examine the tree following the insertion of C_s. For our example we examine tree (h) of Figure 15.10. An inorder traversal of tree (h) yields the sequence (1, 2, 3, 4, 5, 6, 9, 10). Replacing these bottom endpoints with the corresponding wire numbers, we get the sequence (6, 4, 8, 3, 5, 10, 7, 9), which gives the wire permutation following the nine crossings represented in Figure 15.10(h). For the additional two crossings, we insert wire $s = 2$ after the second wire in the sequence to get the new wire sequence (6, 4, 2, 8, 3, 5, 10, 7, 9). The remaining wires 1 through $s - 1$ are added at the front to obtain (1, 6, 4, 2, 8, 3, 5, 10, 7, 9), which is the theX permutation computed in Program 15.13. To obtain theX in this way, we need to rerun part of the code used to compute the k_is, perform an inorder traversal, insert wire s, and add a few wires at the front of the sequence. The time needed for all of these steps is $O(n \log n)$. theA and theB may be obtained from theX in linear time using the last two for loops of Program 15.13.

EXERCISES

23. Write a histogramming program that first inputs the n keys into an array, then sorts this array, and finally makes a left-to-right scan of the array outputting the distinct key values and the number of times each occurs.

24. Write a histogramming program that uses a chained hash table, rather than a binary search tree as in Program 15.10, to store the distinct keys and their frequencies. Compare the run-time performance of your new program with that of Program 15.10.

25. (a) Extend the class DBinarySearchTree by adding the public member removeGreaterThanOrEqual(theKey), which removes the element with smallest key $\geq$ theKey. The removed element is returned.

    (b) Use removeGreaterThanOrEqual (and not getGreaterThanOrEqual) to obtain a new version of bestFitPack.

    (c) Which will run faster? Why?

26. Write the crossing table (see Figure 15.8) for the permutation $C[1 : 10] = [6, 4, 5, 8, 3, 2, 10, 9, 1, 7]$. Compute the top-half and bottom-half permutations A and B that balance the number of crossings in the top and lower halves of the channel.

27. Do Exercise 26 with $C[1 : 10] = [10, 9, 8, 1, 2, 3, 7, 6, 5, 4]$.

28. (a) Use an indexed binary search tree to obtain an $O(n \log n)$ expected time solution for the crossing-distribution problem.

    (b) Test the correctness of your code.

    (c) Compare the actual run time of this solution to that of Program 15.13. Do this comparison using randomly generated permutations C and $n = 1000; 10,000;$ and $50,000$.

29. Write a program to create a concordance for a piece of text (see Exercise 46 in Chapter 11). Use a binary search tree to construct the concordance entries and then perform an inorder traversal of this AVL tree to output the concordance entries in sorted order. Comment on the merits of using a binary search tree versus a hash table. In particular, what can you say about the expected performance of the two approaches when the input text has n words and only $m \leq n$ of these are distinct?

CHAPTER 16

BALANCED SEARCH TREES

BIRD'S-EYE VIEW

This last chapter on trees develops balanced tree structures—tree structures whose height is $O(\log n)$. We develop two balanced binary tree structures, AVL and red black, and one tree structure, B-tree, whose degree is more than 2. AVL and red-black trees are suitable for internal memory applications, and the B-tree is suitable for external memory (e.g., a large dictionary that resides on disk) applications. These balanced structures allow you to perform dictionary operations as well as by-rank operations in $O(\log n)$ time in the worst case. When a linear list is represented as an indexed balanced tree, the *get*, *add*, and *remove* operations take $O(\log n)$ time.

The splay tree is another data structure that is developed in this chapter. Although the height of a splay tree is $O(n)$ and an individual dictionary operation performed on a splay tree takes $O(n)$ time, every sequence of u operations performed on a splay tree takes $O(u \log u)$ time. The asymptotic complexity of a sequence of u operations is the same regardless of whether you use splay trees, AVL trees, or red-black trees.

The following table summarizes the asymptotic performance of the various dictionary structures considered in this text. All complexities are theta of the given function.

Method	Worst Case			Expected		
	Search	Insert	Remove	Search	Insert	Remove
sorted array	$\log n$	n	n	$\log n$	n	n
sorted chain	n	n	n	n	n	n
skip lists	n	n	n	$\log n$	$\log n$	$\log n$
hash tables	n	n	n	1	1	1
binary search tree	n	n	n	$\log n$	$\log n$	$\log n$
AVL tree	$\log n$	$\log n$	$\log n$	$\log n$	$\log n$	$\log n$
red-black tree	$\log n$	$\log n$	$\log n$	$\log n$	$\log n$	$\log n$
splay tree	n	n	n	$\log n$	$\log n$	$\log n$
B-trees	$\log n$	$\log n$	$\log n$	$\log n$	$\log n$	$\log n$

The Java classes `java.util.TreeMap` and `java.util.TreeSet` use red-black trees to guarantee logarithmic performance for the search, insert, and delete operations.

In practice, we expect hashing to outperform balanced search trees when the desired operations are search, insert, and delete (all by key value); therefore, hashing is the preferred method in these applications. When the dictionary operations are done solely by key value, balanced search trees are recommended only in time-critical applications in which we must guarantee that no dictionary operation ever takes more than a specified amount of time. Balanced search trees are also recommended when the search and delete operations are done by rank and for applications in which the dictionary operations are not done by exact key match. An example of the latter would be finding the smallest element with a key larger than k.

The actual run-time performance of both AVL and red-black trees is similar; in comparison, splay trees take less time to perform a sequence of u operations. In addition, splay trees are easier to implement.

Both AVL and red-black trees use "rotations" to maintain balance. AVL trees perform at most one rotation following an insert and $O(\log n)$ rotations following a delete. However, red-black trees perform a single rotation following either an insert or delete. This difference is not important in most applications where a rotation takes $\Theta(1)$ time. It does, however, become important in advanced applications where a rotation cannot be performed in constant time. One such application is the implementation of the balanced priority search trees of McCreight. These priority search trees are used to represent elements with two-dimensional keys. In this case each key is a pair (x, y). A priority search tree is a tree that is simultaneously a min (or max) tree on y and a search tree on x. When rotations are performed in these trees, each has a cost of $O(\log n)$. Since red-black trees perform a single rotation following an insert or delete, the overall insert or delete time remains $O(\log n)$ if we use a red-black tree to represent a priority search tree. When we use an AVL tree, the time for the delete operation becomes $O(\log^2 n)$.

Although AVL trees, red-black trees, and splay trees provide good performance when the dictionary being represented is sufficiently small to fit in our computer's memory, they are quite inadequate for larger dictionaries. When the dictionary resides on disk, we need to use search trees with a much higher degree and hence a much smaller height. An example of such a search tree, the B-tree, is also considered in this chapter.

Although Java codes are not given for any of the data structures developed in this chapter, several codes are available on the Web site as solutions to exercises. The Web site also has material on other search structures such as tries and suffix trees.

This chapter does not have an applications section because the applications of balanced search trees are the same as those of binary search trees (Chapter 15). By using a balanced search tree in these applications, we obtain code whose worst-case asymptotic complexity is the same as the expected complexity when unbalanced binary search trees are used.

16.1   AVL TREES

16.1.1   Definition

We can guarantee $O(\log n)$ performance for each search tree operation by ensuring that the search tree height is always $O(\log n)$. Trees with a worst-case height of $O(\log n)$ are called **balanced trees**. One of the more popular balanced trees, known as an **AVL tree**, was introduced in 1962 by Adelson-Velskii and Landis.

Definition 16.1 *An empty binary tree is an AVL tree. If T is a nonempty binary tree with T_L and T_R as its left and right subtrees, then T is an AVL tree iff (1) T_L and T_R are AVL trees and (2) $|h_L - h_R| \leq 1$ where h_L and h_R are the heights of T_L and T_R, respectively.* ∎

An **AVL search tree** is a binary search tree that is also an AVL tree. Trees (a) and (b) of Figure 15.1 are AVL trees, while tree (c) is not. Tree (a) is not an AVL search tree, as it is not a binary search tree. Tree (b) is an AVL search tree. The trees of Figure 15.3 are AVL search trees.

An **indexed AVL search tree** is an indexed binary search tree that is also an AVL tree. Both the search trees of Figure 15.2 are indexed AVL search trees. In the remainder of this section, we will not consider indexed AVL search trees explicitly. However, the techniques we develop carry over in a rather straightforward manner to such trees. We will use the terms *insert* and *put* as well as the terms *remove* and *delete* interchangeably.

If we are to use AVL search trees to represent a dictionary and perform each dictionary operation in logarithmic time, then we must establish the following properties:

1. The height of an AVL tree with n elements/nodes is $O(\log n)$.

2. For every value of n, $n \geq 0$, there exists an AVL tree. (Otherwise, some insertions cannot leave behind an AVL tree, as no such tree exists for the current number of elements.)

3. An n-element AVL search tree can be searched in $O(height) = O(\log n)$ time.

4. A new element can be inserted into an n-element AVL search tree so that the result is an $n + 1$ element AVL tree and such an insertion can be done in $O(\log n)$ time.

5. An element can be deleted from an n-element AVL search tree, $n > 0$, so that the result is an $n - 1$ element AVL tree and such a deletion can be done in $O(\log n)$ time.

Property 2 follows from property 4, so we will not show property 2 explicitly. Properties 1, 3, 4, and 5 are established in the following subsections.

16.1.2   Height of an AVL Tree

We will obtain a bound on the height of an AVL tree that has n nodes in it. Let N_h be the minimum number of nodes in an AVL tree of height h. In the worst case the height of one of the subtrees is $h - 1$, and the height of the other is $h - 2$. Both these subtrees are also AVL trees. Hence

$$N_h = N_{h-1} + N_{h-2} + 1, \quad N_0 = 0, \quad \text{and} \quad N_1 = 1$$

Notice the similarity between this definition for N_h and the definition of the Fibonacci numbers

$$F_n = F_{n-1} + F_{n-2}, \quad F_0 = 0, \quad \text{and} \quad F_1 = 1$$

It can be shown (see Exercise 9) that $N_h = F_{h+2} - 1$ for $h \geq 0$. From Fibonacci number theory we know that $F_h \approx \phi^h / \sqrt{5}$ where $\phi = (1 + \sqrt{5})/2$. Hence $N_h \approx \phi^{h+2}/\sqrt{5} - 1$. If there are n nodes in the tree, then its height h is at most $\log_\phi(\sqrt{5}(n + 1)) - 2 \approx 1.44 \log_2(n + 2) = O(\log n)$.

16.1.3   Representation of an AVL Tree

AVL trees are normally represented by using the linked representation scheme for binary trees. However, to facilitate insertion and deletion, a balance factor bf is associated with each node. The balance factor $bf(x)$ of a node x is defined as

height of left subtree of $x -$ height of right subtree of x

From the definition of an AVL tree, it follows that the permissible balance factors are -1, 0, and 1. Figure 16.1 shows two AVL search trees and the balance factors for each node.

16.1.4   Searching an AVL Search Tree

To search an AVL search tree, we may use the code of Program 15.4 without change. Since the height of an AVL tree with n elements is $O(\log n)$, the search time is $O(\log n)$.

16.1.5   Inserting into an AVL Search Tree

If we use the strategy of Program 15.5 to insert an element into an AVL search tree, the tree following the insertion may no longer be AVL. For instance, when an element with key 32 is inserted into the AVL tree of Figure 16.1(a), the new search tree is the one shown in Figure 16.2(a). Since this tree contains nodes with balance

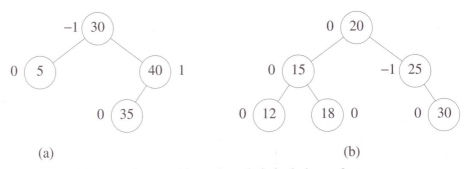

(a)   (b)

The number outside each node is its balance factor

Figure 16.1 AVL search trees

factors other than -1, 0, and 1, it is not an AVL tree. When an insertion into an AVL tree using the strategy of Program 15.5 results in a search tree that has one or more nodes with balance factors other than -1, 0, and 1, the resulting search tree is **unbalanced**. We can restore balance (i.e., make all balance factors -1, 0, and 1) by shifting some of the subtrees of the unbalanced tree as in Figure 16.2(b).

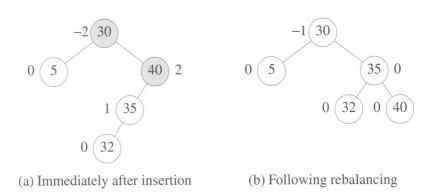

(a) Immediately after insertion   (b) Following rebalancing

Figure 16.2 Sample insertion into an AVL search tree

Before examining the subtree movement needed to restore balance, let us make some observations about the unbalanced tree that results from an insertion. I1 denotes insertion obervation 1.

I1: In the unbalanced tree the balance factors are limited to -2, -1, 0, 1, and 2.

I2: A node with balance factor 2 had a balance factor 1 before the insertion.

Similarly, a node with balance factor -2 had a balance factor -1 before the insertion.

I3: The balance factors of only those nodes on the path from the root to the newly inserted node can change as a result of the insertion.

I4: Let A denote the nearest ancestor of the newly inserted node whose balance factor is either -2 or 2. (In the case of Figure 16.2(a), the A node is the node with key 40.) The balance factor of all nodes on the path from A to the newly inserted node was 0 prior to the insertion.

Node A (see I4) may be identified while we are moving down from the root searching for the place to insert the new element. From I2 it follows that $bf(A)$ was either -1 or 1 prior to the insertion. Let X denote the last node encountered that has such a balance factor. When inserting 32 into the AVL tree of Figure 16.1(a), X is the node with key 40; when inserting 22, 28, or 50 into the AVL tree of Figure 16.1(b), X is the node with key 25; and when inserting 10, 14, 16, or 19 into the AVL tree of Figure 16.1(b), there is no node X.

When node X does not exist, all nodes on the path from the root to the newly inserted node have balance factor 0 prior to the insertion. The tree cannot be unbalanced following the insertion because an insertion changes balance factors by -1, 0, or 1, and only balance factors on the path from the root may change. Therefore, if the tree is unbalanced following the insertion, X exists. If $bf(X) = 0$ after the insertion, then the height of the subtree with root X is the same before and after the insertion. For example, if this height was h before the insertion and if $bf(X)$ was 1, the height of its left subtree X_L was $h-1$ and that of its right subtree X_R was $h-2$ before the insertion (see Figure 16.3(a)). For the balance factor to become 0, the insertion must be made in X_R resulting in an X'_R of height $h-1$ (see Figure 16.3(b)). The height of X'_R must increase to $h-1$ as all balance factors on the path from X to the newly inserted node were 0 prior to the insertion. The height of X remains h, and the balance factors of the ancestors of X are the same before and after the insertion, so the tree is balanced.

The only way the tree can become unbalanced is if the insertion causes $bf(X)$ to change from -1 to -2 or from 1 to 2. For the latter case to occur, the insertion must be made in the left subtree X_L of X (see Figure 16.3(c)). Now the height of X'_L must become h (as all balance factors on the path from X to the newly inserted node were 0 prior to the insertion). Therefore, the A node referred to in observation I4 is X.

When the A node has been identified, the imbalance at A can be classified as either an L (the newly inserted node is in the left subtree of A) or R type imbalance. This imbalance classification may be refined by determining which grandchild of A is on the path to the newly inserted node. Notice that such a grandchild exists, as the height of the subtree of A that contains the new node must be at least 2 for the balance factor of A to be -2 or 2. With this refinement of the imbalance classification, the imbalance at A is of one of the types LL (new node is in the left

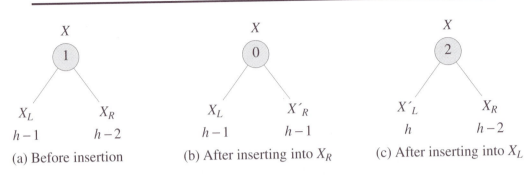

(a) Before insertion   (b) After inserting into X_R (c) After inserting into X_L

Balance factor of X is inside the node
Subtree heights are below subtree names

Figure 16.3 Inserting into an AVL search tree

subtree of the left subtree of A), LR (new node is in the right subtree of the left subtree of A), RR, and RL.

A generic LL type imbalance appears in Figure 16.4. Figure 16.4(a) shows the conditions before the insertion, and Figure 16.4(b) shows the situation following the insertion of an element into the left subtree B_L of B. The subtree movement needed to restore balance at A appears in Figure 16.4(c). B becomes the root of the subtree that A was previously root of, B'_L remains the left subtree of B, A becomes the root of B's right subtree, B_R becomes the left subtree of A, and the right subtree of A is unchanged. The balance factors of nodes in B'_L that are on the path from B to the newly inserted node change as does the balance factor of A. The remaining balance factors are the same as before the rotation. Since the heights of the subtrees of Figures 16.4(a) and (c) are the same, the balance factors of the ancestors (if any) of this subtree are the same as before the insertion. So no nodes with a balance factor other than -1, 0, or 1 remain. A single LL rotation has rebalanced the entire tree! You may verify that the rebalanced tree is indeed a binary search tree.

Figure 16.5 shows a generic LR type imbalance. Since the insertion took place in the right subtree of B, this subtree cannot be empty following the insertion; therefore, node C exists. However, its subtrees C_L and C_R may be empty. The rearrangement of subtrees needed to rebalance appears in Figure 16.5(c). The values of $bf(B)$ and $bf(A)$ following the rearrangement depend on the value, b, of $bf(C)$ just after the insertion but before the rearrangement. The figure gives these values as a function of b. The rearranged subtree is seen to be a binary search tree. Also, since the heights of the subtrees of Figures 16.5(a) and (c) are the same, the balance factors of their ancestors (if any) are the same before and after the insertion. So a single LR rotation at A rebalances the entire tree.

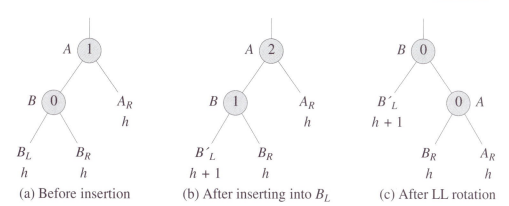

Balance factors are inside nodes
Subtree heights are below subtree names

Figure 16.4 An LL rotation

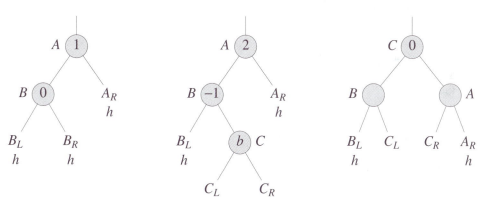

$$b = 0 \Rightarrow bf(B) = bf(A) = 0 \text{ after rotation}$$
$$b = 1 \Rightarrow bf(B) = 0 \text{ and } bf(A) = -1 \text{ after rotation}$$
$$b = -1 \Rightarrow bf(B) = 1 \text{ and } bf(A) = 0 \text{ after rotation}$$

Figure 16.5 An LR rotation

The cases RR and RL are symmetric to the ones we have just seen. The transformations done to remedy LL and RR imbalances are often called **single rotations**, while those done for LR and RL imbalances are called **double rotations**. The transformation for an LR imbalance can be viewed as an RR rotation followed by an LL rotation, while that for an RL imbalance can be viewed as an LL rotation followed by an RR rotation (see Exercise 13).

The steps in the AVL search-tree-insertion algorithm that results from our discussion appear in Figure 16.6. These steps can be refined into Java code that has a complexity of $O(height) = O(\log n)$. *Notice that a single rotation (LL, LR, RR, or RL) is sufficient to restore balance if the insertion causes imbalance.*

Step 1: Find the place to insert the new element by following a path from the root as in a search for an element with the same key. During this process, keep track of the most recently seen node with balance factor -1 or 1. Let this node be A. If an element with the same key is found, the insert fails and the remaining steps are not performed.

Step 2: If there is no node A, then make another pass from the root, updating balance factors. Terminate following this pass.

Step 3: If $bf(A) = 1$ and the new node was inserted in the right subtree of A or if $bf(A) = -1$ and the insertion took place in the left subtree, then the new balance factor of A is 0. In this case update balance factors on the path from A to the new node and terminate.

Step 4: Classify the imbalance at A and perform the appropriate rotation. Change balance factors as required by the rotation as well as those of nodes on the path from the new subtree root to the newly inserted node.

Figure 16.6 Steps for AVL search tree insertion

16.1.6   Deletion from an AVL Search Tree

To delete an element from an AVL search tree, we proceed as in Program 15.6. Let q be the parent of the node that was physically deleted. For example, if the element with key 25 is deleted from the tree of Figure 16.1(b), the node containing this element is deleted and the right-child pointer from the root diverted to the only child of the deleted node. The parent of the deleted node is the root, so q is the root. If instead, the element with key 15 is deleted, its spot is used by the element with key 12 and the node previously containing this element is deleted. Now q is the node that originally contained 15 (i.e., the left child of the root). Since the balance factors of some (or all) of the nodes on the path from the root to q have changed as a result of the deletion, we retrace this path backward from q toward the root.

If the deletion took place from the left subtree of q, $bf(q)$ decreases by 1, and if it took place from the right subtree, $bf(q)$ increases by 1. We may make the following observations (D1 denotes deletion obervation 1):

D1: If the new balance factor of q is 0, its height has decreased by 1; we need to change the balance factor of its parent (if any) and possibly those of its other ancestors.

D2: If the new balance factor of q is either -1 or 1, its height is the same as before the deletion and the balance factors of its ancestors are unchanged.

D3: If the new balance factor of q is either -2 or 2, the tree is unbalanced at q.

Since balance factor changes may propogate up the tree along the path from q to the root (see observation D1), it is possible for the balance factor of a node on this path to become -2 or 2. Let A be the first such node on this path. To restore balance at node A, we classify the type of imbalance. The imbalance is of type L if the deletion took place from A's left subtree. Otherwise, it is of type R. If $bf(A) = 2$ after the deletion, it must have been 1 before. So A has a left subtree with root B. A type R imbalance is subclassified into the types R0, R1, and R-1, depending on $bf(B)$. The type R-1, for instance, refers to the case when the deletion took place from the right subtree of A and $bf(B) = -1$. Similarly, type L imbalances are subclassified into the types L0, L1, and L-1.

An R0 imbalance at A is rectified by performing the rotation shown in Figure 16.7. Notice that the height of the shown subtree was $h+2$ before the deletion and is $h+2$ after. So the balance factors of the remaining nodes on the path to the root are unchanged. As a result, the entire tree has been rebalanced.

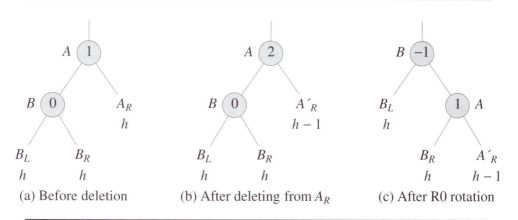

(a) Before deletion   (b) After deleting from A_R (c) After R0 rotation

Figure 16.7 An R0 rotation (single rotation)

Figure 16.8 shows how to handle an R1 imbalance. While the pointer changes are the same as for an R0 imbalance, the new balance factors for A and B are different and the height of the subtree following the rotation is now $h + 1$, which is 1 less than before the deletion. So if A is not the root, the balance factors of some of its ancestors will change and further rotations may be necessary. Following an R1 rotation, we must continue to examine nodes on the path to the root. *Unlike the case of an insertion, one rotation may not suffice to restore balance following a deletion. The number of rotations needed is $O(\log n)$.*

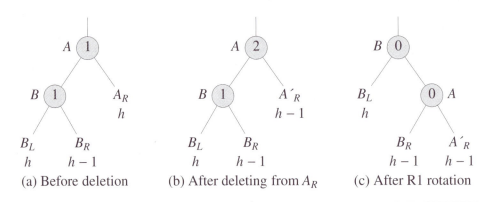

(a) Before deletion   (b) After deleting from A_R (c) After R1 rotation

Figure 16.8 An R1 rotation (single rotation)

The transformation needed when the imbalance is of type R$-$1 appears in Figure 16.9. The balance factors of A and B following the rotation depend on the balance factor b of the right child of B. This rotation leaves behind a subtree of height $h + 1$, while the subtree height prior to the deletion was $h + 2$. So we need to continue on the path to the root.

LL and R1 rotations are identical; LL and R0 rotations differ only in the final balance factors of A and B; and LR and R$-$1 rotations are identical.

EXERCISES

1. Start with an empty AVL search tree and insert the following keys in the given order: 15, 14, 13, 12, 11, 10, 9, 8, 7, 6, 5, 4, 3, 2, 1. Draw figures similar to Figures 16.2 and 16.3 depicting your tree immediately after each insertion and following the rebalancing rotation (if any). Label all nodes with their balance factors and identify the rotation type (if any) that is done.

2. Do Exercise 1 using the insert key sequence: 1, 2, 3, 4, 5, 6, 7, 8, 9, 10, 11, 12, 13, 14, 15.

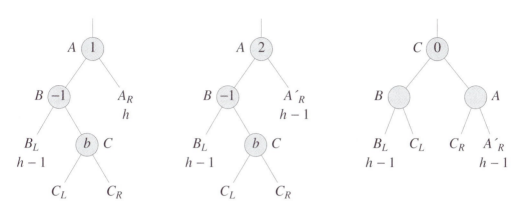

(a) Before deletion   (b) After deleting from A_R (c) After R−1 rotation

$$b = 0 \Rightarrow bf(A) = bf(B) = 0 \text{ after rotation}$$
$$b = 1 \Rightarrow bf(A) = -1 \text{ and } bf(B) = 0 \text{ after rotation}$$
$$b = -1 \Rightarrow bf(A) = 0 \text{ and } bf(B) = 1 \text{ after rotation}$$

Figure 16.9 An R−1 rotation (double rotation)

3. Do Exercise 1 using the insert key sequence: 20, 10, 5, 30, 40, 3, 4, 25, 23, 27, 50.

4. Do Exercise 1 using the insert key sequence: 40, 50, 70, 30, 20, 45, 25, 10, 5, 22, 1, 35.

5. Start with an AVL search tree that is a 15-node full binary tree; the keys are 1–15. Remove the keys in the order 15, 14, 13, $\cdots$, 1. Draw your tree immediately following each deletion and immediately after each rotation that is performed. Label all nodes with their balance factors and identify the rotation type (if any) that is done.

6. Do Exercise 5 but this time remove the keys in the order 1, 2, 3, $\cdots$, 15.

7. Do Exercise 5 but this time remove keys in the order 6, 7, 5, 10, 9, 11, 15, 12, 13, 1, 2, and 3.

8. Do Exercise 5 but this time remove keys in the order 11, 14, 13, 15, 9, 2, 3, 1, 6, 5, and 7.

9. Prove by induction that the minimum number of nodes in an AVL tree of height h is $N_h = F_{h+2} - 1$, $h \geq 0$.

10. Prove observations I1 through I4 regarding an unbalanced tree resulting from an insertion using the strategy of Program 15.5.

11. Draw a figure analogous to Figure 16.3 for the case when $bf(X) = -1$ prior to the insertion.

12. Draw figures analogous to Figures 16.4 and 16.5 for the case of RR and RL imbalances.

13. Start with the LR imbalance shown in Figure 16.5(b) and draw the tree that results when we perform an RR rotation at node B. Observe that an LL rotation on this resulting tree results in the tree of Figure 16.5(b).

14. Draw figures analogous to Figures 16.7, 16.8, and 16.9 for the case of L0, L1, and L−1 imbalances.

★ 15. Develop a Java class AVLtree that includes the binary search tree methods get, put, remove, and ascend. Fully code all your methods and test their correctness. Your implementations for the first three operations must have complexity $O(\log n)$, and that for the last operation should be $O(n)$. Show that this is the case.

★ 16. Do Exercise 15 for the case when the search tree may contain several elements with the same key. Call the new class DAVLtree.

★ 17. Develop a Java class IndexedAVLtree that includes the indexed binary search tree methods get(theKey), put, remove(theKey), get(theIndex), remove-(theIndex), and ascend. Fully code all your methods and test their correctness. Your implementations for the first five operations must have complexity $O(\log n)$ and that for the last operation should be $O(n)$. Show that this is the case.

★ 18. Do Exercise 17 for the case when the search tree may contain several elements with the same key. Call the new class DIndexedAVLtree.

19. Explain how you could use an AVL tree to reduce the asymptotic complexity of our solution to the railroad car rearrangement problem of Section 9.5.3 to $O(n \log k)$.

★ 20. Develop the class LinearListAsIndexedAVLtree that implements the interface LinearList (Program 5.1). See Exercise 21 in Chapter 15 for some clues. Other than the operation indexOf, all operations should run in logarithmic or less time.

21. Replace the use of a binary search tree in Program 15.12 with an AVL search tree with duplicates. Measure the performance of the two versions of the best-fit bin-packing codes.

22. (a) Use an indexed AVL search tree to obtain an $O(n \log n)$ solution for the crossing-distribution problem (Section 15.6.3).

    (b) Test the correctness of your code.

    (c) Compare the actual run time of this solution to that of the $\Theta(n^2)$ solution described in Section 15.6.3 (see Program 15.13). Do this comparison using randomly generated permutations C and $n = 1000$; 10,000; and 50,000.

16.2 RED–BLACK TREES

16.2.1 Definition

A **red-black tree** is a binary search tree in which every node is colored either red or black. The remaining properties satisfied by a red-black tree are best stated in terms of the corresponding extended binary tree. Recall, from Section 13.5.1, that we obtain an extended binary tree from a regular binary tree by replacing every null pointer with an external node. The additional properties are

RB1. The root and all external nodes are colored black.

RB2. No root-to-external-node path has two consecutive red nodes.

RB3. All root-to-external-node paths have the same number of black nodes.

An equivalent definition arises from assigning colors to the pointers between a node and its children. The pointer from a parent to a black child is black and to a red child is red. Additionally,

RB1′. Pointers from an internal node to an external node are black.

RB2′. No root-to-external-node path has two consecutive red pointers.

RB3′. All root-to-external-node paths have the same number of black pointers.

Notice that if we know the pointer colors, we can deduce the node colors and vice versa. In the red-black tree of Figure 16.10, the external nodes are shaded squares, black nodes are shaded circles, red nodes are unshaded circles, black pointers are thick lines, and red pointers are thin lines. Notice that every path from the root to an external node has exactly two black pointers and three black nodes (including the root and the external node); no such path has two consecutive red nodes or pointers.

Let the **rank** of a node in a red-black tree be the number of black pointers (equivalently the number of black nodes minus 1) on any path from the node to any external node in its subtree. So the rank of an external node is 0. The rank of the root of Figure 16.10 is 2, that of its left child is 2, and of its right child is 1.

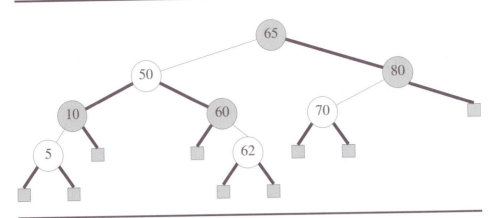

Figure 16.10 A red-black tree

Lemma 16.1 *Let the length of a root-to-external-node path be the number of point-ers on the path. If P and Q are two root-to-external-node paths in a red-black tree, then $length(P) \leq 2length(Q)$.*

Proof Consider any red-black tree. Suppose that the rank of the root is r. From RB1$'$ the last pointer on each root-to-external-node path is black. From RB2$'$ no such path has two consecutive red pointers. So each red pointer is followed by a black pointer. As a result, each root-to-external-node path has between r and $2r$ pointers, so $length(P) \leq 2length(Q)$. To see that the upper bound is possible, consider the red-black tree of Figure 16.10. The path from the root to the left child of 5 has length 4, while that to the right child of 80 has length 2.   ∎

Lemma 16.2 *Let h be the height of a red-black tree (excluding the external nodes), let n be the number of internal nodes in the tree, and let r be the rank of the root.*

(a) $h \leq 2r$

(b) $n \geq 2^r - 1$

(c) $h \leq 2\log_2(n+1)$

Proof From the proof of Lemma 16.1, we know that no root-to-external-node path has length $> 2r$, so $h \leq 2r$. (The height of the red-black tree of Figure 16.10 with external nodes removed is $2r = 4$.)

Since the rank of the root is r, there are no external nodes at levels 1 through r, so there are $2^r - 1$ internal nodes at these levels. Consequently, the total number of internal nodes is at least this much. (In the red-black tree of Figure 16.10, levels 1 and 2 have $3 = 2^2 - 1$ internal nodes. There are additional internal nodes at levels 3 and 4.)

From (b) it follows that $r \leq \log_2(n+1)$. This inequality together with (a) yields (c). ∎

Since the height of a red-black tree is at most $2\log_2(n + 1)$, search, insert, and delete algorithms that work in $O(h)$ time have complexity $O(\log n)$.

Notice that the worst-case height of a red-black tree is more than the worst-case height (approximately $1.44\log_2(n + 2)$) of an AVL tree with the same number of (internal) nodes.

16.2.2 Representation of a Red-Black Tree

Although it is convenient to include external nodes when defining red-black trees, in an implementation null pointers, rather than physical nodes, represent external nodes. Further, since pointer and node colors are closely related, with each node we need to store only its color or the color of the two pointers to its children. Node colors require just one additional bit per node, while pointer colors require two. Since both schemes require almost the same amount of space, we may choose between them on the basis of actual run times of the resulting red-black tree algorithms.

In our discussion of the insert and delete operations, we will explicitly state the needed color changes only for the nodes. The corresponding pointer color changes may be inferred.

16.2.3 Searching a Red-Black Tree

We can search a red-black tree with the code we used to search an ordinary binary search tree (Program 15.4). This code has complexity $O(h)$, which is $O(\log n)$ for a red-black tree. Since we use the same code to search ordinary binary search trees, AVL trees, and red-black trees and since the worst-case height of an AVL tree is least, we expect AVL trees to show the best worst-case performance in applications where search is the dominant operation.

16.2.4 Inserting into a Red-Black Tree

Elements may be inserted using the strategy used for ordinary binary trees (Program 15.5). When the new node is attached to the red-black tree, we need to assign the node a color. If the tree was empty before the insertion, then the new node is the root and must be colored black (see property RB1). Suppose the tree was not empty prior to the insertion. If the new node is given the color black, then we will have an extra black node on paths from the root to the external nodes that are children of the new node. On the other hand, if the new node is assigned the color red, then we might have two consecutive red nodes. Making the new node black is guaranteed to cause a violation of property RB3, while making the new node red may or may not violate property RB2. We will make the new node red.

If making the new node red causes a violation of property RB2, we will say that the tree has become imbalanced. The nature of the imbalance is classified by examining the new node u, its parent pu, and the grandparent gu of u. Observe that since property RB2 has been violated, we have two consecutive red nodes. One of these red nodes is u, and the other must be its parent; therefore, pu exists. Since pu is red, it cannot be the root (as the root is black by property RB1); u must have a grandparent gu, which must be black (property RB2). When pu is the left child of gu, u is the left child of pu and the other child of gu is black (this case includes the case when the other child of gu is an external node); the imbalance is of type LLb. The other imbalance types are LLr (pu is the left child of gu, u is the left child of pu, the other child of gu is red), LRb (pu is the left child of gu, u is the right child of pu, the other child of gu is black), LRr, RRb, RRr, RLb, and RLr.

Imbalances of the type XYr (X and Y may be L or R) are handled by changing colors, while those of type XYb require a rotation. When we change a color, the RB2 violation may propagate two levels up the tree. In this case we will need to reclassify at the new level, with the new u being the former gu, and apply the transformations again. When a rotation is done, the RB2 violation is taken care of and no further work is needed.

Figure 16.11 shows the color changes performed for LLr and LRr imbalances; these color changes are identical. Black nodes are shaded, while red ones are not. In Figure 16.11(a), for example, gu is black, while pu and u are red; the pointers from gu to its left and right children are red; gu_R is the right subtree of gu; and pu_R is the right subtree of pu. Both LLr and LRr color changes require us to change the color of pu and of the right child of gu from red to black. Additionally, we change the color of gu from black to red provided gu is not the root. Since this color change is not done when gu is the root, the number of black nodes on all root-to-external-node paths increases by 1 when gu is the root of the red-black tree.

If changing the color of gu to red causes an imbalance, gu becomes the new u node, its parent becomes the new pu, its grandparent becomes the new gu, and we continue to rebalance. If gu is the root or if the color change does not cause an RB2 violation at gu, we are done.

Figure 16.12 shows the rotations performed to handle LLb and LRb imbalances. In Figures 16.12(a) and (b), u is the root of pu_L. Notice the similarity between these rotations and the LL (refer to Figure 16.4) and LR (refer to Figure 16.5) rotations used to handle an imbalance following an insertion in an AVL tree. The pointer changes are the same. In the case of an LLb rotation, for example, in addition to pointer changes we need to change the color of gu from black to red and of pu from red to black.

In examining the node (or pointer) colors after the rotations of Figure 16.12, we see that the number of black nodes (or pointers) on all root-to-external-node paths is unchanged. Further, the root of the involved subtree (gu before the rotation and pu after) is black following the rotation; therefore, two consecutive red nodes cannot exist on the path from the tree root to the new pu. Consequently, no additional

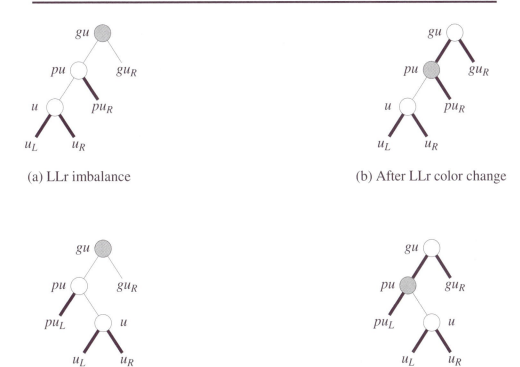

(a) LLr imbalance

(b) After LLr color change

(c) LRr imbalance

(d) After LRr color change

Figure 16.11 LLr and LRr color changes

rebalancing work is to be done. *A single rotation (preceded possibly by $O(\log n)$ color changes) suffices to restore balance following an insertion!*

Example 16.1 Consider the red-black tree of Figure 16.13(a). External nodes are shown for convenience. In an actual implementation, the shown black pointers to external nodes are simply null pointers and external nodes are not represented. Notice that all root-to-external-node paths have three black nodes (including the external node) and two black pointers.

To insert 70 into this red-black tree, we use the algorithm of Program 15.5. The new node is added as the left child of 80. Since the insertion is done into a nonempty tree, the new node is assigned the color red. So the pointer to it from its parent (80) is also red. This insertion does not result in a violation of property RB2, and no remedial action is necessary. Notice that the number of black pointers on all root-to-external-node paths is the same as before the insertion.

Next insert 60 into the tree of Figure 16.13(b). The algorithm of Program 15.5

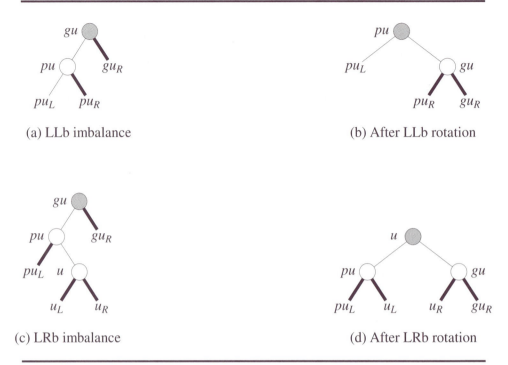

(a) LLb imbalance

(b) After LLb rotation

(c) LRb imbalance

(d) After LRb rotation

Figure 16.12 LLb and LRb rotations for red-black insertion

attaches a new node as the left child of 70, as is shown in Figure 16.13(c). The new node is red, and the pointer to it is also red. The new node is the u node, its parent (70) is pu, and its grandparent (80) is gu. Since pu and u are red, we have an imbalance. This imbalance is classified as an LLr imbalance (as pu is the left child of gu, u is the left child of pu, and the other child of gu is red). When the LLr color change of Figure 16.11(a) and (b) is performed, we get the tree of Figure 16.13(d). Now u, pu, and gu are each moved two levels up the tree. The node with 80 is the new u node, the root becomes pu, and gu is null. Since there is no gu node, we cannot have an RB2 imbalance at this location and we are done. All root-to-external-node paths have exactly two black pointers.

Now insert 65 into the tree of Figure 16.13(d). The result appears in Figure 16.13(e). The new node is the u node. Its parent and grandparent are, respectively, the pu and gu nodes. We have an LRb imbalance that requires us to perform the rotation of Figure 16.12(c) and (d). The result is the tree of Figure 16.13(f).

Finally, insert 62 to obtain the tree of Figure 16.13(g). We have an LRr imbalance that requires a color change. The resulting tree and the new u, pu, and gu nodes appear in Figure 16.13(h). The color change just performed has caused an

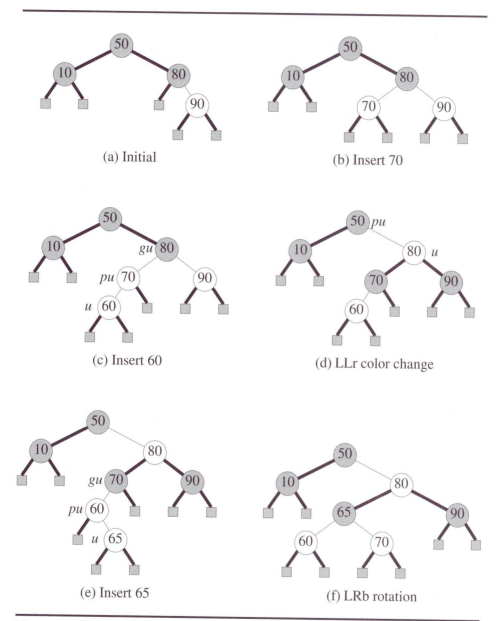

(a) Initial

(b) Insert 70

(c) Insert 60

(d) LLr color change

(e) Insert 65

(f) LRb rotation

Figure 16.13 Insertion into a red-black tree (continues)

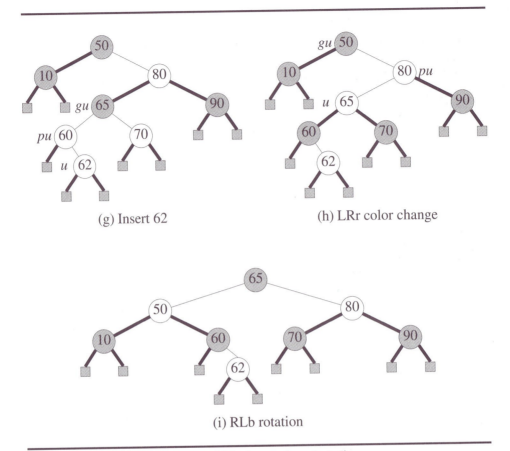

(g) Insert 62

(h) LRr color change

(i) RLb rotation

Figure 16.13 Insertion into a red-black tree (concluded)

RLb imbalance two levels up, so we now need to perform an RLb rotation. The rotation results in the tree of Figure 16.13(i). Following a rotation, no further work is needed, and we are done.   ∎

16.2.5   Deletion from a Red-Black Tree

Deletions are performed by first using the deletion algorithm for ordinary binary search trees (Program 15.6) and then performing remedial color changes and a single rotation if necessary. Consider the red-black tree of Figure 16.14(a). If Program 15.6 is used to delete 70, the node containing 70 is physically removed (deleted) from the tree and we get the tree of Figure 16.14(b). (If pointer colors are represented, we will also need to change the color of 90's left pointer to get this tree.) When 90 is deleted from tree (a), the node that contains 90 is physically removed from the tree, the right-child pointer from its parent is changed to point to the left subtree of the physically removed node, and tree (c) results. The deletion of 65 from tree (a) is done by moving 62 into the root and then physically removing the node that originally contained 62; the result is tree (d). Let y denote the node that takes the place of the node that is physically removed (or deleted). The y nodes for the deletion examples appear in Figure 16.14. In the case of Figure 16.14(b), for example, the left child of 90 was deleted. Its new left child is the external node y.

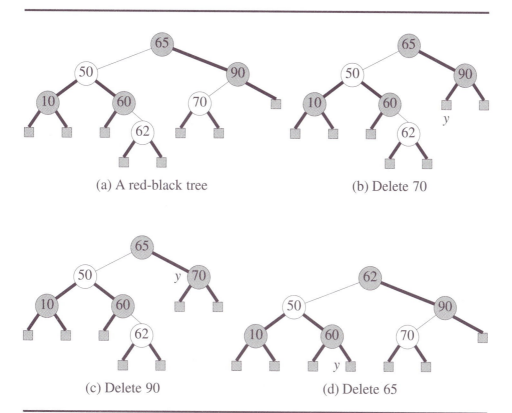

(a) A red-black tree

(b) Delete 70

(c) Delete 90

(d) Delete 65

Figure 16.14 Red-black deletion examples

In the case of tree (b), the deleted node (i.e., the one that contained 70 in tree (a)) was red. Its deletion does not affect the number of black nodes on root-to-external-node paths, and no remedial work is necessary. In tree (c) the deleted node (i.e., the one with 90 in tree (a)) was black, and the number of black nodes (and hence pointers) on paths from the root-to-external-nodes in y is 1 less than before. Since y is not the new root, an RB3 violation occurs. In tree (d) the deleted node was red, and no RB3 violation occurs. *An RB3 violation occurs only when the deleted node was black and y is not the root of the resulting tree.* No other red-black property violations are possible following a deletion using Program 15.6.

When an RB3 violation occurs, the subtree rooted at y is one black node (or equivalently, one black pointer) deficient; therefore, the number of black nodes (and hence pointers) on paths from the root to external nodes in the subtree y is 1 less than on paths to other external nodes. We will say that the tree has become **imbalanced**. We classify the nature of the imbalance by identifying the parent py and sibling v of y. When y is the right child of py, the imbalance is of type R. Otherwise, it is of type L. Observe that since y is one black node deficient, v cannot be an external node. If v is a black node, the imbalance is of type Lb or Rb. When v is red, the imbalance is of type Lr or Rr.

First consider an Rb imbalance. Imbalances of type Lb are handled in a similar way. Rb imbalances may be divided into three subcases on the basis of the number of v's red children. The three subcases are Rb0, Rb1, and Rb2.

When the imbalance type is Rb0, a color change is performed (Figure 16.15). Figure 16.15 shows the two possibilities for the color of py. If py was black prior to the color change, then the color change causes the subtree rooted at py to be one black node deficient. Also, in Figure 16.15(b) the number of black nodes on paths to external nodes in v is 1 less than before the color change. Therefore, regardless of whether the path goes to an external node in v or y, following the color change, it is one black node deficient. If py is the root of the whole red-black tree, nothing more is to be done. If it is not, then py becomes the new y; the imbalance at y is reclassified, and appropriate remedial action occurs at this new y.

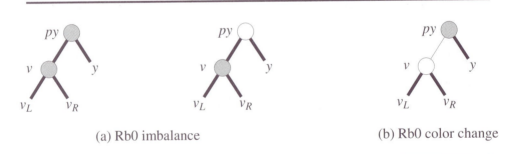

(a) Rb0 imbalance   (b) Rb0 color change

Figure 16.15 Rb0 color change for red-black deletion

When py was red before the color change, the number of black nodes on paths to external nodes in y increases by 1 but is unchanged for those in v. The entire tree becomes balanced, and we are done.

Rotations are performed when the imbalance type is Rb1 or Rb2. These rotations appear in Figure 16.16. A thatched node denotes a node that may be either red or black. The color of such a node is not changed as a result of the rotation. Therefore, in Figure 16.16(b) the root of the shown subtree has the same color before and after the rotation—the color of v in (b) is the same as that of py in (a). You should verify that following the rotation the number of black nodes (and hence black pointers) on paths from the root-to-external-nodes in y is increased by 1 and unchanged on paths from the root to the remaining external nodes. As a result, a rotation rebalances the tree, and no further work is to be done.

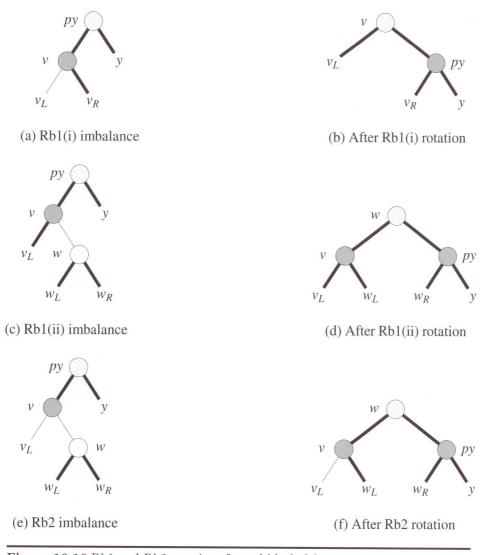

(a) Rb1(i) imbalance

(b) After Rb1(i) rotation

(c) Rb1(ii) imbalance

(d) After Rb1(ii) rotation

(e) Rb2 imbalance

(f) After Rb2 rotation

Figure 16.16 Rb1 and Rb2 rotations for red-black deletion

Next consider imbalances of type Rr. The case of Lr imbalances is symmetric. Since y is one black node deficient and v is red, both v_L and v_R have at least one black node that is not an external node; therefore, both children of v are internal nodes. Rr imbalances may be subdivided into three cases according to the number of red children (0, 1, or 2) that v's right child has. All three cases of an Rr imbalance are handled by a rotation. The rotations appear in Figures 16.17 and 16.18. Once again, you can verify that the shown rotation restores balance to the entire tree.

(a) Rr0 imbalance   (b) Rr0 rotation

Figure 16.17 Rr0 rotation for red-black deletion

Example 16.2 If we delete 90 from the red-black tree of Figure 16.13(i), we get the tree of Figure 16.19(a). Since the deleted node was not the root and was black, we have an imbalance. The imbalance is of type Rb0, and a color change is performed to get the tree of Figure 16.19(b). Since py was originally a red node, this color change rebalances the tree and we are done.

If we now delete 80 from tree (b), tree (c) results. A red node was deleted, so the tree remains balanced. When 70 is deleted from tree (c), we get tree (d). This time a nonroot black node was deleted, and the tree is unbalanced. The imbalance type is Rr1(ii) (the right child w of v has one red pointer, which is itself the right-child pointer of w). Following an Rr1(ii) rotation, tree (e) is obtained. This tree is balanced. ∎

16.2.6   Implementation Considerations and Complexity

The remedial action taken to rebalance a red-black tree following an insertion or deletion requires us to move back on the path taken from the root to the point of insertion or deletion. This backward movement is easy to do if each node has a parent field in addition to data, left child, right child, and color fields. An alternative to adding a parent field to each node is to save, on a stack, pointers to nodes encountered on the downward path from the root to the point of insertion/deletion.

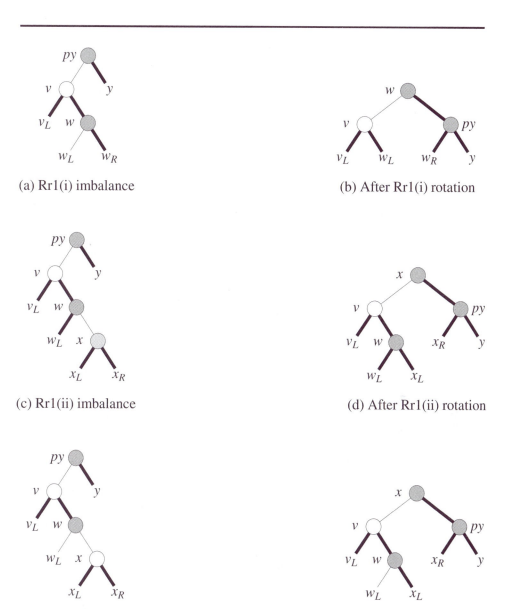

(a) Rr1(i) imbalance

(b) After Rr1(i) rotation

(c) Rr1(ii) imbalance

(d) After Rr1(ii) rotation

(e) Rr2 imbalance

(f) After Rr2 rotation

Figure 16.18 Rr1 and Rr2 rotations for red-black deletion

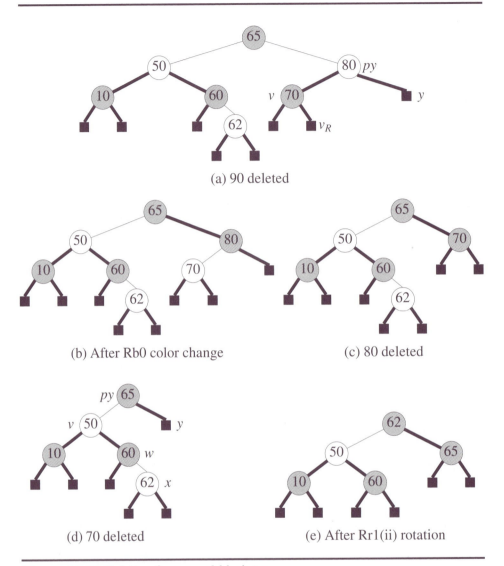

(a) 90 deleted

(b) After Rb0 color change

(c) 80 deleted

(d) 70 deleted

(e) After Rr1(ii) rotation

Figure 16.19 Deletion from a red-black tree

Now we may move back toward the root by performing deletes from the stack of saved pointers. For an n-element red-black tree, the addition of parent fields increases the space requirements by $\Theta(n)$, while the use of a stack increases the space requirements by $\Theta(\log n)$. Although the stack scheme is more efficient on space requirements, the parent-pointer scheme runs slightly faster.

Since the color changes performed following an insert or delete may propogate back toward the root, $O(\log n)$ of these color changes may be performed. Rotations, on the other hand, guarantee to rebalance the tree. As a result, at most one rotation may be performed following each insert/delete. The time needed for each color change or rotation operation is $\Theta(1)$; the total time needed to insert/delete is $O(\log n)$.

EXERCISES

23. Start with an empty red-black tree and insert the following keys in the given order: 15, 14, 13, 12, 11, 10, 9, 8, 7, 6, 5, 4, 3, 2, 1. Draw figures similar to Figure 16.13 depicting your tree immediately after each insertion and following the rebalancing rotation or color change (if any). Label all nodes with their color and identify the rotation type (if any) that is done.

24. Do Exercise 23 using the insert key sequence: 1, 2, 3, 4, 5, 6, 7, 8, 9, 10, 11, 12, 13, 14, 15.

25. Do Exercise 23 using the insert key sequence: 20, 10, 5, 30, 40, 57, 3, 2, 4, 35, 25, 18, 22, 21.

26. Do Exercise 23 using the insert key sequence: 40, 50, 70, 30, 42, 15, 20, 25, 27, 26, 60, 55.

27. Start with a red-black tree that is a 15-node full binary tree; the keys are 1–15. All nodes are black. Remove the keys in the order 15, 14, 13, $\cdots$, 1. Draw your tree immediately following each deletion and immediately after each rotation or color change that is performed. Label all nodes with their colors and identify the rotation type (if any) that is done.

28. Do Exercise 27 but this time remove the keys in the order 1, 2, 3, $\cdots$, 15.

29. Do Exercise 27 but this time remove keys in the order 6, 7, 5, 10, 9, 11, 15, 12, 13, and 2.

30. Do Exercise 27 but this time remove keys in the order 11, 14, 13, 15, 9, 12, 2, 3, and 1.

31. Draw the RRr and RLr color changes that correspond to the LLr and LRr changes of Figure 16.11.

32. Draw the RRb and RLb rotations that correspond to the LLb and LRb changes of Figure 16.12.

33. Draw the Lb0 color change that corresponds to the Rb0 change of Figure 16.15.

34. Draw the Lb1 and Lb2 rotations that correspond to the Rb1 and Rb2 rotations of Figure 16.16.

35. Draw the Lr0, Lr1, and Lr2 rotations that correspond to the Rr0, Rr1, and Rr2 rotations of Figures 16.17 and 16.18.

★ 36. Develop a Java class `RedBlackTree` that implements the interface `BSTree` (Program 15.1). Fully code all your methods and test their correctness. Your implementations for `get`, `put`, and `remove` must have complexity $O(\log n)$, and that for the `ascend` should be $O(n)$. Show that this is the case. The implementations of `put` and `remove` should follow the development in the text.

★ 37. Develop a Java class `DRedBlackTree` that implements the interface `DBSTree` (see Exercise 4). Fully code all your methods and test their correctness. Your implementations for `get`, `put`, and `remove` must have complexity $O(\log n)$, and that for the `ascend` should be $O(n)$. Show that this is the case.

★ 38. Develop a Java class `IndexedRedBlackTree` that implements the interface `IndexedBSTree` (Program 15.2). Fully code all your methods and test their correctness. Your implementations for `get`, `put`, and `remove` must have complexity $O(\log n)$, and that for the `ascend` should be $O(n)$. Show that this is the case.

★ 39. Develop a Java class `DIndexedRedBlackTree` that implements the interface `DIndexedBSTree` (see Exercise 5). Fully code all your methods and test their correctness. Your implementations for `get`, `put`, and `remove` must have complexity $O(\log n)$, and that for the `ascend` should be $O(n)$. Show that this is the case.

★ 40. Develop a Java class `LinearListAsRedBlackTree` that implements the interface `LinearList`. Fully code all your methods and test their correctness.

16.3 SPLAY TREES

16.3.1 Introduction

When either AVL trees or red-black trees are used to implement a dictionary, the worst-case complexity of each dictionary operation is logarithmic in the dictionary size. No known data structures provide a better worst-case time complexity for these operations. However, in many applications of a dictionary, we are less interested in the time taken by an individual operation than we are in the time taken by a sequence of operations. This is the case, for example, for the applications considered at the end of Chapter 15. The complexity of each of these applications depends on the time taken to perform a sequence of dictionary operations, not on the time taken for any one of them.

Splay trees are binary search trees in which the complexity of an individual dictionary operation is $O(n)$. However, every sequence of g *get*, p *put*, and r *remove* operations is done in $O((g + p + r) \log p)$ time, the same asymptotic complexity as when AVL trees or red-black trees are used. Experimental studies indicate that for random sequences of dictionary operations, splay trees are actually faster than AVL trees and red-black trees are. Moreover, splay trees are easier to code.

16.3.2 The Splay Operation

In a splay tree the dictionary operations are performed exactly as they are by the methods of the class `BinarySearchTree` (Section 15.3). However, the operations *get*, *put*, and *remove* are followed by a splay operation that starts at a splay node. At the end of the splay operation, the splay node is the root of the binary search tree. The **splay node** is selected to be the highest level (i.e, deepest) node, in the resulting tree, that was examined (i.e., a comparison was done with the key in this node, the node was newly created, the node was removed, or we moved to the left or right child of the node) during the dictionary operation.

Example 16.3 Consider the binary search tree of Figure 15.4(a). When performing the operation *get*(80), the deepest node examined is the node with key 80; this node is the splay node. When the operation *get*(31) is performed, the deepest node examined is the node with key 31; this node becomes the splay node. The operation *get*(55) follows the path from 30 to 60; the deepest node examined is the one with key 60. So this node becomes the splay node.

A *put* operation might create a new node or overwrite the element in an existing node. When a new node is created, this new node is the deepest node examined. Therefore, this new node becomes the splay node. When an existing element is overwritten, the node containing this overwritten element is the deepest node examined. Therefore, this node becomes the splay node. In the tree of Figure 15.4(a), the splay node for *put*(5, e) is the left child of the root. The splay node for *put*(65, e) is the newly created node, which becomes the right child of 60.

When the binary search tree has an element with key k, the deepest node examined by *remove*(k) is the node that is removed from the tree. This node does not become the splay node because it is not a node in the resulting tree. The parent of the removed node becomes the splay node because it is the deepest of the examined nodes that remain. In the tree of Figure 15.4(a), the splay node for *remove*(33) is the node with key 32, for *remove*(35) the splay node is the node with key 40, for *remove*(40) the splay node is the node with key 32, and for *remove*(30) the splay node is the node with key 5. ∎

The **splay operation** comprises a sequence of **splay steps**. When the splay node is the root of the binary search tree, this sequence of steps is empty. When the splay node is not the root node, each splay step moves the splay node either one level or two levels up the tree. A one-level move is made only when the splay node is at level 2 of the binary search tree.

There are two types of one-level splay steps. One is done when the splay node q is the left child of its parent p; the other is done when the splay node q is the right child of its parent. The first type is called a type L splay step, and the second is a type R step. Figure 16.20 shows a type L splay step. Notice that following the splay step the splay node becomes the root of the binary search tree. A type R splay step is similar.

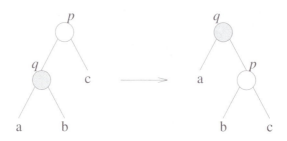

a, b, and c are subtrees
Shaded node is the splay node

Figure 16.20 Type L splay step

Two-level splay steps are done whenever the level of the splay node is > 2. Therefore, when a two-level splay step is done, the splay node q has a parent p and a grandparent gp. There are four types of two-level splay steps: LL, LR, RR, and RL. In an LR splay step, for example, p is the left child of gp, and q is the right child of p. Figure 16.21 shows a type LL and a type LR splay step. In each the splay node is moved two levels up the tree. Splay steps of type RR and LR are similar. Notice the similarity between splay steps and AVL tree rotations (Figures 16.4 and 16.5).

Example 16.4 Consider the binary search tree of Figure 16.22(a). Suppose that a $get(2)$ operation is performed. The shaded node becomes the splay node and a splay operation is initiated. This splay operation will first move the splay node from level 6 to level 4 by using an LL splay step (Figure 16.22(b)); next a type LR splay step moves the splay node to level 2 (Figure 16.22(c)); finally, a type L splay step moves the splay node to level 1. ■

Although we can move the splay node from any level of the binary search tree to level 1 by performing one-level splay steps alone (i.e., types L and R), limiting a splay operation to one-level splay steps does not ensure that every sequence of g *get*, p *put*, and r *remove* operations is done in $O((g+p+r)\log p)$ time. To establish this time bound, it is necessary to use a sequence of two-level splay steps terminated by at most 1 one-level splay step.

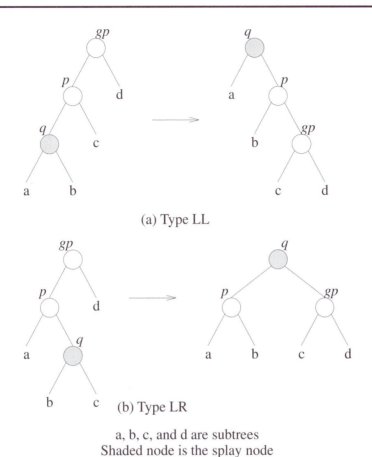

(a) Type LL

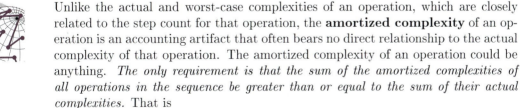

(b) Type LR

a, b, c, and d are subtrees
Shaded node is the splay node

Figure 16.21 Types LL and LR splay steps

16.3.3   Amortized Complexity

Unlike the actual and worst-case complexities of an operation, which are closely related to the step count for that operation, the **amortized complexity** of an operation is an accounting artifact that often bears no direct relationship to the actual complexity of that operation. The amortized complexity of an operation could be anything. *The only requirement is that the sum of the amortized complexities of all operations in the sequence be greater than or equal to the sum of their actual complexities.* That is

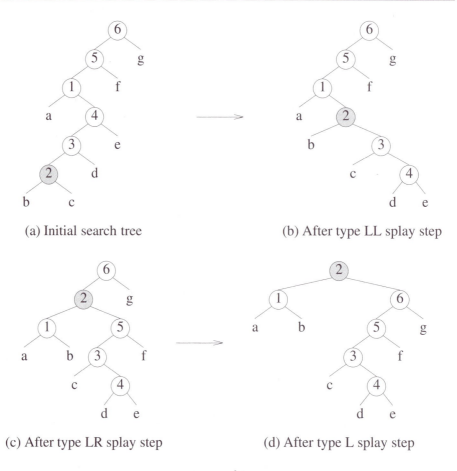

(a) Initial search tree

(b) After type LL splay step

(c) After type LR splay step

(d) After type L splay step

a–g are subtrees
Shaded node is the splay node

Figure 16.22 Sample splay operation

$$\sum_{i=1}^{n} amortized(i) \geq \sum_{i=1}^{n} actual(i) \qquad (16.1)$$

where $amortized(i)$ and $actual(i)$, respectively, denote the amortized and actual complexities of the ith operation in a sequence of n operations. Because of this requirement on the sum of the amortized complexities of the operations in any sequence of operations, we may use the sum of the amortized complexities as an upper bound on the complexity of any sequence of operations.

You may view the amortized cost of an operation as being the amount you charge the operation rather than the amount the operation costs. You can charge an operation any amount you wish so long as the amount charged to all operations in the sequence is at least equal to the actual cost of the operation sequence.

Theorem 16.1 *The amortized complexity of a* get, put, *or* remove *operation performed on a splay tree with* n *elements is* $O(\log n)$.

From Theorem 16.1 and Equation 16.1, it follows that the actual complexity of any sequence of g *get*, p *put*, and r *remove* operations is $O((g + p + r) \log p)$ time.

EXERCISES

41. Start with a splay tree that is a 15-node full binary tree; the keys are 1–15. Search for the keys in the order 15, 14, 13, $\cdots$, 1. Draw your tree after each rotation that is performed and label the rotation type.

42. Do Exercise 41 but this time search for the keys in the order 1, 15, 8, 7, 12, 10, 6, 2, 14.

43. Start with an empty splay tree and insert the following keys in the given order: 20, 10, 5, 30, 40, 25, 8, 35, 7, 23. Draw figures similar to Figures 16.20 through 16.22, depicting your tree immediately after each insertion and following each rotation (if any). Label each rotation with the rotation type.

44. Do Exercise 43 using the insert key sequence: 40, 50, 70, 30, 35, 75, 25, 10, 15, 22, 16, 23.

45. Start with a splay tree that is a 15-node full binary tree; the keys are 1–15. Remove the keys in the order 15, 14, 13, $\cdots$, 1. Draw your tree immediately following each deletion and immediately after each rotation that is performed. Label each rotation with the rotation type.

46. Do Exercise 45 but this time remove the keys in the order 1, 2, 3, $\cdots$, 15.

47. Do Exercise 45 but this time remove keys in the order 6, 7, 5, 10, 9, 11, 15, 12, 13, and 14.

48. Do Exercise 45 but this time remove keys in the order 11, 14, 13, 15, 9, 12, 2, 3, and 1.

49. (a) Draw figures similar to Figures 16.20 and 16.21 for type R, RR, and RL splay steps.

    (b) Draw a figure similar to Figure 16.22 that begins with a binary search tree and performs type RR, RL, and R splay steps on the splay node while moving the splay node from its initial level to level 1.

50. Give an example of an n-node splay tree that has height n. From this conclude that the time of complexity of the *get*, *put*, and *remove* operations for splay trees is $O(n)$.

51. Explain how a splay operation can be used to implement the `split` method of Exercise 12.

52. Develop the class `SplayTree` that implements the interface `BSTree` by using a splay tree. Test the correctness of all methods.

53. Develop the class `DSplayTree` that implements the interface `DBSTree` (see Exercise 4) by using a splay tree. Test the correctness of all methods.

54. Develop the class `IndexedSplayTree` that implements the interface `Indexed-BSTree` by using a splay tree. Test the correctness of all methods.

55. Develop the class `DIndexedSplayTree` that implements the interface `DIndexedBSTree` (see Exercise 5) by using a splay tree. Test the correctness of all methods.

56. Develop the class `LinearListAsSplayTree` that implements the interface `LinearList` by using a splay tree. Test the correctness of all methods.

16.4 B-TREES

16.4.1 Indexed Sequential Access Method (ISAM)

AVL and red-black trees guarantee good performance when the dictionary is small enough to reside in internal memory. For larger dictionaries (called **external dictionaries** or **files**) that must reside on a disk, we can get improved performance using search trees of higher degree. Before we jump into the study of these high-degree search trees, let us take a look at the popular **indexed sequential access method** (ISAM) for external dictionaries. This method provides good sequential and random access.

In the ISAM method the available disk space is divided into blocks, a block being the smallest unit of disk space that will be input or output. Typically, a block is one track long and can be input or output with a single seek and latency delay. The dictionary elements are packed into the blocks in ascending order, and the blocks are used in an order that minimizes the delay in going from one block to the next.

For sequential access the blocks are input in order, and the elements in each block are retrieved in ascending order. If each block contains m elements, the number of disk accesses per element retrieved is $1/m$.

To support random access, an index is maintained. This index contains the largest key in each block. Since the index contains only as many keys as there are blocks and since a block generally houses many elements (i.e., m is usually large), the index is generally small enough to reside in internal memory. To perform a random access of an element with key k, the index is searched for the single block that can contain the corresponding element; this block is retrieved from the disk and searched internally for the desired element. As a result, a single disk access is sufficient to perform a random access.

This technique may be extended to larger dictionaries that span several disks. Now the elements are assigned to disks in ascending order and then to blocks within a disk also in ascending order. Each disk maintains a block index that retains the largest key in each block. Additionally, an overall disk index maintains the largest key in each disk. This index generally resides in memory.

To perform a random access, the disk index is searched to determine the single disk that the desired record might reside on. Next the block index for this disk is retrieved from the appropriate disk and searched for the block that is to be fetched from the disk. The block is then fetched and searched internally. In the extended scheme a random access requires two disk accesses (one to fetch a block index and another to fetch a block).

Since the ISAM method is essentially an array-based representation scheme, it runs into difficulty when inserts and deletes are performed. We can partially alleviate this difficulty by leaving space in each block so that a few inserts can be performed without moving elements across block boundaries. Similarly, we can leave empty space in the block after deletes, rather than perform an expensive shift of the elements across block boundaries to use the new free space.

We can overcome these difficulties with the ISAM method at the expense of making sequential access more expensive. Elements are stored in any arbitrary order, and an index with an entry for each key is maintained. All elements are accessed via this index. The B-tree is a data structure that is suitable for indexes that reside on disk.

16.4.2 m-Way Search Trees

Definition 16.2 *An **m-way search tree** may be empty. If it is not empty, it is a tree that satisfies the following properties:*

1. *In the corresponding extended search tree (obtained by replacing null pointers with external nodes), each internal node has up to m children and between 1 and $m-1$ elements. (External nodes contain no elements and have no children.)*

2. *Every node with p elements has exactly $p+1$ children.*

3. *Consider any node with p elements. Let $k_1, \cdots, k_p$ be the keys of these elements. The elements are ordered so that $k_1 < k_2 < \cdots < k_p$. Let $c_0, c_1, \cdots, c_p$ be the $p+1$ children of the node. The elements in the subtree with root c_0 have keys smaller than k_1, those in the subtree with root c_p have keys*

larger than k_p, and those in the subtree with root c_i have keys larger than k_i but smaller than k_{i+1}, $1 \leq i < p$. ∎

Although it is useful to include external nodes when defining an m-way search tree, external nodes are not physically represented in actual implementations. Rather, a null pointer appears wherever there would otherwise be an external node.

Figure 16.23 shows a seven-way search tree. External nodes are shown as solid squares. All other nodes are internal nodes. The root has two elements (with keys 10 and 80) and three children. The middle child of the root has six elements and seven children; six of these children are external nodes.

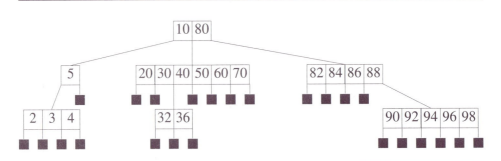

Figure 16.23 A seven-way search tree

Searching an m-Way Search Tree

To search the seven-way search tree in Figure 16.23 for an element with key 31, we begin at the root. Since 31 lies between 10 and 80, we follow the middle pointer. (By definition, all elements in the first subtree have key < 10, and all in the third have key > 80.) The root of the middle subtree is searched. Since $k_2 < 31 < k_3$, we move to the third subtree of this node. Now we determine that $31 < k_1$ and move into the first subtree. This move causes us to fall off the tree; that is, we reach an external node. We conclude that the search tree contains no element with key 31.

Inserting into an m-Way Search Tree

If we wish to insert an element with key 31, we search for 31 as above and fall off the tree at the node [32,36]. Since this node can hold up to six elements (each node of a seven-way search tree can have up to six elements), the new element may be inserted as the first element in the node.

To insert an element with key 65, we search for 65 and fall off the tree by moving to the sixth subtree of the node [20,30,40,50,60,70]. This node cannot accommodate additional elements, and a new node is obtained. The new element is put into this node, and the new node becomes the sixth child of [20,30,40,50,60,70].

Deleting from an m-Way Search Tree

To delete the element with key 20 from the search tree of Figure 16.23, we first perform a search. The element is the first element in the middle child of the root. Since $k_1 = 20$ and $c_0 = c_1 = 0$, we may simply delete the element from the node. The new middle child of the root is [30,40,50,60,70]. Similarly, to delete the element with key 84, we first locate the element. It is the second element in the third child of the root. Since $c_1 = c_2 = 0$, the element may be deleted from this node and the new node configuration is [82,86,88].

When deleting the element with key 5, we have to do more work. Since the element to be deleted is the first one in its node and since at least one of its neighboring children (these children are c_0 and c_1) is nonnull, we need to replace the deleted element with an element from a nonempty neighboring subtree. From the left neighboring subtree (c_0), we may move up the element with largest key (i.e., the element with key 4).

To delete the element with key 10 from the root of Figure 16.23, we may replace this element with either the largest element in c_0 or the smallest element in c_1. If we opt to replace it with the largest in c_0, then the element with key 5 moves up and we need to find a replacement for this element in its original node. The element with key 4 is moved up.

Height of an m-Way Search Tree

An m-way search tree of height h (excluding external nodes) may have as few as h elements (one node per level and one element per node) and as many as $m^h - 1$. The upper bound is achieved by an m-way search tree of height h in which each node at levels 1 through $h - 1$ has exactly m children and nodes at level h have no children. Such a tree has $\sum_{i=0}^{h-1} m^i = (m^h - 1)/(m - 1)$ nodes. Since each of these nodes has $m - 1$ elements, the number of elements is $m^h - 1$.

As the number of elements in an m-way search tree of height h ranges from a low of h to a high of $m^h - 1$, the height of an m-way search tree with n elements ranges from a low of $\log_m(n + 1)$ to a high of n.

A 200-way search tree of height 5, for example, can hold $32 * 10^{10} - 1$ elements but might hold as few as 5. Equivalently, a 200-way search tree with $32 * 10^{10} - 1$ elements has a height between 5 and $32 * 10^{10} - 1$. When the search tree resides on a disk, the search, insert, and delete times are dominated by the number of disk accesses made (under the assumption that each node is no larger than a disk block). Since the number of disk accesses needed for the search, insert, and delete operations are $O(h)$ where h is the tree height, we need to ensure that the height is close to $\log_m(n + 1)$. This assurance is provided by balanced m-way search trees.

16.4.3   B-Trees of Order m

Definition 16.3 *A **B-tree of order** m is an m-way search tree. If the B-tree is not empty, the corresponding extended tree satisfies the following properties:*

1. *The root has at least two children.*

2. *All internal nodes other than the root have at least $\lceil m/2 \rceil$ children.*

3. *All external nodes are at the same level.*   ■

The seven-way search tree of Figure 16.23 is not a B-tree of order 7, as it contains external nodes at more than one level (levels 3 and 4). Even if all its external nodes were at the same level, it would fail to be a B-tree of order 7 because it contains nonroot internal nodes with two (node [5]) and three (node [32,36]) children. Nonroot internal nodes in a B-tree of order 7 must have at least $\lceil 7/2 \rceil = 4$ children. A B-tree of order 7 appears in Figure 16.24. All external nodes are at level 3, the root has three children, and all remaining internal nodes have at least four children. Additionally, it is a seven-way search tree.

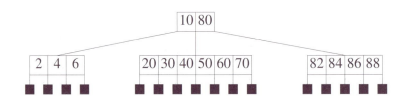

Figure 16.24 A B-tree of order 7

In a B-tree of order 2, no internal node has more than two children. Since an internal node must have at least two children, all internal nodes of a B-tree of order 2 have exactly two children. This observation, coupled with the requirement that all external nodes be on the same level, implies that B-trees of order 2 are full binary trees. As such, these trees exist only when the number of elements is $2^h - 1$ for some integer h.

In a B-tree of order 3, internal nodes have either two or three children. So a B-tree of order 3 is also known as a 2-3 tree. Since internal nodes in B-trees of order 4 must have two, three, or four children, these B-trees are also referred to as 2-3-4 (or simply 2,4) trees. A 2-3 tree appears in Figure 16.25. Even though this tree has no internal node with four children, it is also an example of a 2-3-4 tree. To build a 2-3-4 tree in which at least one internal node has four children, simply add elements with keys 14 and 16 into the left child of 20.

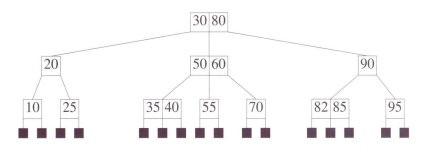

Figure 16.25 A 2-3 tree or B-tree of order 3

16.4.4   Height of a B-Tree

Lemma 16.3 *Let T be a B-tree of order m and height h. Let $d = \lceil m/2 \rceil$ and let n be the number of elements in T.*

(a) $2d^{h-1} - 1 \leq n \leq m^h - 1$

(b) $\log_m(n+1) \leq h \leq \log_d(\frac{n+1}{2}) + 1$

Proof The upper bound on n follows from the fact that T is an m-way search tree. For the lower bound, note that the external nodes of the corresponding extended B-tree are at level $h + 1$. The minimum number of nodes on levels 1, 2, 3, 4, $\cdots$, $h + 1$ is 1, 2, $2d$, $2d^2$, $\cdots$, $2d^{h-1}$, so the minimum number of external nodes in the B-tree is $2d^{h-1}$. Since the number of external nodes is 1 more than the number of elements

$$n \geq 2d^{h-1} - 1$$

Part (b) follows directly from (a).   ■

From Lemma 16.3 it follows that a B-tree of order 200 and height 3 has at least 19,999 elements, and one of the same order and height 5 has at least $2 * 10^8 - 1$ elements. Consequently, if a B-tree of order 200 or more is used, the tree height is quite small even when the number of elements is rather large. In practice, the B-tree order is determined by the disk block size and the size of individual elements. There is no advantage to using a node size smaller than the disk block size, as each disk access reads or writes one block. Using a larger node size involves multiple disk accesses, each accompanied by a seek and latency delay, so there is no advantage to making the node size larger than one block.

Although in actual applications the B-tree order is large, our examples use a small m because a two-level B-tree of order m has at least $2d - 1$ elements. When

m is 200, d is 100 and a two-level B-tree of order 200 has at least 199 elements. Manipulating trees with this many elements is quite cumbersome. Our examples involve 2-3 trees and B-trees of order 7.

16.4.5   Searching a B-Tree

A B-tree is searched using the same algorithm as is used for an m-way search tree. Since all internal nodes on some root-to-external-node path may be retreived during the search, the number of disk accesses is at most h (h is the height of the B-tree).

16.4.6   Inserting into a B-Tree

To insert an element into a B-tree, we first search for the presence of an element with the same key. If such an element is found, the insert fails because duplicates are not permitted. When the search is unsuccessful, we attempt to insert the new element into the last internal node encountered on the search path. For example, when inserting an element with key 3 into the B-tree of Figure 16.24, we examine the root and its left child. We fall off the tree at the second external node of the left child. Since the left child currently has three elements and can hold up to six, the new element may be inserted into this node. The result is the B-tree of Figure 16.26(a). Two disk accesses are made to read in the root and its left child. An additional access is necessary to write out the modified left child.

Next let us try to insert an element with key 25 into the B-tree of Figure 16.26(a). This element is to go into the node [20,30,40,50,60,70]. However, this node is full. *When the new element needs to go into a full node, the full node is split.* Let P be the full node. Insert the new element e together with a null pointer into P to get an overfull node with m elements and $m + 1$ children. Denote this overfull node as

$$m, \ c_0, \ (e_1, c_1), \ \cdots, \ (e_m, c_m)$$

where the e_is are the elements and the c_is are the children pointers. The node is split around element e_d where $d = \lceil m/2 \rceil$. Elements to the left remain in P, and those to the right move into a new node Q. The pair (e_d, Q) is inserted into the parent of P. The format of the new P and Q is

$$P: \ d - 1, \ c_0, \ (e_1, c_1), \ \cdots, \ (e_{d-1}, c_{d-1})$$

$$Q: \ m - d, \ c_d, \ (e_{d+1}, c_{d+1}), \ \cdots (e_m, c_m)$$

Notice that the number of children of both P and Q is at least d.

In our example, the overfull node is

$$7, 0 \ (20,0), \ (25,0), \ (30,0), \ (40,0), \ (50,0), \ (60,0), \ (70,0)$$

and $d = 4$. Splitting around e_4 yields the two nodes

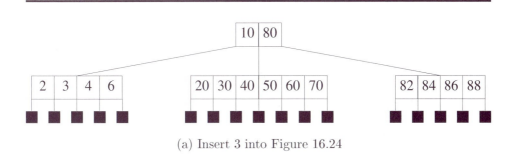

(a) Insert 3 into Figure 16.24

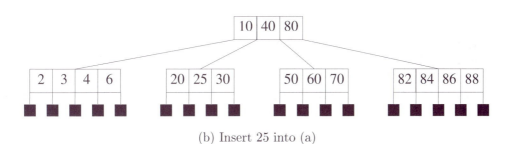

(b) Insert 25 into (a)

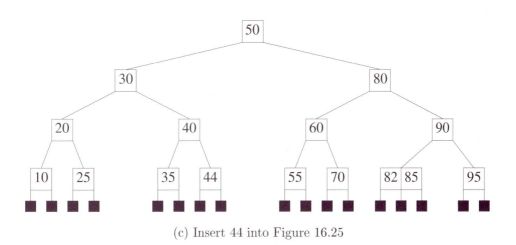

(c) Insert 44 into Figure 16.25

Figure 16.26 Inserting into a B-tree

$$P : 3, 0, (20{,}0), (25{,}0), (30{,}0)$$
$$Q : 3, 0, (50{,}0), (60{,}0), (70{,}0)$$

When the pair $(40, Q)$ is inserted into the parent of P, we get the B-tree of Figure 16.26(b).

To insert 25 into Figure 16.26(a), we need to get the root and its middle child from the disk. Then we write to disk the two split nodes and the modifed root. The total number of disk accesses is 5.

As a final example, consider inserting an element with key 44 into the 2-3 tree of Figure 16.25. This element goes into the node [35,40]. Since the node is full, we get the overfull node

$$3, 0, (35{,}0), (40{,}0), (44{,}0)$$

Splitting around $e_d = e_2$ yields the two nodes

$$P : 1, 0, (35{,}0)$$
$$Q : 1, 0, (44{,}0)$$

When we attempt to insert the pair $(40, Q)$ into the parent A of P, we see that this node is full. Following the insertion, we get the overfull node

$$A : 3, P, (40{,}Q), (50{,}C), (60{,}D)$$

where C and D are pointers to the nodes [55] and [70]. The overfull node A is split to create a new node B. The new A and B are

$$A : 1, P, (40{,}Q) \quad B : 1, C, (60{,}D)$$

Now we need to insert the pair $(50, B)$ into the root. Prior to this insertion, the root has the format

$$R: 2, S, (30{,}A), (80{,}T)$$

where S and T are, respectively, pointers to the first and third subtrees of the root. Following the insertion of the pair $(50, B)$, we get the overfull node

$$R: 3, S, (30{,}A), (50{,}B), (80{,}T)$$

This node is split around the element with key 50 to create a new R and a new node U as below:

$$R: 1, S, (30{,}A)$$
$$U: 1, B, (80{,}T)$$

The pair $(50,U)$ would normally be inserted into the parent of R. However, since R has no parent, we create a new root with the format

$$1, R, (50,U)$$

The resulting 2-3 tree appears in Figure 16.26(c).

Three disk accesses are made to read in nodes [30,80], [50,60], and [35,40]. For each node that splits, two accesses are made to write the modified node and the newly created node. In our case three nodes are split, so six write accesses are made. Finally, a new root is created and written out. This write takes an additional disk access. The total number of disk accesses is 10.

When an insertion causes s nodes to split, the number of disk accesses is h (to read in the nodes on the search path) $+ 2s$ (to write out the two split parts of each node that is split) $+ 1$ (to write the new root or the node into which an insertion that does not result in a split is made). Therefore, the number of disk accesses needed for an insertion is $h + 2s + 1$, which is at most $3h + 1$.

16.4.7   Deletion from a B-Tree

Deletion is first divided into two cases: (1) the element to be deleted is in a node whose children are external nodes (i.e., the element is in a leaf), and (2) the element is to be deleted from a nonleaf. Case (2) is transformed into case (1) by replacing the deleted element with either the largest element in its left-neighboring subtree or the smallest element in its right-neighboring subtree. The replacing element is guaranteed to be in a leaf.

Consider deleting the element with key 80 from the B-tree of Figure 16.26(a). Since the element is not in a leaf, we find a suitable replacement. The possibilities are the element with key 70 (i.e., the largest element in the left-neighboring subtree) and 82 (i.e., the smallest element in the right-neighboring subtree). When we use the 70, the problem of deleting this element from the leaf [20,30,40,50,60,70] remains.

If we are to delete the element with key 80 from the 2-3 tree of Figure 16.26(c), we replace it with either the element with key 70 or that with key 82. If we select the 82, the problem of deleting 82 from the leaf [82,85] remains.

Since case (2) may be transformed into case (1) quite easily, we concern ourselves with case (1) only. To delete an element from a leaf that contains more than the minimum number of elements (1 if the leaf is also the root and $\lceil m/2 \rceil - 1$ if it is not) requires us to simply write out the modified node. (In case this node is the root, the B-tree becomes empty.) To delete 50 from the B-tree of Figure 16.26(a), we write out the modified node [20,30,40,60,70], and to delete 85 from the 2-3 tree of Figure 16.26(c), we write out the node [82]. Both cases require h disk accesses to follow the search path down to the leaf and an additional access to write out the modified version of the leaf that contained the deleted element.

When the element is being deleted from a nonroot node that has exactly the minimum number of elements, we try to replace the deleted element with an element from its nearest-left or -right sibling. Notice that every node other than the root has either a nearest-left sibling or a nearest-right sibling or both. For example, suppose we wish to delete 25 from the B-tree of Figure 16.26(b). This deletion leaves behind the node [20,30], which has just two elements. However, since this node is a nonroot node of a B-tree of order 7, it must contain at least three elements. Its nearest-left sibling, [2,3,4,6], has an extra element. The largest element from here is moved to the parent node, and the intervening element (i.e., with key 10) is moved down to create the B-tree of Figure 16.27(a). The number of disk accesses is 2 (to go from the root to the leaf that contains 25) + 1 (to read in the nearest-left sibling of this leaf) + 3 (to write out the changed leaf, its sibling, and its parent) = 6.

Suppose that instead of checking the nearest-left sibling of [20,30], we had checked its nearest-right sibling, [50,60,70]. Since this node has only three elements, we cannot delete an element. (If the node had four elements or more, we would have moved its smallest element to the parent and moved the element in the parent that lies between these two siblings into the leaf that is one element short.) Now we can check the nearest-left sibling of [20,30]. Performing this check requires an additional disk access, and we are not certain that this nearest sibling will have an extra element. *In the interest of keeping the worst-case disk-access count low, we will check only one of the nearest siblings of a node that is one element short.*

When the nearest sibling that is checked has no extra elements, we merge the two siblings with the element between them in the parent into a single node. Since the siblings have $d - 2$ and $d - 1$ elements, respectively, the merged node has $2d - 2$ elements. As $2d - 2$ equals $m - 1$ when m is odd and $m - 2$ when m is even, there is enough space in a node to hold this many elements.

In our example the siblings [20,30] and [50,60,70] and the element with key 40 are merged into the single node [20,30,40,50,60,70]. The resulting B-tree is that of Figure 16.26(a). This deletion requires two disk accesses to get to the node [20,25,30], another access to read in its nearest-right sibling, and then two more accesses to write out the two nodes that are modified. The total number of disk accesses is 5.

Notice that since merging reduces the number of elements in the parent node, the parent may end up being one element short. If the parent becomes one element short, we will need to check the parent's nearest sibling and either get an element from there or merge with it. If we get an element from the nearest-right (-left) sibling, then the left-most (right-most) subtree of this sibling is also taken. If we merge, the grandparent may become one element short and the process will need to be applied at the grandparent. At worst the shortage will propagate back to the root. When the root is one element short, it is empty. The empty root is discarded, and the tree height decreases by 1.

Suppose we wish to delete 10 from the 2-3 tree of Figure 16.25. This deletion leaves behind a leaf with zero elements. Its nearest-right sibling [25] does not have

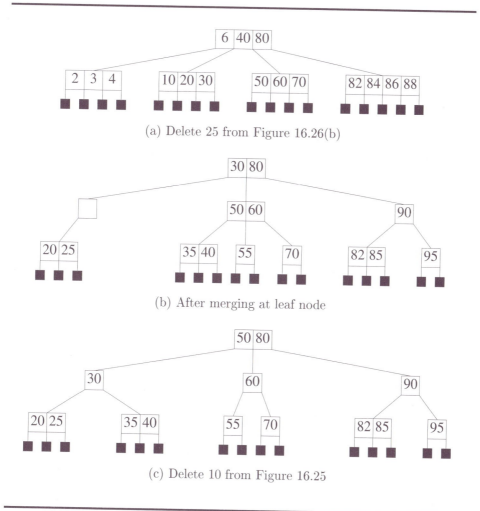

(a) Delete 25 from Figure 16.26(b)

(b) After merging at leaf node

(c) Delete 10 from Figure 16.25

Figure 16.27 Deleting from a B-tree

an extra element. Therefore, the two sibling leaves and the in-between element in the parent (10) are merged into a single node. The new tree structure appears in Figure 16.27(b). We now have a node at level 2 that is an element short. Its nearest-right sibling has an extra element. The left-most element (i.e., the one with key 50) moves to the parent, and the element with key 30 moves down. The resulting 2-3 tree appears in Figure 16.27(c). Notice that the left subtree of the former [50,60] has moved also. This deletion took three read accesses to get to the leaf that contained the element that was to be deleted; two read accesses to get the nearest-right siblings of the level 3 and 2 nodes; and four write accesses to write out the four nodes at levels 1, 2, and 3 that were modified. The total number of disk accesses is 9.

As a final example, consider the deletion of 44 from the 2-3 tree of Figure 16.26(c). When the 44 is removed from the leaf it is in, this leaf becomes short one element. Its nearest-left sibling does not have an extra element, and so the two siblings together with the in-between element in the parent are merged to get the tree of Figure 16.28(a). We now have a node at level 3 that is one element short. Its nearest-left sibling is examined and found to have no extra elements, so the two siblings and the in-between element in their parent are merged. The tree of Figure 16.28(b) is obtained. Now we have a level 2 node that is one element short. Its nearest-right sibling has no extra elements, and we perform another merge to

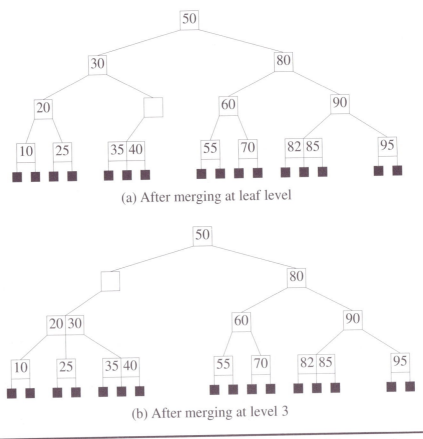

(a) After merging at leaf level

(b) After merging at level 3

Figure 16.28 Deleting 44 from the 2-3 tree of Figure 16.26(c) (continues)

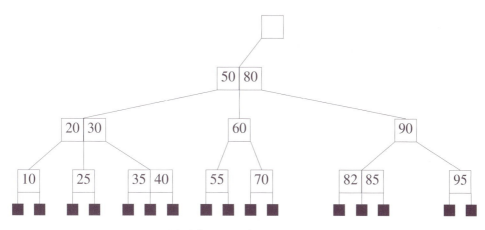

(c) After merging at level 2

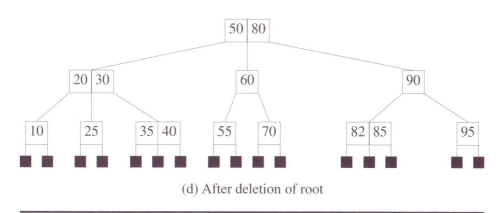

(d) After deletion of root

Figure 16.28 Deleting 44 from the 2-3 tree of Figure 16.26(c) (concluded)

get the tree of Figure 16.28(c). Now the root is an element short. Since the root becomes an element short only when it is empty, the root is discarded. The final 2-3 tree is shown in Figure 16.28(d). Notice that when the root is discarded, the tree height reduces by 1.

We need four disk accesses to find the leaf that contains the element to be deleted, three nearest-sibling accesses, and three write accesses. The total number is 10.

The worst case for a deletion from a B-tree of height h is when merges take place at levels h, $h-1$, $\cdots$, and 3 and we get an element from a nearest sibling at level 2. The worst-case disk access count is $3h$; (h reads to find the leaf with the element to be deleted) + ($h - 1$ reads to get nearest siblings at levels 2 through h) + ($h - 2$ writes of merged nodes at levels 3 through h) + (3 writes for the modified root and 2 level 2 nodes).

16.4.8   Node Structure

Our discussion has assumed a node structure of the form

$$s, \; c_0, \; (e_1, c_1), \; (e_2, c_2), \; \cdots, \; (e_s, c_s)$$

where s is the number of elements in the node, the e_is are the elements in ascending order of key, and the c_is are children pointers. When the element size is large relative to the size of a key, we may use the node structure

$$s, \; c_0, \; (k_1, c_1, p_1), \; (k_2, c_2, p_2), \; \cdots, \; (k_s, c_s, p_s)$$

where the k_is are the element keys and the p_is are the disk locations of the corresponding elements. By using this structure, we can use a B-tree of a higher order. An even higher-order B-tree, called a B'-tree, becomes possible if nonleaf nodes contain no p_i pointers and if, in the leaves, we replace the null children pointers with p_i pointers.

Another possibilty is to use a balanced binary search tree to represent the contents of each node. Using a balanced binary search tree in this way reduces the permissible order of the B-tree, as with each element we need a left- and right-child pointer as well as a balance factor or color field. However, the CPU time spent inserting/deleting an element into/from a node decreases. Whether this approach results in improved overall performance depends on the application. In some cases a smaller m might increase the B-tree height, resulting in more disk accesses for each search/insert/delete operation.

EXERCISES

57. Start with an empty 2-3 tree and insert the keys 20, 40, 30, 10, 25, 28, 27, 32, 36, 34, 35, 8, 6, 2, and 3 in this order. Draw the 2-3 tree following each insert.

58. Insert 2, 1, 5, 6, 7, 4, 3, 8, 9, 10, and 11, in this order, into the 2-3 tree of Figure 16.26(c). Draw the 2-3 tree following each insert.

59. From the 2-3 tree of Figure 16.25, remove the keys 55, 40, 70, 35, 60, 95, 90, 82, 80 in this order. Draw a figure similar to Figure 16.28 showing the different steps in each remove.

60. (a) Remove 10 from the 2-3 tree of Figure 16.26(c). Draw a figure similar to Figure 16.28 showing the different steps in the delete.

(b) Do part (a) but this time remove 70 from Figure 16.26(c).

(c) Do part (a) but this time remove 95 and 85 (in this order) from Figure 16.26(c).

61. What is the maximum number of disk accesses made during a search of a B-tree of order $2m$ if each node is two disk blocks and requires two disk accesses to retrieve? Compare this number with the corresponding number for a B-tree of order m that uses nodes that are one disk block in size. Based on this analysis, what can you say about the merits of using a node size larger than one block?

62. What is the maximum number of disk accesses needed to delete an element that is in a nonleaf node of a B-tree of order m?

63. Suppose we modify the way an element is deleted from a B-tree as follows: If a node has both a nearest-left and nearest-right sibling, then both are checked before a merge is done. What is the maximum number of disk accesses that can be made when deleting from a B-tree of height h?

★ 64. A 2-3-4 tree may be represented as a binary tree in which each node is colored black or red. A 2-3-4 tree node that has just one element is represented as a black node; a node with two elements is represented as a black node with a red child (the red child may be either the left or right child of the black node); a node with three elements is represented as a black node with two red children.

(a) Draw a 2-3-4 tree that contains at least one node with two elements and one with three. Now draw it as a binary tree with colored nodes using the method just described.

(b) Verify that the binary tree is a red-black tree.

(c) Prove that when any 2-3-4 tree is represented as a colored binary tree as described here, the result is a red-black tree.

(d) Prove that every red-black tree can be represented as a 2-3-4 tree using the inverse mapping.

(e) Verify that the color changes and rotations given in Section 16.2.4 for an insertion into a red-black tree are obtainable from the B-tree insertion method using the mapping in (d).

(f) Do part (e) for the case of deletion from a red-black tree.

★ 65. Develop a class TwoThree that implements the interface Dictionary (Program 11.1) using a 2-3 tree. Test the correctness of your code.

★ 66. Develop a class TwoThreeFour that implements the interface Dictionary (Program 11.1) using a 2-3-4 tree. Test the correctness of your code.

16.5 REFERENCES AND SELECTED READINGS

AVL trees were invented by G. Adelson-Velskii and E. Landis in 1962. More material on these and other search trees developed in this chapter can be found in the book *The Art of Computer Programming: Sorting and Searching*, Volume 3, Second Edition, by D. Knuth, Addison-Wesley, Reading, MA, 1998.

Red-black trees were invented by R. Bayer in 1972. However, Bayer called these trees "symmetric balanced B-trees." The red-black terminology is from Guibas and Sedgewick who studied these trees in greater detail in 1978. The pioneering papers are "Symmetric Binary B-Trees: Data Structures and Maintenance Algorithms" by R. Bayer, *Acta Informatica*, 1, 1972, 290–306, and "A Dichromatic Framework for Balanced Trees" by L. Guibas and R. Sedgewick, *Proceedings of the 10th IEEE Symposium on Foundations of Computer Science*, 1978, 8–21.

The application of red-black trees to the implementation of priority search trees is described in the paper "Priority Search Trees" by E. McCreight, *SIAM Journal on Computing*, 14, 2, 1985, 257–276.

Various balanced search-tree structures that have the same asymptotic complexity as do AVL and red-black trees are described in the text *Fundamentals of Data Structures in C++* by E. Horowitz, S. Sahni, and D. Mehta, W. H. Freeman, New York, NY, 1994. This text also has the complexity analysis for splay trees and describes B'-trees and B*-trees, which are variants of B-trees.

You can find a detailed development of amortized complexity in the Web site for this book. And don't forget, you can learn about other search structures, such as tries and suffix trees, by visiting the Web site.

CHAPTER 17

GRAPHS

BIRD'S-EYE VIEW

Congratulations! You have successfully journeyed through the forest of trees. Awaiting you now is the study of the graph data structure. Surprisingly, graphs are used to model literally thousands of real-world problems. Not so surprisingly, we will see only a very small fraction of these problems in the remainder of this book. This chapter covers the following topics:

- Graph terminology including these terms: *vertex, edge, adjacent, incident, degree, cycle, path, connected component,* and *spanning tree.*

- Different types of graphs: undirected, directed, and weighted.

- Common graph representations: adjacency matrix, array adjacency lists, and linked adjacency lists.

- Standard graph search methods: breadth-first and depth-first search.

- Algorithms to find a path in a graph, to find the connected components of an undirected graph, and to find a spanning tree of a connected undirected graph.

- Specifying an abstract data type as an abstract class.

Additional graph algorithms—topological sorting, bipartite covers, shortest paths, minimum-cost spanning trees, max clique, and traveling salesperson—are developed in the remaining chapters of this book.

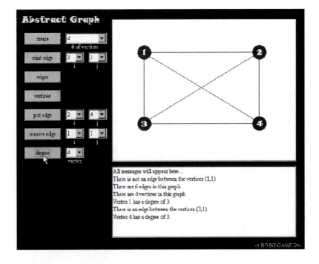

Play with a graph—On the Web

17.1   DEFINITIONS

Informally, a graph is a collection of vertices or nodes, pairs of which are joined by lines or edges. More formally, a **graph** $G = (V,E)$ is an ordered pair of finite sets V and E. The elements of V are called **vertices** (vertices are also called **nodes** and **points**). The elements of E are called **edges** (edges are also called **arcs** and **lines**). Each edge in E joins two different vertices of V and is denoted by the tuple (i,j), where i and j are the two vertices joined by E.

A graph is generally displayed as a figure in which the vertices are represented by circles and the edges by lines. Examples of graphs appear in Figure 17.1. Some of the edges in this figure are oriented (i.e., they have arrow heads), while others are not. An edge with an orientation is a **directed** edge, while an edge with no orientation is an **undirected** edge. The undirected edges (i,j) and (j,i) are the same; the directed edge (i,j) is different from the directed edge (j,i), the former being oriented from i to j and the latter from j to i.[1]

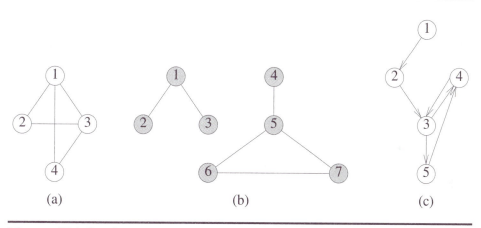

Figure 17.1 Graphs

Vertices i and j are **adjacent** vertices iff (i,j) is an edge in the graph. The edge (i,j) is **incident** on the vertices i and j. Vertices 1 and 2 of Figure 17.1(a) are adjacent, as are vertices 1 and 3; 1 and 4; 2 and 3; and 3 and 4. This graph has no other pairs of adjacent vertices. The edge $(1,2)$ is incident on the vertices 1 and 2 and the edge $(2,3)$ is incident on the vertices 2 and 3.

It is sometimes useful to have a slightly refined notion of adjacency and incidence for directed graphs. The directed edge (i,j) is **incident to** vertex j and **incident from** vertex i. Vertex i is **adjacent to** vertex j, and vertex j is **adjacent from**

---

[1]Some books use the notation i,j for an undirected edge and (i,j) for a directed one. Others use (i,j) for an undirected edge and $<i,j>$ for a directed one. This book uses the same notation, (i,j), for both kinds of edges. Whether an edge is directed or not will be clear from the context.

vertex i. In the graph of Figure 17.1(c), vertex 2 is adjacent from 1, while 1 is adjacent to 2. Edge (1,2) is incident from 1 and incident to 2. Vertex 4 is both incident to and from 3. Edge (3,4) is incident from 3 and incident to 4. For an undirected edge, the refinements "to" and "from" are synonomous.

Using set notation, the graphs of Figure 17.1 may be specified as $G_1 = (V_1, E_1)$; $G_2 = (V_2, E_2)$; and $G_3 = (V_3, E_3)$ where

$$V_1 = \{1,2,3,4\}; \qquad E_1 = \{(1,2), (1,3), (2,3), (1,4), (3,4)\}$$
$$V_2 = \{1,2,3,4,5,6,7\}; \qquad E_2 = \{(1,2), (1,3), (4,5), (5,6), (5,7), (6,7)\}$$
$$V_3 = \{1,2,3,4,5\}; \qquad E_3 = \{(1,2), (2,3), (3,4), (4,3), (3,5), (5,4)\}$$

If all the edges in a graph are undirected, then the graph is an **undirected** graph. The graphs of Figures 17.1(a) and (b) are undirected graphs. If all the edges are directed, then the graph is a **directed** graph. The graph of Figure 17.1(c) is a directed graph.

By definition, a graph does not contain multiple copies of the same edge. Therefore, an undirected graph can have at most one edge between any pair of vertices, and a directed graph can have at most one edge from vertex i to vertex j and one from j to i. Also, a graph cannot contain any **self-edges**; that is, edges of the form (i,i) are not permitted. A self-edge is also called a **loop**.

A directed graph is also called a **digraph**. In some applications of graphs, we will assign a weight or cost to each edge. When weights have been assigned to edges, we use the terms **weighted undirected graph** and **weighted digraph** to refer to the resulting data object. The term **network** is often used to refer to a weighted undirected graph or digraph. Actually, all the graph variants defined here may be regarded as special cases of networks—an undirected (directed) graph may be viewed as an undirected (directed) network in which all edges have the same weight.

17.2   APPLICATIONS AND MORE DEFINITIONS

Graphs are used in the analysis of electrical networks; the study of the molecular structure of chemical compounds (particularly hydrocarbons); the representation of airline routes and communication networks; in planning projects, genetic studies, statistical mechanics, and social sciences; and in many other situations. In this section we formulate some real-world problems as problems on graphs.

Example 17.1 [Path Problems] In a city with many streets, we can say that each intersection is a vertex in a digraph. Each segment of a street that is between two adjacent intersections is represented by either one or two directed edges. Two directed edges, one in either direction, are used if the street segment is two way, and a single directed edge is used if it is a one-way segment. Figure 17.2 shows a hypothetical street map and the corresponding digraph. In this figure there are three streets—1St, 2St, and 3St—and two avenues—1Ave and 2Ave The intersections are labeled 1 through 6. The vertices of the corresponding digraph (Figure 17.2(b)) have the same labels as given to the intersection in Figure 17.2(a).

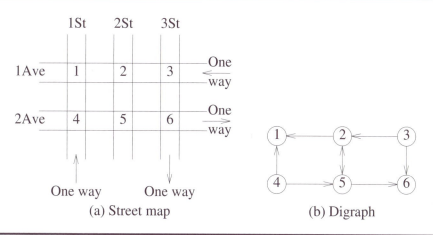

(a) Street map   (b) Digraph

Figure 17.2 Street map and corresponding digraph

A sequence of vertices $P = i_1, i_2, \cdots, i_k$ is an i_1 to i_k **path** in the graph $G = (V, E)$ iff the edge (i_j, i_{j+1}) is in E for every j, $1 \le j < k$. There is a path from intersection i to intersection j iff there is a path from vertex i to vertex j in the corresponding digraph. In the digraph of Figure 17.2(b), 5, 2, 1 is a path from 5 to 1. There is no path from 5 to 4 in this digraph.

A **simple path** is a path in which all vertices, except possibly the first and last, are different. The path 5, 2, 1 is a simple path, whereas the path 2, 5, 2, 1 is not.

Each edge in a graph may have an associated **length**. The length of a path is the sum of the lengths of the edges on the path. The shortest way to get from intersection i to intersection j is obtained by finding a shortest path from vertex i to vertex j in the corresponding network (i.e., weighted digraph). ∎

Example 17.2 [Spanning Trees] Let $G = (V, E)$ be an undirected graph. G is **connected** iff there is a path between every pair of vertices in G. The undirected graph of Figure 17.1(a) is connected, while that of Figure 17.1(b) is not. Suppose that G represents a possible communication network with V being the set of cities and E the set of communication links. It is possible to communicate between every pair of cities in V iff G is connected. In the communication network of Figure 17.1(a), cities 2 and 4 can communicate by using the communication path 2,3,4, while in the network of Figure 17.1(b), cities 2 and 4 cannot communicate.

Suppose that G is connected. Some of the edges of G may be unneccessary in that G remains connected even if these edges are removed. In the graph of

Figure 17.1(a), for example, the graph remains connected even if we remove the edges (2,3) and (1,4).

A graph H is a **subgraph** of another graph G iff its vertex and edge sets are subsets of those of G. A **cycle** is a simple path with the same start and end vertex. For example, 1, 2, 3, 1 is a cycle in the graph of Figure 17.1(a). A connected undirected graph that contains no cycles is a **tree**. A subgraph of G that contains all the vertices of G and is a tree is a **spanning tree** of G. Figure 17.3 gives some of the spanning trees of Figure 17.1(a).

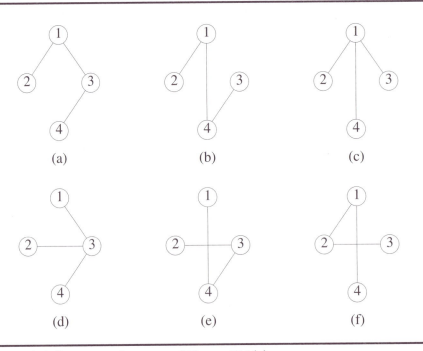

Figure 17.3 Some spanning trees of Figure 17.1(a)

A connected undirected graph with n vertices must have at least $n - 1$ edges. Hence when each link of a communication network has the same construction cost, the construction of all links on any one spanning tree minimizes network construction cost and ensures that a communication path exists between every pair of cities. Further, if the links have different (but nonnegative) costs, then the links on a minimum-cost spanning tree (the cost of a spanning tree is the sum of the costs of the edges on it) are to be constructed. Figure 17.4 shows a graph and two of its spanning trees. ∎

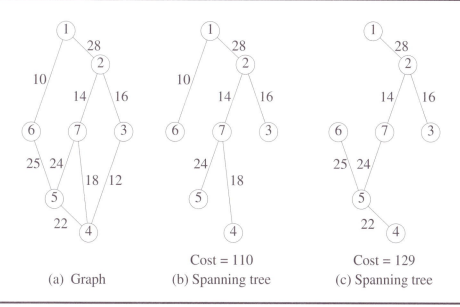

| | Cost = 110 | Cost = 129 |
| (a) Graph | (b) Spanning tree | (c) Spanning tree |

Figure 17.4 Connected graph and two of its spanning trees

Example 17.3 [Interpreters] Suppose that you are planning an international convention. All the speakers at this convention know English only. The remaining participants know one of the languages L1, L2, L3, $\cdots$, Ln. You have available a set of interpreters who can translate between English and some of the other languages. Your task is to select the fewest number of interpreters to do the job.

We can formulate the problem as a graph problem in which the graph has two sets of vertices. One set corresponds to interpreters and the other to languages (Figure 17.5). An edge exists between interpreter i and language Lj iff interpreter i can translate between English and this language. Interpreter i **covers** language Li iff an edge connects the interpreter and the language. We want to find the smallest subset of the interpreter vertices that cover the language vertices.

The graph of Figure 17.5 has an interesting property: We can partition the vertex set into two subsets, A (the interpreter vertices) and B (the language vertices), so that every edge has one endpoint in A and the other in B. Graphs with this property are **bipartite graphs**. ∎

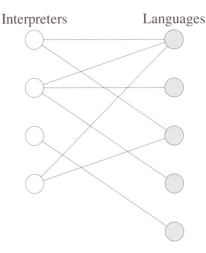

Figure 17.5 Interpreters and languages

EXERCISES

1. Consider the graph of Figure 17.4(b). Which of the following are simple paths? Why?

   (a) 6, 1, 2, 7, 4

   (b) 1, 2, 3, 4

   (c) 7, 2, 3, 2, 1, 6

   (d) 4, 5, 7, 2

2. (a) List all simple paths between vertices 1 and 4 in Figure 17.1(a).

   (b) List all simple paths between vertices 1 and 7 in Figure 17.4(a).

   (c) List all simple paths between vertices 3 and 6 in Figure 17.4(a).

   (d) List all simple paths from vertex 4 to vertex 1 in Figure 17.1(c).

   (e) List all simple paths from vertex 4 to vertex 1 in Figure 17.2(b).

3. Draw all subgraphs of Figure 17.1(a).

4. List all cycles of the graph of Figure 17.4(a).

5. List all cycles of the graph of Figure 17.2(b).

6. Draw two more spanning trees of the graph of Figure 17.4(a). Give the cost of each spanning tree.

7. Anita, Beth, Jack, and Roger have applied for a job at the local bookstore. Anita can work on Monday, Wednesday, and Friday; Beth can work on Monday, Tuesday, and Thursday; Jack can work on Sunday, Monday, and Saturday; and Roger can work on Thursday and Friday. Draw a bipartite graph in which the vertices represent applicants and days of the week, and edges connect applicants to days on which they can work. Select the minimum number of applicants so that all days of the week are covered.

8. Identify two additional real-world situations that may be modeled with a bipartite graph.

17.3 PROPERTIES

The **degree** d_i of vertex i of an undirected graph is the number of edges incident on vertex i. For the graph of Figure 17.1(a), $d_1 = 3$; $d_2 = 2$; $d_3 = 3$; and $d_4 = 2$.

Property 17.1 *Let $G = (V, E)$ be an undirected graph. Let $n = |V|$ and $e = |E|$.*

(a) $\sum_{i=1}^{n} d_i = 2e$

(b) $0 \leq e \leq n(n-1)/2$

Proof To prove (a), note that each edge in an undirected graph is incident on exactly two vertices. Hence the sum of the degrees of the vertices equals two times the number of edges. For (b), observe that the degree of a vertex lies between 0 and $n - 1$, so the sum of the degrees lies between 0 and $n(n - 1)$. From (a), it now follows that e lies between 0 and $n(n - 1)/2$. ∎

An n-vertex undirected graph with $n(n - 1)/2$ edges is a **complete** graph. Figure 17.6 gives the complete undirected graphs for $n = 1, 2, 3$, and 4. The complete undirected graph on n vertices is denoted K_n.

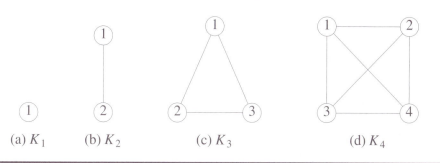

(a) K_1 (b) K_2 (c) K_3 (d) K_4

Figure 17.6 Complete undirected graphs

Let G be a digraph. The **in-degree** d_i^{in} of vertex i is the number of edges incident to i (i.e., the number of edges coming into this vertex). The **out-degree** d_i^{out} of vertex i is the number of edges incident from this vertex (i.e., the number of edges leaving vertex i). For the digraph of Figure 17.1(c), $d_1^{in} = 0$; $d_1^{out} = 1$; $d_2^{in} = 1$; $d_2^{out} = 1$; $d_3^{in} = 2$; and $d_3^{out} = 2$.

Property 17.2 *Let $G = (V, E)$ be a directed graph. Let $n = |V|$ and $e = |E|$.*

(a) $0 \le e \le n(n-1)$

(b) $\sum_{i=1}^{n} d_i^{in} = \sum_{i=1}^{n} d_i^{out} = e$

Proof Exercise 10 asks you to prove this property.   ■

A **complete** digraph (also denoted K_n) on n vertices contains exactly $n(n-1)$ directed edges. Figure 17.7 gives the complete digraphs for $n = 1, 2, 3,$ and 4.

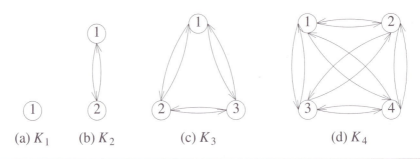

(a) K_1 (b) K_2 (c) K_3 (d) K_4

Figure 17.7 Complete digraphs

In the context of undirected graphs, the terms *in-degree* and *out-degree* may be used as synonyms for the term *degree*. The definitions provided in this section extend to networks in a rather straightforward way.

EXERCISES

9. For each graph in Figure 17.8, determine the following:

   (a) The in-degree of each vertex.

   (b) The out-degree of each vertex.

   (c) The set of vertices adjacent from vertex 2.

   (d) The set of vertices adjacent to vertex 1.

   (e) The set of edges incident from vertex 3.

   (f) The set of edges incident to vertex 4.

   (g) All directed cycles and their lengths.

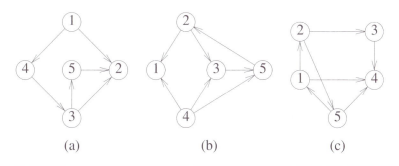

(a)　　　　　　　　(b)　　　　　　　　(c)

Figure 17.8 Digraphs

10. Prove Property 17.2.

11. Let G be any undirected graph. Show that the number of vertices with odd degrees is even.

12. Let $G = (V, E)$ be a connected graph with $|V| > 1$. Show that G contains either a vertex of degree 1 or a cycle (or both).

13. Let $G = (V, E)$ be a connected undirected graph that contains at least one cycle. Let $(i, j) \in E$ be an edge that is on at least one cycle of G. Show that the graph $H = (V, E - \{(i, j)\})$ is also connected.

14. Prove the following:

    (a) For every n there exists a connected undirected graph containing exactly $n - 1$ edges, $n \geq 1$.

    (b) Every n-vertex connected undirected graph contains at least $n - 1$ edges. You may use the results of the previous two exercises.

15. A digraph is **strongly connected** iff it contains a directed path from i to j and from j to i for every pair of distinct vertices i and j.

    (a) Show that for every n, $n \geq 2$, there exists a strongly connected digraph that contains exactly n edges.

    (b) Show that every n vertex strongly connected digraph contains at least n edges, $n \geq 2$.

17.4   THE ADT *Graph*

The abstract data type *Graph* refers to all varieties of graphs, whether directed, undirected, weighted, or unweighted. The abstract data type specification of ADT 17.1 lists only a few of the many operations commonly performed on a graph. As we progress through this text, we will add operations.

AbstractDataType *Graph*
{

    instances
        a set V of vertices and a set E of edges

    operations
            vertices() : return the number of vertices in the graph

              edges() : return the number of edges in the graph

      existsEdge(i, j) : return `true` if edge (i, j) exists; `false` otherwise

   putEdge(*theEdge*) : put the edge *theEdge* into the graph

    removeEdge(i, j) : remove the edge (i, j)

          degree(i) : return the degree of vertex i, defined only for undirected graphs

       inDegree(i) : return the in-degree of vertex i

      outDegree(i) : return the out-degree of vertex i

}

ADT 17.1 Abstract data type specification of a graph

    With graphs it is useful to have a common class from which all of our graph implementation classes derive. This approach is useful because we wish, later, to include nonabstract methods that are to be inherited by all implementations of graphs. Therefore, instead of defining an interface for the ADT *Graph*, we define an abstract class `Graph` as shown in Program 17.1.

    In addition to the ADT methods, we have a method to create an iterator for a vertex of the graph. This iterator will permit us to sequence through the vertices that are adjacent from a specified vertex. Suppose we create an iterator for vertex 5 as below:

```
Iterator vertex5Iterator = iterator(5);
```

Successive executions of `vertex5Iterator.next()` will return vertices j such that $(5, j)$ is an edge of the graph.

```
public abstract class Graph
{
    // ADT methods
    public abstract int vertices();
    public abstract int edges();
    public abstract boolean existsEdge(int i, int j);
    public abstract void putEdge(Object theEdge);
    public abstract void removeEdge(int i, int j);
    public abstract int degree(int i);
    public abstract int inDegree(int i);
    public abstract int outDegree(int i);

    // create an iterator for vertex i
    public abstract Iterator iterator(int i);
}
```

Program 17.1 The abstract class Graph

17.5   REPRESENTATION OF UNWEIGHTED GRAPHS

The most frequently used representation schemes for unweighted graphs are adjacency based: adjacency matrices, array adjacency lists, and linked adjacency lists.

17.5.1   Adjacency Matrix

The **adjacency matrix** of an n-vertex graph $G = (V, E)$ is an $n \times n$ matrix A. Each element of A is either 0 or 1. We will assume that $V = \{1, 2, \cdots, n\}$. If G is an undirected graph, then the elements of A are defined as follows:

$$A(i, j) = \begin{cases} 1 & \text{if } (i, j) \in E \text{ or } (j, i) \in E \\ 0 & \text{otherwise} \end{cases} \tag{17.1}$$

If G is a digraph, then the elements of A are defined as follows:

$$A(i, j) = \begin{cases} 1 & \text{if } (i, j) \in E \\ 0 & \text{otherwise} \end{cases} \tag{17.2}$$

The adjacency matrices for the graphs of Figure 17.1 appear in Figure 17.9.

The validity of the following statements is an immediate consequence of Equations 17.1 and 17.2:

1. $A(i, i) = 0$, $1 \le i \le n$ for all n-vertex graphs.

$$
\begin{array}{c}
\begin{array}{cccccccc}
 & 1 & 2 & 3 & 4 & 5 & 6 & 7 \\
1 & 0 & 1 & 1 & 0 & 0 & 0 & 0 \\
2 & 1 & 0 & 0 & 0 & 0 & 0 & 0 \\
3 & 1 & 0 & 0 & 0 & 0 & 0 & 0 \\
4 & 0 & 0 & 0 & 0 & 1 & 0 & 0 \\
5 & 0 & 0 & 0 & 1 & 0 & 1 & 1 \\
6 & 0 & 0 & 0 & 0 & 1 & 0 & 1 \\
7 & 0 & 0 & 0 & 0 & 1 & 1 & 0
\end{array}
\end{array}
$$

$$
\begin{array}{cccccc}
 & 1 & 2 & 3 & 4 \\
1 & 0 & 1 & 1 & 1 \\
2 & 1 & 0 & 1 & 0 \\
3 & 1 & 1 & 0 & 1 \\
4 & 1 & 0 & 1 & 0
\end{array}
\qquad
\begin{array}{cccccc}
 & 1 & 2 & 3 & 4 & 5 \\
1 & 0 & 1 & 0 & 0 & 0 \\
2 & 0 & 0 & 1 & 0 & 0 \\
3 & 0 & 0 & 0 & 1 & 1 \\
4 & 0 & 0 & 1 & 0 & 0 \\
5 & 0 & 0 & 0 & 1 & 0
\end{array}
$$

(a)   (b)   (c)

Figure 17.9 Adjacency matrices for the graphs of Figure 17.1

2. The adjacency matrix of an undirected graph is symmetric. That is, $A(i,j) = A(j,i)$, $1 \le i \le n$, $1 \le j \le n$.

3. For an n-vertex undirected graph, $\sum_{j=1}^{n} A(i,j) = \sum_{j=1}^{n} A(j,i) = d_i$. (Recall that d_i is the degree of vertex i.)

4. For an n-vertex digraph, $\sum_{j=1}^{n} A(i,j) = d_i^{out}$ and $\sum_{j=1}^{n} A(j,i) = d_i^{in}$, $1 \le i \le n$.

Mapping the Adjacency Matrix into an Array

The $n \times n$ adjacency matrix A may be mapped into an $(n+1) \times (n+1)$ array a of type **boolean** by using the mapping $A(i,j)$ equals 1 iff a$[i][j]$ is **true**, $1 \le i \le n$, $1 \le j \le n$. This mapping requires $(n+1)^2 = n^2 + 2n + 1$ bits. Alternatively, we may use an $n \times n$ array—a$[n][n]$—and the mapping $A(i,j)$ equals 1 iff a$[i-1][j-1]$ is **true**, $1 \le i \le n$, $1 \le j \le n$. Since this alternative requires n^2 bits, the storage requirement is reduced by $2n + 1$ bits.

A further reduction by n bits results if we use the fact that all diagonal entries are 0 and so need not be stored. When the diagonal is eliminated, an upper- and a lower-triangular matrix remain (see Section 8.3.4). These matrices may be compacted into an $(n-1) \times n$ matrix as in Figure 17.10. The shaded entries represent the lower triangle of the original adjacency matrix.

These methods to reduce the storage requirements yield a very small reduction and come at the cost of causing a mismatch between the vertex indexes used in the external and internal representation of a graph. This mismatch has the potential of causing errors in our codes. Further, the reduced storage methods require more time to access an edge. Therefore, we will use the $(n+1) \times (n+1)$ array mapping.

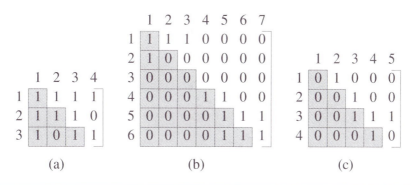

Figure 17.10 Adjacency matrices of Figure 17.9 with diagonals eliminated

For undirected graphs the adjacency matrix is symmetric (see Section 8.3.5), so only the elements above (or below) the diagonal need to be stored explicitly. Hence we need only $(n^2 - n)/2$ bits. By using the method of Section 8.3.5, we reduce the space requirement by about 50 percent. This reduction is significant for large graphs.

When adjacency matrices are used, we need $\Theta(n)$ time to determine the set of vertices adjacent to or from any given vertex. However, we can add or delete an edge in $\Theta(1)$ time.

17.5.2   Linked Adjacency Lists

The **adjacency list** for vertex i is a linear list that includes all vertices adjacent from i. In an **adjacency-list representation** of a graph, we maintain an adjacency list for each vertex of the graph. When these adjacency lists are represented as chains, we get the linked-adjacency-list representation.

We may use an array aList of type Chain to represent all the adjacency lists. aList[i].firstNode points to the first node in the adjacency list for vertex i. If x points to a node in the chain aList[i], then (i, x.element.vertex), where the data type of vertex is int, is an edge of the graph. Figure 17.11 gives some linked-adjacency-list representations.

Since each reference (pointer) and integer is 4 bytes long, the space needed by the linked-adjacency-list representation of an n-vertex graph is $4(n + 1)$ (for the array aList) + $4n$ (for the n firstNode pointers) + $4 * 3 * m$ (m chain nodes, 4 bytes for each of the two fields (next and element) of a chain node, 4 bytes for the vertex field of element) = $4(2n + 3m + 1)$ bytes where $m = 2e$ for an undirected graph, $m = e$ for a digraph, and e is the number of edges.

When e is much less than n^2, the linked-adjacency-list representation takes less space than does the adjacency-matrix representation. For example, a digraph with

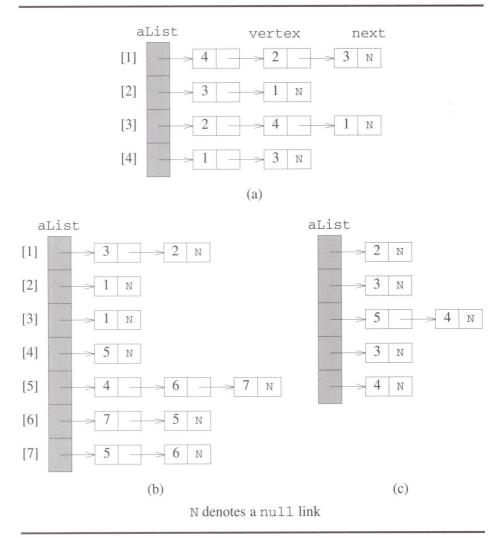

Figure 17.11 Linked adjacency lists for the graphs of Figure 17.1

$e = n$ edges requires $20n + 4$ bytes $= 160n + 32$ bits of space when linked adjacency lists are used; the same digraph requires n^2 bits when an adjacency matrix is used. The linked-list representation takes less space when $n \geq 161$.

When linked adjacency lists are used, we can determine the vertices adjacent from vertex i in time Θ(number of vertices adjacent from vertex i). The time needed to add or delete the edge (i, j) is $O(d_i + d_j)$ or $O(d_i^{out})$, depending on whether the graph is undirected or directed.

17.5.3   Array Adjacency Lists

In the **array-adjacency-list** representation of a graph, each adjacency list is represented by using an array-based linear list representation rather than a chain. So, for example, the data type of the array aList of the linked-adjacency-list representation may now be any of the array-based data types (i.e., classes) developed in Chapter 5. Alternatively, we may use a two-dimensional irregular array (Section 8.1.6) aList[][] with aList[i].length equal to the size of the adjacency list for vertex i. Figure 17.12 gives some array-adjacency-list representations. You may interpret each aList[i] as a one-dimensional array or as an instance of any of the array-based linear list representations developed in Chapter 5.

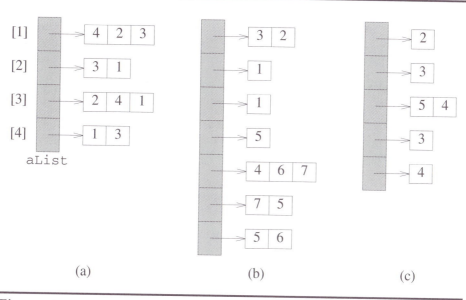

Figure 17.12 Array adjacency lists for graphs of Figure 17.1

The array-adjacency-list representation requires $4m$ bytes of space less than that required by linked adjacency lists, because, in the array-adjacency-list representation, we do not have the m next pointer fields that are present in the linked-adjacency-list representation. Most of the operations commonly performed on a graph can be done in the same asymptotic complexity by using either linked or array adjacency lists. Based on the experimental results of Sections 6.1.6 and 9.4.3, we expect array adjacency lists to outperform linked adjacency lists for most graph applications.

EXERCISES

16. Draw the following representations for the digraph of Figure 17.2(b).

    (a) Adjacency matrix.
    (b) Linked adjacency lists.
    (c) Array adjacency lists.

17. Do Exercise 16 for the graph of Figure 17.4(a).

18. Do Exercise 16 for the graph of Figure 17.5.

19. Do Exercise 16 for the digraph of Figure 17.8(a).

20. Do Exercise 16 for the digraph of Figure 17.8(b).

21. Suppose that the adjacency matrix of a graph is represented using a Boolean array as in Figure 17.10. Note that in this representation, the diagonal of the adjacency matrix is not stored (see Figure 17.10). Write methods `set` and `get` to, respectively, store and retrieve the value of $A(i, j)$. The complexity of each method should be $\Theta(1)$.

22. Do Exercise 21 for the case of an undirected graph for which only the lower triangle is explicitly stored in a one-dimensional `boolean` array `a`.

23. Assume that a directed $n \times n$ adjacency matrix is represented in an $n \times n$ `boolean` array `a`. Write a method to determine the number of edges in the graph. The complexity of your method should be $O(n^2)$. Show that this is the case.

24. Suppose that an undirected graph is represented with the array-adjacency-list representation (see Figure 17.12).

    (a) Write a method to remove the edge (i, j). What is the time complexity of your code?
    (b) Write a method to put an edge into the array-adjacency-list representation. What is the time complexity of your code?

25. Do Exercise 23 for the case when linked adjacency lists (see Figure 17.11) are used.

26. Do Exercise 24 for the case when linked adjacency lists are used.

27. Do Exercise 24 for the case of a directed graph.

28. Let G be an n-vertex e-edge undirected graph. What is the least value of e for which the adjacency-matrix representation of G uses less space than the array-adjacency-list representation uses?

29. Do Exercise 28 for the case of a directed graph G.

17.6   REPRESENTATION OF WEIGHTED GRAPHS

Weighted graphs are generally represented with schemes that are simple extensions of those used for unweighted graphs. The **cost-adjacency-matrix** representation uses a matrix C just like the adjacency-matrix representation does. If $A(i,j)$ is 1, then $C(i,j)$ is the cost (or weight) of the corresponding edge. If $A(i,j)$ is 0, then the corresponding edge is not present and $C(i,j)$ equals null. Figure 17.13 gives possible cost-adjacency matrices for the graphs of Figure 17.1.

$$
\begin{array}{c|cccc}
 & 1 & 2 & 3 & 4 \\
\hline
1 & - & 4 & 7 & 8 \\
2 & 4 & - & 2 & - \\
3 & 7 & 2 & - & 6 \\
4 & 8 & - & 6 & -
\end{array}
$$

(a)

$$
\begin{array}{c|ccccccc}
 & 1 & 2 & 3 & 4 & 5 & 6 & 7 \\
\hline
1 & - & 9 & 5 & - & - & - & - \\
2 & 9 & - & - & - & - & - & - \\
3 & 5 & - & - & - & - & - & - \\
4 & - & - & - & - & 3 & - & - \\
5 & - & - & - & 3 & - & 6 & 4 \\
6 & - & - & - & - & 6 & - & 1 \\
7 & - & - & - & - & 4 & 1 & -
\end{array}
$$

(b)

$$
\begin{array}{c|ccccc}
 & 1 & 2 & 3 & 4 & 5 \\
\hline
1 & - & 8 & - & - & - \\
2 & - & - & 3 & - & - \\
3 & - & - & - & 2 & 7 \\
4 & - & - & 6 & - & - \\
5 & - & - & - & 5 & -
\end{array}
$$

(c)

The small dash (-) denotes a null value

Figure 17.13 Possible cost-adjacency matrices for the graphs of Figure 17.1

We can obtain the adjacency-list representation of a weighted graph from that of the corresponding graph by using chains whose elements have the two fields **vertex** and **weight**. Figure 17.14 shows the representation for the weighted graph that corresponds to the cost-adjacency matrix of Figure 17.13(a). The first component of each node in this figure is **vertex**, and the second is **weight**.

We can obtain the array-adjacency-list representation of a weighted graph from that of the corresponding unweighted graph by replacing each entry with a (vertex, weight) pair. The representation differs from that shown in Figure 17.14 only in that there are no **next** pointers.

EXERCISES

30. Draw the array-adjacency-list representations of the weighted graphs that correspond to the cost-adjacency matrices of Figures 17.13(a) and (b).

31. Draw the linked-adjacency-list representations of the weighted graphs that correspond to the cost-adjacency matrices of Figures 17.13(b) and (c).

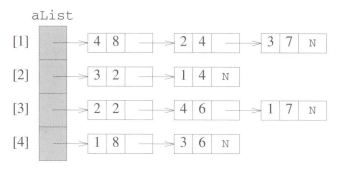

aList

[1]

[2]

[3]

[4]

4 | 8 → 2 | 4 → 3 | 7 | N

3 | 2 → 1 | 4 | N

2 | 2 → 4 | 6 → 1 | 7 | N

1 | 8 → 3 | 6 | N

N denotes a `null` link

Figure 17.14 Linked adjacency lists for weighted graph of Figure 17.13(a)

17.7   CLASS IMPLEMENTATIONS

17.7.1   The Different Classes

For each of the four graph types—unweighted undirected graphs, weighted undirected graphs, unweighted digraphs, and weighted digraphs—we considered three possible representations (matrix, linked, and array) in Sections 17.5 and 17.6. With one Java class for each graph type and representation combination, we will have 12 classes. Only eight of these classes are explicitly considered in this text. We develop the four that correspond to the array-adjacency-list representation in Exercises 37 through 40.

The eight classes we will develop are `AdjacencyGraph` (unweighted undirected graphs using the matrix representation), `AdjacencyWGraph`, `AdjacencyDigraph`, `AdjacencyWDigraph`, `LinkedGraph`, `LinkedWGraph`, `LinkedDigraph`, and `Linked-WDigraph`.

Several pairs of our four graph types have an "IsA" relationship between them. For example, an undirected graph may be viewed as a directed graph in which edge (i, j) is present whenever edge (j, i) is present; as a weighted undirected graph in which all edge weights are 1; or as a weighted digraph in which all edge weights are 1 and edge (j, i) is present whenever edge (i, j) is present. Similarly, a digraph may be viewed as a weighted digraph in which all edge weights are 1.

The presence of these relationships makes it easier to develop the eight classes because we can derive one class from another. Although many IsA relationships exist, we will employ just a few. Figure 17.15 shows the derivation hierarchy we use. The class `AdjacencyGraph`, for example, is derived from the class `AdjacencyDigraph`, and the class `AdjacencyWGraph` is derived from `AdjacencyWDigraph`. The abstract class `Graph` is a common superclass for all our graph classes. We will use this class in later sections to house methods that are implementation independent. These implementation-independent methods are inherited by all of our graph classes.

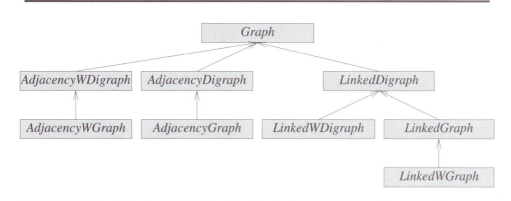

Figure 17.15 Class derivation hierarchy

Our graph classes use the following data types:

- EdgeNode $\cdots$ its lone data member is **vertex** and the data type of this member is **int**.

- WeightedEdgeNode $\cdots$ it has an integer data member **vertex** and a data member **weight** whose data type is **Object**.

- Edge $\cdots$ the data members are **vertex1** and **vertex2**; both are of type **int**, and they represent the endpoints of an edge.

- WeightedEdge $\cdots$ this has two integer data members **vertex1** and **vertex2** and a data member **weight** whose data type is **Object**.

17.7.2   Adjacency-Matrix Classes

The adjacency-matrix classes for weighted edges are similar to those for unweighted edges. The primary difference is that the weighted-edge classes use a two-dimensional array of type **Object**, whereas the classes for unweighted edges use a two-dimensional array of type **boolean**. We describe only the weighted-edge classes **AdjacencyWDigraph** and **AdjacencyWGraph** here. Although only partial code for the class **AdjacencyWDigraph** is given in the book, you can obtain complete codes for all adjacency-matrix classes from the Web site.

The Class `AdjacencyWDigraph`

Program 17.2 gives the code for `AdjacencyWDigraph`.

The first constructor creates the cost-adjacency matrix `a` for a weighted directed graph with n = `theVertices` vertices and zero edges. Note that Java initializes all entries in the two-dimensional array `a` to `null` and initializes e to 0. Therefore, the complexity of the first constructor is $O(n^2)$. The second constructor is the default constructor, which creates a weighted directed graph with zero vertices.

```
public class AdjacencyWDigraph extends Graph
{
   // data members
   int n;           // number of vertices
   int e;           // number of edges
   Object [][] a;   // adjacency array

   // constructors
   public AdjacencyWDigraph(int theVertices)
   {
      // code to validate theVertices comes here
      n = theVertices;
      a = new Object [n + 1] [n + 1];
      // default values are e = 0 and a[i][j] = null
   }

   // default is a 0 vertex graph
   public AdjacencyWDigraph()
      {this(0);}

   // Graph methods

   /** put edge e into the digraph; if the edge is already
     * there, update its weight to e.weight
     * @throws IllegalArgumentException when theEdge is invalid */
   public void putEdge(Object theEdge)
   {
      WeightedEdge edge =  (WeightedEdge) theEdge;
      int v1 = edge.vertex1;
      int v2 = edge.vertex2;
```

Program 17.2 Cost-adjacency matrix for weighted directed graphs (continues)

```
    if (v1 < 1 || v2 < 1 || v1 > n || v2 > n || v1 == v2)
        throw new IllegalArgumentException
                ("(" + v1 + "," + v2 + ") is not a permissible edge");

    if (a[v1][v2] == null)  // new edge
        e++;
    a[v1][v2] = edge.weight;
}

/** remove the edge (i,j) */
public void removeEdge(int i, int j)
{
    if (i >= 1 && j >= 1 && i <= n && j <= n && a[i][j] != null)
    {
        a[i][j] = null;
        e--;
    }
}

/** this method is undefined for directed graphs */
public int degree(int i)
    {throw new NoSuchMethodError();}

/** @return out-degree of vertex i
  * @throws IllegalArgumentException when i is not a valid vertex */
public int outDegree(int i)
{
    if (i < 1 || i > n)
        throw new IllegalArgumentException("no vertex " + i);

    // count out edges from vertex i
    int sum = 0;
    for (int j = 1; j <= n; j++)
        if (a[i][j] != null)
            sum++;

    return sum;
}
```

Program 17.2 Cost-adjacency matrix for weighted directed graphs (continues)

```
/** create and return an iterator for vertex i
 * @throws IllegalArgumentException when i is an invalid vertex */
public Iterator iterator(int i)
{
   if (i < 1 || i > n)
      throw new IllegalArgumentException("no vertex " + i);

   return new VertexIterator(i);
}

private class VertexIterator implements Iterator
{
   // data members
   private int v;    // the vertex being iterated
   private int nextVertex;

   // constructor
   public VertexIterator(int i)
   {
      v = i;
      // find first adjacent vertex
      for (int j = 1; j <= n; j++)
         if (a[v][j] != null)
         {
            nextVertex = j;
            return;
         }

      // no edge out of vertex i
      nextVertex = n + 1;
   }

   // methods
   /** @return true iff there is a next vertex */
   public boolean hasNext()
      {return nextVertex <= n;}
```

Program 17.2 Cost-adjacency matrix for weighted directed graphs (continues)

```
/** @return next adjacent vertex and edge weight
 * @throws NoSuchElementException
 * when there is no next vertex */
public Object next()
{
   if (nextVertex <= n)
   {
      int u = nextVertex;
      // find next adjacent vertex
      for (int j = u + 1; j <= n; j++)
         if (a[v][j] != null)
         {
            nextVertex = j;
            return new WeightedEdgeNode(u, a[v][u]);
         }

      // no next adjacent vertex for v
      nextVertex = n + 1;
      return new WeightedEdgeNode(u, a[v][u]);
   }
   else throw new NoSuchElementException
            ("no next vertex");
}

/** unsupported method */
public void remove()
   {throw new UnsupportedOperationException();}
}
}
```

Program 17.2 Cost-adjacency matrix for weighted directed graphs (concluded)

The code for the methods **vertices**, **edges**, and **existsEdge** is straightforward and is not shown in Program 17.2. The method **putEdge** first verifies that the endpoints of the input edge **theEdge** are in the range [1, n] and that the endpoints are different; that is, the endpoints correspond to vertices of the weighted digraph and the edge is not a self-edge. If the edge **theEdge** that is to be added to the weighted digraph fails this test, an exception of type **IllegalArgumentException** is thrown. If the edge passes the test, we must verify that **theEdge** already exists in the graph. When **theEdge** exists in the graph, we must update the weight of the edge, but not increase the edge count. When **theEdge** is a new edge, we must set the edge weight in **a** and increase the edge count.

removeEdge first verifies that the edge to be removed exists. If the edge exists, the corresponding entry in a is set to null and the edge count reduced by 1. The method degree simply throws an error of type NoSuchMethodError because degree is defined only for undirected graphs (whether weighted or unweighted). The out-degree of vertex i is computed by determining the number of entries a[i][*] that are not null, and the in-degree of vertex i is the number of entries a[*][i] that are not null (the code for inDegree is not shown).

For the iterator methods, we define the class VertexIterator, which is a member class of AdjacencyWDigraph. Recall from our discussion of the abstract class Graph (Section 17.4) that the iterator is to return, one by one, the vertices that are adjacent from the vertex that is being iterated. The data members of VertexIterator are v (the vertex that is being iterated) and nextVertex (the next vertex that is adjacent from vertex v). The constructor of VertexIterator initializes v and nextVertex. To initialize nextVertex we must scan the entries a[v][*] from left to right looking for the first entry that is not null. If no vertex is adjacent from vertex v, nextVertex is set to n+1. The code for hasNext simply checks whether nextVertex is ≤ n. The code for next first verifies that there is a next adjacent vertex, then determines the next value for nextVertex by scanning a[v][nextVertex+1:n], and finally it returns the initial value of nextVertex.

The complexity of existsEdge, vertices, edges, putEdge, removeEdge, degree, and hasNext is $\Theta(1)$. The complexity of outDegree, inDegree, elements, the constructor of VertexIterator, and next is $O(n)$. The complexity of outDegree and inDegree may be reduced to $\Theta(1)$ by keeping an array of out-degree values and an array of in-degree values.

The Class AdjacencyWGraph

Since this class is defined as a subclass of AdjacencyWDigraph, it inherits all the data members and methods of the superclass. We need to override those methods that are to work differently. The method putEdge must set both a[v1][v2] and a[v2][v1] to the weight of theEdge; removeEdge must set both a[i][j] and a[j][i] to null; and degree should be defined to return the number of entries a[i][*] that are not null. The code for the overriding methods is quite similar to code we have already seen for the methods of AdjacencyWDigraph. We do not include this code in the book, but you can get the code from the Web site.

17.7.3 An Extension to the Class Chain

In the linked-list representations of a graph, each object is represented as an array of chains where each chain is of type Chain (Section 6.1). One of the chain operations we need has not been defined yet. This additional operation removeElement(the-Vertex) searches the chain for an element whose vertex equals theVertex. If a matching element is found, it is deleted from the chain. The extension of Chain that includes the new method is called GraphChain.

17.7.4 Linked-List Classes

Program 17.3 gives the data members, constructors, and some of the simple methods of the class `LinkedDigraph`. The complexity of the first constructor is $O(n)$ ($n =$ `theVertices`); that of the second constructor, `vertices`, and `edges` is $\Theta(1)$; and that of `existsEdge(i,j)` is $O(d_i^{out})$.

To put an edge (`v1`, `v2`) into a digraph, we first verify that the edge is not already in the digraph, and then we insert an element of type `EdgeNode` at the front of the chain `aList[v1]` (see Program 17.4). To remove the edge (`i`, `j`) we use `GraphChain.removeElement` to remove the element on the chain `aList[v1]` whose vertex field is `j`. The complexity of `put` is $O(d_{v1}^{out})$, and that of `removeEdge` is $O(d_i^{out})$.

The method `degree` is undefined for a directed graph; its code is similar to that of `AdjacencyWDigraph.degree` (Program 17.2). The out-degree of vertex `i` is just `aList[i].size()`. Since the complexity of `Chain.size` is $\Theta(1)$, the out-degree of a vertex is determined in $\Theta(1)$ time. Computing the in-degree of a vertex is far more expensive. To compute the in-degree of vertex `i`, we must search all the adjacency lists, keeping a count of the number of lists that contain vertex `i` (Program 17.4). The complexity of `inDegree` is $O(n+e)$, where n and e are, respectively, the number of vertices and the number of edges in the digraph; this complexity may be reduced to $\Theta(1)$ by keeping an array of in-degree values.

For a vertex iterator we may simply use the iterator for `Chain`; the iterator for vertex `i` is created by the invocation `aList[i].iterator()`.

Other Linked Classes

The remaining linked classes may be implemented by overriding only those methods of their superclass that must work differently. The codes for these remaining linked classes may be obtained with modest effort and can be found at the Web site.

EXERCISES

32. Write the method `AdjacencyDigraph::input`, which inputs an undirected graph. Assume that the input consists of the number of vertices and edges in the graph together with a list of edges. Each edge is given as a pair of vertices. Since `AdjacencyGraph` is a subclass of `AdjacencyDigraph`, `AdjacencyGraph` inherits the input method you just wrote for `AdjacencyDigraph`. Are undirected graphs correctly input by the inherited method? If not, override the input method by writing a new one for `AdjacencyGraph`.

33. Write the method `AdjacencyWDigraph::input`, which inputs a weighted digraph.

```
public class LinkedDigraph extends Graph
{
   // data members
   int n;                    // number of vertices
   int e;                    // number of edges
   GraphChain [] aList;      // adjacency lists

   // constructors
   public LinkedDigraph(int theVertices)
   {
      // code to validate theVertices comes here
      n = theVertices;
      aList = new GraphChain [n + 1];
      for (int i = 1; i <= n; i++)
         aList[i] = new GraphChain();

      // default value of e is 0
   }

   // default is a 0-vertex graph
   public LinkedDigraph()
      {this(0);}

   // Graph methods
   /** @return number of vertices */
   public int vertices()
      {return n;}

   /** @return number of edges */
   public int edges()
      {return e;}

   /** @return true iff (i,j) is an edge */
   public boolean existsEdge(int i, int j)
   {
      if (i < 1 || j < 1 || i > n || j > n
          || aList[i].indexOf(new EdgeNode(j)) == -1)
         return false;
      else
         return true;
   }
}
```

Program 17.3 Data members and basic methods of LinkedDigraph

```java
/** put theEdge into the digraph */
public void putEdge(Object theEdge)
{
   Edge edge =  (Edge) theEdge;
   int v1 = edge.vertex1;
   int v2 = edge.vertex2;
   if (v1 < 1 || v2 < 1 || v1 > n || v2 > n || v1 == v2)
      throw new IllegalArgumentException
            ("(" + v1 + "," + v2 + ") is not a permissible edge");

   if (aList[v1].indexOf(new EdgeNode(v2)) == -1)  // new edge
   {
      // put v2 at front of chain aList[v1]
      aList[v1].add(0, new EdgeNode(v2));
      e++;
   }
}


/** remove the edge (i,j) */
public void removeEdge(int i, int j)
{
   if (i >= 1 && j >= 1 && i <= n && j <= n)
   {
      Object v = aList[i].removeElement(j);
      if (v != null)  // edge (i,j) did exist
         e--;
   }
}
/** @return in-degree of vertex i */
public int inDegree(int i)
{
   if (i < 1 || i > n)
      throw new IllegalArgumentException("no vertex " + i);

   // count in edges at vertex i
   int sum = 0;
   for (int j = 1; j <= n; j++)
      if (aList[j].indexOf(new EdgeNode(i)) != -1)
         sum++;

   return sum;
}
```

Program 17.4 Additional methods of LinkedDigraph

34. Write the method `LinkedDigraph::input`, which inputs a digraph. The complexity of your method should be linear in the number of vertices and edges in the input graph. Show that this is the case.

35. Write the method `LinkedWDigraph::input`, which inputs a weighted digraph. The complexity of your method should be linear in the number of vertices and edges in the input graph. Show that this is the case.

36. We can speed `LinkedWGraph` and `LinkedWDigraph` if we include a new version of the `indexOf` method in `GraphChain`. The new version updates the element in case it is already in the chain. Develop such an `indexOf` method and modify the `put` methods of `LinkedWGraph` and `LinkedWDigraph` to utilize this new method.

37. Develop the Java class `ArrayDigraph` in which digraphs are represented with array adjacency lists.

38. Develop the Java class `ArrayGraph` in which undirected graphs are represented with array adjacency lists.

39. Develop the Java class `ArrayWDigraph` in which weighted digraphs are represented with array adjacency lists.

40. Develop the Java class `ArrayWGraph` in which weighted undirected graphs are represented with array adjacency lists.

17.8   GRAPH SEARCH METHODS

The operations that are performed on graphs are too numerous to list here. We saw some of these operations (e.g., find a path, find a spanning tree, determine whether the undirected graph is connected) in Section 17.2, and we will see some others later in this book. Many operations require us to visit all vertices that can be reached from a given start vertex. (A vertex u is reachable from vertex v iff there is a (directed) path from v to u.) The two standard ways to search for these vertices are **breadth-first search** (BFS) and **depth-first search** (DFS). Although both search methods are popular, the depth-first method is used more frequently to obtain efficient graph algorithms.

17.8.1   Breadth-First Search

Consider the directed graph of Figure 17.16(a). One way to determine all the vertices reachable from vertex 1 is to first determine the set of vertices adjacent from 1. This set is {2,3,4}. Next we determine the set of new vertices (i.e., vertices not yet reached) that are adjacent from vertices in {2,3,4}. This set is {5,6,7}. The set of new vertices adjacent from vertices in {5,6,7} is {8,9}. No new vertices are adjacent from a vertex in {8,9}; therefore, {1,2,3,4,5,6,7,8,9} is the set of vertices reachable from vertex 1.

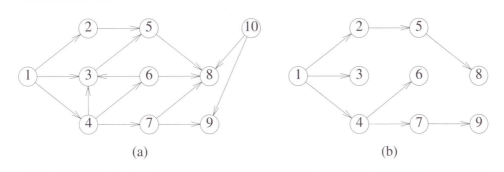

(a)   (b)

Figure 17.16 Breadth-first search

This method of starting at a vertex and identifying all vertices reachable from it is called breadth-first search (BFS). Such a search may be implemented using a queue. A pseudocode version of a possible implementation appears in Figure 17.17. Notice the similarity between BFS and level-order traversal of a binary tree.

If we use the pseudocode of Figure 17.17 on the graph of Figure 17.16(a) with v = 1, then vertices 2, 3, and 4 will get added to the queue (assume that they get added in this order) during the first iteration of the outer `while` loop. In the next iteration of this loop, 2 is removed from the queue, and vertex 5 added to it. Next 3 is deleted from the queue, and no new vertices are added. Then 4 is deleted and 6 and 7 added; 5 is deleted and 8 added; 6 is deleted and nothing added; and 7 is deleted and 9 added. Finally, 8 and 9 are deleted, and the queue becomes empty. The procedure terminates, and vertices 1 through 9 have been marked as reached. Figure 17.16(b) shows the subgraph formed by the edges used to reach the nodes that get visited.

Theorem 17.1 *Let G be an arbitrary graph and let v be any vertex of G. The pseudocode of Figure 17.17 labels all vertices that are reachable from v (including vertex v).*

Proof Exercise 43(a) asks you to prove this theorem.   ∎

17.8.2   Implementation of Breadth-First Search

As indicated by the pseudocode of Figure 17.17, at a suitably high level the manner in which a BFS is performed is independent of whether we are dealing with an undirected graph, digraph, weighted undirected graph, or weighted digraph and

```
breadthFirstSearch(v)
{
    Label vertex v as reached.
    Initialize Q to be a queue with only v in it.
    while (Q is not empty)
    {
        Delete a vertex w from the queue.
        Let u be a vertex (if any) adjacent from w.
        while (u)
        {
            if (u has not been labeled)
            {
                Add u to the queue.
                Label u as reached.
            }
            u = next vertex that is adjacenct from w.
        }
    }
}
```

Figure 17.17 Pseudocode for BFS

is also independent of the particular representation used. However, to implement statements such as

u = next vertex that is adjacent from w

we need to know the implementation in use. We can avoid writing separate code to perform a BFS for each of our implementations by making our BFS method a member of the class **Graph**, which is a superclass of all of the implementation classes, and using graph iterators to go from one adjacent vertex to the next.

The implementation-independent code for BFS (see Program 17.5) closely follows the pseudocode of Figure 17.17. Program 17.5 assumes that **reach[i]** = 0 initially for all vertices and that **label** ≠ 0. All reachable vertices have **reach[i]** set to **label** upon termination.

17.8.3   Complexity Analysis of Graph.bfs

Each vertex that is reachable from the start vertex v is labeled, added to the queue exactly once, deleted from the queue exactly once, and its row in the adjacency matrix or its linked adjacency list traversed exactly once. If s vertices are labeled, then the time for all of these operations is $O(sn)$ when an adjacency matrix is used and $O(\sum_i d_i^{out})$ when a linked adjacency list is used. In the latter case the sum is done over all i where i is a labeled vertex. For an undirected graph the out-degree of a vertex is considered equal to its degree.

```
/** breadth-first search
  * reach[i] is set to label for all vertices reachable
  * from vertex v */
public void bfs(int v, int [] reach, int label)
{
   ArrayQueue q = new ArrayQueue(10);
   reach[v] = label;
   q.put(new Integer(v));
   while (!q.isEmpty())
   {
      // remove a labeled vertex from the queue
      int w = ((Integer) q.remove()).intValue();

      // mark all unreached vertices adjacent from w
      Iterator iw = iterator(w);
      while (iw.hasNext())
      {// visit an adjacent vertex of w
         int u = ((EdgeNode) iw.next()).vertex;
         if (reach[u] == 0)
         {// u is an unreached vertex
            q.put(new Integer(u));
            reach[u] = label; // mark reached
         }
      }
   }
}
```

Program 17.5 Implementation-independent BFS code

At this point we may wonder what the unified BFS code costs compared to codes customized for each representation. We need three customized codes—one is a member of `AdjacencyWDigraph`, another is a member of `AdjacencyDigraph`, and the third is a member of `LinkedDigraph`. The remaining methods inherit the customized code from their superclass. Programs 17.6 and 17.7 give the customized codes for `AdjacencyDigraph` and `LinkedDigraph`, respectively. The customized code for `AdjacencyWDigraph` is obtained from that for `AdjacencyDigraph` by changing the line

```
if (a[w][u] && reach[u] == 0)
```

to

```
if (a[w][u] != null && reach[u] == 0)
```

```java
public void bfs(int v, int [] reach, int label)
{
   ArrayQueue q = new ArrayQueue(10);
   reach[v] = label;
   q.put(new Integer(v));
   while (!q.isEmpty())
   {
      // remove a labeled vertex from the queue
      int w = ((Integer) q.remove()).intValue();

      // mark all unreached vertices adjacent from w
      for (int u = 1; u <= n; u++)
      {
         if (a[w][u] && reach[u] == 0)
         {// u is an unreached vertex
            q.put(new Integer(u));
            reach[u] = label;
         }
      }
   }
}
```

Program 17.6 Direct BFS implementation for `AdjacencyDigraph`

On our 300 MHz Pentium II PC, `Graph.bfs` took 29 milliseconds (ms) to do a BFS on a 100-vertex, unweighted complete undirected graph represented by its adjacency matrix. The corresponding time for `AdjacencyDigraph.bfs` was 0.9 ms. So we pay a 32-fold performance penalty to use the implementation-independent method `Graph.bfs`. For the linked representation the implementation-independent code took 5 ms, while the customized code took 3 ms. The performance penalty for this case is almost twofold.

As indicated above, we can expect to pay a potentially very significant performance penalty when using the implementation-independent BFS code rather than the customized versions. Most of this penalty comes from the use of iterators. However, we should keep in mind that several merits are associated with the implementation-independent code. For example, this single code works with all representations, whereas the customized route requires several codes. Consequently, if we introduce new representations (for example array adjacency lists), we can use the implementation-independent code with no change. When developing code for a new graph application, we can first develop the implementation-independent code.

```
public void bfs(int v, int [] reach, int label)
{
    ArrayQueue q = new ArrayQueue(10);
    reach[v] = label;
    q.put(new Integer(v));
    while (!q.isEmpty())
    {
        // remove a labeled vertex from the queue
        int w = ((Integer) q.remove()).intValue();

        // mark all unreached vertices adjacent from w
        for (ChainNode p = aList[w].firstNode; p != null; p = p.next)
        {
            int u = ((EdgeNode) p.element).vertex;
            if (reach[u] == 0)
            {// u is an unreached vertex
                q.put(new Integer(u));
                reach[u] = label;
            }
        }
    }
}
```

Program 17.7 Direct BFS implementation for `LinkedDigraph`

This approach enables all graph implementations to make use of this application. Then as time and resources permit, we can develop the more efficient customized codes for individual representations.

17.8.4   Depth-First Search

Depth-first search (DFS) is an alternative to BFS. The DFS strategy has already been used in the rat-in-a-maze problem (Section 9.5.6) and is quite similar to pre-order traversal of a binary tree.

Figure 17.18 gives the pseudocode for DFS. Starting at a vertex v, a DFS proceeds as follows: First the vertex v is marked as reached, and then an unreached vertex u adjacent from v is selected. If such a vertex does not exist, the search terminates. Assume that a u as described exists. A DFS from u is now initiated. When this search is completed, we select another unreached vertex adjacent from v. If such a vertex does not exist, then the search terminates. If such a vertex exists, a DFS is initiated from this vertex, and so on.

```
depthFirstSearch(v)
{
    Label vertex v as reached.
    for (each unreached vertex u adjacenct from v)
        depthFirstSearch(u);
}
```

Figure 17.18 Pseudocode for DFS

Let us try out `depthFirstSearch` on the digraph of Figure 17.16(a). If v = 1, then vertices 2, 3, and 4 are the candidates for the first choice of u. Suppose that the first value assigned to u is 2. A DFS from 2 is now initiated. Vertex 2 is marked as reached. The only candidate for u this time is vertex 5, and a DFS from 5 is initiated. Vertex 5 is marked as reached, and then a DFS from 8 is initiated. Next vertex 8 is marked. From 8 there are no unreached adjacent vertices, so the algorithm backs up to vertex 5. There are no new candidates for u here, so we back up to 2 and then to 1.

At this point we have two candidates: vertices 3 and 4 for u. Assume that 4 is selected. A DFS from 4 is initiated, and vertex 4 is marked as reached. Vertices 3, 6, and 7 are now the candidates for u. Assume that vertex 6 is selected. When v = 6, vertex 3 is the only candidate for u. A DFS from 3 is initiated, and vertex 3 gets labeled as reached. No new vertices are adjacent from 3, and we back up to vertex 6. No new vertices are adjacent from here, so we back up to 4. From 4 we initiate a DFS with u = 7. Next we reach vertex 9 from which there are no new adjacent vertices. This time we back up all the way to 1. As there are no new vertices adjacent from 1, the algorithm terminates.

For `depthFirstSearch` we can prove a theorem analogous to Theorem 17.1; `depthFirstSearch` labels vertex v and all vertices reachable from v (Exercise 43(b)).

Theorem 17.2 *Let G be an arbitrary graph and let v be any vertex of G. Procedure* `depthFirstSearch` *labels all vertices that are reachable from v (including vertex v).*

Proof Exercise 43(b) asks you to prove this theorem.   ∎

17.8.5   Implementation of Depth-First Search

Program 17.8 gives the public method `Graph.dfs` as well as the private method `Graph.rDfs`. The code of Program 17.8 assumes that `reach` and `label` are class data members of `Graph`. In the implementation of DFS, it is easier to let u run through all vertices adjacent from v, rather than just through the unreached vertices adjacent from v.

```
/** depth-first search
  * reach[i] is set to label for all vertices reachable
  * from vertex v */
public void dfs(int v, int [] reach, int label)
{
   Graph.reach = reach;
   Graph.label = label;
   rDfs(v);
}

/** recursive dfs method */
private void rDfs(int v)
{
   reach[v] = label;
   Iterator iv = iterator(v);
   while (iv.hasNext())
   {// visit an adjacent vertex of v
      int u = ((EdgeNode) iv.next()).vertex;
      if (reach[u] == 0)  // u is an unreached vertex
         rDfs(u);
   }
}
```

Program 17.8 Depth-first search

17.8.6   Complexity Analysis of `Graph.dfs`

You can verify that the methods `dfs` and `bfs` have the same time and space complexities. However, the instances for which `dfs` takes maximum space (i.e., stack space for the recursion) are those on which `bfs` takes minimum space (i.e., queue space); and the instances for which `bfs` takes maximum space are those on which `dfs` takes minimum space. Figure 17.19 gives the best-case and worst-case instances for `dfs` and `bfs`.

EXERCISES

41. Consider the graph of Figure 17.4(a).

    (a) Draw an adjacency-list representation (either linked or array) for this graph.

    (b) Label the vertices in the order in which they are visited in a BFS that starts at vertex 4. Use your representation of part (a) and the code of Program 17.5.

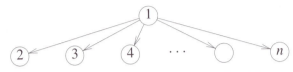

(a) Worst case for `dfs(1)`; best case for `bfs(1)`

(b) Best case for `dfs(1)`; worst case for `bfs(1)`

Figure 17.19 Worst-case and best-case space complexity graphs

(c) Show the subgraph formed by the edges used to reach new vertices during your search of part (b).

(d) Redo parts (b) and (c), but this time do a DFS using the code of Program 17.8.

42. Do Exercise 41 using vertex 7 as the start vertex for the search.

43. (a) Prove Theorem 17.1.

(b) Prove Theorem 17.2.

44. Develop customized DFS codes for `AdjacencyDigraph` and `LinkedDigraph`.

(a) Test the correctness of your codes.

(b) Determine the speedup obtained by the customized codes over the implementation-independent code of Program 17.8 on a complete digraph with 100 vertices.

17.9   APPLICATIONS REVISITED

17.9.1   Finding a Path

We can find a path (see Example 17.1) from a source vertex s to a destination vertex d by starting a search (either breadth first or depth first) at vertex s and terminating the search as soon as we reach vertex d. To actually construct the path, we need to remember the edges used to move from one vertex to the next. For the path problem, the needed set of edges is implicitly stored in the depth-first recursion, so it is easier to develop a path-finding code by using the depth-first strategy. As the recursion unfolds following the labeling of vertex d, the path is constructed backward from d to s. The code for `Graph.findPath` appears in Program 17.9. Program 17.10 gives the code for `rFindPath`.

```
/** find a path from s to d
  * @return the path in an array using positions 0 on up
  * @return null if there is no path */
public int [] findPath(int s, int d)
{
    // initialize for recursive path finder
    int n = vertices();
    path = new int [n];
    path[0] = s;    // first vertex is always s
    length = 0;     // current path length
    destination = d;
    reach = new int [n + 1];
    for (int i = 1; i <= n; i++)
        reach[i] = 0;

    // search for path
    if (s == d || rFindPath(s))
    {// a path was found, trim array to path size
        int [] newPath = new int [length + 1];
        // copy from old space to new space
        System.arraycopy(path, 0, newPath, 0, length + 1);
        return newPath;
    }
    else
        return null;
}
```

Program 17.9 Preprocessor to find a path in a graph

If there is no path from s to d, `findPath` returns `null`; otherwise, it returns an array p that contains the vertices on the path from s to d, p[0] = s, and p[p.length - 1] = d.

`findPath` first initializes the following class data members of `Graph`: `destination`, `path`, `length`, and `reach`. The DFS for the path is actually performed by the private method `Graph.rFindPath`, which returns `false` iff no path to the destination is found. Method `Graph.rFindPath` is a modified DFS. There are essentially two modifications that have been made to a standard DFS: (1) `rFindPath` discontinues the search for reachable vertices as soon as the destination vertex `destination` is reached, and (2) `rFindPath` records the vertices on the path from the source s

```
/** real path finder, performs a depth-first search
  * @param s source vertex not equal to destination
  * @return true iff a path to destination is found */
private boolean rFindPath(int s)
{
   reach[s] = 1;
   Iterator is = iterator(s);
   while (is.hasNext())
   {// visit an adjacent vertex of s
      int u = ((EdgeNode) is.next()).vertex;
      if (reach[u] == 0)    // u is an unreached vertex
      {// move to vertex u
         length++;
         path[length] = u; // add u to path
         if (u == destination) return true;
         if (rFindPath(u))
            return true;
         // no path from u to destination
         length--;            // remove u from path
      }
   }
   return false;
}
```

Program 17.10 Recursive method to find a path in a graph

to the current vertex u in the array `path`. Notice that `rFindPath` is invoked only when s ≠ d. Also, notice that `rFindPath` does not necessarily find a shortest path (i.e., a path with the fewest number of edges) to the destination. When a BFS is used in place of a DFS, a shortest path is found (Exercise 45).

`findPath` and `dfs` have the same complexity.

17.9.2   Connected Graphs and Components

We can determine whether an undirected graph G is connected (see Example 17.2) by performing either a DFS or BFS from any vertex and then verifying that all vertices have been labeled as reached. Although this strategy directly verifies only that there is a path from the start vertex of the DFS or BFS to every other graph vertex, this verification is sufficient to conclude that a path exists between every pair of vertices. To see the validity of this claim, suppose that i is the start vertex of the search and that the search reaches all vertices of the graph. We may construct a path between any two vertices u and v by using the path from i to u in the reverse direction and then the path from i to v. Method `connected` (Program 17.11) returns `false` if the graph is not connected and `true` if it is. Since the notion of connectedness is defined only for undirected graphs, we test that the graph `this` is undirected by invoking the method `Graph.verifyUndirected` (Program 17.12). The code for this method will need to be updated if we later define additional implementations of undirected graphs.

```
/** @return true iff graph is connected */
public boolean connected()
{
   // make sure this is an undirected graph
   verifyUndirected("connected");

   int n = vertices();

   // set all vertices as not reached
   reach = new int [n + 1];
   for (int i = 1; i <= n; i++)
      reach[i] = 0;

   // mark vertices reachable from vertex 1
   dfs(1, reach, 1);

   // check if all vertices marked
   for (int i = 1; i <= n; i++)
      if (reach[i] == 0)
         return false;
   return true;
}
```

Program 17.11 Determine whether an undirected graph is connected

In an undirected graph the set C of vertices that are reachable from a vertex i, together with the edges that connect pairs of vertices in C, is a **connected component**. The undirected graph of Figure 17.1(b) has two connected components. One consists of the vertices $\{1,2,3\}$ and the edges $\{(1,2), (1,3)\}$, and the other consists of the remaining vertices and edges. In the **component-labeling problem**, we are to label the vertices of an undirected graph so that two vertices are assigned the same label iff they belong to the same component. In the example of Figure 17.1(b), vertices 1, 2, and 3 can be labeled 1, and the remaining vertices labeled 2.

```
/** verify that the graph is an undirected graph
 * @throws UndefinedMethodException if graph is directed  */
public void verifyUndirected(String theMethodName)
{
   Class c = getClass();    // class of this
   if (c == AdjacencyGraph.class ||
       c == AdjacencyWGraph.class ||
       c == LinkedGraph.class ||
       c == LinkedWGraph.class)
      return;

   // not an undirected graph
   throw new UndefinedMethodException
      ("Graph." + theMethodName + " is for undirected graphs only");
}
```

Program 17.12 Verifying that a graph is undirected

We can label components by making repeated invocations of either a DFS
or BFS. We start each invocation at an as-yet-unlabeled vertex and perform a
search. For each search a new label is used to mark the vertices that are reached.
So vertices that are in different components have different labels. The method
`Graph.labelComponents` (Program 17.13) solves the component-labeling problem.
It returns the number of components in the undirected graph. The component labels are returned in the array `c[1:n]` where `n` is the number of vertices in the graph.
We may use `dfs` in place of `bfs` in Program 17.13 and obtain the same results. The
complexity of Program 17.13 is $O(n^2)$ when the graph is represented as an adjacency
matrix and $O(n+e)$ when we use the linked-adjacency-list representation.

17.9.3   Spanning Trees

If a BFS is carried out starting from any vertex in a connected undirected graph
or network with `n` vertices, then from Theorem 17.1 we know that all vertices will
get labeled. Exactly `n-1` of these vertices are reached in the inner `while` loop of
`Graph.bfs` (Program 17.5). When a new vertex `u` is reached in this loop, the edge
used to reach `u` is `(w,u)`. The set of edges used in the inner `while` loop to reach
previously unreached vertices is of size `n-1`. Since this set of edges contains a path
from `v` to every other vertex in the graph, it defines a connected subgraph, which
is a spanning tree of G.

Consider the graph of Figure 17.20(a). If a BFS is started at vertex 1, then
the edges {(1,2), (1,3), (1,4), (2,5), (4,6), (4,7), (5,8)} are used to reach previ-

```
/** label the components of an undirected graph
 *   @return the number of components
 *   set c[i] to be the component number of vertex i */
public int labelComponents(int [] c)
{
   // make sure this is an undirected graph
   verifyUndirected("labelComponents");

   int n = vertices();

   // assign all vertices to no component
   for (int i = 1; i <= n; i++)
      c[i] = 0;

   label = 0;  // ID of last component
   // identify components
   for (int i = 1; i <= n; i++)
      if (c[i] == 0)  // vertex i is unreached
      {// vertex i is in a new component
         label++;
         bfs(i, c, label); // mark new component
      }

   return label;
}
```

Program 17.13 Component labeling

ously unreached vertices. This set of edges corresponds to the spanning tree of Figure 17.20(b).

A **breadth-first spanning tree** is any spanning tree obtained in the manner just described from a BFS. We can verify that the spanning trees of Figures 17.20 (b), (c), and (d) are all breadth-first spanning trees of the graph of Figure 17.20 (a); the start vertex for each BFS is the shaded node.

When a DFS is performed in a connected undirected graph or network, exactly n-1 edges are used to reach new vertices. The subgraph formed by these edges is also a spanning tree. Spanning trees obtained in this manner from a DFS are called **depth-first spanning trees**. Figure 17.21 shows some of the depth-first spanning trees of Figure 17.20(a). In each case the start vertex is vertex 1.

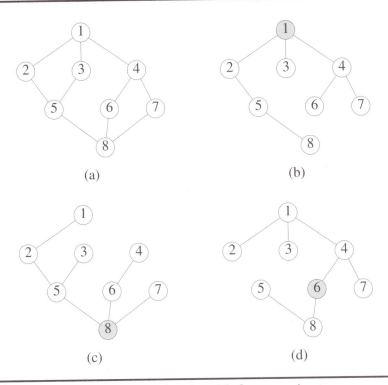

Figure 17.20 A graph and some of its breadth-first spanning trees

EXERCISES

45. Write a version of Program 17.9 that uses a BFS rather than a DFS. Show that this version finds a shortest path from s to d.

46. For the graph of Figure 17.20(a), do the following:

    (a) Draw a breadth-first spanning tree starting at vertex 3.
    (b) Draw a breadth-first spanning tree starting at vertex 7.
    (c) Draw a depth-first spanning tree starting at vertex 3.
    (d) Draw a depth-first spanning tree starting at vertex 7.

47. Do Exercise 46 using the graph of Figure 17.4(a).

48. Write code for the public method Graph.bfSpanningTree(i), which finds a breadth-first spanning tree of a connected undirected graph by initiating a BFS at vertex i. Your code should return null if it fails because there is

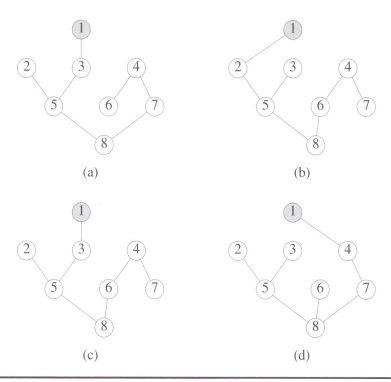

(a)

(b)

(c)

(d)

Figure 17.21 Some depth-first spanning trees of Figure 17.20(a)

no spanning tree (i.e., the graph is not connected). When a spanning tree is found, your method should return an array of edges that make up the spanning tree. The data type of the edge array that is returned is `Edge []`.

49. Do Exercise 48 for the case of `Graph.dfSpanningTree(i)`, which finds a depth-first spanning tree beginning at vertex `i`.

50. Write code for the public method `Graph.cycle()`, which determines whether an undirected graph has a cycle. Base your code on either a DFS or a BFS.

  (a) Prove the correctness of your code.

  (b) Determine the time and space complexities of your code.

51. Let G be an undirected graph. Write code for the method `Graph.bipar-tite()`, which returns `null` if G is not a bipartite graph (see Example 17.3) and an integer array `label` if it is. When G is bipartite, the array `label` is a labeling of the vertices such that `label[i]` $= 1$ for vertices in one subset and

label[i] = 2 for vertices in the other subset. The complexity of your code should be $O(n^2)$ if G has n vertices and is represented as a matrix and $O(n+e)$ if a linked list representation is used. Show that this is the case. (*Hint:* Perform several BFSs, each time beginning at an as-yet-unreached vertex. Assign this unreached vertex to set 1; vertices adjacent from this vertex are assigned to set 2, those adjacent to these set 2 vertices are assigned to set 1, and so on. Also check for conflicting assignments, i.e., the set assignment of a vertex is changed.)

52. Let G be an undirected graph. Its **transitive closure** is a 0/1 valued array tc such that tc[i][j] = 1 iff G has a path with one or more edges from vertex i to vertex j. Write a public method Graph.undirectedTC() to compute and return the transitive closure of G. The time complexity of your method should be $O(n^2)$ where n is the number of vertices in G. (*Hint:* Use component labeling.)

53. Do Exercise 52 for Graph::directedTC(), which is to be used when G is directed. What is the complexity of your algorithm?

CHAPTER 18

THE GREEDY METHOD

BIRD'S-EYE VIEW

Exit the world of data structures. Enter the world of algorithm-design methods. In the remainder of this book, we study methods for the design of good algorithms. Although the design of a good algorithm for any given problem is more an art than a science, some design methods are effective in solving many problems. You can apply these methods to computer problems and see how the resulting algorithm works. Generally, you must fine-tune the resulting algorithm to achieve acceptable performance. In some cases, however, fine-tuning is not possible, and you will have to think of some other way to solve the problem.

Chapters 18 through 22 present five basic algorithm-design methods: the greedy method, divide and conquer, dynamic programming, backtracking, and branch and bound. This list excludes several more advanced methods, such as linear programming, integer programming, neural networks, genetic algorithms, and simulated annealing, that are also widely used. These methods are typically covered in courses dedicated to them.

This chapter begins by introducing the notion of an optimization problem. Next the greedy method, which is a very intuitive method, is described. Although it is usually quite easy to formulate a greedy algorithm for a problem, the formulated algorithm may not always produce an optimal answer. Therefore, *it is essential that we prove that our greedy algorithms actually work.* Even when greedy algorithms do not guarantee optimal answers, they remain useful, as they often get us answers that are close to optimal. We use the greeedy method to obtain algorithms for the container-loading, knapsack, topological-ordering, bipartite-cover, shortest-path, and minimum-cost spanning-tree problems.

18.1   OPTIMIZATION PROBLEMS

Many of the examples used in this chapter and in the remaining chapters are **optimization problems**. In an optimization problem we are given a set of **constraints** and an **optimization function**. Solutions that satisfy the constraints are called **feasible solutions**. A feasible solution for which the optimization function has the best possible value is called an **optimal solution**.

Example 18.1 [Thirsty Baby] A very thirsty, and intelligent, baby wants to quench her thirst. She has access to a glass of water, a carton of milk, cans of various juices, and bottles and cans of various sodas. In all the baby has access to n different liquids. From past experience with these n liquids, the baby knows that some are more satisfying than others. In fact, the baby has assigned satisfaction values to each liquid. s_i units of satisfaction are obtained by drinking 1 ounce of the ith liquid.

Ordinarily, the baby would just drink enough of the liquid that gives her greatest satisfaction per ounce and thereby quench her thirst in the most satisfying way. Unfortunately, there isn't enough of this most satisfying liquid available. Let a_i be the amount in ounces of liquid i that is available. The baby needs to drink a total of t ounces to quench her thirst. How much of each available liquid should she drink?

We may assume that satisfaction is additive. Let x_i denote the amount of liquid i that the baby should drink. The solution to her problem is obtained by finding real numbers x_i, $1 \leq i \leq n$ that maximize $\sum_{i=1}^{n} s_i x_i$ subject to the constraints $\sum_{i=1}^{n} x_i = t$ and $0 \leq x_i \leq a_i$, $1 \leq i \leq n$.

Note that if $\sum_{i=1}^{n} a_i < t$, then there is no solution to the baby's problem. Even if she drinks all the liquids available, she will be unable to quench her thirst.

This precise mathematical formulation of the problem provides an unambiguous specification of what the program is to do. Having obtained this formulation, we can provide the input/output specification, which takes the form:

[Input] n, t, s_i, a_i, $1 \leq i \leq n$. n is an integer, and the remaining numbers are positive reals.

[Output] Real numbers x_i, $1 \leq i \leq n$, such that $\sum_{i=1}^{n} s_i x_i$ is maximum, $\sum_{i=1}^{n} x_i = t$, and $0 \leq x_i \leq a_i$, $1 \leq i \leq n$. Output a suitable message if $\sum_{i=1}^{n} a_i < t$.

The constraints are $\sum_{i=1}^{n} x_i = t$ and $0 \leq x_i \leq a_i$, and the optimization function is $\sum_{i=1}^{n} s_i x_i$. Every set of x_is that satisfies the constraints is a feasible solution. Every feasible solution that maximizes $\sum_{i=1}^{n} s_i x_i$ is an optimal solution. ■

Example 18.2 [Loading Problem] A large ship is to be loaded with cargo. The cargo is containerized, and all containers are the same size. Different containers may have different weights. Let w_i be the weight of the ith container, $1 \leq i \leq n$. The cargo capacity of the ship is c. We wish to load the ship with the maximum number of containers.

This problem can be formulated as an optimization problem in the following way: Let x_i be a variable whose value can be either 0 or 1. If we set x_i to 0, then container i is not to be loaded. If x_i is 1, then the container is to be loaded. We wish to assign values to the x_is that satisfy the constraints $\sum_{i=1}^{n} w_i x_i \leq c$ and $x_i \in \{0, 1\}, 1 \leq i \leq n$. The optimization function is $\sum_{i=1}^{n} x_i$.

Every set of x_is that satisfies the constraints is a feasible solution. Every feasible solution that maximizes $\sum_{i=1}^{n} x_i$ is an optimal solution. ■

Example 18.3 [Minimum-Cost Communication Network] We introduced this problem in Example 17.2. The set of cities and possible communication links can be represented as an undirected graph. Each edge has a cost (or weight) assigned to it. This cost is the cost of constructing the link represented by the edge. Every connected subgraph that includes all the vertices represents a feasible solution. Under the assumption that all weights are nonnegative, the set of feasible solutions can be narrowed to the set of spanning trees of the graph. An optimal solution is a spanning tree with minimum cost.

In this problem we need to select a subset of the edges. This subset must satisfy the following constraint: *The set of selected edges forms a spanning tree.* The optimization function is the sum of the weights of the selected edges. ■

18.2   THE GREEDY METHOD

In the **greedy method** we attempt to construct an optimal solution in stages. At each stage we make a decision that appears to be the best (under some criterion) at the time. A decision made in one stage is not changed in a later stage, so each decision should assure feasibility. The criterion used to make the greedy decision at each stage is called the **greedy criterion**.

Example 18.4 [Change Making] A child buys candy valued at less than \$1 and gives a \$1 bill to the cashier. The cashier wishes to return change using the fewest number of coins. Assume that an unlimited supply of quarters, dimes, nickels, and pennies is available. The cashier constructs the change in stages. In each stage a coin is added to the change. This coin is selected using the greedy criterion: *At each stage increase the total amount of change constructed by as much as possible.* To assure feasiblity (i.e., the change given exactly equals the desired amount) of the solution, the selected coin should not cause the total amount of change given so far to exceed the final desired amount.

Suppose that 67 cents in change is due the child. The first two coins selected are quarters. A quarter cannot be selected for the third coin because such a selection results in an infeasible selection of coins (change exceeds 67 cents). The third coin selected is a dime, then a nickel is selected, and finally two pennies are added to the change.

The greedy method has intuitive appeal in that we construct the change by using a strategy that our intuition tells us should result in the fewest (or at least close to the fewest) number of coins being given out. We can actually prove that the greedy algorithm just described does indeed generate change with the fewest number of coins (see Exercise 1). ∎

Example 18.5 [Machine Scheduling] You are given n tasks and an infinite supply of machines on which these tasks can be performed. Each task has a start time s_i and a finish time f_i, $s_i < f_i$. $[s_i, f_i]$ is the processing interval for task i. Two tasks i and j overlap iff their processing intervals overlap at a point other than the interval start or end. For example, the interval $[1, 4]$ overlaps with $[2, 4]$, but not with $[4, 7]$. A **feasible** task-to-machine assignment is an assignment in which no machine is assigned two overlapping tasks. Therefore, in a feasible assignment each machine works on at most one task at any time. An **optimal assignment** is a feasible assignment that utilizes the fewest number of machines.

Suppose we have $n = 7$ tasks labeled a through g and that their start and finish times are as shown in Figure 18.1(a). The following task-to-machine assignment is a feasible assignment that utilizes seven machines: Assign task a to machine $M1$, task b to machine $M2$, $\cdots$, task g to machine $M7$. This assignment is not an optimal assignment because other assignments use fewer machines. For example, we can assign tasks a, b, and d to the same machine, reducing the number of utilized machines to five.

A greedy way to obtain an optimal task assignment is to assign the tasks in stages, one task per stage and in nondecreasing order of task start times. Call a machine **old** if at least one task has been assigned to it. If a machine is not old, it is **new**. For machine selection, use the greedy criterion: *If an old machine becomes available by the start time of the task to be assigned, assign the task to this machine; if not, assign it to a new machine.*

For the data of Figure 18.1(a), the tasks in nondecreasing order of task start time are a, f, b, c, g, e, d. The greedy algorithm assigns tasks to machines in this order. The algorithm has $n = 7$ stages, and in each stage one task is assigned to a machine. Stage 1 has no old machines, so a is assigned to a new machine (say, $M1$). This machine is now busy from time 0 to time 2 (see Figure 18.1(b)). In stage 2 task f is considered. Since the only old machine is busy when task f is to start, it is assigned to a new machine (say, $M2$). When task b is considered in stage 3, we find that the old machine $M1$ is free at time $s_b = 3$, so b is assigned to $M1$. The availability time for $M1$ becomes $f_b = 7$, and that for M_2 is $f_f = 5$. In stage 4 task c is considered. Since neither of the old machines is available at time

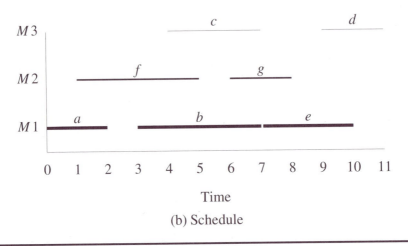

task	a	b	c	d	e	f	g
start	0	3	4	9	7	1	6
finish	2	7	7	11	10	5	8

(a) Seven tasks

(b) Schedule

Figure 18.1 Tasks and a three-machine schedule

$s_c = 4$, task c is assigned to a new machine (say, $M3$). The availability time of this machine becomes $f_c = 7$. Task g is considered in stage 5 and assigned to machine $M2$, which is the first to become available. Task e is assigned in stage 6 to machine $M1$ or $M3$ (assume it is assigned to $M1$), and finally, in stage 7, task d is assigned to machine $M2$ or $M3$ (Figure 18.1(b) assumes task d is assigned to $M3$).

The proof that the described greedy algorithm generates optimal assignments is left as an exercise (Exercise 7). The algorithm may be implemented to have complexity $O(n \log n)$ by sorting the tasks in nondecreasing order of s_i, using an $O(n \log n)$ sort (such as heap sort) and then using a min heap of availability times for the old machines. ∎

Example 18.6 [Shortest Path] You are given a directed network as in Figure 18.2. The length of a path is defined to be the sum of the costs of the edges on the path. You are to find a shortest path from a start vertex s to a destination vertex d.

A greedy way to construct such a path is to do so in stages. In each stage a vertex is added to the path. Suppose that the path built so far ends at vertex q and q is not the destination vertex d. The vertex to add in the next stage is obtained

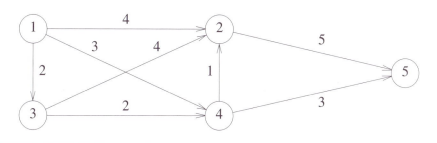

Figure 18.2 Sample digraph

using the greedy criterion: *Select a nearest vertex adjacent from q that is not already on the path.*

This greedy method does not necessarily obtain a shortest path. For example, suppose we wish to construct a shortest path from vertex 1 to vertex 5 in Figure 18.2. Using the greedy method just outlined, we begin at vertex 1 and move to the nearest vertex not already on the path. We move to vertex 3, a distance of only two units. From vertex 3 the nearest vertex we can move to is vertex 4. From vertex 4 we move to vertex 2 and then to the destination vertex 5. The constructed path is 1, 3, 4, 2, 5, and its length is 10. This path is not the shortest 1-to-5 path in the digraph. In fact, several shorter paths exist. For instance, the path 1, 4, 5 has length 6. ■

Now that you have seen three examples of a greedy algorithm, you should be able to go over the applications considered in earlier chapters and identify several of the solutions developed as greedy ones. For example, the Huffman tree algorithm of Section 13.6.3 constructs a binary tree with minimum weighted external path length in $n-1$ stages. In each stage two binary trees are combined to create a new binary tree. This algorithm uses the greedy criterion: Of the available binary trees, combine two with the least weight.

The LPT-scheduling (longest processing time first) rule of Section 13.6.2 is a greedy one. It schedules the n jobs in n stages. First the jobs are ordered by length. Then in each stage a machine is selected for the next job. The machine is selected using the greedy criterion: *Minimize the length of the schedule constructed so far.* This criterion translates into scheduling the job on the machine on which it finishes first. This machine is also the machine that becomes idle first.

Notice that in the case of the machine-scheduling problem of Section 13.6.2, the greedy algorithm does not guarantee optimal solutions. However, it is intuitively appealing and generally produces solutions that are very close in value to the optimal. It uses a rule of thumb that we might expect a human machine scheduler to use in a real scheduling environment. Algorithms that do not guarantee optimal solutions but generally produce solutions that are close to optimal are called **heuristics**. So the LPT method is a heuristic for machine scheduling. Theorem

9.2 states a bound between the finish time of LPT schedules and optimal schedules, so the LPT heuristic has **bounded performance**. A heuristic with bounded performance is an **approximation algorithm**.

Section 14.5.1 stated several bounded performance heuristics (i.e., approximation algorithms) for the bin-packing problem. Each of these heuristics is a greedy heuristic. The LPT method of Section 13.6.2 is also a greedy heuristic. All these heuristics have intuitive appeal and, in practice, yield solutions much closer to optimal than suggested by the bounds given in that section.

The rest of this chapter presents several applications of the greedy method. In some applications the result is an algorithm that always obtains an optimal solution. In others the algorithm is just a heuristic that may or may not be an approximation algorithm.

EXERCISES

1. Show that the greedy algorithm for the change-making problem (Example 18.4) always generates change with the fewest number of coins.

2. Consider the change-making problem of Example 18.4. Suppose that the cashier has only a limited number of quarters, dimes, nickels, and pennies. Formulate a greedy solution to the change-making problem. Does your algorithm always use the fewest number of coins? Prove your result.

3. Extend the algorithm of Example 18.4 to the case when the cashier has $100, $50, $20, $10, $5, and $1 bills in addition to coins and a customer gives u dollars and v cents as payment toward a purchase of x dollars and y cents. Does your algorithm always generate change with the fewest total number of bills and coins? Prove this.

4. Write a Java program implementing the change-making solution of Example 18.4. Assume that the cashier has bills in the denominations $100, $50, $20, $10, $5, and $1 in addition to coins. Your program should include a method to input the purchase amount and the amount given by the customer as well as a method to output the amount of change and a breakdown by denomination.

5. Suppose that some country has coins in the denominations 14, 12, 5, and 1 cents. Will the greedy method of Example 18.4 always generate change with the fewest number of coins? Prove your answer.

6. (a) Show that the greedy algorithm of Example 18.5 always finds an optimal task assignment.

   (b) Program your algorithm so that its complexity is $O(n \log n)$; n is the number of tasks.

★   7. Consider the machine-scheduling problem of Example 18.5. Assume that only one machine is available and that we are to select the largest number of tasks that can be scheduled on this machine. For the example, the largest task selection is $\{a, b, e\}$. A greedy algorithm for this task-selection problem would select the tasks in stages. In each stage one task is selected using the following criterion: *From the remaining tasks, select the one that has the least finish time and does not overlap with any of the already selected tasks.*

(a) Show that this greedy algorithm obtains optimal selections.

(b) Develop an $O(n \log n)$ implementation of this algorithm. (*Hint:* Use a min heap of finish times.)

18.3   APPLICATIONS

18.3.1   Container Loading

A Greedy Solution

The terminology is from Example 18.2. The ship may be loaded in stages; one container per stage. At each stage we need to decide which container to load. For this decision we may use the greedy criterion: *From the remaining containers, select the one with least weight.* This order of selection will keep the total weight of the selected containers minimum and hence leave maximum capacity for loading more containers. Using the greedy algorithm just outlined, we first select the container that has least weight, then the one with the next smallest weight, and so on until either all containers have been loaded or there isn't enough capacity for the next one.

Example 18.7 Suppose that $n = 8$, $[w_1, \cdots, w_8] = [100, 200, 50, 90, 150, 50, 20, 80]$, and $c = 400$. When the greedy algorithm is used, the containers are considered for loading in the order 7, 3, 6, 8, 4, 1, 5, 2. Containers 7, 3, 6, 8, 4, and 1 together weigh 390 units and are loaded. The available capacity is now 10 units, which is inadequate for any of the remaining containers. In the greedy solution we have $[x_1, \cdots, x_8] = [1, 0, 1, 1, 0, 1, 1, 1]$ and $\sum x_i = 6$. ■

Correctness of Greedy Algorithm

Theorem 18.1 *The greedy algorithm generates optimal loadings.*

Proof Let $x = [x_1, \cdots, x_n]$ be the solution produced by the greedy algorithm and let $y = [y_1, \cdots, y_n]$ be any feasible solution. We will show that $\sum_{i=1}^{n} x_i \geq \sum_{i=1}^{n} y_i$. Without loss of generality we may assume that the containers have been ordered so that $w_i \leq w_{i+1}$, $1 \leq i < n$. From the way the greedy algorithm works, we know that there is a k, $0 \leq k \leq n$ such that $x_i = 1$, $i \leq k$, and $x_i = 0$, $i > k$.

We use induction on the number p of positions i such that $x_i \neq y_i$. For the induction base, we see that when $p = 0$, x and y are the same. So $\sum_{i=1}^{n} x_i \geq \sum_{i=1}^{n} y_i$. For the induction hypothesis, let m be an arbitrary natural number and assume that $\sum_{i=1}^{n} x_i \geq \sum_{i=1}^{n} y_i$ whenever $p \leq m$.

In the induction step, we show that $\sum_{i=1}^{n} x_i \geq \sum_{i=1}^{n} y_i$ when $p = m + 1$. Find the least integer j, $1 \leq j \leq n$, such that $x_j \neq y_j$. Since $p \neq 0$, such a j exists. Also, $j \leq k$, as otherwise y is not a feasible solution. Since $x_j \neq y_j$ and $x_j = 1$, $y_j = 0$. Set y_j to 1.

If the resulting y is a feasible solution, let z denote the resulting y. If the resulting y denotes an infeasible solution, there must be an l in the range $[k + 1, n]$ for which $y_l = 1$. Set y_l to 0. Let z denote the resulting y. As $w_j \leq w_l$, z is a feasible loading.

In either case, $\sum_{i=1}^{n} z_i \geq \sum_{i=1}^{n} y_i$, and z differs from x in at most $p - 1 = m$ positions. From the induction hypothesis, it follows that $\sum_{i=1}^{n} x_i \geq \sum_{i=1}^{n} z_i, \geq \sum_{i=1}^{n} y_i$. ∎

Java Implementation

Program 18.1 gives the Java code for the greedy container-loading algorithm since the greedy method loads containers in increasing order of their weight. The data type `Container` has the integer data members `id` (an identifier in the range 1 through number of containers) and `weight` (container weight), and `Container` implements the interface `Comparable` so that container comparison is done by container weight.

Program 18.1 begins by sorting the containers by weights using the heap sort method (Program 13.8). Following the sort, containers are loaded in increasing order of weight. Since the sort takes $O(n \log n)$ time and the remainder of the algorithm takes $O(n)$ time, the overall time complexity of Program 18.1 is $O(n \log n)$.

18.3.2   0/1 Knapsack Problem

Problem Description

In the 0/1 knapsack problem, we wish to pack a knapsack (bag or sack) with a capacity of c. From a list of n items, we must select the items that are to be packed into the knapsack. Each object i has a weight w_i and a profit p_i. In a feasible knapsack packing, the sum of the weights of the packed objects does not exceed the knapsack capacity. An optimal packing is a feasible one with maximum profit. The problem formulation is

$$\text{maximize} \sum_{i=1}^{n} p_i x_i$$

```
/** greedy algorithm for container loading
 * set x[i] = 1 iff container i, i >= 1 is loaded */
public static void containerLoading
        (Container [] c, int capacity, int [] x)
{
   // sort into increasing order of weight
   HeapSort.heapSort(c);

   int n = c.length - 1;   // number of containers
   // initialize x
   for (int i = 1; i <= n; i++)
      x[i] = 0;

   // select objects in order of weight
   for (int i = 1; i <= n && c[i].weight <= capacity; i++)
   {// enough capacity for container c[i].id
      x[c[i].id] = 1;
      capacity -= c[i].weight;  // remaining capacity
   }
}
```

Program 18.1 Loading containers

subject to the constraints

$$\sum_{i=1}^{n} w_i x_i \le c \text{ and } x_i \in \{0,1\}, \ 1 \le i \le n$$

In this formulation we are to find the values of x_i. $x_i = 1$ means that object i is packed into the knapsack, and $x_i = 0$ means that object i is not packed. The 0/1 knapsack problem is really a generalization of the container-loading problem to the case where the profit earned from each container is different. In the context of the knapsack problem, the ship is the *knapsack*, and the containers are *objects* that may be packed into the knapsack.

Example 18.8 You are the first-prize winner in a grocery-store contest, and the prize is a free cart load of groceries. There are n different items available in the store, and the contest rules stipulate that you can pick at most one of each. The cart has a capacity of c, and item i takes up w_i amount of cart space. The cost of item i is p_i. Your objective is to fill the cart with groceries that have the maximum value. Of course, you cannot exceed the cart capacity, and you cannot take two of any item. The problem may be modeled by using the 0/1 knapsack formulation.

The cart corresponds to the knapsack, and the available grocery items correspond
to the objects.   ■

Possible Greedy Strategies

Several greedy strategies for the 0/1 knapsack problem are possible. In each of
these strategies, the knapsack is packed in several stages. In each stage one object
is selected for inclusion into the knapsack using a greedy criterion. One possibility
for this greedy criterion is as follows: *From the remaining objects, select the object
with maximum profit that fits into the knapsack.* Using this criterion, the object
with the largest profit is packed first (provided enough capacity is available), then
the one with next largest profit, and so on. This strategy does not guarantee an
optimal solution. For instance, consider the case $n = 3$, $w = [100, 10, 10]$, $p = [20,
15, 15]$, and $c = 105$. When we are greedy on profit, we obtain the solution $x =
[1, 0, 0]$. The total profit from this solution is 20. The optimal solution is $[0, 1, 1]$.
This solution has profit 30.

An alternative is to be greedy on weight. This time we use the following selection
criterion: *From the remaining objects, select the one that has minimum weight and
also fits into the knapsack.* Although the use of this criterion yields an optimal
solution for the preceding instance, it does not do so in general. Consider the
instance $n = 2$, $w = [10, 20]$, $p = [5, 100]$, and $c = 25$. When we are greedy on
weight, we obtain the solution $x = [1, 0]$, which is inferior to the solution $[0, 1]$.

Yet another possibility is to be greedy on the profit density p_i/w_i. The new
selection criterion is as follows: *From the remaining objects, select the one with
maximum p_i/w_i that fits into the knapsack.* This strategy does not guarantee optimal solutions either. For example, try this strategy on the instance $n = 3$, $w =
[20, 15, 15]$, $p = [40, 25, 25]$, and $c = 30$.

Greedy Heuristics

We should not be too disheartened that none of the considered greedy algorithms
can guarantee optimal solutions. The 0/1 knapsack problem is an NP-hard problem
(see Section 13.6.2 for a discussion of NP-hard problems), and we probably cannot
find a polynomial-time algorithm that solves it. Although packing a knapsack in
nonincreasing order of the ratio p_i/w_i does not guarantee an optimal packing, this
approach is intuitively appealing. We expect it to be a good heuristic and produce
solutions that are very close to optimal most of the time. In an experiment that
involved 600 randomly generated knapsack instances, this greedy heuristic generated
optimal solutions for 239. For 583 instances the generated solution had a value
within 10 percent of optimal, and all 600 solutions were within 25 percent of optimal.
Quite an impressive performance by an algorithm that runs in $O(n \log n)$ time.

We may ask whether the greedy heuristic guarantees solutions that have a value
that is within x percent of the optimal value for some x, $x < 100$. The answer is

no. To see this, consider the instance $n = 2$, $w = [1, y]$, $p = [10, 9y]$, and $c = y$. The greedy solution is $x = [1, 0]$. This solution has value 10. For $y \geq 10/9$, the optimal solution has value $9y$. Therefore, the value of the greedy solution is $(9y - 10)/(9y) * 100$ percent away from the optimal value. For large y this value approaches 100 percent.

We can modify the greedy heuristic to provide solutions within x percent of optimal for $x < 100$. First we place a subset of at most k objects into the knapsack. If this subset has weight greater than c, we discard it. Otherwise, the remaining capacity is filled by considering the remaining objects in decreasing order of p_i/w_i. The best solution obtained considering all possible subsets with at most k objects is the solution generated by the heuristic.

Example 18.9 Consider the knapsack instance $n = 4$, $w = [2, 4, 6, 7]$, $p = [6, 10, 12, 13]$, and $c = 11$. When $k = 0$, the knapsack is filled in nonincreasing order of profit density. First we place object 1 into the knapsack, then object 2. The capacity that remains at this time is five units. None of the remaining objects fits, and the solution $x = [1, 1, 0, 0]$ is produced. The profit earned from this solution is 16.

Let us now try the greedy heuristic with $k = 1$. The subsets to begin with are $\{1\}$, $\{2\}$, $\{3\}$, and $\{4\}$. The subsets $\{1\}$ and $\{2\}$ yield the same solution as obtained with $k = 0$. When the subset $\{3\}$ is considered, x_3 is set to 1. Five units of capacity remain, and we attempt to use this capacity by considering the remaining objects in nonincreasing order of profit density. Object 1 is considered first. It fits, and x_1 is set to 1. At this time only three units of capacity remain, and none of the remaining objects can be added to the knapsack. The solution obtained when we begin with the subset $\{3\}$ in the knapsack is $x = [1, 0, 1, 0]$. The profit earned from this solution is 18. When we begin with the subset 4, we produce the solution $x = [1, 0, 0, 1]$ that has a profit value of 19. The best solution obtained considering subsets of size 0 and 1 is $[1, 0, 0, 1]$. This solution is produced by the greedy heuristic when $k = 1$.

If $k = 2$, then in addition to the subsets considered for $k < 2$, we need to consider the subsets $\{1, 2\}$, $\{1, 3\}$, $\{1, 4\}$, $\{2, 3\}$, $\{2, 4\}$, and $\{3, 4\}$. The last of these subsets represents an infeasible starting point and is discarded. For the remaining, the solutions obtained are $[1, 1, 0, 0]$, $[1, 0, 1, 0]$, $[1, 0, 0, 1]$, $[0, 1, 1, 0]$, and $[0, 1, 0, 1]$. The last of these solutions has the profit value 23, which is higher than that obtained from the subsets of size 0 and 1. This solution is therefore the solution produced by the heuristic.   ∎

The solution produced by the modified greedy heuristic is $k - optimal$. That is, if we remove up to k objects from the solution and put back up to k, the new solution is no better than the original. Further, the value of a solution obtained in this manner comes within $100/(k+1)$ percent of optimal. When $k = 1$, the solutions are guaranteed to have value within 50 percent of optimal; when $k = 2$, they are guaranteed to have value within 33.33 percent of optimal; and so on. The run time of the heuristic increases with k. The number of subsets to be tried is $O(n^k)$, and $O(n)$ time is spent on each. Also, $O(n \log n)$ time is needed to order the objects by p_i/w_i. So the total time taken is $O(n^{k+1})$ when $k > 0$.

The observed performance is far better than suggested by the worst-case bounds. Figure 18.3 summarizes the results of 600 random tests.

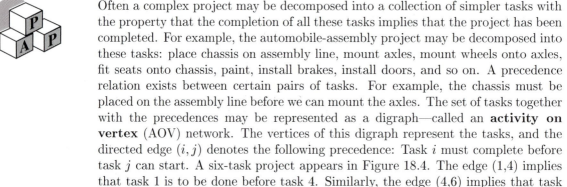

	Percent Deviation				
k	0	1%	5%	10%	25%
0	239	390	528	583	600
1	360	527	598	600	
2	483	581	600		

Figure 18.3 Number of solutions within x percent out of 600

18.3.3   Topological Sorting

Problem Description

Often a complex project may be decomposed into a collection of simpler tasks with the property that the completion of all these tasks implies that the project has been completed. For example, the automobile-assembly project may be decomposed into these tasks: place chassis on assembly line, mount axles, mount wheels onto axles, fit seats onto chassis, paint, install brakes, install doors, and so on. A precedence relation exists between certain pairs of tasks. For example, the chassis must be placed on the assembly line before we can mount the axles. The set of tasks together with the precedences may be represented as a digraph—called an **activity on vertex** (AOV) network. The vertices of this digraph represent the tasks, and the directed edge (i, j) denotes the following precedence: Task i must complete before task j can start. A six-task project appears in Figure 18.4. The edge (1,4) implies that task 1 is to be done before task 4. Similarly, the edge (4,6) implies that task 4 is to be done before task 6. The edges (1,4) and (4,6) together imply that task 1 is to be done before task 6. So the precedence relation is transitive. As a result of this observation, we see that the edge (1,4) is redundant, as the edges (1,3) and (3,4) imply (1,4).

In many situations we must perform the tasks consecutively, for example, to solve the automobile-assembly problem or to put together a consumer product (bicycle, child's swing set, lawn mower, etc.) labeled "some assembly required." We perform the assembly tasks in a sequence dictated by the accompanying instructions. This sequence has the property that for every edge (i, j) in the task digraph for the assembly project, task i comes before task j in the assembly sequence. Sequences that satisfy this property are **topological orders** or **topological sequences**, and

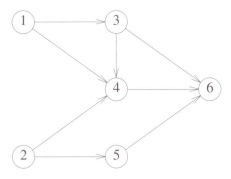

Figure 18.4 A task digraph

the process of constructing a topological order from a task digraph is **topological sorting**.

The task digraph of Figure 18.4 has several topological orders. Three of these orders are 123456, 132456, and 215346. The sequence 142356 is not a topological order, as (for example) task 4 precedes task 3 in this sequence, whereas the task digraph contains the edge (3,4). This sequence violates the precedence dictated by this edge (and others).

A Greedy Solution

We may formulate a greedy algorithm to construct a topological order or sequence. This algorithm constructs the sequence from left to right in stages. In each stage we add a vertex to the sequence. We select the new vertex using the greedy criterion: *From the remaining vertices, select a vertex w that has no incoming edge (v, w) with the property that v hasn't already been placed into the sequence.* Notice that if we add a vertex w that violates this criterion (i.e., the digraph has an edge (v, w) and vertex v is not part of the constructed sequence), then we cannot complete the sequence in a topological order, as vertex v will neccessarily come after vertex w. A high-level statement of the greedy algorithm appears in Figure 18.5. Each iteration of the `while` loop represents a stage of the greedy algorithm.

Let us try out this algorithm on the digraph of Figure 18.4. We start with an empty sequence *theOrder*. In the first stage we select the first vertex for *theOrder*. The digraph has two candidate vertices, 1 and 2, for the first position in the sequence. If we select vertex 2, the sequence becomes *theOrder* = 2 and stage 1 is complete. In stage 2 we select the second vertex for *theOrder*. Applying the greedy criterion with *theOrder* = 2, we see that the candidate vertices are 1 and 5. If we select vertex 5, then *theOrder* = 25. For the next stage vertex 1 is the only candidate for w. Following stage 3 *theOrder* = 251. In stage 4 vertex 3 is the only

Let n be the number of vertices in the digraph.
Let *theOrder* be an empty sequence.
```
while (true)
{
    Let w be any vertex that has no incoming edge (v, w) such that v is not in
        theOrder.
    if there is no such w, break.
    Add w to the end of theOrder.
}
if (theOrder has fewer than n vertices)
    the algorithm fails.
else
    theOrder is a topological sequence.
```

Figure 18.5 Topological sorting

candidate for w. Thus we add vertex 3 to *theOrder* to get *theOrder* = 2513. In the next two stages, we add vertices 4 and 6 to get *theOrder* = 251346.

Correctness of the Greedy Algorithm

To establish the correctness of the greedy algorithm, we need to show (1) that when the algorithm fails, the digraph has no topological sequence and (2) that when the algorithm doesn't fail, *theOrder* is, in fact, a topological sequence. Item (2) is a direct consequence of the greedy criterion used to select the next vertex. For (1) we show in Lemma 18.1 that when the algorithm fails, the digraph has a cycle. When the digraph has a cycle, $q_j q_j + 1 \cdots q_k q_j$, there can be no topological order, as the sequence of precedences defined by the cycle implies that q_j must finish before q_j can start.

Lemma 18.1 *If the algorithm of Figure 18.5 fails, the digraph has a cycle.*

Proof Note that upon failure $|theOrder| < n$ and there are no candidates for inclusion in *theOrder*. So there is at least one vertex, q_1, that is not in *theOrder*. The digraph must contain an edge (q_2, q_1) where q_2 is not in *theOrder*; otherwise, q_1 is a candidate for inclusion in *theOrder*. Similarly, there must be an edge (q_3, q_2) such that q_3 is not in *theOrder*. If $q_3 = q_1$, then $q_1 q_2 q_3$ is a cycle in the digraph. If $q_3 \neq q_1$, there must be a q_4 such that (q_4, q_3) is an edge and q_4 is not in *theOrder*; otherwise, q_3 is a candidate for inclusion in *theOrder*. If q_4 is one of q_1, q_2, or q_3, then again the digraph has a cycle. Since the digraph has a finite number n of vertices, continued application of this argument will eventually detect a cycle. ■

Selection of Data Structures

To refine the algorithm of Figure 18.5 into Java code, we must decide on a representation for the sequence *theOrder*, as well as how to detect candidates for inclusion into *theOrder*. An efficient implementation results if we represent *theOrder* as a one-dimensional array; use a stack to keep track of all vertices that are candidates for inclusion into *theOrder*; and use a one-dimensional array inDegree such that inDegree[j] is the number of vertices i for which (i, j) is an edge of the digraph and i is not a member of *theOrder*. A vertex j becomes a candidate for inclusion in *theOrder* when inDegree[j] becomes 0. *theOrder* is initially the empty sequence, and inDegree[j] is simply the in-degree of vertex j. Each time we add a vertex to x, inDegree[j] decreases by 1 for all j that are adjacent from the added vertex.

For the digraph of Figure 18.4, inDegree[1:6] = $[0, 0, 1, 3, 1, 3]$ in the beginning. Vertices 1 and 2 are candidates for inclusion in *theOrder*, as their inDegree value is 0. Therefore, we start with 1 and 2 on the stack. In each stage we remove a vertex from the stack and add that vertex to *theOrder*. We also reduce the inDegree values of the vertices that are adjacent from the vertex just added to *theOrder*. If vertex 2 is removed from the stack and added to *theOrder* in stage 1, we get theOrder[0] = 2 and inDegree[1:6] = $[0, 0, 1, 2, 0, 3]$. Since inDegree[5] has just become 0, it is added to the stack.

Java Implementation

Program 18.2 gives the resulting Java code. This code is defined as a member method of Graph. Consequently, it can be used for digraphs with and without edge weights. The method topological returns true if a topological order is found and false if the input digraph does not have a topological order. When a topological order is found, the order is returned in theOrder[0:n-1], where n is the number of vertices in the digraph.

Complexity Analysis

The total time spent in the first for loop is $O(n^2)$ if we use an adjacency-matrix representation and $O(n+e)$ if we use a linked-adjacency-list representation. The second for loop takes $O(n)$ time. Of the two nested while loops, the outer one may be iterated at most n times. Each iteration adds a vertex nextVertex to theOrder and initiates the inner while loop. When adjacency matrices are used, this inner while loop takes $O(n)$ time for each nextVertex. When we use linked adjacency lists, this loop takes $d_{nextVertex}^{out}$ time. Therefore, the time spent on the inner while loop is either $O(n^2)$ or $O(n+e)$. Hence the complexity of Program 18.2 is $O(n^2)$ when we use adjacency matrices and $O(n+e)$ when we use linked adjacency lists.

```
public boolean topologicalOrder(int [] theOrder)
{
   // make sure this is a digraph
   verifyDirected("topologicalOrder");
   int n = vertices();
   // compute in-degrees, default initial values are 0
   int [] inDegree = new int [n + 1];
   for (int i = 1; i <= n; i++)
   {// edges out of vertex i
      Iterator ii = iterator(i);
      while (ii.hasNext())
      {// visit an adjacent vertex of i
         int u = ((EdgeNode) ii.next()).vertex;
         inDegree[u]++;
      }
   }
   // stack vertices with zero in-degree
   ArrayStack stack = new ArrayStack(10);
   for (int i = 1; i <= n; i++)
      if (inDegree[i] == 0)
         stack.push(new Integer(i));
   // generate topological order
   int i = 0;   // cursor for array s
   while (!stack.empty())
   {// select from stack
      int nextVertex = ((Integer) stack.pop()).intValue();
      theOrder[i++] = nextVertex;
      // update in-degrees
      Iterator iNextVertex = iterator(nextVertex);
      while (iNextVertex.hasNext())
      {// visit an adjacent vertex of nextVertex
         int u = ((EdgeNode) iNextVertex.next()).vertex;
         inDegree[u]--;
         if (inDegree[u] == 0)
            stack.push(new Integer(u));
      }
   }
   return (i == n);
}
```

Program 18.2 Topological sorting

18.3.4   Bipartite Cover

Problem Description

A bipartite graph (see Example 17.3) is an undirected graph in which the n vertices may be partitioned into two sets A and B so that no edge in the graph connects two vertices that are in the same set (i.e., every edge in the graph has one endpoint in A and the other in B). A subset A' of the set A is said to **cover** the set B (or simply, A' is a cover) iff every vertex in B is connected to at least one vertex of A'. The size of the cover A' is the number of vertices in A'. A' is a minimum cover iff A has no subset of smaller size that covers B.

Example 18.10 Consider the 17-vertex bipartite graph of Figure 18.6. $A = \{1, 2, 3, 16, 17\}$, and $B = \{4, 5, 6, 7, 8, 9, 10, 11, 12, 13, 14, 15\}$. The subset $A' = \{1, 2, 3, 17\}$ covers the set B. Its size is 4. The subset $A' = \{1, 16, 17\}$ also covers B and is of size 3. A has no subset of size less than 3 that covers B. Therefore, $A' = \{1, 16, 17\}$ is a minimum cover of B.   ∎

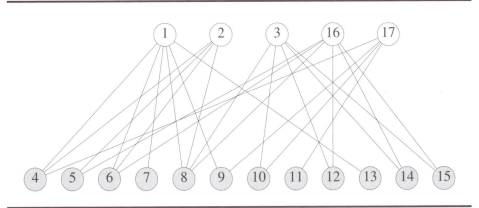

Figure 18.6 Figure for Example 18.10

We will refer to the problem of finding a minimum cover in a bipartite graph as the **bipartite-cover** problem. In the context of Example 17.3, a minimum cover is useful because it identifies the fewest number of interpreters who can handle the translations at the convention. The bipartite-cover problem is identical to the **set-cover** problem. In this latter problem we are given a collection $S = \{S_1, S_2, \cdots, S_k\}$ of k sets. The members of each set S_i are from the universe U. A subset S' of S covers U iff $\cup_{i \in S'} S_i = U$. The number of sets in S' is the size of the cover, and S' is a minimum cover iff there is no cover of U of smaller size. We can transform the set-cover problem into the bipartite-cover problem (and vice versa) by using the vertices in A to represent the sets $S_1, \cdots, S_k$ and the vertices in B to represent the elements of the universe U. An edge exists between a vertex in A and one in B iff the corresponding element of U is in the corresponding set of S.

Example 18.11 Let $S = \{S_1, \cdots, S_5\}$, $U = \{4, 5, \cdots, 15\}$, $S_1 = \{4, 6, 7, 8, 9, 13\}$, $S_2 = \{4, 5, 6, 8\}$, $S_3 = \{8, 10, 12, 14, 15\}$, $S_4 = \{5, 6, 8, 12, 14, 15\}$, and $S_5 = \{4, 9, 10, 11\}$. $S' = \{S_1, S_4, S_5\}$ is a cover of size 3. No smaller cover exists, so it is a minimum cover. The set-cover instance may be mapped into the bipartite graph of Figure 18.6 using vertices 1, 2, 3, 16, and 17 to represent sets S_1, S_2, S_3, S_4, and S_5, respectively. Vertex j represents universe element j, $4 \le j \le 15$.   ∎

A Greedy Heuristic

The set-cover problem is known to be NP-hard. Since the set-cover and bipartite-cover problems are identical, the bipartite-cover problem is also NP-hard. As a result we probably will not be able to develop a fast algorithm to solve it. We can, however, use the greedy method to develop a fast heuristic. One possiblity is to construct the cover A' in stages. In each stage we select a vertex of A for inclusion into the cover. This vertex is selected by using the greedy criterion: *Select a vertex of A that covers the largest number of uncovered vertices of B.*

Example 18.12 Consider the bipartite graph of Figure 18.6. Initially $A' = \phi$, and no vertex of B is covered. Vertices 1 and 16 each covers six uncovered vertices of B; vertex 3 covers five; and vertices 2 and 17 each covers four. Therefore, in the first stage, we add either vertex 1 or vertex 16 to A'. If we add vertex 16, it covers the vertices $\{5, 6, 8, 12, 14, 15\}$. The uncovered vertices are $\{4, 7, 9, 10, 11, 13\}$. Vertex 1 of A covers four of these uncovered vertices ($\{4, 7, 9, 13\}$), vertex 2 covers one ($\{4\}$), vertex 3 covers one ($\{10\}$), vertex 16 covers zero, and vertex 17 covers four. In the next stage, either 1 or 17 is selected for inclusion into A'. If we choose vertex 1, vertices $\{10, 11\}$ remain uncovered. Vertices 1, 2, and 16 cover none of these uncovered vertices; vertex 3 covers one; and vertex 17 covers two. Therefore, we select vertex 17. Now no uncovered vertices remain, and we are done. $A' = \{1, 16, 17\}$.   ∎

A high-level statement of the greedy covering heuristic appears in Figure 18.7. You should be able to show (1) that the algorithm fails to find a cover iff the initial bipartite graph does not have a cover, and (2) that bipartite graphs exist on which the heuristic will fail to find a minimum cover.

Selection of Data Structures and Complexity

To implement the algorithm of Figure 18.7, we need to select a representation for A' and to decide how to keep track of the number of uncovered vertices of B that each vertex of A covers. Since only additions are made to the set A', we can represent A' as a one-dimensional integer array `theCover` and use `coverSize`

$A' = \phi$
while (more vertices can be covered)
   Add the vertex that covers the largest number of uncovered vertices to A'.
if (some vertices are uncovered) fail.
else a cover has been found.

Figure 18.7 High-level statement of greedy covering heuristic

to keep track of the number of elements in A'. We store the members of A' in theCover[0:coverSize-1].

For a vertex i of A, let new_i be the number of uncovered vertices of B that i covers. In each stage we need to select the vertex with maximum new_i and then update the new_is, as some previously uncovered vertices are now covered. For this update we examine the vertices of B that are newly covered by v. Let j be one such vertex. The new_i value of all vertices of A that cover j is to be reduced by 1.

Example 18.13 Consider the graph of Figure 18.6. Initially (new_1, new_2, new_3, new_{16}, new_{17}) = (6, 4, 5, 6, 4). Suppose we select vertex 16 in stage 1, as in Example 18.12. To update the new_is, we examine all the newly covered vertices of B. These vertices are 5, 6, 8, 12, 14, and 15. When we examine vertex 5, we reduce the new_i values of vertices 2 and 16 by 1 because vertex 5 is no longer an uncovered vertex being covered by either 2 or 16. When we examine vertex 6, the counts for vertices 1, 2, and 16 are reduced by 1. Similarly, when we examine vertex 8, the counts of 1, 2, 3, and 16 are reduced by 1. After we examine all the newly covered vertices, the new_i values are (4, 1, 1, 0, 4). In the next stage we select vertex 1. The newly covered vertices are 4, 7, 9, and 13. When we examine vertex 4, new_1, new_2, and new_{17} are reduced by 1; and when we examine vertex 7, only new_1 is reduced by 1 because vertex 1 is the only vertex that covers 7. ∎

To implement the vertex-selection process, we need to know the new_i values and also which vertices have already been covered. We can use 2 one-dimensional arrays for this purpose. newVerticesCovered is an integer array such that newVertices-Covered[i] equals new_i, and covered is a boolean array such that covered[i] equals false if vertex i is not covered and true if it is. We can now refine the high-level statement of Figure 18.7 to obtain the version in Figure 18.8.

The time spent updating newVerticesCovered is $O(e)$ where e is the number of edges in the bipartite graph. It takes $\Theta(n^2)$ time to find the edges of a graph represented by an adjacency matrix and $\Theta(n + e)$ time when we use a linked-adjacency list. The actual update time is either $O(n^2)$ or $O(n + e)$ depending on the graph representation.

The selection of vertex v at the start of each stage takes $\Theta(SizeOfA)$ time where $SizeOfA = |A|$. Since all vertices of A may need to be selected, the number of

```
coverSize = 0; // current size of cover
newVerticesCovered[i] = degree[i] for all i in A.
covered[i] = false for all i in B.
while (newVerticesCovered[i] > 0 for some i in A)
{
    Let v be a vertex with largest newVerticesCovered[i].
    theCover[coverSize++] = v;
    for (all vertices j adjacent from v)
    {
        if (!covered[j])
        {
            covered[j] = true;
            Reduce newVerticesCovered[k] by 1 for all vertices
                adjacent from j.
        }
    }
}
if (some vertices are uncovered)
    fail
else
    a cover has been found
```

Figure 18.8 Refined version of Figure 18.7

stages is $O(SizeOfA)$ and the overall complexity of the cover algorithm is either $O(SizeOfA^2 + n^2) = O(n^2)$ or $O(SizeOfA^2 + n + e)$.

Reducing the Complexity

We can reduce the complexity of selecting vertex v at the start of each stage to $\Theta(1)$ time by using a sorted array of new_i values, a max heap, or a max selection tree. With the sorted-array approach, the new_i values need to be sorted at the end of each stage. This sort takes $\Theta(SizeOfB)$ time ($SizeOfB = |B|$) when we use the bin sort (see bin sort in Section 6.5.1) method. As $SizeOfB$ is generally much larger than $SizeOfA$, the sorted-array approach does not yield an overall improvement.

If we use a max heap, then following each stage we need to restructure the heap to account for the change in newVerticesCovered values. We can do this restructuring each time a newVerticesCovered value is reduced by 1. Such a reduction can cause the reduced newVerticesCovered value to move at most one level down the heap; therefore, this restructuring costs $\Theta(1)$ per newVerticesCovered reduction of 1. The total number of reductions is $O(e)$. Hence over all stages of the algorithm, only

$O(e)$ time is spent maintaining the max heap. Therefore, when we use a max heap, the overall complexity of the cover algorithm is either $O(n^2)$ or $O(n + e)$.

When we use a max winner tree, restructuring the winner tree following the update of each `newVerticesCovered` takes $\Theta(\log SizeOfA)$ time. The best time to do this restructuring is at the end of each stage, rather than after each reduction of a `newVerticesCovered` value by 1. The number of restructurings needed is $O(e)$, so the total restructuring time is $O(e \log SizeOfA)$. This time is larger than the restructuring time for a max heap.

However, we can obtain the same time bound as we do when we use a heap by maintaining bins of vertices with the same `newVerticesCovered` value. Since `newVerticesCovered` values may range from zero to $SizeOfB$, $SizeOfB + 1$ bins are needed. Each bin i is a doubly linked list of vertices that have `newVertices-Covered` value i. At the end of a stage, if `newVerticesCovered[6]`, for example, has changed from 12 to 4, then we need to move it from bin 12 to bin 4. We can make this move in $\Theta(1)$ time using simulated pointers and an array `node` of nodes such that `node[i]` represents vertex i and `node[i].left` and `node[i].right` are the doubly linked list pointers. To move vertex 6 from bin 12 to bin 4, we delete `node[6]` from bin 12 and insert it into bin 4. With this bin scheme the complexity of the covering heuristic is $O(n^2)$ or $O(n + e)$, depending on whether the adjacency matrix or list representation of a graph is used.

The refinement of Figure 18.8 into Java code that uses bins that are doubly linked lists with simulated pointers is available from the Web as the method `Graph.bi-partiteCover`.

18.3.5   Single-Source Shortest Paths

Problem Description

In this problem we are given a weighted graph G with the property that each edge (i, j) has a nonnegative cost (or length) $a[i][j]$. The length of a path is the sum of the costs of the edges on the path. Figure 18.9(a) shows a five-vertex weighted digraph. The number on each edge is its cost. The length of the path 1, 2, 5 from vertex 1 to vertex 5 is $4 + 5 = 9$; the length of the path 1, 5 is 8; and the length of the path 1, 3, 4, 5 is 6.

In the **single-source, all-destinations, shortest-path** problem, we must find a shortest path from a given source vertex to each of the vertices (called destinations) in the graph to which there is a path. Figure 18.9(b) lists the shortest paths from vertex 1 of the digraph of Figure 18.9(a); these paths are listed in increasing order of length. The number preceding each path is its length.

A Greedy Solution

We can solve the shortest-path problem using a greedy algorithm, developed by E. Dijkstra, that generates the shortest paths in stages. In each stage a shortest path to a new destination vertex is generated. The destination vertex for the next

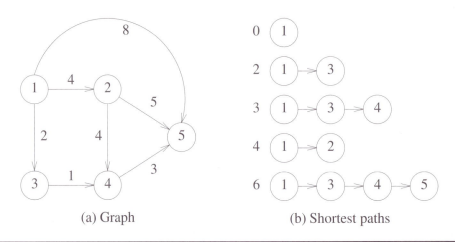

(a) Graph   (b) Shortest paths

Figure 18.9 Shortest-paths example

shortest path is selected using the greedy criterion: *From the vertices to which a shortest path has not been generated, select one that results in the least path length.* In other words, Dijkstra's method generates the shortest paths in increasing order of length.

We begin with the trivial path from the source vertex to itself. This path has no edges and has a length of 0. In each stage of the greedy algorithm, the next shortest path is generated. This next shortest path is the shortest possible one-edge extension of an already generated shortest path (Exercise 31). For the example of Figure 18.9, the second path of (b) is a one-edge extension of the first; the third is a one-edge extension of the second; the fourth is a one-edge extension of the first; and the fifth is a one-edge extension of the third.

This observation results in a convenient way to store the shortest paths. We can use an array `predecessor` such that `predecessor[i]` gives the vertex that immediately precedes vertex `i` on the shortest `sourceVertex` to `i` path. For our example `predecessor[1:5]` = [0, 1, 1, 3, 4]. The path from `sourceVertex` to any vertex `i` may be constructed backward from `i` and following the sequence `predecessor[i]`, `predecessor[predecessor[i]]`, `predecessor[predecessor[predecessor[i]]]`, $\cdots$ until we reach `sourceVertex`. If we begin our example with `i = 5`, we get the vertex sequence `predecessor[i] = 4`, `predecessor[4] = 3`, `predecessor[3] = 1` = `sourceVertex`. Therefore, the path is 1, 3, 4, 5.

To facilitate the generation of shortest paths in increasing order of length, we define `distanceFromSource[i]` to be the length of the shortest one-edge extension of a path already generated so that the extended path ends at vertex `i`. When we start, we have only the path from `sourceVertex` to `sourceVertex` and its length is 0. At this time `distanceFromSource[i]` equals `a[sourceVertex][i]` (a is the cost-adjacency matrix of the digraph) for every vertex i $\neq$ `sourceVertex`; `distanceFromSource[sourceVertex]` = 0. To generate the next path, we need to select a vertex to which a shortest path hasn't already been generated. Of the vertices that satisfy this requirement, the one for which `distanceFromSource[]` is minimum is the one at which the next path terminates. When we obtain a new shortest path, the value of `distanceFromSource[]` may change for some vertices because some of the one-edge extensions of the new shortest paths may yield a smaller value.

Pseudocode for Dijkstra's Greedy Algorithm

Putting these observations together, we get the high-level description of Figure 18.10. Step 1 initializes `predecessor` to `sourceVertex` for all vertices adjacent from `sourceVertex`. This initialization records the best information currently available. That is, the shortest path from `sourceVertex` to i is a one-edge extension of the shortest path from `sourceVertex` to `sourceVertex`. As shorter paths are discovered, `predecessor[i]` will be updated. When the next shortest path is generated, we need to update `distanceFromSource` by looking at the one-edge extensions of this path (step 4). The list `newReachableVertices` contains all vertices that have been determined to be reachable from `sourceVertex` and to which the shortest path is yet to be generated.

Selection of Data Structures and Complexity

We need to choose a data structure for the list `newReachableVertices`. From this list, we need to extract a vertex with least `distanceFromSource` (step 3). This extraction can be done in logarithmic time if `newReachableVertices` is maintained as a min heap (see Section 13.4). Since step 3 is executed $O(n)$ times, the total time spent in step 3 is $O(n \log n)$. However, in step 4 we need to possibly change some `distanceFromSource` values, as some one-edge extensions of the newly generated shortest path may yield a smaller value of `distanceFromSource` for some of the unreached vertices. Although key reduction is not a standard min heap operation, it can be done in logarithmic time. Since the total number of key reductions is $O(\text{number of edges in the digraph}) = O(n^2)$, the key reduction time is $O(n^2 \log n)$.

The time spent in steps 3 and 4 is $O(n^2)$ if `newReachableVertices` is maintained as an unordered chain. Now each execution of step 3 takes $O(|\text{newReachableVertices}|) = O(n)$ time, and each key reduction takes $\Theta(1)$ time. (`distanceFromSource[j]` needs to be reduced, and no change is to be made in the chain.)

Step 1: Initialize `distanceFromSource[i]` = `a[sourceVertex][i]`, $1 \le i \le n$.
Set `predecessor[i]` = `sourceVertex` for all `i` adjacent from `sourceVertex`.
Set `predecessor[sourceVertex]` = 0 and `predecessor[i]` = -1 for all other vertices.
Create a list `newReachableVertices` of all vertices for which `predecessor[i]` > 0 (i.e., `newReachableVertices` now contains all vertices that are adjacent from `sourceVertex`).

Step 2: If `newReachableVertices` is empty, terminate. Otherwise, go to step 3.

Step 3: Delete from `newReachableVertices` the vertex `i` with least value of `distanceFromSource` (ties are broken arbitrarily).

Step 4: Update `distanceFromSource[j]` to `min{distanceFromSource[j]`, `distanceFromSource[i]+a[i][j]}` for all vertices `j` adjacent from `i`. If `distanceFromSource[j]` changes, set `predecessor[j]` = `i` and add `j` to `newReachableVertices` in case it isn't already there. Go to step 2.

Figure 18.10 High-level description of Dijkstra's shortest-path algorithm

Java Implementation

The refinement of Figure 18.10 into the Java method `AdjacencyWDigraph.short-estPaths` appears in Program 18.3. This code uses the class `GraphChain` (Section 17.7.3).

Comments on Complexity

The complexity of Program 18.3 is $O(n^2)$. Any shortest-path algorithm must examine each edge in the graph at least once, since any of the edges could be in a shortest path. Hence the minimum possible time for such an algorithm would be $O(e)$. Since cost-adjacency matrices were used to represent the graph, it takes $O(n^2)$ time just to determine which edges are in the digraph. Therefore, any shortest-path algorithm that uses this representation must take $O(n^2)$. For this representation, then, Program 18.3 is optimal to within a constant factor. Even if a change to adjacency lists is made, only the overall time for the last `for` loop can be brought down to $O(e)$ (because `distanceFromSource` can change only for vertices adjacent from `i`). The total time spent selecting and deleting the minimum-distance vertex from `newReachableVertices` remains $O(n^2)$.

```
public void shortestPaths(int sourceVertex,
            Operable [] distanceFromSource, int [] predecessor)
{
   if (sourceVertex < 1 || sourceVertex > n)
      throw new IllegalArgumentException
            ("source vertex cannot be " + sourceVertex);

   GraphChain newReachableVertices = new GraphChain();

   // initialize
   for (int i = 1; i <= n; i++)
   {
      distanceFromSource[i] = (Operable) a[sourceVertex][i];
      if (distanceFromSource[i] == null)
         predecessor[i] = -1;
      else
      {
         distanceFromSource[sourceVertex] =
                  (Operable) distanceFromSource[i].zero();
         predecessor[i] = sourceVertex;
         newReachableVertices.add(0, new EdgeNode(i));
      }
   }
   predecessor[sourceVertex] = 0;   // source vertex has no predecessor

   // update distanceFromSource and predecessor
   while (!newReachableVertices.isEmpty())
   {// more paths exist
      // find unreached vertex v with least distanceFromSource
      Iterator iNewReachableVertices = newReachableVertices.iterator();
      int v = ((EdgeNode) iNewReachableVertices.next()).vertex;
      while (iNewReachableVertices.hasNext())
      {
         int w = ((EdgeNode) iNewReachableVertices.next()).vertex;
         if (distanceFromSource[w].compareTo(distanceFromSource[v]) < 0)
            v = w;
      }
```

Program 18.3 Shortest-path program (continues)

```
// next shortest path is to vertex v
// delete v from newReachableVertices and
// update distanceFromSource
newReachableVertices.removeElement(v);
for (int j = 1; j <= n; j++)
{
    if (a[v][j] != null && (predecessor[j] == -1 ||
            distanceFromSource[j].compareTo
                (distanceFromSource[v].add(a[v][j])) > 0))
    {
        // distanceFromSource[j] decreases
        distanceFromSource[j] = (Operable) distanceFromSource[v].
                                            add(a[v][j]);
        // add j to newReachableVertices
        if (predecessor[j] == -1)
            // not reached before
            newReachableVertices.add(0, new EdgeNode(j));
        predecessor[j] = v;
    }
}
}
}
```

Program 18.3 Shortest-path program (concluded)

18.3.6   Minimum-Cost Spanning Trees

This problem was considered in Examples 17.2 and 18.3. Since every spanning tree of an n-vertex undirected network G has exactly $n - 1$ edges, the problem is to select $n - 1$ edges in such a way that the selected edges form a least-cost spanning tree of G. We can formulate at least three different greedy strategies to select these $n - 1$ edges. These strategies result in three greedy algorithms for the minimum-cost spanning-tree problem: Kruskal's algorithm, Prim's algorithm, and Sollin's algorithm.

Kruskal's Algorithm

The Method

Kruskal's algorithm selects the $n - 1$ edges one at a time using the greedy criterion: *From the remaining edges, select a least-cost edge that does not result in a cycle when added to the set of already selected edges.* Note that a collection of edges that contains a cycle cannot be completed into a spanning tree. Kruskal's algorithm has up to e stages where e is the number of edges in the network. The e edges are considered in order of increasing cost, one edge per stage. When an edge is considered, it is rejected if it forms a cycle when added to the set of already selected edges. Otherwise, it is accepted.

Consider the network of Figure 18.11(a). We begin with no edges selected. Figure 18.11(b) shows the current state of affairs. Edge (1,6) is the first edge picked. It is included into the spanning tree that is being built, and the graph of Figure 18.11(c) obtained. Next the edge (3,4) is selected and included into the tree (Figure 18.11(d)). The next edge to be considered is (2,7). Its inclusion into the tree being built does not create a cycle, so we get the graph of Figure 18.11(e). Edge (2,3) is considered next and included into the tree (Figure 18.11(f)). Of the edges not yet considered, (7,4) has the least cost. It is considered next. Its inclusion into the tree results in a cycle, so this edge is rejected. Edge (5,4) is the next edge to be added to the tree being built. The new configuration appears in Figure 18.11(g). The next edge to be considered is the edge (7,5). It is rejected, as its inclusion creates a cycle. Finally, edge (6,5) is considered and included into the tree being built. The inclusion of this edge completes the spanning tree (Figure 18.11(h)). The resulting tree has cost 99.

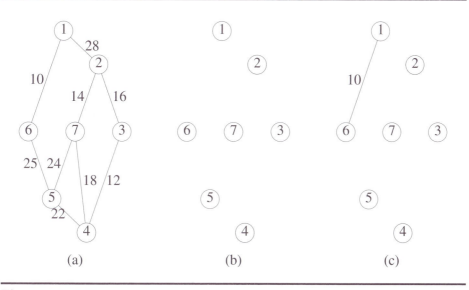

(a)   (b)   (c)

Figure 18.11 Constructing a minimum-cost spanning tree (continues)

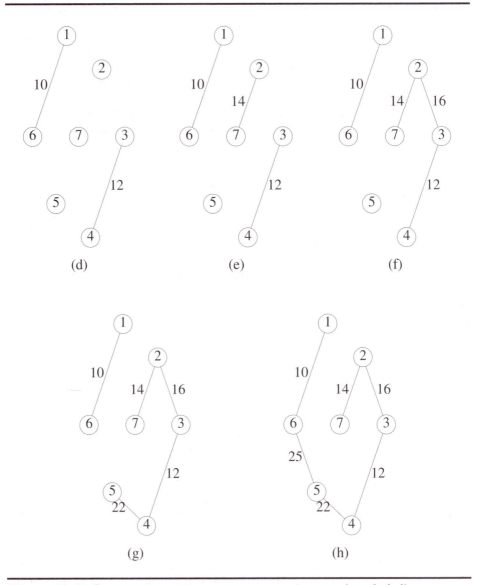

Figure 18.11 Constructing a minimum-cost spanning tree (concluded)

Figure 18.12 gives a high-level statement of Kruskal's algorithm.

```
// Find a minimum-cost spanning tree in an n-vertex network.
    Let T be the set of selected edges. Initialize T = φ.
    Let E be the set of network edges.
    while (E ≠ φ) && (|T| ≠ n − 1)
    {
        Let (u, v) be a least-cost edge in E.
        E = E − {(u, v)}. // delete edge from E
        if ((u, v) does not create a cycle in T)
            Add edge (u, v) to T.
    }
    if (|T| == n − 1)
        T is a minimum-cost spanning tree.
    else
        The network is not connected and has no spanning tree.
```

Figure 18.12 High-level statement of Kruskal's algorithm

Correctness Proof

We need to establish the following: (1) Kruskal's method results in a spanning tree whenever a spanning tree exists, and (2) the spanning tree generated is of minimum cost.

Let G be any weighted undirected graph (i.e., G is an undirected network). From Section 17.9.3 we know that an undirected graph G has a spanning tree iff it is connected. Further, the only edges that get rejected (or discarded) in Kruskal's method are those that are currently on a cycle. The deletion of a single edge that is on a cycle of a connected graph results in a graph that is also connected. Hence if G is initially connected, the set of edges in T and E always forms a connected graph. Consequently, if G is initially connected, the algorithm cannot terminate with $E = \phi$ and $|T| < n - 1$.

Now let us prove that the constructed spanning tree T is of minimum cost. Since G has a finite number of spanning trees, it has at least one of minimum cost. Let $minTrees$ be the set of minimum-cost spanning trees of G. For any $W \in minTrees$, let d_W be the number of edges in T that are also in W. Let k, $k < n$, be $\max\{d_W | W \in minTrees\}$. If $k = n - 1$, $T \in minTrees$. So assume $k < n - 1$. The proof is by contradiction.

Let $U \in minTrees$ be a minimum-cost spanning tree for which $d_U = k$. We add to U one edge, e, from T and remove one edge, f, from U. The edges e and f are selected in the following way:

1. Let e be the least-cost edge in T that is not in U. Such an edge must exist because $k < n - 1$.

2. When e is added to U, a unique cycle is created. Let f be any edge on this cycle that is not in T. Note that at least one of the edges on this cycle is not in T, because T contains no cycles.

From the way e and f are selected, it follows that $V = U + \{e\} - \{f\}$ is a spanning tree and that T has exactly $k + 1$ edges that are also in V. Now if we can show that V is a minimum-cost spanning tree, then we would have a contradiction with the assumption that $k = \max\{d_W | W \in minTrees\}$, and the proof would be complete.

Clearly, the cost of V is the cost of U plus the cost of edge e minus the cost of edge f. If the cost of e is less than the cost of f, then the spanning tree V has a smaller cost than the tree U, which is impossible (U is a minimum-cost spanning tree).

If e has a higher cost than f, then f is considered before e by Kruskal's algorithm. Since f is not in T, Kruskal's algorithm must have discarded f when f was considered for inclusion in T. Hence f together with edges in T having a cost less than or equal to the cost of f must form a cycle. Since e is a least-cost edge of T that is not in U, all edges of T whose cost is less than that of e (and hence all edges of T whose cost is $\leq$ that of f) are also in U. Hence U must also contain a cycle, but it does not because it is a spanning tree. The assumption that e is of higher cost than f therefore is invalid.

The only possibility left is that e and f have the same cost. Hence V has the same cost as U, and so V is a minimum-cost spanning tree.

Choice of Data Structures and Complexity

To select edges in nondecreasing order of cost, we can set up a min heap and extract edges one by one as needed. When there are e edges in the graph, it takes $O(e)$ time to initialize the heap and $O(\log e)$ time to extract each edge.

The edge set T together with the vertices of G define a graph that has up to n connected components. Let us represent each component by the set of vertices in it. These vertex sets are disjoint. To determine whether the edge (u, v) creates a cycle, we need merely check whether u and v are in the same vertex set (i.e., in the same component). If so, then a cycle is created. If not, then no cycle is created. Hence two finds on the vertex sets suffice. When an edge is included in T, two components are combined into one and a union is to be performed on the two sets. The set operations find and union can be carried out efficiently using the tree scheme (together with the weighting rule and path compaction) of Section 12.9.2. The number of finds is at most $2e$, and the number of unions at most $n - 1$ (exactly $n - 1$ if the weighted undirected graph is connected). Including the initialization time for the trees, this part of the algorithm has a complexity that is just slightly more than $O(n + e)$.

The only operation performed on the set T is that of adding a new edge to it. T may be implemented as an array spanningTreeEdges with additions being performed at one end. We can add at most $n-1$ edges to T. So the total time for operations on T is $O(n)$.

Summing up the various components of the computing time, we get $O(n+e\log e)$ as the asymptotic complexity of Figure 18.12.

Java Implementation

Using the data structures just described, Figure 18.12 may be refined into Java code. Program 18.4 gives the resulting code. The method of Program 18.4 is a member of Graph and has been written so as to work with all representations of a weighted undirected graph The class ComparableEdge has the same fields as does WeightedEdge. However, ComparableEdge implements the interface Comparable by comparing the weights of two edges.

The code returns false if there is no spanning tree and true otherwise. Note that when it returns true, a minimum-cost spanning tree is returned in the array spanningTreeEdges.

Prim's Algorithm

Prim's algorithm, like Kruskal's, constructs the minimum-cost spanning tree by selecting edges one at a time. The greedy criterion used to determine the next edge to select is *From the remaining edges, select a least-cost edge whose addition to the set of selected edges forms a tree*. Consequently, at each stage the set of selected edges forms a tree. By contrast, the set of selected edges in Kruskal's algorithm forms a forest at each stage.

Prim's algorithm begins with a tree T that contains a single vertex. This vertex can be any of the vertices in the original graph. Then we add a least-cost edge (u, v) to T such that $T \cup \{(u, v)\}$ is also a tree. This edge-addition step is repeated until T contains $n-1$ edges. Notice that edge (u, v) is always such that exactly one of u and v is in T. A high-level description of Prim's algorithm appears in Figure 18.13. This description also provides for the possibility that the input graph may not be connected. In this case there is no spanning tree. Figure 18.14 shows the progress of Prim's algorithm on the graph of Figure 18.11(a). The refinement of Figure 18.13 into a Java program and its correctness proof are left as Exercise 37.

Prim's algorithm can be implemented to have a time complexity $O(n^2)$ if we associate with each vertex v not in TV a vertex $near(v)$ such that $near(v) \in TV$ and $cost(v, near(v))$ is minimum over all such choices for $near(v)$. The next edge to add to T is such that $cost(v, near(v))$ is minimum and $v \notin TV$.

Sollin's Algorithm

Sollin's algorithm selects several edges at each stage. At the start of a stage, the selected edges together with the n vertices of the graph form a spanning forest. During a stage we select one edge for each tree in this forest. This edge is a

```java
public boolean kruskal(WeightedEdge [] spanningTreeEdges)
{
   verifyWeightedUndirected("kruskal");

   int n = vertices();
   int e = edges();
   // set up array of graph edges
   ComparableEdge [] edge = new ComparableEdge [e + 1];
   int k = 0;         // cursor for edge[]
   for (int i = 1; i <= n; i++)
   {// get all edges incident to i
      Iterator ii = iterator(i);
      while (ii.hasNext())
      {
         WeightedEdgeNode w = (WeightedEdgeNode) ii.next();
         if (i < w.vertex)  // add w to edge array
            edge[++k] = new ComparableEdge(i, w.vertex,
                                   (Comparable) w.weight);
      }
   }
   // put edges in min heap
   MinHeap minHeap = new MinHeap(1);
   minHeap.initialize(edge, e);

   FastUnionFind uf = new FastUnionFind(n); // union/find structure

   // extract edges in cost order and select/reject
   k = 0;  // use as cursor for t now
   while (e > 0  && k < n - 1)
   {// spanning tree not complete & edges remain
      ComparableEdge x = (ComparableEdge) minHeap.removeMin();
      e--;
      int a = uf.find(x.vertex1);
      int b = uf.find(x.vertex2);
      if (a != b)
      {// select edge x
         spanningTreeEdges[k++] = new WeightedEdge
                              (x.vertex1, x.vertex2, x.weight);
         uf.union(a,b);
      }
   }
   return (k == n - 1);
}
```

Program 18.4 Java code for Kruskal's algorithm

```
// Assume that the network has at least one vertex.
   Let T be the set of selected edges. Initialize T = φ.
   Let TV be the set of vertices already in the tree. Set TV = {1}.
   Let E be the set of network edges.
   while (E ≠ φ) && (|T| ≠ n − 1)
   {
        Let (u, v) be a least-cost edge such that u ∈ TV and v ∉ TV.
        if (there is no such edge)
            break.
        E = E − {(u, v)}. // delete edge from E
        Add edge (u, v) to T.
        Add vertex v to TV.
   }
   if (|T| == n − 1)
        T is a minimum-cost spanning tree.
   else
        The network is not connected and has no spanning tree.
```

Figure 18.13 Prim's minimum-spanning-tree algorithm

minimum-cost edge that has exactly one vertex in the tree. The selected edges are added to the spanning tree being constructed. Note that two trees in the forest can select the same edge, so we must eliminate duplicates. When several edges have the same cost, two trees can select different edges that connect them. In this case also, we must discard one of the selected edges. At the start of the first stage, the set of selected edges is empty. The algorithm terminates when only one tree remains at the end of a stage or when no edges remain to be selected.

Figure 18.15 shows the stages in Sollin's algorithm when it begins with the graph of Figure 18.11(a). The initial configuration of zero selected edges is the same as that shown in Figure 18.11(b). Each tree in this spanning forest is a single vertex. The edges selected by vertices $1, 2, \cdots, 7$ are, respectively, $(1, 6), (2, 7), (3, 4), (4, 3),$ $(5, 4), (6, 1), (7, 2)$. The distinct edges in this selection are $(1, 6), (2, 7), (3, 4),$ and $(5, 4)$. Adding these edges to the set of selected edges results in the configuration of Figure 18.15(a). In the next stage the tree with vertex set $1, 6$ selects edge $(6, 5)$, and the remaining two trees select the edge $(2, 3)$. Following the addition of these two edges to the set of selected edges the spanning-tree construction is complete. The constructed spanning tree appears in Figure 18.15(b). The development of Sollin's algorithm into a Java program and its correctness proof are left as Exercise 38.

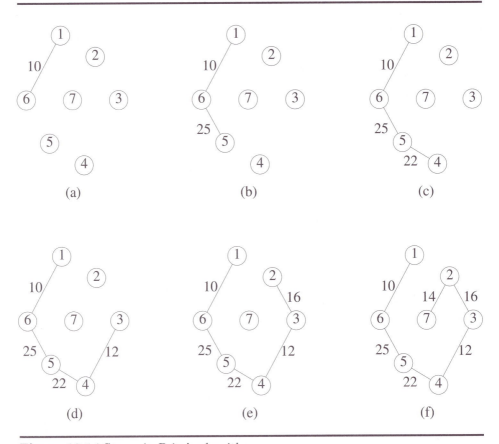

Figure 18.14 Stages in Prim's algorithm

Which Algorithm Should You Use?

We have seen three greedy algorithms for the minimum-cost spanning-tree problem. Since all three always construct a minimum-cost spanning tree, you should select one based on performance criteria. Because the space requirements of all three are approximately the same, the decision is made based on their relative time complexities. The asymptotic complexity of Kruskal's method is $O(n + e \log e)$ and that of Prim's method is $O(n^2)$ (though an $O(e + n \log n)$ implementation is also possible; see the solution to Exercise 37 on the Web site); Sollin's method was not analyzed in this text. Experimental results indicate that Prim's method is generally the fastest. Therefore, this method should be used.

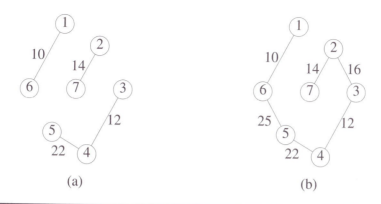

Figure 18.15 Stages in Sollin's algorithm

EXERCISES

8. Extend the greedy solution for the loading problem to the case when there are two ships. Does the algorithm always generate optimal solutions?

9. We are given n tasks to perform in sequence. Suppose that task i needs t_i units of time. If the tasks are done in the order 1, 2, $\cdots$, n, then task i completes at time $c_i = \sum_{j=1}^{i} t_j$. The average completion time (ACT) is $\frac{1}{n} \sum_{i=1}^{n} c_i$.

   (a) Consider the case of four tasks with task times (4, 2, 8, 1). What is the ACT when the task order is 1, 2, 3, 4?

   (b) What is the ACT when the task order is 2, 1, 4, 3?

   (c) The following method constructs a task order that tries to minimize the ACT: *Construct the order in n stages; in each stage select from the remaining tasks one with least task time.* For the example of part (a), this strategy results in the task order 4, 2, 1, 3. What is the ACT for this greedy order?

   (d) Write a Java program that implements the greedy strategy of (c). The complexity of your program should be $O(n \log n)$. Show that this is so.

   (e) Show that the greedy strategy of (c) results in task orders that have minimum ACT.

10. If two people perform the n tasks of Exercise 9, we need an assignment of tasks to each and an order in which each person is to perform his/her assigned tasks. The task completion times and ACT are defined as in Exercise 9. A possible greedy method that aims to minimize the ACT is as follows: *The two workers select tasks alternately and one at a time; from the remaining tasks, one with*

least task time is selected; each person does his/her tasks in the order selected. For the example of Exercise 9(a), if person 1 begins the selection process, he/she selects task 4, person 2 selects task 2, person 1 selects task 1, and finally person 2 selects task 3.

   (a) Write a Java program to implement this strategy. What is its time complexity?

   (b) Does the outlined greedy strategy always minimize the ACT? Prove your answer.

11. (a) Extend the greedy algorithm of Exercise 10 to the case when m persons are available to do the tasks.

   (b) Does your algorithm guarantee optimal solutions? Prove your answer.

   (c) Write Java code for your algorithm. What is its complexity?

12. Consider the stack-folding problem of Example 8.5.

   (a) Develop a greedy algorithm to fold the carton stack into the fewest number of substacks such that no substack is of height more than *height*.

   (b) Does your algorithm guarantee to fold into the fewest number of substacks always? Prove your answer.

   (c) Write Java code for your algorithm of (a).

   (d) What is the time complexity of your code of (c).

13. Write a Java program for the 0/1 knapsack problem using this heuristic: Pack the knapsack in nonincreasing order of profit density.

14. Write a Java program for the 0/1 knapsack problem using the bounded-performance heuristic with $k = 1$.

15. Prove the error bound on the bounded-performance heuristic for the 0/1 knapsack problem for the case $k = 1$.

16. Write a Java program for the 0/1 knapsack problem using the bounded-performance heuristic with $k = 2$.

17. Consider the **continuous-knapsack problem** in which we require $0 \leq x_i \leq 1$, rather than $x_i \in 0, 1$. A possible greedy algorithm is *Consider objects in nonincreasing order of profit density; if there is enough remaining capacity to accommodate the object, put it in; if not, put in a fraction to fill the knapsack.*

   (a) What is the packing obtained for the instance $n = 3$, $w = [100, 10, 10]$, $p = [20, 15, 15]$, and $c = 105$?

   (b) Prove that this greedy algorithm always generates an optimal solution.

   (c) Write a Java program that implements this algorithm.

18. The thirsty-baby problem of Example 18.1 is a generalization of the continuous-knapsack problem of Exercise 17. Extend the greedy method of Exercise 17 to this problem. Does the algorithm guarantee optimal solutions? Prove your answer.

19. [AOE Networks] The task digraph of Figure 18.4 is called an activity on vertex (AOV) network because the vertices of the digraph represent tasks or activities. The activity on edge (AOE) network is a related network in which the edges represent activities (or tasks) and the vertices represent events. One of the vertices of the AOE network represents the start event s, and another vertex represents the finish event f. The in-degree of the start event and the out-degree of the finish event are 0. An event i, other than the start event, occurs when all activities coming into the event (i.e., all activities denoted by edges of the form (j, i)) complete; and activity (i, k) can start only after event i has occurred. In an AOE network several activities can be done in parallel.

Figure 18.16 shows an eight-event, 12-activity AOE network. The number on an edge is the time it takes to complete that activity. So activity (1,4) takes five time units. Vertex 1 is the start event, and vertex 8 is the finish event.

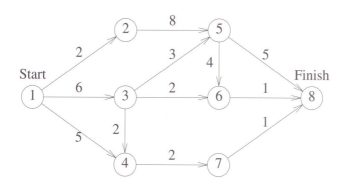

Figure 18.16 An AOE network

By definition, the start event occurs at time 0.

(a) List the events of Figure 18.16 in topological order.

(b) Let $earliestEventTime(i)$, be the earliest time at which event i can occur. Prove that, for i not the start event,

$$earliestEventTime(i) = \max_{(j,i) \in E} \{earliestEventTime(j) + length(j, i)\}$$

$$(18.1)$$

where E is the set of edges of the AOE network and $length(j, i)$ is the time required by activity (j, i). Keep in mind that you can do as many activities as you wish concurrently.

(c) Use Equation 18.1 and the topological order of part (a) to compute the earliest event times for the events of Figure 18.16.

(d) The earliest event time of the finish event is called the **project length**. What is the project length for the project represented by the AOE network of Figure 18.16?

(e) The latest event time $latestEventTime(i)$ of event i is the latest time by which event i must occur; if event i does not occur by this time, then the project cannot complete in time equal to the project length. Clearly, the latest event time for the finish event is the same as its earliest event time. Prove that, for i not the finish event,

$$latestEventTime(i) = \min_{(i,j) \in E} \{latestEventTime(j) - length(i, j)\}$$

(18.2)

(f) Use Equation 18.2 and the reverse of the topological order of part (a) to compute the latest event times for the events of Figure 18.16.

(g) From the definition of an AOE network, it follows that the earliest time, $earliestActivityTime(i, j)$, at which activity (i, j) can commence is $earliestEventTime(i)$; if the activity starts later than

$$latestActivityTime(i, j) = latestEventTime(j) - length(i, j)$$

then the project cannot finish in time equal to the project length. Compute the earliest and latest activity times for the activities of Figure 18.16.

(h) The **slack time**, $slack(i, j)$, of activity (i, j) is

$$latestActivityTime(i, j) - earliestActivityTime(i, j)$$

Compute the slack times for all activities.

(i) A **critical activity** is an activity whose slack is 0. Identify the critical activities of Figure 18.16.

20. Write a program to input an AOE network (see Exercise 19) and output the project length, earliest and latest event and activity times, slack times, and critical activities. The complexity of your program should be $O(n + e)$ where n is the number of events and e is the number of activities. Test your code.

21. (a) Show that the algorithm of Figure 18.7 fails to find a cover iff the input bipartite graph does not have a cover.

    (b) Give a bipartite graph that has a cover and on which the algorithm of Figure 18.7 fails to find a minimum cover.

22. Trace the working of Figure 18.8 on the graph of Figure 18.6.

23. Devise another greedy heuristic for the bipartite-cover problem. This time use the following greedy criterion: *If there is a vertex of B that can be covered by only a single vertex of A, select this vertex; otherwise, select a vertex of A that covers the largest number of uncovered vertices.*

    (a) Write a high-level statement of the greedy heuristic.

    (b) Refine this greedy heuristic into a Java method that is a member of the class `Graph`.

    (c) What is the time complexity of your method?

    (d) Test the correctness of your code.

24. Let G be an undirected graph. A subset S of the vertices of G is a **clique** iff there is an edge between every pair of vertices in S. The size of the clique is the number of vertices in S. A **maximum clique** is a clique of largest size. The problem of finding a maximum clique (i.e., the max-clique problem) in a graph is NP-hard.

    (a) Provide a high-level statement of a possible greedy heuristic for the max-clique problem.

    (b) Give an example of a graph on which your heuristic actually produces a maximum clique and also an example on which it does not.

    (c) Refine the heuristic of (a) into the public method `Graph.maxClique(int [] cliqueVertices)` that returns the size of the largest clique found and puts the vertices of this largest clique into the array `cliqueVertices`.

    (d) What is the time complexity of your code?

25. Let G be an undirected graph. A subset S of the vertices of G is an **independent set** iff no two vertices of S are connected by an edge. A maximum independent set is an independent set with the maximum number of vertices. Finding the maximum independent set of a graph is NP-hard. Do Exercise 24 for the maximum-independent-set problem.

26. A **coloring** of an undirected graph G is an assignment of the labels $\{1, 2, \cdots\}$ to the vertices of G such that no two vertices connected by an edge have the same label. In the graph-coloring problem, we are to color G using the fewest number of distinct colors (labels). The graph-coloring problem is NP-hard. Do Exercise 24 for the graph-coloring problem.

27. List all simple paths from vertex 1 to vertex 3 in the weighted digraph of Figure 18.17. What is the length of each path? Which is the shortest path?

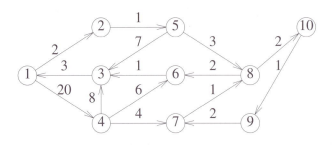

Figure 18.17 A weighted digraph

28. List the shortest paths from vertex 1 to each vertex of Figure 18.17 in ascending order of length. Observe that each path, other than the first, is a one-edge extension of a previous path.

29. (a) For the graph of Figure 18.17, show the initial `distanceFromSource` and `predecessor` arrays for Dijkstra's method (Figure 18.10). Use vertex 1 as the source vertex.

    (b) Now show these two arrays following each iteration of the loop of steps 2, 3, and 4.

    (c) Use the final `predecessor` array to determine the shortest paths from vertex 1.

30. Do Exercise 29 using vertex 5 as the source vertex.

31. Show that when shortest paths are generated in order of length, the next shortest path to be generated is always a one-edge extension of an already generated shortest path.

32. Show that the greedy algorithm of Figure 18.10 may not correctly compute the lengths of the shortest paths in a digraph that has one or more edges with negative cost.

33. Write a method `path(p,s,i)` that uses the p values computed by the method `shortestPaths` and outputs a shortest path from vertex s to vertex i. What is the time complexity of your method?

34. Write a version of Program 18.3 for the case when the weighted digraph is a member of the class `LinkedWDigraph`. Your method should be defined as a member of this class. What is the time complexity of your method?

35. Write a version of Program 18.3 for the case when the weighted digraph is a member of the class `LinkedWDigraph` and has only $O(n)$ edges. This time implement l as a min heap. What is the time complexity of your method?

36. Write a version of Program 18.3 that works for weighted undirected and directed graphs and is independent of the representation that is used. Your method will be a member of `Graph`.

★ 37. (a) Provide a correctness proof for Prim's method (Figure 18.13).

   (b) Refine Figure 18.13 into a Java method `Graph.prim` with complexity $O(n^2)$. (*Hint:* Use a strategy similar to that used in the shortest paths code of Program 18.3.)

   (c) Show that the complexity of your method is indeed $O(n^2)$.

★ 38. (a) Prove that Sollin's algorithm finds a minimum-cost spanning tree for every connected undirected graph.

   (b) What is the maximum number of stages in Sollin's algorithm? Give this as a function of the number of vertices n in the graph.

   (c) Write a Java method, `Graph.sollin`, that finds a minimum-cost spanning tree using Sollin's algorithm.

   (d) What is the complexity of your method?

★ 39. Let T be a tree (not necessarily binary) in which a length is associated with each edge. Let S be a subset of the vertices of T and let T/S denote the forest that results when the vertices of S are deleted from T. We wish to find a minimum-cardinality subset S such that no forest in T/S has a root-to-leaf path whose length exceeds d.

   (a) Develop a greedy algorithm to find a minimum-cardinality S. (*Hint:* Start at the leaves and move toward the root.)

   (b) Prove the correctness of your algorithm.

   (c) What is the complexity of your algorithm? In case it is not linear in the number of vertices in T, redesign your algorithm so that its complexity is linear.

★ 40. Do Exercise 39 for the case when T/S denotes the forest that results from making two copies of each vertex in S. The pointer from the parent goes to one copy, and pointers to the children go from the other copy.

41. A convex polygon (Section 6.5.3) with $n > 2$ vertices is to be triangulated (i.e., partitioned or cut into triangles; each corner of a triangle is a vertex of the polygon). A cut starts at a polygon vertex u and ends at a nonadjacent vertex v. The cost of the cut (u, v) is $c(u, v)$. A total of $n - 2$ cuts are required to triangulate the polygon.

   (a) Formulate a greedy strategy to find a triangulation with minimum cost.

   (b) Does your strategy always find a minimum-cost triangulation? Prove your answer.

   (c) Write a program that implements your strategy. Test your code.

   (d) What is the complexity of your code?

18.4   REFERENCES AND SELECTED READINGS

Greedy approximation algorithms for several problems appear in the paper "A Survey of Approximately Optimal Solutions to Some Covering and Packing Problems" by V. Paschos, *ACM Computing Surveys*, 29, 2, 1997, 171–209. An experimental evaluation of greedy algorithms for the minimum-cost spanning-tree problem appears in the paper "An Empirical Assessment of Algorithms for Constructing a Minimum Spanning Tree" by B. Moret and H. Shapiro, *DIMACS Series in Discrete Mathematics*, 15, 1994, 99–117.

CHAPTER 19

DIVIDE AND CONQUER

BIRD'S-EYE VIEW

The divide-and-conquer strategy so successfully used by monarchs and colonizers may also be applied to the development of efficient computer algorithms. We begin this chapter by showing how to adapt this ancient strategy to the algorithm-development arena. Then we use the strategy to obtain good algorithms for the minmax problem; matrix multiplication; a problem from recreational mathematics—the defective-chessboard problem; sorting; selection; and a computational geometry problem—find the closest pair of points in two-dimensional space.

Since divide-and-conquer algorithms decompose a problem instance into several smaller independent instances, divide-and-conquer algorithms may be effectively run on a parallel computer; the independent smaller instances can be worked on by different processors of the parallel computer.

This chapter develops the mathematics needed to analyze the complexity of frequently occurring divide-and-conquer algorithms and proves that the divide-and-conquer algorithms for the minmax and sorting problems are optimal by deriving lower bounds on the complexity of these problems. The derived lower bounds agree with the complexity of the divide-and-conquer algorithms for these problems.

19.1   THE METHOD

The divide-and-conquer methodology is very similar to the modularization approach to software design. Small instances of a problem are solved using some direct approach. To solve a large instance, we (1) divide it into two or more smaller instances, (2) solve each of these smaller problems, and (3) combine the solutions of these smaller problems to obtain the solution to the original instance. The smaller instances are often instances of the original problem and may be solved by using the divide-and-conquer strategy recursively.

Example 19.1 [Detecting a Counterfeit Coin] You are given a bag with 16 coins and told that one of these coins may be counterfeit. Further, you are told that counterfeit coins are lighter than genuine ones. Your task is to determine whether the bag contains a counterfeit coin. To aid you in this task, you have a machine that compares the weights of two sets of coins and tells you which set is lighter or whether both sets have the same weight.

We can compare the weights of coins 1 and 2. If coin 1 is lighter than coin 2, then coin 1 is counterfeit and we are done with our task. If coin 2 is lighter than coin 1, then coin 2 is counterfeit. If both coins have the same weight, we compare coins 3 and 4. Again, if one coin is lighter, a counterfeit coin has been detected and we are done. If not, we compare coins 5 and 6. Proceeding in this way, we can determine whether the bag contains a counterfeit coin by making at most eight weight comparisons. This process also identifies the counterfeit coin.

Another approach is to use the divide-and-conquer methodology. Suppose that our 16-coin instance is considered a large instance. In step 1, we divide the original instance into two or more smaller instances. Let us divide our 16-coin instance into two 8-coin instances by arbitrarily selecting 8 coins for the first instance (say A) and the remaining 8 coins for the second instance B. In step 2, we need to determine whether A or B has a counterfeit coin. For this step we use our machine to compare the weights of the coin sets A and B. If both sets have the same weight, a counterfeit coin is not present in the 16-coin set. If A and B have different weights, a counterfeit coin is present and it is in the lighter set. Finally, in step 3 we take the results from step 2 and generate the answer for the original 16-coin instance. For the counterfeit-coin problem, step 3 is easy. The 16-coin instance has a counterfeit coin iff either A or B has one. So with just one weight comparison, we can complete the task of determining the presence of a counterfeit coin.

Now suppose we need to identify the counterfeit coin. We will define a "small" instance to be one with two or three coins. Note that if there is only one coin, we cannot tell whether it is counterfeit. All other instances are "large" instances. If we have a small instance, we may identify the counterfeit coin by comparing one of the coins with up to two other coins, performing at most two weight comparisons.

The 16-coin instance is a large instance. So it is divided into two 8-coin instances A and B as above. By comparing the weights of these two instances, we determine whether or not a counterfeit coin is present. If not, the algorithm terminates.

Otherwise, we continue with the subinstance known to have the counterfeit coin. Suppose B is the lighter set. It is divided into two sets of four coins each. Call these sets $B1$ and $B2$. The two sets are compared. One set of coins must be lighter. If $B1$ is lighter, the counterfeit coin is in $B1$ and $B1$ is divided into two sets of two coins each. Call these sets $B1a$ and $B1b$. The two sets are compared, and we continue with the lighter set. Since the lighter set has only two coins, it is a small instance. Comparing the weights of the two coins in the lighter set, we can determine which is lighter. The lighter one is the counterfeit coin.   ■

Example 19.2 [Gold Nuggets] Your boss has a bag of gold nuggets. Each month two employees are given one nugget each for exemplary performance. By tradition, the first-ranked employee gets the heaviest nugget in the bag, and the second-ranked employee gets the lightest. This way, unless new nuggets are added to the bag, first-ranked employees get heavier nuggets than second-ranked employees get. Since new nuggets are added periodically, it is necessary to determine the heaviest and lightest nugget each month. You have a machine that can compare the weights of two nuggets and report which is lighter or whether both have the same weight. As this comparison is time-consuming, we wish to determine the heaviest and lightest nuggets, using the fewest number of comparisons.

Suppose the bag has n nuggets. We can use the strategy used in method `max` (Program 1.29) to find the heaviest nugget by making $n - 1$ comparisons. After we identify the heaviest nugget, we can find the lightest from the remaining $n - 1$ nuggets using a similar strategy and performing an additional $n - 2$ comparisons. The total number of weight comparisons is $2n - 3$. Two alternative strategies appear in Programs 2.24 and 2.25. The first strategy performs $2n - 2$ comparisons, and the second performs at most $2n - 2$ comparisons.

Let us try to formulate a solution that uses the divide-and-conquer method. When n is small, say, $n \leq 2$, one comparison is sufficient to identify the heaviest and lightest nuggets. When n is large (in this case $n > 2$), in step 1 we divide the instance into two or more smaller instances. Suppose we divide the bag of nuggets into two smaller bags A and B, each containing half the nuggets. In step 2 we determine the heaviest and lightest nuggets in A and B. Let these nuggets be H_A (heaviest in A), L_A, H_B, and L_B. Step 3 determines the heaviest overall nugget by comparing H_A and H_B and the lightest by comparing L_A and L_B. We can use the outlined divide-and-conquer scheme recursively to perform step 2.

Suppose $n = 8$. The bag is divided into two bags A and B with four nuggets each (Figure 19.1(a)). To find the heaviest and lightest nuggets in A, the four nuggets in A are divided into two groups $A1$ and $A2$. Each group contains two nuggets. We can identify the heavier nugget H_{A1} and the lighter one L_{A1} in $A1$ with one comparison (Figure 19.1(b)). With another comparison, we can identify H_{A2} and L_{A2}. Now by comparing H_{A1} and H_{A2}, we can identify H_A. A comparison between L_{A1} and L_{A2} identifies L_A. So with four comparisons we have found H_A and L_A. We need another four comparisons to determine H_B and L_B. By comparing H_A and

H_B (L_A and L_B), we determine the overall heaviest (lightest) nugget. Therefore, the divide-and-conquer approach requires 10 comparisons when $n = 8$. In contrast, Program 1.29 requires 13 comparisons, and both Programs 2.24 and 2.25 require up to 14 comparisons.

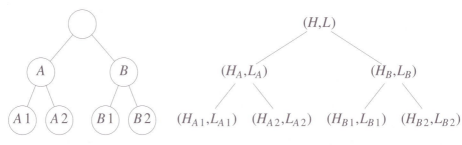

(a) Dividing into smaller bags   (b) Finding heavy and light nuggets in a bag

Figure 19.1 Finding the heaviest and lightest of eight nuggets

Let $c(n)$ be the number of comparisons used by the divide-and-conquer approach. For simplicity, assume that n is a power of 2. When $n = 2$, $c(n) = 1$. For larger n, $c(n) = 2c(n/2) + 2$. Using the substitution method (see Example 2.20), this recurrence can be solved to obtain $c(n) = 3n/2 - 2$ when n is a power of 2. The divide-and-conquer approach uses almost 25 percent fewer comparisons than the alternative schemes suggested in this example use. ∎

Example 19.3 [Matrix Multiplication] The product of two $n \times n$ matrices A and B is a third $n \times n$ matrix C where $C(i, j)$ is given by

$$C(i, j) = \sum_{k=1}^{n} A(i, k) * B(k, j), \quad 1 \le i \le n, \quad 1 \le j \le n \qquad (19.1)$$

If each $C(i, j)$ is computed by using this equation, then the computation of each requires n multiplications and $n - 1$ additions. The total operation count for the computation of all terms of C is therefore $n^3 m + n^2(n - 1)a$ where m denotes a multiplication and a an addition or subtraction.

To formulate a divide-and-conquer algorithm to multiply the two matrices, we need to define a "small" instance, specify how small instances are multiplied, determine how a large instance may be subdivided into smaller instances, state how these smaller instances are to be multiplied, and finally describe how the solutions of these smaller instances may be combined to obtain the solution for the larger instance. To keep the discussion simple, let's assume that n is a power of 2 (i.e., n is one of the numbers 1, 2, 4, 8, 16, $\cdots$).

To begin with, let us assume that $n = 1$ is a small instance and that $n > 1$ is a large instance. We will modify this assumption later if we need to. Since a small matrix is a 1×1 matrix, we can multiply two such matrices by multiplying together the single element in each.

Consider a large instance, that is, one with $n > 1$. We can divide such a matrix A into four $n/2 \times n/2$ matrices A_1, A_2, A_3, and A_4 as shown in Figure 19.2(a). When n is greater than 1 and a power of 2, $n/2$ is also a power of 2. So the smaller matrices satisfy our assumption on the matrix size also. The matrices B_i and C_i, $1 \leq i \leq 4$, are defined in a similar way. The matrix product we are to perform may be represented as in Figure 19.2(b). We may use Equation 19.1 to verify that the following equations are valid:

$$
\begin{array}{rcll}
C_1 & = & A_1 B_1 + A_2 B_3 & (19.2) \\
C_2 & = & A_1 B_2 + A_2 B_4 & (19.3) \\
C_3 & = & A_3 B_1 + A_4 B_3 & (19.4) \\
C_2 & = & A_3 B_2 + A_4 B_4 & (19.5)
\end{array}
$$

These equations allow us to compute the product of A and B by performing eight multiplications and four additions of $n/2 \times n/2$ matrices. We can use these equations to complete our divide-and-conquer algorithm. In step 2 of the algorithm, the eight multiplications involving the smaller matrices are done using the divide-and-conquer algorithm recursively. In step 3 the eight products are combined using a direct matrix addition algorithm (see Program 2.21). The complexity of the resulting algorithm is $\Theta(n^3)$, the same as the complexity of Program 2.22, which uses Equation 19.1 directly. The divide-and-conquer algorithm will actually run slower than Program 2.22 because of the overheads introduced by the instance-dividing and -recombining steps.

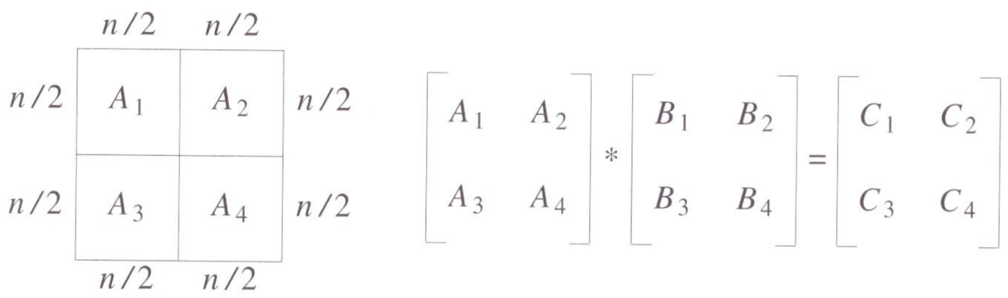

(a) Dividing A into four

(b) $A * B = C$

Figure 19.2 Dividing a matrix into smaller matrices

To get a faster algorithm, we need to be more clever about the instance-dividing and -recombining steps. A scheme, known as Strassen's method, involves the computation of seven smaller matrix products (versus eight in the preceding scheme). The results of these seven smaller products are matrices $D, E, \cdots, J$, which are defined as

$$
\begin{aligned}
D &= A_1(B_2 - B_4) \\
E &= A_4(B_3 - B_1) \\
F &= (A_3 + A_4)B_1 \\
G &= (A_1 + A_2)B_4 \\
H &= (A_3 - A_1)(B_1 + B_2) \\
I &= (A_2 - A_4)(B_3 + B_4) \\
J &= (A_1 + A_4)(B_1 + B_4)
\end{aligned}
$$

The matrices D through J may be computed by performing seven matrix multiplications, six matrix additions, and four matrix subtractions. The components of the answer may be computed by using another six matrix additions and two matrix subtractions as below:

$$
\begin{aligned}
C_1 &= E + I + J - G \\
C_2 &= D + G \\
C_3 &= E + F \\
C_4 &= D + H + J - F
\end{aligned}
$$

Let us try this scheme on a multiplication instance with $n = 2$. Sample A and B matrices together with their product C are given below:

$$
\begin{bmatrix} 1 & 2 \\ 3 & 4 \end{bmatrix} * \begin{bmatrix} 5 & 6 \\ 7 & 8 \end{bmatrix} = \begin{bmatrix} 19 & 22 \\ 43 & 50 \end{bmatrix}
$$

Since $n > 1$, the matrix multiplication instance is divided into four smaller matrices as in Figure 19.2(a); each smaller matrix is a 1×1 matrix and has a single element. The 1×1 multiplication instances are small instances, and they are solved directly. Using the equations for D through J, we obtain the values that follow.

$$\begin{aligned}
D &= 1(6-8) = -2 \\
E &= 4(7-5) = 8 \\
F &= (3+4)5 = 35 \\
G &= (1+2)8 = 24 \\
H &= (3-1)(5+6) = 22 \\
I &= (2-4)(7+8) = -30 \\
J &= (1+4)(5+8) = 65
\end{aligned}$$

From these values the components of the answer are computed as follows:

$$\begin{aligned}
C_1 &= 8 - 30 + 65 - 24 = 19 \\
C_2 &= -2 + 24 = 22 \\
C_3 &= 8 + 35 = 43 \\
C_4 &= -2 + 22 + 65 - 35 = 50
\end{aligned}$$

For our 2×2 instance, the divide-and-conquer algorithm has done seven multiplications and 18 add/subtracts. We could have computed C by performing eight multiplications and four add/subtracts by using Equation 19.1 directly. For the divide-and-conquer scheme to be faster, the time cost of a multiplication must be more than the time cost of 14 add/subtracts.

If Strassen's instance-dividing scheme is used only when $n \geq 8$ and smaller instances are solved using Equation 19.1, then the case $n = 8$ requires seven multiplications of 4×4 matrices and 18 add/subtracts of matrices of this size. The multiplications take $64m + 48a$ operations each, and each matrix addition or subtraction takes $16a$ operations. The total operation count is $7(64m+48a) + 18(16a)$ $= 448m + 624$. The direct method has an operation count of $512m + 448a$. A minimum requirement for Strassen's method to be faster is that the cost of $512 - 448$ multiplications be more than that of $624 - 448$ add/subtracts. Or one multiplication should cost more than approximately 2.75 add/subtracts.

If we consider a "small" instance to be one with $n < 16$, the Strassen's decomposition scheme is used only for matrices with $n \geq 16$; smaller matrices are multiplied using Equation 19.1. The operation count for the divide-and-conquer algorithm becomes $7(512m + 448a) + 18(64a) = 3584m + 4288a$ when $n = 16$. The direct method has an operation count of $4096m + 3840a$. If the cost of a multiplication is the same as that of an add/subtract, then Strassen's method needs time for 7872 operations plus overhead time to do the problem division. The direct method needs time for 7936 operations plus time for the **for** loops and other overhead items in the program. Even though the operation count is less for Strassen's method, it is not expected to run faster because of its larger overhead.

For larger values of n, the difference between the operation counts of Strassen's method and the direct method becomes larger and larger. So for suitably large n, Strassen's method will be faster. Let $t(n)$ denote the time required by Strassen's divide-and-conquer method. Since large instances are recursively divided into smaller ones until each instance becomes of size k or less (k is at least eight and may be larger depending on the implementation and computer characteristics), the recurrence for t is

$$t(n) = \begin{cases} d & n \leq k \\ 7t(n/2) + cn^2 & n > k \end{cases} \tag{19.6}$$

where cn^2 represents the time to perform 18 add/subtracts of $n/2 \times n/2$ matrices as well as the time to divide the instance of size n into the smaller instances. Using the substitution method, this recurrence may be solved to obtain $t(n) = \Theta(n^{\log_2 7})$. Since $\log_2 7 \approx 2.81$, the divide-and-conquer matrix multiplication algorithm is asymptotically faster than Program 2.22.   ∎

Implementation Note

The divide-and-conquer methodology naturally leads to recursive algorithms. In many instances, these recursive algorithms are best implemented as recursive programs. In fact, in many cases all attempts to obtain nonrecursive programs result in the use of a stack to simulate the recursion stack. However, in some instances we can implement the divide-and-conquer algorithm as a nonrecursive program without the use of such a stack and in such a way that the resulting program is faster, by a constant factor, than the natural recursive implementation. The divide-and-conquer algorithms for both the gold nuggets problem (Example 19.2) and the merge sort method (Section 19.2.2) can be implemented without the use of recursion so as to obtain fast programs that do not directly simulate the recursion.

Example 19.4 [Gold Nuggets] The work done by the algorithm of Example 19.2 to find the lightest and heaviest of eight nuggets is described by the binary tree of Figure 19.3. The leaves of this tree denote the eight nuggets (a, b, $\cdots$, h). Each shaded node represents an instance containing all the leaves in its subtree. Therefore, root A represents the problem of finding the lightest and heaviest of all eight nuggets, while node B represents the problem of finding the lightest and heaviest of the nuggets a, b, c, and d. The algorithm begins at the root. The eight-nugget instance represented by the root is divided into 2 four-nugget instances represented by the nodes B and C. At B the four-nugget instance is divided into the two-nugget instances D and E. We solve the two-nugget instance at node D by comparing the nuggets a and b to determine which is heavier. After we solve the problems at D and E, we solve the problem at B by comparing the lighter nuggets from D and E, as well as the heavier nuggets at D and E. We repeat this process at F, G, and C and then at A.

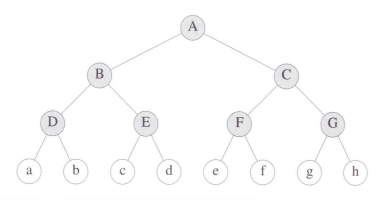

Figure 19.3 Finding the lightest and heaviest of eight nuggets

We can classify the work of the recursive divide-and-conquer algorithm as follows:

1. Divide a large instance into many smaller ones, each of size 1 or 2, during a downward root-to-leaf pass of the binary tree of Figure 19.3.

2. Compare the nuggets in each smaller size 2 instance to determine which nugget is heavier and which is lighter. This comparison is done at nodes D, E, F, and G. For size 1 instances the single nugget is both the smaller and lighter nugget.

3. Compare the lighter nuggets to determine which is lightest. Compare the heavier nuggets to determine which is heaviest. These comparisons are done at nodes A through C.

This classification of the work leads to the nonrecursive code of Program 19.1 to find the locations of the minimum and maximum of the a.length weights a[0:a.length-1], and these locations are returned as a pair of the type MinMaxPair (Program 2.24).

The cases a.length < 1 and a.length = 1 are handled first. If a.length > 1 and odd, the first weight a[0] becomes the candidate for minimum and maximum, and we are left with an even number of weights a[1:a.length-1] to account for in the for loop. When a.length is even, the first two weights are compared outside the for loop and p.min and p.max are set to the location of the smaller and larger weight, respectively. Again, we are left with an even number of weights a[2:a.length-1] to account for in the for loop.

```
public static MinMaxPair minMax(Comparable [] a)
{
   // special cases, a.length <= 1
   if (a.length < 1)
      throw new IllegalArgumentException
                  ("Cannot find min and max of zero elements");
   if (a.length == 1) return new MinMaxPair(0, 0);

   // a.length > 1, initialize Min and Max
   int s = 1;              // start point for loop
   MinMaxPair p;           // current min and max
   if (a.length % 2 == 1)  // a.length is odd
      p = new MinMaxPair(0, 0);
   else
   {// a.length is even, compare first pair
      if (a[0].compareTo(a[1]) > 0) p = new MinMaxPair(1, 0);
      else p = new MinMaxPair(0, 1);
      s = 2;
   }

   // compare remaining pairs
   for (int i = s; i < a.length; i += 2)
   {
      // find larger of a[i] and a[i + 1], then compare larger one
      // with a[p.max] and smaller one with a[p.min]
      if (a[i].compareTo(a[i + 1]) > 0)
      {
         if (a[i].compareTo(a[p.max]) > 0) p.max = i;
         if (a[i + 1].compareTo(a[p.min]) < 0) p.min = i + 1;
      }
      else
      {
         if (a[i + 1].compareTo(a[p.max]) > 0) p.max = i + 1;
         if (a[i].compareTo(a[p.min]) < 0) p.min = i;
      }
   }

   return p;
}
```

Program 19.1 Nonrecursive code to find the min and max in a[0:a.length-1]

In the `for` loop the outer `if` finds the larger and smaller of the pair (`w[i]`,`w[i+1]`) being compared. This work corresponds to the category 2 work in our classification of the work of our divide-and-conquer algorithm. The embedded `if`s find the smallest of the smaller weights and the largest of the larger weights. This work is the category 3 work.

The `for` loop compares the smaller of each pair to the current minimum weight `a[p.min]` and compares the larger to the current maximum weight `a[p.max]`; `p.min` and `p.max` are updated if necessary.

For the complexity analysis, we see that when `a.length` is even, one comparison is made outside the `for` loop and `3(a.length/2-1)` inside. The total number of comparisons is `3a.length/2-2`. When `a.length` is odd, no comparisons are made outside the `for` loop. However, `3(a.length-1)/2` comparisons are made inside. Therefore, regardless of whether `a.length` is odd or even, a total of $\lceil$`3a.length/2`$\rceil - 2$ comparisons are made, `a.length` > 0. In Section 19.4.1 we show that this is the minimum number of comparisons that every algorithm that finds the minimum and the maximum of `a.length` weights must make. ■

EXERCISES

1. Extend the divide-and-conquer method of Example 19.1 to the case of $n > 1$ coins. How many weight comparisons are done?

2. Consider the counterfeit-coin problem of Example 19.1. Suppose that the information "counterfeit coins are lighter than genuine ones" is changed to "counterfeit coins and genuine coins do not have the same weight." Also assume that the coin bag contains n coins.

    (a) Formulate a divide-and-conquer algorithm that either outputs the message "there is no counterfeit coin" or identifies the counterfeit coin. Your algorithm should recursively divide large problem instances into two smaller ones. How many weight comparisons are needed to identify the counterfeit coin (in case such a coin exists)?

    (b) Repeat part (a) with the requirement that large instances are divided into three smaller ones.

3. (a) Write Java programs that implement both schemes of Example 19.2 to find the maximum and minimum of n elements. Use recursion to implement the divide-and-conquer scheme.

    (b) Programs 2.24 and 2.25 are two other codes to find the maximum and minimum of n elements. What are the minimum and maximum number of comparisons made by each?

    (c) Compare the run times of the codes of (a) and (b) as well as the code of Program 19.1 for $n = 100$; 1000; and 10,000. For the code of Program 2.25 use both the average- and worst-case times. The two codes of

(a) and that of Program 2.24 should have the same average- and worst-case times.

(d) Note that unless the comparison cost is very high, the divide-and-conqer algorithm will not outperform the others on worst-case data. Why? Will it ever outperform Program 2.25 on the average-time measure? Why?

4. Show that the divide-and-conquer matrix-multiplication algorithm that results from the direct application of Equations 19.2 through 19.5 has complexity $\Theta(n^3)$. From this analysis conclude that the resulting program will be slower than Program 2.22.

5. Use the substitution method to show that the solution to the recurrence Equation 19.6 is $\Theta(n^{\log_2 7})$.

6. Program Strassen's matrix-multiplication algorithm and experiment with different values of k (see Equation 19.6) to determine which value results in best performance. Now compare the run times of your program with those for Program 2.22. It is sufficient to do this comparison for the case when n is a power of 2.

7. When n is not a power of 2, we may add rows and columns to the matrices to obtain larger matrices whose size is a power of 2. Suppose that the smallest number of rows and columns are added so that the resulting matrix size m is a power of 2.

(a) How large can the ratio m/n be?

(b) What matrix entries should you use for the new rows and columns so that when the new matrices A' and B' are multiplied, the product of the original matrices A and B appears in the top-left corner of C'?

(c) The run time of Strassen's method to multiply A' and B' is $\Theta(m^{2.81})$. What is the run time as a function of n?

19.2   APPLICATIONS

19.2.1   Defective Chessboard

Problem Description

A **defective chessboard** is a $2^k \times 2^k$ board of squares with exactly one defective square. Figure 19.4 shows some of the possible defective chessboards for $k \leq 2$. The defective square is shaded. Note that when $k = 0$, there is only one possible defective chessboard (Figure 19.4(a)). In fact, for any k there are exactly 2^{2k} different defective chessboards.

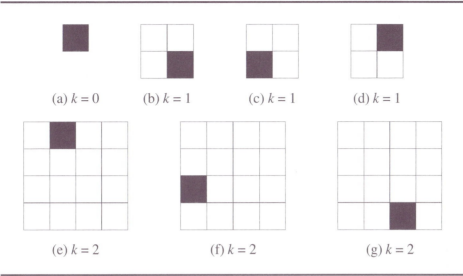

(a) $k = 0$ (b) $k = 1$ (c) $k = 1$ (d) $k = 1$

(e) $k = 2$ (f) $k = 2$ (g) $k = 2$

Figure 19.4 Defective chessboards

In the defective-chessboard problem, we are required to tile a defective chessboard using triominoes (Figure 19.5). In this tiling two triominoes may not overlap, triominoes should not cover the defective square, and triominoes must cover all other squares. With these constraints the number of triominoes to be used becomes $(2^{2k} - 1)/3$. We can verify that $(2^{2k} - 1)/3$ is an integer. A defective chessboard with $k = 0$ is easily tiled, as it has no nondefective squares. The number of triominoes used in the tiling is zero. When $k = 1$, there are exactly three nondefective squares and these squares are covered using a triomino in one of the orientations of Figure 19.5.

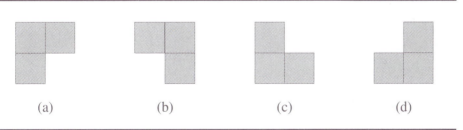

(a)   (b)   (c)   (d)

Figure 19.5 Triominoes with different orientations

Solution Strategy

The divide-and-conquer method leads to an elegant solution to the defective-chessboard problem. The method suggests reducing the problem of tiling a $2^k \times 2^k$ defective chessboard to that of tiling smaller defective chessboards. A natural partitioning of a $2^k \times 2^k$ chessboard would be into four $2^{k-1} \times 2^{k-1}$ chessboards as in Figure 19.6(a). Notice that when such a partitioning is done, only one of the four smaller boards has a defect (as the original $2^k \times 2^k$ board had exactly one defective square). Tiling one of the four smaller boards corresponds to tiling a defective $2^{k-1} \times 2^{k-1}$ chessboard. To convert the remaining three boards to defective boards, we place a triomino at the corner formed by these three. Figure 19.6(b) shows this placement for the case when the defect in the original $2^k \times 2^k$ chessboard falls into the upper left $2^{k-1} \times 2^{k-1}$ board. We can use this partitioning technique recursively to tile the entire $2^k \times 2^k$ defective chessboard. The recursion terminates when the chessboard size has been reduced to 1×1. The chessboard's only square now has a defect, and no triominoes are to be placed.

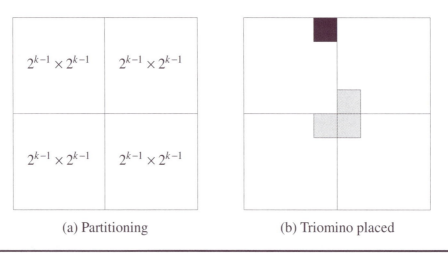

(a) Partitioning   (b) Triomino placed

Figure 19.6 Partitioning a $2^k \times 2^k$ board

Java Implementation

We can code this divide-and-conquer algorithm as the recursive Java method `Chessboard.tileBoard` (Program 19.2). The class `Chessboard` has two data members, `board` and `tile`. `board` is a two-dimensional integer array that represents the chessboard, and `board[0][0]` represents the top-left corner square of the chessboard; `tile`, an integer variable with initial value 1, gives the index of the next tile to use.

```
public void tileBoard(int topRow, int topColumn,
                      int defectRow, int defectColumn, int size)
{
   if (size == 1) return;
   int tileToUse = tile++,
      quadrantSize = size / 2;

   // tile top-left quadrant
   if (defectRow < topRow + quadrantSize &&
      defectColumn < topColumn + quadrantSize)
      // defect is in this quadrant
      tileBoard(topRow, topColumn, defectRow, defectColumn,
             quadrantSize);
   else
   {// no defect in this quadrant
      // place a tile in bottom-right corner
      board[topRow + quadrantSize - 1][topColumn + quadrantSize - 1]
          = tileToUse;
      // tile the rest
      tileBoard(topRow, topColumn, topRow + quadrantSize - 1,
             topColumn + quadrantSize - 1, quadrantSize);
   }

   // code for remaining three quadrants is similar
}
```

Program 19.2 Tiling a defective chessboard

The initial invocation is `tileBoard(0,0,dr,dc,size)` where $size = 2^k$, and `dr` and `dc` give the row and column index of the defect. The number of tiles needed to tile the defective chessboard is $(size^2 - 1)/3$. Method `tileBoard` represents these tiles by the integers 1 through $(size^2 - 1)/3$ and labels each nondefective square of the chessboard with the number of the tile that covers it.

Complexity Analysis

Let $t(k)$ denote the time taken by `tileBoard` to tile a $2^k \times 2^k$ defective chessboard. When $k = 0$, `size` equals 1 and a constant d amount of time is spent. When $k > 0$, four recursive calls are made. These calls take $4t(k-1)$ time. In addition to this time, time is spent testing the `if` conditionals and tiling three nondefective squares.

Let this time be denoted by the constant c. We obtain the following recurrence for t:

$$t(k) = \begin{cases} d & k = 0 \\ 4t(k-1) + c & k > 0 \end{cases} \tag{19.7}$$

We may solve this recurrence using the substitution method (see Example 2.20) to obtain $t(k) = \Theta(4^k) = \Theta(\text{number of tiles needed})$. Since we must spend at least $\Theta(1)$ time placing each tile, we cannot obtain an asymptotically faster algorithm than divide and conquer.

19.2.2   Merge Sort

The Sort Method

We can apply the divide-and-conquer method to the sorting problem. In this problem we must sort n elements into nondecreasing order. The divide-and-conquer method suggests sorting algorithms with the following general structure: If n is 1, terminate; otherwise, partition the collection of elements into two or more subcollections; sort each; combine the sorted subcollections into a single sorted collection.

Suppose we limit ourselves to partitioning the n elements into two subcollections. Now we need to decide how to perform this partitioning. One possibility is to put the first $n-1$ elements into the first subcollection (say, A) and the last element into the second subcollection (say, B). A is sorted using this partitioning scheme recursively. Since B has only one element, it is already sorted. Following the sort of A, we need to combine A and B, using the method **insert** of Program 2.10. Comparing the resulting sort algorithm with **insertionSort** (Program 2.15), we see that we have really discovered the recursive version of insertion sort. The complexity of this sort algorithm is $O(n^2)$.

Another possibility for the two-way partitioning of n elements is to put the element with largest key in B and the remaining elements in A. Then A is sorted recursively. To combine the sorted A and B, we need merely append B to the sorted A. If we find the element with largest key using the function **Max** of Program 1.29, the resulting sort algorithm is a recursive formulation of **selectionSort** (Program 2.7). If we use a bubbling process (Program 2.8) to locate and move the element with largest key to the right-most position, the resulting algorithm is a recursive version of **bubbleSort** (Program 2.9). In either case the sort algorithm has complexity $\Theta(n^2)$. This complexity can be made $O(n^2)$ by terminating the recursive partitioning of A as soon as A is known to be in sorted order (see Examples 2.16 and 2.17).

The partitioning schemes used to arrive at the three preceding sort algorithms partitioned the n elements into two very unbalanced collections A and B. A has $n-1$ elements, while B has only 1 element. Let us see what happens when this partitioning is done in a more balanced way, that is, when A gets a fraction n/k of the elements and B gets the rest. Now both A and B are to be sorted by recursive application of the divide-and-conquer scheme. To combine the sorted A and B, we use a process called *merge*, which combines two sorted sequences into one.

Example 19.5 Consider the eight elements with keys [10, 4, 6, 3, 8, 2, 5, 7]. If we pick $k = 2$, then [10, 4, 6, 3] and [8, 2, 5, 7] are to be sorted independently. The result is [3, 4, 6, 10] and [2, 5, 7, 8]. To merge these two sorted sequences, we begin at the front of each. The smaller element, 2, is moved to the result sequence. Next 3 and 5 are compared, and 3 is moved to the result sequence. Then 4 and 5 are compared, and 4 is placed in the result sequence. Next 6 and 5 are compared, and so on.

If we pick $k = 4$, then the sequences [10, 4] and [6, 3, 8, 2, 5, 7] are to be sorted. The result of sorting these sequences independently is [4, 10] and [2, 3, 5, 6, 7, 8]. When these sorted sequences are merged, we obtain the desired eight-element sorted sequence. ∎

Figure 19.7 is a high-level statement of the divide-and-conquer sort algorithm that results when the number of smaller instances created is 2 and the partitioning is such that A gets n/k elements.

```
public static void sort(E, n)
{// Sort the n elements in E.  k is global.
   if (n >= k)
   {
      i = n / k;
      j = n - i;
      Let A consist of the first i elements in E.
      Let B consist of the remaining j elements in E.
      sort(A, i);
      sort(B, j);
      merge(A, B, E, i, j); // merge from A and B into E
   }
   else
      sort E using insertion sort.
}
```

Figure 19.7 Pseudocode for divide-and-conquer sort

From our brief description of merge, it is evident that n elements can be merged in $O(n)$ time. Let $t(n)$ be the worst-case time of the divide-and-conquer sort algorithm (Figure 19.7). We obtain the following recurrence for t

$$t(n) = \begin{cases} d & n < k \\ t(n/k) + t(n - n/k) + cn & n \geq k \end{cases} \tag{19.8}$$

where c and d are constants. From Equation 19.8 it follows that $t(n)$ is minimum when $t(n/k) + t(n - n/k)$ is minimum.

Theorem 19.1 *Let $f(x)$ satisfy*

$$f(y + d) - f(y) \geq f(z + d) - f(z) \tag{19.9}$$

for all $y \geq z$ and all positive d. For every real number w, $f(w/k) + f(w - w/k)$ is minimum when $k = 2$.

Proof Substituting $z = y - d$ into Equation 19.9, we get

$$f(y + d) - f(y) \geq f(y) - f(y - d)$$

or

$$2f(y) \leq f(y + d) + f(y - d) \tag{19.10}$$

Substituting $d = w/2 - w/k$ when $k \geq 2$, $d = w/k - w/2$ when $k < 2$, and $y = w/2$ into Equation 19.10, we get

$$2f(w/2) \leq f(w/k) + f(w - w/k) \qquad \blacksquare$$

Every sort algorithm has complexity $\Omega(n \log n)$ (see Section 19.4.2). Therefore, $f(n) = t(n)$ satisfies Equation 19.9, and the complexity of Figure 19.7 is minimum when $k = 2$, that is, when the two smaller instances are of approximately the same size. (Actually, a complexity of $\Omega(n)$ is sufficient to satisfy Equation 19.9.) *Divide-and-conquer algorithms usually have optimal performance when the smaller instances created are of approximately the same size.*

Setting $k = 2$ in the recurrence for $t(n)$, we get the following recurrence:

$$t(n) = \begin{cases} d & n \leq 1 \\ t(\lfloor n/2 \rfloor) + t(\lceil n/2 \rceil) + cn & n > 1 \end{cases}$$

The presence of the floor and ceiling operators makes this recurrence difficult to solve. We can overcome this difficulty by solving the recurrence only for values of n that are a power of 2. In this case the recurrence takes the simpler form

$$t(n) = \begin{cases} d & n \leq 1 \\ 2t(n/2) + cn & n > 1 \end{cases}$$

We can solve this recurrence using the substitution method, and the result is $t(n) = \Theta(n \log n)$. Although the recurrence that was solved is valid only when n is a power of 2, the asymptotic bound obtained is valid for all n because $t(n)$ is a nondecreasing function of n. Since $t(n) = \Theta(n \log n)$, this time represents the best- and worst-case complexity of merge sort. Further, since the best- and worst-case complexities are the same, the average complexity of merge sort is also given by $\Theta(n \log n)$.

Java Implementation

Figure 19.7 with $k = 2$ is the sorting method known as **merge sort** (or more precisely **two-way merge sort**). Let us now proceed to refine Figure 19.7 with $k = 2$ (i.e., merge sort) into a Java function to sort n elements. The easiest way to do this refinement is to represent the elements as a chain (i.e., as a member of the class Chain (Section 6.1)). In this case we divide E into two roughly equal lists by moving down to the $(n/2)$th node and breaking the chain. The merge procedure should be capable of merging together two sorted chains. We will not complete the refinement using chains, as we wish to compare the performance of the resulting Java code with those of heap sort and insertion sort. Neither of these latter sorting methods was coded using a linked representation for the collection of elements.

To be compatible with our earlier sort methods, the merge sort method must begin with the element collection E in an array a and return the sorted sequence in the same array. With this requirement the refinement of Figure 19.7 takes the following course. When E is divided in two, we can avoid copying both halves into A and B and simply keep track of the left and right ends of each half. We can then perform the merge with the sequences to be merged in a initially. We can merge the sequences into a new array b and then copy them back into a. The refined version of Figure 19.7 appears in Figure 19.8.

```
public static void mergeSort(Comparable [] a, int left, int right)
{// sort a[left:right]
   if (left < right)
   {// at least 2 elements
      int midddle = (left + right) / 2;
      mergeSort(a, left, middle);
      mergeSort(a, middle + 1, right);
      merge(a, b, left, middle, right); // merge from a to b
      copy(b, a, left, right);          // copy result back to a
   }
}
```

Figure 19.8 Divide-and-conquer sort refinement

We can improve the performance of Figure 19.8 in many ways. For example, we can easily eliminate the recursion. If we examine this program carefully, we see that the recursion simply divides the element list repeatedly until we are left with segments of size 1. The merging that takes place after this division into segments of size 1 is best described for the case when n is a power of 2. The segments of size 1 are merged to get sorted segments of size 2. These segments of size 2 are then merged to get sorted segments of size 4. The merge process is repeated until a single sorted sequence of size n remains. Figure 19.9 shows the merging (and copying) that takes place when $n = 8$. The square brackets denote the start and end of sorted segments.

initial segments	[8]	[4]	[5]	[6]	[2]	[1]	[7]	[3]
merge to b	[4	8]	[5	6]	[1	2]	[3	7]
copy to a	[4	8]	[5	6]	[1	2]	[3	7]
merge to b	[4	5	6	8]	[1	2	3	7]
copy to a	[4	5	6	8]	[1	2	3	7]
merge to b	[1	2	3	4	5	6	7	8]
copy to a	[1	2	3	4	5	6	7	8]

Figure 19.9 Merge sort example

An iterative version of merge sort begins by merging pairs of adjacent segments of size 1, then it merges pairs of adjacent segments of size 2, and so on. We can eliminate virtually all the copying from b to a by merging alternately from a to b and from b to a. The iterative merge sort algorithm appears in Program 19.3.

```
public static void mergeSort(Comparable [] a)
{
    Comparable [] b = new Comparable [a.length];
    int segmentSize = 1;
    while (segmentSize < a.length)
    {
        mergePass(a, b, segmentSize); // merge from a to b
        segmentSize += segmentSize;
        mergePass(b, a, segmentSize); // merge from b to a
        segmentSize += segmentSize;
    }
}
```

Program 19.3 Sort a[0:a.length-1] using merge sort

To complete our sorting code, we need to specify the method `mergePass`. In our Java development, the method `mergePass` (Program 19.4) simply determines the left and right ends of the segments to be merged. The actual merging of a pair of segments is done by the method `merge` (Program 19.5).

```
public static void mergePass(Comparable [] x, Comparable [] y,
                             int segmentSize)
{
   int i = 0;    // start of the next segment
   while (i <= x.length - 2 * segmentSize)
   {// merge two adjacent segments from x to y
      merge(x, y, i, i + segmentSize - 1, i + 2 * segmentSize - 1);
      i = i + 2 * segmentSize;
   }

   // fewer than 2 full segments remain
   if (i + segmentSize < x.length)
      // 2 segments remain
      merge(x, y, i, i + segmentSize - 1, x.length - 1);
   else
      // 1 segment remains, copy to y
      for (int j = i; j < x.length; j++)
         y[j] = x[j];
}
```

Program 19.4 Merge pairs of adjacent segments from x to y

Natural Merge Sort

The merge sort method of Program 19.3 is also known as `straight merge sort`. In a **natural merge sort**, we start by identifying the existing sorted segments within the input sequence. For example, the element list [4, 8, 3, 7, 1, 5, 6, 2] contains the sorted segments [4, 8], [3, 7], [1, 5, 6], and [2]. These segments may be identified by making a left-to-right scan of the element list, looking for positions i such that element i is larger than element $i+1$. Once the initial segments have been identified, we repeatedly merge passes over the segments until only one segment remains.

As noted above, the element list [4, 8, 3, 7, 1, 5, 6, 2] has four segments. Segments 1 and 2 are merged to get [3, 4, 7, 8], and segments 3 and 4 are merged to get [1, 2, 5, 6]. Finally, these two segments are merged to get the single sorted segment [1, 2, 3, 4, 5, 6, 7, 8]. Thus only two merge passes are made over the data. Program 19.3 would begin with segments of size 1 and make three merge passes.

```
public static void merge(Comparable [] c, Comparable [] d,
            int startOfFirst, int endOfFirst, int endOfSecond)
{
    int first = startOfFirst,       // cursor for first segment
        second = endOfFirst + 1,    // cursor for second
        result = startOfFirst;      // cursor for result

    // merge until one segment is done
    while ((first <= endOfFirst) && (second <= endOfSecond))
        if (c[first].compareTo(c[second]) <= 0)
            d[result++] = c[first++];
        else
            d[result++] = c[second++];

    // take care of leftovers
    if (first > endOfFirst)
        for (int q = second; q <= endOfSecond; q++)
            d[result++] = c[q];
    else
        for (int q = first; q <= endOfFirst; q++)
            d[result++] = c[q];
}
```

Program 19.5 Merge two adjacent segments from c to d

The best case for natural merge sort is when the input element list is already sorted. Natural merge sort would identify exactly one sorted segment and make no merge passes, while Program 19.3 would make $\lceil \log_2 n \rceil$ merge passes. So natural merge sort would complete in $\Theta(n)$ time, while Program 19.3 would take $\Theta(n \log n)$ time.

The worst case for natural merge sort is when the input elements are in decreasing order of their keys. With this input, n initial segments are identified; both merge sort and natural merge sort make the same number of passes, but natural merge sort has a higher overhead in keeping track of segment boundaries. The worst-case performance of natural merge sort is worse than that of straight merge sort.

On average, we expect a list of n elements to have $n/2$ segments because, on average, the ith key is larger than the $i + 1$st key with probability 0.5. Starting with half as many segments, natural merge sort is expected to make one fewer merge pass than is made by straight merge sort. However, the time saved is offset by the cost of the initial sorted segment-finding pass and the added cost of keeping track of segment boundaries. Because of these observations, natural merge sort is recommended only in situations where we expect the input data to have few segments.

19.2.3   Quick Sort

The Sort Method

We can also use the divide-and-conquer approach to arrive at another totally different sort method called **quick sort**. In this method the n elements to be sorted are partitioned into three segments (or groups)—a left segment *left*, a middle segment *middle*, and a right segment *right*. The middle segment contains exactly one element; no element in *left* has a key larger than the key of the element in *middle*; and no element in *right* has a key that is smaller than that of the middle element. As a result, the elements in *left* and *middle* can be sorted independently, and no merge is required following the sorting of *left* and *right*. The element in *middle* is called the **pivot** or **partitioning element**. The sort method is described more precisely by the code of Figure 19.10.

```
// Sort a[0:a.length-1] using quick sort.
```
   Select an element from a[0:a.length-1] for *middle*. This element is the pivot.
   Partition the remaining elements into the segments *left* and *right* so that
       no element in *left* has a key larger than that of the pivot and
       no element in *right* has a key smaller than that of the pivot.
   Sort *left* using quick sort recursively.
   Sort *right* using quick sort recursively.
   The answer is *left* followed by *middle* followed by *right*.

Figure 19.10 High-level statement of quick sort

Consider the element list [4, 8, 3, 7, 1, 5, 6, 2]. Suppose we pick the element with key 6 as the pivot. Then 6 is in *middle*; 4, 3, 1, 5, and 2 are in *left*; and 8 and 7 are in *right*. When *left* has been sorted, the keys are in the order 1, 2, 3, 4, 5. When *right* has been sorted, its keys are in the order 7, 8. Putting the elements in *right* after the element in *middle* and those in *left* before the one in *middle*, we get the sorted sequence [1, 2, 3, 4, 5, 6, 7, 8]. The left segment [4, 3, 1, 5, 2], for example, is sorted recursively. We start by selecting a pivot; then the segment is partitioned into the three subsegments *left*, *middle*, and *right*; and the *left* and *right* subsegments are sorted recursively. If 3 is selected as the pivot, *left* contains 1 and 2, *middle* is 3, and *right* contains 4 and 5. When the sorted left segment, the middle segment, and the sorted right segment are concatenated, we get the sorted segment [1, 2, 3, 4, 5].

Java Implementation

The public method `quickSort` (Program 19.6) sets the class data member `Quick-sort.a`, which is an array of type `Comparable`; moves the largest element of the element array `a` to the right-most position of the array; and invokes the private recursive method `quickSort` (Program 19.7), which does the actual sorting. We move the largest element to the right-most position because our element partitioning scheme (Program 19.7) requires that each segment either has its largest element on the right or is followed by an element that is $\geq$ all elements in the segment; in case this condition is not satisfied, the first do loop of Program 19.7 throws an `IndexOutOfBoundsException` when the pivot is the largest element, for example.

```java
/** sort a[0 : a.length - 1] using the quick sort method */
public static void quickSort(Comparable [] a)
{
   QuickSort.a = a;
   if (a.length <= 1) return;
   // move largest element to right end
   MyMath.swap(a, a.length - 1, MyMath.max(a, a.length - 1));
   quickSort(0, a.length - 2);
}
```

Program 19.6 Driver for recursive quick sort method

The partitioning of the element list into *left*, *middle*, and *right* is done in place (Program 19.7). In this implementation the pivot is always the element at the left end of the segment that is to be sorted. Other choices that result in improved performance are possible. One such choice is discussed later in this section.

Program 19.7 remains correct when we change the $<$ and $>$ in the conditionals of the `do-while` statements to `<=` and `>=`, respectively (provided the right-most element of a segment is larger than the pivot). Experiments suggest that the average performance of quick sort is better when it is coded as in Program 19.6. All attempts to eliminate the recursion from this procedure result in the introduction of a stack. The last recursive call, however, can be eliminated without the introduction of a stack. We leave the elimination of this recursive call as Exercise 21.

Complexity Analysis

Let $n = $ `a.length`. Program 19.6 requires $O(n)$ recursion stack space. The space requirements can be reduced to $O(\log n)$ by simulating the recursion using a stack. In this simulation the smaller of the two segments *left* and *right* is sorted first. The boundaries of the other segment are put on the stack.

```
/** sort a[leftEnd:rightEnd], a[rightEnd+1] >= a[leftEnd:rightEnd] */
private static void quickSort(int leftEnd, int rightEnd)
{
   if (leftEnd >= rightEnd) return;

   int leftCursor = leftEnd,          // left-to-right cursor
       rightCursor = rightEnd + 1;  // right-to-left cursor
   Comparable pivot = a[leftEnd];

   // swap elements >= pivot on left side
   // with elements <= pivot on right side
   while (true)
   {
      do
      {// find >= element on left side
         leftCursor++;
      } while (a[leftCursor].compareTo(pivot) < 0);

      do
      {// find <= element on right side
         rightCursor--;
      } while (a[rightCursor].compareTo(pivot) > 0);

      if (leftCursor >= rightCursor) break;  // swap pair not found
      MyMath.swap(a, leftCursor, rightCursor);
   }

   // place pivot
   a[leftEnd] = a[rightCursor];
   a[rightCursor] = pivot;

   quickSort(leftEnd, rightCursor - 1);   // sort left segment
   quickSort(rightCursor + 1, rightEnd);  // sort right segment
}
```

Program 19.7 Recursive quick sort method

The worst-case computing time for quick sort is $\Theta(n^2)$, and it is achieved, for instance, when *left* is always empty. However, if we are lucky and *left* and *right* are always of about the same size, then the complexity is $\Theta(n \log n)$. Therefore, the best-case complexity of quick sort is $\Theta(n \log n)$ (Exercise 24). Surprisingly, the average complexity of quick sort is also $\Theta(n \log n)$.

Theorem 19.2 *The average complexity of* quickSort *is* $\Theta(n \log n)$ *where n is the number of elements to be sorted.*

Proof Let $t(n)$ denote the average time needed to sort an n-element array. When $n \leq 1$, $t(n) \leq d$ for some constant d. Suppose that $n > 1$. Let s be the size of the left segment following the partitioning of the elements. Because the pivot element is in the middle segment, the size of the right segment is $n - s - 1$. The average times to sort the left and right segments are $t(s)$ and $t(n - s - 1)$, respectively. The time needed to partition the elements is bounded by cn where c is a constant. Since s can have any of the n values 0 through $n - 1$ with equal probability, we obtain the following recurrence:

$$t(n) \leq cn + \frac{1}{n} \sum_{s=0}^{n-1} [t(s) + t(n - s - 1)]$$

We can simplify this recurrence as follows:

$$t(n) \leq cn + \frac{2}{n} \sum_{s=0}^{n-1} t(s) \leq cn + \frac{4d}{n} + \frac{2}{n} \sum_{s=2}^{n-1} t(s) \qquad (19.11)$$

Now using induction on n we show that $t(n) \leq kn \log_e n$ for $n > 1$ and $k = 2(c + d)$. Here $e \approx 2.718$ is the base of natural logarithms. The induction base covers the case $n = 2$. From Equation 19.11 we obtain $t(2) \leq 2c + 2d \leq kn \log_e 2$. For the induction hypothesis we assume $t(n) \leq kn \log_e n$ for $2 \leq n < m$ where m is an arbitrary integer that is greater than 2. In the induction step we need to prove $t(m) \leq km \log_e m$. From Equation 19.11 and the induction hypothesis, we obtain

$$t(m) \leq cm + \frac{4d}{m} + \frac{2}{m} \sum_{s=2}^{m-1} t(s) \leq cm + \frac{4d}{m} + \frac{2k}{m} \sum_{s=2}^{m-1} s \log_e s \qquad (19.12)$$

To proceed further we use the following facts:

- $s \log_e s$ is an increasing function of s.

- $\int_2^m s \log_e s\, ds < \frac{m^2 \log_e m}{2} - \frac{m^2}{4}$.

Using these facts and Equation 19.12, we obtain

$$\begin{aligned}
t(m) \quad &< \quad cm + \frac{4d}{m} + \frac{2k}{m} \int_2^m s \log_e s\, ds \\
&< \quad cm + \frac{4d}{m} + \frac{2k}{m} \left[\frac{m^2 \log_e m}{2} - \frac{m^2}{4} \right]
\end{aligned}$$

$$= \quad cm + \frac{4d}{m} + km \log_e m - \frac{km}{2}$$
$$< \quad km \log_e m$$

So the average complexity of `quickSort` is $O(n \log n)$. In Section 19.4.2 we show that the complexity of every comparison sort method (including `quickSort`) is $\Omega(n \log n)$. Therefore, the average complexity of `quickSort` is $\Theta(n \log n)$. ∎

The table of Figure 19.11 compares the average and worst-case complexities of the sort methods developed in this book.

Method	Worst	Average
bubble sort	n^2	n^2
count sort	n^2	n^2
insertion sort	n^2	n^2
selection sort	n^2	n^2
heap sort	$n \log n$	$n \log n$
merge sort	$n \log n$	$n \log n$
quick sort	n^2	$n \log n$

Figure 19.11 Comparison of sort methods

Median-of-Three Quick Sort

Our implementation of quick sort exhibits its worst-case performance when presented with a sorted list. It is distressing to have a sort program that takes more time on a sorted list than on an unsorted one. We can remedy this problem and, at the same time, improve the average performance of quick sort by selecting the pivot element using the **median-of-three rule**.

In a median-of-three quick sort, the pivot is chosen to be the median of the three elements {`a[leftEnd]`, `a[(leftEnd+rightEnd)/2]`, `a[rightEnd]`}. For example, if these elements have keys {5, 9, 7}, then `a[rightEnd]` is used as the value of `pivot`. To implement the median-of-three rule, it is easiest to swap the element in the median position with that at `a[leftEnd]` and then proceed as in Program 19.6. If `a[rightEnd]` is the median element, then we swap `a[leftEnd]` and `a[rightEnd]` just before `pivot` is set to `a[leftEnd]` in Program 19.7 and proceed as in the remainder of the code.

When the median-of-three rule is used, quick sort takes $O(n \log n)$ time when the input list is in sorted order. Moreover, the case when one of the two partitions is empty is eliminated (except when we have duplicates). In other words, the median-of-three rule ensures a better balance between the two partitions. Is this improvement in balance enough to pay for the added cost of computing the pivot? Only an experiment can answer this question.

Performance Measurement

The observed average times for `quickSort` appear in Figure 19.12. These times are for Program 19.6 with the pivot being the first element of the segment. This figure includes the average times for merge, heap, and insertion sort. For each n at least 100 randomly generated integer instances were run. These random instances were constructed by making repeated calls to the method `Math.random`. If the time taken to sort these instances was less than 1 second (see Section 4.4), then additional random instances were sorted until the total time taken was at least this much. The times reported in Figure 19.12 include the time taken to set up the random data. For each n the time taken to set up the data and the time for the remaining overheads included in the reported numbers is the same for all sort methods. As a result, the data of Figure 19.12 is useful for comparative purposes. The data of this figure, for n ≤ 100, is plotted in Figure 19.13.

As Figure 19.13 shows, quick sort outperforms the other sort methods for suitably large n. We see that the break-even point between insertion and quick sort is a little below 20. The exact break-even point can be found experimentally by obtaining run-time data for n = 15, 16, 17, 18, and 19. Let the exact break-even point be `nBreak`. For average performance, insertion sort is the best sort method (of those tested) to use when n ≤ `nBreak`, and quick sort is the best when n > `nBreak`. We can improve on the performance of quick sort for n > `nBreak` by combining insertion and quick sort into a single sort function by replacing the following statement in Program 19.6

```
if (leftEnd >= rightEnd) return;
```

with the code

```
if (rightEnd - leftEnd < nBreak)
{
   insertionSort(a, leftEnd, rightEnd);
   return;
}
```

Here `insertionSort(a, leftEnd, rightEnd)` is a method that sorts a[leftEnd: rightEnd], using the insertion sort method. The performance measurement of the modified quick sort code is left as Exercise 28. Further improvement in performance may be possible by replacing `nBreak` with a smaller value (see Exercise 28).

For worst-case behavior most implementations will show merge sort to be best for n > c where c is some constant. For n ≤ c insertion sort has the best worst-case behavior. The performance of merge sort can be improved by combining insertion sort and merge sort (see Exercise 29).

n	Insert	Heap	Merge	Quick
0	0.09	0.10	0.09	0.09
10	0.12	0.13	0.13	0.12
20	0.14	0.16	0.16	0.15
30	0.18	0.20	0.20	0.18
40	0.22	0.24	0.24	0.22
50	0.27	0.29	0.27	0.26
60	0.33	0.33	0.32	0.31
70	0.40	0.37	0.37	0.33
80	0.48	0.41	0.41	0.37
90	0.56	0.47	0.45	0.41
100	0.65	0.51	0.49	0.44
200	1.99	1.03	0.93	0.86
300	4.08	1.55	1.45	1.29
400	6.90	2.13	1.95	1.75
500	10.70	2.71	2.43	2.23
600	18.15	3.33	3.01	2.73
700	20.60	3.90	3.56	3.50
800	26.90	4.52	4.12	3.67
900	34.35	5.25	4.62	4.38
1000	42.30	5.75	5.20	4.73

Times are in milliseconds

Figure 19.12 Average times for sort methods

The run-time results for the sort methods point out some of the limitations of asymptotic complexity analysis. Asymptotic analysis is not a good predictor of performance for small instances—insertion sort with its $O(n^2)$ complexity is better than all of the $O(n \log n)$ methods for small instances. Programs that have the same asymptotic complexity often have different actual run times.

Java's Sort Method

If you had to develop the sort method `java.util.arrays.sort`, what would you do? The results of Figures 19.12 and 19.13 leave you in a quandary. Should you pick a method that optimizes worst-case performance, or should you pick one that optimizes average performance? Should you limit your choice to a sort method that is stable (i.e., a method that does not alter the relative order of equal elements)?

The developers of Java's sort method opted to optimize average performance and use quick sort when sorting arrays of a primitive data type. To reduce the impact of the quadratic worst-case performance of quick sort, they used a more

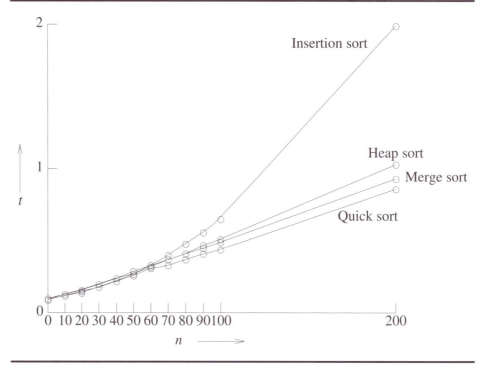

Figure 19.13 Plot of average times (milliseconds)

sophisticated method to determine the pivot. Java's sort method sorts segments of size less than 7 using insertion sort; larger segments are sorted using quick sort. When the segment size is between 7 and 40, the pivot is selected using the median-of-three rule; but when the segment size is more than 40, a pseudo median-of-nine rule is used to select the pivot. In the pseudo median-of-nine rule, nine equally spaced elements are sampled; these nine samples are grouped into three groups of three samples each, and the median of each group is computed. The pivot is the median of the three group medians.

When sorting an array of elements whose data type is a subclass of `Object` (essentially all data types you might define), `java.util.arrays.sort` uses a modified merge sort and so guarantees $O(n \log n)$ performance. The modified merge sort skips the merging of two segments when the last element of the first segment is $\leq$ the first element of the second segment.

So when you sort elements of a primitive data type, you use a sort method that is not stable; but nonprimitive data types are sorted using a stable sort.

19.2.4   Selection

Problem Description

In this problem we are given an array $a[0 : n-1]$ of n elements and are to determine the kth smallest element. This element is the element in position a[k-1] following a sort of the array. Consider the case $n = 8$; each element has the two fields, key and id, where key is an integer and id is a character. Let the eight elements be $[(12, a), (4, b), (5, c), (4, d), (5, e), (10, f), (2, g), (20, h)]$. Then suppose that following a sort we have the array $[(2, g), (4, d), (4, b), (5, c), (5, e), (10, f), (12, a), (20, h)]$. If k = 1, we return the element with id g; if k = 8, we return the element with id h; if k = 6, we return the element with id f; and if k = 2, we return the element with id d. Actually, in this last case we have some flexibility, as the sort could have placed either of the elements with ids d and b into a[1], because both have the same key. Therefore, either may be returned. However, if one element is returned when k = 2, the other should be returned when k = 3.

One application of the selection problem is finding the median element. In this case $k = \lceil n/2 \rceil$. Medians are useful statistical quantities that are reported often in the media, for example, median salary, median age, and median height. Other values of k are also useful. For example, we can divide a population into quartiles by finding the $n/4$, $n/2$, and $3n/4$ elements.

Solution Strategy and Implementation

We can solve the selection problem in $O(n \log n)$ time by first sorting the n elements (for example, using heap sort or merge sort) and then picking off the element in position a[k-1]. We can obtain better average performance by using quick sort (see Figure 19.12), even though this method has an inferior asymptotic complexity of $O(n^2)$.

We can adapt the code of Program 19.6 to the selection problem so as to obtain an even faster solution. If the pivot a[leftEnd] is to be placed in a[j] following the execution of the two while loops, then a[leftEnd] is known to be the j-leftEnd+1th element of a[leftEnd:rightEnd]. If we are looking for the kth element in a[leftEnd:rightEnd] and j-leftEnd+1 equals k, then the answer is a[leftEnd]; if j-leftEnd+1 < k, then the element we are looking for is the k-j+leftEnd-1th element of *right*; otherwise, it is the kth element of *left*. Therefore, we need to make either zero or one recursive call. The code for the new selection program appears in Programs 19.8 and 19.9. A for or while loop can replace the recursive calls made by select (see Exercise 35).

Complexity Analysis

The worst-case complexity of Program 19.8 is $\Theta(n^2)$. This worst case is achieved, for example, when *left* is always empty and the kth element is in *right*. However, if

```
/** @return k'th smallest element in a[0 : a.length - 1] */
public static Comparable select(Comparable [] a, int k)
{
   if (k < 1 || k > a.length)
      throw new IllegalArgumentException
                  ("k must be between 1 and a.length");

   Select.a = a;
   // move largest element to right end
   MyMath.swap(a, a.length - 1, MyMath.max(a, a.length - 1));
   return select(0, a.length - 1, k);
}
```

Program 19.8 Preprocessor to find the kth element

left and *right* are always of the same size or differ in size by at most 1, then we get the following recurrence for the time needed by Program 19.8:

$$t(n) \leq \begin{cases} d & n \leq 1 \\ t(\lfloor n/2 \rfloor) + cn & n > 1 \end{cases} \tag{19.13}$$

If we assume that n is a power of 2, the floor operator may be dropped and the recurrence solved, using the substitution method, to obtain $t(n) = \Theta(n)$. By selecting the partitioning element more carefully, the worst-case time also becomes $\Theta(n)$. The more careful way to select the partitioning element is to use the **median-of-medians** rule in which the n elements of a are divided into $\lfloor n/r \rfloor$ groups for some integer constant r. Each of these groups contains exactly r elements. The remaining $n \bmod r$ elements are not used in the selection of the pivot. Next we find the median of each group by sorting the r elements in each group and then selecting the one in the middle position (i.e., in position $\lceil r/2 \rceil$). The median of these $\lfloor n/r \rfloor$ medians is computed, using the selection algorithm recursively, and is used as the partitioning element.

Example 19.6 [Median of Medians] Consider the case $r = 5$, $n = 27$, and $a = [2, 6, 8, 1, 4, 9, 20, 6, 22, 11, 9, 8, 4, 3, 7, 8, 16, 11, 10, 8, 2, 14, 15, 1, 12, 5, 4]$. These 27 elements may be divided into the five groups $[2, 6, 8, 1, 4]$, $[9, 20, 6, 22, 11]$, $[9, 8, 4, 3, 7]$, $[8, 16, 11, 10, 8]$, and $[2, 14, 15, 1, 12]$. The remaining elements, 5 and 4, are not used when selecting the pivot. The medians of these five groups are 4, 11, 7, 10, and 12, respectively. The median of the elements $[4, 11, 7, 10, 12]$ is 10. This median is used as the partitioning element. With this choice of the pivot, we get *left* $= [2, 6, 8, 1, 4, 9, 6, 9, 8, 4, 3, 7, 8, 8, 2, 1, 5, 4]$, *middle* $= [10]$, and *right* $= [20, 22, 11, 16, 11, 14, 15, 12]$. If we are to find the kth element for $k < 19$, only

```
/** @return k'th element in a[leftEnd:rightEnd] */
private static Comparable select(int leftEnd, int rightEnd, int k)
{
   if (leftEnd >= rightEnd) return a[leftEnd];
   int leftCursor = leftEnd,      // left-to-right cursor
       rightCursor = rightEnd + 1;  // right-to-left cursor
   Comparable pivot = a[leftEnd];

   // swap elements >= pivot on left side
   // with elements <= pivot on right side
   while (true)
   {
      do
      {// find >= element on left side
         leftCursor++;
      } while (a[leftCursor].compareTo(pivot) < 0);

      do
      {// find <= element on right side
         rightCursor--;
      } while (a[rightCursor].compareTo(pivot) > 0);

      if (leftCursor >= rightCursor) break;  // swap pair not found
      MyMath.swap(a, leftCursor, rightCursor);
   }

   if (rightCursor - leftEnd + 1 == k) return pivot;

   // place pivot
   a[leftEnd] = a[rightCursor];
   a[rightCursor] = pivot;

   // recursive call on one segment
   if (rightCursor - leftEnd + 1 < k)
      return select(rightCursor + 1, rightEnd,
                    k - rightCursor + leftEnd - 1);
   else return select(leftEnd, rightCursor - 1, k);
}
```

Program 19.9 Recursive method to find the kth element

left needs to be examined; if $k = 19$, the element is the pivot; and if $k > 19$, the eight elements of *right* need to be examined. In this last case we need to find the $k - 19$th element of *right*. ∎

Theorem 19.3 *When the partitioning element is chosen using the median-of-medians rule, the following statements are true:*

(a) *If $r = 9$, then $\max\{|left|, |right|\} \leq 7n/8$ for $n \geq 90$.*

(b) *If $r = 5$ and all elements of a are distinct, then $\max\{|left|, |right|\} \leq 3n/4$ for $n \geq 24$.*

Proof Exercise 33 asks you to prove this theorem. ∎

From Theorem 19.3 and Program 19.8, it follows that if the median-of-medians rule with $r = 9$ is used, the time $t(n)$ needed to select the kth element is given by the following recurrence:

$$t(n) = \begin{cases} cn \log n & n < 90 \\ t(\lfloor n/9 \rfloor) + t(\lfloor 7n/8 \rfloor) + cn & n \geq 90 \end{cases} \qquad (19.14)$$

where c is a constant. This recurrence assumes that an $n \log n$ method is used when $n < 90$ and that larger instances are solved using divide and conquer with the median-of-medians rule. Using induction, you can show (Exercise 34) that $t(n) \leq 72cn$ for $n \geq 1$. When the elements are distinct, we may use $r = 5$ to get linear-time performance.

19.2.5   Closest Pair of Points

Problem Description

In this problem you are given n points (x_i, y_i), $1 \leq i \leq n$, and are to find two that are closest. The distance between two points i and j is given by the following formula:

$$\sqrt{(x_i - x_j)^2 + (y_i - y_j)^2}$$

Example 19.7 Suppose that n equal-size holes are to be drilled into a sheet of metal. If any two holes are too close, metal failure may occur during the drilling process. By determining the minimum distance between any two holes, we can assess the probabilty of such a failure. This minimum distance corresponds to the distance between a closest pair of points. ∎

Solution Strategy

We can solve the closest-pair-of-points problem in $O(n^2)$ time by examining all $n(n-1)/2$ pairs of points, computing the distance between the points in each pair, and determining the pair for which this distance is minimum. We will call this method the *direct approach*. The divide-and-conquer method suggests the high-level algorithm of Figure 19.14.

```
if (n is small)
{
    Find the closest pair using the direct approach.
    return;
}

// n is large
Divide the point set into two roughly equal parts A and B.
Determine the closest pairs of points in A and B.
Determine the closest point pair such that one point is in A and the other in B.
From the three closest pairs computed, select the one with least distance.
```

Figure 19.14 Finding a closest pair of points

This algorithm uses the direct approach to solve small instances and solves large instances by dividing them into two smaller instances. One instance (say, A) will be of size $\lceil n/2 \rceil$, and the other (say, B) of size $\lfloor n/2 \rfloor$. The closest pair of points in the original instance falls into one of the three categories: (1) both points are in A (i.e., it is a closest pair of A); (2) both points are in B; and (3) one point is in A, and the other in B. Suppose we determine the closest pair in each of these categories. The pair with the least distance is the overall closest pair. The closest pair in category 1 can be determined by using the closest-pair algorithm recursively on the smaller point set A. The closest pair in B can be similarly determined.

To determine the closest pair in category 3, we need a different method. The method depends on how the points are divided into A and B. A reasonable way to do this division is to cut the plane by a vertical line that goes through the median x_i value. All points to the left of this line are in A; all to the right are in B; and those on the line are distributed between A and B so as to meet the size requirements on A and B.

Example 19.8 Consider the 14 points a through n of Figure 19.15(a). These points are plotted in Figure 19.15(b). The median $x_i = 1$, and the vertical line $x = 1$ is shown as a broken line in Figure 19.15(b). The points to the left of this line (i.e., points b, c, h, and n) are in A, and those to the right of the line (i.e., points a, e, f, j, k, and l) are in B. Of the points d, g, and m that are on the line, two are added to A and one to B so that A and B have seven points each. Suppose that d and m are assigned to A, and g is assigned to B. ■

label	a	b	c	d	e	f	g
x_i	2	0.5	0.25	1	3	2	1
y_i	2	0.5	1	2	1	0.7	1
label	h	i	j	k	l	m	n
x_i	0.6	0.9	2	4	1.1	1	0.7
y_i	0.8	0.5	1	2	0.5	1.5	2

(a) The 14 points

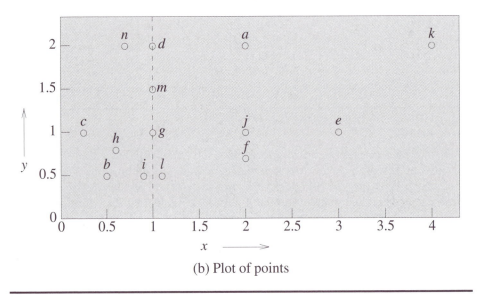

(b) Plot of points

Figure 19.15 Fourteen-point instance

Let δ be the smaller of the distances between the points in the closest pairs of A and B. For a pair in category 3 to be closer than δ, each point of the pair must be less than distance δ from the dividing line. Therefore, we can eliminate from consideration all points that are a distance $\geq \delta$ from this line. The broken line of Figure 19.16 is the dividing line. The shaded box has width 2δ and is centered at the dividing line. Points on or outside the boundary of this box are eliminated. Only the points inside the shaded region need be retained when determining whether there is a category 3 pair with distance less than δ.

Let R_A and R_B, respectively, denote the points of A and B that remain. If there is a point pair (p, q) such that $p \in A$, $q \in B$, and p and q are less than δ apart,

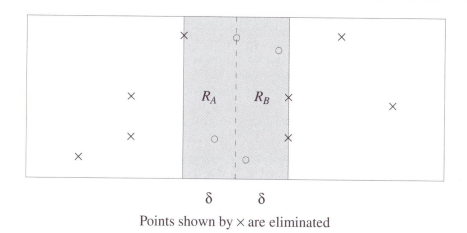

δ δ

Points shown by × are eliminated

Figure 19.16 Eliminating points that are too far from the dividing line

then $p \in R_A$ and $q \in R_B$. We can find this point pair by considering the points in R_A one at a time. Suppose that we are considering point p of R_A and that p's y-coordinate is $p.y$. We need to look only at points q in R_B with y-coordinate $q.y$ such that $p.y - \delta < q.y < p.y + \delta$ and see whether any point is less than distance δ from p. The region of R_B that contains these points q appears in Figure 19.17(a). Only the points of R_B within the shaded $\delta \times 2\delta$ box need be paired with p to see whether p is part of a category **3** pair with distance less than δ. This $\delta \times 2\delta$ region is p's **comparing region**.

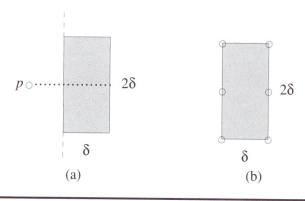

2δ 2δ

δ δ

(a)   (b)

Figure 19.17 Comparing region for p

Example 19.9 Consider the 14 points of Example 19.8. The closest point pair in A (see Example 19.8) is (b, h) with a distance of approximately 0.316. The closest point pair in B is (f, j) with a distance of 0.3. Therefore, $\delta = 0.3$. When determining whether there is a category 3 pair with distance less than δ, all points other than d, g, i, l, and m are eliminated from consideration, as each is $\geq \delta$ distant from the dividing line that has x-cordinate 1. We have $R_A = \{d, i, m\}$ and $R_B = \{g, l\}$. Since there are no points in the comparing regions of d and g, only point i needs to be considered further. The comparing region of i contains only point l. We compute the distance between i and l and find that it is less than δ. (i, l) is therefore the closest pair. ∎

Since all points on the boundary of or inside the $\delta \times 2\delta$ comparing region are at least δ apart, the number of such points cannot exceed six. Figure 19.17(b) shows the only way to place six points while satisfying the minimum distance δ requirement. So each point of R_A is paired with at most six points of R_B when determining a closer category 3 pair.

Choice of Data Structures

To implement the divide-and-conquer algorithm of Figure 19.14, we need to decide what exactly is a "small" instance and also decide how to represent the points. Since the closest pair of a set of fewer than 2 points is not defined, we must ensure that our division process does not create sets of size less than 2. The creation of sets with fewer than two points can be avoided if our divide-and-conquer algorithm considers sets with fewer than four points as small.

Our implementation utilizes four classes to represent points. The class `Point` has two data members x and y to store the x- and y-coordinates of a point, and both x and y are of type `double`. The class `Point1` derives from `Point` and adds the additional data member id, which is of type `int`. The class `Point1` implements the interface `Comparable`, comparing two points by their x-coordinates alone. This implementation of `Comparable` allows us to use merge sort (Program 19.3) to sort the points into ascending order of x-coordinate. The third class for points is `Point2`. This class also derives from `Point`, and adds the integer data member p whose significance is described below. The class `Point2` implements the interface `Comparable` comparing two points by their y-coordinate alone. This implementation of `Comparable` allows us to use merge sort (Program 19.3) to sort the points into ascending order of y-coordinate. The fourth and last point class is `PointPair`. This class has the data members a (first point in the pair), b (second point in the pair), and dist (distance between the points a and b). a and b are of type `Point1`, and dist is of type `double`.

The input points may be represented in an array x of type `Point1`. Suppose that the points in x have been sorted by their x-coordinate. If at any stage of the division process the points under consideration are x[$l : r$], then we may obtain A and B by first computing $m = (l + r)/2$. The points X[$l : m$] are in A, and the remaining points are in B.

After we compute the closest pairs in A and B, we need to compute R_A and R_B and then determine whether there is a closer pair with one point in R_A and the other in R_B. The test of Figure 19.17 may be implemented in a simple way if the points are sorted by their y-coordinate. A list of the points sorted by y-coordinate is maintained in another array using the class Point2. Notice that for this class, the methods of Comparable have been implemented so as to facilitate sorting by y-coordinate. The field p is used to index back to the same point in the array x.

Java Implementation

With the necessary data structures determined, let us examine the resulting code. First we define a method dist (Program 19.10) that computes the distance between two points a and b. Notice that Program 19.10 may also be used to compute the distance between points of type Point1 and Point2 because the class Point is the superclass of Point1 and Point2.

```
public static double dist(Point u, Point v)
{
    double dx = u.x - v.x;
    double dy = u.y - v.y;
    return Math.sqrt(dx * dx + dy * dy);
}
```

Program 19.10 Computing the distance between two points

The public method closestPair (Program 19.11) returns null if the number of points is fewer than 2. When the number of points exceeds 1, the method returns the closest pair of points. Method closestPair begins by verifying that we have at least two points. Then the points in x are sorted by x-coordinate, using mergeSort (Program 19.3). Next the points are copied into an array y and sorted by y-coordinate. Following this sort, $y[i].y \le y[i+1].y$, and for each i, $y[i].p$ gives point i's location in the array x. After this preprocessing, we invoke the private method closestPair (Program 19.12), which does the actual determination of the closest pair.

The private method closestPair (Program 19.12) determines the closest pair from among the points $x[l:r]$. These points are assumed to be sorted by their x-coordinate. $y[l:r]$ is the same points sorted by their y-coordinate. $z[l:r]$ is available as space for temporary results. Upon completion the closest pair of points is returned as an instance of PointPair, and the array y is restored to its input status. The method does not modify the array x.

We begin by taking care of small instances; that is, instances with fewer than four points. Since no instance of size less than two is created by the division process,

```
/** @return closest pair of points in array x
  * @return null if fewer than two points in x */
public static PointPair closestPair(Point1 [] x)
{
    if (x.length < 2) return null;

    // sort on x-coordinate
    MergeSort.mergeSort(x);

    // create a point array sorted on y-coordinate
    Point2 [] y = new Point2 [x.length];
    for (int i = 0; i < x.length; i++)
        // copy point i from x to y and index it
        y[i] = new Point2(x[i].x, x[i].y, i);
    MergeSort.mergeSort(y);  // sort on y-coordinate

    // create a temporary array
    Point2 [] z = new Point2 [x.length];

    // find closest pair
    return closestPair(x, y, z, 0, x.length - 1);
}
```

Program 19.11 The public method ClosestPoints.closestPair

we need to handle the cases of two and three points. These cases are handled by trying out all possibilities. When the number of points exceeds 3, the instance is divided into two smaller instances A and B by computing m = (l+r)/2. The points x[l:m] are in A, and the points x[m+1:r] are in B. The corresponding sorted-by-y lists are created in z[l:m] and z[m+1:r] from the sorted-by-y list y[l:r] by scanning the list y from left to right and determining which points are in A and which in B. The roles of the arrays y and z are interchanged, and two recursive calls are made to obtain the closest pairs in A and B. Upon return from these recursive calls, array z is guaranteed to be unaltered, but array y is not. However, only y[l:r] may have changed. y[l:r] is reconstructed from z[l:r] by merging (Program 19.5) the sublists corresponding to A and B.

To implement the test of Figure 19.17, we first scan the array segment y[l:r] that contains the points under consideration sorted by y and accumulate points that are $< \delta$ from the dividing line (see Figure 19.16) in sorted order of y-coordinate in another array z[l:k-1]. The pairing of each point p of R_A with all points in its comparing region of R_B is divided into two parts: (1) pairing with points in the

```
/** @param x[l:r] points sorted by x-coordinate, r > 1
 * @param y[l:r] points sorted by y-coordinate
 * @param z[l:r] is used for work space
 * @return closest pair of points in x[l:r] */
private static PointPair closestPair(Point1 [] x, Point2 [] y,
                                     Point2 [] z, int l, int r)
{
   if (r - l == 1)  // only two points
      return new PointPair(x[l], x[r], dist(x[l], x[r]));

   if (r - l == 2)
   {// three points
      // compute distance between all pairs
      double d1 = dist(x[l], x[l + 1]);
      double d2 = dist(x[l + 1], x[r]);
      double d3 = dist(x[l], x[r]);
      // find closest pair
      if (d1 <= d2 && d1 <= d3)
         return new PointPair(x[l], x[l + 1], d1);
      if (d2 <= d3)
         return new PointPair(x[l + 1], x[r], d2);
      else
         return new PointPair(x[l], x[r], d3);
   }

   // more than three points, divide into two
   int m = (l + r) / 2;     // x[l:m] in A, rest in B

   // create sorted-by-y lists in z[l:m] & z[m+1:r]
   int f = l,       // cursor for z[l:m]
       g = m + 1;   // cursor for z[m+1:r]
   for (int i = l; i <= r; i++)
      if (y[i].p > m) z[g++] = y[i];
      else z[f++] = y[i];

   // solve the two parts
   PointPair best = closestPair(x, z, y, l, m);
   PointPair right = closestPair(x, z, y, m + 1, r);

   // make best closer pair of the two
   if (right.dist < best.dist)
      best = right;
```

Program 19.12 Determination of closest pair of points (continues)

```
MergeSort.merge(z, y, l, m, r);    // reconstruct y

// put points within best.d of midpoint in z
int k = 1;                          // cursor for z
for (int i = 1; i <= r; i++)
   if (Math.abs(y[m].x - y[i].x) < best.dist)
      z[k++] = y[i];

// search for closer category 3 pair
// by checking all pairs from z[1:k-1]
for (int i = 1; i < k; i++)
{
   for (int j = i + 1; j < k && z[j].y - z[i].y < best.dist; j++)
   {
      double dp = dist(z[i], z[j]);
      if (dp < best.dist) // closer pair found
         best = new PointPair(x[z[i].p], x[z[j].p], dp);
   }
}
return best;
}
```

Program 19.12 Determination of closest pair of points (concluded)

comparing region of R_B that have y-coordinate $\geq$ p.y and (2) pairing with points that have y-coordinate $\leq$ p.y. These two parts may be implemented by pairing each point z[i], $1 \leq$ i $<$ k (regardless of whether it is in R_A or R_B) with a point z[j], i $<$ j, for which z[j].y-z[i].y $< \delta$. For each z[i] the points that get examined lie inside the $2\delta \times \delta$ region shown in Figure 19.18. Since the points in each $\delta \times \delta$ subregion are at least δ apart, the number in each subregion cannot exceed four. So the number of points z[j] that each z[i] is paired with is at most seven.

Complexity Analysis

Let $t(n)$ denote the time taken by the private method closestPair on a set of n points. When $n < 4$, $t(n)$ equals some constant d. When $n \geq 4$, it takes $\Theta(n)$ time to divide the instance into two parts, reconstruct y after the two recursive calls, eliminate points that are too far from the dividing line, and search for a better category 3 pair. The recursive calls take $t(\lceil n/2 \rceil)$ and $t(\lfloor n/2 \rfloor)$ time, respectively.

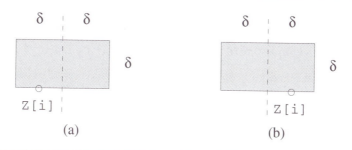

(a)   (b)

Figure 19.18 Region of points paired with z[i]

Therefore, we obtain the recurrence

$$t(n) = \begin{cases} d & n < 4 \\ t(\lfloor n/2 \rfloor) + t(\lceil n/2 \rceil) + cn & n \geq 4 \end{cases}$$

which is the same as the recurrence for merge sort. Its solution is $t(n) = \Theta(n \log n)$. The additional work done by the public method closestPair consists of sorting x, creating y and z, and sorting y. The total time for this additional work is also $\Theta(n \log n)$. The overall time complexity of the divide-and-conquer closest-pair code is $\Theta(n \log n)$ under the assumption that no exception is thrown.

EXERCISES

8. Write a complete program for the defective-chessboard problem. Include modules to welcome the user to the program; input the chessboard size and location of the defect; and output the tiled chessboard. The output is to be provided on a color monitor using colored tiles. No two tiles that share a common boundary should be colored the same. Since the chessboard is a planar figure, it is possible to color the tiles in this way using at most four colors. However, for this exercise, it is sufficient to devise a greedy coloring heuristic that attempts to use as few colors as possible.

9. Solve the recurrence of Equation 19.7 using the substitution method.

10. Does $f(x) = \sqrt{x}$ satisfy Equation 19.9?

11. Show that $f(x) = x^a \log^b x$ satisfies Equation 19.9 for all $a \geq 1$, all integer $b \geq 0$, and all $x \geq 1$.

12. Start with the array [11, 2, 8, 3, 6, 15, 12, 0, 7, 4, 1, 13, 5, 9, 14, 10] and draw a figure similar to Figure 19.9 that shows the steps involved in a merge sort.

13. Do Exercise 12 using the array $[11, 3, 8, 7, 5, 10, 0, 9, 4, 2, 6, 1]$.

14. Write a merge sort code that works on chains of elements. The output should be a sorted chain. Make your sort method a member of the class `Chain` or of a class that extends `Chain` (Section 6.1).

15. Start with the array $[2, 3, 6, 8, 11, 15, 0, 7, 12, 1, 4, 13, 5, 9, 10, 14]$ and draw a figure similar to Figure 19.9 that shows the steps invovled in a natural merge sort.

16. Do Exercise 15 using the array $[11, 3, 8, 5, 7, 10, 0, 9, 2, 4, 6, 1]$.

17. Write the method `NaturalMergeSort` that implements a natural merge sort. The input and output configurations are the same as for Program 19.3.

18. Write a natural merge sort code that sorts a chain of elements. Your function should be a member of the class `Chain` or of a class that extends `Chain` (Section 6.1).

19. Start with the segment $[5, 3, 8, 4, 7, 1, 0, 9, 2, 10, 6, 11]$ and draw a figure to show the status of this segment following each swap that is done in the `while` loop of Program 19.7. Also show the segment after the pivot is properly placed. Use 5 as the pivot.

20. Do Exercise 19 using the array $[7, 3, 6, 8, 11, 14, 0, 2, 12, 1, 4, 13, 5, 9, 10, 15]$. Use 7 as the pivot.

21. Replace the last recursive call to `quickSort` in Program 19.6 with a `while` loop. Compare the average run time of the resulting sort method with that of Program 19.6.

22. Rewrite Program 19.6 using a stack to simulate the recursion. The new code should stack the boundaries of only the larger of the segments *left* and *right*.

    (a) Show that the stack space needed is $O(\log n)$.

    (b) Compare the average run time of Program 19.6 with that of the new code.

23. Show that the worst-case time complexity of `quickSort` is $\Theta(n^2)$.

24. Suppose that the partitioning into *left*, *middle*, and *right* is always such that *left* and *right* have the same size when n (n is the number of elements in the segment being sorted) is odd and *left* has one element more than *right* when n is even. Show that under this assumption, the time complexity of Program 19.6 is $O(n \log n)$.

25. Show that $\int s \log_e s \, ds = \frac{s^2 \log_e s}{2} - \frac{s^2}{4}$. Use this result to show that $\int_2^m s \log_e s \, ds < \frac{m^2 \log_e m}{2} - \frac{m^2}{4}$.

26. Compare the worst-case and average times of Program 19.6 when the median-of-three rule is used to the times when it is not used. Do this comparison experimentally; use suitable test data and $n = 10, 20, \cdots, 100, 200, 300, 400, 500, 1000$.

27. Do Exercise 26 using a random number generator rather than the median-of-three rule to select the pivot element.

28. At the end of the quick sort section, we suggested combining two sort methods: quick sort and insertion sort. The combined algorithm is essentially a quick sort that reverts to an insertion sort when the size of a segment is less than or equal to `changeOver` = `nBreak`. Can we obtain a faster algorithm by using a different value for `changeOver`? Why? Modify Program 19.6 to use the median-of-three rule; experiment with different values of `changeOver` and see what happens. Determine the best value of `changeOver` for the case of average performance. After you have optimized your quick sort code, compare the average performance of your code and that of `arrays.sort`.

29. In this exercise we will develop a sort procedure with best worst-case performance.

    (a) Compare the worst-case run times of insertion, bubble, selection, heap, merge, and quick sort. The worst-case input data for insertion, bubble, selection, and quick sort are easy to generate. For merge sort, write a program to generate the worst-case data. This program will essentially unmerge a sorted sequence of n elements. For heap sort, estimate the worst-case time using random permutations.

    (b) Use the results of part (a) to obtain a composite sort function that has the best worst-case performance. More likely than not, your composite procedure will include only merge and insertion sort.

    (c) Run an experiment to determine the worst-case run time of your composite function. Compare the performance with that of the original sort procedures and of `arrays.sort`.

    (d) Plot the worst-case times of the eight sort methods on a single graph sheet.

30. Start with the array [4, 3, 8, 5, 7, 10, 0, 9, 2, 11, 6, 1] and draw a figure to show the progress of Programs 19.8 and 19.9 when started with $k = 7$. You should show the segment to be searched following each partitioning pass and also give the new k value.

31. Do Exercise 30 using the array [7, 3, 6, 8, 11, 15, 0, 2, 12, 1, 4, 13, 5, 9, 10, 14] and $k = 5$.

32. Use the substitution method to solve Equation 19.13 for the case when n is a power of 2.

★   33. Prove Theorem 19.3.

★   34. Use induction to show that Equation 19.14 implies $t(n) \leq 72cn$ for $n \geq 1$.

35. Programs 19.8 and 19.9 need $O(\texttt{a.length})$ space for the recursion stack. This space can be entirely eliminated by replacing the recursive calls with a `while` or `for` loop. Rewrite the code in this way. Compare the run time of the two versions of the selection code.

36. (a) Recode Program 19.9 using a random number generator to select the partitioning element. Conduct experiments to compare the average performance of the two codes.

(b) Recode Program 19.9 using the median-of-medians rule with $r = 9$.

37. In an attempt to speed Program 19.12, we might eliminate the square root operator from the computation of the distance between two points and instead work with the square of the distance. Finding the closest pair is the same as finding a pair with minimum squared distance. What changes need to be made to Program 19.12? Experiment with the two versions and measure the performance improvement you can achieve.

38. Devise a faster algorithm to find the closest pair of points when all points are known to lie on a straight line. For example, suppose the points are on a horizontal line. If the points are sorted by x-coordinate, then the nearest pair contains two adjacent points. Although this strategy results in an $O(n \log n)$ algorithm if we use `mergeSort` (Program 19.3), the algorithm has considerably less overhead than Program 19.11 has and so runs faster.

39. Consider the closest-pair-of-points problem. Suppose that instead of sorting the points by x-coordinate initially, we use method `select` (Program 19.8) to find the median x_i and divide the points into A and B.

(a) Write a high-level description of the resulting algorithm for the closest-pair problem.

(b) What is the complexity of your algorithm?

(c) Comment on whether or not you expect the new algorithm to be faster than Program 19.12.

19.3   SOLVING RECURRENCE EQUATIONS

Several techniques—substitution, induction, characteristic roots, and generating function—are available to solve recurrence equations. You can find a detailed development of these methods in the Web site for this book. In this section, we describe a table look-up method that can be used to solve many recurrences associated with divide-and-conquer algorithms.

The complexity of many divide-and-conquer algorithms is given by a recurrence of the form

$$t(n) = \begin{cases} t(1) & n = 1 \\ a * t(n/b) + g(n) & n > 1 \end{cases} \tag{19.15}$$

where a and b are known constants. We will assume that $t(1)$ is known and that n is a power of b (i.e., $n = b^k$). Using the substitution method (see the Web site), we can show that

$$t(n) = n^{\log_b a}[t(1) + f(n)] \tag{19.16}$$

where $f(n) = \sum_{j=1}^{k} h(b^j)$ and $h(n) = g(n)/n^{\log_b a}$.

Figure 19.19 tabulates the asymptotic value of $f(n)$ for various values of $h(n)$. This table allows us to easily obtain the asymptotic value of $t(n)$ for many of the recurrences we encounter when analyzing divide-and-conquer algorithms.

$h(n)$	$f(n)$
$O(n^r)$, $r < 0$	$O(1)$
$\Theta((\log n)^i)$, $i \geq 0$	$\Theta(((\log n)^{i+1})/(i+1))$
$\Omega(n^r)$, $r > 0$	$\Theta(h(n))$

Figure 19.19 $f(n)$ values for various $h(n)$ values

Let us solve a few recurrences using this table. The recurrence for binary search when n is a power of 2 is

$$t(n) = \begin{cases} t(1) & n = 1 \\ t(n/2) + c & n > 1 \end{cases}$$

Comparing this recurrence with Equation 19.14, we see that $a = 1$, $b = 2$, and $g(n) = c$. Therefore, $\log_b(a) = 0$, and $h(n) = g(n)/n^{\log_b a} = c = c(\log n)^0 = \Theta((\log n)^0)$.

From Figure 19.19, we obtain $f(n) = \Theta(\log n)$. Therefore, $t(n) = n^{\log_b a}(c + \Theta(\log n))$ $= \Theta(\log n)$.

For the merge sort recurrence, we obtain $a = 2$, $b = 2$, and $g(n) = cn$. So $\log_b a = 1$, and $h(n) = g(n)/n = c = \Theta((\log n)^0)$. Hence $f(n) = \Theta(\log n)$ and $t(n)$ $= n(t(1) + \Theta(\log n)) = \Theta(n \log n)$.

As another example, consider the recurrence

$$t(n) = 7t(n/2) + 18n^2, \ n \geq 2 \text{ and a power of } 2$$

that corresponds to the recurrence for Strassen's matrix-multiplication method (Equation 19.6) with $k = 1$ and $c = 18$. We obtain $a = 7$, $b = 2$, and $g(n) = 18n^2$. Therefore, $\log_b a = \log_2 7 \approx 2.81$, and $h(n) = 18n^2/n^{\log_2 7} = 18n^{2 - \log_2 7} = O(n^r)$ where $r = 2 - \log_2 7 < 0$. Therefore, $f(n) = O(1)$. The expression for $t(n)$ is

$$t(n) = n^{\log_2 7}(t(1) + O(1)) = \Theta(n^{\log_2 7})$$

as $t(1)$ is assumed to be a constant.

As a final example, consider the following recurrence:

$$t(n) = 9t(n/3) + 4n^6, \ n \geq 3 \text{ and a power of } 3$$

Comparing this recurrence with Equation 19.14, we obtain $a = 9$, $b = 3$, and $g(n) = 4n^6$. Therefore, $\log_b a = 2$ and $h(n) = 4n^6/n^2 = 4n^4 = \Omega(n^4)$. From Figure 19.13 we see that $f(n) = \Theta(h(n)) = \Theta(n^4)$. Therefore,

$$t(n) = n^2(t(1) + \Theta(n^4)) = \Theta(n^6)$$

as $t(1)$ may be assumed constant.

EXERCISES

40. Use the substitution method to show that Equation 19.16 is the solution to the recurrence 19.15.

41. Use the table of Figure 19.19 to solve the following recurrences. In each case assume $t(1) = 1$.

    (a) $t(n) = 10t(n/3) + 11n$, $n \geq 3$ and a power of 3.

    (b) $t(n) = 10t(n/3) + 11n^5$, $n \geq 3$ and a power of 3.

    (c) $t(n) = 27t(n/3) + 11n^3$, $n \geq 3$ and a power of 3.

    (d) $t(n) = 64t(n/4) + 10n^3 \log^2 n$, $n \geq 4$ and a power of 4.

(e) $t(n) = 9t(n/2) + n^2 2^n$, $n \geq 2$ and a power of 2.

(f) $t(n) = 3t(n/8) + n^2 2^n \log n$, $n \geq 8$ and a power of 8.

(g) $t(n) = 128t(n/2) + 6n$, $n \geq 2$ and a power of 2.

(h) $t(n) = 128t(n/2) + 6n^8$, $n \geq 2$ and a power of 2.

(i) $t(n) = 128t(n/2) + 2^n/n$, $n \geq 2$ and a power of 2.

(j) $t(n) = 128t(n/2) + \log^3 n$, $n \geq 2$ and a power of 2.

19.4   LOWER BOUNDS ON COMPLEXITY

$f(n)$ is an **upper bound** on the complexity of a problem iff at least one algorithm solves this problem in $O(f(n))$ time. One way to establish an upper bound of $f(n)$ on the complexity of a problem is to develop an algorithm whose complexity is $O(f(n))$. Each algorithm developed in this book established an upper bound on the complexity of the problem it solved. For example, until the discovery of Strassen's matrix-multiplication algorithm (Example 19.3), the upper bound on the complexity of matrix multiplication was n^3, as the algorithm of Program 2.22 was already known and this algorithm runs in $\Theta(n^3)$ time. The discovery of Strassen's algorithm reduced the upper bound on the complexity of matrix multiplication to $n^{2.81}$.

$f(n)$ is a **lower bound** on the complexity of a problem iff every algorithm for this problem has complexity $\Omega(f(n))$. To establish a lower bound of $g(n)$ on the complexity of a problem, we must show that *every* algorithm for this problem has complexity $\Omega(g(n))$. Making such a statement is usually quite difficult as we are making a claim about all possible ways to solve a problem, rather than about a single way to solve it.

For many problems we can establish a trivial lower bound based on the number of inputs and/or outputs. For example, every algorithm that sorts n elements must have complexity $\Omega(n)$, as every sorting algorithm must examine each element at least once or run the risk that the unexamined elements are in the wrong place. Similarly, every algorithm to multiply two $n \times n$ matrices must have complexity $\Omega(n^2)$, as the result contains n^2 elements and it takes $\Omega(1)$ time to produce each of these elements, and so on. Nontrivial lower bounds are known for a very limited number of problems.

In this section we establish nontrivial lower bounds on two of the divide-and-conquer problems studied in this chapter—finding the minimum and maximum of n elements and sorting. For both of these problems, we limit ourselves to **comparison algorithms**. These algorithms perform their task by making comparisons between pairs of elements and possibly moving elements around; they do not perform other operations on elements. The minmax algorithms of Chapter 2, as well as those proposed in this chapter, satisfy this property, as do all the sort methods studied in this book except for bin sort and radix sort (Sections 6.5.1 and 6.5.2).

19.4.1   Lower Bound for the Minmax Problem

Program 19.1 gave a divide-and-conquer function to find the minimum and maximum of n elements. This function makes $\lceil 3n/2 \rceil - 2$ comparisons between pairs of elements. We will show that every comparison algorithm for the minmax problem must make at least $\lceil 3n/2 \rceil - 2$ comparisons between the elements. For purposes of the proof, we assume that the n elements are distinct. This assumption does not affect the generality of the proof, as distinct element inputs form a subset of the input space. In addition, every minmax algorithm must work correctly on these inputs as well as on those that have duplicates.

The proof uses the **state space method**. In this method we describe the start, intermediate, and finish states of every algorithm for the problem as well as how a comparison algorithm can go from one state to another. Then we determine the minimum number of transitions needed to go from the start state to the finish state. This minimum number of transitions is a lower bound on the complexity of the problem. The start, intermediate, and finish states of an algorithm are abstract entities, and there is no requirement that an algorithm keep track of its state explicitly.

For the minmax problem the algorithm state can be described by a tuple (a, b, c, d) where a is the number of elements that the minmax algorithm still considers candidates for the maximum and minimum elements; b is the number of elements that are no longer candidates for the minimum, but are still candidates for the maximum; c is the number of elements that are no longer candidates for the maximum, but are still candidates for the minimum; and d is the number of elements that the minmax algorithm has determined to be neither the minimum nor the maximum. Let A, B, C, and D denote the elements in each of the preceding categories.

When the minmax algorithm starts, all n elements are candidates for the min and max. So the start state is $(n,0,0,0)$. When the algorithm finishes, there are no elements in A, one in B, one in C, and $n - 2$ in D. Therefore, the finish state is $(0, 1, 1, n - 2)$. Transitions from one state to another are made on the basis of comparisons between pairs of elements. When two elements from A are compared, the smaller element can be placed in C and the larger in B. (Recall that all elements are distinct, so we cannot get an equal compare.) The following state transition is possible:

$$(a, b, c, d) \rightarrow (a - 2, b + 1, c + 1, d)$$

Other possible transitions follow.

- When comparisons between elements of B are made, the possible transition is

$$(a, b, c, d) \rightarrow (a, b - 1, c, d + 1)$$

- When comparisons between elements of C are made, the possible transition is

$$(a, b, c, d) \rightarrow (a, b, c - 1, d + 1)$$

- When an element of A is compared with an element of B, the possible transitions are

$(a, b, c, d) \rightarrow (a - 1, b, c, d + 1)$ (the A element is greater than the B element)
$(a, b, c, d) \rightarrow (a - 1, b, c + 1, d)$ (the A element is smaller than the B element)

- When an element of A is compared with an element of C, the possible transitions are

$(a, b, c, d) \rightarrow (a - 1, b, c, d + 1)$ (the A element is smaller than the C element)
$(a, b, c, d) \rightarrow (a - 1, b + 1, c, d)$ (the A element is greater than the C element)

Although other comparisons are possible, none of these comparisons can guarantee a state change. Examining the possible state changes, we see that when n is even, the quickest way to go from the start state $(n,0,0,0)$ to the finish state $(0, 1, 1, n - 2)$ is to do $n/2$ comparisons between elements in A, $n/2 - 1$ between those in B, and $n/2 - 1$ between those in C. The total number of comparisons is $3n/2 - 2$. When n is odd, the fastest way to go from the start state to the finish state is to make $\lfloor n/2 \rfloor$ comparisons between elements in A, $\lfloor n/2 \rfloor - 1$ comparisons between elements in B, $\lfloor n/2 \rfloor - 1$ comparisons between elements in C, and up to two more comparisons involving the remaining element of A. The total count is $\lceil 3n/2 \rceil - 2$.

Since no comparison algorithm for the minmax problem can go from the start state to the finish state making fewer than $\lceil 3n/2 \rceil - 2$ comparisons between pairs of elements, this number is a lower bound on the number of comparisons every minmax comparison algorithm must make. Hence Program 19.1 is an optimal comparison algorithm for the minmax problem.

19.4.2   Lower Bound for Sorting

A lower bound of $n \log n$ on the worst-case complexity of every comparison algorithm that sorts n elements can be established by using the state space method. This time the algorithm state is given by the number of permutations of the n elements that are still candidates for the output permutation. When the sort algorithm starts, all $n!$ permutations of the n elements are candidates for the sorted output and when the algorithm terminates, only one candidate permutation remains. (As for the minmax problem, we assume the n elements to be sorted are distinct.)

When two elements a_i and a_j are compared, the current set of candidate permutations is divided into two groups—one group retains permutations that are consistent with the outcome $a_i < a_j$, and the other set retains those that are consistent with the outcome $a_i > a_j$. Since we have assumed that the elements are distinct, the outcome $a_i = a_j$ is not possible. For example, suppose that $n = 3$ and that the first comparison is between a_1 and a_3. Prior to this comparison, as far as the algorithm is concerned, all six permutations of the elements are candidates for the sorted permutation. If $a_1 < a_3$, then the best the algorithm can do is eliminate the permutations (a_3, a_1, a_2), (a_3, a_2, a_1), and (a_2, a_3, a_1). The remaining three permutations must be retained as candidates for the output.

If the current candidate set has m permutations, then a comparison produces two groups, one of which must have at least $\lceil m/2 \rceil$ permutations. A worst-case execution of the sort algorithm begins with a candidate set of size $n!$, reduces this set to one of size at least $n!/2$, then reduces the candidate set further to one of size at least $n!/4$, and so on until the size of the candidate set becomes 1. The number of reduction steps (and hence comparisons needed) is at least $\lceil \log n! \rceil$.

Since $n! \geq \lceil n/2 \rceil^{\lceil n/2 \rceil - 1}$, $\log n! \geq (n/2 - 1) \log(n/2) = \Omega(n \log n)$. Hence every sort algorithm that is a comparison algorithm must make $\Omega(n \log n)$ comparisons in the worst case.

We can arrive at this same lower bound from a **decision-tree** proof. In such a proof we model the progress of an algorithm by using a tree. At each internal node of this tree, the algorithm makes a comparison and moves to one of the children based on the outcome of this comparison. External nodes are nodes at which the algorithm terminates. Figure 19.20 shows the decision tree for `insertionSort` (Program 2.15) while sorting the three-element sequence `a[0:2]`. Each internal node has a label of the type `i:j`. This label denotes a comparison between `a[i]` and `a[j]`. If `a[i] < a[j]`, the algorithm moves to the left child. A right child move occurs when `a[i] > a[j]`. Since the elements are distinct, the case `a[i] = a[j]` is not possible. The external nodes are labeled with the sorted permutation that is generated. The left-most path in the decision tree of Figure 19.20 is followed when `a[1] < a[0]`, `a[2] < a[0]`, and `a[2] < a[1]`; the permutation at the left-most external node is `(a[2],a[1],a[0])`.

Notice that each leaf of a decision tree for a comparison sort algorithm defines a unique output permutation. Since every correct sorting algorithm must be able to produce all $n!$ permutations of n inputs, the decision tree for every correct comparison sort algorithm must have at least $n!$ external nodes. Because a tree whose height is h has at most 2^h external nodes, the decision tree for a correct comparison sort algorithm must have a height that is at least $\lceil \log_2 n! \rceil = \Omega(n \log n)$. Therefore, every comparison sort algorithm must perform $\Omega(n \log n)$ comparisons in the worst case. Further, since the average height of every binary tree that has $n!$ external nodes is also $\Omega(n \log n)$ (Exercise 47), the average complexity of every comparison sort algorithm is also $\Omega(n \log n)$.

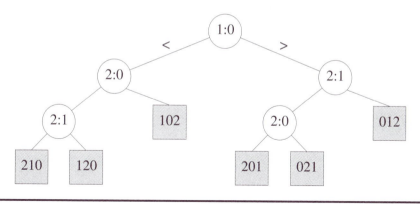

Figure 19.20 Decision tree for `insertionSort` when n = 3

The preceding lower-bound proof shows that heap sort and merge sort are optimal worst-case sort methods (as far as asymptotic complexity is concerned) and that heap sort, merge sort, and quick sort are optimal average-case methods.

EXERCISES

42. Use the state space method to show that every comparison algorithm that finds the maximum of n elements makes at least $n - 1$ comparisons between pairs of elements.

43. Show that $n! \geq \lceil n/2 \rceil^{\lceil n/2 \rceil - 1}$.

44. Draw the decision tree for `insertionSort` when $n = 4$.

45. Draw the decision tree for `mergeSort` (Program 19.3) when $n = 4$.

46. Let $a_1, \cdots, a_n$ be a sequence of n elements. Elements a_i and a_j, $i < j$, are **inverted** iff $a_i > a_j$. The number of pairs (i, j) such that a_i and a_j are inverted is the **inversion number** of the element sequence.

    (a) What is the inversion number of the sequence 6, 2, 3, 1?

    (b) What is the maximum inversion number possible for a sequence of n elements?

    (c) Suppose that a sort method compares only pairs of adjacent elements and then possibly swaps them (this is essentially what bubble, selection, and insertion sorts do). Show that sort methods of this type must perform $\Omega(n^2)$ comparisons in the worst case.

47. Let T be an extended binary tree with n internal nodes; let I, the internal path length of T, be the sum of the lengths of the paths from the root to each of the internal nodes; let E, the external path length of T, be the sum of the lengths of the paths from the root to each of the external nodes.

(a) Show that $E = I + 2n$.

(b) Show that I is minimized when T is a complete binary tree.

(c) Show that when T is a complete binary tree, $I = (n + 1)p - 2^{p+1} + 2$ where $p = \lfloor \log_2(n + 1) \rfloor$.

(d) Use the results of parts (a), (b), and (c) to determine the minimum value of E.

(e) From the result of part (d), conclude that the average external path length of every binary tree that has n internal nodes is $\Omega(\log n)$.

CHAPTER 20

DYNAMIC PROGRAMMING

BIRD'S-EYE VIEW

Dynamic programming is arguably the most difficult of the five design methods we are studying. It has its foundations in the principle of optimality. We can use this method to obtain elegant and efficient solutions to many problems that cannot be so solved with either the greedy or divide-and-conquer methods. After describing the method, we consider its application to the solution of the knapsack, matrix multiplication chains, shortest-path, and noncrossing subset of nets problems. Additional applications (e.g., image compression and component folding) are developed on the Web site. You should study these as well as the exercise solutions to gain mastery of dynamic programming.

20.1   THE METHOD

In dynamic programming, as in the greedy method, we view the solution to a problem as the result of a sequence of decisions. In the greedy method we make irrevocable decisions one at a time, using a greedy criterion. However, in dynamic programming we examine the decision sequence to see whether an optimal decision sequence contains optimal decision subsequences. Some examples that illustrate this point are given below.

Example 20.1 [Shortest Path] Consider the digraph of Figure 18.2. We wish to find a shortest path from the source vertex $s = 1$ to the destination vertex $d = 5$. We need to make decisions on the intermediate vertices. The choices for the first decision are 2, 3, and 4. That is, from vertex 1 we may move to any one of these vertices. Suppose we decide to move to vertex 3. Now we need to decide on how to get from 3 to 5. If we go from 3 to 5 in a suboptimal way, then the 1-to-5 path constructed cannot be optimal, even under the restriction that from vertex 1 we must go to vertex 3. For example, if we use the suboptimal path 3, 2, 5 with length 9, the constructed 1-to-5 path 1, 3, 2, 5 has length 11. Replacing the suboptimal path 3, 2, 5 with an optimal one 3, 4, 5 results in the path 1, 3, 4, 5 of length 9.

For this shortest-path problem, suppose that our first decision gets us to some vertex v. Although we do not know how to make this first decision we do know that the remaining decisions must be optimal for the problem of going from v to d. ■

Example 20.2 [0/1 Knapsack Problem] Consider the 0/1 knapsack problem of Section 18.3.2. We need to make decisions on the values of $x_1, \cdots, x_n$. Suppose we are deciding the values of the x_is in the order $i = 1, 2, \cdots, n$. If we set $x_1 = 0$, then the available knapsack capacity for the remaining objects (i.e., objects 2, 3, $\cdots$, n) is c. If we set $x_1 = 1$, the available knapsack capacity is $c - w_1$. Let $r \in \{c, c - w_1\}$ denote the remaining knapsack capacity.

Following the first decision, we are left with the problem of filling a knapsack with capacity r. The available objects (i.e., 2 through n) and the available capacity r define the *problem state* following the first decision. Regardless of whether x_1 is 0 or 1, $[x_2, \cdots, x_n]$ must be an optimal solution for the problem state following the first decision. If not, there is a solution $[y_2, \cdots, y_n]$ that provides greater profit for the problem state following the first decision. So $[x_1, y_2, \cdots, y_n]$ is a better solution for the initial problem.

Suppose that $n = 3$, $w = [100, 14, 10]$, $p = [20, 18, 15]$, and $c = 116$. If we set $x_1 = 1$, then following this decision, the available knapsack capacity is 16. $[x_2, x_3] = [0, 1]$ is a feasible solution to the two-object problem that remains. It returns a profit of 15. However, it is not an optimal solution to the remaining two-object problem, as $[x_2, x_3] = [1, 0]$ is feasible and returns a greater profit of 18. So $x = [1, 0, 1]$ can be improved to $[1, 1, 0]$. If we set $x_1 = 0$, the available capacity for the two-object instance that remains is 116. If the subsequence $[x_2, x_3]$ is not an optimal solution for this remaining instance, then $[x_1, x_2, x_3]$ cannot be optimal for the initial instance. ∎

Example 20.3 [Airfares] A certain airline has the following airfare structure: From Atlanta to New York or Chicago, or from Los Angeles to Atlanta, the fare is $100; from Chicago to New York, it is $20; and for passengers connecting through Atlanta, the Atlanta to Chicago segment is only $20. A routing from Los Angeles to New York involves decisions on the intermediate airports. If problem states are encoded as (origin, destination) pairs, then following a decision to go from Los Angeles to Atlanta, the problem state is *We are at Atlanta and need to get to New York.* The cheapest way to go from Atlanta to New York is a direct flight with cost $100. Using this direct flight results in a total Los Angeles–to–New York cost of $200. However, the cheapest routing is Los Angeles–Atlanta–Chicago–New York with a cost of $140, which involves using a suboptimal decision subsequence for the Atlanta–to–New York problem (Atlanta–Chicago–New York).

If instead we encode the problem state as a triple (*tag, origin, destination*) where *tag* is 0 for connecting flights and 1 for all others, then once we reach Atlanta, the state becomes (0, Atlanta, New York) for which the optimal routing is through Chicago. ∎

When optimal decision sequences contain optimal decision subsequences, we can establish recurrence equations, called **dynamic-programming recurrence equations**, that enable us to solve the problem in an efficient way.

Example 20.4 [0/1 Knapsack] In Example 20.2 we saw that for the 0/1 knapsack problem, optimal decision sequences were composed of optimal subsequences. Let $f(i, y)$ denote the value of an optimal solution to the knapsack instance with remaining capacity y and remaining objects $i, i + 1, \cdots, n$. From Example 20.2 it follows that

$$f(n, y) = \begin{cases} p_n & y \geq w_n \\ 0 & 0 \leq y < w_n \end{cases} \tag{20.1}$$

and

$$f(i, y) = \begin{cases} \max\{f(i + 1, y), f(i + 1, y - w_i) + p_i\} & y \geq w_i \\ f(i + 1, y) & 0 \leq y < w_i \end{cases} \tag{20.2}$$

By making use of the observation that optimal decision sequences are made up of optimal subsequences, we have obtained a recurrence for f. $f(1, c)$ is the value of the optimal solution to the knapsack problem we started with. Equation 20.2 may be used to determine $f(1, c)$ either recursively or iteratively. In the iterative approach, we start with $f(n, *)$, as given by Equation 20.1, and then obtain $f(i, *)$

in the order $i = n-1, n-2, \cdots, 2$, using Equation 20.2. Finally, $f(1, c)$ is computed by using Equation 20.2.

For the instance of Example 20.2, we see that $f(3, y) = 0$ if $0 \le y < 10$, and 15 if $y \ge 10$. Using Equation 20.2, we obtain $f(2, y) = 0$ if $0 \le y < 10$, 15 if $10 \le y < 14$, 18 if $14 \le y < 24$, and 33 if $y \ge 24$. The optimal solution has value $f(1, 116) = \max\{f(2,116), f(2, \ 116 - w_1) + p_1\} = \max\{f(2,116), f(2, 16) + 20\} = \max\{33, 38\} = 38$.

To obtain the values of the x_is, we proceed as follows: If $f(1, c) = f(2, c)$, then we may set $x_1 = 0$ because we can utilize the c units of capacity getting a return of $f(1, c)$ from objects $2, \cdots, n$. In case $f(1, c) \ne f(2, c)$, then we must set $x_1 = 1$. Next we need to find an optimal solution that uses the remaining capacity $c - w_1$. This solution has value $f(2, c - w_1)$. Proceeding in this way, we may determine the value of all the x_is.

For our sample instance we see that $f(2, 116) = 33 \ne f(1, 116)$. Therefore, $x_1 = 1$, and we need to find x_2 and x_3 so as to obtain a return of $38 - p_1 = 18$ and use a capacity of at most $116 - w_1 = 16$. Note that $f(2, 16) = 18$. Since $f(3, 16) = 15 \ne f(2, 16)$, $x_2 = 1$; the remaining capacity is $16 - w_2 = 2$. Since $f(3, 2) = 0$, we set $x_3 = 0$. ∎

The **principle of optimality** states that no matter what the first decision, the remaining decisions must be optimal with respect to the state that results from this first decision. This principle implies that an optimal decision sequence is comprised of optimal decision subsequences. Since the principle of optimality may not hold for some formulations of some problems, it is necessary to verify that it does hold for the problem being solved. *Dynamic programming cannot be applied when this principle does not hold.*

The steps in a dynamic-programming solution are

- Verify that the principle of optimality holds.

- Set up the dynamic-programming recurrence equations.

- Solve the dynamic-programming recurrence equations for the value of the optimal solution.

- Perform a **traceback** step in which the solution itself is constructed.

It is very tempting to write a simple recursive program to solve the dynamic-programming recurrence. *However, as we will see in subsequent sections, unless care is taken to avoid recomputing previously computed values, the recursive program will have prohibitive complexity.* When the recursive program is designed to avoid this recomputation, the complexity is drastically reduced. The dynamic-programming recurrence may also be solved by iterative code that naturally avoids recomputation of already computed values. Although this iterative code has the same time complexity as the "careful" recursive code, the former has the advantage of not requiring additional space for the recursion stack. As a result, the iterative code generally runs faster than the careful recursive code.

20.2   APPLICATIONS

20.2.1   0/1 Knapsack Problem

Recursive Solution

The dynamic-programming recurrence equations for the 0/1 knapsack problem were developed in Example 20.4. A natural way to solve a recurrence such as Equation 20.2 for the value $f(1, c)$ of an optimal knapsack packing is by a recursive program such as Program 20.1. The invocation `knapsack(p,w,c)` returns the value of $f(1, c)$. Although Program 20.1 is written for integer profits and weights, by changing the data type of `theProfit` and/or `theWeight` in the `knapsack` method header, we can obtain code for any desired primitive data type (e.g., `long`, `float`, and `double`).

Let $t(n)$ be the time this code takes to solve an instance with n objects. We see that $t(1) = a$ and $t(n) \le 2t(n-1) + b$ for $n > 1$. Here a and b are constants. This recurrence solves to $t(n) = O(2^n)$.

Example 20.5 Consider the case $n = 5$, $p = [6, 3, 5, 4, 6]$, $w = [2, 2, 6, 5, 4]$, and $c = 10$. To determine $f(1, 10)$, method f is invoked as $f(1,10)$. The recursive calls made are shown by the tree of Figure 20.1. Each node has been labeled by the value of y. Nodes on level j have $i = j$. So the root denotes the invocation $f(1,10)$. Its left and right children, respectively, denote the invocations $f(2,10)$ and $f(2,8)$. In all, 28 invocations are made. Notice that several invocations redo the work of previous invocations. For example, $f(3, 8)$ is computed twice, as are $f(4, 8)$, $f(4, 6)$, $f(4, 2)$, $f(5, 8)$, $f(5, 6)$, $f(5, 3)$, $f(5, 2)$, and $f(5, 1)$. If we save the results of previous invocations, we can reduce the number of invocations to 19 because we eliminate the shaded nodes of Figure 20.1. ■

Recursive Solution without Recomputations

As observed in Example 20.5, Program 20.1 is doing more work than necessary. To avoid recomputing the same $f(i, y)$ value, we may keep a list of $f(i, y)$s that have already been computed. The elements of this list are triples of the form $(i, y, f(i, y))$. Before making an invocation $f(i,y)$, we see whether the list contains a triple of the form $(i, y, *)$ where $*$ denotes a wildcard. If so, $f(i, y)$ is retrieved from the list. If not, the invocation is made and then the triple $(i, y, f(i, y))$ added to the list. The list of triples may be implemented as a hash table (see Section 11.5) or as a binary search tree (see Chapter 16).

When the weights are integer, we may use an integer array `fArray[i][y]` such that `f[i][y]` equals -1 iff $f(i, y)$ has not been computed before. Program 20.2 gives the recursive code that avoids recomputation of previously computed f values. This code assumes that `fArray` is an $(n + 1) \times (c + 1)$ integer array, which is a class data member that has been initialized to -1 by the public method `knapsack`, which invokes method f.

```
public class RecursiveDPKnapsack
{
   static int [] profit;
   static int [] weight;
   static int numberOfObjects;

   public static int knapsack(int [] theProfit, int [] theWeight,
                              int knapsackCapacity)
   {
      profit = theProfit;
      weight = theWeight;
      numberOfObjects = theProfit.length - 1;
      return f(1, knapsackCapacity);
   }

   /** recursive method to solve dynamic programming recurrence
     * @return f(i,theCapacity) */
   private static int f(int i, int theCapacity)
   {
      if (i == numberOfObjects)
         return (theCapacity < weight[numberOfObjects])
                 ? 0 : profit[numberOfObjects];
      if (theCapacity < weight[i])
         return f(i + 1, theCapacity);
      return Math.max(f(i + 1, theCapacity),
                      f(i + 1, theCapacity - weight[i]) + profit[i]);
   }
}
```

Program 20.1 Recursive method for knapsack problem

To determine the time complexity of Program 20.2, we will use an accounting scheme in which we charge different components of the total time to different $f(i, y)$s and then add up the amounts charged to each $f(i, y)$. When computing an $f(i, y)$, the cost of an invocation f(i+1,z) is charged to $f(i + 1, z)$ if $f(i + 1, z)$ has not been computed and to $f(i, z)$ otherwise. (This $f(i + 1, z)$ in turn offloads the cost of computing new $f(*, *)$s to the individual $f(*, *)$s that are computed.) The cost of the remainder of Program 20.2 is charged to $f(i, y)$. This remaining cost is $\Theta(1)$. The total amount charged to each $f(i, y)$ is constant, and the number of $f(i, y)$s is $(c + 1)(n + 1)$. Therefore, the total time is $O(cn)$ (recall that c denotes the knapsack capacity and n is the number of objects). By avoiding the recomputation

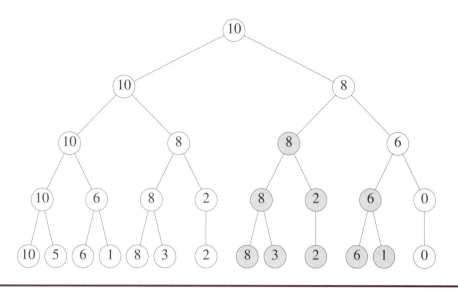

Figure 20.1 Tree of recursive calls

of previously computed $f(i, y)$s, we have cut the running time of the recursive code from an impractical $O(2^n)$ to a very practical $O(cn)$!

Iterative Solution with Integer Weights

We can devise a fairly simple iterative algorithm (Program 20.3) to solve for $f(1, c)$ when the weights are integer. This algorithm, based on the strategy outlined in Example 20.4, computes each $f(i, y)$ exactly once. Program 20.3 uses a two-dimensional array `f[][]` to store the values of the function f. Program 20.4 gives the code for the traceback needed to determine the x_i values that result in the optimal filling.

Example 20.6 Figure 20.2 shows the `f` array computed by Program 20.3 using the data of Example 20.5. The data are computed by rows from top to bottom and within a row from left to right. The value `f[1][10] = 15` is not shown.

   To determine the x_i values, we begin with x_1. Since $f(1, 10) \neq f(2, 10)$, $f(1, 10)$ must equal $f(2, 10-w_1)+p_1 = f(2, 8)+6$. Therefore, $x_1 = 1$. Since $f(2, 8) \neq f(3, 8)$, $f(2, 8)$ must equal $f(3, 8 - w_2) + p_2 = f(3, 6) + 3$ and $x_2 = 1$. $x_3 = x_4 = 0$ because $f(3, 6) = f(4, 6) = f(5, 6)$. Finally, since $f(5, 4) \neq 0$, $x_5 = 1$. ∎

   The complexity of the iterative `knapsack` code is $\Theta(nc)$ and that of `traceback` is $\Theta(n)$.

```
private static int f(int i, int theCapacity)
{
   // check if already computed
   if (fArray[i][theCapacity] >= 0)
      return fArray[i][theCapacity];

   // not yet computed
   if (i == numberOfObjects)
   {// use Equation 20.1
      // compute and save f(i,theCapacity)
      fArray[i][theCapacity] = (theCapacity < weight[numberOfObjects])
                               ? 0 : profit[numberOfObjects];
      return fArray[i][theCapacity];
   }
   // use Equation 20.2
   if (theCapacity < weight[i])
      // object i does not fit
      fArray[i][theCapacity] = f(i + 1, theCapacity);
   else
      // object i fits, try both possibilities
      fArray[i][theCapacity] = Math.max(f(i + 1, theCapacity),
                   f(i + 1, theCapacity - weight[i]) + profit[i]);

   return fArray[i][theCapacity];
}
```

Program 20.2 Recursive method for knapsack problem with no recomputations

i	\multicolumn{11}{c}{y}
	0	1	2	3	4	5	6	7	8	9	10
5	0	0	0	0	6	6	6	6	6	6	6
4	0	0	0	0	6	6	6	6	6	10	10
3	0	0	0	0	6	6	6	6	6	10	11
2	0	0	3	3	6	6	9	9	9	10	11

Figure 20.2 f function/array for Example 20.6

```
public static void knapsack(int [] profit, int [] weight,
                            int knapsackCapacity, int [][] f)
{
   int numberOfObjects = profit.length - 1;

   // initialize f[numberOfObjects][]
   int yMax = Math.min(weight[numberOfObjects] - 1, knapsackCapacity);
   for (int y = 0; y <= yMax; y++)
      f[numberOfObjects][y] = 0;
   for (int y = weight[numberOfObjects]; y <= knapsackCapacity; y++)
      f[numberOfObjects][y] = profit[numberOfObjects];

   // compute f[i][y], 1 < i < numberOfObjects
   for (int i = numberOfObjects - 1; i > 1; i--)
   {
      yMax = Math.min(weight[i] - 1, knapsackCapacity);
      for (int y = 0; y <= yMax; y++)
         f[i][y] = f[i + 1][y];
      for (int y = weight[i]; y <= knapsackCapacity; y++)
         f[i][y] = Math.max(f[i + 1][y],
                        f[i + 1][y - weight[i]] + profit[i]);
   }

   // compute f[1][knapsackCapacity]
   f[1][knapsackCapacity] = f[2][knapsackCapacity];
   if (knapsackCapacity >= weight[1])
      f[1][knapsackCapacity] = Math.max(f[1][knapsackCapacity],
               f[2][knapsackCapacity-weight[1]] + profit[1]);
}
```

Program 20.3 Iterative computation of f

Tuple Method *(Optional)*

The code of Program 20.3 has two drawbacks. First, it requires that the weights be integer. Second, it is slower than Program 20.1 when the knapsack capacity is large. In particular, if $c > 2^n$, its complexity is $\Omega(n2^n)$. We can overcome both of these shortcomings by using a tuple approach in which for each i, $f(i, y)$ is stored as an ordered list $P(i)$ of pairs $(y, f(i, y))$ that correspond to the y values at which the function f changes. The pairs in each $P(i)$ are in increasing order of y. In addition, since $f(i, y)$ is a nondecreasing function of y, the pairs are also in increasing order of $f(i, y)$.

```
public static void traceback(int [][] f, int [] weight,
                             int knapsackCapacity, int [] x)
{
   int numberOfObjects = weight.length - 1;

   for (int i = 1; i < numberOfObjects - 1; i++)
      if (f[i][knapsackCapacity] == f[i+1][knapsackCapacity])
         // do not include object i
         x[i] = 0;
      else
      {// include object i
         x[i] = 1;
         knapsackCapacity -= weight[i];
      }
   x[numberOfObjects] = (f[numberOfObjects][knapsackCapacity] > 0)
                        ? 1 : 0;
}
```

Program 20.4 Iterative computation of x

Example 20.7 Consider the f function of Figure 20.2. When $i = 5$, the function f is completely specified by the pairs $P(5) = [(0, 0), (4, 6)]$. The pairs $P(i)$ for $i = 4, 3,$ and 2 are $[(0, 0), (4, 6), (9, 10)]$, $[(0, 0), (4, 6), (9, 10), (10, 11)]$, and $[(0, 0), (2, 3), (4, 6), (6, 9), (9, 10), (10, 11)]$.

To compute $f(1, 10)$, we use Equation 20.2, which yields $f(1, 10) = \max\{f(2, 10), f(2, 8) + p_1\}$. From $P(2)$ we get $f(2, 10) = 11$, and $f(2, 8) = 9$ ($f(2, 8) = 9$ comes from the pair $(6, 9)$). Therefore, $f(1, 10) = \max\{11, 15\} = 15$.

To determine the x_i values, we begin with x_1. Since $f(1, 10) = f(2, 6) + p_1$, $x_1 = 1$. Since $f(2, 6) = f(3, 6 - w_2) + p_2 = f(3, 4) + p_2$, $x_2 = 1$. $x_3 = x_4 = 0$ because $f(3, 4) = f(4, 4) = f(5, 4)$. Finally, since $f(5, 4) \neq 0$, $x_5 = 1$.   ∎

If we examine the pairs in each $P(i)$, we see that each pair $(y, f(i, y))$ corresponds to a different combination of 0/1 assignments to the variables $x_i, \cdots, x_n$. Let (a, b) and (c, d) be pairs that correspond to two different 0/1 assignments to $x_i, \cdots, x_n$. If $a \geq c$ and $b < d$, then (a, b) is dominated by (b, c). Dominated assignments do not contribute pairs to $P(i)$. If two or more assignments result in the same pair, only one is in $P(i)$.

Under the assumption that $w_n \leq c$, $P(n) = [(0, 0), (w_n, p_n)]$. These two pairs correspond to x_n equal to 0 and 1, respectively. For each i, $P(i)$ may be obtained from $P(i + 1)$. First, compute the ordered set of pairs Q such that (s, t) is a pair of Q iff $w_i \leq s \leq c$ and $(s - w_i, t - p_i)$ is a pair of $P(i + 1)$. Now Q has the pairs with $x_i = 1$, and $P(i+1)$ has those with $x_i = 0$. Second, merge Q and $P(i+1)$ eliminating dominated as well as duplicate pairs to get $P(i)$.

Example 20.8 Consider the data of Example 20.7. $P(5) = [(0, 0), (4, 6)]$, so $Q = [(5, 4), (9, 10)]$. When merging $P(5)$ and Q to create $P(4)$, the pair $(5, 4)$ is eliminated because it is dominated by the pair $(4, 6)$. As a result, $P(4) = [(0, 0), (4, 6), (9, 10)]$. To compute $P(3)$, we first obtain $Q = [(6, 5), (10, 11)]$ from $P(4)$. Next merging with $P(4)$ yields $P(3) = [(0, 0), (4, 6), (9, 10), (10, 11)]$. Finally, to get $P(2)$, $Q = [(2, 3), (6, 9)]$ is computed from $P(3)$. Merging $P(3)$ and Q yields $P(2) = [(0, 0), (2, 3), (4, 6), (6, 9), (9, 10), (10, 11)]$. ∎

Since the pairs in each $P(i)$ represent different $0/1$ assignments to $x_i, \cdots, x_n$, no $P(i)$ has more than 2^{n-i+1} pairs. When computing $P(i)$, Q may be computed in $\Theta(|P(i+1)|)$ time. The time needed to merge $P(i+1)$ and Q is also $\Theta(|P(i+1)|)$. So all the $P(i)$s may be computed in $\Theta(\sum_{i=2}^{n} |P(i+1)|) = O(2^n)$ time. When the weights are integer, $|P(i)| \le c + 1$. In this case the complexity becomes $O(\min\{nc, 2^n\})$.

20.2.2   Matrix Multiplication Chains

Problem Description

An $m \times n$ matrix A and an $n \times p$ matrix B can be multiplied in $\Theta(mnp)$ time (see Exercise 2.24). We will use mnp as a measure of the time needed to multiply the two matrices. Suppose we are to multiply three matrices A, B, and C. There are two ways in which we can accomplish this task. In the first, we multiply A and B to get the product matrix D and then multply D and C to get the desired result. This multiplication order can be written as $(A * B) * C$. The second way is $A * (B * C)$. Although both multiplication orders obtain the same result, one may take a lot more computing time than the other.

Example 20.9 Suppose that A is a 100×1 matrix, B is a 1×100 matrix, and C is a 100×1 matrix. Then the time needed to compute $A * B$ is 10,000. Since the result is a 100×100 matrix, the time needed to perform the multiplication with C is 1,000,000. The overall time needed to compute $(A * B) * C$ is therefore 1,010,000. $B * C$ can be computed in 10,000 units of time. Since the result is a 1×1 matrix, the time needed for the multiplication with A is 100. The total time needed to compute $A * (B * C)$ is therefore 10,100! Furthermore, when computing $(A * B) * C$, we need 10,000 units of space to store $A * B$; however, when $A * (B * C)$ is computed, only one unit of space is needed for $B * C$.

As an example of a real problem that can benefit from computing the matrix product $A*B*C$ in the proper order, consider the registration of 2 three-dimensional images. In the registration problem, we are to determine the amount by which one image needs to be rotated, translated, and shrunk (or expanded) so that it approximates the second. One way to perform this registration involves doing about

100 iterations of computation. Each iteration computes the following 12×1 vector T:

$$T = \sum A(x, y, z) * B(x, y, z) * C(x, y, z)$$

Here A, B, and C are, respectively, 12×3, 3×3, and 3×1 matrices. (x, y, z) gives the coordinates of a voxel, and the sum is done over all voxels. Let t be the number of computations needed to compute $A(x, y, z) * B(x, y, z) * C(x, y, z)$ for a single voxel. Assume that the image is of size $256 \times 256 \times 256$ voxels. In this case the total number of computations needed for the 100 iterations is approximately $100 * 256^3 * t \approx 1.7 * 10^9 t$. When the three matrices are multiplied from left to right, $t = 12 * 3 * 3 + 12 * 3 * 1 = 144$. When we multiply from right to left, $t = 3 * 3 * 1 + 12 * 3 * 1 = 45$. The left-to-right computation requires approximately $2.4 * 10^{11}$ operations, while the right-to-left computation requires about $7.5 * 10^{10}$ operations. On a computer that can do 100 million operations per second, the first scheme would take 40 minutes and the second would take 12.5 minutes.   ■

When we are to compute the matrix product $A * B * C$, only two multiplication orders are possible (left to right and right to left). We can determine the number of operations each order requires and go with the cheaper one. In a more general situation, we are to compute the matrix product $M_1 \times M_2 \times \cdots \times M_q$ where M_i is an $r_i \times r_{i+1}$ matrix, $1 \le i \le q$. Consider the case $q = 4$. The matrix product $A * B * C * D$ may be computed in any of the following five ways:

$$A * ((B * C) * D) \qquad A * (B * (C * D))$$
$$(A * B) * (C * D) \qquad ((A * B) * C) * D \qquad (A * (B * C)) * D$$

The number of different ways in which the product of q matrices may be computed increases exponentially with q. As a result, for large q it is not practical to evaluate each multiplication scheme and select the cheapest.

Dynamic-Programming Formulation

We can use dynamic programming to determine an optimal sequence of pairwise matrix multiplications to use. The resulting algorithm runs in $O(q^3)$ time. Let M_{ij} denote the result of the product chain $M_i \times \cdots \times M_j$, $i \le j$, and let $c(i, j)$ be the cost of the optimal way to compute M_{ij}. Let $kay(i, j)$ be such that the optimal computation of M_{ij} computes $M_{ik} \times M_{k+1,j}$. An optimal computation of M_{ij} therefore comprises the product $M_{ik} \times M_{k+1,j}$ preceded by optimal computations of M_{ik} and $M_{k+1,j}$. The principle of optimality holds, and we obtain the dynamic-programming recurrence that follows.

$$c(i,i) \;=\; 0, 1 \le i \le q$$
$$c(i,i+1) \;=\; r_i r_{i+1} r_{i+2} \text{ and } kay(i,i+1) = i, \; 1 \le i < q$$
$$c(i,i+s) \;=\; \min_{i \le k < i+s} \{ c(i,k) + c(k+1, i+s) + r_i r_{k+1} r_{i+s+1} \},$$
$$1 \le i \le q-s, \; 1 < s < q$$
$$kay(i,i+s) \;=\; \text{value of } k \text{ that obtains the above minimum}$$

The above recurrence for c may be solved recursively or iteratively. $c(1,q)$ is the cost of the optimal way to compute the matrix product chain, and $kay(1,q)$ defines the last product to be done. The remaining products can be determined by using the kay values.

Recursive Solution

As in the case of the 0/1 knapsack and image-compression problems, any recursive solution must be implemented so as to avoid computing the same $c(i,j)$ and $kay(i,j)$ values more than once otherwise, the complexity of the algorithm is too high.

Example 20.10 Consider the case $q = 5$ and $r = (10, 5, 1, 10, 2, 10)$. The dynamic-programming recurrence yields

$$c(1,5) \;=\; \min\{c(1,1) + c(2,5) + 500, c(1,2) + c(3,5) + 100, \qquad (20.3)$$
$$c(1,3) + c(4,5) + 1000, c(1,4) + c(5,5) + 200\}$$

Four of the needed cs have $s = 0$ or 1. Their values are immediately computable from the dynamic-programming equations. We get $c(1,1) = c(5,5) = 0$; $c(1,2) = 50$; $c(4,5) = 200$. For $c(2,5)$, we get

$$c(2,5) \;=\; \min\{c(2,2) + c(3,5) + 50, c(2,3) + c(4,5) + 500, \qquad (20.4)$$
$$c(2,4) + c(5,5) + 100\}$$

$c(2,2) = c(5,5) = 0$; $c(2,3) = 50$; and $c(4,5) = 200$. For $c(3,5)$ and $c(2,4)$ we need to use the recurrences

$$c(3,5) \;=\; \min\{c(3,3) + c(4,5) + 100, c(3,4) + c(5,5) + 20\}$$
$$=\; \min\{0 + 200 + 100, 20 + 0 + 20\}$$
$$=\; 40$$

and

$$\begin{aligned} c(2,4) &= \min\{c(2,2)+c(3,4)+10, c(2,3)+c(4,4)+100\} \\ &= \min\{0+20+10,\ 50+0+20\} \\ &= 30 \end{aligned}$$

These computations also yield $kay(3,5) = 4$ and $kay(2,4) = 2$. Now we know all the values needed to compute $c(2,5)$. Substituting these values in Equation 20.4, we get

$$c(2,5) = \min\{0+40+50, 50+200+500, 30+0+100\} = 90$$

and so $kay(2,5) = 2$. To use Equation 20.3 to compute $c(1,5)$, we still need values for $c(3,5)$, $c(1,3)$, and $c(1,4)$. Proceeding as above, we obtain the values 40, 150, and 90. The corresponding kay values are 4, 2, and 2. Substituting into Equation 20.3, we get

$$\begin{aligned} c(1,5) &= \min\{0+90+500, 50+40+100, 150+200+1000, \\ &\qquad 90+0+200\} = 190 \end{aligned}$$

and $kay(1,5) = 2$.

The optimal multiplication sequence has cost 190. The sequence can be determined by examining $kay(1,5)$, which equals 2. So the last multiplication to perform is $M_{12} \times M_{35}$. Since both M_{12} and M_{35} are to be computed optimally, the kay values may be used to figure out how. $kay(1,2) = 1$, so M_{12} is computed as $M_{11} \times M_{22}$. Also, since $kay(3,5) = 4$, M_{35} is optimally computed as $M_{34} \times M_{55}$. M_{34} in turn is computed as $M_{33} \times M_{44}$, so the optimal multiplication sequence is

Multiply M_{11} and M_{22} to get M_{12}
Multiply M_{33} and M_{44} to get M_{34}
Multiply M_{34} and M_{55} to get M_{35}
Multiply M_{12} and M_{35} to get M_{15} ■

The recursive code to determine $c(i,j)$ and $kay(i,j)$ appears in Program 20.5. This code assumes that the one-dimensional integer array r and the two-dimensional integer array kay are class data members. The code computes the value of $c(i,j)$ and also sets kay[a][b] $= kay(a,b)$ for all a and b for which $c(a,b)$ is computed during the computation of $c(i,j)$. The method traceback uses the kay values computed by the method c to determine the optimal multiplication sequence.

```
/** return c(i,j) and compute kay[i][j] = kay(i,j) */
private static int c(int i, int j)
{
   if (i == j)
      return 0;  // one matrix
   if (i == j - 1)
   {// two matrices
      kay[i][i + 1] = i;
      return r[i] * r[i + 1] * r[i + 2];
   }

   // more than two matrices
   // set u to min term for k = i
   int u = c(i,i) + c(i + 1, j) + r[i] * r[i + 1] * r[j + 1];
   kay[i][j] = i;

   // compute remaining min terms and update u
   for (int k = i + 1; k < j; k++)
   {
      int t = c(i, k) + c(k + 1, j) + r[i] * r[k + 1] * r[j + 1];
      if (t < u)
      {// smaller min term found, update u and kay[i][j]
         u = t;
         kay[i][j] = k;
      }
   }

   return u;
}

/** output best way to compute Mij */
public static void traceback(int [][] kay, int i, int j)
{
   if (i == j)  // only one matrix
      return;
   traceback(kay, i, kay[i][j]);
   traceback(kay, kay[i][j] + 1, j);
   System.out.println("Multiply M " + i + ", " + kay[i][j] +
           " and M " + (kay[i][j] + 1) + ", " + j);
}
```

Program 20.5 Recursive computation of $c(i,j)$ and $kay(i,j)$

Let $t(q)$ be the complexity of method c when $j - i + 1 = q$ (i.e., when M_{ij} is composed of q matrices). We see that when q is 1 or 2, $t(q) = d$ where d is a constant. When $q > 2$, $t(q) = 2\sum_{k=1}^{q-1} t(k) + eq$ where e is a constant. For $q > 2$, $t(q) > 2t(q-1) + e$. So $t(q) = \Omega(2^q)$. The complexity of method traceback is $O(q)$.

Recursive Solution without Recomputations

By avoiding the recomputation of c (and hence kay) values previously computed, the complexity can be reduced to $O(q^3)$. To avoid the recomputation, we need to save the values of the $c(i, j)$s in a two-dimensional array c[][] whose initial values are 0. Program 20.6 gives the new recursive code for method c.

To analyze the complexity of the new method c (Program 20.6), we will again use the cost amortization method. Observe that the invocation c(1,q) causes each $c(i, j)$, $1 \le i \le j \le q$ to be computed exactly once. For $s = j - i > 1$, the computation of each requires s amount of work in addition to the work done computing the needed $c(a, b)$s that haven't as yet been computed. This additional work is charged to the $c(a, b)$s that are being computed for the first time. These $c(a, b)$s, in turn, offload some of this charge to the first-time cs that need to be computed during the computation of $c(a, b)$. As a result, each $c(i, j)$ is charged s amount of work. For each s, $q - s + 1$ $c(i, j)$s are computed. The total cost is therefore $\sum_{s=1}^{q-1} s(q - s + 1) = O(q^3)$.

Iterative Solution

The dynamic-programming recurrence for c may be solved iteratively, computing each c and kay exactly once, by computing the $c(i, i+s)$s in the order $s = 2, 3, \cdots$, $q - 1$.

Example 20.11 Consider the five-matrix instance of Example 20.10. We begin by initializing $c(i, i)$ to 0, $1 \le i \le 5$. Next we compute $c(i, i+1)$ for $i = 1, \cdots, 4$. $c(1, 2)$ $= r_1 r_2 r_3 = 50$, $c(2, 3) = 50$, $c(3, 4) = 20$, and $c(4, 5) = 200$. The corresponding kay values are 1, 2, 3, and 4.

When $s = 2$, we get

$$
\begin{aligned}
c(1,3) &= \min\{c(1,1) + c(2,3) + r_1 r_2 r_4, c(1,2) + c(3,3) + r_1 r_3 r_4\} \\
&= \min\{0 + 50 + 500, 50 + 0 + 100\} = 150
\end{aligned}
$$

and $kay(1, 3) = 2$. $c(2, 4)$ and $c(3, 5)$ are computed in a similar way. Their values are 30 and 40. The corresponding kay values are 2 and 3.

When $s = 3$, we compute $c(1, 4)$ and $c(2, 5)$. All the values needed to compute $c(2, 5)$ (see Equation 20.4) are known. Substituting these values, we get $c(2, 5) = 90$ and $kay(2, 5) = 2$. $c(1, 4)$ is computed from a similar equation. Finally, when $s = 4$, only $c(1, 5)$ is to be computed. The equation is 20.3. All quantities on the right side are known. ∎

```
private static int c(int i, int j)
{
   // check if already computed
   if (c[i][j] > 0)  // c(i,j) was computed earlier
      return c[i][j];

   // c(i,j) not computed before, compute it now
   if (i == j)
      return 0;  // one matrix
   if (i == j - 1)
   {// two matrices
      kay[i][i + 1] = i;
      c[i][j] = r[i] * r[i + 1] * r[i + 2];
      return c[i][j];
   }

   // more than two matrices
   // set u to min term for k = i
   int u = c(i,i) + c(i + 1, j) + r[i] * r[i + 1] * r[j + 1];
   kay[i][j] = i;

   // compute remaining min terms and update u
   for (int k = i + 1; k < j; k++)
   {
      int t = c(i, k) + c(k + 1, j) + r[i] * r[k + 1] * r[j + 1];
      if (t < u)
      {// smaller min term found, update u and kay[i][j]
         u = t;
         kay[i][j] = k;
      }
   }

   c[i][j] = u;
   return c[i][j];
}
```

Program 20.6 Computing $c(i, j)$ without recomputations

The iterative code to compute the c and kay values is method `matrixChain`
(Program 20.7). Its complexity is $O(q^3)$. We can use a traceback to determine the
optimal multiplication sequence following the computation of kay.

```java
public static void matrixChain(int [] r, int [][] c, int [][] kay)
{
   int q = r.length - 2;    // number of matrices

   // initialize c[i][i], c[i][i+1], and kay[i][i+1]
   for (int i = 1; i < q; i++)
   {
      c[i][i] = 0;
      c[i][i + 1] = r[i] * r[i + 1] * r[i + 2];
      kay[i][i + 1] = i;
   }
   c[q][q] = 0;

   // compute remaining c's and kay's
   for (int s = 2; s < q; s++)
      for (int i = 1; i <= q - s; i++)
      {// min term for k = i
         c[i][i+s] = c[i][i] + c[i + 1][i + s]
                     + r[i] * r[i + 1] * r[i + s + 1];
         kay[i][i + s] = i;

         // remaining min terms
         for (int k = i + 1; k < i + s; k++)
         {
            int t = c[i][k] + c[k + 1][i + s]
                    + r[i] * r[k + 1] * r[i + s + 1];
            if (t < c[i][i + s])
            {// smaller min term, update c and kay
               c[i][i + s] = t;
               kay[i][i + s] = k;
            }
         }
      }
}
```

Program 20.7 Iterative computation of c and kay

20.2.3 All-Pairs Shortest Paths

Problem Description

In the **all-pairs shortest-path problem**, we are to find a shortest path between every pair of vertices in a directed graph G. That is, for every pair of vertices (i, j), we are to find a shortest path from i to j as well as one from j to i. These two paths are the same when G is undirected.

When no edge has a negative length, the all-pairs shortest-path problem may be solved by using Dijkstra's greedy single-source algorithm (Section 18.3.5) n times, once with each of the n vertices as the source vertex. This process results in an $O(n^3)$ solution to the all-pairs problem. The dynamic-programming soultion we develop in this section, called Floyd's algorithm, runs in $\Theta(n^3)$ time. Floyd's algorithm works even when the graph has negative-length edges (provided there are no negative-length cycles). Also, the constant factor associated with Floyd's algorithm is smaller than that associated with Dijkstra's algorithm. Therefore, Floyd's algorithm takes less time than the worst-case time for n applications of Dijkstra's algorithm.

Dynamic-Programming Formulation

We permit negative-length edges but require that G not contain any negative-length cycles. Under this assumption, every pair of vertices (i, j) always has a shortest path that contains no cycle. When the graph has a cycle whose length is less than 0, some shortest paths have length $-\infty$, as they involve going around the negative-length cycle indefinitely.

Let the n vertices of G be numbered 1 through n. Let $c(i, j, k)$ denote the length of a shortest path from i to j that has no intermediate vertex larger than k. Hence $c(i, j, 0)$ is the length of the edge (i, j) in case this edge is in G. It is 0 if $i = j$ and ∞ otherwise. $c(i, j, n)$ is the length of a shortest path from i to j.

Example 20.12 For the digraph of Figure 18.17, $c(1, 3, k) = \infty$ for $k = 0, 1, 2, 3$; $c(1, 3, 4) = 28$; $c(1, 3, k) = 10$ for $k = 5, 6, 7$; and $c(1, 3, k) = 9$ for $k = 8, 9, 10$. Hence the shortest 1-to-3 path has length 9. ∎

How can we determine $c(i, j, k)$ for any k, $k > 0$? There are two possibilities for a shortest i-to-j path that has no intermediate vertex larger than k. This path may or may not have k as an intermediate vertex. If it does not, then its length is $c(i, j, k-1)$. If it does, then its length is $c(i, k, k-1) + c(k, j, k-1)$. $c(i, j, k)$ is the smaller of these two quantities. So we obtain the recurrence

$$c(i, j, k) = \min\{c(i, j, k-1), c(i, k, k-1) + c(k, j, k-1)\}, \quad k > 0$$

The above recurrence formulates the solution for one k in terms of the solutions for $k - 1$. Obtaining solutions for $k - 1$ should be easier than obtaining those for k directly.

Recursive Solution

If the above recurrence is solved recursively, the complexity of the resulting procedure is excessive. Let $t(k)$ be the time needed to solve the recurrence recursively for any i, j, k combination. From the recurrence, we see that $t(k) = 3t(k - 1) + c$. Using the substitution method, we obtain $t(n) = \Theta(3^n)$. So the time needed to obtain all the $c(i, j, n)$ values is $\Theta(n^2 3^n)$.

Iterative Solution

The values $c(i, j, n)$ may be obtained far more efficiently by noticing that some $c(i, j, k-1)$ values get used several times. By avoiding the recomputation of $c(i, j, k)$s that were computed earlier, all c values may be determined in $\Theta(n^3)$ time. This strategy may be implemented recursively as we did for the matrix chain problem (see Program 20.6) or iteratively. We will develop only the iterative code. Our first attempt at developing this iterative code results in the pseudocode of Figure 20.3.

```
// Find the lengths of the shortest paths.
   // initialize c(i,j,0)
   for (int i = 1; i <= n; i++)
      for (int j = 1; j <= n; j++)
```
$$c(i, j, 0) = a(i, j); \text{ // a is the cost adjacency matrix}$$

```
   // compute c(i,j,k) for 0 < k <= n
   for (int k = 1; k <= n; k++)
      for (int i = 1; i <= n; i++)
         for (int j = 1; j <= n; j++)
```
$$\text{if } (c(i, k, k - 1) + c(k, j, k - 1) < c(i, j, k - 1))$$
$$c(i, j, k) = c(i, k, k - 1) + c(k, j, k - 1);$$
```
            else
```
$$c(i, j, k) = c(i, j, k - 1);$$

Figure 20.3 Initial shortest-paths algorithm

Observe that $c(i, k, k) = c(i, k, k - 1)$ and that $c(k, i, k) = c(k, i, k - 1)$ for all i. As a result, if $c(i, j)$ replaces $c(i, j, *)$ throughout Figure 20.3, the final value of $c(i, j)$ will be the same as $c(i, j, n)$.

Java Implementation

With this observation Figure 20.3 may be refined into the Java code of Program 20.8. This refinement uses the class **AdjacencyWDigraph** defined in Program 17.2. Method **allPairs** returns, in c, the lengths of the shortest paths. In case there is no path from i to j, c[i][j] is set to null. This method also computes kay[i][j] such that kay[i][j] is the largest k that is on a shortest i-to-j path. The kay values may be used to construct a shortest path from one vertex to another (see method outputPath of Program 20.9).

```
public void allPairs(Operable [][] c, int [][] kay)
{
   // initialize c[i][j] = c(i,j,0)
   Operable notNull = null;   // eventually a nonnull element
   for (int i = 1; i <= n; i++)
      for (int j = 1; j <= n; j++)
      {
         c[i][j] = (Operable) a[i][j];
         if (c[i][j] != null)
            notNull = c[i][j];
         kay[i][j] = 0;
      }
   if (notNull == null) // graph has no edges
      return;
   for (int i = 1; i <= n; i++)
      c[i][i] = (Operable) notNull.zero();

   // compute c[i][j] = c(i,j,k)
   for (int k = 1; k <= n; k++)
      for (int i = 1; i <= n; i++)
         for (int j = 1; j <= n; j++)
         {
            Operable t1 = c[i][k];
            Operable t2 = c[k][j];
            Operable t3 = c[i][j];
            if (t1 != null && t2 != null &&
               (t3 == null || t3.compareTo(t1.add(t2)) > 0))
            {// smaller value for c[i][j] found
                  c[i][j] = (Operable) t1.add(t2);
                  kay[i][j] = k;
            }
         }
}
```

Program 20.8 Computation of c and kay

The time complexity of Program 20.8 is readily seen to be $\Theta(n^3)$. Program 20.8 takes $O(n)$ time to output a shortest path.

```
/** output shortest path from i to j */
public static void outputPath(Operable [][] c, int [][] kay,
                              int i, int j)
{
   if (c[i][j] == null)
      System.out.println("There is no path from " + i + " to " + j);
   else
   {
      System.out.print("The path is " + i + " ");
      outputPath(kay, i, j);
      System.out.println();
   }
}

/** actual code to output i to j path */
public static void outputPath(int [][] kay, int i, int j)
{
   if (i == j)
      return;
   if (kay[i][j] == 0)  // no intermediate vertices on path
      System.out.print(j + " ");
   else
   {// kay[i][j] is an intermediate vertex on the path
      outputPath(kay, i, kay[i][j]);
      outputPath(kay, kay[i][j], j);
   }
}
```

Program 20.9 Output a shortest path

Example 20.13 A sample cost array a appears in Figure 20.4(a). Figure 20.4(b) gives the c array computed by Program 20.8, and Figure 20.4(c) gives the kay values. From these kay values we see that the shortest path from 1 to 5 is the shortest path from 1 to kay[1][5] = 4 followed by the shortest path from 4 to 5. The shortest path from 4 to 5 has no intermediate vertex on it, as kay[4][5] = 0. The shortest path from 1 to 4 goes through kay[1][4] = 3. Repeating this process, we determine that the shortest 1-to-5 path is 1, 2, 3, 4, 5. ∎

0	1	4	4	8
3	0	1	5	9
2	2	0	1	8
8	8	9	0	1
8	8	2	9	0

(a)

0	1	2	3	4
3	0	1	2	3
2	2	0	1	2
5	5	3	0	1
4	4	2	3	0

(b)

0	0	2	3	4
0	0	0	3	4
0	0	0	0	4
5	5	5	0	0
3	3	0	3	0

(c)

Figure 20.4 Shortest-paths example

20.2.4   Single-Source Shortest Paths with Negative Costs

Introduction

Do graphs with negative edge costs actually arise in practice? They must; otherwise, we would not study such graphs. Consider a graph in which vertices represent cities, and an edge cost gives the cost of renting a car in one city and dropping it off in another. Most edge costs are positive. However, if there is a net migration into Florida, then Florida will have a surplus of cars and cities that are losing population will have no cars. To fix this imbalance in rental cars, the rental company will actually pay you to drive a car from a select Florida city to one that is short of cars. So some edges have a negative cost. The Web site shows how to solve a scheduling problem and a system of difference equations by finding shortest paths in a graph that has negative edge costs.

The single-source, all-destinations, greedy algorithm developed in Section 18.3.5 cannot be used to obtain the shortest paths when the digraph has one or more edges whose cost is less than 0 (see the solution to Exercise 32). However, the dynamic-programming all-pairs shortest-path algorithm of Section 20.2.3 works as long as the graph/digraph has no cycle whose length/cost is less than 0. As pointed out in Section 20.2.3, the shortest-path problem is not well-defined when we have cycles whose length/cost is negative, because now some shortest paths have an infinite number of edges on them. Therefore, it is reasonable to assume that the graph/digraph we are dealing with has no cycle whose length/cost is negative.

Since the dynamic-programming algorithm of Section 20.2.3 finds shortest paths in a graph/digraph that has edges whose cost is less than 0 (but no cycle whose cost is less than 0) in $\Theta(n^3)$ time, the single-source all-destinations algorithm that we develop should run in less time to be a useful algorithm. The complexity of the algorithm we will develop here is $O(n^3)$ when the adjacency-matrix representation is used and is $O(ne)$ when the adjacency-list representation is used (e is the number of edges). Therefore, the new algorithm has a run-time advantage over the algorithm of Section 20.2.3 when we are interested in finding the shortest paths from a single source vertex. The new algorithm is due to Bellman and Ford and is known as the Bellman-Ford algorithm.

Dynamic-Programming Formulation

Since the graph/digraph has no negative length/cost cycles, we can assume that all shortest paths have at most $n - 1$ edges. Note that a path with n or more edges must contain a cycle; this cycle has length/cost ≥ 0, and so the path that remains following the deletion of this cycle is no longer than the original path. Therefore, between any two connected vertices there is always a shortest path that has no cycle and hence has at most $n - 1$ edges.

As in Sections 18.3.5 and 20.2.3, we first assume that we are interested only in the lengths of the shortest paths. Let $d(v, k)$ be the length of a shortest path from the source vertex to vertex v under the constraint that the path has at most k edges. We see that $d(v, n - 1)$ is the length of a shortest path from the source vertex to vertex v under no constraint and is the answer we seek. Further, $d(v, 0)$ is the length of a shortest path from the source vertex to vertex v using at most zero edges. Therefore, $d(v, 0)$ is 0 when $v = s$ and is infinity otherwise. For $k > 0$, the shortest path has between 0 and k edges. When the number of edges on this shortest path is at least 1,

$$d(v, k) = \min\{d(u, k - 1) + cost(u, v)|(u, v) \text{ is an edge of the graph}\}$$

where u denotes the vertex just before vertex v on this shortest path. We, therefore, obtain the following dynamic-programming recurrence

$$d(v, k) = \min\{d(v, 0), \min\{d(u, k - 1) + cost(u, v)|(u, v) \text{ is an edge of the graph}\}\}$$

This recurrence can be used to compute $d(*, n - 1)$ by computing the ds in the order $d(*, 1), d(*, 2), \cdots, d(*, n - 1)$.

Iterative Solution

Although we can solve the dynamic-programming recurrence for d recursively or recursively without recomputations, an iterative solution results in the least run time. Figure 20.5 gives the pseudocode for the iterative algorithm.

Figure 20.6 gives a refinement of Figure 20.5 in which the computation is done in place, that is, using a d that has only one subscript.

Notice that while the in-place computation does not have $d(*) = d(*, k)$ at the end of each iteration of the outer loop, the value of $d(*)$ on termination is $d(*, n-1)$. Basically, the original code computes the min function $n-1$ times at each vertex and ensures that in the end there is no vertex whose $d(v)$ can be reduced by performing the min function again at this vertex. The modified in-place code does this also. The assurance that no further reduction in d is possible follows from the fact that the graph/digraph has no cycle with negative cost. In fact, on termination we can check each $d(v)$ to see whether it can be reduced by applying the min operation of

```
initialize d(*,0);
```

$$\text{initialize } d(*,0);$$

```
// compute remaining d(*,k)s
for (int k = 1; k < n; k++)
{
    d(v,k) = d(v,0) for all v;
    for (each edge (u,v))
        d(v,k) = min{d(v,k), d(u,k-1) + cost(u,v)};
}
```

Figure 20.5 Pseudocode for Bellman-Ford algorithm

```
initialize d(*) = d(*,0);
```

```
// compute d(*) = d(*,n-1)s
for (int k = 1; k < n; k++)
    for (each edge (u,v))
        d(v) = min{d(v), d(u) + cost(u,v)};
```

Figure 20.6 Refined pseudocode for Bellman-Ford algorithm

the pseudocode. If any d can be reduced, the original graph has a cycle of negative length/cost.

Two other observations that can be used to reduce the computation time are (1) if for some k, $d(v)$ does not change for any v, then we can abort the outer **for** loop, and (2) the inner **for** loop need be done only for those edges (u, v) for which $d(u)$ changed on the previous iteration of the outer loop. Figure 20.7 gives the pseudocode for the Bellman-Ford algorithm with these observations incorporated.

Java Implementation

When implementing the pseudocode of Figure 20.7, it is useful to maintain an array `inList2` such that `inList2[v]` is true iff vertex `v` is in `list2`. This array needs to be reset to `false` at the end of each iteration of the outer **for** loop. This resetting is done efficiently by going through the vertices that are in `list2` and resetting only the corresponding array values.

Although any list structure that permits constant time insertion and deletion may be used (for example, a stack or a queue), we will use `ArrayLinearList` because we have defined an enumerator for this class and because this class has better best-

initialize $d(*) = d(*, 0)$;
put the vertices that are adjacent from the source vertex onto a list $list1$;

```
// compute d(*) = d(*, n − 1)
put the source vertex into list1;
for (int k = 1; k < n; k++)
{
    // see if there are vertices whose d value has changed
    if (list1 is empty) break;    // no such vertex
    while (list1 is not empty)
    {
        delete a vertex u from list1;
        for (each edge (u, v))
        {
            d(v) = min{d(v), d(u) + cost(u, v)};
            if (d(v) has changed and v is not on list2) add v to list2;
        }
        list1 = list2;
        make list2 empty;
    }
}
```

Figure 20.7 Final pseudocode for Bellman-Ford algorithm

case performance than any of the other linear list classes we have developed. Using the enumerator, we can reset the array `inList2` easily at the end of each iteration of the outer `for` loop.

Program 20.10 gives our implementation of the Bellman-Ford algorithm. This code includes the predecessor array `p` as used in shortest-path code of Program 18.3. Using the terminal `p` values, we can construct the shortest paths as described in the solution to Exercise 33.

Complexity Analysis

At the start of each iteration of the `for (int k ...)` loop, there are $O(n)$ vertices in `list1`. Therefore, the innermost `while` loop iterates $O(e)$ (e is the number of edges) times for each value of `k`. So each iteration of the `for (int k ...)` loop takes $O(n^2)$ time when the adjacency-matrix representation is used and $O(e)$ time when the adjacency-list representation is used. Therefore, the overall complexity is $O(n^3)$ when the adjacency-matrix representation is used and $O(ne)$ when the adjacency-list representation is used.

```
public void bellmanFord(int s, Operable [] d, int [] p,
                        Operable theZero)
{
   verifyWeighted("bellmanFord");

   int n = vertices();
   if (s < 1 || s > n)
      throw new IllegalArgumentException
                 ("illegal source vertex" + s);

   // define two lists for vertices whose d has changed
   ArrayLinearList list1 = new ArrayLinearList();
   ArrayLinearList list2 = new ArrayLinearList();
   // define an array to record vertices that are in List2
   boolean [] inList2 = new boolean [n+1];

   // initialize p[1:n] = 0; inList2[1:n] = false by default
   for (int i = 0; i <= n; i++)
      p[i] = 0;

   // set d[s] = d^0(s) = 0
   d[s] = (Operable) theZero.zero();
   p[s] = s;  // p[i] != 0 means vertex i has been reached
              // will later reset p[s] = 0

   // initialize list1
   list1.add(0, new Integer(s));

   // do n - 1 rounds of updating d
   for (int k = 1; k < n; k++)
   {
      if (list1.isEmpty())
         break;  // no more changes possible
      // process vertices on list1
      Iterator ilist1 = list1.iterator();
```

Program 20.10 Bellman-Ford algorithm (continues)

```
      while (ilist1.hasNext())
      {
         // get a vertex u whose d value has changed
         int u = ((Integer) ilist1.next()).intValue();

         // update d for the neighbors v of u
         Iterator iu = iterator(u);
         while (iu.hasNext())
         {
            WeightedEdgeNode vEdge = (WeightedEdgeNode) iu.next();
            if (p[vEdge.vertex] == 0 ||
               ((Operable) d[u].add(vEdge.weight)).
                 compareTo(d[vEdge.vertex]) < 0)
            {
               // this is either the first path to vEdge.vertex
               // or is a shorter path than earlier ones
               d[vEdge.vertex] = (Operable) d[u].add(vEdge.weight);
               p[vEdge.vertex] = u;
               // put vEdge.vertex into list2 unless it is already there
               if (!inList2[vEdge.vertex])
               {// put at end of list
                  list2.add(list2.size(), new Integer(vEdge.vertex));
                  inList2[vEdge.vertex] = true;
               }
            }
         }
      }

      // set list1 and list2 for next update round
      list1 = list2;
      list2 = new ArrayLinearList();

      // reset inList2[1:n] to false
      ilist1 = list1.iterator();
      while (ilist1.hasNext())
         inList2[((Integer) ilist1.next()).intValue()] = false;
   }
   p[s] = 0;  // s has no predecessor
}
```

Program 20.10 Bellman-Ford algorithm (concluded)

20.2.5   Noncrossing Subset of Nets

Problem Description

In the crossing-distribution problem of Section 15.6.3, we are given a routing channel with n pins on either side and a permutation C. Pin i on the top side of the channel is to be connected to pin C_i on the bottom side, $1 \leq i \leq n$. The pair (i, C_i) is called a **net**. In all we have n nets that are to be connected or routed. Suppose that we have two or more routing layers of which one is a *preferred layer*. For example, in the preferred layer it may be possible to use much thinner wires, or the resistance in the preferred layer may be considerably less than in other layers. Our task is to route as many nets as possible in the preferred layer. The remaining nets will be routed, at least partially, in the other layers. Since two nets can be routed in the same layer iff they do not cross, our task is equivalent to finding a maximum noncrossing subset (MNS) of the nets. Such a subset has the property that no two nets of the subset cross. Since net (i, C_i) is completely specified by i, we may refer to this net as net i.

Example 20.14 Consider the example of Figure 15.7 that has been redrawn as Figure 20.8. The nets (1,8) and (2,7) (or equivalently, the nets 1 and 2) cross and so cannot be routed in the same layer. The nets (1,8), (7,9), and (9,10) do not cross and so can be routed in the same layer. These three nets do not constitute an MNS, as a larger subset of noncrossing nets exists. The set of four nets (4,2), (5,5), (7,9), (9,10) is an MNS of the routing instance given in Figure 20.8. ∎

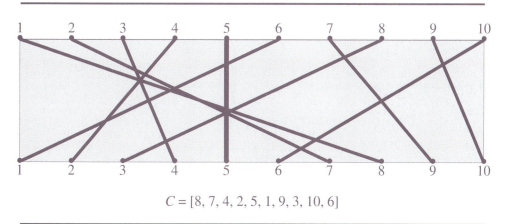

$$C = [8, 7, 4, 2, 5, 1, 9, 3, 10, 6]$$

Figure 20.8 A wiring instance

Dynamic-Programming Formulation

Let $MNS(i,j)$ denote an MNS under the constraint that all pairs (u, C_u) in the MNS have $u \le i$ and $C_u \le j$. Let $size(i,j)$ be the size (i.e., number of nets) of $MNS(i,j)$. Note that $MNS(n,n)$ is an MNS for the input instance and that $size(n,n)$ is its size.

Example 20.15 For the example of Figure 20.8, $MNS(10,10)$ is the answer we seek. As pointed out in Example 20.14, $size(10,10) = 4$. Nets $(1,8)$, $(2,7)$, $(7,9)$, $(8,3)$, $(9,10)$, and $(10,6)$ cannot be members of $MNS(7,6)$ because either their top pin number is greater than 7 or their bottom pin number is greater than 6. So we are left with four nets that are eligible for membership in $MNS(7,6)$. These nets appear in Figure 20.9. The subset $(3,4)$, $(5,5)$ is a noncrossing subset of size 2. There is no noncrossing subset of size 3. So $size(7,6) = 2$. ∎

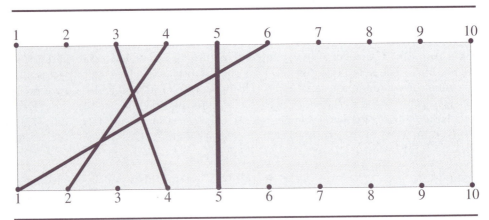

Figure 20.9 Nets of Figure 20.8 that may be in $MNS(7,6)$

When $i = 1$, the net $(1, C_1)$ is the only candidate for membership in $MNS(1,j)$. This net can be a member only when $j \ge C_1$. So we obtain

$$size(1,j) = \begin{cases} 0 & \text{if } j < C_1 \\ 1 & j \ge C_1 \end{cases} \tag{20.5}$$

Next consider the case $i > 1$. If $j < C_i$, then the net (i, C_i) cannot be part of $MNS(i,j)$. In this case all nets (u, C_u) in $MNS(i,j)$ have $u < i$ and $C_u < j$. Therefore

$$size(i,j) = size(i-1,j), \quad j < C_i \tag{20.6}$$

If $j \geq C_i$, then the net (i, C_i) may or may not be in $MNS(i,j)$. If it is, then no nets (u, C_u) such that $u < i$ and $C_u > C_i$ can be members of $MNS(i,j)$, as nets of this form cross (i, C_i). All other nets in $MNS(i,j)$ must have $u < i$ and $C_u < C_i$. The number of such nets in $MNS(i,j)$ must be M_{i-1,C_i-1}; otherwise, $MNS(i,j)$ doesn't have the maximum number of nets possible. If (i, C_i) is not in $MNS(i,j)$, then all nets in $MNS(i,j)$ have $u < i$; therefore, $size(i,j) = size(i-1,j)$. Although we do not know whether the net (i, C_i) is in $MNS(i,j)$, of the two possibilities, the one that gives the larger MNS must hold. Therefore

$$size(i,j) = \max\{size(i-1,j), size(i-1,C_i-1)+1\}, \quad j \geq C_i \qquad (20.7)$$

Iterative Solution

Although Equations 20.5 through 20.7 may be solved recursively, our earlier examples have shown that the recursive solution of dynamic-programming recurrences is inefficient even when we avoid recomputation of previously computed values. So we consider only an iterative solution. For this iterative solution, we use Equation 20.5 to first compute $size(1,j)$. Next we compute $size(i,j)$ for $i = 2, 3, \cdots, n$ in this order of i using Equations 20.6 and 20.7. Finally, we use a traceback to determine the nets in $MNS(n,n)$.

Example 20.16 Figure 20.10 shows the $size(i,j)$ values obtained for the example of Figure 20.8. Since $size(10,10) = 4$, we know that the MNS for this instance has four nets. To find these four nets, we begin at $size(10,10)$. $size(10,10)$ was computed using Equation 20.7. Since $size(10,10) = size(9,10)$, it follows from the reasoning used to obtain Equation 20.7 that there is an MNS of size 4 that does not include net 10. We must now find $MNS(9,10)$. Since $size(9,10) \neq size(8,10)$, $MNS(9,10)$ must include net 9. The remainder of the nets in $MNS(9,10)$ also constitute $MNS(8, C_9 - 1) = MNS(8,9)$. Since $size(8,9) = size(7,9)$, net 8 may be excluded from the MNS. So we proceed to determine $MNS(7,9)$, which must include net 7 as $size(7,9) \neq size(6,9)$. The remainder of the MNS is $MNS(6, C_7-1) = MNS(6,8)$. Net 6 is excluded as $size(6,8) = size(5,8)$. Net 5 is added to the MNS, and we proceed to determine $MNS(4, C_5 - 1) = MNS(4,4)$. Net 4 is excluded, and then net 3 is added to the MNS. No other nets are added. The traceback yields the size 4 MNS $\{3, 5, 7, 9\}$.

Notice that the traceback does not require $size(10,j)$ for values of j other than 10. We need not compute the values that are not required. ∎

Java Implementation

Program 20.11 gives the iterative codes to compute the $size(i,j)$s and then the MNS. Method mns computes the $size(i,j)$ values in a two-dimensional array size.

i					j					
	1	2	3	4	5	6	7	8	9	10
1	0	0	0	0	0	0	0	1	1	1
2	0	0	0	0	0	0	1	1	1	1
3	0	0	0	1	1	1	1	1	1	1
4	0	1	1	1	1	1	1	1	1	1
5	0	1	1	1	2	2	2	2	2	2
6	1	1	1	1	2	2	2	2	2	2
7	1	1	1	1	2	2	2	2	3	3
8	1	1	2	2	2	2	2	2	3	3
9	1	1	2	2	2	2	2	2	3	4
10	1	1	2	2	2	3	3	3	3	4

Figure 20.10 $size(i, j)$s for the instance of Figure 20.8

The mapping is $size(i, j) = $ `size[i][j]`. `size[i][j]` $= size(i, j)$ is computed for $1 \le i < n$, $0 \le j \le n$ as well as for $i = j = n$. The time taken by this computation is $\Theta(n^2)$. Method `traceback` (Program 20.12) returns, in `net[0:sizeOfMNS]`, the nets that form an MNS. This method takes $\Theta(n)$ time, so the total time taken by the dynamic-programming algorithm for the MNS problem is $\Theta(n^2)$.

EXERCISES

1. Let $n = 5$, $p = [7, 3, 5, 2, 4]$, $w = [3, 1, 2, 1, 2]$, and $c = 6$. Draw a figure similar to Figure 20.1 that shows the recursive class made by Program 20.1. Label each node by the y value and shade nodes that represent the recomputation of a previously computed value.

2. Use the data of Exercise 1 and arrive at a table similar to that of Figure 20.2. Use the iterative method of Program 20.3. Now trace back from $f(1, c)$ and detemine the x_i values.

3. Modify Program 20.1 so that it also computes the values of the x_is that result in an optimal packing.

4. Write Java code implementing the tuple method. You code should determine the x_i values that define an optimal packing.

5. [0/1/2 Knapsack] Define the 0/1/2 knapsack problem to be

$$\text{maximize} \sum_{i=1}^{n} p_i x_i$$

```
public static void mns(int [] theC, int [][] size)
{
    int numberOfNets = theC.length - 1;
    // initialize size[1][*]
    for (int j = 0; j < theC[1]; j++)
        size[1][j] = 0;
    for (int j = theC[1]; j <= numberOfNets; j++)
        size[1][j] = 1;

    // compute size[i][*], 1 < i < numberOfNets
    for (int i = 2; i < numberOfNets; i++)
    {
        for (int j = 0; j < theC[i]; j++)
            size[i][j] = size[i - 1][j];
        for (int j = theC[i]; j <= numberOfNets; j++)
            size[i][j] = Math.max(size[i - 1][j],
                             size[i - 1][theC[i] - 1] + 1);
    }

    size[numberOfNets][numberOfNets] =
        Math.max(size[numberOfNets - 1][numberOfNets],
              size[numberOfNets - 1][theC[numberOfNets] - 1] + 1);
}
```

Program 20.11 Compute $size(i, j)$ for all i and j

subject to the constraints

$$\sum_{i=1}^{n} w_i x_i \le c \text{ and } x_i \in \{0, 1, 2\},\ 1 \le i \le n$$

Let f be as defined for the 0/1 knapsack problem.

(a) Determine equations similar to Equations 20.1 and 20.2 for the 0/1/2 knapsack problem.

(b) Assume that the ws are integer. Write a method similar to Program 20.3 to compute f as a two-dimensional array and then to determine an optimal assignment of values for x.

(c) What is the complexity of your method?

```
/** put max noncrossing subset in net[0:sizeOfMNS-1]
 * @return size of MNS */
public static int traceback(int [] theC, int [][] size, int [] net)
{
    int numberOfNets = theC.length - 1;
    int maxAllowed = numberOfNets;    // max bottom pin number allowed
    int sizeOfMNS = 0;
    for (int i = numberOfNets; i > 1; i--)
        // is net i in MNS?
        if (size[i][maxAllowed] != size[i - 1][maxAllowed])
        {// yes, net i is in the MNS
            net[sizeOfMNS++] = i;
            maxAllowed = theC[i] - 1;
        }

    // is net 1 in MNS?
    if (maxAllowed >= theC[1])
        net[sizeOfMNS++] = 1;   // yes

    return sizeOfMNS;
}
```

Program 20.12 Find a maximum noncrossing subset of nets

6. [Two-dimensional Knapsack] The two-dimensional 0/1 knapsack problem is defined as

$$\text{maximize} \sum_{i=1}^{n} p_i x_i$$

subject to the constraints

$$\sum_{i=1}^{n} v_i x_i \le c, \ \sum_{i=1}^{n} w_i x_i \le d, \ \text{and} \ x_i \in \{0, 1\}, \ 1 \le i \le n$$

Let $f(i, y, z)$ denote the value of an optimal solution to the two-dimensional knapsack problem with objects i through n, $c = y$, and $d = z$.

(a) Determine equations similar to Equations 20.1 and 20.2 for $f(n, y, z)$ and $f(i, y, z)$.

(b) Assume that the vs and ws are integer. Write a method similar to Program 20.3 to compute f as a three-dimensional array and then to determine an optimal assignment of values for x.

(c) What is the complexity of your method?

7. Use the dynamic-programming recurrence for the matrix chains problem to compute $c(i, j)$ and $kay(i, j)$, $1 \leq i \leq j \leq q$ for $q = 5$ and $r = (100, 10, 100, 2, 50, 4)$. What is the cost of the best way to multiply the q matrices? Use the kay values to determine that best way to mulitiply the q matrices.

8. Do Exercise 7 using $q = 6$ and $r = (2, 100, 4, 100, 2, 200, 3)$.

9. Show that $\sum_{s=1}^{q-1} s(q - s + 1) = O(q^3)$.

10. Only the upper triangle of the arrays c and kay are used when solving the matrix multiplication recurrence. Rewrite the code of Program 20.7, defining c and kay to be members of the class UpperTriangularMatrix (see Section 8.3.4). Comment on the merits of using two-dimensional arrays versus upper-triangular matrices for this program.

11. Use the dynamic-programming recurrence equations for the all-pairs shortest-path problem to determine all $c(i, j, k)$ values for the graph of Figure 18.9. Present your results as a sequence of matrices $c(*, *, k)$, one matrix for each k. Also, give the final kay array computed by Floyd's algorithm.

12. Do Exercise 11 using the undirected graph that corresponds to the digraph of Figure 18.9 (this graph is obtained by replacing each directed edge with an undirected edge).

13. Write a version of Program 20.8 that will work on members of the class LinkedWDigraph. The asymptotic complexity of your code should be the same as that of Program 20.8.

14. Let G be a weighted directed acyclic graph with n vertices. Assume that the vertices in G have been labeled 1 through n such that if (i, j) is an edge of G, then $i < j$. Let $l(i, j)$ be the length of the edge (i, j).

(a) Use dynamic programming to obtain a method that determines the length of a longest path in G. Your method should work in $O(n + e)$ time where e is the number of edges in G.

(b) Write a method that uses the results of your method for part (a) and constructs the longest possible path. The complexity of your new method should be $O(p)$ where p is the number of vertices on the longest path.

15. [Reflexive Transitive Closure] Modify Program 20.8 so that it starts with an adjacency matrix of a directed graph and computes its reflexive transitive

closure matrix `rtc`. `rtc[i][j]` = 1 if there is a directed path from vertex i to vertex j that uses zero or more edges. `rtc[i][j]` = 0 otherwise. The complexity of your code should be $O(n^3)$ where n is the number of vertices in the graph.

16. Use Equations 20.5 through 20.7 to compute the *size* values for the case when $C = [4, 2, 6, 8, 9, 3, 1, 10, 7, 5]$. Present your results as is shown in Figure 20.10. Use these results to determine an MNS.

17. In Section 18.3.3 we saw that a project may be decomposed into several tasks and that these tasks may be performed in topological order. Let the tasks be numbered 1 through n so that task 1 is done first, then task 2 is done, and so on. Suppose that we have two ways to perform each task. Let $C_{i,1}$ be the cost of doing task i the first way, and let $C_{i,2}$ be the cost of doing it the second way. Let $T_{i,1}$ be the time it takes to do task i the first way, and let $T_{i,2}$ be the time when the task is done the second way. Assume that the Ts are integers. Develop a dynamic-programming algorithm to determine the least-cost way to complete the entire project in no more than t time. Assume that the cost of the project is the sum of the task costs and the total time is the sum of the task times. (*Hint:* Let $c(i, j)$ be the least cost with which tasks i through n can be completed in time j.) What is the complexity of your algorithm?

18. A machine has n components. For each component, there are three suppliers. The weight of component i from supplier j is $W_{i,j}$, and its cost is $C_{i,j}$, $1 \le j \le 3$. The cost of the machine is the sum of the component costs, and its weight is the sum of the component weights. Write a dynamic-programming algorithm to determine from which supplier to buy each component so as to have the lightest machine with cost no more than c. Assume that the costs are integer. (*Hint:* Let $w(i, j)$ be the least-weight machine composed of components i through n that costs no more than j.) What is the complexity of your algorithm?

19. Do Exercise 18 but this time define $w(i, j)$ to be the least-weight machine, with components 1 through i, that costs no more than j.

20. [Longest Common Subsequence] String s is a subsequence of string a if s can be obtained from a by deleting some of the characters in a. The string "onion" is a subsequence of "recognition." s is a common subsequence of a and b iff it is a subsequence of both a and b. The length of s is its number of characters. Develop a dynamic-programming algorithm to find a longest common subsequence of the strings a and b. (*Hint:* Let $a = a_1 a_2 \cdots a_n$ and $b = b_1 b_2 \cdots b_m$. Define $l(i, j)$ to be the length of a longest common subsequence of the strings $a_i \cdots a_n$ and $b_j \cdots b_m$.) What is the complexity of your algorithm?

21. Do Exercise 20 but this time define $l(i, j)$ to be the length of a longest common subsequence of the strings $a_1 \cdots a_i$ and $b_1 \cdots b_j$.

22. [Longest Sorted Subsequence] Write an algorithm to find a longest sorted subsequence (see Exercise 20) of a sequence of integers. What is the complexity of your algorithm?

23. Let x_1, x_2, $\cdots$, be a sequence of integers. Let $sum(i, j) = \sum_i^j x_k$. Write an algorithm to find i and j for which $sum(i, j)$ is maximum. What is the complexity of your algorithm?

24. [String Editing] In the **string-editing problem**, you are given two strings $a = a_1 a_2 \cdots a_n$ and $b = b_1 b_2 \cdots b_m$ and three cost functions C, D, and I. $C(i, j)$ is the cost of changing a_i to b_j, $D(i)$ is the cost of deleting a_i from a, and $I(i)$ is the cost of inserting b_i into a. String a may be changed to string b by performing a sequence of change, delete, and insert operations. Such a sequence is called an **edit sequence**. For example, we could delete all the a_is and then insert the b_is, or when $n \geq m$, we could change a_i to b_i, $1 \leq i \leq n$, and then delete the remaining a_is. The cost of a sequence of operations is the sum of the individual operation costs. Write a dynamic-programming algorithm to determine a least-cost edit sequence. (*Hint:* Define $c(i, j)$ to be the cost of a least-cost edit sequence that transforms $a_1 \cdots a_i$ into $b_1 \cdots b_j$.) What is the complexity of your algorithm?

25. Do Exercise 41 in Chapter 18 using dynamic programming.

20.3   REFERENCES AND SELECTED READINGS

An $O(n \log n)$ algorithm for the matrix multiplication chains problem may be found in the papers "Computation of Matrix Chain Products" parts I & II by T. Hu and M. Shing, *SIAM Journal on Computing*, 11, 1982, 362–372 and 13, 1984, 228–251.

The dynamic-programming algorithm for the noncrossing subset of nets problem is based on the work reported in the paper "Finding a Maximum Planar Subset of a Set of Nets in a Channel" by K. Supowit, *IEEE Transactions on Computer-Aided Design of Integrated Circuits and Systems*, 6, 1, 1987, 93–94.

Chapters 21 and 22 are available from the Web site for this book. The URL for this site is

`http://www.mhhe.com/sahnijava`

INDEX